MODELS AND THEORIES

Models and theories are of central importance in science, and scientists spend substantial amounts of time building, testing, comparing and revising models and theories. It is therefore not surprising that the nature of scientific models and theories has been a widely debated topic within the philosophy of science for many years.

The product of two decades of research, this book provides an accessible yet critical introduction to the debates about models and theories within analytical philosophy of science since the 1920s. Roman Frigg surveys and discusses key topics and questions, including:

- What are theories? What are models? And how do models and theories relate to each other?
- The linguistic view of theories (also known as the syntactic view of theories), covering different articulations of the view, its use of models, the theory-observation divide and the theory-ladenness of observation, and the meaning of theoretical terms.
- The model-theoretical view of theories (also known as the semantic view of theories), covering its analysis of the model-world relationship, the internal structure of a theory, and the ontology of models.
- Scientific representation, discussing analogy, idealisation, and different accounts of representation.
- Modelling in scientific practice, examining how models relate to theories and what models are, classifying different kinds of models, and investigating how robustness analysis, perspectivism, and approaches committed to uncertainty-management deal with multi-model situations.

Models and Theories is the first comprehensive book-length treatment of the topic, making it essential reading both for advanced undergraduate and graduate students, researchers, and professional philosophers working in philosophy of science and philosophy of technology. It will also be of interest to philosophically minded readers working in physics, computer sciences, and STEM fields more broadly.

Roman Frigg is Professor of Philosophy in the Department of Philosophy, Logic and Scientific Method at the London School of Economics and Political Science, UK. He is the winner of the Friedrich Wilhelm Bessel Research Award of the Alexander von Humboldt Foundation and a permanent visiting professor in the Munich Centre for Mathematical Philosophy of the Ludwig-Maximilians-University Munich, Germany. His current work focuses on the nature of scientific models and theories, the foundations of statistical mechanics, and decision making under uncertainty.

MODELS AND THEORIES

A Philosophical Inquiry

Roman Frigg

Routledge
Taylor & Francis Group

LONDON AND NEW YORK

Cover image: Getty Images

First published 2023
by Routledge
4 Park Square, Milton Park, Abingdon, Oxon OX14 4RN

and by Routledge
605 Third Avenue, New York, NY 10158

Routledge is an imprint of the Taylor & Francis Group, an informa business

© 2023 Roman Frigg

The right of Roman Frigg to be identified as author of this work has been
asserted by him in accordance with sections 77 and 78 of the Copyright,
Designs and Patents Act 1988.

British Library Cataloguing-in-Publication Data
A catalogue record for this book is available from the British Library

Library of Congress Cataloging-in-Publication Data
Names: Frigg, Roman, author.
Title: Models and theories : a philosophical inquiry / Roman Frigg.
Description: Abingdon, Oxon ; New York, NY : Routledge, 2022. |
    Includes bibliographical references and index.
Identifiers: LCCN 2022000857 (print) | LCCN 2022000858 (ebook) |
Subjects: LCSH: Science—Methodology. | Science—Philosophy.
Classification: LCC Q175 .F896 2022 (print) | LCC Q175 (ebook) |
    DDC 507.2/1—dc23/eng20220419
LC record available at https://lccn.loc.gov/2022000857
LC ebook record available at https://lccn.loc.gov/2022000858

ISBN: 978-1-844-65490-1 (hbk)
ISBN: 978-1-844-65491-8 (pbk)
ISBN: 978-1-003-28510-6 (ebk)

DOI: 10.4324/9781003285106

Typeset in Times New Roman
by Apex CoVantage, LLC

For my wife Benedetta, my mother Margrit, and in memory of my father Martin

CONTENTS

PART III

PART IV

PREFACE

Models and theories are of central importance in science. Scientists spend substantial amounts of time building, testing, comparing and revising models and theories, and significant parts of many journal articles are concerned with exploring their features. It is therefore not surprising that the nature of scientific models and theories has been a widely debated topic within the philosophy of science for many years. The aim of this book is to provide an accessible and yet critical introduction to the debates about models and theories within analytical philosophy of science since the 1920s. The book is intended to be intelligible to advanced undergraduate students in philosophy, as well as to philosophically-minded scientists. I hope, however, that it will also be of interest to professional philosophers. The book presupposes no formal training, but it requires casual familiarity with formal logic and a recollection of the broad contours of high school science. I briefly explain logical and scientific concepts when they are first invoked, but these explanations are intended as reminders and do not double as introductions to the subject.

The book has been in the works for the better part of the last two decades, and during this time I have acquired debts that are uncomfortably high. The book has its origins in my PhD thesis, which was written under the supervision of Nancy Cartwright and Carl Hoefer. Their support and encouragement were crucial not only for completing the thesis but also for deciding to write this book. Andreas Achen, Margherita Harris, James Nguyen, Lorenzo Sartori and James Wills deserve gallantry awards for reading substantial parts of the manuscript and providing comments on it. Two anonymous referees for the publisher have provided extensive reports on the manuscript. I would like to thank them for their careful and constructive comments, which were helpful when making revisions. At various points in its protracted development Nancy Cartwright, Mark Colyvan, Erik Curiel, Neil Dewar, José Díez, Stephan Hartmann, Laurenz Hudetz, David

Lavis, Simon Le-Druillennec, Anna Mahtani, Michela Massimi, James Nguyen, and Martin Zach read chapters of the manuscript and offered feedback. I am grateful to them for sharing their knowledge and insight with me. Chapters 3 to 6 were discussed in a reading group at the University of Barcelona, and Chapters 11 and 12 were presented in the joint work-in-progress seminar of Ghent University and the Vrije Universiteit Brussels. I would like to thank the participants of the reading group and the seminar for many helpful comments and suggestions. I am also grateful for helpful discussions on the topics of this book with Rachel Ankeny, Joseph Berkovitz, Richard Bradley, Seamus Bradley, Otávio Bueno, Jeremy Butterfield, Craig Callender, Jordi Cat, Hasok Chang, Foad Dizadji-Bahmani, Stephen Downes, Catherine Elgin, Enno Fischer, Steven French, Stacie Friend, Mathias Frisch, Manuel García-Carpintero, Peter Godfrey-Smith, Till Grüne-Yanoff, Rom Harré, Casey Helgeson, Carl Hoefer, Tarja Knuuttila, Elaine Landry, Sabina Leonelli, Arnon Levy, Olimpia Lombardi, Pablo Lorenzano, Sebastian Lutz, Genoveva Martí, Hernán Miguel, Mary Morgan, Margaret Morrison, Fred Muller, Wayne Myrvold, Tom Philp, Christopher Pincock, Stathis Psillos, Miklós Rédei, Alan Richardson, Michael Redhead, Julian Reiss, Bryan Roberts, Joe Roussos, Fiora Salis, Lenny Smith, Dave Stainforth, Katie Steele, Max Steuer, David Teira, Paul Teller, Erica Thompson, Martin Thomson-Jones, Adam Toon, Thomas Uebel, Ioannis Votsis, Michael Weisberg, Wang Wei, Charlotte Werndl, Philipp Wichardt, John Worrall, and Lena Zuchowski, as well as all those whom I hope will forgive me for forgetting to mention them. It is self-evident that the responsibility for the final text is my own. The comments from my interlocutors made the book better than it would have been otherwise, and it is none of their fault if I was unable to make good on every flaw that they pointed out to me, nor, indeed, if I stubbornly insisted on keeping them.

Chapters 6 and 9, as well as parts of Chapter 8 draw on ideas that I developed in collaboration with James Nguyen. James and I have been cooperating closely over the last decade, co-authoring a double-digit number of papers and two books. I have largely lost track of which ideas were his and which were mine, if indeed such a distinction can meaningfully be drawn. Wherever possible I reference joint publications, indicating where the ideas were first published.

I have benefitted from research assistance from Andrew Goldfinch, who helped me organise bibliographical references and readings, and who generously offered to proofread the final manuscript. Tony Bruce and Adam Johnson from Routledge accompanied the project over the years. Their constructive advice and their ability to gently nudge in the right moments were instrumental to pushing this project over the finishing line. Ramachandran Vijayaragavan and his team copyedited the entire manuscript and turned an amorphous pile of files into a book. Heartfelt thanks to all of them for their help and support.

I have spent my entire academic adult life at LSE, which provided an ideal environment to write the book. I am grateful to my colleagues in the Department of Philosophy, Logic and Scientific Method and in the Centre for Philosophy of Natural and Social Science for creating a supportive and collegiate environment in which my work could flourish. Over extended periods of time, the manuscript was simmering quietly on the backburner. This changed when I received a Friedrich Wilhelm Bessel Research Award from the Alexander von Humboldt Foundation, which provided a teaching buyout that freed up a sufficient amount of time to get the manuscript close to its final state.

Last but not least, I'm deeply grateful to my family for their ceaseless and unconditional support. When, just after receiving my "diploma" (something like an MRes) in physics, I told my parents that I would now become a philosopher rather than get a job and earn a living, they remained admirably composed and actively supported the decision. My father started reading my papers and called me on Sunday mornings to press me on my arguments. His calls would usually end with a genial, yet earnest, reminder that writing "the book" ought to be my first priority. It is one of the irredeemable regrets in my life that I have not been able to finish it before his untimely death. I met my wife, Benedetta, shortly after my father's passing, and in what must have been a clandestine operation of pre-established harmony, she immediately made it one of her missions to focus my straying mind on "the book". Her support for the project remained unwavering when book writing turned Sundays into "Sundays" and holidays into "holidays", and even when she had to put up with a grumpy and despondent incarnation of me because nothing seemed to advance. Her love and support were invaluable, and the book would not have made it on the home stretch without her.

INTRODUCTION

The unknown captivates. Ever since antiquity, humans have devised methods and techniques to uncover what is hidden. In modern science, models and theories play an indispensable role in this endeavour. Many scientific disciplines develop theories that are used both to discover, explore, and control phenomena and to systematise, organise, and summarise our knowledge about them. Mastering a field often requires understanding its theories. Quantum theory, relativity theory, electromagnetic theory, and evolutionary theory are examples of theories that are central in their respective domains. But theories are not the only means by which scientists push the boundaries of knowledge. Models play prominent roles in many disciplines. The billiard ball model of the gas, the Bohr model of the atom, the Lotka-Volterra model of predator-prey interaction, general circulation models of the atmosphere, and agent-based models of social systems are examples of models that are foundational in their fields.

What are theories? What are models? And how do models and theories relate to each other? These are the core questions that this book is concerned with. They are time-honoured questions. Since the beginning of the last century an impressive body of literature has emerged that is concerned with the nature of models and theories. Unsurprisingly, different schools of thought have given different answers to these questions and, indeed, interpreted the questions themselves differently. Readers encounter a bewildering array of positions that are often difficult to pin down and map out.

This book aims to offer guidance in this unwieldy territory in three ways. First, it provides an introduction to the problems, issues, and challenges that have shaped the field, as well as an introduction to the philosophical positions that have driven the discussions about models and theories. Second, it presents a guide to the literature, documenting what has been said when and by whom, and locating individual contributions in the wider intellectual context. Third, it takes stock and

DOI: 10.4324/9781003285106-1

assesses where the different debates stand. What has been achieved, what has fallen by the wayside, and what can we learn from failed attempts? Occasionally, the first and second aims are in tension with each other. On the one hand, points can be made without extensive referencing, and those who are primarily interested in the arguments themselves may find references distracting. On the other hand, those who are interested in how debates have unfolded, and, indeed, in further reading, will not be satisfied with a decontextualised abstract argument. I have tried to mitigate this conflict by using in-text references only for direct quotations and when I explicitly discuss a particular position. All other references are in the endnotes. These endnotes anchor arguments in debates, and they provide additional readings for those who wish to pursue a matter further.

Throughout the book, I illustrate arguments and positions with examples to make abstract points palpable. There is a temptation to be original in the choice of examples and use one's own favourites in lieu of cases that have become standard points of reference. Wherever possible I have resisted this temptation, and I have stuck with the well-known cases that are discussed in the literature. This is a deliberate choice rather than intellectual lethargy. First, in keeping with the aim of providing a guide to the literature, the book seeks to acquaint the reader with cases that have actually been discussed in the literature rather than with a collection of personal favourites. Second, standard cases serve as touchstones. Accounts and arguments need to make sense of, and be tested against, accepted paradigm cases. A discussion based on previously unseen (and possibly idiosyncratic) examples would rightly arouse suspicions of cherry-picking or shifting goal posts. Third, the more intriguing the examples, the more likely they are to divert attention away from the main problems and issues. Keeping cases within the boundaries of the expected is therefore also a means to focus attention on the conceptual issues. Once a point is clear, readers can replace the book's examples with their own.

In particular, in the first two parts of the book, the examples are largely taken from physics. This choice is primarily owed to the fact that the views discussed in these parts have been schooled and developed with examples from physics. This said, I admit to having done little to resist this concentration on physics, which aligns with my own interests and, more importantly, competences. Had a philosopher of biology or economics written this book, they might have made different choices. The choices should, however, not present an obstacle to reading the book. The knowledge of physics required to understand the philosophical points rarely, if ever, goes beyond the high school curriculum, and those who spent their formative years studying Homer's epics rather than Newton's axioms will be able to glean enough physics to follow the examples by spending a little time on a relevant Wikipedia page.

Goodman famously noted that "[f]ew terms are used in popular and scientific discourse more promiscuously than 'model'" (1976, 171). Goodman is spot on. It is therefore worth briefly reviewing some of the meanings of "model" and setting aside those that are irrelevant in the current context. The word "model" derives from the Latin "modulus", which means "measure" or "standard". It reappears in the 16th century in Italian as "modello" and in English as "model", where it designates architectural plans or drawings representing the proportions of a building, or, more generally, a likeness that is made to scale. The notion of a model as a true-to-scale replica is still a possible usage of the term in modern-day science, although, as we shall see, it is by no means the only one. The same cannot be said about the many other usages of the term. We expressly exclude the following as intended uses of "model" in this book. First, occasionally "model" is used as a synonym for "theory", for instance when physicists call their best theory of elementary particles "the standard model", or when the Bohr model of the atom is referred to as the "Bohr theory of the atom". It makes little sense to ask, as we do in this book, how models and theories relate to one another unless models and theories are considered to be different, and so we set aside a use of the term "model" that takes models to be theories. Second, phrases like "it's just a model" indicate either that scientists take a cautious attitude towards a certain proposition which they regard as speculative or provisional, or that something is known to be false and entertained only for heuristic purposes. To what extent a product of scientific thought is supported by fact is an important question. Indeed, this question is so important that it has its own subfield within the philosophy of science, namely confirmation theory. Our question is prior to the question of confirmation theory. We ask: what is the thing about which one can later ask whether, and if so to what degree, it is confirmed by evidence? For this reason, we do not use "model" as a qualifier of evidential support.

Other uses of "model" are so obviously out of line with the topic of this book that there should be no danger of confusion. "Model" can be used as a synonym for "notion" or "conception", for instance when we speak of the "the ancient model of the atom" or "the enlightenment model of free speech". A model can be something that serves as a template for the production of something else, for instance when we say that medieval guilds provided the model for the first universities in the 11th and 12th centuries. A model can also be a method or recipe for achieving something, for instance when we say that contractarianism is the justificatory model in social systems governed by social rules. The department's "model student" is an example to be emulated. Ford's *Model T* and the latest model of the *MacBook Air* are particular products. Little Jimmy's model railway is a toy. And then there are models who do not wake up for less than ten thousand dollars a day. Regimenting language is neither possible nor desirable, but it ought to be clear that "model" is not used in any of these meanings in this book.

"Theory" descends from the ancient Greek term *theōría*, which is closely related to *theōrós* (spectator). So *theōría* literally means something like *the spectator's view* and evokes the acts of *watching* or *observing*. It has subsequently been used to mean *consideration* and *speculation*. In the 16th century "theory" came to refer to the conceptual basis of a subject area of study and the principles of a field. This is a workable first indication of the meaning of "theory" in the context of contemporary science, and we will develop this conception further in this book. However, like "model", "theory" has also acquired a number of divergent and, at least in the current context, unhelpful meanings, which we have to set aside. In a reversal of the tentative character supposedly expressed by "model", a theory is sometimes seen as something with a secure foundation, or as a true description of reality.[1] Usage, however, is not uniform and "theory" can also have the exact opposite meaning. Before making an MRI scan, doctors have a theory that a tumour is benign, but they will be able to confirm this only once they have the results; you can have a theory that your neighbour does not pay his taxes; and scientist urge caution by exclaiming "oh, well, that's just a theory!". Whichever way one wants to use "theory", as previously noted, degrees of confirmation are not our concern here and so we set these uses of "theory" aside.

Sometimes "theory" is contrasted with "practice". Something is said to be a "theory" if it belongs to the realm of unsullied contemplation and if it is antithetical to action. When confronted with an impractical suggestion an engineer might dismiss it as something that "works only in theory"; branding a claim as "correct in theory" is tantamount to saying that it is unworkable; and halfway through the exam period a student may become resigned to the view that there is now "only a theoretical possibility" of still getting a first-class honours degree. While not infrequent in idiomatic expressions, the use of "theory" as a euphemism for the unachievable is irrelevant to our discussion. And, as an afterthought, we might add that it is often also unjustified – the history of many technical innovations (just think of radio transmission and GPS) testifies to the fact that there is nothing more practical than a good theory!

Now that we have identified the relevant senses of "model" and "theory", we are in a position to ask what models and theories are and how they operate. Our discussion of these questions begins with the movement of logical empiricism which gained prominence in the 1920s.[2] There is a degree of arbitrariness to every cut-off, and my own is no exception. One could have begun the discussion with Poincaré, Duhem and Mach, or with the great "philosophical physicists" of the late 19th century, Boltzmann, Hertz, Kelvin, and Maxwell. Or maybe with Mill and Hume, or . . . . There is something to be said for each of these potential choices. However, while undoubtedly these authors made important contributions, the focus on theories and models as we know it from current debates only crystallised in the work of the logic empiricists. It is only through their work that "models and theories" became a recognisable subfield of the philosophy of science. This motivates my choice to take logical empiricism as the starting point of the discussion.

The arrangement of the material in the book is broadly chronological, beginning with logical empiricism and ending with topics that have emerged only relatively recently. This could give the impression that this is a historical book. It is not. The focus of the discussion is systematic: it is concerned with the tenability of arguments and the cogency of accounts, rather than with historical figures and their intellectual trajectories. The broadly historical arrangement of the material is a ploy to make the arguments easier to follow because certain positions become intelligible only when contrasted with their predecessors and when discussed against certain backgrounds. The qualification "broadly" is essential. Throughout the book I make a conscious effort to emphasise how historical positions bear on contemporary problems. It is indeed one of the theses of this book that positions that have long been assigned to the dust bin of history turn out to be surprisingly relevant to contemporary concerns when given a fresh reading. Readers will be confronted with current problems and concerns from the outset, and they will not have to fight their way through long chapters dealing with material that is only of historical interest to finally get "back to the future" at the end of the book.

The book is divided into four parts, and every part has four chapters. I will now introduce the content and objectives of the four parts, and then give an overview of the individual chapters.

Part I is concerned with what I call the *Linguistic View of Theories* (the *Linguistic View*, for short), broadly the view that a scientific theory is a description of its subject matter in a formal language. The Linguistic View is better known as the "syntactic view of theories", but, as we will see, this is a misnomer and I prefer the descriptively more accurate label "Linguistic View of Theories". The view is closely associated with logical empiricism and is widely believed to have departed for good when logical empiricism perished in the 1960s. So some readers may wonder: why begin a book on models and theories with a discussion of a philosophical position that is long gone?

The answer is that reports of the death of the Linguistic View have been premature. Engaging in an extensive discussion of the Linguistic View is not an act of philosophical necrophilia; it is an expression of the conviction that there is much of contemporary interest to be learned from it. Specifically, it is one of the contentions of this book that the divide between linguistic and non-linguistic conceptions of theories is a false dichotomy, and that the anti-linguistic turn that happened in the philosophy of science around 1960 was a mistake.[3] Theories have both linguistic and non-linguistic elements, and the challenge for an analysis of theories is to show how they work together and how they can be integrated into a consistent whole. A reflection on the Linguistic View is a starting point for this project. Readers who remain unconvinced that topics and positions associated with the Linguistic View have much life left in them should find these chapters useful for another reason. Love it or hate it, the modern discussion about the nature of models and theories has its origins in logical empiricism, and the positions and doctrines of the logical empiricists still provide the backdrop against which many debates unfold. Familiarity with these positions and doctrines is therefore a *sine qua non* for everybody who wishes to partake in contemporary discussions. Those who remain unconvinced of the systematic value of the Linguistic View may read these chapters as providing the necessary background for what is to follow.

The demise of the Linguistic View marks a branching point in the discussion. Those who shared the logical empiricists' emphasis on formal analysis but thought that this analysis had to proceed along different lines gathered under the umbrella of the *Model-Theoretical View of Theories* (*Model-Theoretical View*, for short), broadly the view that a scientific theory is a family of models. The proponents of this view usually self-identify as contributing to the "semantic view of theories", but for reasons that will become clear later, "semantic view of theories" is no less misleading than "syntactic view of theories" and is therefore a label that is best avoided. We discuss the Model-Theoretical View in Part II.

Those who not only disagreed with how the logical empiricists put formal methods to use but also regarded the emphasis on formal methods as unhelpful to begin with took a different route. While sharing the Model-Theoretical View's emphasis on models, they intended to avoid the view's reliance on formal methods and aimed to develop a philosophical account of models through an analysis of scientific practice. We discuss this approach in Part IV. Philosophers working in that paradigm never formed a cohesive school of thought, and there is no umbrella notion under which they all could be subsumed. This is not accidental. Writers working in this tradition were committed to developing their views in close proximity to scientific practice and were generally wary of overarching programmes and rational reconstructions. A certain degree of disunity is the inevitable consequence of this philosophical outlook. Writing about a movement that is by its very nature dispersive is difficult, and so there is a temptation to group the ungroupable. Occasionally this is done by subsuming philosophers working in this intellectual tradition under the umbrella of the "models as mediators programme". This is not entirely fortunate. "Models as mediators" was the name of a particular research project on models carried out at LSE in the 1990s, as well as the title of an influential book that came out of the project. While the project is located squarely within this intellectual tradition, the tradition itself goes back to the 1950s and has a longer and more diverse history than the "models as mediators" project. If one had to coin a label, then *Models in Scientific Practice Programme* would probably be a fitting option, and the models as mediators project would be a particular project falling under that label.

The discussions of the Model-Theoretical View in Part II and the Models in Scientific Practice Programme in Part IV are connected by a discussion of scientific representation, which is the focus of Part III. The reason for placing a discussion of scientific representation in-between the discussions of the two main approaches to models is that the question of how models represent their target systems has already become a focal point in various places in Part II, and important points of contention between the Model-Theoretical View and the Models in Scientific Practice Programme turn on how the relation between models and their targets is construed. So Part III both brings a discussion that started in Part II to a conclusion and lays the groundwork for the discussion of the Models in Scientific Practice Programme in Part IV. Beyond this strategic role, Part III deals with an important topic in its own right: how models relate to the parts or aspects of the world that they are about. This problem has a universal and a specific aspect. The universal aspect concerns a discussion of scientific representation in general, and we will discuss a number of different accounts of scientific representation. The specific aspect concerns particular model-world relations that play an important role in applications: analogy, idealisation, abstraction and approximation. Understanding these relations is crucial, and a large portion of Part III is dedicated to analysing them.

Now that we are clear on the content of, and the relations between, the four parts, let us have a look at the core arguments of the individual chapters.[4] The four chapters of Part I discuss different aspects of the Linguistic View. In Chapter 1 we articulate the Linguistic View and defend it against a number of criticisms which, if successful, would immediately undermine the view. We glean the basic tenets of the Linguistic View by looking at how Newton developed his mechanics in his *Philosophiae Naturalis Principia Mathematica*, and we then work our way toward a general formulation of the view, which has become known as the Received View of Theories. We then discuss four objections against the view: that it is committed to kind of logic that is too weak to capture any serious mathematics; that it regards theories as purely syntactical items; that it is committed to absurd identity criteria for theories; and that it fails to illuminate how theories operate in scientific practice. We will see that these objections miss their target. It is therefore justified to take the Linguistic View seriously and see how its various aspects can be developed.

In Chapter 2 we discuss what role models play in the Received View. We begin by distinguishing between two different types of models: representational models and logical models. The former are representations of a target system; the latter are items that make a formal sentence true if the sentence is interpreted as describing the model. The Received View employs the latter notion and sees models as alternative interpretations of a theory's formalism. This notion of a model provides the entry ticket to formal semantics, which plays an important role both in the discussion of the Received View and in the development of the Model-Theoretical View. We discuss the notion of a set-theoretical structure on which this semantics is based, along with the notion of two structures being isomorphic. This leads to a discussion of the expressive power of first-order logic, which also involves a discussion of two famous results in formal logic, the Löwenheim-Skolem theorem and Gödel's first incompleteness theorem. Insights gained in this discussion will also be important when assessing the Model-Theoretical View in Chapter 5.

After this discussion of the formal aspects of a theory, we turn to the relation between theory and observation. In Chapter 3 we see that understanding this relation led logical empiricists to bifurcate a theory's vocabulary into observation terms and theoretical terms. The former are terms like "red" that refer to observables, while the latter are terms like "electron" that (purportedly) refer to unobservables. This bifurcation faces three important objections: that the *epistemic* distinction between observables and unobservables fails to translate into a *linguistic* distinction between different terms; that there is no clear line between what is observable and what is unobservable; and that observation is always theory-laden. These are serious objections, and the most promising way to circumvent them is to bifurcate a theory's vocabulary differently, namely between antecedently understood and new terms. Observations are often made and recorded in the form of data, and the raw data gathered in experiments are processed to form data models. We study how observations are distilled into data models, and we get clear on what this process involves.

As we have seen, the Received View relies on a bifurcation of a theory's vocabulary into observation terms and theoretical terms. While it seems clear, at least prima facie, what the meaning of observation terms is, the same cannot be said of theoretical terms. In Chapter 4 we address the question of how theoretical terms acquire meaning. We begin our discussion with verificationism, and then go through the important empiricist responses to the problem: explicit definitions, implicit definitions, reduction sentences, interpretative systems, meaning from models, elimination either through Craig's theorem or the Ramsey sentence, the Carnap sentence, Hilbert's ε-operator, and definite descriptions. We then turn to the alternative realist programme, which regards theoretical terms as being on par with observation terms: both refer to things in the world. We end the chapter with a discussion of the causal-historical theory of reference, which explains how exactly terms can do this.

As we have seen previously, the Linguistic View was followed by the Model-Theoretical View, which is the focus of the chapters in Part II. Chapter 5 begins with a detailed discussion of Suppes' structuralist version of the Model-Theoretical View, which regards a theory as a family of models and models are taken to be set-theoretical structures. This helps structuring the discussion in this part of the book because other formulations of the view build on Suppes' account in various ways. One of the core issues in the Model-Theoretical View is the role of language. The view construes theories as non-linguistic entities, and by banning language from theories it aims to excise the issues we encountered in Chapters 2 to 4. The question of when two theories are identical provides a conundrum for this view, and through a discussion of this issue we will reach the conclusion that language is an important part of a theory that cannot be omitted. The challenge for a tenable account of theories is therefore to integrate linguistic and non-linguistic elements in a cogent way. In the last section of the Chapter, I sketch an account that tries to do this, which I call the "dual view" of theories.

In Chapter 6 we raise the question of how an account that regards a theory as a family of models, understood as set-theoretical structures, analyses the relation of a theory to its intended subject matter. This is the fundamental problem of scientific representation: how do the models of a theory represent their target systems? We start our discussion of this question with a reflection on the problem itself because on closer inspection it becomes clear that there is no such thing as "the" problem of scientific representation. We distinguish between five different questions that an account of representation must answer, and we formulate five conditions of adequacy that a successful answer to these questions must meet. This provides the lens through which we analyse the two accounts of representation that are implicit in the structuralist version of the Model-Theoretical View: the Data Matching Account and the Morphism Account. The former says that models must have substructures that are isomorphic to data models of the kind we encountered in Chapter 3; the latter says that target systems themselves have structures and models are isomorphic to them. We conclude that neither provides a satisfactory account of representation: the Data Matching Account conflates evidential support with representation, and the Morphism Account only provides incomplete answers to the problems of representation. So the issue of representation is left unresolved in the structuralist version of the Model-Theoretical View.

In Chapter 7 we look at the internal organisation of a theory. The basic posit of the Model-Theoretical View is that a theory is a family of models. But not any collection of models is theory, and so far little has been said about what binds this family together. What are the "family ties" between the models of a theory? The most detailed answer to this question has been given in a research programme known as *Munich Structuralism*. This programme offers a comprehensive answer to the question of what connects the models of a theory. We articulate this answer and introduce the programme's core notion of a theory-net. As an added benefit, this analysis of the internal organisation of theories offers a new perspective on the problem of theory-ladenness of observation. We discuss what this perspective involves and relate it back to the discussion in Chapter 3.

The versions of the Model-Theoretical View discussed in Chapters 5 to 7 are structuralist versions because they regard the models of a theory as set-theoretical structures and analyse both how models represent and how models relate to one another in structural terms. In Chapter 8 we discuss two alternative accounts. The first regards models as abstract entities and analyses representation in terms of similarity: a model represents its target due to being similar to it. Using the five questions and five conditions for an account of representation from Chapter 6, we scrutinise the similarity account of representation and find it wanting in various ways. The second alternative account regards models as abstract replicas and explicates representation in terms of idealisation and abstraction. This proposal moves the debate in an interesting direction, but remains too skeletal to provide a tenable account of representation. So, again, the issue of representation is left unresolved.

An important conclusion that emerges from the discussion in Part II is that even though scientific representation is a core problem for any account of models and theories, no tenable account of representation has emerged from the Model-Theoretical View. The chapters in Part III focus on this problem. Chapter 9 is dedicated to an examination of alternative accounts of representation that have emerged in recent discussions. We introduce and discuss the positions that sail under the flags of General Griceanism, direct representation, inferentialism, representation-as, and DEKI. Some of these offer promising alternatives to the accounts we have discussed in Part II.

Many of the accounts of representation discussed in Chapter 9 are "overarching" accounts. They pin down the general structure of how representation works, but they require as inputs in various places specific model-world relationships. The three chapters that follow provide analyses of some of the most important relations of this kind. Chapter 10 discusses analogies and analogical models. We begin by offering a general characterisation of analogies and then discuss some important kinds of analogies, chief among them formal analogies, material analogies and functional analogies. We then turn to different uses of analogies and discuss first analogical models – models that relate to their target systems by analogy – and then review the heuristic use of analogies in theory construction. We end with a discussion of the relation between analogies and metaphors.

The next two chapters discuss idealisations. Chapter 11 begins by distinguishing between the closely related, but as we will see different, concepts of idealisation, approximation, and abstraction. In doing so we provide analyses of abstraction and approximation. Idealisation turns out to be more difficult to circumscribe, and an extensive discussion of attempts to define idealisations leads us to the conclusion that there is no unified definition. As a result, a discussion of idealisation has to proceed in a piecemeal manner, introducing different kinds of idealisations and analysing them one by one. This is the project for Chapter 12, where we discuss two important types of idealisations: limit idealisations and factor exclusions. Limit idealisations push a certain property to an extreme, for instance by regarding a slippery surface as frictionless; a factor exclusion amounts to omitting a certain factor entirely, for instance by disregarding the collision of particles in a gas. After providing some mathematical background on limits, we present an analysis of limit idealisations and factor exclusions, and we discuss their consequences for our understanding of what information we can gain from idealised models about their target systems.

The chapters in Part IV of the book are concerned with models as they are used in scientific practice. Chapter 13 reconsiders the relation between models and theories. As we have seen, the Linguistic View and the Model-Theoretical View both see models as subordinate to theories, albeit in very different ways. For the Linguistic View, they are alternative interpretations of a theory's formalism; for the Model-Theoretical View, they are the building blocks of theories. Neither of these visions does justice to the way models operate in practice, where they can stand in different and complex relations to theories. We discuss a number of model-theory relations ranging from total independence to close alliance, and we then ask whether, and how, the Model-Theoretical View could account for these relations.

If models are divorced from theory, the question of what models are appears in a new light. This is the topic of Chapter 14. We begin our discussion by distinguishing between an ontological and functional reading of the question. On the former, the question is what kind of things model objects are; on the latter, the question is what it means for something for function as a model. We discuss different answers and come to the sober conclusion that there is no definition of what a model is, neither ontologically nor functionally. Nevertheless, it is an interesting question what kinds of things usually do serve as models. To put the question into focus, we formulate five desiderata that an account of model objects must satisfy. These desiderata are less pressing in the case of material models, physical objects like ship-shaped blocks of wood and systems of waterpipes and reservoirs. However, they become important in the context of non-material models. We discuss set-theoretical structures, abstract objects, descriptions, mathematical objects, equations, computational structures, fictional objects, and artefacts as potential model objects, and we conclude that upon closer analysis there are only two kinds of models: mathematical models and fictional models. We then formulate an account of fictional models that meets the challenges.

In many contexts, scientific communities end up producing a multiplicity of models of the same target system. Nuclear physics and climate science are paradigmatic examples of disciplines where this happens. This is puzzling: why do scientists do this and how to they handle these "multi-model situations"? In Chapter 15 we first discuss the motivations for constructing multiple models of the same target, and then discuss different ways of approaching the resulting "model ensembles": robustness analysis, perspectivism, and uncertainty management. We identify the situations in which they are appropriate and discuss their pros and cons.

Models proliferate. Those delving into the literature on scientific models will find a bewildering array of model types. A recent, but almost certainly incomplete, count returned over 120 different model types. This is disorientating and perplexing. Chapter 16 aims to impose some order on this "model muddle" by briefly introducing each model type, explaining how different model types relate to one another, and sorting the different types into broad groups. This will make the collection of models easier to understand and handle.

The book ends with an Envoi.

Space constraints rendered it impossible to include discussions of theory change, inter-theory relations, laws of nature, scientific explanation, scientific understanding, confirmation, thought experiments, measurement theory, mechanisms, computer simulations, and the roles of models in the special sciences in this book. I hope that the richness of the material covered in the book compensates for these, and indeed other, omissions.

There is nothing pleonastic about noting that the chapters of this book have been written as book chapters. They were not previously published as papers, and they are designed to build on each other and to contribute to an unfolding narrative. This said, I have tried to make the chapters self-contained, and so they are also readable in isolation. Unfortunately, the linearity of writing does not always do justice to the winding paths of thought and to the complex interrelations of various topics. I have tried to mitigate the tension between the linear progression of a text and the complexity of the relations between ideas by adding signposts and cross references, indicting how the materials in different parts of the book are related.

Some sections in the book are technically more demanding than others in that they rely on results from formal logic or make extensive use of symbolic notation. Sections of this kind are marked with an asterisk. Readers with limited enthusiasm for logic and formal material can skip these sections without losing the thread because the book is written so that nothing in later parts builds on material in the asterisked sections. Finally, as is common in analytic philosophy, I use "iff" as a shorthand for "if and only if", and " := " indicates a definition (with the definiendum on the side of the colon).

Notes

1 This conception of "theory" can also be found in the philosophical literature. See, for instance, Achinstein's (1968, 215), Hesse's (1967, 355–356), Redhead's (1980, 147), and Wimsatt's (1987, 23).
2 There is a question concerning labels. I here follow Creath (2017) in using "logical empiricism" as an umbrella term covering the entire movement, including the Vienna Circle. Sometimes the label "logical positivism" is used to refer to the philosophy of Vienna Circle, and distinguished from the "logical empiricism" of the Berlin Society for Scientific Philosophy (Salmon 2000, 233). Other times the line between the two is drawn along continental boundaries: "logical positivism" is taken to denote what happened in Europe before World War II and "logical empiricism" is taken to refer what became of that movement in North America after the war. However, as Creath (2017, Sec. 1) notes, fundamentally the term "logical empiricism" has no precise boundaries, and there is little to distinguish it from "logical positivism".
3 Or, if one follows Rorty (1967) in seeing the *linguistic turn* as one of the major developments in early 20th century philosophy, then one might describe the events around 1960 as the anti-linguistic U-turn.
4 What follows is not a complete synopsis of each chapter. I focus on the main line of argument of each chapter with the aim of making visible how the chapters hang together.

References

Achinstein, P. 1968. *Concepts of Science: A Philosophical Analysis*. Baltimore: Johns Hopkins Press.
Creath, R. 2017. Logical Empiricism. In E. N. Zalta (ed.), *The Stanford Encyclopedia of Philosophy*. https://plato.stanford.edu/archives/fall2017/entries/logical-empiricism/.
Goodman, N. 1976. *Languages of Art* (2nd ed.). Indianapolis and Cambridge: Hacket.
Hesse, M. B. 1967. Models and Analogy in Science. In P. Edwards (ed.), *Encyclopedia of Philosophy*. New York: Macmillan, pp. 354–359.
Redhead, M. 1980. Models in Physics. *The British Journal for the Philosophy of Science* 31: 145–163.
Rorty, R. M. (ed.) 1967. *The Linguistic Turn. Essays in Philosophical Method*. Chicago: Chicago University Press.
Salmon, W. C. 2000. Logical Empiricism. In W. H. Newton-Smith (ed.), *A Companion to the Philosophy of Science*. Malden: Blackwell, pp. 233–242.
Wimsatt, W. C. 1987. False Models as Means to Truer Theories. In M. H. Nitecki and A. Hoffman (eds.), *Neutral Models in Biology*. New York and Oxford: Oxford University Press, pp. 23–55.

PART I

1

THEORY AND LANGUAGE

1.1 Introduction

Theories lie at the heart of many scientific disciplines. But what kind of objects are scientific theories? In this chapter we discuss a family of approaches that take theories to be linguistic objects: descriptions of their subject matter. To introduce and motivate the view, we begin by looking at Newtonian mechanics, one of the most important and successful theories in the history of science. Following Newton's own discussion, we get acquainted with the broad outlines of a linguistic understanding of theories (Section 1.2). The picture of theories implicit in Newton's discussion can be summarised in what I call the Linguistic View of Theories. What has become known as the Received View of Theories, the vision of theories developed by logical empiricists, is a specific version of the Linguistic View of Theories according to which a theory is an interpreted axiomatic system (Section 1.3). The Received View faces a number of difficult questions, and it has been confronted with a number of criticisms. In the second half of this chapter we review a number of objections to the Received View that would immediately pull the rug from underneath the view if they were successful. The objections are that the view is committed to a system of logic that is too weak to capture the mathematics that most scientific theories rely on (Section 1.4); that the view regards theories as purely syntactical items bare of any semantics and that it both hinders and misconstrues scientific progress (Section 1.5); that it is committed to absurd identity criteria for theories (Section 1.6*); and that it is untenable because it fails to capture what theories look like in scientific practice (Section 1.7). We will see that these objections are based on misunderstandings, misattributions, and non-sequiturs, and that they fail to undermine the Received View. This justifies taking the view seriously and following some of its important developments closely (Section 1.8).

DOI: 10.4324/9781003285106-3

1.2 A Glimpse at Newtonian Mechanics

Newton's *Philosophiae Naturalis Principia Mathematica* (*Principia*, for short) is one of the most significant contributions to science of all time (the Latin title means "the mathematical principles of natural philosophy"). It presents what we nowadays call *Newtonian mechanics*. First published in 1687 (with second and third editions in 1713 and 1726 respectively), it had a tremendous influence on the course of modern physics, and its core ideas remain influential today. For this reason, *Principia* is a good place to look for an answer to the question of what a scientific theory is.

Principia begins with a chapter entitled "Definitions". In this chapter Newton presents eight definitions in which he defines the central terms of his theory.[1] In the first definition he introduces the notion of the "quantity of matter" (1726/1999, 49), which we now call *mass*. The second definition presents the notion of the "quantity of motion", which he defines as "a measure of motion that arises from the velocity and the quantity of matter jointly" (*ibid.*, 50).[2] In modern terminology this is the definition of *momentum p*, which is the product of the mass m and the velocity v of a particle: $p = mv$. The other six definitions concern different kinds of forces. The eight definitions are followed by a *Scholium* (an explanatory comment) in which Newton explains that "[t]hus far it has seemed best to explain the senses in which less familiar words are to be taken in this treatise" (*ibid.*, 54). He immediately adds that the definitions do not cover all words that he will use because he does not define words that are "very familiar to everyone" (*ibid.*, 54). Newton thinks that "space", "time", "place", and "motion" are words that are very familiar to everyone, and he adds that "the meanings of words are to be defined by usage" (*ibid.*, 59). Hence, Newton took the meaning of these words to be manifest to his readers.

The second chapter is called "Axioms, or the Laws of Motion". In this chapter Newton formulates his famous laws of motion, which are still an integral part of every textbook of mechanics. The first law is the *law of inertia*: "Every body perseveres in its state of being at rest or of moving uniformly straight forward except insofar as it is compelled to change its state by forces impressed" (*ibid.*, 62). The second law says: "A change in motion is proportional to the motive force impressed and takes place along the straight line in which that force is impressed" (*ibid.*, 62). In modern notion the second law is the equation $\vec{F} = m\vec{a}$, where $\vec{F}$ is the force acting on the particle (the arrow indicates that the force is a vector, i.e. has direction in space) and $\vec{a}$ is the object's acceleration (which is also a vector). The second law is nowadays also known as *Newton's equation of motion*. The third law is the *action-reaction principle*: "To any action there is always an opposite and equal reaction; in other words, the actions of two bodies upon each other are always equal and always opposite in direction" (*ibid.*, 63). In the *Scholium* at the end of the chapter Newton observes that these laws are "confirmed by experiments of many kinds" (*ibid.*, 70).

The next chapter states a number of "lemmas" (a lemma is a subsidiary or intermediate theorem). These lemmas are mainly geometrical propositions, which are not concerned with forces or motion. However, they are useful in derivations because, as Newton puts it, "[w]hat has been demonstrated concerning curved lines and the [plane] surfaces comprehended by them is easily applied to curved surfaces and their solid contents." (*ibid.*, 87). In other words, the lemmas of pure geometry can be used to describe the physical situations Newton is interested in.

With the lemmas in place, Newton states various "propositions". Some of the propositions are "problems", but most of them are "theorems" (*ibid.*, 90ff.). Theorems are propositions that can be inferred from definitions, axioms, lemmas and other propositions that have been stated earlier. The first theorem, for instance, states that "[t]he areas which bodies made to move in orbits describe by radii drawn to an unmoving center of forces lie in unmoving planes and are proportional to the times" (*ibid.*, 90). In the proof Newton appeals to his first law of motion and the third lemma. To prove his theorems, Newton tacitly appeals to a background logic that allows him to deduce propositions from other propositions.

The bulk of *Principia* (after the first theorem there are still over 500 pages to come!) is by and large concerned with deducing results from previously established propositions and axioms. Some of the most celebrated of these appear towards the end where Newton establishes the law of general gravity (*ibid.*, 448–460), which says that two bodies are attracted to each other by a force that is proportional to the product of the masses of the two bodies and inversely proportional to the square of the distance. In contemporary notation the law reads $\vec{F} = \vec{e}\,Gm_1 m_2 / r^2$, where m_1 and m_2 are the masses of the two objects, r is the distance between the two, G is the constant of gravitation, and $\vec{e}$ is the vector pointing from the first to the second body. From this Newton derives a theorem saying that "[t]he planets move in ellipses that have a focus in the center of the sun, and by radii drawn to that center they describe areas proportional to the times" (*ibid.*, 463). This is in fact a statement of Kepler's first and second laws of planetary motion, which Newton managed to derive from his own laws of motion and the law of gravity.

To derive Kepler's laws, Newton (tacitly) assumes that the gravitational interaction between the sun and the planet is the only force relevant to the planet's motion and that all other forces, most notably the gravitational interaction between the planet and other objects in the universe, are negligible. It is furthermore assumed that both the sun and the planet are perfect spheres with a homogenous mass distribution (meaning that the mass is evenly distributed within the sphere), which implies that the gravitational interaction between the planet and the sun behaves as if the entire mass of each object was concentrated in its centre.[3] Since the sun's mass is vastly larger than the mass of the planet, the calculations also assume that the sun is at rest and the planet orbits around it. With these assumptions in place, the result can be derived. The set of these assumptions, or the fictionalised object to which these assumptions refer, are now known as the Newtonian model of planetary motion.

1.3 The Linguistic View and the Received View

Although Newton does not articulate an explicit account of the nature of scientific theories, there is a view of the structure of scientific theories implicit in his presentation of mechanics. For Newton, a theory is a linguistic entity. He begins his discussion by defining terms and reflecting on their meaning, and he then formulates "propositions" and "theorems". But not any linguistic entity is a theory. A newspaper article, no matter how detailed, is not a theory; and neither is a traveller's account of her journey. Plausibly, one can identify three conditions on a theory in Newton's discussion:

(L1) The language in which the theory is formulated has a logical structure that allows scientists to derive propositions from other propositions and to formulate proofs of theorems.

(L2) A theory contains general principles, or axioms, which are the theory's laws.

(L3) The language of the theory contains terms that are understood prior to the formulation of the theory, as well as technical terms that are introduced in the context of the theory (and are therefore intelligible only in that context).

A short version of (L3) says that the language of the theory is divided into "old" and "new" terms, where the old terms are known and understood before the theory is formulated while the new terms originate in the theory itself. For obvious reasons I call this the *Linguistic View of Theories* (*Linguistic View*, for short). This view provides the starting point for our discussion of theories.

As we have seen, Newton also mentions that his laws are confirmed by experiments. This raises the question of whether having empirical support, or being confirmed, ought to be part of the notion of a scientific theory. There are arguments either way, but not including confirmation in the *notion* of a scientific theory is the more natural choice. This makes room for a scientific theory to be confirmed or unconfirmed, to be still under investigation, or indeed to have been disconfirmed or even refuted. If scientific theories were *ipso facto* confirmed, then there could never be a question concerning the evidential support for a scientific theory; nor could a scientific theory ever turn out to be false. Such a usage of the term would not sit well with the way in which scientists speak about theories.

Newtonian mechanics is not a special case. In fact, at least as far as physics is concerned, theories generally conform to the picture of theories that arises from *Principia*. Maxwell's theory of electromagnetism, the special theory of relativity, the general theory of relativity, quantum mechanics, thermodynamics, and at least certain formulations of quantum field theory (most notably axiomatic quantum field theory) all fit the mould of the Linguistic View: they use a mathematical language that provides the inferential resources to make deductions and formulate proofs; they have at their core general equations that are the axioms or laws of the theory (Maxwell's equations, the Lorentz transformations, Einstein's field equation, the Schrödinger equation, and so on); and the terms of their language are a mixture of descriptive terms that were understood prior to the formulation of the theory and technical terms that are specific to the theory.

An early explicit philosophical analysis of scientific theories arose in the philosophical movement of *logical empiricism*. The movement's epicentre was the Vienna Circle in the 1920s and 1930s, but groups contributing to the movement were active in other places around Europe, most notably Berlin.[4] The analysis of the nature of scientific theories that arose in logical empiricism is nowadays known under many different names, most notably as the "received view" and as the "syntactic view".[5] For reasons that will soon become clear, "syntactic view" is a misnomer and so I will use "received view" throughout (and I will capitalise it to indicate that the term is used as a name).

The Received View is a qualification and elaboration of the Linguistic View. This is no coincidence. Logical empiricists were firmly committed to a scientifically informed philosophy and had the declared aim of producing philosophical views that were not only in line, but in fact continuous, with science. We now introduce the Received View with reference to the Linguistic View, making explicit where it builds on it and where it goes beyond it.[6]

Let us begin with (L1). In his proofs and derivations Newton made use of certain principles of logical inference, but the appeal to these principles was tacit, and Newton did not articulate what the principles were. Logical empiricists regarded logic as crucial for the analysis of philosophical problems, and the reliance on logic was a declared part of their philosophical programme, hence the "logical" in "logical empiricism". In this they were in line with the broader programme of analytical philosophy, which was crucially linked to advances in formal logic and which saw logic as a crucial tool in discussions of philosophical problems. Ordinary language was seen as marred with imprecisions and ambiguities, and formulating a philosophical problem in a precise formal language was seen as a necessary step towards a solution. For this reason, the logical empiricists stipulated that a scientific theory had be expressed in a system of formal logic.[7] Logical empiricists remained non-committal about the precise nature of this system and only insisted that there had to be *a* formal system. We will return to the issue of the choice of a formal system in the next section.

In line with the Linguistic View's (L2), the Received View posits that at the heart of a scientific theory lie general principles. Since the entire theory has to be formulated in a language of formal logic, the general principles themselves are also formulated in that language. This brings us to a qualification. For Newton "law" and "axiom" could be used interchangeably. In modern logic, however, axioms are understood as purely formal items: they are well-formed strings of symbols in the formal language of the logical system. An axiom thus understood is not a law. A formal sentence becomes a law only when the symbols occurring in the sentence are *interpreted* in terms of the theory's subject matter (more about interpretation soon). The string "$\vec{F} = m\vec{a}$" is a law of mechanics only if "$\vec{F}$" is interpreted as force, "m" as mass, and "$\vec{a}$" as acceleration. Without such an interpretation " $\vec{F} = m\,\vec{a}$ " would be merely a string of symbols. A formal axiom becomes a law when it is endowed with a physical interpretation (Carnap 1938, 199).[8]

There are two related reasons for the requirement that a theory must have laws. The first reason is that laws make general statements about a subject matter. They lay bare relations between properties and describe these relations in an efficient way. The world contains a myriad of moving objects: falling stones, orbiting planets, oscillating pendula, accelerating rockets, and so on. A description of each individual motion, even if it could somehow be produced, would be unmanageably long and would provide little, if any, insight into how objects move and why they move in the way in which they do. Newtonian mechanics subsumes all instances of motion under one simple law, $\vec{F} = m\,\vec{a}$. In this way it accounts for what all motions have in common and provides an explanation for their dynamical behaviour. Depending on one's interpretation of these general statements, they either "govern" what happens in the world, or they provide the most effective summary of the processes in the theory's domain.[9] Either way, laws provide a systematic and general statement of the interconnections between relevant physical properties and thereby provide a compact statement of the core propositions of a theory.

The second reason for having laws has to do with the formal aspect of laws, their axiomatic character. Earlier we said that axioms are strings of symbols in the formal language of the theory's logical system. This is true, but they are strings that have a special feature. Consider a set S of sentences formulated in the language of the theory. The so-called deductive closure $D(S)$ of S contains all sentences that can be deduced from S with the rules of logic contained in the language. If, for instance, S contains statements "p" and "if p then q", and the language contains *modus ponens*,[10] then $D(S)$ also contains "q" because "q" logically follows from "p" and "if p then q". S is *deductively closed*, iff forming the deductive closure does not "add" anything to S; that is, if taking S's deductive closure returns S itself: $S = D(S)$. We can then say that a theory, in formal terms, is a deductively closed set of sentences. That is, a theory T must satisfy the requirement $T = D(T)$ (Machover 1996, 216).

A set of axioms for a theory T is then not just any set of formal statements, but a set that satisfies $T = D(A)$: the theory is the deductive closure of the axioms. That is, if you take the axioms and deduce everything from them that the theory's language and its deductive apparatus permit, then you get the entire theory. Having a set of axioms is not per se a big deal. Trivially, a theory follows from itself and so a full statement of T is always also a set of axioms. To be interesting, A must be "smaller than" T and generate the entire theory from a small set of axioms. There is a good question concerning what "small" means, but at the very least it means that A should be finitely specifiable (Machover 1996, 238). Hence, we say that a theory T is axiomatisable if there exists a set A that can be specified by a *finite recipe* such that $T = D(A)$. If we have such recipe, then we see how everything follows from a small set of assumptions, and this offers great insight into the theory because we know what is guaranteed by the axioms.[11]

The most important part of the Received View is its articulation of (L3), which is also the aspect in which it diverges most from the Linguistic View. The crucial point in (L3) is that the terms of a theory fall into different groups that need to be dealt with differently. Logical empiricists agree with this broad idea, but see the relevant dividing line in a different place than Newton.

To formulate the problem properly, we first have to get clear on what kind of terms there are in a theory. The symbols of a formal language fall into two groups. The first group, *logical terms*, contains variables, connectives, quantifiers, and, if we work in logic with equality, the equality symbol. The second group, *extralogical terms* (sometimes *nonlogical terms*), contains individual constants, predicate and relation symbols, and function symbols. We call the bifurcation of the symbols into logical and extralogical the *first bifurcation*. This bifurcation matters to the development of the Received View because the two kinds of symbols raise different issues. Extralogical symbols have to be given an empirical interpretation. By contrast, logical symbols need no such interpretation. They are studied by logic and as far as the use of a logical system in the empirical sciences is concerned, they can be taken for granted.

The challenge then is to come to grips with extralogical symbols. Newton's distinction between terms that are "very familiar to everyone" and terms that have to be defined within a theory pertains to what the Received View calls extralogical terms. In principle, the logical empiricists could have stuck with Newton's distinction, but they drew the line in a different place. In fact, in drawing this line the "empiricism" in "logical empiricism" becomes relevant. Broadly speaking, *empiricism* is the doctrine that experience is the only source of knowledge. Everything we know ultimately stems from what we see, hear, touch, smell and taste. In other words, knowledge is *a posteriori*. Empiricism contrasts with rationalism according to which there are important ways to gain knowledge independently of experience. For rationalists there is *a priori* knowledge, and hence at least some truths about nature can be discovered by introspection. Empiricists, by contrast, insist that experience is the *sole* source of information about nature and reject the idea that there are facts about nature that can be recognised through reason alone. Accordingly, empiricists hold that the meaning of extralogical terms must be analysed in terms of experiences we make. A term acquires meaning by being connected to experience; terms that cannot, in one way or another, be connected to experience are meaningless.

Let us illustrate this basic idea with Hume's classic account of causality.[12] Causal claims form an important part of both science and everyday life. As an example, consider the claim "aspirin causes headaches to wane". Hume argues that we cannot experience causal relations in themselves: we see people take aspirins and soon thereafter we see them reporting that their headaches have gone, but the causal relation as such has no correlate in our sense experience. For this reason, Hume argues, we have to find the experiential basis of causal claims. In his analysis, causality is nothing but temporal succession, spatiotemporal contiguity and constant conjunction. He illustrates this with the example of a billiard ball crashing into another billiard ball and setting it in motion. The first ball colliding into the second ball is the cause of the second ball's motion because the motion of the first ball precedes the motion of the second ball; in the moment of the collision the two are spatiotemporally contiguous; and we see the same pattern repeat itself every time two balls collide. Hence the unobservable property of something causing something else has been traced back to the observable properties of succession, contiguity, and constant conjunction. And this is all that we can say about causation. No amount of introspection will teach us anything about causes beyond what we glean from experience, and the term "cause" has no meaning beyond the meaning it receives from the combination of "succession", "contiguity", and "constant conjunction".

The logical empiricists therefore took the relevant dividing line between different extralogical terms to be between terms whose application can be determined directly by observation and terms for which this is not possible. Terms of the former kind are called *observation terms*; terms of the latter kind are called *theoretical terms*.[13] In Hume's example, "temporal succession", "spatiotemporal contiguity", and "constant conjunction" are observation terms, and "cause" is a theoretical term. So rather than dividing terms into ones that are "very familiar to everyone" and ones that must be defined, logical empiricists divided terms into observation terms and theoretical terms.[14] This is the *second bifurcation*.

Observation terms are anchored in observation, but what are theoretical terms anchored in? The Received View postulates that theoretical terms are related to observation terms by so-called *correspondence rules*.[15] In general, correspondence rules connect a term that is not directly related to experience to a term, or terms, that are so related. In effect, Hume has introduced the explicit definition "C causes E iff E temporally succeeds C, C and E are spatiotemporally contiguous, and there is a constant conjunction between C and E". This is a correspondence rule because it connects the theoretical term "cause" to the observation terms "temporally succeeds", "spatiotemporally contiguous", and "constant conjunction" through a definition. As we will see later (in Chapter 4), explicit definitions are only a special kind of correspondence rule, and most of these rules have a different form. But for now we can take explicit definitions as our paradigm example of correspondence rule and use it to boost intuitions.

The observation terms of a theory taken together form the *observation vocabulary* of the theory, and the theoretical terms taken together form the theory's *theoretical vocabulary*. We obtain the *observation language* of the theory by adding a logical structure to the observation vocabulary (for instance by adding logical connectives like "and" and inferential rules like modus ponens). Likewise, we get a theory's *theoretical language* by adding a logical structure to the theoretical vocabulary (Suppe 1977, 50). Finally, the *formalism of a theory* is the logical system of a theory together with the (uninterpreted) axioms.

Gathering these elements, we can now give a statement of the basic tenets of the Received View. According to that view, a theory T is a linguistic entity that satisfies the following criteria:

(R1) T is formulated in an appropriate system of formal logic.

(R2) T contains axioms, which, when interpreted, are the theory's laws.

(R3)   The terms of T are divided into logical and extralogical terms (first bifurcation). The extralogical terms are further divided into observation terms and theoretical terms (second bifurcation). Observation terms are interpreted in terms of something that is given by observation. Theoretical terms are connected to observation terms by correspondence rules.

The Received View is sometimes summed up in the slogan that a theory is an interpreted axiomatic system, where "system" is owed to (R1), "axiomatic" to (R2) and "interpreted" to (R3).[16] Feigl (1970, 6) illustrated the view in the now-famous diagram reproduced in Figure 1.1. At the bottom is the "soil" of experience that is captured in "empirical concepts" (which are expressed through observation terms). In the upper part of the diagram there is the formalism of the theory, which consists of theoretical concepts that are connected to each other through postulates (our "axioms"). Some theoretical concepts are primitive (like Newton's

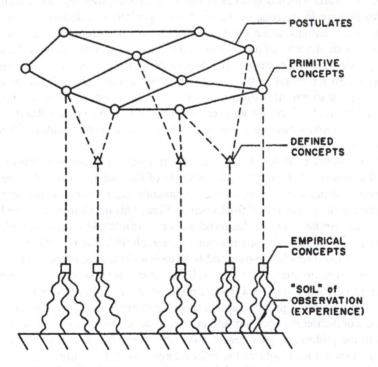

POSTULATES

PRIMITIVE
CONCEPTS

DEFINED
CONCEPTS

EMPIRICAL
CONCEPTS

"SOIL" of
OBSERVATION
(EXPERIENCE)

FIGURE 1.1 The Received View according to Feigl.

"force"), while others are defined through primitive concepts (for instance when we say that momentum is equal to mass times velocity). The theoretical concepts are connected to observation concepts through correspondence rules, which are symbolised by the dashed lines.

These are the broad outlines of the Received View as developed most prominently by Carnap and Hempel, as well as by Braithwaite, Nagel, and Schlick (see the references in Endnote 6).

The Received View is seen as inextricably linked to logical empiricism, and, so the story goes, when logical empiricism perished in the 1960s, the Received View perished with it. Craver captures the gist of this narrative when he refers to the view as the "once received view" (2002, 55). We will examine the arguments against the Received View in the chapters to come, but it is important to add a corrective to this narrative immediately. Analyses of theories *very much like* the Received View have been held – and keep being held – by philosophers who have no association with logical empiricism. For instance, in the third chapter of his *The Logic of Scientific Discovery*, entitled "Theories", Popper dedicates an entire section to the problem of "interpreting a system of axioms" (1959, 51–54), and throughout his work he emphasised the importance of testing observable consequences of theories. This requires an understanding of a theory as an interpreted axiomatic system. Likewise, at the heart of the so-called "best systems analysis" of laws of nature, which originates in the work of Mill, Ramsey, and Lewis, lies the idea that our knowledge of the world is organised in a deductive axiomatic system whose axioms strike the best balance between simplicity and strength. The axioms are the laws of nature and truths about the world follow as deductive consequence from the system.[17] The picture of a theory as an axiomatic logical system is also important in the scientific realism debate. One of the important articulations of structural realism works with the so-called *Ramsey Sentence* of a theory (Worrall 2007). As we will see in Section 4.6, appeal to the Ramsey Sentence requires understanding a theory as an axiomatic system with a bifurcated vocabulary.

This list is not complete by any means. It should be sufficient, however, to show that reports of the death of an analysis of theories in terms of interpreted axiomatic systems may well have been premature. We referred to such views as ones that are "very much like" the Received View. This needs to be qualified. The main differences between the Received View as formulated by logical empiricists and the views mentioned in the previous paragraph lie in their explication of the notion of an interpretation, most notably in their articulation, or indeed rejection, of the second bifurcation. There are substantial controversies around the issues of where to draw the line between the observable and the unobservable, and of whether such a line ought to be drawn at the level of language, as well as around the nature of theoretical concepts and their relation to observation. These are core issues in the philosophy of science, and they go right to the heart of the matter. But let us not lose sight of the relevant contrast. All positions mentioned so far are in agreement that theories are interpreted axiomatic systems, and there is no suggestion that theories are families of models, set-theoretic or otherwise, as the Model-Theoretical View has it. The disagreement concerns the articulation of details, not the broad contours of the view.

This is possible because the Received View is a special version of the Linguistic View. Arguments against the Received View are not *ipso facto* arguments against the Linguistic View, and even opponents of the Received View can still endorse the Linguistic View.[18] Indeed, there is a multitude of possible positions between the relatively broad Linguistic View and the relatively specific Received View, and those who reject, say, correspondence rules can still formulate a version of the Linguistic View that does not include correspondence rules.

In the remainder of this chapter, we discuss a number of immediate objections to the Received View. If these objections were successful, they would right away undermine the Received View and make further discussions superfluous. We will see that this is not the case. These objections are based on misattributions (Sections 1.4 and 1.6), misunderstandings (Section 1.5), or hasty conclusions (Sections 1.7). This clears the way for an examination of the serious issues that the Received View, and indeed the Linguistic View, face. In Chapter 2 we introduce models and discuss what role they play in the Received View. In Chapter 3 we discuss in detail the separation of a theory's vocabulary into observational and theoretical terms, and the dividing lines between observation and theory more generally. In Chapter 4 we discuss the role and function of theoretical terms, and how their meaning should be understood.

1.4 Exhaustive Axiomatisation and the First-Order Rumour

As we have seen in the previous section, the deductive closure of a set A of axioms for a theory must be the theory: $T = D(A)$. So far we intended a theory's axioms to be general statements like Newton's three laws of motion. There is an immediate problem with this way of thinking about axioms, namely that nothing much follows from Newton's laws of motion *on their own* and that therefore the deductive closure of Newton's laws would not be identical to what we usually regard as Newtonian mechanics. The source of the problem is obvious: Newton made extensive use of various mathematical background theories, which provided the relevant mathematical concepts and rules to run derivations and formulate proofs. Without these background theories the three Axioms are next to useless. One might say that this is little more than a matter of presentation. All we have to do to rectify the problem is to recognise a mathematical background theory B as one of the axioms to restore the picture: $T = D(A \& B)$. The exact nature of B would depend on the theoretical context, but would in most cases include elements of number theory, analysis, measure theory, probability theory, and algebra.

Suppes argues that this route is foreclosed to the Received View because the requirement of axiomatisation forces the view to explicitly write down the axioms of every mathematical concept that occurs in the theory. Discussing what he calls the "standard formalisation", he claims that axioms concerning "the joint occurrence of two events", "axioms about the real numbers", and "axioms that belong just to probability theory" all have to be explicitly written down in the axiomatisation of the theory (1992, 207; cf. 2002, 27). Lutz (2012, 88) calls this the requirement of "exhaustive axiomatisation". This requirement, Suppes argues, is undesirable because in "this welter of axioms" one loses sight of those that are specific to the theory at hand and because "it is senseless and uninteresting continually to repeat these general axioms on sets and on numbers whenever we consider formalizing a scientific theory"; indeed, the result of such an axiomatic reconstruction is "is too awkward and ungainly a theory to be of any use" (*ibid.*, 207–208).

Lutz takes Suppes to task for imposing a requirement on the Received View that it neither is, nor need to be, committed to (*ibid.*, 89–91). He argues that the Received View can appeal to background theories, and possibly even packages of theories, and that it can assume these as a background *without* explicitly listing them. Newtonian mechanics can assume number theory, algebra, analysis, and whatever else it needs as a given and it is under no obligation to write everything down explicitly. The Received View is not committed to starting *ab ovo* every time it axiomatises a theory. It can focus on those parts of the material that are specific to the theory and pack the "rest" into the background B, which is assumed to be developed elsewhere. This is standard scientific practice (a textbook on mechanics rarely, if ever, includes a chapter on, say, number theory), and the Received View can in principle adopt this practice without detriment.

The qualification "in principle" is crucial. The issue is that to be able to pack the background into a "B" that appears as a premise in arguments, the background must be available in a suitable axiomatic form, and there is a question about whether this is the case. To see what the worry is, we need to say more about the logic that is used in a theory. Neither (L1) nor (R1) are specific about the nature of the logical system in which a theory ought to be formulated. It has become part of the philosophical folklore to attribute to the Received View a firm commitment to first-order logic, a logic in which quantifiers only range over individuals. On this reading, (R1) should really say that T is formulated in first-order logic.[19]

The problem is that first-order logic has important limitations, and in as far as the Received View is committed to first-order logic it inherits these limitations. An important limitation is that many mathematical concepts cannot be expressed in first-order logic. As Barwise and Feferman note, notions like *continuous function, random variable, having probability greater than some real number r, countable set, infinite set*, and *set of measure zero* cannot be expressed in first-order logic (1985, 5–6).[20]

This is a problem for the requirement that a theory be axiomatised. If notions like *continuous function*, and *random variable* cannot be formalised in first-order logic, then B cannot be formalised in first-order logic and so the expression "$D(A \& B)$" is meaningless because there is no B in the theory's language to plug into it. From this it follows that scientific theories that use any of the formal tools that are beyond the grasp of first-order logic cannot be axiomatised in a first-order language. Since almost any theory makes use of such tools, it is concluded that almost no theory can be so axiomatised.[21]

If the Received View were indeed committed to first-order logic, this would be a serious problem. But it is not. The claim that the Received View is committed to first-order logic is a rumour for which there is neither a systematic reason nor historical evidence. Regarding the first point, there is nothing in what has been said so far about scientific theories that would force first-order logic on us, and pinning first-order logic to the Received View (or indeed the Linguistic View) is an unmotivated stipulation. Any formal system that allows scientists to carry out derivations and run proofs can in principle be used to systematise a theory, and any additional requirements must be grounded in other considerations.[22]

As regards the second point, there is no textual evidence that the logical empiricists insisted on analysing theories in terms of first-order logic. They often singled out the logic of Russell and Whitehead's *Principia Mathematica* as the logic of a scientific theory.[23] But neither is the logic of *Principia Mathematica* first-order;[24] nor is there any evidence that the logical empiricists were strongly committed to that particular version of logic. The logic of *Principia Mathematica* was widely regarded as the best system of logic in the early parts of the 20th Century, and it seemed reasonable to base an analysis of science on the best logic available. But Carnap in particular remained non-committal about logical systems. The language he used in his first major work, *Der Logische Aufbau der Welt* (1928), was not a first-order language (Lutz 2012, 83), and neither was the language in his 1954 Introduction to Symbolic Logic (*ibid.*).[25] In his (1956, 42) Carnap noted that logical or causal modalities could be introduced into a system if needed, and in his (1958) he explicitly took scientific languages to be higher-order languages. Since 1958 Carnap made frequent use of the Ramsey sentence, which is a sentence that can only be formulated in second-order logic (we discuss the Ramsey sentence in Section 4.6). In a lecture delivered in 1959 he said explicitly that a scientific language "contains a comprehensive logic including the whole of mathematics, either in set-theoretic form or in type-theoretic form" (quoted in Psillos 2000, 159). Furthermore, neither Nagel's (1961, Chs. 5–6) nor Hempel's (1966, Ch. 6) discussions of the Received View make reference to any particular formal system, and there is certainly no suggestion that the logic of scientific theories has to be first-order logic.[26]

In sum, neither the Linguistic View nor the Received View are committed to first-order logic, and both are free to use any logic that is deemed appropriate in a certain context. But having freedom of choice does not absolve the view from actually making a choice, and this is where things get tricky. Many difficult considerations arise when making a choice, and there are no easy answers. We return to this problem in Sections 2.8–2.10 after having introduced models.

1.5 Rosetta Stones and Stumbling Blocks

Hanson banishes the Received View because he takes it to regard a theory as an empty formalism without content. He accuses logical empiricists of having "invited us to think of a *theory* as a totally uninterpreted Rosetta Stone discovered in the semantical desert arid of meaning" (1969, 63, original emphasis) and later complains that "[t]o chop theories apart into *formalism* and *interpretation* – and then to identify only the formalism with the 'theory' – is the simple mistake of misplaced discreteness" (*ibid.*, 77, original emphasis). Its rhetorical allure notwithstanding, this criticism betrays a complete misunderstanding of the Received View. As we have seen in the last section, the Received View defines a theory as an *interpreted* formalism. An interpretation is an integral part of a theory, and no one ever said that a "bare" formalism was a theory. This mistake is, however, encouraged by the label "syntactic view", which suggests that a theory is a syntactic item. Liu therefore rightly notes that "syntactic view" is a misnomer because it gives the mistaken impression that the view "only consider the uninterpreted and highly abstract calculus . . . as a theory, which is in fact not the case. Interpretations and correspondence rules are also essential components of a theory" (1997, 151).

Another criticism is that the Received View is a stumbling block for scientific progress.[27] The claim is that axiomatising a theory in effect puts a freeze on it and prevents it from evolving: axiomatisation obstructs creativity and puts an end to the process of investigation. For this reason, axiomatisation is disadvantageous and should be avoided. This criticism is unfounded. Axioms are not set in stone and if they become unfit for purpose they can be changed. There is also no historical evidence that axiomatised theories suffer from underdevelopment. Geometry flourished after Euclid axiomatised the theory, and Newtonian mechanics has been developed in numerous ways in the centuries after Newton (and, indeed, developments are ongoing). Axioms can make basic claims of a theory explicit, bring hidden assumptions to the fore, and reveal gaps in an argument. Euclid's infamous fifth postulate has been a major driver of advances in geometry, and the scrutiny of Newton's equation of motion has eventually led to new forms of mechanics (classical and nonclassical). Schlimm (2006) offers an extensive discussion of the role of axioms in 20th century science and points out that axioms were in fact instrumental to progress in many parts of mathematics and physics, thereby disproving the claim that axioms are an impediment to progress.[28]

A related criticism is that the Received View is descriptively inadequate because, as Craver puts it, the view "neglects or distorts the *dynamics* of scientific theories – the protracted process of generating, evaluating, revising, and replacing theories over time" (2002, 60, original emphasis). Craver in fact mentions two separate points. Let us begin with "neglect". To address this point, we need to draw a distinction between two different kinds of philosophical accounts of theories. A *synchronic account* describes a theory at a given instant of time and explains what parts it has, how the parts work, how they interact with each other, and how all parts come together to form an operational whole. A *diachronic account* describes how a theory changes over time and explains how the parts and their functions evolve, how their interactions adjust, and how the whole theory transforms. To make this distinction more palpable, consider the same distinction in the context of a building. A synchronic account of, say, the Tower Bridge in London explicates the engineering of the bridge by spelling out what parts it has and how they are integrated to form a stable structure, which involves specifying the carrying capacity of the pillars, the static properties of the suspension, and so on. A diachronic account of the bridge describes how the bridge has changed over the years, what modifications have been made, what revisions it has undergone, and so on. It is clear that the Received View offers a synchronic account of theories and not a diachronic account. But why would this choice amount to "neglect"? Theory change is an important topic, but there is no imperative that every account of theories must address it. To accuse the Received View of neglect is to accuse it of not having done something that it never intended to do. It is like accusing a structural engineer who gives an account of the static properties of Tower Bridge of neglect for not also explaining the bridge's history.

Craver's second point is that the Received View "distorts" the dynamics of theories. In particular in the wake of Kuhn's *The Structure of Scientific Revolutions* (1970), theory change became a major topic in the philosophy of science, and the view that scientific progress is a more or less linear accumulation of knowledge was replaced by an account that sees scientific progress as going through revolutionary phases in which one paradigm is replaced by another, incommensurable, paradigm.[29] The charge then is that the Received View is committed to a wrong, and outdated, view of scientific progress. This is unfounded in two ways. First, the Received View is not committed to any view of scientific progress, and hence it cannot be committed to a "distorted" view. Indeed, it is difficult to see how the Received View could be *at once* be guilty of neglecting the diachronic development of theories *and* of promulgating a distorted view of that development! Second, Richardson (2007) offers a historical analysis of the charge and points out that the logical empiricists were in no way hostile to a Kuhnian picture of scientific progress. Carnap commented approvingly on Kuhn's work, and, indeed, Kuhn's (1970) was originally published as a monograph in the series *Foundations of the Unity of Science*, which was co-edited by Carnap (Richardson 2007, 354–355). Hence neither does the view itself embody any particular account of progress nor is there historical evidence that (at least the leading) logical empiricists were opposed to a Kuhnian understanding of scientific progress.

1.6* Identity in Crisis?

Newton's mechanics correctly describes the motion of medium-size objects (at least to a good degree of approximation), but it is difficult to apply to certain situations, for instance when objects move under external constraints. For instance, the motion of a trolley on a helter skelter is difficult to calculate with Newton's equation. To get around this problem, Lagrange reformulated Newtonian mechanics in a way that treats constraints differently and makes them more manageable. This reformulation is now known as Lagrangean Mechanics. So we have in front of us what looks like two different formulations of the same theory. About 250 years later, the quantum revolution took place. In 1925 Heisenberg presented matrix mechanics, and in 1926 Schrödinger formulated wave mechanics. Both theories addressed the same set of problems and were applied to the same systems, and Schrödinger soon argued that the two theories were identical in the sense that they were actually the same theory just formulated in different ways. This argument was borne out in 1932, when von Neumann presented a unified formulation of quantum theory based on the mathematics of Hilbert spaces.[30]

Cases like these raise the question of identity criteria for theories: what conditions have to obtain for two theories to be identical? To discuss this question, we need to distinguish between a theory and a theory formulation. A *theory formulation* Φ is given in a particular language. It is what we encounter when we read a textbook or a scientific paper. The theory itself is *expressed* by a set of sentences that constitutes a formulation. Let $T(\Phi)$ be the theory that the formulation Φ expresses. A theory is independent of a particular formulation and it can be expressed through different formulations. Assume now that we are given two different formulations Φ_1 and Φ_2. Under what conditions do two formulations express the same theory? An answer to this question has the following general form:[31]

Φ_1 is equivalent to Φ_2 iff $T(\Phi_1)$ is identical with $T(\Phi_1)$

Let us call this the *identity schema*. The schema regiments terminology: "equivalent" applies to theory formulations and "identical" to theories. The schema says that two theories are identical if their formulations are equivalent. Since it is a bi-conditional, one can use the truth or falsity of one side of the bi-conditional to determine the truth or falsity of the other side. However, we usually have access to theories only through their formulations and the only way to decide whether two theories are identical is to decide whether the formulations are equivalent.

Critics of the Received View claim that the view is committed to individuating theories syntactically, which has the consequence that every change in the description leads to a new theory.[32] Suppe illustrates this with the example of a translation (1977, 204). Consider that a theory is first formulated in English and then translated into French. The English formulation and the French formulation consist of different sentences. If theories are collections of sentences, then the translation into French produces a new theory. But this is the wrong verdict, because the English and the French sentences express the same theory. Translations between different ordinary languages are of course only an illustration. The same problem arises with the examples we mentioned above. Newtonian and Lagrangean mechanics use a different formalism; the strings of symbols that result when the theories are written down are different; and therefore, claims Suppe, the Received View is forced to consider them as different theories. And for the same reason matrix mechanics and wave mechanics have to come out as different theories.

Suppe is of course correct in pointing out that the English formulation of a theory and its French translations express the same theory, but he is mistaken in believing that the Received View cannot return this verdict. His criticism is based two assumptions. First, he claims that the Received View collapses the distinction between a theory formulation and a theory itself, thereby identifying a theory with its formulation: $T(\Phi) = \Phi$. Second, he claims that the Received View is committed to a purely syntactic equivalence criterion according to which two theory formulations are equivalent iff they are *syntactically* identical; that is, iff they consists of identical strings of symbols. This is why even the smallest change in the formulation of a theory yields a new theory.

Let us have a look at these assumptions. The first is difficult to assess. There is little, if any, explicit discussion of the distinction between theory formulations and theories in the literature in which the Received View originates, and it is a matter of interpretation whether one wants to attribute to the Received View the claim that $T(\Phi) = \Phi$. Suppe bases this attribution on the claim that, according to the Received View, theories are "linguistic entities" (1989, 3). But that theories are linguistic entities does not imply that theories are identical with their formulations. Propositions are linguistic entities and yet they are not identical with the sentences that expresses them; and meanings are linguistic entities and yet they are not identical with the expressions that carry them. Suppe might reply that this muddies the waters because propositions and meanings are not linguistic entities. If so, then we need a more precise definition of what counts as a linguistic entity (and an argument for the conclusion that theories are linguistic entities in the sense of that more precise definition).

Be this as it may. The real problem with Suppe's argument lies with the second assumption, that two theory formulations are equivalent iff they are syntactically identical. This criterion is wildly implausible. His own case of linguistic translation brings the problem into focus. Consider a well-worn example: "snow is white", "la neige est blanche" and "雪是白的" express the same matter of fact, but they do so in different languages. If we take these to be the formulations of our theory of snow, a purely syntactical criterion of theoretical equivalence has to regard them as non-equivalent because they are not syntactically identical. This is clearly the wrong verdict. The root of the problem is that there is more to language than syntax, and there is no reason to take *syntactical identity* to be a criterion for *linguistic equivalence*. Indeed, as Worrall notes, "the sensible axiomatiser is not the prisoner or any particular language" because the choice of a language to express a theory is only made on "the ground of suitability and convenience without any claim being made that this is the 'true' language of the theory" (1984, 72). Likewise, Halvorson observes that no advocate of the Received View has ever advocated anything like Suppe's criterion and that there is nothing in the Received View that would force such a criterion on us (2016, 588).

A number of plausible alternatives are available. Hendry and Psillos suggest that two theory formulations are equivalent iff they have identical truth conditions (2007, 137). Rosenberg submits that two theory formulations are equivalent iff they express the same propositions (2000, 99).[33] Quine argues that two formulations are equivalent iff both theories are empirically equivalent and the two formulations can be rendered identical by switching predicates in one of them (1975, 320). Worrall observes that formulations of a theory can be regarded as equivalent if they are logically equivalent or if there is a wider language in which the primitive terms of both theories become defined terms (1984, 72). Glymour proposes that two formulations are equivalent iff they are definitionally equivalent (1971, 279), which, roughly, means that the vocabulary that is used by one theory can be defined in the other theory and vice versa. Further criteria have emerged in a recent debate about theory identity that got started by Halvorson's (2012), which we review in Section 5.5.

There is no need to adjudicate between these proposals here. The point is that all these options are available to the Received View, which is therefore in no way forced to accept the absurd view that theories are individuated by the syntax of their formulation.

Another alleged source of difficulties with identity criteria are correspondence rules. Since the theory incorporates correspondence rules, the theory changes every time the correspondence rules change.[34] Correspondence rules can change when the observational basis changes. If, for instance, mercury thermometers are replaced by infrared thermometers, the correspondence rule linking "temperature" to observations changes, thereby changing the theory. This is deemed implausible because theories do not change when we introduce new observational techniques.

It is true that a theory changes as result of alterations of the correspondence rules, but it is not *prima facie* clear that this is either an implausible or an undesirable result. Insofar as theories are based in observations (the basic posit of empiricism!), we should expect theories to change when observations change. The air of implausibility that attaches to the idea that there is a concomitant theoretical change when the observational basis changes has a lot to do with a faulty understanding of "new". If novelty is understood as an all-or-nothing matter, then the claim is indeed implausible: we do not get a completely new or a completely different theory by adding a new observational technique. But if one sees novelty as something that comes in degrees, one can say that the kind of changes we have been discussing only bring about a very small change, which does not seem to be implausible at all. That temperature is something that cannot only be measured with mercury columns but also with infrared radiation has some influence on the concept of temperature, and a fortiori on the theories in which temperature plays a role. We discuss the relation between observational and theoretical concepts at length in Chapter 4. At this point we merely note that there is nothing obviously absurd in the admission that there can be theoretical changes as a result of changes in a theory's observational basis.

1.7 The Alleged Ravages of Rational Reconstruction

A common objection to the Received View is that theories as formulated by practicing scientists do not look like an interpreted axiomatic system. Suppe claims that "[t]urning to science itself, axiomatization occurs only infrequently, and then usually in foundational studies of well-developed theories" (2000a), and Carver observes that the Received View "is not typically defended as an accurate description of theories in the wild" (2002, 58).

This is only partially true. As we have seen in Sections 1.1 and 1.2, Newton's development of his mechanics comes close the picture of theories that the Received View canvasses, and other theories in physics conform, at least broadly, to Newton's picture. So the Received View is more than just a philosopher's pipe dream. This said, it is true that the presentation of theories in scientific practice does not always conform to the prescriptions of the Received View, or, indeed, the Linguistic View. Someone who opens a textbook on solid-state physics, nuclear physics, elementary particle physics, astrophysics or chaos theory is unlikely to find an axiomatic development of the theory.

This should not come as a great surprise; nor should it be a cause for alarm. The Received View was never meant to be a factual description of "theories in the wild". A theory that is presented under the form of the Received View has undergone a *rational reconstruction*.[35] So the Received View provides a normative rather than a descriptive account of theories, informing us how theories should look like after rational reconstruction rather than how we should expect to find them in textbooks and research papers. The idea of logical reconstruction was widely discussed among neo-Kantians in the early 20th Century, and it became the core of the philosophical programme in Carnap's *Der Logische Aufbau der Welt*.[36] In the preface to the second edition Carnap offers the following characterisation:

> By rational reconstruction is here meant the searching out of new definitions for old concepts. The old concepts did not ordinarily originate by way of deliberate formulation, but in more or less unreflected and spontaneous development. The new definitions should be superior to the old in clarity and exactness, and, above all, should fit into a systematic structure of concepts. Such a clarification of concepts, nowadays frequently called "explication," still seems to me one of the most important tasks of philosophy, especially if it is concerned with the main categories of human thought.
>
> *(Carnap 1967, v)*

The suggestion that theories should be rationally reconstructed does not imply that scientist have done their job badly. The construction and exploration of a theory are creative acts, which can leave certain issues unresolved: the definitions of core concepts can be opaque, the connection of theoretical postulates to observation can be tenuous, and so on. An approach committed to rational reconstruction sees the task of philosophy in replacing vague or imprecise pronouncements with transparent and explicit formulations.[37]

Rational reconstructions are not only a philosopher's ploy. When the foundations of a scientific theory (or discipline) turn out to be unclear or controversial, scientists themselves may offer reconstructions of theories. Quantum Mechanics is a case in point. In response to the many difficult issues that arose in the connection with quantum theory, von Neumann (1932/1955) offered an axiomatic formulation of the theory that fits Carnap's mould in many respects, and the project of rationally reconstructing quantum mechanics with the aim of better understanding its conceptual structure continues to this day.[38] Reconstructive projects also exist for other theories in physics, most notably statistical mechanics, thermodynamics, relativity theory, and quantum field theory, and beyond physics for evolutionary theory, phylogenetics, and the theory of rational decision-making, to mention just a few.

Rational reconstruction is not universally popular. An early attack came from Quine, who argues that it is "[b]etter to discover how science is in fact developed and learned than to fabricate a fictitious structure" (1969, 78). Philosophy of science, then, should describe theories as they appear in the practice of science and an analysis of theories should be descriptive. This outlook has garnered support and many philosophers of science nowadays see themselves as analysing the practice of science, tracing the historical development of ideas, and looking at the social structure of scientific communities. However, as noted in the previous paragraph, the dismissal of rational reconstruction is by no means universal, and reconstructive projects keep being pursued in many parts of philosophy of science (in fact, the now-dominant Model-Theoretical View, which we discuss in Part II, also proffers a philosophical programme that is based on the rational reconstruction of theories).[39] This is not the place to review all the pros and cons of rational reconstruction. The point we are making is a more modest one: that a view is a rational reconstruction, or that a philosophical programme involves rational reconstruction, is not *ipso facto* a refutation of that view or that programme.

A different line of criticism would leave the central ideas of rational reconstruction intact but insist that the Received View asks for a reconstruction of the wrong kind. This seems to be Suppe's line when he challenges proponents of the Received View to show that every clear-cut example of a scientific theory can be axiomatised in a *fruitful way* (1977, 62–66). An axiomatisation is fruitful if it "will reduce the content of the theory to a compact axiomatic basis in such a way as to display the systematic interconnections between the various concepts in pre-axiomatic versions of the theory" (*ibid.*, 64). His verdict is that the Received View fails this test because such axiomatisations are available at best for a small class of theories:

> It is manifest that the systematic interconnections among the concepts occurring in any of the following theories at present are insufficiently well known or understood to admit of fruitful axiomatisation: Hebb's theory of the nervous system, Darwinian theory of evolution, Hoyle's theory of the beginning of the universe, Pike's tagmemic theory of language structure, Freud's psychology, Heyerdahl's theory about the origin of human life on Easter Island or the theory that all Indo-European languages have a common ancestor language, proto-Indo-European. Furthermore, it is manifest that most theories in cultural anthropology; most sociological theories about the family; theories about the origin of the American Indian; most theories in palaeontology; theories of phylogenetic descent; most theories in histology, cellular and microbiology, and comparative anatomy; natural history

theories about the decline of the dinosaur and other prehistoric animals; and theories about the higher processes in psychology, all are such at present that any attempts at axiomatization would be premature and fruitless since they are insufficiently developed to permit their reduction to a highly systematic basis.

(Suppe 1977, 64–65)

Suppe, or any proponent of the Model-Theoretical View, is ill-placed to put much weight on such examples. It is true that these theories are not interpreted formalisms. But they are not families of models either; nor is it obvious that they can be fruitfully reconstructed as such. But let us set this aside for now. A hard-nosed reply to Suppe's challenge might regard axiomatic reconstructability as a criterion for the maturity of a discipline and reject as immature, or even unscientific, theories that cannot be brought into the relevant axiomatic form (Baur 1990, 327). This would tie in with Suppe's observation that "at present" the said theories cannot be axiomatised; that attempts to axiomatise them would be "premature"; and that these theories are "insufficiently developed" to be reduced to a systematic basis (*op. cit.*).

While there are legitimate concerns about the credentials of some items on Suppe's list (Freudian psychology, for instance), we would be ill-advised to discard evolutionary theory, microbiology, and comparative anatomy as immature, or even unscientific. This leaves the Received View with two options. The first is to restrict the scope of the analysis and claim that only *some* theories have (or can be brought into) the form of an interpreted axiomatic system, while other theories have a different structure not captured by the Received View. The second is to insist that Suppe has declared defeat prematurely and that axiomatic forms exist for the said theories.

At the end of the day, it is a factual question whether theories can be fruitfully axiomatised, and a great deal will depend on what one takes "fruitful" to mean.[40] However it seems relatively safe to think that some theories are not like Newtonian mechanics, and that attempts to recast them so that they meet the criteria of the Received View seem to get started on the wrong foot. Classificatory sciences like Linné's taxonomy of plants, genealogical theories like accounts of the origin of European languages, and historical accounts of single event such as the extinction of the dinosaurs would seem to be unlikely to ever fit the mould of the Received View.[41] So it seems reasonable to limit the scope of the Received View to theories that are like Newtonian mechanics in that they are built around overarching principles that aim to subsume a large number of cases under the same theoretical framework.[42] As long as the Received View captures the structure of these theories, it seems to have achieved its goal.

The question then is what "these" theories are. Is there anything beyond a few theories in fundamental physics that fall within the scope of the Received View? Opinions on this matter diverge. Beatty (1981) argues that the Received View is untenable because theories in biology cannot be reconstructed within its framework. The problem, says Beatty, is that the Received View presupposes a notion of law that sees laws as both universal and necessary. An example of a law in biology is the Hardy-Weinberg law in genetics. Yet this law is neither universal nor necessary. And the lesson generalises: other laws in biology are not universal and necessary either. Since the Received View requires a theory to have universal and necessary laws, it is incompatible with biology.[43] For the sake of argument let us assume that Beatty's analysis of laws in biology as non-necessary and non-universal is correct. How much of a problem is this for the Received View? Savage (1998, 5–6) points out that Beatty misses the mark because the Received View does not make any such requirements. That laws be either necessary or universal is not part of the Received View, and the existence of disciplines that have no such laws is no threat to the Received View.[44] In line with Savage's conclusion, a discussion of the relative advantages of the Model-Theoretical View (which he refers to as the "semantic view") and the Received View leads Ereshefsky to the conclusion that "[a]dopting the semantic view of theories will not make our attempts to fully represent such laws easier" (1991, 76–77), and Collier concludes that "the syntactic approach must be as good as any other approach" when it comes to capturing the nature of laws in population genetics (Collier 2002, 292). Hence, whether theories in biology fit the mould of the Received View is an open question, and the same can probably be said about theories in other domains.

Finally, an entirely different reading of "fruitful" emerges from von Fraassen's discussion of the Received View. He notes that "[i]n many texts and treatises on quantum mechanics, for instance, we find a set of propositions called the 'axioms of quantum theory'. They do not look very much like what a logician expects axioms to look like" (1980, 65). So van Fraassen's charge is that we're guilty of equivocating on "axiom" when we call general principles like Newton's equation "axioms" because the kind of axioms that one finds in formal systems are of a different kind than the axioms of scientific theory. For this reason, it is "simply a mistake" to think that when seeing the axioms of quantum theory in a textbook that the "theory is here presented axiomatically in the sense that Hilbert presented Euclidean geometry, or Peano arithmetic" (*ibid.*). But if scientific axioms are different from the axioms of a formal system, then axiomatising a theory in a formal system cannot be fruitful. This is a serious charge, but we are not yet in a position to assess it. First we have to say more about the formal systems in which theories are formulated (so far we only said that they need not be first-order logic), and about the nature of scientific axioms. We return to these issues in Chapters 2 and 5.

1.8 Conclusion

The Received View is not the obvious non-starter that many opponents have claimed it is. A number of criticisms are unsuccessful because they either shoot at straw men or draw conclusions too hastily. This by itself does not, of course, establish that the Received View is the correct analysis of theories, but it does motivate the project of delving deeper into the many difficult problems that the precise articulation of the theory raises, most notably its use of models and the choice of an adequate logical system (Chapter 2), the separation of a theory's vocabulary into observational and theoretical terms (Chapter 3), and the meaning of theoretical terms (Chapter 4).

Notes

1 For a discussion of the nature of Newton's definitions, see Cohen's (2002).
2 I omit editorial footnotes in quotations throughout. Definitions and laws are italicised in the translation I use, but I reproduce the text in normal script to avoid conflation with italics in the rest of the book, where they are used either to indicate emphasis or to mark Latin expressions.
3 Newton is not very explicit about these assumptions. However, he speaks of the "diameter" of planets like Jupiter (see, for instance, *ibid.*, 444), which indicates that the regards them as spheres. In Corollary 3 he sets out to determine the density of planets by considering the properties of "homogeneous spheres" (*ibid.*, 460).
4 See endnote 2 in the Introduction for an explanation of my use of "logical empiricism". For an overview of the core ideas of logical empiricism, see Creath's (2017); for in-depth discussions see, for instance, Kraft's (1953), Richardson's (1997), Stadler's (2001), Uebel's (2007), and the essays gathered in Richardson and Uebel's (2007).
5 The label "received view" is due to Putnam's (1962, 215). The qualifier "syntactic" is van Fraassen's, who calls it the "syntactic approach" or the "syntactic picture of a theory" (1980, 44). Other labels include "orthodox view" or "standard view" (Feigl 1970, 3), "statement view" (Moulines 2002, 5; Stegmüller 1979, 4); "statement conception" (Savage 1998, 3), "hypothetico-deductive account of theories" (Rosenberg 2000, 76), "sentential view" (Churchland 1989, 153), "axiomatic system construal" (Ackermann 1966, 312), "classical view" (Giere 2000, 515), "standard conception" (Glymour 1992, 118), "standard construal" or "standard analysis" (Hempel 1973, 367), "formal-linguistic view" (Muller 2011, 91), and "once received view" (Craver 2002, 55; Rickles 2020, 143).
6 Early statements of the Received View are Carnap's (1923) and Schlick's (1925). Full developments can be found in Carnap's (1938, Sec. 23), Braithwaite's (1953, Chs. 1–3, 1954), Nagel's (1961, Ch. 5), and Hempel's (1966, Ch. 6, 1969, 1970). For a discussion of the historical development of the received view in logical empiricism, see Mormann's (2007).
7 Sometimes this language is referred to as a "calculus"; see, for instance Hempel's (1970, 145) and Braithwaite's (1954, 156, 1962, 124). I do not use this term to avoid confusion with mathematics, where "calculus" refers to the subfield of mathematics that studies the differentiation and integration of functions.
8 Sometimes laws are also referred to as "theoretical principles" or "T-postulates".
9 For the view that laws "govern", see, for instance, Armstrong's (1983); for the view that laws summarise, see, for instance, Lewis' (1994).
10 Modus ponens is the rule that q can be inferred from the premises p and $p \rightarrow q$ (in words: "if p then q").
11 For a discussion of the details of what is meant by a finite recipe and of the values of axiomatisation, see Smith's (2013), in particular Chapter 4.
12 See Hume's (1748/2007, Secs. IV–VII). For the sake of illustration, I here adopt a radical interpretation of Hume's views. Different interpretations are discussed in Strawson's (2014).
13 In what follows I stick to common usage and call terms (purportedly) referring to unobservables "theoretical terms". However, as we will see in Section 3.2, this choice of words can be misleading.

14 I here set aside the question whether observation terms refer to physical or "autopsy-chological" objects, which was the subject of heated debate in the Vienna Circle. See Cat's (2006) and Uebel's (2007) for discussions.

15 Correspondence rules are *mixed sentences* because they contain both observation terms and theoretical terms. They are also referred to as "correspondence postulates" (Carnap 1956, 47), "co-ordinating definitions" (Hanson 1969, 62), "coordinating definitions" (Reichenbach 1929, 155) or "coordinative definitions" (*ibid.*, 161), "C-rules" (Hempel 1965, 195), "semantic rules" or "epistemic correlations" or "rules of interpretation" (Nagel 1961, 93), "interpretative principles" (Hempel 1970, 146), and "dictionary" (Campbell 1920, 122). Occasionally correspondence rules are also referred to as "bridge principles" (Schaffner 1969, 280). This is unfortunate because bridge princi-ples, or "bridge laws", are also appealed to in Nagelian reduction where they establish a connection between the between the terms of a theory and the terms of another theory to which it is reduced. For a discussion of bridge laws, see Dizadji-Bahmani et al. (2010).

16 See, for instance, Hempel's (1970, 145). Nagel's (1961, 90), also includes models in the definition of a theory. This, however, has not become customary. The role of models in the Received View will be discussed in Chapter 2.

17 For a discussion of the best systems analysis and further references, see Cohen and Callender's (2009).

18 Lutz makes this claim by drawing a contrast between what he calls "syntactic approaches" and the Received View. All "frameworks that rely on formalizations in predicate logic of first or higher order" are instances of a syntactic approach, while "the Received View is a specific syntactic approach that *additionally* assumes a bipar-tition of the vocabulary and allows a direct interpretation only of the observational terms" (Lutz 2014, 1476, original emphasis). He notes that this distinction is important because "[s]yntactic approaches have often been dismissed with reference to criticisms of the Received View" (*ibid.*; cf. Lutz 2017, 323–325). Lutz's "syntactic approaches" are, roughly, what I call the Linguistic View. A similar point is made by Mundy, who insists that an understanding of a theory as an interpreted calculus must be dissociated "from the positivist themes with which it has misleadingly come to be associated" (1987, 173).

19 See, for instance, Churchland's (1989, 153), Suppe's (1977, 16, 50), Suppes' (2002, 4, 27–29), Thompson's (1989, 26), and van Fraassen's (1985, 302). The claim has trickled down to encyclopaedias, reference works, and surveys, where it is reported as a matter of fact. See, for instance, Craver's (2002, 55–60), Lloyd's (2006, 822), Morgan and Morrison's (1999, 2), Morrison's (2016, 381–382), and Winther's (2016, Sec. 3).

20 For a detailed assessment, see Shapiro's (1991, Ch. 5) and our discussion in Section 2.8 and Section 2.9.

21 See, for instance, Lloyd's (2006, 824), Stegmüller's (1979, 4–7) and Suppes' (1967, 58, 1992, 207).

22 Azzouni (2014, 2994) makes this point explicitly. Some philosophers, notably Quine (1953, Ch. 6), have advanced what Barwise and Feferman call the "first-order thesis": "logic is first-order logic, so that anything that cannot be defined in first-order logic is outside the domain of logic" (1985, 5). The motivations for this thesis are numerous and varied, with nominalism and the rejection of abstract entities featuring prominently among them. However, the Received View need not follow Quine in endorsing the first-order thesis. For a review of issues surrounding higher order logic, see Linnebo's (2011).

23 See, for instance, Kraft's (1950).

24 For a historical discussion of the emergence of first-order logic, see Moore's (1988).

25 See Leitgeb's (2011) for a discussion of the philosophical programme in Carnap's *Aufbau*.

26 For a discussion of Hempel's stance on the issue, see Lutz's (2012, 84–87). Meyer (2002) provides further arguments against what he calls the "first-orderizability thesis", the view that scientific theories ought to, and can, be formalised in first order logic.

27 See Craver's (2002, 61) and references therein; see also Rosenberg's (2000, 100), which mentions the criticism without endorsing it.

28 Schlimm (2013) further notes that even in mathematics axioms should not be, an in practice are not, regarded as unchangeable self-evident truths, and in his (2011) he examines in detail the creative role axioms played in the discovery of lattices.

29 For extensive discussion of Kuhn's account of theory change, see Bird's (2000) and Hoyningen-Huene's (1993).

30 The case of Newtonian and Lagrangean mechanics is discussed in every advanced textbook of classical mechanics; see, for instance, Goldstein's (1980). For a discussion of the case of quantum mechanics, see, for instance, Muller's (1997a, 1997b).

31 Thanks to Laurenz Hudetz for suggesting this schema to me. For a recent survey of different approaches to theoretical equivalence, see Weatherall's (2019a, 2019b).

32 See Suppe's (1977, 204–205, 1989, 3–4, 82, 1998, 345, 2000c, 103, 2000b, 525). See also da Costa and French's (2003, 24), French's (2008, 271), and Giere's (1988, 84).

33 Thomson-Jones (2012) makes a similar suggestion in the context of a discussion of models.

34 See, for instance, Da Costa and French's (2003, 24) and Suppe's (1989, 4–5, 2000b, 525).

35 Proponents of the Received View were explicit about this. See, for instance, Hempel's (1969, 20, 1970, 148) and Feigl's (1970, 13).

36 The German title means "The Logical Structure of the World". For a discussion of Carnap's use of rational reconstruction, see Demopoulos' (2007) and Richardson's (1997).

37 For a discussion of Carnap's notion of explication, see Dutilh Novaes and Reck's (2017), Kitcher's (2008), and Lutz's (2012, Sec. 5).

38 A recent contribution to this project is Hardy's (2011). For a discussion of von Neumann's axioms, see Rédei and Stöltzner's (2006) and Stöltzner's (2001).

39 For an overview of issues in connection with rational reconstruction, see Richardson's (2006).

40 Recall that $T = D(T)$, and so any theory can be trivially axiomatised simply by declaring every sentence of the theory an axiom. Such an axiomatisation would not be fruitful. But there are many options in-between declaring the entire theory an axiom set and finding a small number of core axioms. Where exactly the right – or "fruitful" – middle ground lies is unclear, and a response to this issue may well be context-dependent.

41 Even in the "hard" sciences, it can be a matter of controversy whether a certain field has successfully been axiomatised, or whether it can be so aximomatised. As an example, see the controversy between Hettema and Kuipers (1988) on one side and Scerri (1997) on the other side on the axiomatisation of the periodic table.

42 To accept this limitation is not tantamount to renouncing *all* elements of the Received View. Classificatory systems, genealogical accounts, and historical narratives are still linguistic entities, and could therefore be accommodated in generalised linguistic view that drops the requirements of axioms and formalisation.

43 Similar claims have also been made by Lloyd (1994, 2–5) and Craver (2002, 62); for a brief survey of the discussion about laws in biology, see Odenbaugh's (2008, 513–515).

44 Savage points out that restrictions to laws *can* be formulated in the Received View, and she argues that the Received View is not threatened by Giere's problem of provisos either (1988, 6–8).

References

Ackermann, R. J. 1966. Confirmatory Models of Theories. *The British Journal for the Philosophy of Science* 16: 312–326.

Armstrong, D. 1983. *What Is a Law of Nature?* Cambridge: Cambridge University Press.

Azzouni, J. 2014. A New Characterization of Scientific Theories. *Synthese* 191: 2993–3008.

Barwise, J. and S. Feferman (eds.) 1985. *Model-Theoretic Logics*. New York and Berlin: Springer.

Baur, M. 1990. On the Aim of Scientific Theories in Relating to the World: A Defence of the Semantic Account. *Dialogue* 29: 323–333.

Beatty, J. 1981. What's Wrong with the Received View of Evolutionary Theory? In P. Asquith and R. Giere (eds.), *Philosophy of Science (Proceedings)* (Vol. 2). East Lansing: Philosophy of Science Association, pp. 397–426.

Bird, A. 2000. *Thomas Kuhn*. Princeton: Princeton University Press.

Braithwaite, R. B. 1953. *Scientific Explanation*. Cambridge: Cambridge University Press.

Braithwaite, R. B. 1954. The Nature of Theoretical Concepts and the Role of Models in an Advanced Science. *Theoria* 2: 155–157.

Braithwaite, R. B. 1962. Models in the Empirical Sciences. In E. Nagel, P. Suppes, and A. Tarski (eds.), *Logic, Methodology and Philosophy of Science*. Standford: Stanford University Press, pp. 224–231.

Campbell, N. R. 1920. *Physics: The Elements*. Cambridge: Cambridge University Press (Reprinted as *Foundations of Science*. New York: Dover 1957).

Carnap, R. 1923. Über Die Aufgabe Der Physik Und Die Anwendung Des Grundsatzes Der Einfachstheit. *Kant Studien* 28: 90–107.

Carnap, R. 1928. *Der Logische Aufbau Der Welt*. Hamburg: Felix Meiner 1998.

Carnap, R. 1938. Foundations of Logic and Mathematics. In O. Neurath, C. Morris, and R. Carnap (eds.), *International Encyclopaedia of Unified Science* (Vol. 1). Chicago: University of Chicago Press, pp. 139–213.

Carnap, R. 1956. The Methodological Character of Theoretical Concepts. In H. Feigl and M. Scriven (eds.), *The Foundations of Science and the Concepts of Phsychologz and Psychoanalysis* (Vol. I, Minnesota Studies in the Philosophy of Science). Minneapolis: University of Minnesota Press, pp. 38–76.

Carnap, R. 1958. Beobachtungssprache Und Theoretische Sprache. *Dialectica* 12: 236–248.

Carnap, R. 1967. *The Logical Structure of the World and Pseudoproblems in Philosophy* (R. A. George, Trans., Reprint 2005). Chicago and La Salle: Open Court.

Cat, J. 2006. Protocol Sentences. In S. Sarkar and J. Pfeifer (eds.), *The Philosophy of Science. An Encyclopedia*. New York: Taylor & Francis, pp. 610–613.

Churchland, P. M. 1989. *A Neurocomputational Perspective: The Nature of Mind and the Structure of Science*. Cambridge, MA: MIT Press.

Cohen, B. I. 2002. Newton's Concepts of Force and Mass, with Notes on the Laws of Motion. In B. I. Cohen and G. E. Smith (eds.), *The Cambridge Companion to Newton*. Cambridge and New York: Cambridge University Press, pp. 57–84.

Cohen, J. and C. Callender 2009. A Better Best System Account of Lawhood. *Philosophical Studies* 145: 1–34.

Collier, J. D. 2002. Critical Notice: Paul Thompson, the Structure of Biological Theories. *Canadian Journal of Philosophy* 22: 287–298.

Craver, C. 2002. Theories and Models. In P. Machamer and M. Silberstein (eds.), *The Blackwell Guide to the Philosphy of Science*. Malden, MA and Oxford: Blackwell, pp. 55–79.

Creath, R. 2017. Logical Empiricism. In E. N. Zalta (ed.), *The Stanford Encyclopedia of Philosophy*. https://plato.stanford.edu/archives/fall2017/entries/logical-empiricism/.

Da Costa, N. C. A. and S. French 2003. *Science and Partial Truth: A Unitary Approach to Models and Scientific Reasoning*. Oxford: Oxford University Press.

Demopoulos, W. 2007. Carnap on the Rational Reconstruction of Scientific Theories. In M. Friedman and R. Creath (eds.), *The Cambridge Companion to Carnap*. Cambridge: Cambridge University Press, pp. 248–272.

Dizadji-Bahmani, F., R. Frigg, and S. Hartmann 2010. Who's Afraid of Nagelian Reduction. *Erkenntnis* 73: 393–412.

Dutilh Novaes, C. and E. Reck 2017. Carnapian Explication, Formalisms as Cognitive Tools, and the Paradox of Adequate Formalization. *Synthese* 194: 195–215.

Ereshefsky, M. 1991. The Semantic Approach to Evolutionary Theory. *Biology and Philosophy* 6: 59–80.

Feigl, H. 1970. The 'Orthodox' View of Theories: Remarks in Defense as Well as Critique. In M. Radner and S. Winokur (eds.), *Analyses of Theories and Methods of Physics and Psychology* (Vol. IV, Minnesota Studies in the Philosophy of Science). Minneapolis: University of Minnesota Press, pp. 3–16.

French, S. 2008. The Structure of Scientific Theories. In S. Psillos and M. Curd (eds.), *The Routledge Companion to Philosophy of Science*. London and New York: Routledge, pp. 269–280.

Giere, R. N. 1988. *Explaining Science: A Cognitive Approach*. Chicago: Chicago University Press.

Giere, R. N. 2000. Theories. In W. H. Newton-Smith (ed.), *A Companion to the Philosophy of Science*. Oxford: Wiley-Blackwell, pp. 515–524.

Glymour, C. 1971. Theoretical Realism and Theoretical Equivalence. In R. C. Buck and R. Cohen (eds.), *Proceeding of the 1970 Biennial Meeting Philosophy of Science Association* (Vol. VIII, Boston Studies in the Philosophy of Science). Dordrecht: Reidel, pp. 275–288.

Glymour, C. 1992. *Realism and the Nature of Theories* (Introduction to the Philosophy of Science). Indianapolis and Cambridge: Hackett.

Goldstein, H. 1980. *Classical Mechanics*. Reading, MA: Addison Wesley.

Halvorson, H. 2012. What Scientific Theories Could Not Be. *Philosophy of Science* 79: 183–206.

Halvorson, H. 2016. Scientific Theories. In P. Humphreys (ed.), *The Oxford Handbook of Philosophy of Science*. Oxford: Oxford University Press, pp. 585–608.

Hanson, N. R. 1969. Logical Positivism and the Interpretation of Scientific Theories. In P. Achinstein and S. F. Barker (eds.), *The Legacy of Logical Positivism*. Baltimore: Johns Hopkins Press, pp. 57–84.

Hardy, L. 2011. Reformulating and Reconstructing Quantum Theory. *arXiv:1104.2066v3*. https://arxiv.org/abs/1104.2066.

Hempel, C. G. 1965. *Aspects of Scientific Explanation and Other Essays in the Philosophy of Science*. New York: Free Press.

Hempel, C. G. 1966. *Philosophy of Natural Science*. Princeton: Princeton University Press.

Hempel, C. G. 1969. On the Structure of Scientific Theories. In C. G. Hempel (ed.), *The Isenberg Memorial Lecture Series*. East Lansing: Michigan State University Press, pp. 11–38.

Hempel, C. G. 1970. On the 'Standard Conception' of Scientific Theories. In M. Radner and S. Winokur (eds.), *Minnesota Studies in the Philosophy of Science Vol. 4*. Minneapolis: University of Minnesota Press, pp. 142–163.

Hempel, C. G. 1973. The Meaning of Theoretical Terms: A Critique of the Standard Empiricist Construal. In P. Suppes, L. Henkin, A. Joja, and G. C. Moisil (eds.), *Logic, Methodology and Philosophy of Science Vol. IV*. Amsterdam: North Holland, pp. 367–378.

Hendry, R. F. and S. Psillos 2007. How to Do Things with Theories: An Interactive View of Language and Models in Science. In J. Brzezinski, A. Klawiter, T. A. F. Kuipers, K. Łastowski, K. Paprzycka, and P. Przybysz (eds.), *The Courage of Doing Philosophy: Essays Dedicated to Lezek Nowak*. Amsterdam and New York: Rodopi, pp. 123–157.

Hettema, H. and T. A. F. Kuipers 1988. The Periodic Table – Its Formalization, Status, and Relation to Atomic Theory. *Erkenntnis* 28: 387–408.

Hoyningen-Huene, P. 1993. *Reconstructing Scientific Revolutions: Thomas S. Kuhn's Philosophy of Science*. Chicago: Chicago University Press.

Hume, D. 1748. *An Enquiry Concerning Human Understanding*. Oxford: Oxford University Press, 2007.

Kitcher, P. 2008. Carnap and the Caterpillar. *Philosophical Topics* 36: 111–127.

Kraft, V. 1950. *Der Wiener Kreis. Der Ursprung Des Neopositivismus*. Wien: Springer.

Kraft, V. 1953. *The Vienna Circle: The Origins of Neo-Positivism*. New York: Philosophical Library.

Kuhn, T. S. 1970. *The Structure of Scientific Revolutions* (2nd ed.). Chicago: Chicago University Press.

Leitgeb, H. 2011. New Life for Carnap's *Aufbau*? *Synthese* 180: 265–299.

Lewis, D. K. 1994. Humean Supervenience Debugged. *Mind* 103: 473–490.

Linnebo, Ø. 2011. Higher-Order Logic. In L. Horsten and R. Pettigrew (eds.), *The Continuum Companion to Philosophical Logic*. London and New York: Continuum International Publishing Group, pp. 105–127.

Liu, C. 1997. Models and Theories I: The Semantic View Revisited. *International Studies in the Philosophy of Science* 11: 147–164.

Lloyd, E. A. 1994. *The Structure and Confirmation of Evolutionary Theory*. Princeton: Princeton University Press.

Lloyd, E. A. 2006. Theories. In S. Sarkar and J. Pfeifer (eds.), *The Philosophy of Science: An Encyclopedia*. New York: Routledge, pp. 822–828.

Lutz, S. 2012. On a Straw Man in the Philosophy of Science: A Defence of the Received View. *HOPOS* 2: 77–120.

Lutz, S. 2014. What's Right with the Syntactic Approach to Theories and Models? *Erkenntnis* 79: 1475–1492.

Lutz, S. 2017. What Was the Syntax-Semantics Debate in the Philosophy of Science About? *Philosophy and Phenomenological Research* 95: 319–352.

Machover, M. 1996. *Set Theory, Logic and Their Limitations*. Cambridge: Cambridge University Press.

Meyer, U. 2002. Is Science First – Order? *Analysis* 62: 305–308.

Moore, G. H. 1988. The Emergence of First-Order Logic. In W. Aspray and P. Kitcher (eds.), *History and Philosophy of Modern Mathematiacs. Minnesota Studies in the Philosophy of Science Vol XI*. Minnesota: University of Minnesota Press, pp. 95–135.

Morgan, M. S. and M. Morrison (eds.) 1999. *Models as Mediators: Perspectives on Natural and Social Science*. Cambridge: Cambridge University Press.

Mormann, T. 2007. The Structure of Scientific Theories in Logical Empiricism. In A. Richardson and T. Uebel (eds.), *The Cambridge Companion to Logical Empiricism*. Cambridge: Cambridge University Press, pp. 136–162.

Morrison, M. 2016. Models and Theories. In P. Humphreys (ed.), *The Oxford Handbook of Philosophy of Science*. Oxford: Oxford University Press, pp. 378–396.

Moulines, C.-U. 2002. Introduction: Structuralism as a Program for Modelling Theoretical Science. *Synthese* 130: 1–11.

Muller, F. A. 1997a. The Equivalence Myth of Quantum Mechanics – Part I. *Studies in History and Philosophy of Modern Physics* 28: 35–61.

Muller, F. A. 1997b. The Equivalence Myth of Quantum Mechanics – Part II. *Studies in History and Philosophy of Modern Physics* 28: 219–241.

Muller, F. A. 2011. Reflections on the Revolution at Stanford. *Synthese* 183: 87–114.

Mundy, B. 1987. Scientific Theory as Partially Interpreted Calculus. *Erkenntnis* 27: 173–196.

Nagel, E. 1961. *The Structure of Science*. London: Routledge and Keagan Paul.

Newton, I. 1726. *The Principia. Mathematical Principles of Natural Philosophy. The Authoritative Translation by I. Bernard Cohen and Anne Whitman Assisted by Julia Budenz* (A. Motte, Trans.). Oakland: University of California Press, 1999.

Odenbaugh, J. 2008. Models. In S. Sarkar and A. Plutynski (eds.), *A Companion to the Philosophy of Biology*. Malden, MA: Wiley-Blackwell, pp. 506–534.

Popper, K. R. 1959. *The Logic of Scientific Discovery*. London: Routledge, 2002.

Psillos, S. 2000. Rudolf Carnap's 'Theoretical Concepts in Science'. *Studies in History and Philosophy of Science* 31: 151–172.

Putnam, H. 1962. What Theories Are Not. In E. Nagel, P. Suppes, and A. Tarski (eds.), *Logic, Methodology, and the Philosophy of Science*. reprinted in *Hilary Putnam: Mathematics, Matter and Method. Philosophical Papers Vol. 1*. Cambridge: Cambridge University Press, pp. 215–227.

Quine, W. V. O. 1953. *From a Logical Point of View*. Cambridge, MA: Harvard University Press.

Quine, W. V. O. 1969. *Ontological Relativity and Other Essays*. New York: Columbia University Press.

Quine, W. V. O. 1975. On Empirically Equivalent Systems of the World. *Erkenntnis* 9: 313–328.

Rédei, M. and M. Stöltzner 2006. Soft Axiomatisation: John Von Neumann on Method and Von Neumann's Method in the Physical Sciences. In E. Carson and R. Huber (eds.), *Intuition and the Axiomatic Method*. Dordrecht: Springer, pp. 235–249.

Reichenbach, H. 1929. The Aims and Methods of Physical Knowledge. In M. Reichenbach and R. Cohen (eds.), *Selected Writings 1909–1953* (Vol. 2). Dordrecht: Reidel, 1953, pp. 120–225.

Richardson, A. 1997. *Carnap's Construction of the World: The Aufbau and the Emergence of Logical Empiricism*. Cambridge: Cambridge University Press.

Richardson, A. 2006. Rational Reconstruction. In S. Sarkar and J. Pfeifer (eds.), *The Philosophy of Science. An Encyclopedia*. New York and London: Routledge, pp. 681–685.

Richardson, A. 2007. 'That Sort of Everyday Image of Logical Positivism' Thomas Kuhn and the Decline of Logical Empiricist Philosophy of Science. In A. Richardson and T. Uebel (eds.), *The Cambridge Companion to Logical Empiricism*. Cambridge: Cambridge University Press, pp. 346–369.

Richardson, A. and T. Uebel (eds.) 2007. *The Cambridge Companion to Logical Empiricism*. Cambridge: Cambridge University Press.

Rickles, D. 2020. *What Is Philosophy of Science?* Cambridge: Polity Press.

Rosenberg, A. 2000. *Philosophy of Science: A Contemporary Introduction*. London: Routledge.

Savage, C. W. 1998. *The Semantic (Mis)Concdeption of Theories*. http://citeseerx.ist.psu.edu/viewdoc/download?doi=10.1.1.14.6280&rep=rep1&type=pdf.

Scerri, E. R. 1997. Has the Periodic Table Been Successfully Axiomatised? *Erkenntnis* 47: 229–243.

Schaffner, K. F. 1969. Correspondence Rules. *Philosophy of Science* 36: 280–290.

Schlick, M. 1925. *Allgemeine Erkenntnislehre* (2nd ed.). Berlin: Springer.

Schlimm, D. 2006. Axiomatics and Progress in the Light of 20th Century Philosophy of Science and Mathematics. In B. Löwe, V. Peckhaus, and T. Räsch (eds.), *Foundations of the Formal Sciences IV: The History of the Concept of the Formal Sciences*. London: College Publications, pp. 233–253.

Schlimm, D. 2011. On the Creative Role of Axiomatics. The Discovery of Lattices by Schröder, Dedekind, Birkhoff, and Others. *Synthese* 183: 47–68.

Schlimm, D. 2013. Axioms in Mathematical Practice. *Philosophia Mathematica* 21: 37–92.

Shapiro, S. 1991. *Foundations without Foundationalism: A Case for Second-Order Logic*. Oxford: Oxford University Press.

Smith, P. 2013. *An Introduction to Gödel's Theorems* (2nd ed.). Cambridge: Cambridge University Press.

Stadler, F. 2001. *The Vienna Circle: Studies in the Origins, Development and Influence of Logical Empiricism*. Berlin and New York: Springer.

Stegmüller, W. 1979. *The Structuralist View of Theories: A Possible Analogue of the Bourbaki Programme in Physical Science*. New York and Berlin: Springer.

Stöltzner, M. 2001. Opportunistic Axiomatics – Von Neumann on the Methodology of Mathematical Physics. In M. Rédei and M. Stöltzner (eds.), *John Von Neumann and the Foundation of Quantum Physics*. Dordrecht: Kluwer, pp. 235–249.

Strawson, G. 2014. *The Secret Connexion. Causation, Realism, and David Hume* (2nd ed.). Oxford: Oxford University Press.

Suppe, F. 1977. The Search for Philosophical Understanding of Scientific Theories. In F. Suppe (ed.), *The Structure of Scientific Theories*. Urbana and Chicago: University of Illinois Press, pp. 3–241.

Suppe, F. 1989. *The Semantic Conception of Theories and Scientific Realism*. Urbana and Chicago: University of Illinois Press.

Suppe, F. 1998. Theories, Scientific. In E. Craig (ed.), *Routledge Encyclopedia of Philosophy* (Vol. 2008). London: Routledge, pp. 344–355.

Suppe, F. 2000a. Axiomatization. In W. H. Newton-Smith (ed.), *A Companion to the Philosophy of Science*. Oxford: Wiley-Blackwell, pp. 9–11.

Suppe, F. 2000b. Theory Identity. In W. H. Newton-Smith (ed.), *A Companion to the Philosophy of Science*. Oxford: Wiley-Blackwell, pp. 525–527.

Suppe, F. 2000c. Understanding Scientific Theories: An Assessment of Developments, 1969–1998. *Philosophy of Science* 67: 102–115.

Suppes, P. 1967. What Is a Scientific Theory. In S. Morgenbesser (ed.), *Philosophy of Science Today*. New York: Basic Books, pp. 66–67.

Suppes, P. 1992. Axiomatic Methods in Science. In M. E. Carvallo (ed.), *Nature, Cognition and System II. Current Systems-Scientijic Research on Natural and Cognitive Systems. Volume 2: On Complementarity and Beyond*. Dordrecht: Springer, pp. 205–232.

Suppes, P. 2002. *Representation and Invariance of Scientific Structures*. Stanford: CSLI Publications.

Thompson, P. 1989. *The Structure of Biological Theories*. Albany: State University of New York Press.

Thomson-Jones, M. 2012. Modeling without Mathematics. *Philosophy of Science* 79: 761–772.

Uebel, T. 2007. *Empiricism at the Crossroads: The Vienna Circle's Protocol-Sentence Debate*. Chicago: Open Court.

van Fraassen, B. C. 1980. *The Scientific Image*. Oxford: Oxford University Press.

van Fraassen, B. C. 1985. Empiricism in the Philosophy of Science. In P. M. Churchland and C. A. Hooker (eds.), *Images of Science*. Chicago: Chicago University Press, pp. 245–308.

von Neumann, J. 1932. *Mathematical Foundations of Quantum Mechanics*. Princeton: Princeton University Press, 1955.

Weatherall, J. O. 2019a. Part 1: Theoretical Equivalence in Physics. *Philosophy Compass* 14(5): e12592: 1–11.

Weatherall, J. O. 2019b. Part 2: Theoretical Equivalence in Physics. *Philosophy Compass* 14(5): e12591: 1–12.

Winther, R. G. 2016. The Structure of Scientific Theories. In E. N. Zalta (ed.), *The Stanford Encyclopedia of Philosophy*. https://plato.stanford.edu/archives/win2016/entries/structure-scientific-theories/.

Worrall, J. 1984. An Unreal Image. *The British Journal for the Philosophy of Science* 34: 65–80.

Worrall, J. 2007. Miracles and Models: Why Reports of the Death of Structural Realism May Be Exaggerated. In A. O'Hare (ed.), *Philosophy of Science*. Cambridge: Cambridge University Press, pp. 125–154.

2
MODELS IN THE RECEIVED VIEW

2.1 Introduction

Models play an important role in science, and so an analysis of the structure of scientific theories must say what models are and identify their place in the edifice of science. We begin by distinguishing between two basic types of models: representational models and logical models (Section 2.2). This allows us to explicate the role of models in the Received View, which sees models as alternative interpretations of a theory's formalism (Section 2.3), and to ask the question of what the value is of having such models (Section 2.4). The Received View's conception of models has faced fierce criticism (Section 2.5). We then introduce set-theoretical structures and formal semantics (Section 2.6), and we discuss what it means for two structures to be isomorphic (Section 2.7). With this formal machinery in place, we can turn to the limitations of first-order logic. We begin by discussing limitations that are rooted in the restricted expressive power of first-order languages (Section 2.8*) and then turn to limiting results for first-order theories, focusing on the Löwenheim-Skolem theorem and on Gödel's first incompleteness theorem (Section 2.9*). We conclude by pointing out that these limitations are not ipso facto arguments against the Received View (Section 2.10).

2.2 Logical Models and Representational Models

Models matter. In his entry on models in the 10th edition of the *Encyclopaedia Britannica*, Boltzmann noted that "[m]odels in the mathematical, physical and mechanical science are of the greatest importance" (1911/1974, 213), and few would disagree with him. Unfortunately, the confusion about the nature of models is even greater than their importance. As we have seen in the Introduction, Goodman aptly noted that few terms are used as promiscuously as "model" and that

DOI: 10.4324/9781003285106-4

therefore almost anything can, in some sense, be referred to as a model. Much of this book will be concerned with identifying and unpacking the various uses of the term "model", and with understanding the roles different kinds of models play in science. The first crucial distinction is between logical models and representational models.[1] These two types of models will accompany us throughout the book, and they will play key roles in many different contexts. Indeed, they will provide the backdrop against which much of what is to come will be discussed, and so it is worth introducing them in some detail.

A *logical model* is a collection of objects, which have properties and stand in certain relations to each other, that make a formal sentence true if the terms of the sentence are interpreted as referring to these objects along with their properties and relations. Hence, being a logical model is a relational attribute that something has with respect to a formal sentence and an interpretation. An example will help to clarifying this idea. Consider the sentence "*Fa & Ga*". The syntax of the logical language we use is such that lower case letters like "*a*" refer to objects, upper case letters like "*F*" and "*G*" designate properties, and "*Fa*" indicates that the object designated by "*a*" has property designated by "*F*" (and likewise for "*Ga*"). So the sentence "*Fa & Ga*" says "object *a* has property *F* and object *a* has property *G*". At this level this is a purely formal sentence because it is not specified what object and what properties the sentence is about; the sentence is really just an "empty shell". An *interpretation* specifies what objects and properties the nonlogical terms in a formal sentence refer to. We can, for instance, interpret "*a*" as referring to the Tower of London, "*F*" as referring to the property of being founded in the year 1066, and "*G*" as referring to the property of being the venue of the execution of Lady Jane Grey. Under this interpretation, "*Fa & Ga*" says "the Tower of London was founded in 1066 and it was the venue of the execution of Lady Jane Grey". This is true, and hence the Tower of London together with the two properties mentioned are a logical model of "*Fa & Ga*".

Semantics is concerned with the relationship between symbols and what they stand for. A logical model is what is denoted by the symbols of a formal sentence under a certain interpretation, and so one can say that the model offers a *semantics* for the sentence. Models are not unique, and the same sentence can have many different models. Immanuel Kant together with the properties of being born in Königsberg and being the author of the *Critique of Pure Reason* is a model of "*Fa & Ga*", and so is South America with the properties of being cone-shaped and having most of its land mass south of the equator. There are no limits to what a logical model can be. In fact, anything can be a logical model if the terms of a formal sentence are interpreted so that they denote objects along with their properties and relations in a way that makes the sentence come out true.

The same idea is sometimes expressed in terms of the notion of *satisfaction*: a model is said to be a class of objects and relation that satisfy a certain formal sentence. In this context "satisfaction" is a technical term and simply means "making a sentence true under a certain interpretation". In the context of a discussion of scientific theories the relevant formal sentences are stated in the language of the formalism of a theory, and hence logical models are sometimes referred to as "models of a theory" or "models for a theory".[2] This is also the terminology common in formal logic, where formalisms are considered to be theories and logical models are models of such theories. The terminology is not entirely felicitous because, as we have seen in Section 1.3, a theory is more than just a formalism, and, as we will see below in Section 2.3, the Received View adds a further requirement for something to be a model of a scientific theory.

A *representational model* is an item that represents something else. The miniature replica of a cruise liner in the window of the travel agent is a model of RMS Laconia. The wooden reproduction in the aviation museum is a model of the *Spirit of St. Louis*, the single-engine monoplane in which Lindbergh completed the first solo transatlantic flight. The cardboard structure in the developer's showroom is a model of the block of flats that they are building. The US Army Corps of Engineer's San-Francisco-Bay-shaped hydraulic system is a model of the San Francisco Bay. The so-called logistic map is a model of the growth of a population of animals. A string of beads connected by springs is a model of a polymer. Pieces on a checkerboard are a model of social segregation. The Bohr model is a model of the hydrogen atom. And so on. What all these models have in common is that they are representations of something beyond themselves, and this is what makes them representational models.[3] It is common to refer to the part or aspect of the world that is represented by a model as the model's *target system*.[4] At this stage we operate with an intuitive notion of representation, and there is no harm in doing so. Nothing in the notion of a representational model depends on a particular analysis of representation. We will keep using the term in this way until Chapter 6, where we start analysing in detail what it involves for something to represent something else.

The notions of a logical model and a representational model are independent of one another. Something can be a logical model without also being a representational model, and vice versa. Under a particular interpretation of "a", "P", and "G" the Tower of London is a logical model of the sentence "$Fa \& Ga$", but this does not imply that the Tower is a representation of something else. Of course, the Tower *could* be taken to represent something else (maybe the horrors of capital punishment), but any such representation relation is wholly independent of the Tower's function as a logical model of "$Fa \& Ga$". Likewise, the miniature replica in the travel agent's window represents RMS Laconia irrespective of whether it also is a logical model of some formal sentence. Being a logical model and being a representational model are not intrinsic properties of objects; they are functions that objects perform in a certain context. Sometimes objects function as an interpretation of a formal sentence; sometimes objects function as a representation of something else; and sometimes objects do neither one nor the other.

Independence is not incompatibility, and nothing prevents the two concepts from cooccurring. In fact, as Hesse (1967, 354) points out, many models in science are at once logical and representational models. Newton's model of planetary motion is a case in point. At the end of Section 1.2 we noted that Newton derived

Kepler's first and second laws of planetary motion from his equation of motion and the law of gravity. To do so he constructed a model. The model is an imagined object that consists of two perfect spheres with a homogenous mass distribution that gravitationally interact with each other but nothing else (i.e. the spheres are gravitationally isolated from the rest of the universe). The assumption of homogeneity allowed him to run calculations as if all the mass was concentrated in the spheres' centres. Newton also assumed that gravity was the only force between the two spheres. The large sphere's mass is vastly larger than the small sphere's and so he assumed that the large sphere was at rest and that the small sphere orbited around it. With these assumptions in place he turned to $\vec{F} = m\vec{a}$. Taking $\vec{F}$ to be the gravitational force exerted on the small sphere by the large sphere, m the mass of the small sphere, and $\vec{a}$ the acceleration of the small sphere, he could calculate the trajectory of the small sphere and show that it was an ellipse.

Newton's determination of a planetary orbit involves both a logical and a representational model. To run his calculations Newton introduced an imaginary system consisting of two homogenous perfect spheres that interact gravitationally with each other and nothing else, with the larger sphere occupying a fixed position. Let us call this imaginary system the Newtonian model of planetary motion ("Newtonian model", for short).[5] The Newtonian model is a logical model of the equation of motion because the terms of the equation – $\vec{F}$, m, and $\vec{a}$ – have been interpreted as referring to features of the model and the equation is true under this interpretation. So the Newtonian model is to "$\vec{F} = m\vec{a}$" what the Tower of London is to "$Fx \& Gx$". But there is more to Newton's model. Interpreting an equation in terms of two homogenous perfect spheres does not create a model of anything else, let alone planetary motion. For the Newtonian model to be *about* the solar system, the model must also be a representational model: the two spheres must be taken to represent the sun and a planet. Therefore, the two spheres are to the sun and the planet what the miniature replica is to RMS Laconia. Thus, the example of Newton's model shows that, and how, the same object can at once be a logical model and a representational model.

2.3 Models in the Received View

As we have seen in Section 1.3, the Received View takes a theory to be a logical system with axioms whose non-logical vocabulary is interpreted either in terms of something observable or in terms of something unobservable with the aid of correspondence rules. Let us call the theory's logical system together with its (uninterpreted) axioms the theory's *formalism*. In other words, a theory's formalism is what one gets when one strips away the interpretation from the theory. The formalism is like "$Fa \& Ga$": it is an "empty shell" and *per se* it is not about anything. Confronted with a formal sentence one can always look for a set of objects and properties that make the sentence true if its terms are interpreted as referring to those objects and properties. In other words, one can always look for a logical model. A theory's formalism is no exception. Given a formalism, one can try to find a logical model of the formalism. As we have seen above, logical models are not unique and so there are, at least in principle, many logical models. So one can set oneself the task of finding an interpretation of a theory's formalism that is not the interpretation given by the original formulation of the theory, and thereby construct a logical model of the theory's formalism that is *different* from the standard interpretation of the theory.

Within the Received View, models are basically just that: alternative logical models for the theory's formalism (a qualification will follow shortly). Braithwaite says that a model is a "second interpretation of the calculus" (1954, 156) or "another interpretation of the theory's calculus" (1962, 225), whereby his "calculus" is synonymous with my "formalism".[6] Hence, to get a model we take a theory, strip it of its interpretation, and then reinterpret the theory's formalism in terms of something other than the theory's "standard" domain of application.

In principle there are no constraints on the choice of a logical model, and an indefinite number of logical models for a given theory can be found. However, an aimless proliferation of logical models contributes nothing to our understanding of a theory. For a model to be useful it must have a crucial feature: the model must be familiar to us. That is, the formalism must be interpreted in terms of something recognisable. Or, in Hesse's words, "a model is drawn from a familiar and well-understood process" (1961, 21).[7] This requirement applies to all terms of the formalism, in particular the terms that were considered theoretical terms under the standard interpretation of the theory. These terms were given an "indirect" interpretation via correspondence rules, which made them difficult to grasp intuitively. These terms now also receive a direct interpretation in terms of something familiar to us. In other words, then, a *model of a scientific theory* is a *recognisable* logical model. Or, in other words, it is a reinterpretation of the theory's *entire* nonlogical vocabulary in terms of something familiar.[8]

As an example, consider the kinetic theory of gases. The theory takes a gas to consist of a large number of molecules that move freely unless they either collide with each other or the walls of the vessel containing the gas. A description of the gas' manifest behaviour (for instance that it spreads when a confining wall is removed) is derived as a theorem from the axioms of the theory. Since molecules and their motions are unobservable, and since terms like "gas molecule" and "trajectory of a molecule" are theoretical terms, the theory is not easy to comprehend. To get an intuitive grip on the theory, we can find a familiar model. One way of doing this is to re-interpret the theory in terms of billiard balls. The terms that were formerly interpreted as referring to molecules are now interpreted as referring to billiard balls; the terms that were interpreted as referring to the trajectories of molecules are now interpreted as referring to the trajectory of billiard balls; and so on. A bunch of billiard balls is a logical model of the theory's formalism because they make claims of the theory true,[9] and, since we are familiar with billiard balls, they are also a model of the kinetic theory of gases. Other well-known examples of models of this kind are water waves as a model of the acoustic theory of sound waves, and the solar system as a model of the Bohr theory of the atom.[10]

Models as construed in the Received View are not used representationally, and they play no role in bringing about, or even understanding, the theory's relation to the world. The theory relates to its subject matter through observation terms and correspondence rules, and models are immaterial in this.

2.4 Why Have Models?

The first and obvious advantage of having a model for a scientific theory is that it provides intuitive access to a potentially complicated and confusing theory because a model is a familiar object. Nagel thinks that this advantage is so considerable that in practice theories are often presented through their models rather than in the form of an axiomatic logical system with correspondence rules. Writing about atomic theory, he observes that

> [t]he Bohr theory is usually not presented as an abstract set of postulates, augmented by an appropriate number of rules of correspondence for the uninterpreted nonlogical terms implicitly defined by the postulates. It is customarily expounded . . . by way of relatively familiar notions . . . at least part of whose content can be visually imagined. Such a presentation is adopted, among other reasons, because it can be understood with greater ease than can an inevitably longer and more complicated purely formal exposition.
>
> *(1961, 95)*

One of the chief advantages of an intuitively graspable model is that it serves the purpose of scientific exploration. Both Nagel (1961, 107–117) and Braithwaite (1962, 229–230) emphasised the heuristic role of models in the construction of theories, the exploration of the implications of a theory, and the extension of a theory into new domains. Models serve this purpose in part because they provide the entry ticket to *as-if* reasoning: we can think about hydrogen atoms as if they were a little solar systems; we can think about gases as if they were collections of billiard balls; and so on (Braithwaite 1953, 93). This helps scientists to think through situations that would otherwise not be easily graspable, and it allows them to do things with theories that they might not be able to do if they operated solely at the formal level.

Yet, models also bear perils. Nagel brands a model "a potential intellectual trap" (1961, 115) and Braithwaite warns that "[t]he price of the employment of models is eternal vigilance" (1953, 93). The main pitfall is that scientists get too cosy with models and eventually identify objects in the model with objects of the theory. The issue is not so much that anybody would commit the basic error of literally identifying, say, a gas with a collection of billiard balls. The problem is that we may be tempted to carry over properties of the model to the objects of the theory that cannot be so carried over. The crucial point is that only those properties that the model possesses *in virtue of being an interpretation* of the formalism can be projected onto the domain of the theory. Models usually have a great many properties other than those grounding the reinterpretation of a formalism, and the reinterpretation does not justify projecting these properties onto the objects of the theory. We can infer from the billiard ball model that when a gas molecule collides with the wall of the vessel the angle of incidence is equal to the angle or reflection, but we cannot infer that molecules are coloured and have numbers written on them. In actual practice the line between properties that are part of the interpretation of the formalism and ones that are not is not always straightforward to draw, which may give rise to controversies (we return to this issue in Chapter 10).

A further function of models is that they can be used to establish the consistency of a theory's formalism. Formal logic teaches us that a formalism is consistent if it has a model. Braithwaite (1953, 93, 1962, 227) rightly points out that this furnishes a valuable tool to check whether a formalism is consistent.

Nagel's and Braithwaite's largely positive assessment of models contrasts with Carnap's and Hempel's deflationary attitude. Neither of them denies the pedagogical, psychological, heuristic, and even logical value of models, but they insist that eventually models are dispensable. Carnap's assessment of the value of modelling is clear and unrepentant:

> When abstract, nonintuitive formulas, as, e.g., Maxwell's equations of electromagnetism, were proposed as new axioms, physicists endeavoured to make them "intuitive" by constructing a "model", i.e., a way of representing electromagnetic micro-processes by analogy to known macro-processes, e.g., movements of visible things. Many attempts have been made in this direction, but without satisfactory results. It is important to realize that the discovery of a model has no more than an aesthetic or didactic or at best heuristic value, but it is not at all essential for a successful application of the physical theory.
>
> *(1938, 209–210)*

Later, Carnap warned that that a "physicist must always guard against taking a visual model as more than a pedagogical device or makeshift help" (Carnap 1966, 174). Hempel's discussion of models is somewhat more sympathetic, but he also insists that models "add nothing to the content of the theory and are, thus, logically dispensable" (1970, 157).[11]

As Bailer-Jones points out, this attitude about models is hardly surprising given Carnap's and Hempel's commitment to rational reconstruction (1999, 26). As we have seen in Section 1.7, authors committed to the ideal of rational reconstruction see their task in finding a cleaned-up version of a theory that provides clear definitions of previously vague concepts and makes the logical structure of the theory transparent. The study of a historical process of investigation, of how scientists actually proceed, and of what heuristics are used, is seen as a subject matter for psychology rather than for philosophy. So Carnap's and Hempel's disinterest in models is not the result of an erroneous understanding of scientific practice; it is a consequence of their approach to philosophy of science.

Before turning to criticisms, a further purported function of models should be mentioned. As we have seen in Section 1.3, the Received View sees theoretical discourse as dependent on discourse about observations, which raises the issue of the meaning of theoretical terms. If a theoretical term is nothing but a complicated abbreviation of a description of something observable, what do theoretical terms mean? It has been suggested that theoretical terms get their meaning from a model of a scientific theory rather than from correspondence rules and implicit definitions. We will discuss this suggestion in Section 4.5.

2.5 Criticisms

Spector (1965, 126–128) thinks that the Received View's notion of a model is too liberal because certain undesirable items get classified as models. The first item on his list are Platonic entities. A formalism can often be interpreted in terms of Platonic entities such as perfect geometrical shapes or numbers. Yet, Spector says, these are not a model of a theory. It is, however, unclear whether the Received View must invoke Platonic entities as models. Logical empiricists would not recognise such entities and hence deny that there is something to begin with that could serve as a model. And even if they did admit Platonic entities into their ontology, they could argue that Platonic entities do not meet the criterion of familiarity, which is prerequisite for something to be a model.

The second item on Spector's list (*ibid.*) are alternative theories. Two theories can use the same formalism and yet be about completely different subject matters. Indeed, logical empiricists have offered what they saw as an alternative definition to the definition we have seen in Section 2.3, according to which models are different theories based on the same formalism. Brodbeck says that "[i]f the laws of one theory have the same form as the laws of another theory, then one may be said to be a *model* for the other" (1959, 379, original emphasis), and Braithwaite states that "a *model for a theory* T is another theory M which corresponds to the theory T in respect of deductive structure" (1962, 225). Braithwaite takes this definition to be "equivalent" to the definition in Section 2.3 (*ibid.*).[12] Spector takes issue with this notion of model. He discusses the example of acoustic theory and electric circuit theory, which are about different things and yet use the same formal structure. By that token, the Received View should regard one theory as a model of the other. This is a conclusion Spector wants to resist on grounds that there is no unity of the theories' subject matter. Similarly, Achinstein (1964, 332–334, 1965, 111) argues that the logical empiricists' definition of a model leads to an implausible proliferation of models because not every instance of shared formalism should be regarded as a model.[13]

This proliferation is not an unintended consequence of the Received View's notion of a model, and proponents of the view explicitly embrace the proposition that theories which share a formalism are models of each other. Hence, Spector and Achinstein cannot appeal to "unintended consequences" internal to the Received View, and they must reject the Received View's notion of a model for reasons that are external to the view. The reason proffered is an appeal to scientific practice. Spector (*ibid.*) refers to what physicists would recognise as models, and Achinstein (*ibid.*) argues that the logical empiricists' notion of a model does not do justice to the examples of models one finds in the sciences. Proponents of the Received View would have been unimpressed by this criticism because they see neither an analysis of what physicists think nor an analysis of examples in scientific practice as being within the purview of philosophy of science. To make this criticism stick, a meta-philosophical discussion must be had about the aims and methods of philosophical analysis, which brings us back to the discussion about rational reconstruction in Section 1.7.

A criticism pointing in a similar direction is that models in science are not logical models. Achinstein (1964, 330–334, 1972, 236), Spector (1965, 130–135), and Swanson (1966, 302–303) argued that models, rather than being an interpretation of a formalism, should be seen as items that bear a substantive relation to a part of the world.[14] This substantive relation has often been identified as analogy, important physical similarities that hold between the model and the system that the model is about. In effect this criticism urges that models in science are not logical models but representational models. This begs the question against the Received View, at least if no further argument is given for why models must be representational models. Such an argument would, presumably, be based on scientific practice, which would bring us back to the point in the previous paragraph.

2.6 Logical Models and Structures

In Section 2.2 we introduced the notion of a logical model as something that makes a formal sentence true. Our example was the Tower of London, which is a logical model of the formal sentence "$Fa \& Ga$" if the two predicate variables are interpreted, respectively, as referring to the properties of being founded in the year 1066 and being the venue of the execution of Lady Jane Grey. This is all we need as far as the use of models within the Received View is concerned, and we could simply leave it at that and move on. However, the notion has been further developed in logic, and this development has turned out to be crucial both for the formulation of the Model Theoretical View, which we discuss in Part II, and for the criticisms that this view levelled against the Received View. We will discuss this development now so that we have the requisite tools later in the book. The development in question is the advent of structural models and the sub-discipline of logic called *model theory*.[15] In the broadest sense, model theory is the study of the interpretation of formal languages in terms of structures.

As we have seen in Section 2, the Tower of London is not the only model of the sentence "$Fa \& Ga$". Immanuel Kant, South America, and countless other objects are also models of "$Fa \& Ga$". While the material constitution of the models matters in some contexts, it is irrelevant in others. From a logical point of view, there is often little interest in the objects and properties and relations themselves, and what matters is the "formal structure" of the models. What the models of "$Fa \& Ga$" we have seen so far have in common is that they consist of one object with two properties instantiated by the object, and it is obvious that *any* object with two properties is a model of "$Fa \& Ga$". What matters from a formal point of view is only that there is an object (in this context often referred to as an *individual*); it does not matter whether the object is a castle, a philosopher, or a continent. These "material" characterisations can be stripped away, and we end up with dummies or placeholders: objects whose only feature is "being an object". There are no such objects in our world; they are mathematical abstractions, and we consider them because they are useful for formal analysis. In what follows we use italicised lowercase Roman letters with subscripts to denote such objects. For instance, a_1, a_2, a_3 denote three such objects.

Objects have properties. The Tower of London was built in 1066. Relations hold between objects; they define how objects are to one another. Examples are *standing to the right of, being in love with,* and *being nicer than.* These are examples of binary relations because they hold between two objects. There are relations for any natural number n. *Standing in-between* is a ternary relation (because one thing stands between two other things), and so on. The *arity* of a relation is the number n of objects that enter into the relation, and we speak of an *n-ary* relation if n objects enter into it.[16] Once we have the notion of arity at hand, a property is simply a relation with arity 1, and for this reason it is common in logic not to distinguish between properties and relations, and to take the term "relation" to also include properties. I will follow this convention.

The things between which a relation holds is its *extension*. The extension of "blue" is the class of all blue things; the extension of *hotter than* is the collection of all pairs of objects where the first has a higher temperature than the second; and so on. Two relations are *coextensive* if they have the same extension. That two relations are coextensive does not mean that the relations themselves are the same. *Being with heart* and *being with stomach* are coextensive because all creatures who have a heart also have a stomach and vice versa; and yet the two properties are not identical because having a heart and having a stomach are different things.

A "deflationary" move similar to the one we made in the case of objects is now also needed for relations. From a formal point of view, it does not matter what the relation "in itself" is, and one only cares about which objects enter into the relation. Russell makes this point succinctly in his *Introduction to Mathematical Philosophy*:

> For mathematical purposes . . . the only thing of importance about a relation is the cases in which it holds, not its intrinsic nature. Just as a class may be defined by various different but co-extensive concepts – e.g. "man" and "featherless biped" – so two relations which are conceptually different may

> hold in the same set of instances. . . . From the mathematical point of view, the only thing of importance about the relation "father" is that it defines this set of ordered couples.
>
> *(1919/1993, 60)*

That is to say that relations are specified purely extensionally – a relation is nothing over and above its extension. And to specify an extension we only need the kind of dummy objects we have just introduced, not "real" physical things.

This idea can be expressed more elegantly if we introduce the notion of an ordered *n-tuple* ("tuple" for short). A *n*-tuple is an *ordered* list of *n* objects. It is a convention to list the elements of a tuple in parentheses. If we swap two objects in the list, we get a different tuple. Hence the 3-tuples (a_1, a_2, a_3) and (a_1, a_3, a_2) are different tuples. We can then define an *n-ary* relation r as a set of *n*-tuples. For instance, the set $r = \{(a_1, a_2), (a_2, a_3)\}$ defines a particular binary relation on three objects. This definition satisfies Russell's requirement because nothing has been said about what the relation "intrinsically" is, nor indeed what the objects "intrinsically" are. The three objects could be three women – Jane, Nora, and Lily – and the relation could be *mother of*. The definition of r then says that the relation holds between Jane and Nora, and between Nora and Lily. But the objects could also be bricks and the relation could be *being placed directly on top of*. There is a myriad of possibilities. The crucial point is that these possibilities do not matter for a purely extensionally defined relation.

Relations thus understood can only have formal properties, i.e. properties that pertain to their extension. An example of such property is *asymmetry*. A binary relation is asymmetric iff it is the case that whenever it holds of a tuple (a_1, a_2) it does not hold of the "inverted" tuple (a_2, a_1). This property can be *illustrated* with the above example: *mother of* is asymmetric because if Jane is the mother of Nora, then Nora cannot also be the mother of Jane. But we do not need *mother of*, or indeed any substantive relation, to *define* asymmetry, which can be introduced at the purely formal level. From the point of view of extensionally defined relations, there is no difference between *mother of* and *being placed directly on top of*: they are both asymmetric binary relations.

With these notions in place, we can now define a *structure*: a structure S is a composite entity consisting of (i) a non-empty set U of objects called the *domain* (or universe) of the structure and (ii) an indexed set R (i.e. an ordered list) of relations on U.[17] The qualification that R be an indexed set simply means that relations are labelled and we can speak of the first or the fifth relation, which will be convenient later on when we define an isomorphism between structures. So we say that a structure is the tuple $S = (U, R)$. As a simple example of a structure of this kind consider a structure that has a domain $U = \{a_1, a_2, a_3\}$ with three objects and a set $R = (r_1, r_2, r_3)$ of relations consisting of a binary relation $r_1 = \{(a_1, a_2), (a_2, a_3), (a_1, a_3)\}$ and two unary relations (i.e. properties) $r_2 = \{a_1, a_2, a_3\}$ and $r_3 = \{a_2\}$.[18]

The structures we have defined in the previous paragraph might more aptly be called "abstract structures", "mathematical structures", or "set-theoretical structures" to emphasises that they consist of nothing but dummy objects and extensionally defined relations. In these terms, Russell points out that abstract structures are all that we need for the purposes of mathematics, and indeed logic and set-theory; insofar as these disciplines study structures, they study abstract structures. As Redhead notes, abstract structures can be contrasted with what he calls "concrete structures" (2001, 74). Examples of concrete structures are "a pile of bricks, timbers and slates, which are then 'fitted together' to make a house, or brush strokes which 'relate' to form a picture" (*ibid.*). In Russell's terms, a concrete structure is one in which both the objects and the relations have specified "intrinsic natures"; abstract structures are ones in which this is not the case. The structure with domain $U = \{$Jane, Nora, Lily$\}$ and an set $R = ($*mother of*$)$ is a concrete structure because it is specified that the objects of the domain are three specific women and the relation between them is *mother of*. The structure that consists of the domain $U = \{a_1, a_2, a_3\}$ and the set $R = (r_1)$ with $r_1 = \{(a_1, a_2), (a_2, a_3)\}$ is an abstract structure, because neither the objects nor the relation have an intrinsic nature. There is an interesting philosophical question about what it takes for a physical thing – a pile of bricks or a group of women – to be a concrete *structure* as opposed to a "bare" entity, and will discuss this in some detail in Section 6.5. For now we rely on an intuitive understanding of what a concrete structure is (which we can do without detriment because there is nothing wrong with our intuitive understanding, which, as we will see, will need unpacking but not revision). In what follows I adopt the convention that "structure" (when used without qualifier) means abstract structure; when I refer to concrete structures I will say so explicitly.

Two variants of our definition of a structure have to be mentioned because they play a role in various contexts and will be used in later chapters. The first variant defines structures so that they also include operations.[19] An n-place operation (or function) o on a class A is a map from the set of n-tuples that can be formed with elements of A to A.[20] If $a_1, ..., a_n \in A$ then the value of the operation is denoted by $o(a_1, ..., a_n)$. Like relations, operations are defined purely extensionally, simply by listing which n-tuples get mapped onto which element. It is obvious that operations can be reduced to relations because the n-place operation o is equivalent to the $n+1$-ary relation formed of the tuples $(a_1, ..., a_n, o(a_1, ..., a_n))$. Operations are sometimes introduced despite being strictly speaking redundant. The reason for this is that structural reconstructions of scientific theories come out looking more natural in a framework with operations because operations are ubiquitous in science and recasting them as relations ends up looking contrived. We will see examples of this in Chapter 5. In case one includes operations, a structure is a triple $S = (U, R, O)$ where U and R are as above, and O is an ordered set of operations on U.[21]

The second variant will play an important role when we discuss conditions of theory identity in Section 5.5. As defined so far, a structure contains only objects and relations (and possibly operations). Some authors use a broader definition of a structure, one that also includes certain linguistic constituents: *constants, relation symbols*, and *operation symbols*. Specifically, for every object in a in U there is a linguistic symbol, usually called a *constant* σ_a, that is interpreted as denoting a; for every relation r in the structure there is a relation symbol σ_r that is interpreted as denoting r, and for every operation o in the structure there is an operation symbol σ_o that is interpreted as denoting o. An *interpretation I* (sometimes *interpretation function*) is an assignment of symbols to parts of the structure (that is, an interpretation amounts to a specification of which symbol refers to which parts of the structure).[22] The collection of these symbols is known as the *signature* of S and is denoted by Σ. A structure then is defined as the triple (S, I, Σ). On this definition, a structure consists of set-theoretical structure plus a set of symbols and an interpretation. Following Hudetz (2019) I call such structures *model-theoretical structures*,[23] and the study of the relation between symbols in a formal language and structures is known as *formal semantics*.

By way of illustration, consider again the above example of $S = (U, R)$ with $U = \{a_1, a_2, a_3\}$, $R = (r_1, r_2, r_3,)$, and $r_1 = \{(a_1, a_2), (a_2, a_3), (a_1, a_3)\}$, $r_2 = \{a_1, a_2, a_3\}$ and $r_3 = \{a_2\}$. If nothing else is added, this is a set-theoretical structure. Now consider the signature $\Sigma = \{\sigma_{a_1}, \sigma_{a_2}, \sigma_{a_3}, \sigma_{r_1}, \sigma_{r_2}, \sigma_{r_3}\}$ and the interpretation I saying: symbol σ_{a_1} refers to element a_1, symbol σ_{r_1} refers to relation r_1, etc. Σ is the signature of S, and the triple (S, I, Σ) is a model-theoretical structure.

Hence, model-theoretical structures contain symbols denoting parts of the structure. What such a structure does not contain are syntactic elements that would allow us to form sentences or formulate an argument: there are no connectives, no quantifiers, and no rules of inference. So the structure contains a rudimentary language that allows us to refer to parts of the structure, but not to formulate claims about it.

The crucial point, and this brings us back to our point of departure, is that set-theoretical structures can be logical models. In fact, it is a crucial move in modern logic that we interpret the symbols occurring in formal sentences as referring to the elements of a structure (and if we define structures so that they contain symbols, then the sentences we form in a language employ these symbols).[24] Consider again our sentence *"Fa & Ga"*. We can interpret the symbols in this sentence as referring to parts of the above example structure. For instance, we can interpret *"a"* as referring to object a_2, *"F"* as referring to r_2, and *"G"* as referring to r_3. Under this interpretation *"Fa & Ga"* is true (because a_2 has both properties r_2 and r_3). Hence, S is a (logical) model of the sentence. If, by contrast, we interpret *"a"* as referring to object a_1, while leaving the interpretations of *"F"* and *"G"* unaltered, the sentence is wrong (because a_1 does not have property r_3). Under this interpretation S is not a model of the sentence.

The fact that a certain model-theoretical structure (S, I, Σ) makes a sentence p true is expressed by saying that "(S, I, Σ) satisfies p". In symbolic notation this is written using the so-called double turnstile: $(S, I, \Sigma) \vDash p$. This way of thinking about models and languages goes back to Tarski, which is why what we have been describing so far is also known as *Tarskian semantics* and the structures it employs are sometimes called *Tarskian models*.[25]

A distinction that will be useful later on (in particular in Chapter 5) is the one between object-language and meta-language. An *object language* is a language that talks directly about the subject matter. In the above example we interpreted the symbols of the sentence "*Fx & Gx*" as referring to parts of the structure *S*. Since *S* is the object of study, "*Fa & Ga*" is a sentence in the object-language. In the context of arithmetic, the Arabic numeral "7" is a symbol in the object-language that refers to the number seven, and in the context of Newtonian mechanics "*v*" is symbol in the object-language that refers to the velocity of an object. A *meta-language* is a language that is used to describe the object language. When interpreting "*Fa & Ga*" we said "the symbol '*a*' refers to object a_2 ". This is a sentence in a meta-language because it talks about the language itself (it specifies the reference of a symbol). The statement "the sentence '*Fa & Ga*' is true" is also a sentence in a meta-language because it concerns the sentence "*Fa & Ga*" itself.

2.7   Isomorphic Structures

Structures can bear relations to each other. Such relations are crucial to understanding the limitations of formalisms, to which we turn later in this chapter, and to formulating identity criteria for theories, which we discuss in Chapter 5. The most important relation into which two structures can enter is isomorphism. The word "isomorph" is composed of the Greek words for "equal" and "shape", and literally means "of equal shape". So two structures are isomorphic if they have the same shape. Intuitively, two structures have the same shape if their domains have the same number of elements and one can pair up the elements of the two structures with each other so that the paired-up elements in both structures enter into the same relations. Formally, then, two structures $S^{(1)} = (U^{(1)}, R^{(1)})$ and $S^{(2)} = (U^{(2)}, R^{(2)})$ are *isomorphic* iff there is a mapping $f : U^{(1)} \rightarrow U^{(2)}$ so that (i) f is bijective (one-to-one) and (ii) f preserves the system of relations of the structure.

Let us unpack these conditions, beginning with (i). A mapping f is bijective iff it is injective and surjective. It is injective iff it never maps distinct elements of $U^{(1)}$ to the same element of $U^{(2)}$: $f(x) \neq f(y)$ for all $x \neq y$. A mapping f is surjective iff each element of $U^{(2)}$ is mapped to by at least one element of $U^{(1)}$: for every z in $U^{(2)}$ there exists an x in $U^{(1)}$ so that $z = f(x)$. Colloquially speaking, a surjective mapping "hits" the entire codomain $U^{(2)}$. Hence, a bijective mapping pairs up all elements of $U^{(1)}$ and $U^{(2)}$ so that no element in either domain is left out and so that no element is paired up with more than one element. Turning to (ii), f preserves a system of relations if the following is the case. For all relations r in $R^{(1)}$, the n-tuple $(a_1, ..., a_n)$ of elements of $U^{(1)}$ satisfies the relation r iff the n-tuple $(f(a_1), ..., f(a_n))$ of elements of $U^{(2)}$ satisfies the relation s in $R^{(2)}$ where s is the relation in $R^{(2)}$ that corresponds to r in $R^{(1)}$, and *vice versa*.[26, 27] It remains to be said what we mean by "corresponding" relations and operations. Recall that $R^{(1)}$ and $R^{(2)}$ are *indexed* sets (i.e. ordered lists).

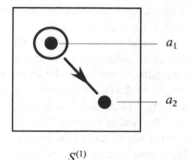

$S^{(1)}$

FIGURE 2.1 Illustration of structure $S^{(1)}$.

So the notion of a relation in $R^{(1)}$ corresponding to a relation in $R^{(2)}$ means that the two have the same index, where both structures have the same index set (and therefore contain the same number of relations) and corresponding relations have the same arity; for instance, r_3 in $R^{(1)}$ corresponds s_3 in $R^{(2)}$ and not to s_2. If a mapping satisfies all these conditions, then it is an *isomorphism*.

To make this definition more intuitive, let us illustrate visually what it means for two structures to be isomorphic. Take $S^{(1)}$ to be a simple structure that consists of a domain with two objects, $U^{(1)} = \{a_1, a_2\}$, and an indexed set $R^{(1)}$ that contains a property $\{a_1\}$ and a binary relation $\{(a_1, a_2)\}$ (where the property has index 1 and the relation index 2). This structure is illustrated in Figure 2.1. The dots symbolise the objects of the domain (the dotted lines are used to indicate which dot is a_1 and which is a_2); the circle symbolises the property (i.e. the dot being encircled means that the object has the property); and the arrow symbolises the binary relation (i.e. the two dots being connected by the arrow means that the relation holds between them). In Figure 2.2 we see again $S^{(1)}$, now accompanied by three other structures $S^{(2)}$, $S^{(3)}$, and $S^{(4)}$, which are symbolised in the same way. To indicate that they are different structures with different objects, properties, and relations, we use squares, triangles, and hexagons to symbolise the objects, and different stroke styles for the circles and arrows.

In Figure 2.3 we check whether there is an isomorphism between $S^{(1)}$ and the other structures. At the top of the figure we see that $S^{(1)}$ and $S^{(2)}$ are indeed isomorphic. The structures meet condition (i) because their objects stand in a bijective relation, which is indicated by the thin arrows between the elements of the two structures; and the way that objects are paired up meets condition (ii) because it preserves the system of properties and relations, which is indicated by the "wavy" arrows which connect the property and the relation in $S^{(1)}$ with the property and the relation $S^{(2)}$. In the middle of the figure we try to set up an isomorphism between at $S^{(1)}$ and $S^{(3)}$, but we fail to do so because the first object of $S^{(3)}$ has no property (there is no circle around it!), and so there is nothing in $S^{(3)}$ that would correspond to the property of the first object of $S^{(1)}$. So condition (ii) fails and the two structures are not isomorphic. At the bottom of the figure we

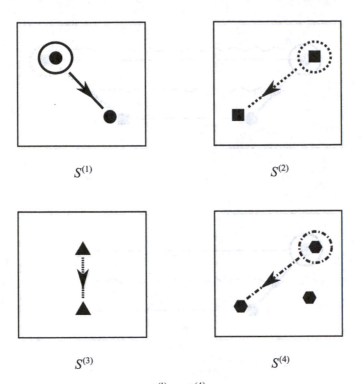

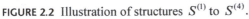

FIGURE 2.2 Illustration of structures $S^{(1)}$ to $S^{(4)}$.

see that $S^{(1)}$ is not isomorphic to $S^{(4)}$ either because there is no object in $S^{(1)}$ that could be mapped onto the third object in $S^{(4)}$, which means that condition (i) fails.

In effect two structures being isomorphic means that they are identical as far as their structural properties are concerned, which is why mathematicians often identify isomorphic structures with each other. We may call two structures by different names, or they may originate in different contexts, and for these reasons we may think that they are different. But if they turn out to be isomorphic, then are not different after all, at least from a structural point of view. Note that the notion of isomorphism as introduced here is symmetric (if $S^{(1)}$ is isomorphic to $S^{(2)}$, then $S^{(2)}$ is isomorphic to $S^{(1)}$), reflexive (every structure is isomorphic to itself) and transitive (if $S^{(1)}$ is isomorphic to $S^{(2)}$, and $S^{(2)}$ is isomorphic to $S^{(3)}$, then $S^{(1)}$ is isomorphic to $S^{(3)}$).

Isomorphism is not the only one kind of mapping between structures, and many other mappings have been defined and studied. We collectively refer to all these mappings as *morphisms*. We are not dwelling on alternative mappings here because they will play only a marginal role in the remainder of the book, but two deserve to be mentioned briefly. A mapping is an *embedding* iff it isomorphically maps $S^{(1)}$ onto a substructure of $S^{(2)}$, where substructure of $S^{(2)}$ is a part of that structure that

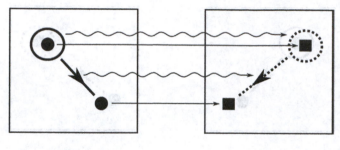

$S^{(1)}$ $S^{(2)}$

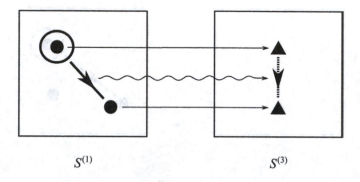

$S^{(1)}$ $S^{(3)}$

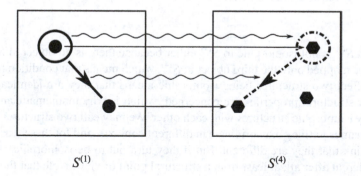

$S^{(1)}$ $S^{(4)}$

FIGURE 2.3 Illustration of isomorphic and non-isomorphic structures.

satisfies all requirements of a structure. A mapping is a *homomorphism* iff it satis-fies all requirements of an isomorphism except that it need not be one-to-one.[28]

With these tools in hand, one can now study the class of models of a theory. Consider a set of formal sentences of the kind we discussed in Section 2.2. In keeping with the spirit of the Received View we consider this set a theory and denote it by T. We can then define the class C_T of all structures that are models of T (that is, C_T contains all structures that make all the sentences in T true under some interpretation of the terms in T). This raises the question of what this class looks like. What kind of structures do we find in this class and how do these structures relate to one another? In special cases it can happen that all models of a theory are isomorphic. Since isomorphic models are (as we have seen above) identical to each other from a structural point of view, such a theory effectively only has one model. A theory with this feature is called *categorical*.

Many theories are not categorical. As a simple example consider the sentence "$\forall x(Px)$", where "$\forall$" is the universal quantifier that expresses that what follows holds for all objects x. So the sentence says "all objects x have property P". Then assume our theory consist only of that sentence. This theory is obviously true of structures with a different number of elements (and which are therefore not isomorphic), and hence is not categorical.

This brings us to the notion of an unintended model. In some applications one may have a particular structure in mind and then look for a set of axioms that effectively describes this structure. So rather than starting with a sentence (or class of sentences) and then ask "which structures are models of this sentence?", one can start with a model (or class of models) and then look for an effective description of this model. If this happens, the model we start from is the *intended model*. If it then turns out that the sentence also has other models – ones that one did not have in mind when picking the sentence – then these models are *unintended models*.

The *cardinality* of a set is a measure of the number of elements in the set, or the set's size. If a set has a finite number of elements, its cardinality is simply the number of elements that it contains. So the cardinality of the domain of the first structure in Figure 2.2 is 2. Things get more complicated when we deal with infinite sets because not all infinities are the same.[29] The "smallest" kind of an infinite cardinality is the kind we find in the natural numbers. This cardinality is denoted by $\aleph^0$ (say "aleph-zero"). Roughly speaking, a set has the cardinality $\aleph^0$ if its elements are countable. In a famous argument Cantor showed that the set of the rational numbers (i.e. the set of all fractions) has cardinality $\aleph^0$ and that the real numbers have a cardinality that is larger than $\aleph^0$. The continuum hypothesis says that the cardinality of the real numbers is $\aleph^1$. The higher cardinals ($\aleph^2$, $\aleph^3$, . . .) are constructs that have no intuitive explanation in terms of either counting or real numbers. The alephs are known as *infinite cardinalities*.

The cardinality of a structure is the cardinality of its domain. For obvious reasons it is a necessary condition for two structures to be isomorphic that they have the same cardinality (because if they have a different cardinality there is no bijective mapping between them). If a theory (understood as a sentence in a formal language) has models of different cardinalities, then the theory is not categorical.

2.8* Speakable and Unspeakable in First-Order Languages

In Section 1.4 we mentioned that first-order logic is reported to be too weak to provide an adequate formal framework for scientific theories. In the remainder of this chapter we discuss wherein these limitations lie.[30]

We have encountered the universal quantifier "$\forall$" earlier in this chapter. The other important quantifier is the existential quantifier "$\exists$", which expresses "there exists". So the sentence "$\exists x(Px)$" says "there exists an object x that has property P". Returning to our previous example with structure $S^{(1)} = (U^{(1)}, R^{(1)})$, the sentence "$\exists x(Px)$" is true in that structure if we interpret P as referring to the property $\{a_1\}$ because there is an object that has the property to which "P" refers, namely a_1. The hallmark of first-order logic is that "$\forall$" and "$\exists$" can be put *only* in front of variables that range over individuals, i.e. the objects in the domain of a structure; they cannot be in front of predicate symbols. So "$\exists x(Px)$" and "$\forall x(Px)$" are first-order sentences while sentences beginning with "$\forall P$"and "$\exists P$" are disallowed. The result of this rule is that first-order logic only allows for quantification over individuals and rules out quantification over relations (and recall that relations, as defined in the current context, include properties). This changes when we move to so-called second-order logic, where sentences with "$\forall P$"and "$\exists P$" are legitimate, and, therefore, quantification over relations is allowed. In second-order logic we can therefore not only say things like "there is an object such that . . ." or "all objects are such that . . ." but also "there is a relation such that . . ." or "all relations are such that . . .".[31]

In Section 1.7 we discussed rational reconstruction and pointed out that the fact that the Recevied View is a rational reconstruction is not ipso facto a reason to reject it. This argument, however, falters if a reconstruction turns out to be impossible, and opponents of the Recevied View have argued that this is the case. Suppes offers a clear statement of this position:

> A major point I want to make is that a simple standard formalization of most theories in the empirical sciences is not possible. The source of the difficulty is easy to describe. Almost all systematic scientific theories of any interest or power assume a great deal of mathematics as part of their formal background. There is no simple or elegant way to include this mathematical background in a standard formalization that assumes only the apparatus of elementary logic. This single point has been responsible for the lack of contact between much of the discussion of the structure of scientific theories by philosophers of science and the standard scientific discussions of these theories.
>
> *(2002, 27)*

By "standard formalization" Suppes means a formalisation in first-order logic. The worry Suppes expresses is somewhat difficult to pin down because what counts as "simple or elegant" may depend on context and, indeed, taste. Despite this, the worry is one that ought to be taken seriously because it is a fact of scientific practice that first-order formulations of theories tend to be rare. There are notable exceptions such as Montague's (1974) first-order axiomatisation of deterministic theories and the first-order axiomatisation of special relativity due to Andréka et al. (2012). But, on the whole, scientists seem to prefer to work in some (informal) version of higher order logic, which would suggest that they find that framework more convenient.

A more radical version of Suppes' worry is that first-order formulations not only fail to be "simple or elegant"; they are not possible *tout court*. We have encountered this claim in Section 1.4, where we saw Barwise and Feferman saying that important notions like *continuous function* and *random variable* cannot be expressed in first-order logic. The reason for this is that the limitations of first-order languages make them too weak to be able to capture certain crucial mathematical concepts.

At this point the reader may wonder why the entire discussion got so hung up on first-order logic. If working in, say, second-order logic is more convenient, then why not simply work in second-order logic? The reason for this is that first-order logic has a particular property that is really important and that second-order logic lacks, namely completeness. Let Φ be any set of formulas formulated in the language of first-order logic, and let α be a formula in the same language. Recall (from Section 2.2) that an interpretation specifies what individuals and relations the nonlogical terms in a formal sentence refer to. We then say that Φ semantically entails α iff *every* interpretation that makes all elements of Φ true also makes α true. If that is the case, we write $\Phi \vDash \alpha$ (where, as we have seen in Section 2.6, " $\vDash$" is the double turnstile). Semantic entailment (sometimes also called "logical consequence") contrasts with deducibility. The formula α is deducible from Φ iff α can be derived from Φ using the rules of inference in the logical system. If that is the case we write $\Phi \vdash \alpha$ (where "$\vdash$" is the single turnstile). Deducibility per se has nothing to do with truth; it just concerns the formal notion of one formula being deducible from another one. A theory is complete if every semantic entailment is also deducible in the theory: if $\Phi \vDash \alpha$ then $\Phi \vdash \alpha$.[32] In a complete logic, all entailments are also deducible. This is a crucial feature because much work with a theory is concerned with deducing sentences from a set of premises. Completeness guarantees that we do not "miss" any entailments: it cannot be the case that Φ entails α while α is not deducible from Φ. In an incomplete theory exactly this can happen: there can be entailments that are not "mirrored" at the level of deduction. This means that it can be the case that Φ entails α while at the same time α is not deducible from Φ, and that's a worry for those who run proofs. For this reason, completeness is a *very* desirable feature.

In sum, first-order logic is complete while second-order logic is not. To see that this is a serious problem think of Φ as the axioms of a theory (which we always can because Φ can be *any* set of formulas) and of α as a proposition of the theory. In second-order logic it can then happen that α is true in the theory (in the sense that it is entailed by the axioms) and yet it is not provable (in the sense that it is not deducible from the axioms). This limits the power of the formalism.[33]

Where do these considerations leave us? We have seen that first-order logic has limitations but also advantages. So there is a serious question of what formal framework one wants to use to formulate a theory, and it is by no means a foregone conclusion that first-order logic is a non-starter. It really depends on how one weighs the pros and cons of different kinds of logics against each other, and this may well depend on context. We will return to this issue on Section 5.8.

2.9* Limiting Results in First-Order Logic

In this section we have a look at two important limiting results in first-order logic: the Löwenheim-Skolem theorem and Gödel's first incompleteness theorem.[34]

The brief discussion of cardinalities in Section 2.7 paved the ground to state the Löwenheim-Skolem theorem, which plays an important role in arguments against the Received View. Consider a theory T in the form of a countable set of sentences in a first-order language. Then the following is true: if T has a model of a particular infinite cardinality, then T also has models of all other infinite cardinalities. Or phrased in terms of alephs, if the theory has a model whose cardinality is a particular aleph, then, for *any* aleph, the theory has a model whose cardinality is that aleph. This means that one cannot formulate a first-order theory that is such that it has only models of a certain infinite cardinality. Hence, first-order logic is unable to control the cardinality of its infinite models, which implies (trivially) that no first-order theory with an infinite model is categorical.

To get an understanding of the implications of this theorem let us have a look at arithmetic, the study of the natural numbers. We can perform elementary operations on these numbers, for instance adding or multiplying two numbers. The rules of how to manipulate numbers are laid down in the laws of arithmetic. These laws are either encoded in the axioms of arithmetic, or they follow from these axioms as theorems. One of the most important axiomatisations of arithmetic is Peano Arithmetic (see, for instance, Machover 1996, Ch. 10). Unsurprisingly the natural numbers are a model of Peano Arithmetic – in fact they are the *intended* model of Peano Arithmetic because the axioms have been formulated with the express purpose of describing these numbers. However, Peano arithmetic is formulated in first-order logic and the Löwenheim-Skolem tells us that the theory not only has models of cardinality $\aleph^0$, as we would expect, but also one of cardinality $\aleph^1$, the cardinality of the real numbers, and, indeed, of *any* other infinite cardinality! These "extra" models are "unintended models" in the sense that Peano Arithmetic was intended to be a theory of the natural numbers and it is an accident of logic, as it were, that it is also a theory of models that are not isomorphic to the natural numbers.[35]

Since almost any scientific theory relies on counting things, it will involve the axioms of arithmetic, and hence has unintended models of the sort we just described. This means that first-order theories are typically unable to pin down the class of models that they are intended to apply to. This means that they are not able to pin down their subject matter because they end up being true of domains that are not only unintended, but also very different from the intended domains. Proponents of the Model-Theoretical View argue that this is a major problem for the Received View and offer a solution to it. We will discuss their reasons for thinking so along with the proposed solution in Section 5.6. At this point we just note that the problem is a genuine first-order problem: second-order logic can pin down the cardinality of its models and therefore avoid the problem. But, as we have seen, in the last section, this comes at the price of being incomplete. So, once again, we're faced with a trade-off.

The second limiting result that is said to be a problem for the received view is Gödel's first incompleteness theorem. Consider a system of arithmetic such as Peano Arithmetic, and let Φ be the axioms of that system. Then let α be any proposition that can be formulated in the language of arithmetic – so α is some claim about numbers. It would then seem to be reasonable to expect that the axioms "fix" the correctness of α in the sense that either α or its negation, $\neg\alpha$, should be deducible from the axioms. That is, one would expect either $\Phi \vdash \alpha$ or $\Phi \vdash \neg\alpha$ to be the case. A theory that has this feature for every α in the language of the theory is *negation-complete*. Our expectation then is that aritmetic is negation complete. Gödel's first incompleteness theorem tells us that this expectation is false.[36] More specifically, the theorem says that every theory of arithmetic that is strong enough to express the standard facts about arithmetic is negation-incomplete: there is a sentence α in the language of arithmetic such that neither $\Phi \vdash \alpha$ nor $\Phi \vdash \neg\alpha$ is the case. Sentences of this kind are referred to as *Gödel sentences*. In fact, the theorem says something even stronger. It says that it not just so happens that we have forgotten to include something in the theory, which would mean that we could complete the theory by including what has been left out initially. Gödel's theorem says that the theory is *negation-incompletable*: no matter how much one adds to the initial theory, what results will be another negation-incomplete theory.[37] The sentence α will be true in the intended model of Φ, which is why Gödel's theorem is sometimes paraphrased as the claim that there are unprovable but true sentences. This is claimed to be a challenge for a formalisation of theories based on first-order logic because every claim in the theory has to be either provable or disprovable based on the axioms.

The Löwenheim-Skolem theorem has played an important role in arguments against the Received View and in favour of the Model-Theoretical View. The role of Gödel's theorem in this debate is rather less clear. None of the main arguments either against the Received View or in support of the Model-Theoretical View build on it. However, Anapolitanos (1989, 210) briefly mentions several arguments of that kind based on Gödel's theorem, and it is instructive to have a brief look at what he regards as the most important problem. Anapolitanos' problem is that Gödel's theorem tells us that "there may exist a sentence in the language of the theory, true in the real world but not provable by the theory". For this reason, "any theory viewed as a deductive system does not and cannot capture the whole picture of the world". This, Anapolitanos argues, "gives a decisive blow to the syntactic approach", i.e. the Received View, and leaves "as the only viable alternative to it a model-theoretic one".

In as far as it is an argument against the Received View, one might wonder why one should expect a scientific theory to provide every truth about the world. Scientific theories are by their nature incomplete and subject to revision. But even if one dares to dream of a final theory that contains everything, why think that Gödel sentences of the theory are scientifically relevant statements? The known examples of Gödel sentences are very specific and unintuitve number-theoretical statements, and there is at least a question why biologists or economists would worry about these. In as far as Anapolitanos' argument is an argument in favour of the Model-Theoretical View, it is unclear what the epistemology behind it is. Anapolitanos seems to think that, from a model-theoretical perspective, we can somehow directly recognise these sentences as either true or false without relying on arguments in the form of proofs. In general this would seem to be over-optimistic. Interesting scientific propositions are not easily recognised as true or false, and their truth or falsity has to be established by long and intricate arguments. These arguments will be couched in stronger metatheory. This metatheory will again involve statements, in which case the argument does not single out the Model-Theoretical View "as the only viable alternative". We return to the role of a metatheory in Section 5.8.

2.10 Conclusion

We have drawn a distinction between representational models and logical models, and we have seen that the Received View relies on the latter notion when it says that models are alternative interpretations of a formalism. By abstracting from the material constitution of a system one gets to the notion of a structure, which is the thing in terms of which sentences in formal logic are usually interpreted. With this formal machinery in place, we have seen that first-order logic faces a number of limitations: its language does not seem to be strong enough to formalise essential mathematical concepts and there are limiting results within it that seem to cast doubt on its suitability for a rational reconstruction of theories.

The Model-Theoretical View promises to solve these problems by shifting to an altogether different framework for analysing theories. We discuss this view in Chapter 5 and we therefore postpone a full evaluation of the gravity and consequences of these problems until then. Readers who are particularly interested in this issue can fast forward to Chapter 5 now and return to Chapters 3 and 4 at a later stage.

At this point I would like to reiterate the point that the Received View is not committed to first-order logic, and that therefore arguments against first-order logic are not *ipso facto* arguments against the Received View (or any other version of the linguistic view). Indeed, the Received View is not committed to any particular formal framework at all. Relatedly, as a number of commentators have pointed out, the Received View is not committed to a ban on model theory. Earman asks why the syntactic view should not be allowed to move from axioms to models, and ponders the option that "a proponent of the traditional view is not allowed to make the shift because the traditional view is a 'syntactic view' of theories". His verdict on this view is scathing: "It is hard to believe that anyone can repeat this answer while keeping a straight face, but I assure the reader that I have observed such behavior. Labeling the traditional view the 'syntactic view' is one of the chief tactics of proponents of the semantic/models view. It is pure slander." (2005, 8). This is because moving from a deductively closed set of sentences to the class of models of these sentences "is not a move to a different conception of theories but just a refocusing of attention to the flip side of the traditional view" (*ibid.*, 9).

Other commentators argue historically. Lutz (2014a) points out that Przełęcki (1974) made extensive use of model theory in his reconstruction of theories and yet regarded himself as being a proponent of the Received View. Halvorson (2016, 585) sees the reason why the impression was created that the Received View bans model-theory in the history of the field. There was no formal semantics in the 1920s and 1930s when most of the foundational publications of logical empiricism appeared, and philosophers placed emphasis on "syntax" because the study of semantics was considered to belong to psychology. This was later misinterpreted as a rejection of model theory and formal semantics, but in truth the emphasis on syntax really only was an emphasis on formal rigour – and formal rigour can of course be had with model theory!

Not being committed to something undesirable is one thing; having a viable alternative is another thing. So far the latter is still missing. As noted, we return to the issue of an adequate formal framework to reconstruct theories in Chapter 5, where we will see that the liberal Received View is in fact indistinguishable from a liberal Model-Theoretical View, and that such a liberal view is a plausible candidate for a tenable framework.

Notes

1 The term "logical model" is Hesse's (1967, 354). She refers to what I call representational models as "replicas, scale models, and analogues" (*ibid.*). As we will see in Part III, being a replica, a scale model or an analogue are different ways of being a representation, and so I prefer the more general term "representational model". The distinction between logical and representational models is discussed, or at least mentioned, in Achinstein's (1964, 329), Balzer et al. (1987, 2), Harré's (2004, 50), Hesse's (1967, 354), and Thomson-Jones' (2006). Hodges' (2018, Sec. 5) offers a historical sketch of how the term acquired this dual meaning.

2 See, for instance, Braithwaite's (1954, 156, 1962, 225).

3 It is sometimes added that models are simplified, idealised, or distorted representations. We will discuss this point in Section 14.2, where we will see that it is unnecessary.

4 Throughout we assume that scientists are able to identify target systems. For a discussion of the process of target system specifications, see Elliott-Graves' (2020).

5 I note that that there is a controversy concerning which among the many things that occur in Newton's determination of planetary orbits should be called "model". I discuss this issue in Chapter 14.

6 The notion of a model as an alternative interpretation of a theory's formalism is widely shared among proponents of the Received View. Further statements can be found in Braithwaite's (1953, 89–90, 1962, 227), Carnap's (1938, 209–210), Hempel's (1965, 434–435), Hutten's (1956, 82), Nagel's (1961, 90), and Spector's (1965, 124–125). These authors also emphasise the familiarity aspect of models, to which we turn soon. An exception is Ackermann (1966, 315) who defines a model as a theory's observation language.

7 In a similar vein Meyer notes that "[s]cientists use mental pictures of 'models' as we shall call them from now on, which tend to make the ideas embodied in their theories intuitively clear" (1951, 112–113). But familiarity is not to be equated with observability. The alternative interpretation that constitutes the model can be in terms of something unobservable if we are – for whatever reasons – familiar with it (Braithwaite 1962, 227).

8 Many authors often use "model" and "analogy" interchangeably (see, for instance, Nagel 1961, Ch. 6). As we will see in Chapter 11, two objects stand in the relation of *formal analogy* if they are interpretations of the same formalism. Hence logical models are formally analogous to each other. However, the concept of analogy extends beyond formal analogies and so I will not speak of logical models as analogies.

9 Strictly speaking this is true only if we make a few idealising assumptions, for instance that the balls move without friction and collide elastically.

10 For a discussion of the Bohr theory, see Nagel's (1961, 90–97), Braithwaite's (1953, 93), Spector's (1965, 125), and Hempel's (1969, 32, 1970, 157). For a discussion of water and sound waves, see Hesse's (1963, Chs. 1–2). Examples of models of this kind are not confined to historical cases. So-called dumb holes are a modern-day example; see Dardashti et al. (2017) for further discussions.

11 See also Hempel's (1965, 434–435, 440, 1969, 33). For a discussion of Carnap's and Hempel's attitude toward models, see Lutz's (2012, 92–99).

12 There is subtle difference though: on the first definition the model is the object that satisfies the theory; on the second definition the model also includes the formalism itself and the interpretation. For our current purposes this difference is immaterial. However, as we will see in Section 5.5, in certain context the difference between an understanding of models that takes them to include a language and one that sees them as "mere objects" matters.

13 Girill (1971) accuses Achinstein of a gross misunderstanding of the notion of a model. Achinstein (1972) replies robustly, and Girill (1972) reiterates his accusation. This ill-spirited exchange largely turns on points that are tangential to contemporary interests and I therefore set it aside.

14 Farre (1967) criticises Swanson's account of models as empty and essentially urges a return to the Received View's original notion of models.

15 Classical introductions to model theory are Hodges' (1997) and Chang and Keisler's (1990).

16 The term "arity" comes from the endings of "bin*ary*", "tern*ary*", and so on.

17 See, for instance, Boolos and Jeffrey's (1989, 98–99), Bourbaki's (1957, 12), Muller's (2004, 716, 2011, 103), Rickart's (1995, 17), Shapiro's (2000, 259), and Solomon's (1990, 168). More precisely, what we have introduced here are first-order structures. Higher order structures are defined through Bourbaki's echelon construction (1968, Ch. 4); see also Hudetz's (2019). For the most part we will work with first-order structures; higher order structures will briefly play a role in Section 5.8.

18 The ontology of structures is a contentious issue. Some think of them as *ante rem* universals (Resnik 1997; Shapiro 1983); some take them to be isomorphism classes of concrete objects (Redhead 2001); and yet others see them as modal objects (Hellman 1989). We leave this issue to the philosophy of mathematics.

19 See, for instance, Bell and Machover's (1977, 9) and Machover's (1996, 148).

20 The set of n-tuples that can be formed with elements of A is standardly denoted by A^n.

21 A structure without operations is sometimes called a relational structure, and one with operations is called an algebraic structure (Hodges 1997, 5).

22 See, for instance, Hodges's (1997, 2–4).

23 Terminology varies. Lutz calls set-theoretical structures "indexed structures" (2017, 330) or "pure structures" (2014b, 1481), and he refers to model-theoretical structures as "labelled structures" (2017, 330).

24 Indeed, the second variant builds this fact already into the definition of a structure by making symbols and an interpretation part of it.

25 See, for instance, Tarski's (1953), where he says: "A possible realization in which all valid sentences of a theory T are satisfied is called a model of T" (*ibid.*, 11).

26 *Vice versa* here means that for all relations s in $R^{(2)}$, the n-tuple $(f(a_1), ..., f(a_n))$ of elements of $U^{(2)}$ satisfies the relation s in $R^{(2)}$ iff the n-tuple $(a_1, ..., a_n)$ of elements of $U^{(1)}$ satisfies the relation r where s is the relation in $R^{(2)}$ that corresponds to r in $R^{(1)}$.

27 If one works with a structure that also contains operations, the following condition is added: for all operations o in $O^{(1)}$, $o(a_1, ..., a_n) = a_{n+1}$ iff $p(f(a_1), ..., f(a_n)) = f(a_{n+1})$ where p is the relation in $O^{(2)}$ that corresponds to o in $O^{(1)}$, and *vice versa*, where vice versa is explained, *mutatis mutandis*, as in the previous endnote.

28 As defined here, homomorphism involves a biconditional. This is in line with how homomorphisms are defined in Enderton's (2001, 94). There are, however, definitions that only involve a conditional; see, for instance, Hodges' (1997, 5). For a discussion of different definitions of various mappings, see Pero and Suárez's (2016).

29 What follows is only a rough intuitive sketch. For a rigorous discussion of cardinals, see, for instance, Machover's (1996, Ch. 6).

30 The discussion in this section and the next is informal and relatively brief. This is so by necessity because the limiting results are complex, and even a half-way rigorous discussion would require a book-length exposition. Bell and Machover's (1977), Machover's (1996), Enderton's (2001), and Smith's (2003) offer comprehensive introductions to logic; Button and Walsh's (2018), Krause and Arenhart's (2017), and Smith's (2013) provide in-depth discussions of limiting results and their philosophical consequences.

31 I am grateful to Laurenz Hudetz and James Nguyen for many helpful discussions about the arguments in this section and the next, and for comments on earlier drafts.

32 A closely related property is soundness: if $\Phi \vdash \alpha$, then $\Phi \vDash \alpha$. So one can say that soundness is the "converse" of completeness.

33 Throughout I assume that we work with standard semantics. Things get more involved when one also considers so-called many-sorted logics. For an overview of issues in many-sorted logics, see Väänänen's (2020); for in-depth discussions, see, for instance, Barrett and Halvorson's (2017), Manzano's (1996), and the contributions to Meinke and Tucker's (1993).

34 There are also a number of issues that arise in connection with the effective axiomatisability of theories and the effective decidability of claims. But a discussion of these issues would take us too far into technical details. Readers can find an introduction to these notions in Smith's (2013).

35 In the context of arithmetic these are often referred to as "non-standard models".

36 Gödel's second incompleteness theorem says, roughly, that theories that are strong enough to express basic arithmetic cannot prove their own consistency.

37 To avoid confusion, notice that the notion of completeness at work in Gödel's theorem is different from the one that is appealed to when we said in the previous section that first-order logic was complete. First-order logic is complete in the sense that if $\Phi \vDash \alpha$, then $\Phi \vdash \alpha$. The theories of arithmetic considered in Gödel's theorem are complete *in that sense*. They are incomplete in the sense of not being *negation-complete*, meaning that neither $\Phi \vdash \alpha$ nor $\Phi \vdash \neg\alpha$ is the case.

References

Achinstein, P. 1964. Models, Analogies, and Theories. *Philosophy of Science* 31: 328–350.

Achinstein, P. 1965. Theoretical Models. *The British Journal for the Philosophy of Science* 16: 102–120.

Achinstein, P. 1972. Models and Analogies: A Reply to Girill. *Philosophy of Science* 39: 235–240.

Ackermann, R. J. 1966. Confirmatory Models of Theories. *The British Journal for the Philosophy of Science* 16: 312–326.

Anapolitanos, D. A. 1989. Theories and Their Models. *Journal for General Philosophy of Science* 20: 201–211.

Andréka, H., J. X. Madarász, I. Németi, and G. Székely 2012. A Logic Road from Special Relativity to General Relativity. *Synthese* 186: 633–649.

Bailer-Jones, D. M. 1999. Tracing the Development of Models in the Philosophy of Science. In L. Magnani, N. J. Nersessian, and P. Thagard (eds.), *Model-Based Reasoning in Scientific Discovery*. New York: Kluwer Academic; Plenum Publishers, pp. 23–40.

Balzer, W., C.-U. Moulines, and J. D. Sneed 1987. *An Architectonic for Science: The Structuralist Program*. Dordrecht: Reidel Publishing Company.

Barrett, T. W. and H. Halvorson 2017. Quine's Conjecture on Many-Sorted Logic. *Synthese* 194: 3563–3582.

Bell, J. and M. Machover 1977. *A Course in Mathematical Logic*. Amsterdam: North-Holland.

Boltzmann, L. 1911. Model. In B. McGuinness (ed.), *Theoretical Physics and Philosophical Problems: Selected Writing*. Dordrecht and Boston: Reidel, 1974, pp. 213–220.

Boolos, G. S. and R. C. Jeffrey 1989. *Computability and Logic* (3rd ed.). Cambridge: Cambridge University Press.

Bourbaki, N. 1957. *Eléments De Mathémathique XXII. Livre I: Théorie Des Ensembles*. Paris: Hermann.

Bourbaki, N. 1968. *Theory of Sets*. Reading, MA: Addison-Wesley.

Braithwaite, R. B. 1953. *Scientific Explanation*. Cambridge: Cambridge University Press.

Braithwaite, R. B. 1954. The Nature of Theoretical Concepts and the Role of Models in an Advanced Science. *Theoria* 2: 155–157.

Braithwaite, R. B. 1962. Models in the Empirical Sciences. In E. Nagel, P. Suppes, and A. Tarski (eds.), *Logic, Methodology and Philosophy of Science*. Standford: Stanford University Press, pp. 224–231.

Brodbeck, M. 1959. Models, Meaning, and Theories. In L. Gross (ed.), *Symposium on Sociological Theory*. New York: Harper and Row, pp. 373–403.

Button, T. and S. Walsh 2018. *Philosophy and Model Theory*. Oxford: Oxford University Press.

Carnap, R. 1938. Foundations of Logic and Mathematics. In O. Neurath, C. Morris, and R. Carnap (eds.), *International Encyclopaedia of Unified Science* (Vol. 1). Chicago: University of Chicago Press, pp. 139–213.

Carnap, R. 1966. *An Introduction to the Philosophy of Science*. New York: Dover 1995 (Reprint of *Philosophical Foundations of Physics: An Introduction to the Philosophy of Science*. New York: Basic Books, 1966).

Chang, C. C. and H. J. Keisler 1990. *Model Theory* (3rd ed.). Amsterdam: North-Holland.

Dardashti, R., K. P. Y. Thébault, and E. Winsberg 2017. Confirmation Via Analogue Simulation: What Dumb Holes Could Tell Us About Gravity. *The British Journal for the Philosophy of Science* 68: 55–89.

Earman, J. 2005. The Emperor's New Theory: The Semantic/Models View of Theories. *Draft*.

Elliott-Graves, A. 2020. What Is a Target System? *Biology and Philosophy* 35: Article 28.

Enderton, H. B. 2001. *A Mathematical Introduction to Logic* (2nd ed.). San Diego and New York: Harcourt.

Farre, G. L. 1967. Remarks on Swanson's Theory of Models. *The British Journal for the Philosophy of Science* 18: 140–144.

Girill, T. R. 1971. Formal Models and Achinstein's Analogies. *Philosophy of Science* 38: 96–104.

Girill, T. R. 1972. Analogies and Models Revisited. *Philosophy of Science* 39: 241–244.

Halvorson, H. 2016. Scientific Theories. In P. Humphreys (ed.), *The Oxford Handbook of Philosophy of Science*. Oxford: Oxford University Press, pp. 585–608.

Harré, R. 2004. *Modeling: Gateway to the Unknown*. Amsterdam: Elsevier.

Hellman, G. 1989. *Mathematics without Numbers: Towards a Modal-Structural Interpretation*. Oxford: Oxford University Press.

Hempel, C. G. 1965. *Aspects of Scientific Explanation and Other Essays in the Philosophy of Science*. New York: Free Press.

Hempel, C. G. 1969. On the Structure of Scientific Theories. In C. G. Hempel (ed.), *The Isenberg Memorial Lecture Series*. East Lansing: Michigan State University Press, pp. 11–38.

Hempel, C. G. 1970. On the 'Standard Conception' of Scientific Theories. In M. Radner and S. Winokur (eds.), *Minnesota Studies in the Philosophy of Science Vol. 4*. Minneapolis: University of Minnesota Press, pp. 142–163.

Hesse, M. B. 1961. *Forces and Fields. The Concept of Action at a Distance in the History of Physics*. London and Edinburgh: Thomas Nelson and Sons.

Hesse, M. B. 1963. *Models and Analogies in Science*. London: Sheed and Ward.

Hesse, M. B. 1967. Models and Analogy in Science. In P. Edwards (ed.), *Encyclopedia of Philosophy*. New York: Macmillan, pp. 354–359.

Hodges, W. 1997. *A Shorter Model Theory*. Cambridge: Cambridge University Press.

Hodges, W. 2018. Model Theory. In E. N. Zalta (ed.), *The Stanford Encyclopedia of Philosophy*. https://plato.stanford.edu/archives/fall2018/entries/model-theory/.

Hudetz, L. 2019. The Semantic View of Theories and Higher-Order Languages. *Synthese* 196: 1131–1149.

Hutten, E. H. 1956. *The Language of Modern Physics: An Introduction to the Philosophy of Science* (2nd ed.). London: Novello.

Krause, D. and J. R. B. Arenhart 2017. *The Logical Foundations of Scientific Theories: Languages, Structures, and Models*. New York and London: Routledge.

Lutz, S. 2012. On a Straw Man in the Philosophy of Science: A Defence of the Received View. *HOPOS* 2: 77–120.

Lutz, S. 2014a. The Semantics of Scientific Theories. In A. Brożek and J. Jadacki (eds.), *Księga Pamiątkowa Marianowi Przełęckiemu W Darze Na 90-Lecie Urodzin*. Lublin: Norbertinum, pp. 33–67.

Lutz, S. 2014b. What's Right with the Syntactic Approach to Theories and Models? *Erkenntnis* 79: 1475–1492.

Lutz, S. 2017. What Was the Syntax-Semantics Debate in the Philosophy of Science About? *Philosophy and Phenomenological Research* 95: 319–352.

Machover, M. 1996. *Set Theory, Logic and Their Limitations*. Cambridge: Cambridge University Press.

Manzano, M. 1996. *Extensions of First Order Logic*. Cambridge: Cambridge University Press.

Meinke, K. and J. V. Tucker (eds.) 1993. *Many-Sorted Logic and Its Applications*. Chichester and New York: John Wiley and Sons.

Meyer, H. 1951. On the Heuristic Value of Scientific Models. *Philosophy of Science* 18: 111–123.

Montague, R. 1974. Deterministic Theories. In R. H. Thomason (ed.), *Formal Philosophy. Selected Papers of Richard Montague*. New Haven and London: Yale University Press, pp. 303–359.

Muller, F. A. 2004. Review of Patrick Suppes' "Representation and Invariance in Scientific Structures". *Studies in History and Philosophy of Modern Physics* 35: 713–720.

Muller, F. A. 2011. Reflections on the Revolution at Stanford. *Synthese* 183: 87–114.

Nagel, E. 1961. *The Structure of Science*. London: Routledge and Keagan Paul.

Pero, F. and M. Suárez 2016. Varieties of Misrepresentation and Homomorphism. *European Journal for Philosophy of Science* 6: 71–90.

Przełęcki, M. 1974. A Set Theoretic Versus a Model Theoretic Approach to the Logical Structure of Physical Theories. *Studia Logica* 33: 91–105.

Redhead, M. 2001. The Intelligibility of the Universe. In A. O'Hear (ed.), *Philosophy at the New Millennium*. Cambridge: Cambridge University Press, pp. 73–90.

Resnik, M. D. 1997. *Mathematics as a Science of Patterns*. Oxford: Oxford University Press.

Rickart, C. E. 1995. *Structuralism and Structure: A Mathematical Perspective*. Singapore: World Scientific.

Russell, B. 1919. *Introduction to Mathematical Philosophy*. London and New York: Routledge, 1993.

Shapiro, S. 1983. Mathematics and Reality. *Philosophy of Science* 50: 523–548.

Shapiro, S. 2000. *Thinking About Mathematics*. Oxford: Oxford University Press.

Smith, P. 2003. *An Introduction to Formal Logic* (2nd ed.). Cambridge: Cambridge University Press.

Smith, P. 2013. *An Introduction to Gödel's Theorems* (2nd ed.). Cambridge: Cambridge University Press.

Solomon, G. 1990. What Became of Russell's Relation-Arithmetic? *Russell* 9: 168–173.

Spector, M. 1965. Models and Theories. *The British Journal for the Philosophy of Science* 16: 121–142.

Suppes, P. 2002. *Representation and Invariance of Scientific Structures*. Stanford: CSLI Publications.

Swanson, J. W. 1966. On Models. *The British Journal for the Philosophy of Science* 17: 297–311.

Tarski, A. 1953. *Undecidable Theories*. Amsterdam: North-Holland Publishing Company.

Thomson-Jones, M. 2006. Models and the Semantic View. *Philosophy of Science* 73: 524–535.

Väänänen, J. 2020. Second-Order and Higher-Order Logic. In E. N. Zalta (ed.), *The Stanford Encyclopedia of Philosophy*. https://plato.stanford.edu/archives/fall2020/entries/logic-higher-order/.

3

DELINEATING THE OBSERVABLE

3.1 Introduction

The leading idea of logical empiricism is that observation provides a neutral basis against which theories are both formulated and tested. To serve this purpose, observation must be objective and free from presuppositions and interpretations. The Received View gives this idea a precise formulation by positing that a theory's descriptive vocabulary is bifurcated into observation terms and theoretical terms (in Section 1.3 we called this the second bifurcation). For observation terms it is "possible, under suitable circumstances, to decide by means of direct observation whether the term does or does not apply to a given situation" (Hempel 1965, 178). "Round", "green", "ball", "liquid", "wheel", "hot", "longer than", and "contiguous with", are examples of observation terms. By contrast, we cannot decide by means of direct observation whether terms like "electron", "orbital", "electromagnetic field", "gene", "quantum jump", and "rate of inflation" apply, and so these are examples of theoretical terms.[1]

The second bifurcation has been confronted with three families of criticism. The first criticism is that the *epistemic* distinction between what we can and cannot observe does not translate into a *linguistic* distinction between terms of different kinds (Section 3.2). The second criticism is that there is no clear boundary between what is observable and what is unobservable. Therefore, even if the vocabulary could be bifurcated as envisaged by the Received View, it would be unclear where the line between observation terms and theoretical terms should be drawn (Section 3.3). The third criticism concerns the question whether there ever is such a thing as theory-neutral observation. Critics argue that observation is theory-laden because theories are always implicated in observations (Section 3.4). At least partially in response to these criticisms, Hempel proposed a different bifurcation that draws the line historically between antecedently understood

DOI: 10.4324/9781003285106-5

terms and new terms rather than between observation terms and theoretical terms (Section 3.5). Throughout the discussion of the three families of criticism, little is said about how the outcomes of observations are registered and processed. In scientific contexts, making observations often takes the form of performing measurements with measurement-devices, and these measurements produce quantitative data as outputs. How are data collected, processed, regimented, and put into a useable form? We analyse the process of gathering data in experiments and their transformation into a data model, which is the form in which they are confronted with theories (Section 3.6). We conclude that articulating the empiricist idea that knowledge comes from experience raises important issues that have not yet been fully resolved (Section 3.7).

3.2 Disambiguating Distinctions

Putnam argues that the second bifurcation, which separates the non-logical vocabulary of a theory into theoretical terms and observation terms, starts off on the wrong foot:

> A theoretical term, properly so-called, is one which comes from a scientific *theory*. . . . In this sense (and I think it the sense important for discussions of science) "satellite" is, for example, a theoretical term (although the things it refers to are quite observable . . .) and "dislikes" clearly is not.
>
> *(1962, 219, original emphasis)*

Putnam makes two points. The first is that that "theoretical" should be taken to mean that a term originates in a theory, rather than that the term (putatively) refers to something unobservable. If we retain the traditional use of "theoretical" that comes from logical empiricism and add Putnam's to it, then "theoretical" is ambiguous. On the one hand, it can mean "unobservable"; on the other hand, it can also mean "originating in a theory". "Observable" is then ambiguous in the same way because it can mean both "being accessible to observation" and "not originating in a theory". This shows that there are two distinctions where we thought that there was only one: the *epistemic* distinction between terms that designate something observable and terms that (putatively) designate something unobservable, and the *genealogical* distinction between terms that derive from a theory and ones that have no theoretical pedigree. In what follows I refer to them as the observable/unobservable distinction and the non-theoretical/theoretical distinction, respectively.[2]

One might say that this ambiguity is harmless because these distinctions line up: terms that designate observables are also non-theoretical, and terms that designate unobservables are also theoretical. For example, terms like "green", "table", and "tree" designate observables and are non-theoretical; and terms like "electron", "superstring", and "gene" designate unobservables and are theoretical. Generalising from these examples one might say that all terms are like this and that the two distinctions therefore draw the line between terms at the same place.

Putnam's second point is that this is wrong because there are theoretical terms that designate observables and, vice versa, there are terms that designate unobservable and that yet are not theoretical. Putnam's example for the former is "satellite", which, he says, both designates something observable and is theoretical. The example may not be entirely felicitous because it is not clear in which theory "satellite" originates. But the observation stands, and other examples easily come to mind: "antenna" originates in classical electrodynamics, "Geiger counter" originates in atomic theory, and "tectonic plate" originates in the theory of plate tectonics, and yet all of them are objects that can be seen with our bare eyes. Putnam's example for the latter is "dislikes", which, he says, is non-theoretical and yet designates something unobservable. Presumably other terms conveying people's attitudes and feelings, like "loves", "hates", and "desires", would be classified in the same way.

Following Bird (1998, 86), we can present the situation in the form of the matrix of scientific terms shown in Figure 3.1. Putnam's second point can then be phrased as the realisation that the matrix has entries not only on the diagonal (running from top left to bottom right), but also in the off-diagonal fields.

Let us now have a look at the four fields and evaluate their implications for the Received View. The field at the bottom right contains terms that are theoretical in both senses. These terms conform to the picture canvassed in Section 1.3 and hence pose no further problem. Unfortunately, things get more involved in the other fields. Take the field at the top right. Here we have terms that designate observables even though they are theoretical. This does not sit well with the logical empiricists' view that observations provide a neutral basis on which theories

Epistemology \ Genealogy	Non-Theoretical	Theoretical
Observable	green table tree	satellite antenna tectonic plate
Unobservable	dislikes loves desires	electron superstring gene

FIGURE 3.1 Matrix of scientific terms.

are built, and against which they are tested. To serve this purpose, observations have to be free from presuppositions and interpretations, and in particular from theories. Observation is where nature "speaks for itself", as it were, and theories have to take nature's pronouncements at face value. However, if terms originate in theories, they carry "theoretical baggage" in that at least part of their meaning and their conditions of applicability will be determined by their ancestral theories. It is not enough for something to be an antenna that it is a metal rod placed in an elevated position relative to its immediate environment. It also has to be able to emit or receive radio signals, and whether or not this is the case can be adjudicated only with reference to electromagnetic theory. Hence, even though "antenna" refers to an observable object, its meaning and its conditions of application depend on a theory. This does not sit well with the idea that observation is the theory-free foundation on which theories are built. If the terms in which we describe observations originate in theories and are meaningful only against the background of the original theories, then observation reports are not theory-free. The phenomenon that observations depend on theories, and that the reports we give of observations use theory-dependent language, has become known as the *theory-ladenness of observation*. Theory-ladenness presents a serious challenge to the Received View. We return to this challenge in Section 3.4.

Let us now explore the column with non-theoretical terms, starting with the top left field of the matrix. Putnam raises an issue also for this field. Colour terms like "red" are the kind of terms that logical empiricists would readily classify as observation terms. As Putnam notes, Newton postulated that red light was made up of red corpuscles (1962, 218). Yet, the colour of corpuscles is unobservable. Or if modern microscopes might have rendered Newton's corpuscles observable, then other examples are readily at hand: we speak of the vibration of a superstring, the diameter of an atom, the shape of a molecule, and the frequency of a gene in a population. In all these cases, terms that one would readily classify as observational – vibration, diameter, shape, frequency – are applied to unobservable objects. This means that the properties designated by these terms are, in the cases at hand, also unobservable (at least in the sense of "unobservable" intended in the Received View). This puts us in the awkward position of having observation terms that designate something unobservable.[3]

One can respond to this in two ways. The first response reverts back to Hempel and stresses that Hempel defines a term as observational if the property it designates can be observed *under suitable circumstances*. "Red" is an observation term because if my eyes are open, my vision is normal, and the light is on, I can decide through direct observation whether the curtains are red. That I cannot see whether a corpuscle is red is therefore not an issue because observing a corpuscle does not qualify as a suitable circumstance, and that I cannot see the corpuscle to be red does therefore not undermine the status of "red" as an observation term. One may now wonder, however, on what basis this decision is made. Which circumstances count as suitable? Indeed, the vagueness of the notion of the right circumstances would also allow for the opposite reaction. Rather than salvaging the status of "red" as an observation term by declaring the circumstances unsuitable, one might say that there are suitable circumstances where the redness of corpuscle would actually be observable and so far we just have not managed to get ourselves into these circumstances. Hence, first appearances notwithstanding, under the right circumstances the shape of a molecule and even the vibration of a superstring would be observable. This would make the notion of the unobservable otiose, and would obliterate the need for the observable/unobservable distinction. So in effect we have traded the problem of saying what is observable for the problem of saying what suitable circumstances are, and it is not clear that the latter is easier to solve than the former.

The second response is to "split" terms and distinguish between observable and unobservable versions of terms. One would then, for instance, distinguish between red_1, which applies to observable objects, and red_2, which applies to unobservable objects (Andreas 2017, Sec. 2.1). This would amount to replacing the ancestral language of science with a highly artificial language with split terms. In principle, this is compatible with the programme of rational reconstruction, and resolving philosophical problems through a revision of language has an important pedigree.[4] Nevertheless, it would seem that splitting the vocabulary of a theory in this way would stretch reconstruction beyond breaking point, and the result of such an endeavour would be too far removed from the original theory to shed light on its workings. Furthermore, it would leave the problem of how terms like red_2 acquire their meaning unresolved.

Let us finally turn to the bottom left field of the matrix. Here we find non-theoretical terms that designate unobservables. Putnam's examples are taken from the vocabulary we use to describe people's feelings and intentions. These examples would, however, seem to be controversial. Can I really not see that someone is angry? If I can, then the "angry" would have to be reclassified as non-theoretical and observable. Or if one insists that we really cannot see that the someone is angry, then do we really not appeal to any theory when I judge someone to be angry? The ascription of attitudes and feelings to people seems to require appeal to *folk psychology* (see, for instance, Horgan and Woodward 1985). Folk psychology may not be a good theory, but it is a theory nevertheless. If so, then terms like "angry" would have to be reclassified as unobservable and theoretical. Is this a problem of the specific example? Maybe. Yet, it does not seem to be easy to find clear-cut examples of non-theoretical yet unobservable terms.[5] Be this as it may, the other elements of the matrix spell enough trouble for the Received View, and a strategy for dealing with these problems will have to be found.

The conclusion we draw from the discussion in this section is that the *epistemic* distinction between observable and unobservable does not straightforwardly translate into a *linguistic* distinction between different kinds of terms.

Before turning to potential responses to this difficulty, we must discuss two further issues. In drawing the matrix of scientific terms, we assumed that there are sharp divisions. Drawing the horizontal line presupposes that there is a sharp division between observable and unobservable. Drawing the vertical line presupposes that there is a sharp division between the theoretical and the non-theoretical. Both presuppositions have been called into question. We discuss the division between observable and the unobservable in the next section and turn to the division between the theoretical and the non-theoretical in Section 3.4.

3.3 Blurred Boundaries

Some things are clearly observable, and some are not. We see that the water in the lake is frozen, but we do not see that the H_2O molecule has a triangular shape with an H-O-H angle of 104.5 degrees. But things are not always so clear. Do we observe a refraction index when we see a ray of light changing its direction when entering into water? Do we observe charges when we touch a wire and feel an electric shock? And do we observe the velocity of a train when we see it pass by?

The way we have discussed the problem so far presupposes that a sharp line can be drawn between the observable and the unobservable. Maxwell (1962) submits that this presupposition is wrong. He argues, first, that there is no non-arbitrary distinction between observable and unobservable and, second, that this is no cause for alarm because the distinction is irrelevant for our understanding of science. Let us call these the *unattainability charge* and the *irrelevancy charge* respectively.[6]

Maxwell offers two arguments in support of unattainability. The first is what I call the *continuum argument*. Maxwell puts it thus:

> The point I am making is that there is, in principle, a continuous series beginning with looking through a vacuum and containing these as members: looking through a windowpane, looking through glasses, looking through binoculars, looking through a low-power microscope, looking through a high-power microscope, etc., in the order given. The important consequence is that, so far, we are left without criteria which would enable us to draw a nonarbitrary line between "observation" and "theory".
>
> *(1962, 1055–1056)*

Most would agree that we see through a windowpane and through ordinary spectacles. Does the transition from using spectacles to using binoculars mark the transition from observable to unobservable? That is, does something that can only be seen through binoculars count as unobservable? Or does the transition take place when we proceed from using binoculars to using a low-power microscope? Or . . .? Alternatively, as Maxwell points out, one could also consider a sequence of objects (*ibid.*, 1056–1057): very small molecules (such as those of hydrogen), medium size molecules (such as those of fatty acids and proteins), and finally extremely large molecules (such as crystals of salt). Large molecules are observable with the naked eye. The other molecules are not: they are visible only with microscopes of different kinds. In both cases there is a gradual transition from observable to unobservable, and there is no non-arbitrary way of drawing a line between observable and unobservable entities.

Maxwell's second argument for unattainability is what I call the *argument from observer-relativity*. The argument aims to establish that even if we were able to draw a line between what is observable and what is unobservable in a non-arbitrary way, the place where this line would come to lie would essentially depend on the capabilities of humans. That we cannot see distant stars without optical instruments and that we cannot see molecules without an electron microscope is owed to the limitations of human faculties, but it has nothing to do with the observability of things *per se*. To make his case, Maxwell asks us to consider a human mutant with the ability to observe ultraviolet radiation and X-rays in the same way we observe light (*ibid.*, 1058).[7] These creatures could observe many things concealed from ordinary humans, for instance viruses, strands of DNA, and protein molecules. So what counts as observable and unobservable depends on contingent facts about the observer, and hence, again, there is no non-arbitrary distinction between observable and unobservable things.

Let us discuss these arguments in reverse order. Van Fraassen (1980, 17–19) objects to the argument from observer-relativity that Maxwell changes the rules of the game. Of course, the human body has certain limitations, and it is exactly these limitations that the "able" in "observable" refers to: "I have a mortar and a pestle made of copper and weighing about a kilo. Should I call it breakable just because a giant could break it? Should I call the Empire State Building portable?" (*ibid.*, 17). These are rhetorical questions, and the answer is "no". The point van Fraassen is making here is that observability cannot possibly be an absolute concept. What is observable is always relative to an epistemic community, and, in the current context, the relevant epistemic community is humans with all their limitations. Humans may mutate and this may change the face of science, or we may extend the community to include other creatures. But this will only change or extend the community; it does not eliminate dependence on an epistemic community. Van Fraassen points out, rightly, that science is knowledge from and for creatures with "certain inherent limitations" (*ibid.*), and what they can and cannot know depends on these limitations. Saying that different creatures could observe different things is therefore beside the point, and not everything is observable simply because there may be other (mostly fictional!) creatures who can observe things that humans cannot observe.

Even if we assume that the line between the observable and the unobservable has to be drawn for humans, where should it be drawn? The continuum argument says that there is no non-arbitrary answer to this question. A first reply to the argument points out that our ambiguity tolerance is higher than Maxwell suggests. In fact, logical empiricists themselves noted that the distinction is not a sharp one, and they insisted that we did not need it to be sharp either. Carnap acknowledged the existence of borderline cases and admitted that the place where one draws the line between observable and unobservable can be "somewhat arbitrary" (quoted in Psillos 2000, 158).[8] Yet Carnap insisted that "from a practical point of view, the distinction is clear enough between terms like 'blue', 'red', 'hard', 'soft', 'cold', etc. on the one hand . . . and on the other hand terms like 'electro-magnetic field', 'electric charge', 'protons', 'neutrons', and so on" (*ibid.*). In case of doubt he recommends taking a liberal stance and to regard as observable everything that is "either directly observable by the senses or measurable by relatively simple techniques" (1966, 226). The implication for Maxwell's example would be that the line between observable and unobservable would presumably have to be drawn somewhere between a strong light microscope and an electron microscope, because the electron microscope uses quantum theory to reconstruct an image from scattering data, which are then visualised on a digital computer. This process cannot be understood as an extension of ordinary vision, and hence no observation is made through an electron microscope.

One might counter that an appeal to direct observability or observability by relatively simple techniques removes little of the initial ambiguity and insist that it is an ambiguity that we cannot tolerate. It remains unclear, one might continue, that we really do not see through devices like an electron microscope because to posit that observation is limited to the lightly aided senses is as arbitrary as to posit that it is limited to the unaided senses. Furthermore, this stance would involve denying that we make observations with the aid of night-vision equipment based on thermal imaging, through X-ray machines, and through magnetic resonance tomographs. Not only would such a denial be theoretically controversial; it would also not sit well with many common practices. Security forces use night-vision equipment to stop intruders, and medics employ X-ray machines to inspect broken bones and tomographs to detect tumours.

Problems of this kind can be avoided if we shift focus from what *is* observed to what *can be* observed in the right circumstances. Introducing this idea, van Fraassen proposes the following criterion of observability: "*X* is observable if there are circumstances which are such that, if *X* is present to us under those circumstances, then we observe it" (1980, 16). On this criterion, the moons of Jupiter, which we see through a telescope, are observable because "astronauts will no doubt be able to see them as well from close up" (*ibid.*). And, presumably, the criterion for whether we see correctly through the telescope is whether what astronauts will see when they are close up coincides with what observers on earth see through the telescope. This move also successfully deals with the cases in the previous paragraph: the security guard could see the intruder if he switched on the light, and the surgeon could see the broken bones and tumours through an incision in the body. Cases like these, says van Fraassen, are different from the purported observation of a micro-particle through a trace in the cloud chamber because there are no circumstances under which a human could observe the particle directly (*ibid.*, 17). So there is, after all, a principled line to be drawn between what is observable and what is unobservable.

This reply faces two problems. The first is that, as we have noted in the previous section, the notion of observation under the right circumstances is difficult to unpack. While van Fraassen's example with the astronaut and the micro-particle has some intuitive plausibility, it is difficult to pin down what exactly the distinction comes down to. Does a heavenly object that is so far away that no human could travel there in their lifetime still qualify as observable? If we respond that we can consider fictionalised humans that live longer than we actually do, why can we not also consider fictionalised humans who have better eyes than we have and are able to see micro-particles?

The second problem is that van Fraassen's criterion, while superior to previous criteria, is essentially just a cunning reformulation of the classical empiricist notion that the boundaries of perceptual experience are at once the boundaries of observation. But, as Shapere points out (1969, 1982) this notion of observation is at odds with how observation is understood in modern science, where observation crucially relies on ever more elaborate equipment and direct sense perception is relegated to the periphery of enquiry.[9] High-tech instrumentation is epistemically significant in many domains of science where observations are made with elaborate machines like the Large Hadron Collider at CERN. Hence, Shapere concludes, insisting on a notion of observation that is closely tied to direct perception is a regress.

It is undoubtedly true that advanced instruments are an indispensable aspect of the experimental practices in many sciences. This, however, does not solve, or render irrelevant, the question of whether, and if so how, we observe with these instruments. One may not agree with van Fraassen's principle of observation and wish to draw the line somewhere else. But everybody either has to draw a line somewhere and take a stand on what observation is and where its boundaries lie, or else argue why no such line can be drawn and justify why observations made with instruments are veridical. These questions have been debated extensively in the context of scientific realism, where particular attention has been paid to the case of microscopes. Do we see through microscopes, and is what we see a veridical image of an object that is just too small to see with the naked eye? Unsurprisingly, the answers given to these questions diverge. Van Fraassen has revisited the issue of observation in recent publications but keeps insisting that the images produced by microscopes are "public hallucinations" (2001, 155, 2008, 101). Hacking (1981, 1983) disagrees and argues that we see through microscopes. Alspector-Kelly (2004) and Teller (2001) offer sustained criticisms of van Fraassen's position, while Kusch (2015) provides a qualified defence. Be this as it may, the point is that the fact that observations are commonly made with the aid of complex instruments neither shows that no division between observable and unobservable can be drawn; nor does it show that the question of whether, and if so how, we make observations through these instruments is obsolete.

Let us now turn to Maxwell's second indictment, the irrelevancy charge. Maxwell submits that drawing a distinction between observable and unobservable is not only unattainable; it is also irrelevant. Maxwell is primarily interested in the reality of the entities postulated by science. What we can and cannot observe is "an accident and a function of our psychological makeup, our current state of knowledge, and the instruments we happen to have available" and for this reason it "has no ontological significance whatever" (*ibid.*, 1061–1062). Entities do not come into existence because we can see them, and they do not cease to exist if they lie outside the reach of our senses.

It is of course true that the existence of an entity does not depend on whether we can observe it; things exist irrespective of our ability to see them (at least as long as we assume a broadly realist picture of science). But Maxwell's argument conflates metaphysics and epistemology. There is no God's eye perspective from which we can first see what objects exist in the world and then turn to science for their exact description. Science has to produce *evidence* for the existence of certain objects, and the nature of the evidence offered depends on whether a purported entity is observable. We believe that we see molecules through electron microscopes, but we do not believe that we observe the souls of the deceased through a medium (or so I assume). We have evidence for the existence of molecules but not for the existence of the souls of the deceased (or at any rate not from the medium). That we believe so has a lot to do with what we take to be observable and how, and brushing issues of observability aside as irrelevant obscures this important fact. The irrelevancy charge fails.

In sum, the distinction between observable and unobservable is neither irrelevant, nor impossible to draw. However, the question of where, and how, the line ought to be drawn is more complicated than the Received View had suggested, and it involves understanding how complicated instruments are used in the service of observation. We turn to this question in the next section.

3.4   The Theory-Ladenness of Observation

As we have seen in Section 3.2, observation terms like "antenna" and "Geiger counter" are theory-laden in that their meaning and conditions of application depend on a theory. The thesis of the *theory-ladenness of observation* says that these are no exceptions: all observations are inextricably entangled with theory and that there is no such thing as theory-free observation. As Hanson puts it: there is no "immaculate perception" (1969, 74). Every observation involves elements that are not given to us by our senses, and there is no observation that does not go beyond what is given by "experience itself". The claim gained prominence in the late 1950s and early 1960s through the writings of Hanson, Kuhn, and Feyerabend, and it has since been discussed extensively in particular among philosophers of science and cognitive scientists.[10]

A look at the relevant literature reveals that "theory-ladenness" is an umbrella term covering a number of different phenomena, and the predicate "theory-laden" is applied to a heterogeneous variety of things including concepts, facts, perception, descriptions, and the process of observation itself. The task for this section is to identify and analyse different kinds of theory-ladenness, and to assess how much of a problem they are for the empiricist ideal that observations should be recorded in a language that is untarnished by our preconceptions and theoretical commitments. We distinguish between five kinds of theory-ladenness: perceptual theory-ladenness, expectation bias, theory-directed attention, operational theory-ladenness, and conceptual theory-ladenness.[11] It is important that those interested in the nature of observation have a good understanding of these kinds of theory-ladenness in order to assess how much of a problem they pose for science. I will therefore discuss them in some detail. Based on this discussion, I will argue that the first four are something that the empiricist ideal can accommodate, and which therefore does not threaten an empiricist understanding of science. The same cannot be said of the fifth kind of theory-ladenness, which requires a re-thinking of the relation between theory and observation.

The first kind of theory-ladenness concerns the presence of theory in conscious visual experience, and I refer to it as *perceptual theory-ladenness*. To motivate the view that observation is theory-laden both Hanson (1958) and Kuhn (1970) make reference to Gestalt psychology, which finds that what we see in a given visual array depends, at least in part, on our expectations and not only on the visual array in front of us. The point can be illustrated with images that can be seen in different ways. Some of the often-used images are shown below.[12] Figure 3.2a shows the so-called Necker cube. Someone sees a cube from above while someone else sees a cube from below. Figure 3.2b is known as the duck-rabbit illusion because the same lines that look like duck to one person look like a rabbit to another person. Figure 3.2c is called "my wife and my mother-in-law" because the drawing can be seen as showing an old lady looking down and as a young lady turning away from the spectator.

The point of these drawings is that even though everybody perceives exactly the same lines, different people see different objects in them. What someone sees in them, so the argument continues, depends on what is on their mind: on their expectations and on their knowledge. Perception and cognition are inseparably intertwined. The argument then draws an analogy between drawings of this kind and scientific research: what we see in a certain situation depends on our background knowledge and our theoretical commitments just like what we see in these images depends on our psychological dispositions and expectations.

Phenomena like these sparked a heated discussion about the theory-ladenness of perception. Fodor (1984) strongly resisted such a position on grounds that visual perception is independent of higher-level beliefs. Churchland (1988) disagreed with Fodor and argued for a thoroughgoing theory-ladenness of perception. Bewer and Lambert (2001) argue that Churchland is essentially right. Raftopoulos (2001b, 2001a) grants Churchland that observation involves some top-down processing, but he maintains that a substantial amount of perceptual information is theory-neutral because perception is cognitively impenetrable. Pylyshyn (2003) argues that humans have a highly complex information processing system called "early vision" which individuates a scene and computes the spatial layout of visible surfaces and which functions wholly independently of actors' believes. Votsis (2015) urges that perception should be "unladened" and argues that perception and observation are largely veridical.[13]

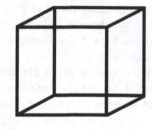

(a)

(b)

(c)

FIGURE 3.2 Ambiguous images: (a) the Necker cube; (b) the duck-rabbit illusion; (c) "my wife and my mother-in-law".

While interesting in its own right, the issue of perception being theory-laden is largely tangential to the concerns about the relation between theories and the world in the context of science. As we have seen in the last section, as science progresses instrumentation increases, and empirical information is rarely gained through perceptual observation. And even where data are gathered through perception, it would seem unlikely that the resulting data patterns provoke illusions of the kind we experience in the duck-rabbit picture. However, as noted previously, those who used images like the ones seen in Figure 3.2, were not saying that observation, literally, functions like duck-rabbit pictures; they use these pictures as an analogy to motivate the claim that the conceptual framework of a theory affects the way in which experiments are made and observations interpreted. But motivations are not arguments. We will need an analysis of what this purported influence of theory on observation is, and then the claim can be evaluated. The next four senses of theory-ladenness that we discuss in this section can be seen as attempts to do so.

A second and closely related sense of theory-ladenness draws attention to the role of expectations in the interpretation of perceptions. In a notorious study, oenologists Morrot et al. (2001) artificially coloured a white wine red with an odourless dye and then gave the coloured wine to 54 wine students who were asked to give an olfactory description of the wine. The shocking result was that the expert tasters overwhelmingly described the dyed white wine as they would describe red wine. Hence the visual information (they *saw* a red liquid in their glasses) ended up overriding the olfactory information, thereby leading to a perceptual illusion. Kuhn (1970, 62–63) draws attention to a similar phenomenon when he points out that expectations can be so strong that they even make us "see" things that are not there at all. For instance, anomalous playing cards (such as black hearts) were "seen" as one of the normal cards (such as black spade) known to us by previous experience.

Not only wine lovers and card players can be misled by their expectations. Brewer and Lambert (2001, 179–180) report an episode from laboratory science where scientists were misled by their expectations in much the same way. Shortly after the discovery of X-rays, French physicist Blondlot reported that he had discovered a new form of radiation, which he called N-rays. The discovery was celebrated as a major breakthrough and within a few years hundreds of papers on N-rays were published. The experimental technique to detect N-rays relied on subtle perceptual discriminations such as the visual detection of an increased activity of sparks. The discovery was debunked when it turned out the experimentalists would still "see" the relevant visual patters even if the apparatus was disturbed in a way that made the presence of N-rays impossible. So observers were seduced by their expectations into seeing the relevant patterns even if they were not there.

The wine tasting and N-ray episodes are examples of *expectation bias*, which is our second sense of theory-ladenness.[14] An expectation bias occurs when an individual's expectations about an outcome influence the individual's perceptions of events (Williams et al. 2012, 1). Morrot's students did not describe the white wine in red wine terms because they had a theory about it; they did so because they expected to get red wine. Likewise, it was not N-ray theory itself that led Blondlot and the physicists around him to see an increased activity of sparks (which was taken to be indicative of N-rays); it was their subjective expectation that N-ray theory was correct and that the pattern would be seen that mislead their perceptions. The problem of expectation bias is well-known, and experimentalists are painfully aware of it. Indeed, much thought goes into the development of experimental designs that minimise, or even completely eliminate, expectation bias. Double-blind clinical trials are an example of such a design.[15]

Furthermore, as Brewer and Lambert point out (2001, 179), cases like the "detection" of N-rays are ones where the bottom-up evidence is weak: stimuli are ambiguous, signals are degraded, and the perceptual judgement required is difficult. In such cases top-down factors can have an influence on perception, and in extreme cases even override bottom-up information. But science can avoid such situations. Blondlot could have constructed an experiment that was designed to avoid expectation bias, for instance one that required experimenters to taking a meter reading of a spark intensity measurement rather than asking them to make a visual judgment about intensity of sparks. It is unlikely that experimenters would have been misled by their expectations if all they had to do was to register whether the needle pointed to "5" or to "10" on the dial.

The third kind of theory-ladenness is what I call *theory-directed attention*. As many authors have noted, our theoretical understanding of the world guides our attention and helps us select what we do and what we focus on.[16] It is neither possible nor desirable to make observations randomly and try to comprehensively screen the entire world. We have to be selective in what we direct our attention to, and often it is a theory that tell us which issues are important enough to deserve our consideration, that draws our attention to particular phenomena, that tells us which variables to measure, and that predicts the range of values where interesting effects are expected to occur. Theories make certain parts or aspects of the world salient. Without Einstein's predictions from his Theory of General Relativity, Eddington would hardly have travelled to the island of Príncipe off the west coast of Africa to observe a solar eclipse; and without the predictions from Quantum Theory no one would ever have built a machine like the Large Hadron Collider in CERN.

A particular aspect of this is that a theory may tell us what to focus our attention on even if we look at one particular system. Kuhn points out that even if Galileo and Aristotle had looked at exactly the same pendulum, they would not have focused on the same aspects or properties (1970, 123–124). Aristotle would have measured the weight of the pendulum bob, the vertical height, and the time it takes the pendulum to return to rest; he would have ignored the radius, the angular displacement, and the period, which were the salient features for Galileo. Issues of "selective focus" also occur in contemporary science. Brewer and Lambert (2001, 180) report that after the official discovery of an astronomical entity, scientists often go through previous observations again and are often able to identify the object in the data even though it had gone unnoticed before. For instance, reviewing astronomical data after the discovery of Uranus revealed 22 "pre-discovery-sightings" of the planet.

The attention-focusing capacity of theories is undeniable and important, but at the same time unproblematic as far as the relation of theory and observation is concerned. The empiricist ideal requires that there be observations described in observation terms, but it does not specify how these observations are made, nor does it rule out that theoretical considerations can motivate how an experiment is designed and which aspects one focuses on. Using theories as guides in the practice of experimentation is wholly compatible with understanding the relation between theory and observation in the way in which the Received View does.

The fourth variety of theory-ladenness arises in connection with experimental design, and I call it *operational theory-ladenness*. As we have seen at end of the previous section, scientific observations are made mostly not with our naked eyes, but with instruments. Heavenly bodies are observed through telescopes; the structure of molecules can be seen through microscopes; brain function is studied with magnetic resonance imaging; and so on. "Machine aided observation" is ubiquitous in science. The crucial question is what warrants observers to believe that the outputs of such devices provide veridical information. What justification does, say, an astronomer have to believe that she really sees a galaxy through her telescope?

Sometimes justification comes from theory.[17] Instruments often depend on theories, both for their construction and for their operation, and the observer's confidence in the output of the device is grounded in her confidence in these theories. Kosso refers to such theories as *accounting theories* (1992, 117). Such theories are embedded in an experimental setup and "describe the chain of interaction from the specimen to the observer" (*ibid.*). These theories warrant that the observations are a truthful reflection of the specimen's properties, and they sanction the observation's reliability and accuracy. We trust machine-aided observations only if the experts who develop and build the machines have a solid theoretical framework. We trust the telescope because we accept the theory of linear optics on which it is based; we trust the electron microscope because we trust quantum theory; and so on. When accounting theories are unavailable, we often do not, and should not, trust the observations made. For instance, we do not trust the "observations" of divination or tasseography because there are no accounting theories that link occurrences in crystal balls or patterns in coffee grounds to a person's future.

The appeal to accounting theories introduces an irreducible dependence on theory into observations. Observations made through instruments are therefore theory-laden in the sense that the instrument relies on an accounting theory. How problematic is this kind of theory-dependence? At this point we have to distinguish between two cases. The first is when the theory under investigation is independent from the accounting theory. The theory that planets move in elliptical orbits is independent from the theories that underlie the telescope astronomers used to confirm that theory. Franklin (1986, 109) and Kosso (1988, 463–463, 1989, 147–148) argue that if this independence is given, then there is no problem because the accounting theories are not the theories at stake in a given experiment. These accounting theories will usually have been tested prior to, and independently of, any application in an apparatus, and they are used as accounting theories only if they are deemed to be reliable (at least on the relevant scale). The use of accounting theories *relativises* observations to these theories, but it does not lead to the kind of profound entanglement of theory and observation that would make a separation of theory and observation impossible. An archaeologist can use the radiocarbon dating method to test her theory that a particular wooden mallet is from the early Middle Ages; and the outcome of this test will depend on the correctness of the atomic theory on which the method is based. But this does not introduce worrisome circularities into her theorising because her observations and her theories are clearly separated.

The second case is if the accounting theory and the theory-to-be-tested are the same or share important parts. This would happen, for instance, if we were to use observations of masses and forces to confirm Newtonian mechanics because the measurement of masses and forces presupposes Newtonian mechanics. The worry is that we are basically guaranteed to get the result that the theory predicts because the experiment is described in terms of the theory. The good news is that this confirmatory circularity can be avoided. To see how exactly it can be avoided, we must have a more detailed look at how experiments relate to theory, and indeed at how different layers of theory relate to one another. We return to this issue in Section 7.4.[18]

The fifth and final form of theory-ladenness is what I call *conceptual theory-ladenness*. This is the sort of theory-ladenness that we encountered in the top-right field in the matrix in Section 3.2 and which is exemplified in terms like "antenna" and "Geiger counter". The core of this kind of theory-ladenness is that the terms that are used in observation statements are theory-laden because their meaning depends on the theory in which they appear. Consider a physicist who reports that she observed the resistance of the solenoid to be 120 Ohms. The physicist does not provide an observation report in a theory-neutral language; in fact that language of the report is theory-dependent because terms like "solenoid", "Ohm", and even "resistance" as used here make sense only against a theoretical background.

Feyerabend argued that this phenomenon is universal and that there are no theory-neutral descriptions of an observation because the meanings of terms we use in such descriptions are always, at least in part, determined by theories. He submits that "[t]he meaning of every term we use depends upon the theoretical context in which it occurs", and he argues that "[w]ords do not 'mean' something in isolation; they obtain their meaning by being part of a theoretical system" (1965, 180).[19] In this vein, Feyerabend claims that the notion of temperature in thermodynamics is incommensurable with the notion of temperature in the kinetic theory of gases (1981, 79), which means that the term "temperature" has a different meaning depending on the theoretical context in which it appears. The same holds true for the term "entropy", which also has a different meaning in thermo-dynamics than it has in the kinetic theory of gases (*ibid.*). Likewise, the terms "mass", "length", and "duration" have different meanings depending on whether they occur in the context of classical mechanics or in Einstein's Theory of Special Relativity (*ibid.*, 81). This meaning variance not only manifests itself in theoreti-cal terms but also in observation terms. Hence, both observation and theoreti-cal terms get (at least part of) their meaning from the role they play in wider theoreti-cal context, and hence every description of an observation is at once a theoreti-cal statement. This renders a neat separation of theoretical and observation terms impossible.

Kuhn sees theories as pertaining to paradigms, and therefore speaks of a "par-adigm-embodied experience" (1970, 128) that scientists make when they make observations. He notes that attempts to rescue the ideal of theory-neutral experi-ence "through the introduction of a neutral language of observations now seem to me hopeless" (*ibid.*, 126) and an observation language therefore "embodies a host of expectations about nature and fails to function the moment these expectations are violated" (*ibid.*, 127). Proponents of the caloric theory of heat, for instance, give a different description of phenomena than those who see heat as form of kinetic energy. Crucially, this involvement of theory in observation reports is ine-liminable. There is nothing one can say about the world that does not go beyond what is given through immediate experience. Every attempt to describe what hap-pens around us involves a certain language and certain concepts that are not given to us by direct experience. An attempt to make theory-free statement must result in complete silence. Observation, and the sentences we produce to report these observations, are therefore theory-laden.[20]

Hanson invites us to consider Tycho and Kepler standing on a hill watching the dawn (1958, 5).[21] Kepler regarded the sun as fixed and the earth as moving around the sun. Tycho, by contrast, adhered to the view that the earth is fixed and other celestial bodies move around it. Hanson then asks the question: do Kepler and Tycho see the same thing? His answer is that they do not. One sees the sun move around the earth, and the other sees the earth move around the sun. Hanson of course does not deny that Tycho and Kepler had the same stimuli on their retinas. But Hanson insists that retinal stimulation and seeing are different things.

> People, not their eyes, see. Cameras, and eye-balls, are blind. . . . That Kepler and Tycho do, or do not, see the same thing cannot be supported by reference to the physical states of their retinas, optical nerves or visual cortices: there is more to seeing than meets the eyeball.
>
> (*ibid.*, 6–7)

And he concludes that "saying that Kepler and Tycho see the same thing at dawn just because their eyes are similarly affected is an elementary mistake: there is a difference between a physical state and a visual experience" (*ibid.*, 8) This is because the theoretical background of an observer is *constitutive* of her observations: without a theory she does not see, and what she sees depends on the conceptual scheme that her theory embodies.

Hanson further illustrates this with an imagined episode of Sir Lawrence Bragg and an Eskimo baby seeing an X-ray tube (*ibid.*, 15). He insists that someone can see an X-ray tube only once she understands the basic physics behind it and has at least a rough idea of how it works and what kind of object it is: "[t]o see an X-ray tube is at least to see that, were it dropped on stone, it would smash" (*ibid.*, 21). And he insists that we *see* that the X-ray tube would break (*ibid.*, 21); we do not infer this after having identified the object as an X-ray tube. Therefore, Bragg sees an X-ray tube while the Eskimo baby does not, even though they are both visually aware of the same object. The Eskimo baby is blind to what the physicist sees. Just like a metal rod placed in an elevated position becomes an antenna only against the background of electrodynamics, a glass tube containing metal plates can be qualified as an X-ray tube only against a certain theoretical background. So even though antennas and X-ray tubes are observable objects, the concept of an antenna and the concept of an X-ray tube have an essential theoretical component that cannot be reduced to something observable. If we were to take all theory out of the notion of an X-ray tube, we would not "free" the concept from theoretical "contamination"; we would dismantle the concept.

Conceptual theory-ladenness presents a serious challenge. If observation is inextricably intertwined with theory because there are neither theory-neutral observations against which theoretical claims could be tested nor a theory-neutral language in which observational findings could be reported, then the empiricist ideal of observation being the forum in which nature speaks for itself, uncoerced by our theoretical predilections, is a pipe dream. The consequences of this are potentially severe. The worry is that theory-ladenness leads to what one might call the *problem of confirmatory circularity*. Observations are supposed to be the touchstone of theories. If, however, observations always involve theory, then it is unclear how observations can provide a test for a theory and offer an objective basis on which to choose between competing theories. If theory is already part of observations, and if theories in fact select their own evidence, then theory testing becomes circular and positive test results would seem to be guaranteed because what is being tested is already in the observation. Referring to observations to confirm a theory would then be like someone wearing green sunglasses referring to her experiences to confirm her theory that the world is inherently green.

If true, this leads to a thorough-going relativism. Observation would not be able to decide between competing theories, and observers would end up observing what conforms with the theories that have already been adopted before making observations, and which cannot possibly be debunked by observations.

Unsurprisingly, not everybody is willing to countenance these conclusions and conceptual theory-ladenness has prompted robust responses. Dretske (1969, Ch. 2) responded that the point turns on a conflation of an epistemic and a non-epistemic way of seeing: *seeing that* an object *x* has property *P* and *seeing x tout court*. The former sense of seeing involves theories; the latter does not. So Tycho and

Kepler both saw the same sun; but one saw *that* it revolved around the earth while the other saw *that* it was at rest and the earth revolved around it. Van Fraassen (1980, 15) turns Dreskes distinction between two ways of seeing into a distinction between two ways of observing and submits that examples like the one with the sun are a confusion of *observing* and *observing that*. Discussing the example of a Stone Age person seeing a tennis ball (which leads to the same issues as Hanson's Eskimo baby seeing the X-ray tube) he concludes that to "say that he does not see the same things and events as we do . . . is just silly; it is a pun which trades on the ambiguity between seeing and seeing that" (*ibid*).

This, however, does not seem to be sufficient to put these worries to rest. Even if we assume that the distinction between observing *that* and observing *tout court* is sound and that there is a sense in which onlookers with different theoretical backgrounds see the same thing, many of the issues raised by conceptual theory-ladenness remain. Noting, say, that Kepler and Tycho see the same object does not go to the heart of the matter. Insofar as theory-testing is concerned, the crucial point is that Kepler sees that the earth moves around the sun while Tycho sees that the sun moves around the earth. It's seeing that, rather than seeing *tout court* that matters. A more thoroughgoing response is needed. We work our way to such a response in the next section.

3.5   Redrawing the Boundary

The discussion so far proceeded under the assumption that there is a binary opposition between observation and theory, and the question was how and where the boundary should be drawn. The discussions in the last three sections shed considerable doubt on our ability to draw such a line, or indeed on there being such a line at all. This suggests that we may have got off on the wrong foot, and that we should try another approach. In this section we discuss one such alternative approach, and we sketch how this approach avoids the problems faced by previous approaches.

Somewhat surprisingly, we have already encountered the core idea of an alternative approach earlier in the book. In Section 1.2 we have seen that Newton bifurcated his theory's vocabulary by distinguishing between terms that are "very familiar to everyone" and terms that needed to be defined in the theory, rather than by distinguishing between observation terms and theoretical terms. In effect this amounts to introducing a historical distinction between the accepted state of knowledge that serves as the background against which a theory is formulated and the novel elements that the theory introduces. In his later work in the 1960s and 1970s, Hempel made the same move when he proposed to distinguish between terms that are understood before the theory is formulated and terms that are newly introduced by a theory:

> the requirement of an observational interpretation base for scientific theories is unnecessarily artificial. The phenomena which a theory is to explain as well as those by reference to which it is tested are usually described in

terms which are by no means observation in a narrow intuitive sense, but which have a well-established use in science and are employed by investigators in the field with high intersubjective agreement. I shall say that such terms belong to the *antecedently available vocabulary*. Often, such terms will have been introduced into the language of science in the context of an earlier theory. . . . It seems reasonable, therefore, to construe the interpretation base of a theory as consisting, not of observational predicates, but of antecedently available ones.

(1973, 372–373, original emphasis)

On this view, the pertinent bifurcation is not between observational and theoretical terms, but between *antecedently available* terms and *new* terms, and there is no presupposition that antecedently understood terms have to be observational.[22] Hempel gives the example of early atomic theory (the Bohr-Sommerfeld theory), where the new terms like "spectral line" are explicated by means of previously available terms like "radiation" and "wave length". These terms were understood and accepted before the Bohr-Sommerfeld theory was introduced, but they are not observation terms in anything like the sense discussed in previous sections; they were provided by earlier theories, among them Maxwell's electromagnetic theory.

This is a sweeping proposal, which, if successful, offers a response to the problems we encountered in the previous sections. If the terms that are taken for granted (and that figure in an explication of a theory's specific vocabulary) are themselves theoretical terms, just ones that originate in antecedently accepted theories, then no precise line has to be drawn between observable and unobservable, which makes the issues we discussed in Sections 3.2 and 3.3 largely obsolete. Rather than looking for an absolute line between the observable and the unobservable, which turns out to be difficult to draw, Hempel's distinction embraces context-relativity and historical contingency, which has the advantage that it makes it possible to draw a line in a given situation. Theory-ladenness is embraced rather than exorcised because theories are not seen as being tested against theory-free observation reports, but rather against theoretical statements formulated in antecedently available scientific vocabulary,[23] which takes the teeth out of conceptual theory-ladenness. This largely takes care of the issues discussed in Sections 3.4.

The reason to still have a bifurcation (rather than renouncing completely the idea that a theory's vocabulary has to be split into two groups) is that Hempel saw it as a crucial task for a theory to explain its own specific vocabulary. He notices that "[i]f the characteristic vocabulary represents 'new' concepts, not previously employed, . . . then it seems reasonable, and indeed philosophically important, to inquire into how their meaning is specified" (1970, 149). So when faced with a new theory we have to identify the theory's particular vocabulary and the theory has to give these terms meaning, for instance by offering correspondence rules that connect the new terms to the antecedently understood terms. We discuss in detail how new terms are defined through previously available ones in the next chapter.

Suppe (1972, 10–11) points to a further reason for keeping a bifurcation. When a new theory is formulated, its claims have not yet been subjected to testing and neither the truth of its theoretical posits nor the accuracy of its predictions have been established. They have to be established by testing them against the available evidence, and this evidence consists precisely of claims that can be formulated in the previously available vocabulary. But, and this is the crucial point, to serve as an evidential basis against which theoretical claims are tested, the facts, regularities, and laws that are formulated in the previously available vocabulary need not be observable. As Suppe notes, all that is required for these to serve as evidence is that they can be "considered unproblematic *relative* to the theory or law which provides the prediction or explanation" (*ibid.*, 10, emphasis added). So the "hard" data against which a theory is tested are hard in the sense that they are established independently of the theory-to-be-tested; they are not hard in the sense that they are directly observable.

On this approach, successive scientific theories form a historically ordered layer-structure, whereby every layer of theory is built upon the previous layer of theory, like every line of bricks in a wall is built upon of the previous line of bricks. Hempel is explicit that being antecedently understood is a relational notion: the concepts of a theory have that status relative to the concepts of another theory. Theories are formulated at some point and, if successful, get accepted. New theories are tested against existing theories, and if they are successful, they form the foundation for future theories. And so on.

This proposal rightly identifies theories formulated in an antecedently understood vocabulary as the touchstone for new theories, but the idea that what separates antecedently understood and theoretical vocabulary is the historical order in which concepts enter the scene is problematic. Consider the example of temperature. The term "temperature" is antecedently understood in the context of assigning temperatures to liquids using mercury thermometers, and it can then be used in the description of the empirical bases against which other claims are tested. The Boyle-Charles law says that the product of the pressure and the volume of a gas is proportional to its temperature. This law is tested against a language that contains the previously understood concepts of pressure, volume, and temperature. Now shift context and turn to thermodynamics. In that context temperature is highly theoretical and an important part of the theory is concerned with the introduction and justification of the temperature scale. So "temperature" is antecedently understood in one context but not in other contexts. And, crucially, the historical order of these contexts is not as Hempel's account would suggest. On the "layer account" one would expect terms to *first* make an appearance as the terms that are to be explained through antecedently available vocabulary to *then* turn into the antecedently available vocabulary for the next theory. But in the case of temperature the order is reversed. The Boyle-Charles law was formulated at the beginning of the 19th Century while thermodynamics was formulated only in the second half of the 19th century, and yet "temperature" was considered an antecedently available term in the former but not in the latter. And temperature is no exception.

Similar points could also be made about terms like "mass", "force", "particle", and "light".

What matters is not the historical order in which terms have entered the scene, but the theoretical context in which they appear, and the way in which they function in that context. What makes a term antecedently available or theoretical must depend on its use in a particular theoretical context rather on the historical sequence of events that saw its introduction. The question is what exactly this means: how does a term have to be used in a theory to count as either theoretical or antecedently available in that theory?

An interesting answer to this question has been proposed by Sneed (1971) and elaborated by Balzer et al. (1987). The authors speak of T-theoretical and T-non-theoretical concepts rather than of new and antecedently available concepts, but the intuition they aim to capture is the same. To draw the line between T-theoretical and T-non-theoretical concepts they argue we should focus on the *application* of concepts. We understand a concept when we know how to apply it, and if we can distinguish situations in which it applies from situations which it does not. For instance, we understand the concept "red" when can successfully apply it and separate things into ones that are red and ones that are not. One can then say that a term is T-theoretical iff *all* methods of determining the extension of the term presuppose at least one law of the theory T. In other words, a term is T-theoretical if it cannot be applied without using the theory. A term is T-non-theoretical if it is not T-theoretical. If the term is such that it has numerical magnitudes (as, for instance, *mass* and *force* have), then being T-theoretical also means that at least one law of T must be used on every occasion where the numerical value of the magnitude is determined.

As a simple example, consider the notion of pressure. If T is thermodyanamics, then pressure is T-non-theoretical because no law of thermodynamics is needed to determine the pressure of a gas. If, by contrast T is classical mechanics, then pressure is T-theoretical because the determination of the pressure of gas requires measuring the force that the gas exerts on piston, and this requires the laws of mechanics. Or, to take a more advanced example, Newtonian mechanics takes over from Galilean kinematics the notions of *time*, *position*, and *trajectory*, and Newtonian mechanics is not needed to apply these concepts, which are therefore T-non-theoretical (if T is Newtonian mechanics). This is the modern-day version of Newton's remark that these notions were familiar to everyone. By contrast, the notion of force originates in Newtonian mechanics and an analysis of the theory shows that any determination of a force presupposes a law of Newtonian mechanics. Force is therefore T-theoretical.

These examples show that a concept can be T-theoretical with respect to one theory and not with respect to another theory. The notion of a trajectory, for instance, is Newtonian-mechanics-non-theoretical while at the same time being Galilean-kinematics-theoretical. This makes good on the requirement that whether a term is antecedently available or new must depend on the theoretical context in which it is used.

This is a promising approach which deals with the problems we have previously encountered in this section. A remaining question is how exactly this approach deals with the worry (discussed in Section 3.4) that theory-ladenness leads to confirmatory circularity because if theories are used in the production of evidence (through an application of their laws), then outcomes of tests would seem to be guaranteed because what is being tested is already in the observations. We will discuss in Section 7.4 how this issue plays out in Balzer, Moulines, and Sneed's approach, where, as we will see, this kind of circularity is successfully avoided.

3.6   Observation and Data Models

So far we have analysed a number of problems that arise in connection with observation. Throughout these discussions we have talked about observations in largely qualitative terms, for instance as the process of seeing that the ball is be red. While this "qualitative" sense of observation is relevant in some scientific disciplines, in many contexts making observations amounts to performing measurements with measurement-devices, and these measurements produce numerical data as outputs. A simple example is the measurement of temperature with a thermometer. The thermometer is the measurement device and the outcome of the measurement is a number, which reflects the temperature of the object.[24] The outcomes of measurements are referred to as *data*.[25] We now want to turn our attention to how data are gathered, processed, and presented, and to how they are eventually compared to theories.

There are different stages in the production and the processing of data. When an astronomer observes the motion of the moon, she chooses a coordinate system and measures the position of the moon in this coordinate system at consecutive instants of time. This is the process of *data acquisition*. Her data are the coordinates of the moon at certain given instants of time. She records the data in a laboratory report. What she notes in her laboratory report are *raw data*, the immediate and unprocessed outcome of an observation. The report can take different forms. She can write down a string of sentences of the form "at time t the moon was in position x", or she can record them in a table or a chart. At the level of the laboratory report, the format in which data are recorded is a choice of convenience. The format becomes a matter of methodological significance further down the line. Raw data are rarely, if ever, used as evidence and compared directly to the relevant theory. No experimental procedure is perfect. Some measurements may be the result of a malfunctioning of the equipment or of human error, and such data points have to be eliminated from the record before the data are used. Even when points are not faulty, the equipment only works at a certain level of precision and to use data one has to know what that precision is, which is usually done by specifying error bars. The data are then processed and put into an orderly form in which they are more useful, a process known as *data reduction*.[26] This means that certain mathematical operations are carried out on the data to produce an adequate summary of the data. The end result of this procedure is a *model of data*, or simply *data model*. So we can say that that a data model is a processed, corrected, rectified, regimented, and in many instances idealised, summary of the data we gain from immediate observation, the raw data.[27]

It is one of the tasks of statistics to describe and summarise a body of data in a compact and useful way, and so the construction of a data model is the province of statistics.[28] In principle any statistical technique can be used in the construction of a data model. In simple cases data reduction can mean that we fit a smooth curve through a finite collection of discrete points using, for instance, a linear regression; it can mean that we calculate the average and the standard deviation of individual data points; or it can mean that we construct a histogram. In more complex cases, it can mean that we perform multiple regressions, or it can mean that we first construct a family of models and choose one model from this family using a model selection criterion like the Akaike information criterion.[29] The point that matters here is that those who construct a data model have, in principle, all the techniques of statistics at their disposition. What operations we perform on the data and which technique we choose depends on the nature of the data, the research interests of the modelers, and the broader context of the investigation. There is no single right way to construct a data model, and the data themselves dictate neither the form of the data model nor what statistical techniques scientists should use to construct it.[30]

Let us illustrate all this with an example. The city of Venice is regularly subject to intense flooding. This raises the question of whether there is a pattern to these floodings that would allow the city to take necessary precautions, and whether there is an identifiable overall trend. To this end, data are collected in a measurement station at Punta della Salute in the centre of the city. The station makes hourly recordings of the sea levels with a tide gauge. The data are collected and made available through by the *Permanent Service for Mean Sea Level* (PSMSL), the global data bank for long-term sea-level information.[31] Data are available for the period from 1909 to 2000. Traditionally, tide gauges were paper-based: the float of the gauge was connected to a pen that drew a line on a piece of paper mounted on a drum rotating at a constant rate. In this way the line drawn reflected the level of the tide at a certain point. The thus marked up pieces of paper contains the raw data. The PSMSL operates a quality control system, called "buddy checking", whereby the outputs of a gauge are checked against the output of neighbouring stations. This leads to a flagging, and potential elimination, of questionable data.

In 2001 the PSMSL, in collaboration with the British Oceanographic Data Centre and the University of Hawaii Sea Level Center, initiated the GLOSS data archaeology and rescue project. The quality controlled and digitised paper records from nearly 100 tide gauges were made available, which resulted in data records of hourly tidal data. In the case of Venice, this means that a long list has been produced which shows the tidal level at full hours between January 1909 and December 2000. In our language, this long list is a data model: it is a condensed, rectified, simplified, and processed version of the paper records that were produced on the rotating drum of the gauge. This data model is, however, still too unwieldy for most purposes, so the PSMSL condensed the hourly data into monthly and then annual averages. Plots of these averages are available for download on its website, and they are reproduced below in Figure 3.3. The records are only 94% complete, which is reflected in gaps in the plots. Tidal levels are shown with respect to the so-called *Revised Local Reference*, which is defined to be 7000mm below mean sea level.

The three data models we have encountered so far – the list with hourly data and the plots with monthly and annual averages – are not the only possible data models. One could also fit a straight line through these, for instance by using a linear regression, and one could continue to include a 95% confidence interval.[32] And of course one does not have to stop here. One could fit curves other than

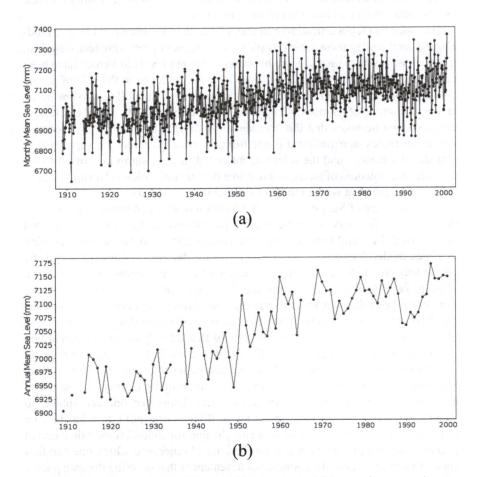

(a)

(b)

FIGURE 3.3 Venetian sea levels: (a) monthly averages and (b) annual averages (source PSMSL).

straight lines to the data; one could calculate the median rather than the average; one could fit a curve through seasonal maxima; and so on.

This example not only illustrates the steps we have described at the beginning of the section; it also shows that data processing often is an iterative process whereby one step builds on the next. First, lines on paper are transformed into digitised hourly values; then monthly averages are calculated from the hourly values; and finally a straight line is fitted to the monthly averages. This, as Harris notes (2003, 1511), can sometimes lead to confusions about what is what, and data can be referred to as raw data when they are in fact a data model. It would seem natural, for instance, to think that the hourly sea levels in the list are the raw data (just imagine that someone took a reading every full hour), when the list is in fact a data model that is constructed from paper plots. Hence, a careful look at the process of measurement and data production is needed to get clarity on what the raw data are and on how data models are created.

Data models play a crucial role in confirming theories because it is data models, and not the often messy and complex raw data, that theories are tested against. If a scientist wants to test, say, the hypothesis that sea levels in Venice have been rising over the 20th century, she will not look for evidence in the pile of papers that have come off the rotating drum in the observatory; she will turn to one of the graphs in Figure 3.2. Suppes is explicit about the role of data models in testing theories when he notes that the "maddeningly diverse and complex experience which constitutes an experiment is not the entity which is directly compared with a model of a theory" and the scientists make "[d]rastic assumptions of all sorts" to reduce the outcome of an experiment to a data model which is "a simple entity ready for comparison with a model of the theory" (1960, 20).

To make sense of Suppes' notion that a data model is compared to a model of the theory, we first have to make explicit that the notion that data are recorded in numerical form and then subjected to mathematical transformations resulting in a data model does not sit well with a picture that sees theories as linguistic all the way down. According to the Received View (as standardly understood), a theory faces reality by first deducing observation sentences from it, and then examining the truth or falsity of these sentences through observations by comparing these observation sentences, which should be true according to the theory, to observation sentences describing observations that actually happened. According to this picture, rather than drawing the graph we see in Figure 3.3b, we would write down a string of sentences like "the annual mean sea level in Punta della Salute in 1909 was 6904mm". But this would not only be clumsy, it would also be unhelpful because sentences are not the sort things that one can subject to statistical analysis. As we have seen, one of things one would do with the data in the graphs in Figure 3.3 is to fit a straight line (or indeed some other curve) to them. But sets of sentences are not the kind of objects to which one can fit a curve. One fits curves to data points, not to sentences that describe the data points. It is of course possible to re-describe the process of data processing so that it all comes down to the manipulation of sentences, but this seems to be awkward and ungainly because the real work is not done at the level of these sentences but at the level of the objects that the sentences describe. And the same comments apply to raw data. Rather than drawing a line on a piece of paper mounted on a rotating drum, one could write down a long string of sentences of the form "the reading of the tide gauge in Punta della Salute was x mm at time t". But the processing of the information contained in these sentences, to produce, say, a chart with annual averages proceeds on the numbers themselves rather than the sentences. While it is in principle possible to present and process data in linguistic form, doing so is not only unwieldy; it also obscures what is really going on in data processing and is out of sync with scientific practice.

This is where Suppes' suggestion becomes relevant. Rather than operating at the linguistic level and deal with descriptions of the data, Suppes urges us to compare models of theory with data models. We have encountered models of theory in Section 2.6, where we have seen that they are set-theoretical structures that make the formal sentences of a theory true. The crucial point to realise now is that data models, from a formal point of view, are also set-theoretical structures of the same kind. For instance, if the data points are numerical and the data model is a smooth curve through these points, then this is, from a formal point of view, a relation over $\mathbb{R}^n$ (for some n), or subsets thereof, and hence the data model is a structure $(\mathbb{R}^n, c)$, where c is the curve. Hence, data models and models of a theory are the same kind of objects, and one can therefore compare them with each other. This, Suppes submits, is a more productive way of thinking about how models face the outcomes of experiments than translating everything into sentences.

One can only agree with Suppes on this, and if the Received View indeed was committed to do all data processing at the level of sentences, the view would not have a compelling account of the relation between theory and data. However, as we have seen in Section 2.10, the Received View is not committed to a "no models policy". Indeed, it is perfectly natural to refocus attention on the models of the linguistic formulation of the theory rather than being focused on the linguistic formulation itself, and so the Received View can avail itself of all the techniques of data processing that we have discussed in this section, and it can analyse the relation between theory and observation in terms of the comparison of theoretical models with data models rather than in terms of sentences. Hence, the role data models play in theory testing is not a *reductio* of the Received View, but it shows that the Received View must be used in a liberal version which assigns models a systematic place.

What we have discussed so far is what one could call the traditional picture of data. This picture has recently attracted some criticism. The thrust of the criticism is not so much that the picture is wrong, but that it is too narrow. Three strands of criticism can be identified. The first strand is that not all data are numerical. Leonelli notes that plant phenotyping "relies heavily on the analysis of large sets of imaging data, which are produced at a fast rate and high volume through automated systems comprising several cameras, each geared to capture different signals (ranging from the visible to the infrared spectrum of light" (2019, 8). She points out that statistical techniques are unsuited, or at least insufficient, for the analysis of such data and that other techniques are required. She then gives a detailed account of how data are processed in the case of plant phenotyping (*ibid.*, 8–15). There is no claim that the methods that work for plant phenotyping also work in other domains, but they illustrate that a picture of data processing focused on statistical analysis does not capture how certain disciplines work with data.

The second strand of criticism is that both data processing and the use of data in the practice of science is more complicated than the traditional picture suggests. Data, Leonelli (2019, 15–18) points out, are prepared in a complicated process that involves not only biologists, but also laboratory technicians, image specialists, computer scientists, and data managers, and "same" data are in fact something different to each of these groups. So the idea that there is a once-and-for-all statistical process that produces the data model that then serves as the fixed and immutable touchstone to test a theory is too simple in many cases.[33]

The third strand of criticism can be summarised in the slogan "it takes more than just statistics". In cases where data are scarce, models of the target system are used to "complete" the data. Rather than "filling the gaps" by fitting a smooth curve to the data point using a statistical method, the gaps can be filled by model calculations. This practice is common in atmospheric science. In that context, methods of data processing that are "model based" are known as *data assimilation*. These methods combine observations (for instance, measurements from ground-based stations, ships, airplanes, and satellites) with numerical outputs of weather models with the aim of turning a gappy set of observations into a complete specification of the system's state. When data assimilation is applied to historical records to construct long-term datasets for past periods, which are then usually used in climate research, the process is known as *reanalysis*.[34] The models that are used for this process are sometimes referred to as *reanalysis models*, and they are part of large group of models called *data analysis models*, which are the models used to process historical weather and climate records (Edwards 2010, xv). Bokulich says that data models produced with model-based methods end up being "model-laden" and therefore prefers to refer to them as "data sets" rather than "data models" (2020, 794). Focusing specifically on models in the geosciences, she then distinguishes seven different kinds of model-ladenness of data, of which assimilation is one kind. She lists: data conversion, data correction, data interpolation, data scaling, data fusion, data assimilation, and synthetic data.[35] She also points out that even though these techniques are often discussed in the context of climate science, they are not limited to climate science and are actually used in other domains.

Sometimes the problem is the opposite: data are abundant rather than scarce. Indeed, data production has increased enormously over the last decade, and IBM estimates that humans now create around 2.5 quintillion bytes of data every day (Lyon 2016, 744). This has led to a boom of so-called *big data*. Some of these data are in the commercial sector, and we see large corporations like Google and Amazon scrambling to get as much data as they possibly can. But big data also play an increasingly important role in science. Astronomers, biologists, and physicists gather large amounts of data which are collected in large data bases. The processing and analysis of data in such databases is often referred to as *data mining* (Leonelli 2016, 88). It is often not possible to analyse and process these data with conventional statistical techniques, and so researchers turn to machine learning methods based on artificial intelligence and neural networks. These new techniques are powerful, and some have gone so far to say that they define a new era of science. In part, such claims are motivated by the idea that while in the traditional picture the main purpose of data was to test theories, when big data are combined with machine learning methods the algorithms generate the new insights "bottom up" from the data. In this way the combination of big data plus machine learning provides insights without needing a "top down" theory, and without aiming to test such a theory. This approach raises many interesting questions, and the philosophical engagement with big data is still in its infancy.[36]

In sum, the notion of a data model, as well as the uses of data, have evolved and expanded significantly over the last two or three decades, but without thereby making the traditional picture obsolete.

3.7   Conclusion

Observation is crucial to every field of science. Nevertheless, unpacking the empiricist dictum that knowledge comes from experience raises important issues. In this chapter we have seen what these issues are and how one might deal with them. Some of the problems we have encountered were artefacts of the Received View's doctrine that the non-logical vocabulary of theory has to be bifurcated into observation terms and theoretical terms. But not all problems can be dismissed in this way. Every epistemology of science will have to take a stand on what we can and what we cannot observe, and deal with the issue that observation is theory-laden. Likewise, every epistemology of science will have to explain how data are gathered, processed, and used to test theories. These questions will remain with us also in Part II of the book.

Notes

1   See also Carnap's (1936, 454–455, 1956, 41, 63) and Hempel's (1969,14, 1973, 371). In the scientific realism debate, the predicate "theoretical" is not only applied to terms, but also to (putative) entities to which theoretical terms (putatively) refer (see, for instance, Psillos 1999, Ch. 1). So "electron" is a theoretical term while an electron is a theoretical entity.

2   I also follow Putnam in discussing the issues pertaining to observability and theoreticity at the level of terms. An alternative would be to discuss the problem at the level of sentences. Carnap (1932) introduced the notion of a *protocol sentence*. These sentences are reports of an individual's direct experience, and hence are couched in observation terms. A simple example is "red here now". Whether a protocol sentence is true or false must be decidable by appeal to direct experience. This of course raises the ques-

tions that we have just seen. The content and form of an observation report was the subject matter of a heated debate in the Vienna Circle in the early 1930s, and there was no agreement as regards the credentials required to qualify as a protocol sentence. The debate is now known as the "protocol-sentence debate". See Cat's (2006), Gillies' (1993, Ch. 6) and Uebel's (2007) for discussions.

3 This criticism focuses on the observation dimension. One could also focus on the theory dimension and argue that first appearances notwithstanding, even simple colour terms like "white" require a background theory for their correct application. For a discussion of colours, see, for instance, Cohen's (2009).

4 For a discussion, see, for instance, Lutz' (2012).

5 Terms referring to objects and places that are too far away from us to see ("the centre of Andromeda"), too far in the past ("the first human being"), or otherwise inaccessible to us ("the centre of the sun") do not seem to fit the bill because there is a least a question whether they are non-theoretical, and, as we will see in the next section, some empiricists would count them as observable.

6 A different argument against the observational-unobservable distinction is that it cannot be drawn on the basis of the ordinary usage of scientific terms. This argument is discussed and dismissed in Suppe's (1972, 2–9).

7 In the same vein, and to the same end, Churchland (1982, 420) suggests a thought experiment featuring a new race of humanoid creatures that have all faculties of humans, but in addition are equipped with a biologically constituted electron microscope above the left eye.

8 See also Carnap's (1936, 455, 1966, 255–259), Hempel's (1969, 14–17), and Nagel's (1961, 80).

9 Indeed, Carnap himself noted that the philosophical notion of observation is different from the scientific notion of observation (1966, Ch. 23). See also Franklin's (1986, Ch. 6) and Torretti's (1990, Ch. 1). Torretti also introduces the notion of an "impersonal observation" which is based on the physical interaction between target and a recording device, rather than human observer.

10 References to the works of Hanson, Kuhn, and Feyerabend will be given later in this section. Gillies points out that early discussions of what we now call the theory-ladenness of observation can already be found in Duhem, Neurath and Popper (1993, Ch. 7). Votsis notes that the term "theory-ladenness" originates in the Ryle's "Dilemmas" (2015, 563). For an introduction and overview, see Schindler's (2013a).

11 Different kinds of theory-ladenness are not mutually exclusive and more than one of them can be present in a given situation. The five types are the result of going over the extant literature and trying to systematise the phenomena that are described under the heading of theory ladenness. One could add further types if one also took the presence of values in science into account (see, for instance, Douglas 2009). Alternative taxonomies of different kinds of theory-ladenness can be found in Brewer and Lambert's (2001), Heidelberger's (2003), Kuipers' (2001, Sec. 2.3), Kusch's (2015), Schindler's (2013a), and Schurz's (2015).

12 Variants of (a) and (c) are used by Hanson (1958, Ch. 1); (b) is discussed by Kuhn (1970, Ch. 10).

13 For reviews of the extensive debate about perceptual theory-ladennedss, see Brewer's (2012, 2015), Estany's (2001), Fridland's (2015), Lupyan's (2015), McCauley's (2015), and Raftopoulos' (2015). For a discussion of how one might test theory-ladenness empirically, see Votsis' (2018, 2020).

14 See Jeng's (2006) for a discussion of expectation bias in physics. Expectation bias is related to, but subtly different from, what psychologists call "experimenter bias", which results when experimenters unintentionally influence their subjects to give them the response they want (Rosenthal and Fode 1963, 183). See Teira's (2013) for

a discussion of experimenter bias, and Schindler's (2013b) for a discussion of theory-ladenness in experiments.

15 For a discussion, see, for instance, Williams et al. (2012) and Worrall's (2007).

16 The *locus classicus* for this view is Popper's (1959). He emphasised that science progresses by theory testing, and that it is theory that dictates were we look for tests. See also Brewer and Lambert's (2001, 180–181), Kosso's (1992, 114–115), and Kuhn's (1970, 126).

17 This is not always be the case. The justification for the workings of microscopes, at least initially, was based on experimental practice rather than theory. See Kusch's (2015) for a discussion.

18 The problem also arises in connection with measurement devices, for instance if one uses a mercury thermometer to test the theory that objects expand when heated (Franklin 2015, 156). Here the operation of the apparatus we use to make the observation, the thermometer, depends on the hypothesis under test, and so one might fear that there is no real comparison of theory and observation and that this prevents the theory from being properly tested. For a discussion of measurement, see, for instance, Chang's (2004) and Tal's (2016); for a survey of problems concerning measurement, see Tal's (2013).

19 The point has in fact been anticipated in Nagel's (1961, 83), and similar arguments can also be found in Achinstein's (1965).

20 It is interesting to note that Kuhn, at least in his (1970), does not use the term "theory-laden" to describe these phenomena. For detailed discussions of Kuhn's views on this issue, see Bird's (2000, Chs. 4 and 5) and Hoyningen-Huene's (1993, Chs. 3 and 4).

21 For an in-depth discussion of Hanson's views, see Lund's (2010, Ch. 3); Feyerabend's (1960) is a rather amusing review of Hanson's (1958).

22 See also Hempel's (1966, 79–80, 1969, 13–15, 1970, 149, 1977, 250–251). The old versus new term distinction is also used in Lewis' (1970, 1972).

23 This conclusion is also reached in Lakatos' (1970, 130).

24 Space constraints prevent me from saying more about the process of measurement. For an elementary introduction, see Brown's (1999, Ch. 4); for an in-depth discussion, see Krantz et al. (1971); for a discussion of the history of the discussions about measurement, see Díez's (1997a, 1997b); for a review of contemporary issues in measurement, see Tal's (2017); and for a discussion of the relation between measurement and representation, see Padovani's (2017).

25 The term comes from the Latin word "dare" which means to give. A "datum" is a given, and "data" is the plural of it. So, strictly speaking, the outcome of single measurement is a datum, although the term rarely seems to be used in singular.

26 Terminology varies. This process is also known as "data cleaning" or "data preparation".

27 See, for instance, Suppes' (1960, 20, 1962, 31) and Harris' (2003, 1509). For further discussions of data models, see also Mayo's (1996, Ch. 5), Suppes' (2007), and van Fraassen's (2008, Ch. 7). For a discussion of data models in finance, see Ippoliti's (2017, 2019).

28 Woodward (2010, 798) distinguishes between *descriptive* and *inferential* uses of statistics and sees describing data as the task of descriptive statistics. At the most general level, one can say that a statistical model is a mathematical representation of the observed data (Stobierski 2019). In this vein, Draper and Smith, after introducing a simple regression equation, say that this equation is a "*model* of what we believe" (1966, 10, original emphasis). So, indeed, statistical models are the philosopher of science's data models.

29 For a comprehensive discussion of statistical techniques, see, for instance, Wasserman's (2004); for a philosophical discussion, see Romeijn's (2017). The core idea of the Akaike information criterion is to choose a curve that strikes the best balance between simplicity and goodness-of-fit. The criterion has been introduced into the philosophical

debate in Forster and Sober's (1994). For further discussions, see Forster's (2002), Myrvold and Harper's (2002), and Sober's (2002, 2004). Sober's (2015) is a book-length discussion of parsimony-reasoning from antiquity to modern science.

30 This has been widely acknowledged in the literature on data models. See, for instance, Harris' (2003, 1511), Wolfson's (1970, 249), and Woodward's (2010, 798).

31 For a description of these data, see Holgate et al. (2013). The monthly and annual averages are available from PSMSL's website at www.psmsl.org/data/obtaining/stations/168.php. For details on the Revised Local Reference, see www.psmsl.org/data/obtaining/rlr.php.

32 This is described in Davison's (2003, Ch. 5) and a plot of this can be seen at https://tidesandcurrents.noaa.gov/sltrends/sltrends_station.shtml?id=270-054.

33 See Leonelli's (2016) for a detailed discussion of how data are used in plant biology. Cristalli and Sánchez-Dorado (2021) discuss how data are integrated in models that consist of different components.

34 For a discussion of data assimilation and reanalysis, see Parker's (2016). Edwards' (2010, Ch. 12) traces the history of reanalysis and provides an account of how the process works in practice.

35 Bokulich and Oreskes' (2017) offers a synoptic discussion of models in geoscience. For further discussion of data in climate science, see Bokulich and Parker's (2021) and Parker's (2020).

36 For synoptic discussions of philosophical issues that arise in connection with big data and machine learning, see, for instance, Floridi's (2012), Lyon's (2016), and Nickles' (2021). For a discussion of the problem of dealing with big data in medicine, see, Williamson's (2017).

References

Achinstein, P. 1965. The Problem of Theoretical Terms. *American Philosophical Quarterly* 2: 193–203.

Alspector-Kelly, M. 2004. Seeing the Unobservable: Van Fraassen and the Limits of Experience. *Synthese* 140: 331–353.

Andreas, H. 2017. Theoretical Terms in Science. In E. N. Zalta (ed.), *The Stanford Encyclopedia of Philosophy*. https://plato.stanford.edu/archives/fall2017/entries/theoretical-terms-science/.

Balzer, W., C.-U. Moulines, and J. D. Sneed 1987. *An Architectonic for Science: The Structuralist Program*. Dordrecht: Reidel Publishing Company.

Bird, A. 1998. *Philosophy of Science*. London: Routledge.

Bird, A. 2000. *Thomas Kuhn*. Princeton: Princeton University Press.

Bokulich, A. 2020. Towards a Taxonomy of the Model-Ladenness of Data. *Philosophy of Science* 87: 793–806.

Bokulich, A. and N. Oreskes 2017. Models in Geosciences. In L. Magnani and T. Bertolotti (eds.), *Springer Handbook of Model-Based Science*. Dordrecht, Heidelberg, London, and New York: Springer, pp. 891–911.

Bokulich, A. and W. S. Parker 2021. Data Models, Representation and Adequacy-for-Purpose. *Europen Journal for Philosophy of Science* 11: Article 31.

Brewer, W. F. 2012. The Theory Ladenness of the Mental Processes Used in the Scientific Enterprise: Evidence from Cognitive Psychology and the History of Science. In R. W. Proctor and E. J. Capaldi (eds.), *Psychology of Science: Implicit and Explicit Processes* (Vol. 68). Oxford: Oxford University Press, pp. 289–334.

Brewer, W. F. 2015. Perception Is Theory Laden: The Naturalized Evidence and Philosophical Implications. *Journal for General Philosophy of Science* 46: 121–138.

Brewer, W. F. and B. L. Lambert 2001. The Theory-Ladenness of Observation and the Theory-Ladenness of the Rest of the Scientific Process. *Philosophy of Science* 68: 176–186.

Brown, J. R. 1999. *Philosophy of Mathematics: An Introduction to the World of Proofs and Pictures*. London: Routledge.

Carnap, R. 1932. Über Protokollsätze. *Erkenntnis* 3: 215–228.

Carnap, R. 1936. Testability and Meaning. *Philosophy of Science* 3: 419–471.

Carnap, R. 1956. The Methodological Character of Theoretical Concepts. In H. Feigl and M. Scriven (eds.), *The Foundations of Science and the Concepts of Phsychologz and Psychoanalysis* (Vol. I, Minnestota Studies in the Philosophy of Science). Minneapolis: University of Minnesota Press, pp. 38–76.

Carnap, R. 1966. *An Introduction to the Philosophy of Science*. New York: Dover 1995 (Reprint of *Philosophical Foundations of Physics: An Introduction to the Philosophy of Science*. New York: Basic Books, 1966).

Cat, J. 2006. Protocol Sentences. In S. Sarkar and J. Pfeifer (eds.), *The Philosophy of Science. An Ecyclopedia*. New York: Tayolr & Francis, pp. 610–613.

Chang, H. 2004. *Inventing Temperature: Measurement and Scientific Progress*. Oxford: Oxford University Press.

Churchland, P. M. 1982. The Ontological Status of Observables: In Praise of the Superempirical Virtues. In D. Rothbarth (ed.), *Science, Reason, and Reality. Issues in the Philosophy of Science*. Philadelphia: Harcourt Brace, 1998, pp. 413–422.

Churchland, P. M. 1988. Perceptual Plasticity and Theoretical Neutrality: A Reply to Jerry Fodor. *Philosophy of Science* 55: 167–187.

Cohen, J. 2009. *The Red and the Real. An Essay on Color Ontology*. Oxford: Oxford University Press.

Cristalli, C. and J. Sánchez-Dorado 2021. Colligation in Modelling Practices: From Whewell's Tides to the San Francisco Bay Model. *Studies in History and Philosophy of Science* 85: 1–15.

Davison, A. C. 2003. *Statistical Models*. Cambridge: Cambridge University Press.

Díez, J. A. 1997a. A Hundred Years of Numbers. An Historical Introduction to Measurement Theory 1887–1990. Part I. *Studies in History and Philosophy of Science* 28: 167–185.

Díez, J. A. 1997b. A Hundred Years of Numbers. An Historical Introduction to Measurement Theory 1887–1990. Part II. *Studies in History and Philosophy of Science* 28: 231–265.

Douglas, H. E. 2009. *Science, Policy, and the Value-Free Ideal*. Pittsburgh: University of Pittsburgh Press.

Draper, N. R. and H. Smith 1966. *Applied Regression Analysis*. New York: John Wiley & Sons.

Dretske, F. 1969. *Seeing and Knowing*. London: Routledge and Keagan Paul.

Edwards, P. N. 2010. *A Vast Machine. Computer Models, Climate Data, and the Politics of Global Warming*. Cambridge, MA: MIT Press.

Estany, A. 2001. The Thesis of Theory-Laden Observation in the Light of Cognitive Psychology. *Philosophy of Science* 68: 203–217.

Feyerabend, P. K. 1960. Patterns of Discovery. *The Philosophical Review* 69: 247–252.

Feyerabend, P. K. 1965. Problems of Empiricism. In R. G. Colodny (ed.), *Beyond the Edge of Certainty*. Englewood Cliffs, NJ: Prenctice Hall, pp. 145–260.

Feyerabend, P. K. 1981. Explanation, Reduction and Empiricism. Philosophical Papers, Volume 1. In P. K. Feyerabend (ed.), *Realism, Rationalism and Scientific Method*. Cambridge: Cambridge University Press, pp. 44–96.

Floridi, L. 2012. Big Data and Their Epistemological Challenge. *Philosophy and Technology* 25: 435–437.

Fodor, J. 1984. Observation Reconsidered. *Philosophy of Science* 51: 23–43.

Forster, M. R. 2002. Predictive Accuracy as an Achievable Goal of Science. *Philosophy of Science* 69.

Forster, M. R. and E. Sober 1994. How to Tell When Simpler, More Unified, or Less Ad Hoc Theories Will Provide More Accurate Predictions. *The British Journal for the Philosophy of Science* 45: 1–35.

Franklin, A. 1986. *The Neglect of Experiment*. Cambridge: Cambridge University Press.

Franklin, A. 2015. The Theory-Ladenness of Experiment. *Journal for General Philosophy of Science* 46: 155–166.

Fridland, E. R. 2015. Skill, Nonpropositional Thought, and the Cognitive Penetrability of Perception. *Journal for General Philosophy of Science* 46: 105–120.

Gillies, D. 1993. *Philosphy of Science in the Twetieth Century. Four Central Themes*. Oxford: Blackwell.

Hacking, I. 1981. Do We See through a Microscope? *Pacific Philosophical Quarterly* 62: 305–322.

Hacking, I. 1983. *Representing and Intervening*. Cambridge: Cambridge University Press.

Hanson, N. R. 1958. *Patterns of Discovery*. Cambridge: Cambdridge University Press.

Hanson, N. R. 1969. Logical Positivism and the Interpretation of Scientific Theories. In P. Achinstein and S. F. Barker (eds.), *The Legacy of Logical Positivism*. Baltimore: Johns Hopkins Press, pp. 57–84.

Harris, T. 2003. Data Models and the Acquisition and Manipulation of Data. *Philosophy of Science* 70: 1508–1517.

Heidelberger, M. 2003. Theory-Ladenness and Scientific Instruments in Experimentation. In H. Radder (ed.), *The Philosophy of Scientific Experimentation*. Pittsburgh: Pittsburgh University Press, pp. 138–151.

Hempel, C. G. 1965. *Aspects of Scientific Explanation and Other Essays in the Philosophy of Science*. New York: Free Press.

Hempel, C. G. 1966. *Philosophy of Natural Science*. Princeton: Princeton University Press.

Hempel, C. G. 1969. On the Structure of Scientific Theories. In C. G. Hempel (ed.), *The Isenberg Memorial Lecture Series*. East Lansing: Michigan State University Press, pp. 11–38.

Hempel, C. G. 1970. On the 'Standard Conception' of Scientific Theories. In M. Radner and S. Winokur (eds.), *Minnesota Studies in the Philosophy of Science Vol. 4*. Minneapolis: University of Minnesota Press, pp. 142–163.

Hempel, C. G. 1973. The Meaning of Theoretical Terms: A Critique of the Standard Empiricist Construal. In P. Suppes, L. Henkin, A. Joja, and G. C. Moisil (eds.), *Logic, Methodology and Philosophy of Science Vol. IV*. Amsterdam: North Holland, pp. 367–378.

Hempel, C. G. 1977. Formulation and Formalization of Scientific Theories. In F. Suppe (ed.), *The Structure of Scientific Theories*. Urbana and Chicago: University of Illinois Press, pp. 244–254.

Holgate, S. J., A. Matthews, P. L. Woodworth, L. J. Rickards, M. E. Tamisiea, E. Bradshaw, et al. 2013. New Data Systems and Products at the Permanent Service for Mean Sea Level. *Journal of Coastal Research* 29: 493–504.

Horgan, T. and J. Woodward 1985. Folk Psychology Is Here to Stay. *The Philosophical Review* 94: 197–226.

Hoyningen-Huene, P. 1993. *Reconstructing Scientific Revolutions: Thomas S. Kuhn's Philosophy of Science*. Chicago: Chicago University Press.

Ippoliti, E. 2017. Dark Data. Some Methodological Issues in Finance. In E. Ippoliti and P. Chen (eds.), *Methods and Finance*. Cham: Springer, pp. 179–194.

Ippoliti, E. 2019. Models and Data in Finance: *Les Liaisons Dangereuses*. In Á. Nepomuceno-Fernández, L. Magnani, F. J. Salguero-Lamillar, C. Barés-Gómez, and M. Fontaine (eds.), *Model-Based Reasoning in Science and Technology. Inferential Models for Logic, Language, Cognition and Computation*. Cham: Springer, pp. 393–406.

Jeng, M. 2006. A Selected History of Expectation Bias in Physics. *American Journal of Physics* 74: 578–583.

Kosso, P. 1988. Dimensions of Observability. *The British Journal for the Philosophy of Science* 39: 449–467.

Kosso, P. 1989. *Observability and Observation in Physical Science*. Dordrecht: Kluwer Academic Publishers.

Kosso, P. 1992. *Reading the Book of Nature: An Introduction to the Philosophy of Science*. Cambridge: Cambridge University Press.

Krantz, D. H., R. D. Luce, P. Suppes, and A. Tversky 1971. *Foundations of Measurement: Volume I, Additive and Polynomial Representations*. New York and London: Academic Press.

Kuhn, T. S. 1970. *The Structure of Scientific Revolutions* (2nd ed.). Chicago: Chicago University Press.

Kuipers, T. A. F. 2001. Structures in Science. Heuristic Patterns Based on Cognitive Structures. An Advanced Textbook in Neo-Classical Philosophy of Science. In J. Hintikka (ed.), *Synthese Library*. Dordrecht: Springer, pp. 3–24.

Kusch, M. 2015. Microscopes and the Theory-Ladenness of Experience in Bas Van Fraassen's Recent Work. *Journal for General Philosophy of Science* 46: 167–182.

Lakatos, I. 1970. Falsificationism and the Methodology of Scientific Research Programmes. In I. Lakatos and A. Musgrave (eds.), *Criticism and the Growth of Knowledge*. Cambridge: Cambridge University Press, pp. 91–196.

Leonelli, S. 2016. *Data- Centric Biology: A Philosophical Study*. Chicago and London: University of Chicago Press.

Leonelli, S. 2019. What Distinguishes Data from Models? *European Journal for Philosophy of Science* 9: Article 22.

Lewis, D. K. 1970. How to Define Theoretical Terms. *The Journal of Philosophy* 67: 427–446.

Lewis, D. K. 1972. Psychophysical and Theoretical Identifications. *Australasian Journal of Philosophy* 50: 249–258.

Lund, M. D. 2010. *N. R. Hanson. Observation, Discovery, and Scientific Change*. New York: Humanity Books.

Lupyan, G. 2015. Cognitive Penetrability of Perception in the Age of Prediction: Predictive Systems Are Penetrable Systems. *Review of Philosophy and Psychology* 6: 547–569.

Lutz, S. 2012. Artificial Language Philosophy of Science. *European Journal for Philosophy of Science* 2: 181–203.

Lyon, A. 2016. Data. In P. Humphreys (ed.), *The Oxford Handbook of Philosophy of Science*. Oxford: Oxford Univeristy Press, pp. 738–758.

Maxwell, G. 1962. The Ontological Status of Theoretical Entities. In M. Curd and J. A. Cover (eds.), *Philosophy of Science: The Central Issues*. New York and London: Norton, 1998, pp. 1052–1062.

Mayo, D. 1996. *Error and the Growth of Experimental Knowledge*. Chicago: University of Chicago Press.

McCauley, R. N. 2015. Maturationally Natural Cognition, Radically Counter-Intuitive Science, and the Theory-Ladenness of Perception. *Journal for General Philosophy of Science* 46: 183–199.

Morrot, G., F. Brochet, and D. Dubourdieu 2001. The Color of Odors. *Brain and Language* 79: 309–320.

Myrvold, W. C. and W. L. Harper 2002. Model Selection, Simplicity, and Scientific Inference. *Philosophy of Science* 69.

Nagel, E. 1961. *The Structure of Science*. London: Routledge and Keagan Paul.

Nickles, T. 2021. Whatever Happened to the Logic of Discovery? From Transparent Logic to Alien Reasoning. In W. J. González (ed.), *Current Trends in Philosophy of Science: A Prospective for the Near Future* (Synthese Library). Cham: Springer, pp. TBA.

Padovani, F. 2017. Coordination and Measurement: What We Get Wrong About What Reichenbach Got Right. In M. Massimi, R. Jan-Willem, and S. Gerhard (eds.), *Epsa15 Selected Papers: The 5th Conference of the European Philosophy of Science Association in Düsseldorf* (Vol. 49–60). Cham: Springer.

Parker, W. S. 2016. Reanalyses and Observations. What's the Difference? *Bulletin of the American Meteorological Society* 97: 1565–1572.

Parker, W. S. 2020. Local Model-Data Symbiosis in Meteorology and Climate Science. *Philosophy of Science* 97: 807–818.

Popper, K. R. 1959. *The Logic of Scientific Discovery*. London: Routledge, 2002.

Psillos, S. 1999. *Scientific Realism: How Science Tracks Truth*. London: Routledge.

Psillos, S. 2000. Rudolf Carnap's 'Theoretical Concepts in Science'. *Studies in History and Philosophy of Science* 31: 151–172.

Putnam, H. 1962. What Theories Are Not. In E. Nagel, P. Suppes, and A. Tarski (eds.), *Logic, Methodology, and the Philosophy of Science*. reprinted in *Hilary Putnam: Mathematics, Matter and Method. Philosophical Papers Vol. 1*. Cambridge: Cambridge University Press, pp. 215–227.

Pylyshyn, Z. 2003. *Seeing and Visualizing. It's Not What You Think*. Cambridge, MA: MIT Press.

Raftopoulos, A. 2001a. Is Perception Informationally Encapsulated? The Issue of the Theory-Ladenness of Perception. *Cognitive Science* 25: 423–451.

Raftopoulos, A. 2001b. Reentrant Neural Pathways and the Theory-Ladenness of Perception. *Philosophy of Science* 68: 187–199.

Raftopoulos, A. 2015. The Cognitive Impenetrability of Perception and Theory-Ladenness. *Journal for General Philosophy of Science* 46: 87–103.

Romeijn, J.-W. 2017. Philosophy of Statistics. In E. N. Zalta (ed.), *The Stanford Encyclopedia of Philosophy*. https://plato.stanford.edu/archives/spr2017/entries/statistics/.

Rosenthal, R. and K. L. Fode 1963. The Effect of Experimenter Bias on the Performance of the Albino Rat. *Behavioural Science* 8: 183–189.

Schindler, S. 2013a. Observation and Theory-Ladenness. In B. Kaldis (ed.), *Encyclopedia of Philosophy and the Social Sciences*. Los Angeles: Sage, pp. 694–697.

Schindler, S. 2013b. Theory-Laden Experimentation. *Studies in History and Philosophy of Science* 44: 89–101.

Schurz, G. 2015. Ostensive Learnability as a Test Criterion for Theory-Neutral Observation Concepts. *Journal for General Philosophy of Science* 46: 139–153.

Shapere, D. 1969. Notes Towards a Post-Positivistic Interpretation of Science. In P. Achinstein and S. F. Barker (eds.), *The Legacy of Logical Positivism*. Baltimore: Johns Hopkins Press, pp. 115–160.

Shapere, D. 1982. The Concept of Observation in Science and Philosophy. *Philosophy of Science* 49: 485–525.

Sneed, J. D. 1971. *The Logical Structure of Mathematical Physics* (2nd revised ed.). Dordrecht: Reidel.

Sober, E. 2002. Instrumentalism, Parsimony, and the Akaike Framework. *Philosophy of Science* 69.

Sober, E. 2004. Likelihood, Model Selection, and the Duhem-Quine Problem. *The Journal of Philosophy* 101: 221–241.

Sober, E. 2015. *Ockham's Razors: A User's Manual*. Cambridge: Cambridge University Press.

Stobierski, T. 2019. What Is Statistical Modelling for Data Analysis. *Northeastern University Graduate Programs Blog*. www.northeastern.edu/graduate/blog/statistical-modeling-for-data-analysis/.

Suppe, F. 1972. What's Wrong with the Received View on the Structure of Scientific Theories? *Philosophy of Science* 39: 1–19.

Suppes, P. 1960. A Comparison of the Meaning and Uses of Models in Mathematics and the Empirical Sciences. In P. Suppes (ed.), *Studies in the Methodology and Foundations of Science: Selected Papers from 1951 to 1969*. Dordrecht: Reidel, 1969, pp. 10–23.

Suppes, P. 1962. Models of Data. In P. Suppes (ed.), *Studies in the Methodology and Foundations of Science: Selected Papers from 1951 to 1969*. Dordrecht: Dordrecht, 1969, pp. 24–35.

Suppes, P. 2007. Statistical Concepts in Philosophy of Science. *Synthese* 154: 485–496.

Tal, E. 2013. Old and New Problems in Philosophy of Measurement. *Philosophy Compass* 8: 1159–1173.

Tal, E. 2016. Making Time: A Study in the Epistemology of Measurement. *British Journal for the Philosophy of Science* 67: 297–335.

Tal, E. 2017. Measurement in Science. In E. N. Zalta (ed.), *The Stanford Encyclopedia of Philosophy*. http://plato.stanford.edu/archives/sum2015/entries/measurement-science/.

Teira, D. 2013. A Contractarian Solution to the Experimenter's Regress. *Philosophy of Science* 80: 709–720.

Teller, P. 2001. Whither Constructive Empiricism. *Philosophical Studies* 106: 123–150.

Torretti, R. 1990. *Creative Understanding: Philosophical Reflections on Physics*. Chicago: The University of Chicago Press.

Uebel, T. 2007. *Empiricism at the Crossroads: The Vienna Circle's Protocol-Sentence Debate*. Chicago: Open Court.

van Fraassen, B. C. 1980. *The Scientific Image*. Oxford: Oxford University Press.

van Fraassen, B. C. 2001. Constructive Empiricism Now. *Philosophical Studies* 106: 151–171.

van Fraassen, B. C. 2008. *Scientific Representation: Paradoxes of Perspective*. Oxford: Oxford University Press.

Votsis, I. 2015. Perception and Observation Unladened. *Philosophical Studies* 172: 563–585.

Votsis, I. 2018. Putting Theory-Ladenness to the Test. *Cognitive Science Society Proceedings*: 2630–2635.

Votsis, I. 2020. Theory-Ladenness: Testing the 'Untestable'. *Synthese* 197: 1447–1465.

Wasserman, L. 2004. *All of Statistics: A Concise Course in Statistical Inference*. New York: Springer.

Williams, J. B., D. Popp, K. A. Kobak, and M. J. Detke 2012. The Power of Expectation Bias. *European Psychiatry* 27: 1.

Williamson, J. 2017. Models in Systems Medicine. *Disputatio* 9: 429–469.

Wolfson, R. J. 1970. Points of View, Scientific Theories and Econometric Models. *Philosophy of Science* 37: 249–260.

Woodward, J. 2010. Data, Phenomena, Signal, and Noise. *Philosophy of Science* 182: 792–803.

Worrall, J. 2007. Why There's No Cause to Randomize. *The British Journal for the Philosophy of Science* 58: 451–488.

4

FRAMING THE THEORETICAL

4.1 Introduction

In Chapter 1 we have seen that the Received View divides the non-logical vocabulary of a theory into observation terms and theoretical terms. Observation terms are terms whose application can be determined through direct observation, while theoretical terms have no immediate connection to experience. This raises the question of how we should understand the semantics of theoretical terms. Broadly speaking, semantics concerns the relation between symbols and the objects that they are symbols for. If we focus on terms (rather than sentences), semantics is the study of the meaning and reference (or denotation) of terms. If theoretical terms have no direct connection to experience, what do they mean and how do they refer? The Received View is committed to the idea that theoretical terms have to be connected to observation terms by correspondence rules. This raises two questions: what is the nature of this connection and what kind of semantics do correspondence rules provide us with?[1]

Before delving into the details, let us firm up our intuitions about meaning and reference with a classical example due to Frege (1892). The term "Venus" *refers* to planet Venus, the second planet from the Sun in our solar system. It turns out that the expressions "the morning star" and "the evening star" also refer to Venus.[2] The three terms have the same referent, namely the planet Venus. Yet they have different *meanings*. "Morning star" conveys that the heavenly body that the term refers to is visible in the morning; "evening star" expresses that the body appears in the sky in the evening; and "Venus" bears the imprint of a mythical age when celestial phenomena pertained to deities.[3] This raises important questions. What is the meaning of an expression? How does a term refer to something? And what is the relation between meaning and reference? Important parts of analytical philosophy are concerned with shedding light on these questions.[4] The aim of this chapter is to discuss how these questions have been answered for theoretical terms like "electron".

DOI: 10.4324/9781003285106-6

A pervasive intuition about meaning is that the meaning of an expression is closely connected to the way in which we tell whether the expression applies to something. If I have no idea how to ascertain whether or not something is a violin, then I do not know what the term "violin" means. This intuition is enshrined in the slogan "meaning is the method of verification", which is the core of verificationism (Section 4.2). Articulating verificationism requires us to discuss the analytic-synthetic distinction and the nature of explicit definitions. This gets us deeper into the philosophy of language than those interested in models and theories would usually care for, and, at first blush, the issues that arise would seem to be rather removed from the concerns of philosophy of science. I appeal to readers' forbearance and ask them to stay with me in this section. I discuss the issues of verification, analyticity, and definitions as briefly as possible (in fact, experts will no doubt deem it too brief). The points we discuss in this section will also be crucial later in the chapter when we turn to more recent approaches to theoretical terms based on the Carnap Sentence, Hilbert's ε-operator, and Lewis' definite descriptions.

As we have seen in Section 1.3, explicit definitions are the simplest and most convenient kind of correspondence rules because they effectively eliminate theoretical vocabulary from theoretical statements. Unfortunately, explicit definitions suffer from a number of problems, and much of the discussion about theoretical terms that follows can be seen as an attempt to circumvent these problems by replacing explicit definitions with other kinds of correspondence rules. The first attempt was Carnap's introduction of so-called reduction sentences, which offer implicit rather than explicit definitions of theoretical terms (Section 4.3). Hempel noted that reduction sentences were still too restrictive and replaced them with what he called interpretative systems (Section 4.4). A different approach reverts to the notion of a model as an alternative interpretation of a theory's formalism and sees the semantics of theoretical terms as given by models (Section 4.5). None of these approaches is satisfactory, and so one might wonder whether it would be better to eliminate theoretical terms altogether because this would make the problem of their semantics obsolete. Two receipes to that effect have been proposed: Craig's theorem and the Ramsey Sentence (Section 4.6).

Elimination turns out to have its own problems, and so the subsequent discussion tried to come to grips with the semantics of theoretical terms through new techniques, most notably the Carnap sentence (Section 4.7*), Hilbert's ε-operator, and Lewis' definite descriptions (Section 4.8*). The distinction between analytic and synthetic statements, introduced in Section 4.2, played an important role in the discussion of theoretical terms. However, the distinction met with resistance, most notably from Quine who argued that it is untenable. We discuss Quine's arguments and a number of responses to it (Section 4.9). Feigl renounces the empiricist principle that theoretical terms have to be explicated through observation terms and proposes a realist analysis of theoretical terms which regards them as being on par with observation terms: theoretical terms are about objects in the world and describe their properties and relations (Section 4.10). This leaves open the question of *how* terms refer to their objects. A recent proposal aims to fill this gap by formulating a semantics of theoretical terms within the framework of the causal-historical theory of reference (Section 4.11). We conclude that none of the proposals discussed in this chapter is entirely satisfactory and that understanding the meaning of theoretical terms remains an open problem (Section 4.12).

4.2 Verificationism, Analyticity, and Explicit Definitions

An important doctrine associated with logical empiricism is the *verification theory of meaning* (VTM), which can be encapsulated in the slogan "the meaning of a sentence is the method of its verification".[5] We verify a statement when we produce evidence showing that the statement is either true or false.[6] Hence VTM says that we grasp the meaning of a sentence if we know what experiences are required in order to be able to affirm the truth or falsehood of the sentence. The emphasis is on method. The meaning of a sentence is specified by saying how one would go about checking whether the sentence is true; it is not sufficient to merely say what state of affairs would serve as a truth maker for the sentence. Consider the sentence "the peak of Mont Blanc is 4810 meters above sea level". According to VTM, it is not enough to say that the sentence is true if the state of affairs of the peak of Mont Blanc being 4810 above sea level obtains in the world. We have to say what technique we would employ to measure the height of the mountain, for instance that we perform a particular set of operations with a GPS system.

It is important that "verification" in VTM refers to *verifiability in principle* and not actual verification. Consider the sentence "there is life on Mars". No one currently has the means to actually verify this sentence. But this does not make the sentence meaningless because one can describe what, in principle, it would take to verify it. This qualification is important because many interesting scientific hypotheses make statements that cannot currently be verified, and to produce circumstances that make a verification possible is seen as a challenge to which science aims to rise, for instance by designing specific experiments that allow us to put hypotheses to test.

If no methods of verification can be stated for a sentence, then the sentence is meaningless. And the verdict of meaninglessness is to be taken literally. A sentence that has no method of verification is not merely unknowable, too abstract, or beyond the reach of empirical science. It is literally meaningless. Such a sentence has the same meaning as "@b€k7*±p^" or "balabala", namely none. To illustrate the point, Carnap describes a thought experiment in which someone describes an object as being "teavy" (Carnap 1931/1996, 14). The person claims that it is a fact that some objects are teavy while others are not. Alas, there are no empirical manifestations of teavyness and the human mind is never able to uncover the secret of which things are teavy and which are not. Carnap dismisses "teavy" as empty verbiage. If no method of verification for the sentence "this object is teavy" can be specified, then nothing is asserted and the sentence is meaningless. Meaningless sentences are "pseudo-statements" (*ibid.*, 11). Since metaphysical statements are by their very nature not empirically verifiable, metaphysics consists of pseudo-sentences. In this way, VTM dismisses metaphysics as devoid of meaning, and hence as a pointless enterprise that ought to be abandoned. Much could be said about the logical positivist's dismissal of metaphysics, but our focus here is on the meaning of scientific discourse.

The requirement of verifiability in principle leaves open how sentences are verified. This issue needs some attention because not all sentences are of the same kind. Consider the sentences (1) "bachelors are unmarried men" and (2) "bachelors live with their mothers". The truth of the first sentence does not depend on matters of fact, and no empirical investigation is needed to ascertain its truth. In fact, we can ascertain its truth on grounds that being unmarried is part of the concept of being a bachelor.[7] A sentence that is true (or false) solely due to the meaning of its constituent terms is *analytic*. (1) is analytic and so no empirical investigation is needed to know that it is true. By contrast, it is not part of the concept of a bachelor that bachelors live with their mothers, and whether it is true that they do depends on facts about bachelors in the world. If it so happens that all bachelors live with their mothers, then (2) is true; if there is a bachelor who does not live with his mother, then (2) is false. Sentences like (2) whose truth depends on how the world is are *synthetic*.

If the truth or falsity of a sentence can be known independently of experience, then it is known *a priori*. If a proposition can only be found to be either true or false by recourse to experience, then it is known *a posteriori*. Which sentences can be known *a priori* and which sentences require appeal to experience? It is a fundamental posit of logical empiricism that *all a priori* knowledge is analytical and *all a posteriori* knowledge is synthetic. The quantifier "all" is crucial. It amounts to denying the existence of synthetic *a priori* knowledge, which some idealists (most notably Kant in the *Critique of Pure Reason*) regarded as possible. In fact, the denial of the possibility of synthetic *a priori* knowledge can be seen as the defining tenet of logical empiricism.[8]

Among the truths that can be known *a priori* are truths of logic. This is because logical empiricists regard truths of logic as analytic (see, for instance, Carnap 1966, 259). Consider the sentence "if no bachelor is a happy man, then no happy man is a bachelor". One does not even need to understand the descriptive terms in it to be able to ascertain its truth. We could replace the terms by placeholders – thus getting "if no B is H, then no H is a B" – and we would still be able to ascertain the truth of the sentence. This because its truth is a matter of pure logic, or, as Carnap would say, a matter of the meanings of the logical connectives "if", "then", "no" and "is" (1966, 259).

Hence, if we wish to ascertain whether a sentence is meaningful, we have two options:

(a) If the sentence is analytic, then we ascertain its truth or falsity *a priori* (and if it is true due to the meaning of the connectives then it is a truth of logic).

(b) If the sentence is synthetic, then its truth or falsity has to be established *a posteriori*, i.e. by appeal to experience.

Posits (a) and (b) taken together provide a criterion for a sentence to be meaningful. Especially in the earlier literature on the topic, the expression "cognitive significance" was used instead of "meaning". Posits (a) and (b) were then referred to as the *criterion of cognitive significance* (CCS).[9] The label *verificationism* is an umbrella term to refer either to VTM or CCS, or to both.

CCS needs further unpacking. First, it relies on a hitherto only intuitively introduced separation of sentences into analytic and synthetic sentences, and nothing has been said about how this separation is explicated. We set this issue aside for now and return to it in Section 4.9. Second, the criterion relies on the notion of establishing the truth of a synthetic sentence by appeal to experience. Let us focus on *elementary sentences*, i.e. sentences of the form "*a* is *P*", where "*a*" refers to an object and "*P*" to a property.[10] In some cases, the referents of both terms are directly observable. If so, the truth or falsity of the sentence can be determined by consulting direct experience. Consider the sentence "the table is green". Assuming that I can see the table and perceive colours, I can assert directly whether the sentence is true or not, and the meaning of the sentence (as per VTM) is something like: identify the table, observe its colour when there is light in the room, and check whether the colour is green. If the truth of a sentence can be ascertained through direct experience, then it is an *observation sentence*.[11]

Unfortunately, many elementary sentences we encounter in scientific contexts are not observation sentences. A sentence like "the electron has a charge of $1.60217662 \times 10^{-19}$ coulombs" cannot be tested directly against experience because it involves terms like "electron" and "charge" whose (putative) referents are not accessible to direct observation. If verification against direct experience is the only option, such sentences must be declared meaningless. This would force us to declare large parts of science to be meaningless, which is a conclusion that scientists would regard as absurd and which the logical empiricists were therefore reluctant to draw.

To avoid this conclusion, Carnap suggested that scientific terms that impede a verification of the sentences in which they occur should be defined through terms for which a verification is possible (Carnap 1931/1996, 12–14).[12] His example is "arthropod". It is not directly observable whether an animal is an arthropod, and so sentences like "arthropods live on all continents" are not verifiable through direct experience. However, one can define "arthropod" as "animal with a segmented body and jointed legs". Assuming that "animal", "segmented body" and "jointed legs" refer to directly observable properties, one can now verify "arthropods live on all continents" by appeal to experience, which makes the sentence meaningful. In general, the prescription is that for every term τ that is such that we cannot decide by appeal to direct experience whether something is a τ, we have to formulate a sentence of the form $\forall x(\tau x \leftrightarrow \omega x)$, where ω is an term related to a method of verification (and "τx" means that term τ applies to object x, "ωx" means that term ω applies to object x, and "$\leftrightarrow$" is the biconditional which can be read as "if and only if"). This sentence says that for all objects, the object is a τ if, and only if, it is an ω. The sentence $\forall x(\tau x \leftrightarrow \omega x)$ is an *explicit definition*, and it states both necessary and sufficient conditions for the application of a term. Explicit definitions render initially unverifiable sentences verifiable because they allow us to replace the problematic terms by their observational definitions, which transforms the original sentence into one in which only terms that refer to directly observable objects or properties occur.

This connects directly to the vision of theories discussed in Section 1.3. Postulate (R3) of the Received View required that theoretical terms be connected to observation terms by correspondence rules, but the nature of these rules was left open. The doctrine of verificationism now fills this gap with the requirement that correspondence rules be explicit definitions. Hence, a correspondence rule has the form $\forall x(\tau x \leftrightarrow \omega x)$, where τ is a theoretical term and ω is an observation term.[13] A theoretical term is then really nothing more than a convenient abbreviation for a (possibly complicated) observation term. Hence, theoretical discourse, in as far as it is meaningful, is just observational discourse in disguise: assertions about putative unobservable entities are in fact assertions about observable entities. Theoretical terms are a mere expedient for economy of thought that can, in principle, be eliminated any time by substituting definitions wherever they occur.[14]

Before turning to problems with this view, there is an item of housekeeping we need to attend to. VTM is a principle that specifies the meaning of *sentences*, but it remains silent about the meaning of *terms*. However, we started our discussion by enquiring into the semantics of theoretical terms, and so we require an additional resource to answer our question. This resource is the *principle of compositionality*: "the meaning of a sentence is determined by the meanings of the words that constitute it and by the way those words are put together, by the syntactic structure of the sentence" (Devitt and Hanley 2006, 3). One can now try to exploit this fact to extract the meaning of terms from the meaning of a sentence in which they occur. The general principle leaves the details of such an analysis underdetermined, but the following is at least prima facie plausible. When testing "*a* is *P*" we have to give definitions of "*a*" and "*P*" in terms of observables (unless, of course, "*a*" and "*P*" are observation terms). The contribution of each term to the meaning of the sentence therefore is the observable definition associated with it because this definition makes it possible to state a method of verification. Given this, it is natural to say that the meaning of a theoretical term is its explication in terms of observables: the meaning of τ is ω. If a term is an observation term, its meaning is the observable property it refers to.

This view faces three challenges. The first comes from Braithwaite, who objects that giving explicit definitions of theoretical terms will "*ossify*" the scientific theory in which they occur" because "there would be no hope of extending the theory to explain more generalisations than it was originally designed to explain" (1954b, 36, original emphasis, cf. 1954a, 155). Braithwaite assumes that definitions, once they are made, are immutable. It is, however, unclear why this would be so. One can always replace a definition with a new altered and expanded definition. However, and that is the grain of truth in Braithwaite's remark, such a replacement would, in effect, produce a new theory because if correspondence rules are part of the theory, then changing the rules changes the theory. It is worth noting, though, that this point is not specific to explicit definitions and every account that sees the theoretical apparatus of a theory as being tied to experience through correspondence rules will face this problem.

The second challenge is what one could call the *problem of multiple definitions*. Verificationism demands that a theoretical term is defined through of a concrete method of verification. The theoretical term *temperature*, for instance, will be defined by the condition "for all x, x has temperature $\theta \leftrightarrow$ a mercury thermometer shows θ when brought in contact with x". The problem is that one also can measure temperature with an alcohol thermometer, a bi-metal strip, an infrared detector, and indeed countless other methods, and each of these methods gives rise to a different definition of temperature. And temperature is no exception: many theoretical terms are associated with multiple measurement methods. But how are we to define a term if different yet equally viable definitions are available?

Operationalism denies that this is a problem and submits that different measurement procedures literally define different terms. The position originates with Bridgman (1927) who, when discussing length, submits that "the concept of length . . . is fixed when the operations by which length is measured are fixed" and more generally that "we mean by any concept nothing more than a set of operations; *the concepts is synonymous with the corresponding set of operations*" (*ibid.*, 5, original emphasis). According to operationalism it is wrong to say that there are different ways to measure temperature. There is no such thing as temperature per se. There is only temperature as measured by a mercury thermometer, temperature as measured by an alcohol thermometer, etc. Bridgman regards these as different concepts, and sees lumping them together as a mistake.

Operationalism faces serious difficulties.[15] The first is that it renders meaningless the attribution of a property to an object if the magnitude of the property is off the range of available measurement devices. For instance, it is meaningless to say that the temperature of the universe a split-second after the big bang was 10^{32} K because there are no instruments able to measure such a temperature. The second difficulty is that operationalism's proliferation of concepts is fundamentally at odds with scientific practice. Different measurement procedures are treated as measuring the *same* quantity and theories formulate laws about these quantities. Thermodynamics recognises only one concept of temperature, and incorporating concepts like temperature-as-measured-by-a-mercury-thermometer and temperature-as-measured-by-an-infrared-device would require a fundamental revision of the theory, and that revision would be completely out of sync with how the theory is used in practice.

An alternative response to the problem of multiple definitions is that verificationism does not demand that separate definitions be given for each method and that we are free to merge them all into one large disjunctive definition. Temperature would then be defined by the disjunction "for all x, x has temperature $\theta \leftrightarrow$ a mercury thermometer shows θ when brought in contact with x, or a bi-metal thermometer shows θ when brought in contact with x, or . . .". This option has not received much attention in the literature on scientific theories, but a parallel problem appears in the Nagelian account of inter-theoretical reduction, where certain bridge laws are disjunctive in the same way as the correspondence rule for temperature. The issue of disjunctive bridge laws has been controversial, and no consensus on whether disjunctive bridge laws are acceptable has emerged. So it would seem to be an open question whether disjunctive correspondence rules are admissible.[16]

The third challenge arises in connection with disposition terms (Carnap 1936, 440). Disposition terms describe what would happen if certain conditions were in place. Something is fragile if it breaks when struck. The observation term ω for disposition terms takes the form of a conditional. Let "sx" stand for "x is struck", and "bx" for "x breaks", and let $\omega x := (sx \rightarrow bx)$, where "$\rightarrow$" is the material conditional "if . . . then . . .". The disposition term φ, being fragile, is then defined by $\forall x(\varphi x \leftrightarrow \omega x)$.[17] In this context s is known as the *test condition* of φ, b as the *observable response*, and the conditional $sx \rightarrow bx$ as the *scientific indicator* (Psillos 1999, 3). So this definition says that for every object x, x is fragile iff the following is true: if x is subjected to the test condition of being struck, then it shows the observable response of breaking.

This definition has an undesirable consequence: every object that does *not* satisfy the test condition possesses the dispositional property automatically. A brand-new football, for instance, comes out as fragile under this definition simply because it has never been struck. The source of the problem is that the scientific indicator is a material conditional, and hence is true whenever sx is false. The problem could be circumvented by adding the clause that sx must be true. This would undercut the problem with the false antecedent, but only at the price of introducing a new one: we are now forced to say that unless an object has actually been struck, it does not possess the dispositional property φ. This means that unless the porcelain vase has actually been struck it is not fragile. This conclusion is equally undesirable and so adding an existential clause does not solve the problem.

One might try to mitigate the force of this objection by arguing that issues with dispositional terms are a marginal problem because what we are really interested in are theoretical terms in scientific theories, which is a different problem. This falls short of solving the problem because many theoretical terms in fact function like disposition terms.[18] Saying, as we did above, that x has temperature θ iff a mercury thermometer shows θ when brought in contact with x in fact amounts to making a dispositional statement, the dispositional aspect being the clause "when brought in contact with x". A proper definition of temperature would be: "for all x, x has temperature θ $\leftrightarrow$ (x is put in contact with a mercury thermometer $\rightarrow$ the thermometer shows θ)", which has the form of the above definition of dispositional terms.[19]

An effective way around these difficulties would be to replace the material conditional in the scientific indicator with a counterfactual conditional. The scientific indicator would then say "if x were struck, then it would break" (or, in the notation of modal logic, $sx \square\!\rightarrow bx$). The problem with this suggestion is that counterfactual conditionals come with a host of problems of their own,[20] and even if we were willing to set these aside, we would still be left with the problem of multiple definitions to which counterfactuals offer no solution.

These three challenges offer no conclusive proof that theoretical terms cannot be given an explicit definition (indeed, we will revisit explicit definitions in Section 4.8*). However, they cast doubt on the viability of the project to such an extent that Carnap (1936) concluded that a new approach was needed. We now turn to this approach.

4.3 Reduction Sentences and Implicit Definitions

Carnap suggested replacing explicit definitions with a kind of correspondence rules that he called *reduction sentences*. Let τ be the theoretical term that we want to reduce to something observable. As in the discussion of disposition terms in the previous section, we consider both test conditions and observational responses for τ. In their most general form, reduction sentences come as pairs, now known as *reduction pairs* (1936, 441–442): $\forall x(s_1 x \rightarrow (b_1 x \rightarrow \tau x))$ and $\forall x(s_2 x \rightarrow (b_2 x \rightarrow \neg\tau x))$.[21] In the first sentence, s_1 is the test condition required to see whether τ applies and b_1 is the observable response one expects after s_1. In the second sentence, b_1 is the test condition required to see whether τ fails to apply, and b_2 is the observable response one expects after s_2. In most cases one uses the same test condition to see whether τ does or does not apply (that is, $s_1 = s_2$) and b_2 is the negation of b_1 (that is, $b_2 = \neg b_1$). The reduction pair is then logically equivalent to the *bilateral reduction sentence* (ibid., 442–443): $\forall x(sx \rightarrow (bx \leftrightarrow \tau x))$, where, for ease of notation, we set $s := s_1 = s_2$ and $b := b_1 = \neg b_2$. This sentence says that for all objects x, if x is subjected to the test condition s, then τ applies to x iff it shows the observable response b. Using the above example of an object being fragile, the bilateral reduction sentence says that for every object x, if x is subjected to test condition of being struck, then: x shows the observable response b iff x is fragile.

Bilateral reduction sentences and explicit definitions have a different logical form. An explicit definition of τ says $\forall x(\tau x \leftrightarrow (sx \rightarrow bx))$, while a bilateral reduction sentence for τ is $\forall x(sx \rightarrow (bx \leftrightarrow \tau x))$. This is of course by design: bilateral reduction sentences do not provide explicit definitions of a theoretical term τ. Carnap saw them as providing a "conditioned definition" (ibid., 443). This is because the sentence can be seen as being composed of an explicit definition, namely $bx \leftrightarrow \tau x$, which is made conditional on sx. The conditional is true whenever the antecedent sx is false no matter what the truth-value of the consequent $bx \leftrightarrow \tau x$. Hence, in such cases it is unspecified whether τ applies, which leaves the meaning of τ partially indeterminate. For this reason, reduction sentences are said to provide only a *partial interpretation* of theoretical terms (Carnap 1956b, 46).[22]

Bilateral reduction sentences solve two problems of explicit definitions. First, as we have seen in the previous section, explicit definitions imply that an object which has never been subjected to test condition s automatically has the theoretical property τ (the brand-new football comes out as being fragile). Reduction sentences avoid this conclusion because if the test conditions are not instantiated, then they just remain silent about τ. The reduction sentence just leaves open whether or not the football is breakable. Second, as we have also seen in the previous section, explicit definitions have a problem accommodating multiple test conditions for the same theoretical property. Reduction sentences avoid this problem because they only state what happens if the test conditions are realised and remain silent about what happens if they are not. For this reason one can have several test conditions, and formulate a reduction sentence for every test condition, without them being in conflict with each other. We can, for instance, have a reduction sentence for "fragile" that has "being struck" as a test condition and another one that has "being smashed" as a test condition, and both can be part of the same theoretical system. One can then see τ as introduced jointly by all reduction sentences.

An important consequence of replacing explicit definitions with reduction sentences is that theoretical terms are now no longer eliminable. If a term is given an explicit definition in terms of observables, then it is in principle always possible to replace the term with the definition and thus translate a theoretical statement into an observation statement. This option is no longer available if a term is introduced with a reduction sentence. As a consequence, the maxim that theoretical discourse is just observational discourse in disguise has to be renounced.

This has an important consequence. If theoretical discourse is not completely reducible to observational discourse, then the meaning of theoretical discourse is not fully accounted for by the meaning of observational discourse. So at least part of the meaning of a theoretical term comes from a source other than experience. What is this source? A plausible possibility is that a term's "non experiential meaning" is provided by the theoretical context in which the term appears.[23] The question then is how this basic idea can be articulated. Hempel suggests that this is best done by appeal to *implicit definitions*: "the meanings of theoretical terms are determined in part by the postulates of the calculus, which serve as 'implicit definitions' for them; and in part by the correspondence rules, which provide them with empirical content" (1970, 149).[24] The idea of implicit definitions of terms has been introduced into logical empiricism through Schlick's (1925, 29–36), who attributes to Hilbert (in *Die Grundlagen der Geometrie*) the view that the axioms of geometry provide implicit definitions of the basic terms of geometry. Discussing the introduction of undefinable basic concepts, Schlick notes that "according to Hilbert [this problem] is solved by stipulating that basic concepts are *defined* by their satisfying the axioms" and he refers to this way of introducing terms as "definition by axioms, or definition by postulates, or implicit definition" (*ibid.*, 31; original emphasis; my translation). As Schlick points out, "the implicit definition has no connection to reality; it deliberately rejects such a connection; it operates in the realm of concepts" (*ibid.*, 35, my translation). On this view, basic geometrical notions like "point" and "straight line" are introduced by the axioms of geometry – statements like "for any two distinct points there is exactly one straight line that passes through both points" – and there is nothing more to being a point or a straight line than satisfying these axioms. Implicit definitions are important in the current context because they endow terms with meaning. If we ask what the term "point" means, an answer is given by appeal to the axioms: "point" means exactly what the axioms say that points are.

According to the Received View, scientific theories are axiomatised, and therefore theoretical terms in scientific theories can also be seen as introduced with implicit definitions. The axioms of a theory like classical mechanics establish systematic connections between the theory's theoretical terms like "mass" and "force" in much the same way in which the axioms of geometry establish connections between basic concepts of geometry like "point" and "line", and so one can see theoretical terms as implicitly defined by the laws of the theory in which they appear. In this way, implicit definitions can be used to provide the part of the meaning of theoretical terms that is not given through experience. That is the idea Hempel appeals to when, in the above quote, he says that the meaning of theoretical terms is determined in part by a theory's calculus and in part by the correspondence rules.

The view that the meaning of theoretical terms is pinned down jointly by reduction sentences and implicit definitions faces a number of challenges. Some of them have to do with the logical and semantic difficulties that attach to implicit definitions.[25] But by far the most significant problem is that it jars with scientific practice. As Hempel himself notes (1952, 32–33), an approach based on reduction sentences is committed to introducing theoretical terms one-by-one because each term gets its own reduction sentence (or sentences). But many theoretical terms cannot be introduced in such a piecemeal manner.[26] Theoretical terms like "mass" and "force" in classical mechanics, "absolute temperature" and "Carnot process" in thermodynamics, and "wave function" in quantum mechanics are not introduced by linking them *individually* to observational conditions. These terms form part of web of theoretical concepts, which cannot be dissociated from one another. They are part of a package that only functions as a whole, and empirical predictions are generated for the most part by the interplay between these concepts and the entire system in which they occur. Indeed, some concepts may not have direct empirical manifestations at all.

4.4 Hempel's Interpretative Systems

To avoid this problem with reduction sentences, Hempel introduced the notion of an *interpretative system*.[27] The leading idea is to drop two assumptions that have shaped previous accounts. The first assumption is that theoretical terms are connected to experience in a piecemeal manner by specifying empirical conditions individually for every theoretical term. Hempel argues that this out of sync with scientific practice, where theories face experience "wholesale". Rather than formulating sentences connecting individual terms to experiential conditions, we should formulate a set of sentences that connects the entire theory to experience. An empirical interpretation applies to a theoretical system as a whole. The second assumption is that correspondence rules must have a particular logical form (for instance, that they must be reduction sentences). Hempel explicitly rejects this view and submits that to interpret a theory one can employ "any sentences, of whatever logical form, which contain theoretical and observational terms" (1965, 208).

Let T be the theoretical postulates of the theory (Section 1.3). Hempel then offers the following definition of an interpretative system (1965, 130, 208): an interpretative system I is a finite set of sentences which (i) are not a truth of logic; (ii) are consistent with T; (iii) contain no extra-logical terms other than the theoretical terms of the theory along with its observation terms; and (iv) are such that every term of both the theoretical and the observation language appears *essentially*. The last clause says that I is not logically equivalent to a set of sentences in which some terms do not occur (this means that I contains no redundancies). I can contain definitions or reduction sentences, but it is not limited to sentences of that form. In this sense interpretative systems are a generalisation of previous approaches.

Like reduction sentences, interpretative systems offer only an implicit definition of theoretical terms. The account is also openly holistic in that the meaning of a theoretical term is seen as depending on the entire theoretical context in which it occurs. The interpretative system's main function is to licence the inference of observation sentences from the theory. T and I together imply observable propositions that T alone would not, and so I renders T testable by experience. But in contrast with reduction sentences, this testability need not be term-by-term. A testable sentence can be the consequence of the interplay of the entire theory, which makes it impossible to correlate the observation sentence with one particular theoretical term.

This approach improves on Carnap's reduction sentences in that it does not require a one-by-one specification of theoretical terms, but it still suffers from the semantic difficulties that pertain to implicit definitions.

4.5   Meaning From Models

The leading idea of all accounts discussed so far was to explicate the meaning of a theoretical term through its connection to observables, and, where this can be achieved only partially, through its place in the edifice of the theory. Schaffner argues that such accounts got started on the wrong foot altogether. He argues that theoretical terms are meaningful "prior to the establishment of correspondence rules" and that "the function of . . . correspondence rules is not to confer 'meaning' on 'meaningless' symbols by relating them to terms – usually 'observational' – which are antecedently understood" but rather to "allow an antecedently meaningful theory to provide an explanation . . . and to permit the further testing of this antecedently understood theory" (1969, 280). Theories are "meaningful *per se*" and are not at the mercy of correspondence rules to infuse them with content. Correspondence rules, rather than contributing to the meaning of the theory's terms, render the theory testable through "laboratory experience" (*ibid.*, 284).

If theoretical terms are not meaningless before they are embedded in a theoretical system with correspondence rules, where does their meaning come from? As we have seen in Section 2.3, a model is an alternative interpretation of a theory's formalism in terms of something familiar. If, for instance, we interpret the formalism of the kinetic theory of gases in terms of billiard balls and their motions, we present a model of the theory. Schaffner (1969, 282–284) submits that theoretical terms get their meaning from models. The term "electron", say, does not become meaningful because the formalism in which it occurs is endowed with correspondence rules. Rather, it is meaningful because there is model interpreting the term. Quoting from Lorentz's *The Theory of Electrons*, where electrons are paraphrased as "extremely small particles, charged with electricity", Schaffner submits that it is through this alternative interpretation of the calculus that theoretical terms acquire their "antecedent theoretical meaning" on which theories build.[28]

This view has pedigree. Hesse (1967, 357, 1969, 93) attributes to Campbell (1920) the view that the "semantics" of a theory is "given by the model", and that theoretical terms get their meaning from models rather than from their connection to observables. In the same vein, Hutten notes that "the model gives a possible interpretation to the symbols" of an equation, which "thereby acquire a meaning" (1956, 82).

This theory of meaning is not without merit. Theoretical terms like "molecule" and "electron" do seem to get at least part of their meaning from alternative interpretations, and theoretical terms like "superstring", "black hole", "tunnel effect", "space-time worm", "polymer chain", "energy level", and "potential barrier" seem to be consciously chosen so that they invoke alternative interpretations.[29] But taken as a full-fledged theory of meaning it seems implausible. The theoretical statement "an electron trapped between two potential barriers has a non-zero minimum energy" would then mean something like "a small particle charged with electricity that has been locked in between two fences does not lose all its vigour to move around". It is doubtful that this paraphrase really captures the meaning of the theoretical proposition (which can be found in any introduction to quantum mechanics). Nagel, after introducing the idea that theoretical terms are introduced with models, warns that "adventitious features of a model may mislead us concerning the actual content of the theory" because "a theory may receive alternative interpretations by way of different models" (1961, 96–97). Indeed, we have seen in Section 2.3 that the same formal sentence can have different interpretations, and hence different models, and if meaning is bestowed on a theory by models, each alternative model gives a different meaning to the theory. But what the terms of, say, quantum mechanics mean should not depend on, or change with, our choices of models.

4.6 Eliminativism

Eliminativism is the doctrine that theoretical terms should be eliminated from theories. This would make the problem of defining them (implicitly or explicitly) redundant: if there are no theoretical terms, there is no problem concerning their semantics. Two ways to eliminate theoretical terms have been discussed in the literature: Craig's theorem and the Ramsey sentence.

Let T be the theory's axiom system, C its correspondence rules, $\theta_1, ..., \theta_m$ its theoretical terms and $\omega_1, ..., \omega_n$ its observation terms. TC is the conjunction of T and C, and TC_O the set of all theorems of TC that contain only observational non-logical vocabulary. *Craig's theorem* establishes that there exists an axiomatised theory TC^* such that (a) $\omega_1, ..., \omega_n$ are the only non-logical terms of TC^* and (b) the theorems of TC^* are exactly the sentences in TC_O.[30] In other words, there is an axiomatised theory TC^* formulated solely in observation terms which has exactly the same observational consequences as the original interpreted theory TC.

This suggests an effective way of dissolving the problem of theoretical terms: replace TC by TC^* and thereby get rid of all theoretical terms without losing any of the theory's empirical consequences. Since the new theory has no theoretical terms anymore, there is no question about their meaning and reference. However, TC^* axiomatises the observational consequences of TC only in a twisted way, namely by effectively turning every observational consequence of TC into an axiom of TC^*. So TC^* is just a long list of all observable consequences of the original theory. This is not an insightful way of axiomatising a set of sentences. Axioms are supposed to present a theory in a condensed form, identifying central principles as axioms from which the other sentences of the theory follow. This is crucial to how we understand a theory; it matters to how we test, improve, and expand a theory; and it is vital to how we use a theory when generating explanations or designing experiments. All this is lost in a "Craig style" axiomatisation, which renders theoretical connections and systematic dependencies invisible. The price for the elimination of theoretical terms is that the theory is turned into an amorphous string of sentences without theoretic structure. This is too high a price to pay, which is why Field dismisses Craig style axiomatisations as "bizarre trickery" (1980, 8).

Another version of eliminativism employs the so-called *Ramsey Sentence* of a theory.[31] The idea behind the Ramsey Sentence is to eliminate the theoretical predicates by replacing them with existentially quantified variables. Let $TC(\theta_1, ..., \theta_m, \omega_1, ..., \omega_n)$ be the interpreted theory. The theory's *Ramsey Sentence* is $TC_R = \exists X_1, ..., \exists X_m TC(X_1, ..., X_m, \omega_1, ..., \omega_n)$, where $TC(X_1, ..., X_m, \omega_1, ..., \omega_n)$ is the theory's *realisation formula*. TC_R says that there exists a set of entities $e_1, ..., e_m$ such that the realisation formula is true if X_1 is interpreted as referring to e_1, and so on. We use the term "entity" in a broad sense so that it covers both individuals and properties. The entities $e_1, ..., e_m$ are then said to *realise* $TC(X_1, ..., X_m, \omega_1, ..., \omega_n)$. Since there are no theoretical terms in TC_R, replacing TC by TC_R amounts to eliminating the theory's theoretical terms. Where the full theory says things like "particles have mass, and mass times acceleration is equal to the force acting on the particle", the theory's Ramsey Sentence says "There are X_1 and X_2 such that particles have X_1, and X_1 times acceleration is equal to X_2 acting on the particle" (where we assumed that "mass" and "force" are theoretical terms).

An important property of the Ramsey Sentence is that it has the same observational consequences as T itself. That is, for any sentence p that contains solely observational vocabulary it is the case that: $TC \vdash p$ iff $TC_R \vdash p$. Hence, the theory's Ramsey Sentence has the full *observational content* of the theory itself, and therefore the same predictive power. At the same time the Ramsey Sentence contains no theoretical terms because they have been replaced by variables. But if there are no theoretical terms, there is no problem concerning the meaning of such terms. So it seems that replacing TC by TC_R makes problems associated with theoretical terms go away without impairing empirical discourse.

But "quantifying away" theoretical terms does not eliminate forces and electrons themselves, and the theory is still seen as referring to these entities. As Carnap notes, through its existential quantifiers, the Ramsey Sentence asserts the existence of something in the external world that has all the properties that physics ascribes to it (1966, 252). So the Ramsey Sentence does not question the existence of the theoretical entities; it merely talks about them without using theoretical terms.[32] For this reason, as Hempel observes, the Ramsey Sentence avoids commitment to theoretical entities "only in the letter" (1965, 216).

The Ramsey sentence would seem to offer a peculiar "resolution" of the problem of theoretical terms. Recall that these terms were regarded as problematic in the first place because of the verificationist maxim that we must be able to establish (or at least test) the truth of a synthetic sentence by appeal to experience. The Ramsey Sentence eliminates the terms at the cost of committing to the existence of exactly those entities that were seen as rendering the terms (purportedly) referring to them suspicious in the first place. This solution makes the problem worse rather than better. Claims about unobservables are unverifiable irrespective of whether they are formulated as unreconstructed theoretical claims ("the force changes the particle's state of motion") or as existential claims in a Ramsey Sentence ("there exists an X such that X changes the particle's state of motion"). In as far as one is concerned about theoretical terms because they (putatively) refer to objects and properties that are beyond the reach of experience, replacing the theory with its Ramsey Sentence offers no consolation.

Beyond the intrinsic difficulties of eliminativism, one might worry that eliminating theoretical concepts puts scientific practice in jeopardy. Scientists introduce these terms because they find them useful to systematise and develop a theory, to connect a theory to experiments, and for providing explanations. These abilities seem to get lost if theoretical terms are eliminated, which is why scientists do not formulate theories in an eliminativist way.[33] Indeed, eliminativism is a backward-looking programme that reformulates theories that have already been formulated, but that does not provide a positive heuristic to advance science.

4.7* The Carnap Sentence

Eliminativism is a dead end, and the problem of the semantics of theoretical terms is back on the table. In Section 4.2 we have seen that meaning and analyticity are closely connected in that sentences that are true solely due to the meaning of their constituent concepts are analytic and can be known *a priori*, while sentences that are synthetic need to be tested against experience and hence can be known only *a posteriori*. Hence, to test a theory, we have to know which part of a theory is analytic and which is synthetic. Where and how should this line be drawn? We now discuss Carnap's solution to this problem.[34]

In preparation of a discussion of Carnap's approach, it is important to note that analyticity is preserved under logical consequence: if a sentence follows logically from an analytical truth, then that sentence is itself analytical. "bachelors are unmarried men" and "unmarried men have no wives" are both analytically true. It follows that "bachelors have no wives" is analytically true too because it is a logical consequence of the previous two sentences.

Carnap offers different articulations of analyticity for observation languages and for theoretical languages. Analyticity in an observation language is given by the language's *meaning postulates, analyticity postulates*, or *A-postulates* (Carnap 1966, 261–264). Some A-postulates are specifications like "the term 'animal' designates the conjunction of the following properties : . . .", where the ellipsis would contain a full list of all definitory properties of animals. But not all A-rules have to be full definitions. Some can also specify meaning relations between terms without defining them. "All birds are animals" is a rule of this kind. It defines neither "bird" nor "animal" but specifies a relation between the extensions of both terms. Carnap notes that a complete system of A-rules may not be forthcoming for ordinary languages because there may be too many rules to state and terms may be ambiguous in various ways. But he thinks that the method works for artificial observation languages where the A-postulates settle meaning relations "by fiat" (*ibid*, 262). A complete system of A-postulates pins down all conceptual connections between the descriptive terms of a theory. Since analyticity is preserved under logical consequence, one can then say that a sentence (in the observation language) is analytic exactly if it follows logically from the A-postulates.

Analyticity in a theoretical language is more difficult to define. The first approach Carnap considers is that analyticity in such a theoretical language can be defined in the same way as in an observation language when the theory's axiom system T is taken to play the role of the theory's A-postulate. He immediately dismisses this as too weak because T is only an "uninterpreted structure of pure mathematics", and "[u]ntil the abstract mathematical structure has been in interpreted . . . the semantic problem of distinguishing analytic from synthetic sentences does not even arise" (1966, 267). A partial interpretation of T is provided by C (the set of correspondence rules) and so one might ask whether the interpreted theory TC would be able play the role of the theory's A-postulate. It does not. TC contains too much information to serve as an A-postulate. In fact, TC is the entire theory and taking the entire theory as an A-postulate amounts to saying that the *entire* theory is analytic. This has the consequence that a theory has no factual content and all its theorems are true due the meaning of its terms (*ibid.*, 268). This is absurd. A scientific theory must make claims whose truth depends on how the world is. That planets revolve around the sun in elliptical orbits is a claim that is true or false in virtue of how actual planets behave and not in virtue of the meanings of the terms "sun", "planet", "orbit", and "elliptical".

So a theory's A-postulate must contain "more" than just T and "less" than TC. The problem then is how to "split" TC into a factual part and an analytical part so that the analytical part only contains sentences that are true in virtue of the terms' meanings and the factual part only contains sentences that are true in virtue of matters of fact? Carnap's solution to this quandary builds on the Ramsey Sentence. As we have seen in the previous section, the Ramsey Sentence has the same observational consequences as the full theory. Furthermore, one can prove that the full theory implies its Ramsey Sentence ($TC \vdash TC_R$) but not vice versa. These two observations provide the crucial clues. Since TC_R has the same observational consequences as TC, it holds the entire observational content of the theory; and since $TC \vdash TC_R$ but not $TC_R \vdash TC$ it follows that TC_R is a proper part of TC. This justifies identifying the factual part of the theory with TC_R. That is, TC_R is the synthetic part of the theory! Since the synthetic and the analytic part together have to make up the entire theory, the analytic part is now TC "minus" TC_R: the analytic part of the theory is the "smallest bit" that one has to add to TC_R in order to obtain TC. This "smallest bit" is the conditional $TC_R \to TC$ because $TC_R \ \& \ (TC_R \to TC)$ is the smallest conjunct that implies TC. Hence the analytic part of the theory is the conditional $TC_R \to TC$ (*ibid.*, 270–272). This conditional is now known as the *Carnap Sentence*.[35] The Carnap sentence gives meaning to the theoretical terms of the theory. It in effect says that if are there such and such entities in the world, we now label them with the theoretical terms of the theory.

The Carnap Sentence is not a truth of logic, but it is factually empty because it has no observable consequences. As noted, the sentence says that *if* there is a class of entities that make TC_R true, *then* the theoretical terms of the theory refer to the entities in this class. It does not tell us whether TC_R is true; it assigns terms their referents under the assumption that the referents exist. A sentence is then analytical exactly if it is a logical consequence of the Carnap sentence.[36]

Díez (2005, 81) casts doubt on Carnap's assumption that the entire synthetic content of the theory is contained in TC_R. The problem arises with mixed sentences, i.e. sentences that contain both observation and theoretical terms. Some of these sentences are neither a consequence of the Carnap Sentence nor of the Ramsey Sentence and so they would qualify neither as analytic nor as synthetic. An example is TC itself, which cannot be derived either from $TC_R \to TC$ or of TC_R. However, we have already ruled out that TC can be analytic; and since a sentence must be either analytic or synthetic, it must be synthetic. If so, TC_R does not contain the entire synthetic content of the theory. It is an open question how Carnap's account can deal with such cases.

The most serious challenge comes from the *multiple realisability* of the realisation formula. The Ramsey Sentence says that there are entities $e_1, ..., e_m$ such that $TC(X_1, ..., X_m, \omega_1, ..., \omega_n)$ comes out true if the variables are interpreted as referring to the entities. However, the Ramsey sentence only requires that there are such entities. It does not require that that these entities are unique, and there is the possibility that there are different sets of entities that all make the realisation formula true. As an example, consider the simple theory "an atom has discrete energy levels" (and for sake of the example assume that "discrete energy levels" is an observation term). The realisation formula of this theory is "X_1 has discrete energy levels". There are atoms and so the Ramsey sentence (which says that there is an X_1 such that X_1 has discrete energy levels) is true. But quantum harmonic oscillators and quantum particles trapped in boxes also have discrete energy levels. So the realisation formula can also be made true by harmonic oscillators and particles in boxes, and hence the theoretical term in the theory that was intended to be a theory about atoms can end up referring to harmonic oscillators and particles in boxes. This is odd because the theory we started with was a theory about atoms and not about other things.

Is the simplicity of our little theory to blame for its multiple realisability, and would the problem go away if more details were added to it? It is certainly true that one can easily amend our little theory so that harmonic oscillators and particles in boxes would no longer make the realisation formula true (for instance, by adding something like "and atoms contain of nucleons"). Unfortunately, the success of this move is undercut by what is now known as "Newman's Theorem". Newman, in a review of Russell's *The Analysis of Matter*, proved a theorem to the effect that that "[a]ny collection of things can be organised so as to have structure W, provided there are the right number of them" (1928, 144).[37] The proof of the theorem is fairly trivial. In Section 2.6 we have seen that properties and relations in structures are defined purely extensionally, and hence the objects of a structure can always be arranged into sets that define certain relations, as long as there are enough objects. This has the consequence that the Ramsey Sentence is always true as long as the theory is empirically adequate and the theory has a model that has the same cardinality as the theory's target domain. This is an extremely weak requirement because theories are designed to be empirically adequate and cardinality constraints are easily met. The Carnap Sentence postulates that the theory's theoretical terms refer to the entities that make the Ramsey Sentence true, and if these entities can be completely artificial set-theoretical constructs, then the theory's theoretical terms can end up referring to these. To undercut this conclusion, one has to start restricting the allowable relations in the domain, for instance by only allowing relations that are natural kinds. Ainsworth (2009) provides a discussion of the many suggestions of this sort that have been made. But even a cursory look at the array of options reveals a problem: each involves substantive assumptions about the domain of unobservables, and hence requires exactly what the original empiricism wanted to avoid: commitment to objects and relations beyond experience.

4.8* Explicit Definitions After All?

The approaches discussed in Sections 4.3 to 4.7 all attempted to avoid explicit definitions, and they have all run up against difficulties. Motivated at least in part by these problems, Carnap himself, and later Lewis, returned to the idea of explicit definitions and endeavoured to articulate a new account of explicit definitions for theoretical terms, albeit one that is very different from the approach we discussed in Section 4.2.

An explicit definition of a term states the conditions that something has to meet for the term to apply. The explicit definitions we encountered in Section 4.2 defined one predicate through a set of other predicates, for instance by stipulating that an object has temperature θ iff a mercury thermometer shows θ when brought in contact with the object. As Hempel noted (Section 4.4), this piecemeal introduction of theoretical terms is at odds with scientific practice and it is more realistic to see a term as defined through the entire theory in which it occurs. Carnap's innovation was to formalise this idea in a way that results in an explicit definition. As above, the theory is given by the sentence $TC(\theta_1,...,\theta_m,\omega_1,....,\omega_n)$. The term for which we seek an explicit definition is θ_1. To construct such a definition we first turn the theory into a predicate by replacing the term to be defined by a blank, yielding $TC(\_\_,...,\theta_m,\omega_1,....,\omega_n)$.[38] We then define the term by saying that something is a θ_1 iff $TC(\_\_,...,\theta_m,\omega_1,....,\omega_n)$ applies to it. Consider again our little theory about atoms from the previous section. The predicate corresponding to this theory is "__ has discrete energy levels". With this predicate we can state an explicit definition of "atom": something is an atom iff "__ has discrete energy levels" applies to it.

This idea can be restated with the realisation formula of the theory's Ramsey Sentence. To say that we apply the predicate $TC(\_\_,...,\theta_m,\omega_1,....,\omega_n)$ to something is tantamount to saying that $TC(X_1,...,X_m,\omega_1,....,\omega_n)$ is true if we interpret the variable X_1 as referring to that something. As we have seen previously, the problem is that the realisation formula may be multiply realisable. Carnap understood that multiple realisability was an obstacle for explicit definitions and suggested dealing with the problem using a logical technique called the *Hilbert ε-operator*.[39] The operator is an *indefinite description* operator. Assume that there is a class of things that have property P. The operator picks an arbitrary member of that class and the sentence "$\varepsilon x Px$" refers to that arbitrarily chosen member, which we call the class' representative (Carnap in Psillos 2000b, 169). For this reason, Hilbert also called εx the *selection operator*. If, for instance, P is "__ is a member of the London Symphony Orchestra", then $\varepsilon x Px$ refers to an arbitrarily selected member of the orchestra. In cases where P is not a monadic property but an n-ary relation symbol the operator chooses an arbitrary sequence of objects $e_1,...,e_n$ that satisfy the relation.

The formula $\theta_1 := \varepsilon_{X_1} \exists X_2...\exists X_m T(X_1,...,X_m,\omega_1,...,\omega_n)$ then provides an explicit definition of the term θ_1, and *mutatis mutandis* for all other theoretical terms. In effect this definition says that θ_1 refers to the first element of an arbitrarily chosen representative of the class of sequences of entities that satisfy the theory's realisation formula. This now provides the analytic part of the theory, and one can prove that this new meaning postulate implies the Carnap sentence (Carnap in Psillos 2000b, 170). The synthetic part is still given by the Ramsey sentence.

The use of the ε-operator does not solve the problem of multiple realisability we encountered in the previous section. Rather, it aims to render the problem benign by embedding it in a logical framework. The term "atom" is defined as ε_{X_1} (X_1 has discrete energy levels), where ε_{X_1} simply picks an arbitrary entity to which "__ has discrete energy levels" applies as the term's referent. As we have seen in the previous section, the predicate ends up applying not only to harmonic oscillators and particles in boxes (something that one might avoid by extending the theory), but, via Newman's Theorem, also to all kinds of set theoretical constructs, and any of these can now be the referent of "atom".

Lewis criticised this indeterminacy in Carnap's approach as unsatisfactory and urged that "[w]e should insist on unique realisation as a standard of correctness" (1970, 433). If the theory has a unique realisation, then its theoretical terms name the components of that realisation; if there is no unique realisation, then the terms have no denotation at all.[40] So if a theory is not uniquely realised, then its terms are undefined. The term "atom" in our little theory refers to nothing. If a theory is multiply realised, the theory itself is therefore false. Yet, the theory's Ramsey Sentence is still true, and so the theory's Carnap Sentence is false too (because the conditional has a true antecedent and a false consequent). But a meaning postulate cannot be false, and so under Lewis's interpretation the Carnap Sentence cannot be the correct meaning postulate. For this reason, Lewis replaces the Carnap Sentence with three new postulates which, taken together, form the meaning postulates of the theory (*ibid.*, 434–435). The first postulate says that if the theory is uniquely realised, the realisers of the theory are the entities named by the theory. The second postulate says that if the theory is not realised at all, then its terms do not name anything. The third postulate says that if the theory is multiply realised, then the terms do not name anything either.

The quantifier $\exists!$ signifies unique existence: "$\exists!x(Px)$" says that there is exactly one object which has property P. One can then define $TC_{RU} = \exists!X_1,...,\exists!X_m TC(X_1,...,X_m,\omega_1,....,\omega_n)$, which is the unique realisation version of the Ramsey sentence (and the letter "U" has been added to the subscript to indicate that unique realisation is required). Percival (2000, 503) points out that Lewis' meaning postulates can then be condensed into the formula $TC_{RU} \leftrightarrow TC$, which he calls the *Lewis Sentence*. The operator ι is the definite description operator: "$\iota x(Px)$" refers to the object that has property P. If P is "being the author of the Critique of Pure Reason", then $\iota x(Px)$ refers to Immanuel Kant. If we replace $\exists$ in Carnap's explicit definition by $\exists!$ and the ε-*operator* by the definite description operator, we get a new explicit definition (1970, 438): $\theta_1 := \iota X_1 \exists!X_2...\exists!X_m TC(X_1,...,X_m,\omega_1,...,\omega_n)$. The definition says that θ_1 is the first element of the sequence of entities that uniquely realise the theory's realisation formula. All other theoretical terms are defined *mutatis mutandis*.

The main challenge for this view comes once again from Newman's theorem. Even if there is only one "intended" or "natural" realisation, there are likely to be many others that can be constructed "Newman style". This upsets the uniqueness requirement and Lewis then has to conclude that the terms do not refer. As we have seen at the end of the previous section, to block Newmanian multiple realisation, one has to restrict allowable realisers, for instance by introducing natural kinds. Lewis himself may have been content with this. In his discussion of materialism, he assumes that there are "natural properties" and that "[t]he world is as physics says it is", where "physics" is "something not too different from present-day physics, though presumably somewhat improved", and such a physics would be "a comprehensive theory of the world, complete as well as correct" (Lewis 1999, 33–34). If a somewhat improved version of present-day physics correctly identifies the true fundamental properties of the world, then Newmanian multiple realisability is blocked. It pays noting, however, that this position implies a thoroughgoing realism, and as such it is a far cry from the empiricism that motivated Carnap and Hempel to define theoretical terms through observation terms.

Bedard (1993, 502) and Díez (2005, 83) hint at another, less committal, escape route. As we have seen in the introductory example with planet Venus, terms can be seen as having both meaning and reference. This opens the possibility to saying that when a theory is not uniquely realised and reference fails, its terms can still have meaning. As Díez puts it, "even if the description is denotationless as a consequence of multiple realizability, its sense/meaning is perfectly determined" (*ibid.*). By way of illustration, let us extend Frege's example and consider "Vulcan". Vulcan was hypothesised to be a planet in an orbit between Mercury and the Sun. However, it turned out that Vulcan does not exist. So the term "Vulcan" has no denotation. Yet it still has a meaning, which is something like "a planet moving in an orbit between Mercury and the Sun". The proposal then is that terms in theories that are either multiply realised or not realised at all, can still have meaning in something like the way in which "Vulcan" has meaning. This, however, would require a theory of meaning that is independent from a theory of reference, and nothing of this kind has been provided so far.

Bedard (*ibid.*) mentions that Lewis endorsed a theory of meaning that explicates meaning in terms of reference in possible worlds. This, however, would have to be articulated in more detail to put the above worries about the consequences of multiple realisation to rest.

4.9 Renouncing Analyticity?

In Section 4.2 we have seen that CCS, which is the driving force behind most accounts of theoretical terms that we have discussed so far, relies on separating statements into analytic and synthetic statements. Quine (1951) argued that there is no such separation and any attempt to articulate a distinction between analytic and synthetic statements is in vein. This, if true, pulls the rug from underneath

CCS. Knowledge, says Quine, forms a "web of belief" in which all propositions are connected and no proposition can be isolated from the rest. The web contains everything from simple observation statements, to theoretical principles, to truths of logic. Statements in science are revisable in the light of new evidence. Normally such revisions are made in the empirical part of a theory. But, as Quine puts it, "our statements about the external world face the tribunal of sense experience not individually but only as a corporate body (*ibid.*, 41).[41] Therefore, *any* statement can be revised to restore consistency between theory and evidence, if necessary even principles at the core of the web such as the principles of logic and mathematics. One could, for instance, revise logic in the light of quantum mechanics.[42] The difference between analytic and synthetic statements is not rooted in the meanings of terms; rather, it is a function of a statement's location in the web of belief. Propositions commonly regarded as analytical are at the centre or the web of belief while observation statements lie at the periphery. Sentences at the core of the web are less easily revisable than ones at the periphery, which explains why analytic statements appear to be unassailable. The distinction, however, is gradual, and there is no non-arbitrary way to draw a line between analytic and synthetic statements. This renders the analytic/synthetic distinctions otiose.

Quine's argument has been extremely influential, and it sparked a number of interesting reactions. It is impossible to review the different positions in this debate here, but (unsurprisingly) no consensus has been reached.[43] Those who followed Quine embarked on projects rethinking the notions of meaning, intension, synonymity, necessity, and *a priori* knowledge, while those who remained unconvinced by Quine's arguments kept pursuing a sound articulation of the analytic/synthetic distinction. Carnap was among those who remained unconvinced. A decade and half after Quine's dismissal, Carnap reasserts that, in his view, "a sharp analytic-synthetic distinction is of supreme importance for the philosophy of science" (1966, 257).[44] Carnap had good reasons to resist Quine. In fact, as Psillos (2000b, 154–157) points out, Quine's argument begs the question against Carnap. At the beginning of Quine's argument lies a subtle shift in the definition of analyticity. Traditionally, analyticity is defined as truth in virtue of meaning. Quine recasts this definition as justifiability independently of experience, and uses unrevisability in the light of experience as the litmus test for analyticity. Analytical statements are then seen as absolute and unrevisable truths. But Carnap never thought of analyticity as unrevisability. On the contrary, it is part and parcel of Carnap's empiricism that any statement can be abandoned in the interest of resolving conflict with experience. As early as 1937, Carnap noted that "no rule of physical language is definite" and that "all rules are laid down with the reservation that they may be altered as soon as it seems expedient to do so", and he is explicit that this includes the rules of logic and mathematics (1937/2000, 318).[45] There are no sacrosanct rules; it is just that "certain rules are more difficult to renounce than others" (*ibid.*). In effect Carnap anticipated Quine's argument, but he drew the exact opposite conclusion: rather than renouncing analyticity, he thought that analyticity was always defined relative to a certain theory and a certain logical system, and as such it was open to revisions. Psillos therefore expresses bewilderment that Quine simply ignored Carnap's theory of analyticity and went on in later writings to assert that there was no clear distinction to be drawn (*ibid.*, 155).

What are the implications of this for the Received View, and a linguistic understanding of theories more generally? Suppe (1977, 67–80) submits that the Received View is untenable because it incorporates the analytic-synthetic distinction. This is too quick in two ways. First, as we have just seen, views on whether the analytic-synthetic distinction is untenable diverge, and there is no consensus that the distinction has been shown to be untenable. So the Received View cannot be brushed aside with argument that it relies on the distinction. Second, not all versions of the linguistic view presuppose the analytic-synthetic distinction; there are ways to articulate a linguistic analysis of theories that are based on an understanding of language that does not require the analytic-synthetic distinction. Indeed, Quine himself took theories to be linguistic objects (see, for instance, his 1975).

4.10 Semantic Realism

Even if one sees no need to give up the analytic/synthetic distinction, the views we have discussed so far all face serious issues, and these issues are all rooted in the empiricist doctrine that theoretical discourse is somehow suspect and that theoretical terms, in one way or another, have to be reduced to observation terms. Given all the problems that this raises, some have seen a case for revising this basic assumption. Feigl proposed turning the tables on the semantics of theoretical terms and set out to "make realism a little more tempting and palatable than it has hitherto been" (1950, 38). His reasons were the weight of the internal difficulties of attempts to explicate theoretical discourse in terms of observable discourse, as well as the intrinsic advantages of a realist position, which he sees in realism's contribution to the economy of thought and the heuristic power of theories. *Semantic realism* regards theoretical discourse as *sui generis* and rejects attempts to explicate the semantics of theoretical terms by means of observation terms as unfounded. Theoretical discourse is like observational discourse in that it aims to talk about objects in the world and describe their properties and relations. Both kinds of discourse have the same purpose, and they function in the same way. Feigl characterises semantic realism as the position that theoretical terms have "factual reference" (*ibid.*, 48, 50), which he also equates with the "surplus meaning" of theoretical terms (the meaning that terms have over and above what is empirically given). A physicist uses the term "electron" to refer to particles (invisible to the human eye) and describes their properties in the same manner in which an engineer uses the term "bridge" to refer to a certain construction and to talk about its features. Semantic realism submits that we have to take theoretical statements at face-value and regard them as literal descriptions of the target domain which can be true or false.

Semantic realism is part and parcel of *scientific realism*. Psillos (1999, xvii) defines scientific realism as the conjunction of the following three theses. First, the metaphysical thesis that the world has a mind-independent natural-kind structure. Second, the semantic thesis that theories provide a literal and truth-conducive description of their subject matter. Third, the epistemic thesis that mature and predictively successful theories give us an approximately true picture of their target domain. The second of Psillos' theses is of course just semantic realism, which shows that semantic realism is an integral component of scientific realism. But the idea that scientific theories provide literal descriptions of real unobservable structures was unpalatable to Feigl's contemporaries, who remained committed to the idea that the unobservable somehow had to be accounted for in terms of the observable.[46] However, Feigl thought that sematic realists were not forced to be scientific realists, arguing that semantic realism was independent both of metaphysical and epistemic claims. He emphasised the difference between "the semantical relation of *designation* (i.e. reference)" and "epistemic reduction (i.e. the evidential basis)" (*ibid.*, 48), thereby driving a wedge between semantic realism and Psillos' third thesis. The connection between semantic realism and Psillos' metaphysical thesis is severed by Feigl's insistence that semantic realism does not lead us back into the "perplexities of traditional transcendent realism and metaphysics" and that "[t]he semantic conception of reference does not justify (demonstrate) realism" (*ibid.*, 50).

Thirty years later, the separation of semantics from epistemic and metaphysical issues became a cornerstone of van Fraassen's *constructive empiricism*. Van Fraassen insists on a "literal construal of the language of science", rejects any attempt to translate scientific claims into an observation language, and avers that "[i]f the theory's statements include 'There are electrons', then the theory says that there are electrons". At the same time he urges that "[n]ot every philosophical position concerning science which insists on a literal construal of the language of science is a realist position" (1980, 11).[47] Van Fraassen's empiricism manifests itself not in the demand to paraphrase away theoretical language, but in the imperative to adopt a certain epistemic attitude toward theoretical claims. He calls this position *constructive empiricism*.[48] According to constructive empiricism, we have to interpret theories literally. But we do not have to believe all claims of a theory. In fact, the right attitude toward a theory is not belief in its truth, but only belief in its empirical adequacy: we should *believe* what a theory says about observables while we should merely *accept* (and not believe) what it says about unobservables. So the right epistemic attitude to a theory as a whole is agnosticism rather than belief (*ibid.*, 11–12). This identifies van Fraassen's position as an anti-realist position, but one of a very different kind than the empiricism of Carnap and Hempel.[49]

Semantic realism as formulated so far, irrespective of whether it is put into the service of realism or antirealism, remains a largely programmatic position. It indicates the broad outlines of a position, but it leaves crucial questions open. How is reference to unobservable entities established? What is the meaning of theoretical terms? And is meaning really, as Feigl thought, to be equated with reference? A recent attempt to address these questions appeals to the so-called causal-historical theory. We now discuss this approach.

4.11   The Causal-Historical Theory

Accounts of reference that have emerged in the literature on the philosophy of language can be divided into two main families: descriptivist accounts and direct reference accounts. Descriptivist accounts originate in Frege's (1892).[50] According to these accounts, terms, both singular and general, are associated with a description. In our introductory example, "Venus" is associated with the description "the second planet from the Sun in our solar system". The content of the description associated with a term is the term's meaning. An important aspect of descriptivism is that meaning is seen as determining reference: the meaning of a term (together with the context of utterance) will determinate what it refers to (on that occasion). Any two terms with the same meaning will therefore have the same reference. The meaning of a term accounts for its cognitive import: it is how the user of a term thinks of the term's referent. This accounts for the difference between terms with the same referents but different meaning, and it makes identity statements non-tautological. As we have seen in the introduction, "morning start" and "evening star" have different meanings and yet they refer to the same object, namely planet Venus. The sentence "the morning star is the evening star" expresses this fact without being tautological (as the sentence "the morning star is the morning star" would be) because the different meanings of the two terms lead to different ways of conceiving of Venus.

The accounts we have discussed so far are descriptivist accounts.[51] This is obvious with explicit definitions (Section 4.2). Explicit definitions associate with each theoretical term an observation term and thereby give the term descriptive content. The posit that "for all x, x has temperature $\theta \leftrightarrow$ a mercury thermometer shows θ when brought in contact with x" endows the term θ with meaning in much the same way in which "Venus is the second planet from the Sun in our solar system" endows "Venus" with meaning. The descriptions associated with terms become more complex in later accounts, and in Lewis' approach (Section 4.8*) the relevant description is provided by the entire theory. Significant differences in the details notwithstanding, the leading idea throughout Sections 4.2–4.3 and 4.7*-4.8* was that the meaning of theoretical terms is specified by the descriptive content of the theory and that their meaning fixes their reference: the referents of the terms are whatever makes the descriptive content of the terms true.[52] The posit that, say, "electron" refers to whatever makes a theory of electrons true is like saying that "Venus" refers to whatever makes the description "the second planet from the Sun in our solar system" true.

This account of the semantics of terms not only faces the problems that we have discussed in previous sections; it also faces a number of in-principle objections. This is not the place to review these objections,[53] but one issue deserves mention. The more advanced approaches we have discussed in Sections 4.4, 4.7* and 4.8* are not only descriptivist; they are also holistic in the sense that terms get their meaning not in isolation but through their place in an *entire* theoretical system. The immediate consequence of this is that a term's meaning changes every time the theory changes. This is a problem when theories evolve historically because it would imply that Bohr and Schrödinger meant different things when they used the word "atom", and since meaning determines reference, there would be no guarantee that terms even refer to the same thing. Some philosophers – most notably Feyerabend (1965), Hanson (1958), and Kuhn (1970) – welcomed the conclusion that theoretical change is inseparable from meaning change and embraced the relativistic consequences of this view. However, many remained unconvinced and tried to salvage constancy of reference and meaning, and with it objectivity, through theory change.

An important move in this realist quest was a shift from a descriptivist account of the semantics of terms to a so-called direct reference theory. The direct reference theory goes back to Mill's (1843/1974), who submitted that proper names work like *tags* on objects: they refer to their bearers *directly* and without the mediation of an associated description. The contemporary version of this view, due to Barcan Marcus' (1961), Kripke's (1980), and Putnam's (1973), is known as the *causal-historical theory*. According to this approach, a theory of reference consists of two parts. The first part, reference-fixing, explains how the reference of a term is fixed when the term is introduced. The second part, reference-transmission, explains how reference is propagated throughout a group of language users. On this account, at some point an astronomer introduced the term "Venus", for instance by pointing to the planet when looking through the telescope and saying "this is Venus"; and other astronomers uttering "Venus" used the term referentially because they could borrow the reference that has been established by the first astronomer. The core idea of the second part, therefore, is that transmission happens through a causal-historical process (which gives the account its name): after a person has bestowed reference on the term, this reference is passed on to other users who effectively "borrow" the reference that the initial user has fixed. This process is historical in so far as the term gets its reference from an initial act of reference fixing and subsequent referential uses of the term utilise the reference fixed in that initial act; it is causal in so far as a speaker's referential use of the term depends on there being a nexus between their use and the original introduction, presumably through passing on the term form user to user. Much can be said about this process, but there is no categorical difference between the transmission of ordinary language terms and of scientific terms, and so a theory of the reference of scientific terms can build on whatever account of transmission seems the most palatable option.

Things are more involved in the first part, which is concerned with reference-fixing. The paradigmatic case of reference fixing is an act consisting of ostension plus dubbing: we point toward an object, or exhibit the object, and then say "this is called τ", where τ is the term we wish to introduce. Babies get their names when, at some point, their parents point to them and say something like "let's call him Martin". The baby gets his name in this initial act of baptism. Procedures like these work for many terms referring to objects from buildings to countries, and even for term referring to natural kinds. Thus introduced, names refer to their objects without the mediation of a description, and the problems that attach to the use of descriptions are avoided. In a recent paper Hoefer and Martí (2020) argue that the causal-historical theory is the correct theory of reference for theoretical terms and they see the account's ability to avoid the relativism that is associated with meaning change (when meaning is associated with descriptions that are based on theories) as one of the main selling points of the account.

The problem is that many entities that appear in scientific theories are not ostensible in the way in which babies are, and when introducing terms that are supposed to refer to unobservables we cannot simply point to the objects in question and say "these are called Boson" and "these are called genes". Kripke recognises this difficulty and submits that reference-fixing can also be done by dint of descriptions. His example is "Neptune", which was introduced by Le Verrier *before* Neptune was observed as "the planet which caused such and such discrepancies in the orbits of certain other planets" (1980, 79). This prescription readily generalises to other terms referring to unobservables, which can also be introduced through identifying descriptions. "Electron", for instance, could be introduced as "the particle that produces a spiral path when shot into a bubble chamber in a magnetic field". In general, then, reference-fixing in the case of unobservable entities is done through a description rather than through ostension, while reference-transmission works through the same *causal-historical* chains as in observable cases.

At this point one wonders, though: have we not come full circle? We left descriptions behind to avoid to the problems of descriptivism, but we now reintroduce descriptions as tools for reference-fixing. The answer is "yes and no". "No" insofar as a description is used only for the *initial* act of reference fixing. If we introduce "Neptune" through Le Verrier's description, then "Neptune" refers to whatever object that description picks out. Our views, theories, and beliefs about Neptune may change, and the current theory of Neptune may have little in common with Le Verrier's; yet the term keeps referring to the same thing that Le Verrier identified with his description. This avoids the relativist conclusions because this view is not committed to saying that a term refers to whatever it is that makes the current version of a theory true. Hoefer and Martí appeal to this stability when they note that

> once a term is introduced . . . the capacity to refer is passed on, and maintained through the subsequent chain of users of the term, so that even if theories later change (as happened in the case of electrons), it is easy to maintain that users of the term are still talking about the same things.
>
> *(2020, 13)*[54]

The answer to our question is "yes" insofar as it has to be the case that the initial description successfully identifies a referent, and that this referent is the correct referent. As we have seen above, this is not trivial. If the description is multiply realisable and therefore applies to things other than the intended objects, then it can happen that terms refer to the wrong things (as we have seen, "atom" can end up referring to harmonic oscillators). While one may try to rectify this problem by enriching descriptions, it remains a question what such an enrichment would look like and how successful such a move would be.

Setting the problem of multiple realisability aside, there is a worry that reference is too easy to come by on this account. As Papineau notes, "the causal theory threatens to ascribe referents to a number of intuitively non-referring terms, such as 'phlogiston' and 'spirit possession', whereas in reality these terms lack reference" (1996, 4). The history of science is usually read as saying that Priestly's theory was wrong and that phlogiston does not exist. But, if we introduce, as Priestly could have, the term "phlogiston" through the description "the chemical substance that is responsible for combustion", then "phlogiston" has reference: it refers to oxygen. Examples of this kind suggest that more substantive descriptions are needed to introduce terms. But what does "more substantive" mean? This question has given rise to a number of proposals, and the issue is the subject matter of ongoing debates. A number of proposals focus on the causal connection between the unobservables that the theoretical terms are supposed to refer to and the phenomena that they produce, while others focus on the epistemic access scientists have to objects.[55] This is a fruitful area for future research.

4.12   Conclusion

We have discussed different ways to analyse the semantics of theoretical terms. We have distinguished between descriptivist approaches and direct reference views, and we have seen that most accounts that have been proposed are descriptivist. The direct reference view, in the concrete form of the causal-historical approach, promises to avoid the pitfalls of descriptivism, but, as we just have seen, it cannot do away with descriptions entirely and so the question arises about what characteristics a description must have to refer successfully to the intended target. This is still an active field of research.

Notes

1   Throughout the chapter, I focus on the Received View's distinction between observation terms and theoretical terms. *Mutatis mutandis*, the discussion equally covers the Linguistic View's distinction between terms that are understood before the theory is formulated and terms that originate in the theory itself (Section 1.3) and Hempel's distinction between antecedently understood terms and new terms (Section 3.5).

2 I here follow Frege's use of "reference". Russell (1905) denied that definite descriptions like "the morning star" refer. For an introductory discussion of this issue, see Michaelson and Reimer's (2019, Sec. 4).

3 Although one might argue that the mythical origins of "Venus" are not part of the meaning of the term and merely belong to the term's connotation. For what follows, nothing hangs on how this is resolved.

4 Contemporary introductions to the problems of meaning and reference can be found in Horwich's (2006) and Lycan's (2008); Devitt and Hanley's (2006) offers a collection of survey papers.

5 VTM has a complex history. It is usually attributed to Schlick (see, for instance, Miller 2007, 95), and Schlick indeed advocated VTM (see, for instance, his 1936, 341). An early version was mentioned in Carnap's (1928/2003, 289), and VTM occupied centre stage in Carnap's "The Elimination of Metaphysics Through Logical Analysis of Language" (1931/1996). Waismann reports that VTM was enunciated by Wittgenstein in personal conversations in 1929 and 1930 (McGuinness 1979, 79). Ayer (1936/1946, Ch. 1) and Lycan (2008, Ch. 8) provide accessible discussions. For extended discussions of VTM and its roots, see Miller's (2007, Ch. 3), Scheffler's (1957a, 1957b), Skorupski's (1997), and Uebel's (2019).

6 Language jars at this point. To "verify" a sentence literally means to establish its truth. But VTM does not say that a sentence is meaningful only if its truth can be established, as this would have the absurd consequence that false sentences are meaningless. In the current context, being able to verify a sentence means that we are able to establish that it is either true or false.

7 It is now common in the philosophy of language to distinguish between terms and concepts. Concepts are the basic building blocks of thought, while terms are linguistic objects. Accordingly, concepts are said to have content and terms to have meaning. However, many of the historical actors that I quote in this chapter did not follow this (modern) distinction, and neither do many contemporary philosophers of science. I follow this slightly looser convention and use "concept" and "term" interchangeably.

8 For a discussion of this point, see Fetzer's (2021, Sec. 2).

9 See, for instance, Hempel's (1951, 61). Hempel also refers to the criterion as the "empiricist criterion of cognitive meaning" (1950, 41), and he says that if a sentence can be tested it has "empirical meaning or significance" (1951, 61), supporting the view that "meaning" and "significance" are used interchangeably. CPP had a chequered history and underwent numerous reformulations. See Justus' (2006) for an account of its history. It is part of the received wisdom of analytical philosophy that the criterion was proven to be untenable. Justus (2014) pushes back against this and argues that the standard criticisms have no force against Carnap's later, more sophisticated, formulation of the criterion. VTM and CCS are often either run together, or not distinguished at all. As presented here, VTM is the fundamental principle, and CCS follows from VTM together with empiricist principle that there is no *a priori* synthetic knowledge. CCS can be seen as an operational procedure to decide whether a given sentence has meaning. I am grateful to Thomas Uebel for helpful discussions on this issue.

10 Many of the most serious difficulties of CPP arise when it is applied to non-elementary sentences. In particular, as Carnap notes (1936, 425–427), general propositions like laws can never be verified. For this reason, he suggested replacing verification with confirmation. For a discussion of problems with other complex sentences, see Justus' (2006). While these problems are important for a comprehensive assessment of verificationism, they are tangential to our current concern, which is the semantics of theoretical terms.

11 See Carnap's (1931/1996). Observation sentences are closely related to protocol sentences. As we have briefly noted in Section 3.2, the form and content of protocol sentences became the subject matter of heated debate in the Vienna Circle in the 1930s.

Cat's (2006), Gillies' (1993, Ch. 6), and Uebel's (2007) provide accounts of this now so-called "protocol-sentence debate".

12 This view in fact goes back to Carnap's earlier work; see his (1923, 99–100) and (1928/2003, 82–83). Braithwaite (1953, 52, 1954b, 35) attributes such a view to Russell's doctrine of logical construction.

13 The observation term can of course also be a complex expression based on several simple notions.

14 The definition of theoretical terms through observation terms need not be direct. Science will have terms that are far removed from experience and are defined in terms of other theoretical terms. This is no problem as long as there are definitions for these terms that eventually (possibly through a long cascade of definitions) tie them to something directly observable.

15 Hempel (1965, Ch. 5, 1966, Ch. 7) offers an assessment of operationalism. For a general discussion of operationalism, see Gillies' (1972).

16 Nagel's account of reduction is formulated in Chapter 11 of his (1961); for a discussion and re-statement, see Dizadji-Bahmani et al. (2010). Arguments against disjunctive laws are given, for instance, by Kim (1999); a defence of such laws is given, for instance, by Sober (1999). Disjunctive laws are closely connected to the multiple realisability of properties. Klein (2013) argues that while multiple realisability threatens the Linguistic View, it is not an issue in the Model-Theoretical View.

17 For ease of presentation, I omit reference to instants of time. See Carnap's (1936, 440–441) for a definition of disposition terms that includes instants of time.

18 The early Carnap thought that all (or at any rate almost all) theoretical terms could be characterised along the lines of disposition terms. Later he rejected this identification and distinguished between the two (1956b, 62–69). But driving a wedge between the two does not solve the problem for disposition terms, and so the explicit definition view of theoretical terms needs to be reviewed anyway.

19 For detailed discussion of the case of temperature, see Chang's (2004).

20 For an overview, see Starr's (2019).

21 As in the previous section, I omit time for ease of presentation. See Carnap's (1936, 441–444) for a statement that includes time.

22 See also Hempel's (1952, 26–27) and Feigl's (1970, 7). For a discussion of partial interpretation, see Achinstein's (1963), Putnam's (1962, 220–224), Suppe's (1971, 1972, 1977, 86–95), and Winnie's (1965).

23 This is a version of the thesis of *semantic holism*. For a discussion, see, for instance, Andreas' (2010, 525), Papineau's (1996, 2), and Psillos' (1999, 13).

24 See also Braithwaite's (1953, 51–53, 76–78), Hempel's (1969, 34, 1973, 369), and Nagel's (1961, 91–93) for a statement and discussion. Quine (1964), Wilson (1964), and Winnie (1967) offer general accounts of implicit definitions; Butterfield and Gomes (2021, Sec. 6) discuss the use of implicit definitions in geometry.

25 Winnie (1967) argues that the approach is not strong enough to ensure that the theory's terms refer to the intended objects or properties in the world, and Psillos and Christopoulou (2009) argue that the approach has problems separating the analytic and the synthetic content of a theory.

26 It ought to be noted that this is a problem also for explicit definitions, which are piecemeal in the same way as reduction sentences.

27 See Hempel's (1965, 206–210, 130–133, 1973, Secs. 4–5). Hempel traces his own account back to Campbell's (1920) notion of a "dictionary" (Hempel 1965, 207). For further discussions, see Suppe's (1977, 24–27).

28 Schaffner's view has an additional element, namely that scientists often use antecedent meanings to create novel terms by combining available terms in radically new ways (1969, 83). This, however, is possible only because the terms that serve as the building blocks have previously acquired meaning through models.

29 In fact, they are frozen metaphors. For a discussion of the relation between metaphors and models, see Section 10.6.

30 For a statement of the assumptions of the theorem and a proof, see Craig's (1953). Craig's (1956) provides a less technical discussion, and Craig's (2008) contains further developments. Ketland's (2006) and Suppe's (2000) offer short introductions. Discussions of the theorem can be found in Cornman's (1972, 85–108), English's (1973, 454–457), Hempel's (1965, 210–215), Putnam's (1965), Scheffler's (1957b, 619–624), Suppe's (1977, 30–32), and Tuomela's (1973, Ch. 2).

31 The Ramsey sentence originates in Ramsey's (1929/1950). An early application to the problem of theoretical terms is Braithwaite's (1953, Ch. 3). Carnap's (1966, Ch. 26) provides detailed discussion. An account of the history of the Ramsey sentence can be found in Psillos' (2000a, 2006); for discussions of the logical properties of the sentence, see English's (1973, 457–462) and Ketland's (2004). Berent (1973) offers a version of Ramsey's method that operates in the meta-language. Braddon-Mitchell and Nola (1997) defend Ramseyfication against the charge that it leads to inconsistencies.

32 Scheffler (1968, 270) goes even further and argues that TC_R is stronger than TC because TC_R carries with it an ontological commitment to the existence of theoretical entities that TC itself does not have. Bohnert (1968) replies that this is so only if one reads the original theory nominalistically, which one need not do. Díez (2005, 76–77) takes an intermediate position according to which both TC and TC_R are committed to the existence of individuals but only TC_R is committed to the existence of properties.

33 For a discussion of arguments of along these lines, see Cornman's (1972), Gaifman et al. (1990), and Tuomela's (1973, Ch. 6).

34 The approach has its origins in Carnap's (1952) and receives its first explicit formulated in his (1958), which is translated into English as his (1975). The presentation here follows the final version in Carnap's (1966).

35 For further discussions of the Carnap sentence, see, for instance, Demopoulos' (2013) and Friedman's (2011).

36 The Carnap sentence defines the analytical relations between theoretical terms without stating explicit definitions, and so it can be seen as a formal statement of the implicit definition of these terms. For a discussion of the Carnap sentence as an implicit definition, see Psillos and Christopoulou's (2009, 2018–2020) and references therein.

37 To the best of my knowledge Carnap did not discuss this result. It was brought to the attention to contemporary philosophy of science by Demopoulos and Friedman (1985). For a review of the now extensive discussions of Newman's Theorem, see Frigg and Votsis' (2011). Winnie (1967) makes a point that is closely related to Newman's theorem. Uebel (2011) and Friedman (2011) examine responses to the problem that are in Carnap's spirit. Conclusions of the same kind have also been reached via Putnam's so-called model-theoretic argument. For a review of the discussions of this argument, see Button and Walsh's (2018) and Hale and Wright's (2017).

38 $TC(\_,...,\theta_m,\omega_1,....,\omega_n)$ is also called an *open sentence*.

39 The first use of this operator is in a lecture held in Santa Barbara in 1959, published as a part of Psillos' (2000b); it is further developed in Carnap's (1961). Avigad and Zach's (2016) provides an introduction; for a discussion of the ε-operator in the philosophy of mathematics, see Schiemer and Gratzl's (2016) and Gratzl and Schiemer's (2017).

40 In his discussion, Lewis does not bifurcate the vocabulary into observable and unobservable terms, but into old and new terms (see Section 3.5). Nothing in what follows depends on how the vocabulary is bifurcated. The position is further developed in Lewis' (1972). Bedard (1993) argues that Lewis' position is too radical because the terms in unrealised or multiply realised theories can have "partial denotation". Papineau (1996) extends the approach to cases in which the theory is only imprecisely specified.

41 Quine's argument resembles Duhem's (1906) thesis that claims are never tested in isolation. See Gillies' (1993) for a discussion of the relation between Quine's and Duhem's arguments.

42 Indeed, this is the project of so-called quantum logic. For a discussion of quantum logic, see, for instance, Rédei's (1998).

43 Rey's (2018) and Russell's (2007) offer concise overviews; Juhl and Loomis' (2010) provides a book-length discussion.

44 Carnap's reply to Quine is in his (1956a, 222–229), and his reply to Hempel, who, like Quine, rejected the analytic/synthetic distinction, is in Schilpp's (1963, 962–966).

45 He reaffirms the point in his (1966, 261).

46 Feigl's paper appeared in the January issue of *Philosophy of Science* in 1950. The April issue of the same year featured a symposium on Feigl's paper with commentaries from Churchman, Frank, Hempel, Nagel, and Ramsperger, as well as a reply from Feigl himself. These papers document the conflict between semantic realism and a positivist approach to theoretical terms.

47 Van Fraassen adopts the Model-Theoretical View of theories, which we discuss in Chapters 5 and 6. However, his semantic realism is independent of that view and hence can be discussed independently of it.

48 For a discussion the epistemic attitudes in van Fraassen's constructive empiricism, see Halvorson's (2020) and Okruhlik's (2014).

49 Rosen (1994) argues that constructive empiricism is in fact a brand of fictionalism, the view that accepting a theory is an act of pretence analogous to the pretence we engage in when reading literary fiction. Van Fraassen's (1994) is a reply to Rosen, and Kalderon's (2005) offers an overview of different fictionalist programmes.

50 As we have seen previously, Russell (1905) also held a descriptivist account of names, but he denied that definite descriptions refer and instead thought that they denote. As above, I stick with Frege's use of "refer" here.

51 Although they differ from Frege's account in that they aim to describe predicates (like "having temperature θ") rather than singular expressions (like "Venus" or "the morning star").

52 In the case of predicates, this can be spelt out in different ways. One might say that the referent of a predicate is the extension of the predicate, i.e. all objects to which the predicate applies. An alternative is to posit the existence of universals and say that the predicate refers to a universal.

53 For an overview of these problems, see Braun's (2008, Sec. 4) and Lycan's (2008, Chs. 2 and 3). Hoefer and Martí discuss these objections with special focus on scientific languages and note that cluster descriptivism, an advanced version of the descriptive account, does not circumvent these problems (2020, Sec. 3); for further discussions with a special focus on H_2O, see their (2019) and Chang's (2012, Ch. 4).

54 Andersen criticises this trait of the account as "too restrictive" because "referential change is totally precluded" (2001, 52).

55 Kroon (1985, 1987) and Psillos (2012) focus on causation; Hoefer and Martí (2020) formulate an account in terms of what they call "epistemic handles". For Further discussions of reference fixing in the causal-historical theory, see Enč's (1976) and Nola's (1980).

References

Achinstein, P. 1963. Theoretical Terms and Partial Interpretation. *The British Journal for the Philosophy of Science* 14: 89–105.

Ainsworth, P. 2009. Newman's Objection. *The British Journal for the Philosophy of Science* 60: 135–171.

Andersen, H. 2001. Reference and Resemblance. *Philosophy of Science* 68: 50–61.

Andreas, H. 2010. Semantic Holism in Scientific Language. *Philosophy of Science* 77: 524–543.

Avigad, J. and R. Zach 2016. The Epsilon Calculus. In E. N. Zalta (ed.), *The Stanford Encyclopedia of Philosophy.* https://plato.stanford.edu/archives/sum2016/entries/epsilon-calculus/.

Ayer, A. J. 1936. *Language, Truth and Logic* (2nd ed.). New York: Dover, 1946.

Barcan Marcus, R. 1961. Modalities and Intensional Languages. *Synthese* 13: 303–322.

Bedard, K. 1993. Partial Denotations of Theoretical Terms. *Nous* 27: 499–511.

Berent, P. 1973. Theoretical Terms in Infinite Theories. *Philosophy of Science* 40: 129.

Bohnert, H. G. 1968. In Defense of Ramsey's Elimination Method. *The Journal of Philosophy* 65: 275–281.

Braddon-Mitchell, D. and R. Nola 1997. Ramsification and Glymour's Counterexample. *Analysis* 57: 167–169.

Braithwaite, R. B. 1953. *Scientific Explanation.* Cambridge: Cambridge University Press.

Braithwaite, R. B. 1954a. The Nature of Theoretical Concepts and the Role of Models in an Advanced Science. *Theoria* 2: 155–157.

Braithwaite, R. B. 1954b. The Nature of Theoretical Concepts and the Role of Models in an Advanced Science. *Revue Internationale de Philosophie* 8: 34–40.

Braun, D. 2008. Names and Natural Kind Terms. In E. Lepore and B. Smith (eds.), *The Oxford Handbook in Philosophy of Language.* Oxford: Oxford University Press, pp. 490–515.

Bridgman, P. W. 1927. *The Logic of Modern Physics.* New York: Macmillan.

Butterfield, J. and H. Gomes 2021. Functionalism as a Species of Reduction. Forthcoming in C. Soto (ed.), *Current Debates in Philosophy of Science: In Honor of Roberto Torretti.* Cham: Springer.

Button, T. and S. Walsh 2018. *Philosophy and Model Theory.* Oxford: Oxford University Press.

Campbell, N. R. 1920. *Physics: The Elements.* Cambridge: Cambridge University Press (Reprinted as *Foundations of Science.* New York: Dover, 1957).

Carnap, R. 1923. Über Die Aufgabe Der Physik Und Die Anwendung Des Grundsatzes Der Einfachstheit. *Kant Studien* 28: 90–107.

Carnap, R. 1928. *The Logical Structure of the World and Pseudoproblems in Philosophy.* Chicago and La Salle: Open Court, 2003.

Carnap, R. 1931. The Elimination of Metaphysics through Logical Analysis of Language. In S. Sarkar (ed.), *Logical Empiricism at Its Peak Schlick. Carnap, and Neurath.* New York and London: Garland Publishing, 1996, pp. 10–32.

Carnap, R. 1936. Testability and Meaning. *Philosophy of Science* 3: 419–471.

Carnap, R. 1937. *Logical Syntax of Language.* London: Routledge, 2000.

Carnap, R. 1952. Meaning Postulates. *Philosophical Studies* 3: 65–73.

Carnap, R. 1956a. *Meaning and Necessity: A Study in Semantics and Modal Logic* (2nd ed.). Chicago and London: Chicago University Press.

Carnap, R. 1956b. The Methodological Character of Theoretical Concepts. In H. Feigl and M. Scriven (eds.), *The Foundations of Science and the Concepts of Phsychologz and Psychoanalysis* (Vol. I, Minnestota Studies in the Philosophy of Science). Minneapolis: University of Minnesota Press, pp. 38–76.

Carnap, R. 1958. Beobachtungssprache Und Theoretische Sprache. *Dialectica* 12: 236–248.

Carnap, R. 1961. On the Use of Hilbert's E-Operator in Scientific Theories. In Y. Bar-Hillel, E. I. J. Poznanski, M. O. Rabin, and A. Robinson (eds.), *Essays on the Foundations of Mathematics.* Jerusalem: Magnes Press, pp. 156–164.

Carnap, R. 1966. *An Introduction to the Philosophy of Science*. New York: Dover, 1995 (Reprint of *Philosophical Foundations of Physics: An Introduction to the Philosophy of Science*. New York: Basic Books, 1966).

Carnap, R. 1975. Observation Language and Theoretical Language. In J. Hintikka (ed.), *Rudolf Carnap, Logical Empiricist. Materials and Perspectives*. Dordrecht: Reidel, pp. 75–85.

Cat, J. 2006. Protocol Sentences. In S. Sarkar and J. Pfeifer (eds.), *The Philosophy of Science: An Ecyclopedia*. New York: Tayolr & Francis, pp. 610–613.

Chang, H. 2004. *Inventing Temperature: Measurement and Scientific Progress*. Oxford: Oxford University Press.

Chang, H. 2012. *Is Water H2O? Evidence, Realism and Pluralism*. Dordrecht: Springer.

Cornman, J. W. 1972. Craig's Theorem, Ramsey-Sentences, and Scientific Instrumentalism. *Synthese* 25: 82–128.

Craig, W. 1953. On Axiomatizability within a System. *The Journal of Symbolic Logic* 18: 30–32.

Craig, W. 1956. Replacement of Auxiliary Expressions. *The Philosophical Review* 65: 38–55.

Craig, W. 2008. The Road to Two Theorems of Logic. *Synthese* 164: 333–339.

Demopoulos, W. 2013. *Logicism and Its Philosophical Legacy*. Cambridge: Cambridge University Press.

Demopoulos, W. and M. Friedman 1985. Bertrand Russell's the Analysis of Matter: Its Historical Context and Contemporary Interest. *Philosophy of Science* 52: 621–639.

Devitt, M. and R. Hanley (eds.) 2006. *The Blackwell Guide to the Philosophy of Language*. Oxford: Blackwell.

Díez, J. A. 2005. The Ramsey Sentence and Theoretical Content. In M. J. Frápolli (ed.), *F.P. Ramsey: Critical Reassessments*. London and New York: Continuum Publishing Group, pp. 70–103.

Dizadji-Bahmani, F., R. Frigg, and S. Hartmann 2010. Who's Afraid of Nagelian Reduction. *Erkenntnis* 73: 393–412.

Duhem, P. 1906. *La Théorie Physique, Son Objet Et Sa Structure* (2nd ed.). Paris: Chevalier and Rivière, 1914 (Engl. trans. by Philip P. Wiener: *The aim and Structure of Physical Theory*. Princeton, 1954).

Enç, B. 1976. Reference of Theoretical Terms. *Nous* 10: 261–282.

English, J. 1973. Underdetermination: Craig and Ramsey. *The Journal of Philosophy* 70: 453–462.

Feigl, H. 1950. Existential Hypotheses. Realistic Versus Phenomenalistic Interpretations. *Philosophy of Science* 17: 35–62.

Feigl, H. 1970. The 'Orthodox' View of Theories: Remarks in Defense as Well as Critique. In M. Radner and S. Winokur (eds.), *Analyses of Theories and Methods of Physics and Psychology* (Vol. IV, Minnesota Studies in the Philosophy of Science). Minneapolis: University of Minnesota Press, pp. 3–16.

Fetzer, J. 2021. Carl Hempel. In E. N. Zalta (ed.), *The Stanford Encyclopedia of Philosophy*. https://plato.stanford.edu/archives/spr2021/entries/hempel/.

Feyerabend, P. K. 1965. Problems of Empiricism. In R. G. Colodny (ed.), *Beyond the Edge of Certainty*. Englewood Cliffs, NJ: Prenctice Hall, pp. 145–260.

Field, H. 1980. *Science without Numbers*. Princeton: Princeton University Press.

Frege, G. 1892. Über Sinn Und Bedeutung. *Zeitschrift für Philosophie und philosophische Kritik* 100: 25–50.

Friedman, M. 2011. Carnap on Theoretical Terms: Structuralism without Metaphysics. *Synthese* 180: 249–263.

Frigg, R. and I. Votsis 2011. Everything You Always Wanted to Know About Structural Realism But Were Afraid to Ask. *European Journal for Philosophy of Science* 1: 227–276.

Gaifman, H., D. N. Osherson, and S. Weinstein 1990. A Reason for Theoretical Terms. *Erkenntnis* 32: 149–159.

Gillies, D. 1972. Operationalism. *Synthese* 25: 1–24.

Gillies, D. 1993. *Philosphy of Science in the Twetieth Century: Four Central Themes*. Oxford: Blackwell.

Gratzl, N. and G. Schiemer 2017. Two Types of Indefinites: Hilbert & Russell. *IfCoLog Journal of Logics and their Applications* 4: 333–348.

Hale, B. and C. Wright 2017. Putnam's Model-Theoretic Argument against Metaphysical Realism. In B. Hale, C. Wright, and A. Miller (eds.), *A Companion to the Philosophy of Language* (2nd ed.). New York: John Wiley & Sons, pp. 703–733.

Halvorson, H. 2020. Concluding Unscientific Image. *Metascience* 29: 177–185.

Hanson, N. R. 1958. *Patterns of Discovery*. Cambridge: Cambdridge University Press.

Hempel, C. G. 1950. Problems and Changes in the Empiricist Criterion of Meaning. *Revue International de Philosophie* 11: 41–63.

Hempel, C. G. 1951. The Concept of Cognitive Significance: A Reconsideration. *Proceedings of the American Society of Arts and Science* 80: 61–77.

Hempel, C. G. 1952. *Fundamentals of Concept Formation in Empirical Science* (Vol. 2.7, International Encyclopedia of Unified Science). Chicago and London: University of Chicago Press.

Hempel, C. G. 1965. *Aspects of Scientific Explanation and Other Essays in the Philosophy of Science*. New York: Free Press.

Hempel, C. G. 1966. *Philosophy of Natural Science*. Princeton: Princeton University Press.

Hempel, C. G. 1969. On the Structure of Scientific Theories. In C. G. Hempel (ed.), *The Isenberg Memorial Lecture Series*. East Lansing: Michigan State University Press, pp. 11–38.

Hempel, C. G. 1970. On the 'Standard Conception' of Scientific Theories. In M. Radner and S. Winokur (eds.), *Minnesota Studies in the Philosophy of Science Vol. 4*. Minneapolis: University of Minnesota Press, pp. 142–163.

Hempel, C. G. 1973. The Meaning of Theoretical Terms: A Critique of the Standard Empiricist Construal. In P. Suppes, L. Henkin, A. Joja, and G. C. Moisil (eds.), *Logic, Methodology and Philosophy of Science Vol. IV*. Amsterdam: North Holland, pp. 367–378.

Hesse, M. B. 1967. Models and Analogy in Science. In P. Edwards (ed.), *Encyclopedia of Philosophy*. New York: Macmillan, pp. 354–359.

Hesse, M. B. 1969. Positivism and the Logic of Scientific Theories. In P. Achinstein and S. F. Barker (eds.), *The Legacy of Logical Positivism*. Baltimore: Johns Hopkins Press, pp. 85–114.

Hoefer, C. and G. Martí 2019. Water Has a Microstructural Essence after All. *European Journal for Philosophy of Science* 9: 1–15.

Hoefer, C. and G. Martí 2020. Realism, Reference & Perspective. *European Journal for Philosophy of Science* 10: 1–22.

Horwich, P. 2006. The Nature of Meaning. In M. Devitt and R. Hanley (eds.), *The Blackwell Guide to the Philosophy of Language*. Oxford: Blackwell, pp. 43–57.

Hutten, E. H. 1956. *The Language of Modern Physics. An Introduction to the Philosophy of Science* (2nd ed.). London: Novello.

Juhl, C. and E. Loomis 2010. *Analyticity*. London: Routledge.

Justus, J. 2006. Cognitive Significance. In S. Sarkar and J. Pfeifer (eds.), *The Philosophy of Science. An Encyclopedia*. New York and London: Routledge, pp. 131–140.

Justus, J. 2014. Carnap's Forgotten Criterion of Empirical Significance. *Mind* 123: 415–436.

Kalderon, M. E. (ed.) 2005. *Fictionalism in Metaphysics*. Oxford: Clarendon Press.

Ketland, J. 2004. Empirical Adequacy and Ramsification. *The British Journal for the Philosophy of Science* 55: 287–300.

Ketland, J. 2006. Craig's Theorem. In D. Borchert (ed.), *Encyclopedia of Philosophy* (Vol. 2, 2nd revised ed.), Farmington Hills, MI: Macmillan, pp. 583–584.

Kim, J. 1999. Making Sense of Emergence 95. *Philosophical Studies* 95: 3–36.

Klein, C. 2013. Multiple Realizability and the Semantic View of Theories. *Philosophical Studies* 163: 683–695.

Kripke, S. 1980. *Naming and Necessity*. Cambridge, MA: Harvard University Press.

Kroon, F. W. 1985. Theoretical Terms and the Causal View of Reference. *Australasian Journal of Philosophy* 63: 143–166.

Kroon, F. W. 1987. Causal Descriptivism. *Australasian Journal of Philosophy* 65: 1–17.

Kuhn, T. S. 1970. *The Structure of Scientific Revolutions* (2nd ed.). Chicago: Chicago University Press.

Lewis, D. K. 1970. How to Define Theoretical Terms. *The Journal of Philosophy* 67: 427–446.

Lewis, D. K. 1972. Psychophysical and Theoretical Identifications. *Australasian Journal of Philosophy* 50: 249–258.

Lewis, D. K. 1999. *Papers in Metaphysics and Epistemology*. Cambridge: Cambridge University Press.

Lycan, W. G. 2008. *Philosophy of Language. A Contemporary Introduction* (2nd ed.). New York and London: Routledge.

McGuinness, B. (ed.) 1979. *Ludwig Wittgenstein and the Vienna Circle. Conversations Recorded by Friedrich Waismann*. Oxford: Basil Blackwell.

Michaelson, E. and M. Reimer 2019. Reference. In E. N. Zalta (ed.), *The Stanford Encyclopedia of Philosophy*. https://plato.stanford.edu/archives/spr2019/entries/reference/.

Mill, J. S. 1843. Of Names. In J. M. Robson (ed.), *He Collected Works of John Stuart Mill* (Vol. VII). Toronto: University of Toronto Press and Routledge & Keagan Paul, 1974, pp. 24–45.

Miller, A. 2007. *Philosophy of Language* (2nd ed.). London and New York: Routledge.

Nagel, E. 1961. *The Structure of Science*. London: Routledge and Keagan Paul.

Newman, M. H. A. 1928. Mr. Russell's 'Causal Theory of Perception'. *Mind* 37: 137–148.

Nola, R. 1980. Fixing the Reference of Theoretical Terms. *Philosophy of Science* 47: 505–531.

Okruhlik, K. 2014. Bas Van Fraassen's Philosophy of Science and His Epistemic Voluntarism. *Philosophy Compass* 9: 653–661.

Papineau, D. 1996. Theory-Dependent Terms. *Philosophy of Science* 63: 1–20.

Percival, P. 2000. Theoretical Terms: Meaning and Reference. In W. H. Newton-Smith (ed.), *A Companion to the Philosophy of Science*. Oxford: Wiley-Blackwell, pp. 495–514.

Psillos, S. 1999. *Scientific Realism: How Science Tracks Truth*. London: Routledge.

Psillos, S. 2000a. Carnap, the Ramsey Sentence and Realistic Empiricism. *Erkenntnis* 52: 253–279.

Psillos, S. 2000b. Rudolf Carnap's 'Theoretical Concepts in Science'. *Studies in History and Philosophy of Science* 31: 151–172.

Psillos, S. 2006. Ramsey's Ramsey-Sentences. In M. C. Galavotti (ed.), *Cambridge and Vienna: Frank P. Ramsey and the Vienna Circle* (Vienna Circle Institute Yearbook, Vol. 12). Berlin: Springer, pp. 67–90.

Psillos, S. 2012. Causal Descriptivism and the Reference of Theoretical Terms. In A. Raftopoulos and P. Machamer (eds.), *Perception, Realism and the Problem of Reference*. Cambridge: Cambridge University Press, pp. 212–238.

Psillos, S. and D. Christopoulou 2009. The a Priori: Between Conventions and Implicit Definitions In N. Kompa, C. Nimtz, and C. Suhm (eds.), *The a Priori and Its Role in Philosophy*. Paderborn: Mentis, pp. 205–220.

Putnam, H. 1962. What Theories Are Not. In E. Nagel, P. Suppes, and A. Tarski (eds.), *Logic, Methodology, and the Philosophy of Science*. reprinted in *Hilary Putnam: Mathematics, Matter and Method. Philosophical Papers Vol. 1*. Cambridge: Cambridge University Press, pp. 215–227.

Putnam, H. 1965. Craig's Theorem. *The Journal of Philosophy* 62: 251–260.

Putnam, H. 1973. Meaning and Reference. *The Journal of Philosophy* 70: 699–611.

Quine, W. V. O. 1951. Two Dogmas of Empiricism. *The Philosophical Review* 60: 20–43.

Quine, W. V. O. 1964. Implicit Definition Sustained. *The Journal of Philosophy* 61: 71–74.

Quine, W. V. O. 1975. On Empirically Equivalent Systems of the World. *Erkenntnis* 9: 313–328.

Ramsey, F. P. 1929. Theories. In R. Braithwaite (ed.), *The Foundations of Mathematics and Other Logical Essays* (2nd ed.). London: Routlege and Kegan Paul, 1950, pp. 212–236.

Rédei, M. 1998. *Quantum Logic in Algebraic Approach*. Dordrecht: Springer.

Rey, G. 2018. The Analytic/Synthetic Distinction. In E. N. Zalta (ed.), *The Stanford Encyclopedia of Philosophy*. https://plato.stanford.edu/archives/win2020/entries/analytic-synthetic/.

Rosen, G. 1994. What Is Constructive Empiricism? *Philosophical Studies* 74: 143–178.

Russell, B. 1905. On Denoting. *Mind* 14: 479–493.

Russell, G. 2007. Fictional Characters. *Philosophy Compass* 2: 712–729.

Schaffner, K. F. 1969. Correspondence Rules. *Philosophy of Science* 36: 280–290.

Scheffler, I. 1957a. Prospects of a Modest Empiricism, I. *Review of Metaphysics* 10: 383–400.

Scheffler, I. 1957b. Prospects of a Modest Empiricism, II. *Review of Metaphysics* 10: 602–625.

Scheffler, I. 1968. Reflections on the Ramsey Method. *The Journal of Philosophy* 65: 269–274.

Schiemer, G. and N. Gratzl 2016. The Epsilon-Reconstruction of Theories and Scientific Structuralism. *Erkenntnis* 81: 407–432.

Schilpp, P. A. (ed.) 1963. *The Philosophy of Rudolf Carnap* (Vol. XI, The Library of Living Philosophers). La Salle: Open Court.

Schlick, M. 1925. *Allgemeine Erkenntnislehre* (2nd ed.). Berlin Springer.

Schlick, M. 1936. Meaning and Verification. *The Philosophical Review* 45: 339–369.

Skorupski, J. 1997. Meaning, Use, Verification. In B. Hale and C. Wright (eds.), *A Companion to the Philosophy of Language*. Oxford: Blackwell, pp. 29–59.

Sober, E. 1999. Multiple Realizability Argument against Reductionism. *Philosophy of Science* 66: 542–564.

Starr, W. 2019. Counterfactuals. In E. N. Zalta (ed.), *The Stanford Encyclopedia of Philosophy*. https://plato.stanford.edu/archives/fall2019/entries/counterfactuals/.

Suppe, F. 1971. On Partial Interpretation. *The Journal of Philosophy* 68: 57–76.

Suppe, F. 1972. What's Wrong with the Received View on the Structure of Scientific Theories? *Philosophy of Science* 39: 1–19.

Suppe, F. 1977. The Search for Philosophical Understanding of Scientific Theories. In F. Suppe (ed.), *The Structure of Scientific Theories*. Urbana and Chicago: University of Illinois Press, pp. 3–241.

Suppe, F. 2000. Craig's Theorem. In W. H. Newton-Smith (ed.), *A Companion to the Philosophy of Science*. Oxford: Wiley-Blackwell, pp. 65–67.

Tuomela, R. 1973. *Theoretical Concepts*. Wien and New York: Springer.

Uebel, T. 2007. *Empiricism at the Crossroads: The Vienna Circle's Protocol-Sentence Debate*. Chicago: Open Court.

Uebel, T. 2011. Carnap's Ramseyfication Defended. *European Journal for Philosophy of Science* 1: 71–87.

Uebel, T. 2019. Verificationism and (Some of) Its Discontents. *Journal for the History of Analytical Philosophy* 7: 1–32.

van Fraassen, B. C. 1980. *The Scientific Image*. Oxford: Oxford University Press.

van Fraassen, B. C. 1994. Gideon Rosen on Constructive Empiricism. *Philosophical Studies* 74: 179–192.

Wilson, F. 1964. Implicit Definitions Once Again. *The Journal of Philosophy* 62: 364–374.

Winnie, J. A. 1965. Theoretical Terms and Partial Definitions. *Philosophy of Science* 32: 324–328.

Winnie, J. A. 1967. The Implicit Definition of Theoretical Terms. *The British Journal for the Philosophy of Science* 18: 223–229.

PART II

PART II

5

THINKING THROUGH STRUCTURES

5.1 Introduction

A radical way of dealing with the challenges faced by the Received View is to wipe the slate clean and start afresh. This is the approach chosen by the Model-Theoretical View of Theories. This view is best known as the "Semantic View of Theories", but for reasons that we will discuss later, this is a misnomer and I will use the label "Model-Theoretical View of Theories" ("Model-Theoretical View", for short) instead. The view comes in different versions, and we will encounter many of them in this part of the book. The original version was formulated by Suppes in the late 1950s and early 1960s, and later versions build on it in various ways. For this reason, we begin with a detailed discussion of Suppes' version of the Model-Theoretical View (Section 5.2). We then give a survey of other views that fall under the umbrella of the Model-Theoretical View (Section 5.3) and review the hopes and promises associated with the Model-Theoretical View (Section 5.4). Next we embark on a detailed discussion of the role of language in the Model-Theoretical View and of what it means for two theories to be equivalent (Section 5.5). Unintended models are claimed to be a problem for the Received View, and we discuss how the Model-Theoretical View deals with this issue (Section 5.6*). "Quietism" is a position according to which many of the problems we have been struggling with so far can be avoided simply by remaining quiet about what theories are. We introduce the position and argue that the philosophical problems we have been wrestling with so far cannot be exorcised in this way, and that we have to tackle these problems head on (Section 5.7). We proceed to discuss what I call the Dual View of theories, which offers a positive suggestion of how this can be done (Section 5.8). We end by taking stock and commenting on alternative ways of analysing theories (Section 5.9).

DOI: 10.4324/9781003285106-8

5.2 Suppes' Structuralism

Suppes urges the philosophical community to abandon the Received View's concentration on the language of a theory and instead focus on the theory's models. He lamented "a strong tendency on the part of many philosophers" to discuss the logical structure of a theory "in purely syntactical terms" and urged that "it is pertinent and natural from a logical standpoint to talk about the models of the theory" (Suppes 2002, 3, cf. 1967, 57). After collecting quotations about models from scientists working in the physical sciences, the biological sciences, the social sciences, mathematical statistics, and applied mathematics, Suppes says:

> I claim that the concept of model in the sense of Tarski may be used without distortion as a fundamental concept in all of the disciplines from which the above quotations are drawn. In this sense I would assert that (the meaning of) the concept of model is the same in mathematics and the empirical sciences.
>
> *(2002, 20–21, cf. 1960, 12–17, 1962, 24–25)*

In Section 2.6 we have seen that a model in the sense of Tarski is a set-theoretical structure S that is used as a logical model, meaning that the terms of a formal sentence (or set of sentences) are interpreted as referring to elements of the structure so that the claims of the formal sentence come out true. The set of sentences is what the Received View considers to be the theory. We have also seen that considering models in addition to formal sentences can shed light on important aspects of formal systems, and Suppes recommends that we make use of the insight of model theory when analysing scientific theories.

But Suppes aims to do more than just bring a subfield of formal logic to the attention of philosophers of science. He urges a complete reversal of the traditional way of thinking about scientific theories. The Received View thinks of a theory as a formal system interpreted in terms of its subject matter and thereby assigns the linguistic formal system centre stage. Suppes regards this as a mistake and submits that what is important about a theory is its models and not its expression in a formal language. This has important implications for how a theory is analysed. The traditional method of studying the models of a theory T would be to first axiomatise T and then look at the structures that satisfy T. Suppes suggests that we bypass the formulation of a theory in a formal language by describing the class (or family) of models of theory T directly, without first presenting a set of axioms.

To make this idea clear we have to introduce two crucial concepts of Suppes' philosophy: the dichotomy between intrinsic and extrinsic characterisations of a theory and the notion of a set-theoretical predicate. If a theory is presented as a logical calculus in first-order logic, then the theory is given an *intrinsic characterisation* (2002, 5, 28). Suppes refers to this as a "standard formalization" of a theory because the intrinsic characterisation is the formal characterisation of a theory attributed to the Received View.[1] An alternative approach is to define the class of intended models of a theory *directly*, without a "detour" through a first-order calculus. Such a specification is an *extrinsic characterisation* of the theory.

To give an extrinsic characterisation amounts to formulating a *set-theoretical predicate* (now sometimes also called a *Suppes predicate*).[2] A set-theoretical predicate τ is applied to theoretical structures, and the structures that satisfy the predicate form the class C_τ. The predicate itself is defined in set-theoretical terms. Suppes points out that nothing depends on which particular version of set theory we choose: we can choose, for instance, Zermelo-Fraenkel set theory, or we can operate in naïve (or informal) set theory.[3] Since mathematical concepts can be defined in terms of set theory, one can also use mathematical concepts when writing down set-theoretical predicates (as they will have been defined previously and one can presuppose these definitions). So in effect we can use the entire apparatus of set theory and mathematics to formulate a set-theoretical predicate.

As an example, consider the set-theoretical predicate *quasi-ordering* (Suppes 1957, 250).[4] Let Q be that predicate and $Q(S)$ be the statement that structure S is a quasi-ordering. As we have seen in Section 2.6, a structure is a tuple $S = (U, R)$, where U is the domain of the structure and R is an indexed set of relations on U. The predicate Q is then defined as follows: $Q(S)$ iff there is a binary relation $r \in R$ that is reflexive and transitive.[5] This predicate applies to some structures but not to others, and C_Q is the class of structures to which Q applies.

Giving an extrinsic characterisation of a theory T amounts to defining a set-theoretical predicate τ such that C_τ is the class of models of the theory. Suppes also refers to the definition of τ as the *extrinsic axiomatisation* of T (2002, 28) and sums up the core of his view in the slogan "to axiomatize a theory is to define a set-theoretical predicate" (*ibid.*, 30, cf. 1957, 249).[6] In the context of an extrinsic axiomatisation there is no uninterpreted formal sentence (of the kind we have seen in Chapter 2) whose terms are then interpreted as referring to elements of the structure, and so the original definition of a model as a structure that makes a formal sentence true does not sit well with an extrinsic axiomatisation (in fact the notion belongs to an intrinsic axiomatisation). For this reason Suppes offers an alternative definition, namely that "[w]hen a theory is axiomatised by defining a set-theoretical predicate, by a *model* for the theory we mean simply an entity which satisfies the predicate" (1957, 253). So the models of the theory are now the elements of the class C_τ.

There are now three different items on the table: intrinsic characterisations, extrinsic characterisations (via a set-theoretical predicate τ), and the class C_τ to which the set-theoretical predicate τ applies. Suppes does not address the question of what constitutes a theory directly and his position on this issue is somewhat elusive (we return to this issue in the next section). However, talk of theories "being defined" by set-theoretical predicates (2002, 30) indicates that Suppes regards the classes defined by set-theoretical predicates as crucial for an analysis of theories, while the intrinsic characterisation of a theory through a logical formalism is seen as secondary (and receives hardly any attention). This primacy of set-theoretical considerations is encapsulated in the slogan that mathematics, not meta-mathematics, is the right tool for the analysis of theories.[7]

This is the core of the *Model-Theoretical View of Theories*. As we noted at the beginning of this chapter, the view is standardly referred to as the "Semantic View of Theories". This label is owed to the fact that the structures in C_r are logical models. Such models are the things in terms of which formal sentences can be interpreted, and providing such an interpretation amounts to giving a semantics. However, calling this view "semantic" is a misnomer for at least two reasons.[8] First, as we have seen in Chapter 2, a semantics requires sentences in a formal language, an interpretation function, and an object in terms of which sentences are interpreted. But a class of models does not come equipped with either formal sentences or an interpretation function. So a theory in Suppes' sense offers a semantics only in the very minimal sense that it consists of the kind of objects that could, in principle, be taken to be the referents of terms in a formal language, but any object could do this. Second, and more importantly, the label "semantic" could easily be misunderstood as indicating that the models themselves have a semantics, that is, that they are representational models. They are not. The elements of C_r are set-theoretical structures, and as such they are pieces of mathematics without any representational function. In fact, the representation in the sense of a model representing a physical system has not entered the scene yet.

Suppes and collaborators analysed Newtonian particle mechanics in great detail. In fact, the extrinsic axiomatisation of mechanics was one of Suppes' motivations to develop the Model-Theoretical View in the first place.[9] He submits that the analysis of Newtonian mechanics in terms of a formal calculus offered in Chapter 1 is wrongheaded and urges that we have a fresh look at the theory from his vantage point. In what follows $\mathbb{R}$ are the real numbers; $\mathbb{R}^+$ are the positive real numbers including zero; and $\mathbb{R}^3$ is a three-dimensional Euclidean space. N is the set-theoretical predicate "being a system of classical particle mechanics". For simplicity, we now work with a structure that also contains operations (see Section 2.6). On Suppes' analysis, a structure $S = (U, R, O)$ is an N iff its domain U consists of the sets P, θ, M, L, and F; the set R of relations is empty; the set O contains the operations l, m, and f; and the constituents of U and O satisfy the following axioms:

Axiom 1: The set P is finite and non-empty.
Axiom 2: The set θ is an interval of $\mathbb{R}$.
Axiom 3: L is $\mathbb{R}^3$ and the operation $l : P \times \theta \to L$ is twice differentiable in θ.
Axiom 4: M is $\mathbb{R}^+$ and there is an operation
Axiom 5: F is $\mathbb{R}^3$ and the operation $f : P \times P \times \theta \to F$ is such that $f(p,q,t) = -f(q,p,t)$ for all p and q in P and for all t in θ.
Axiom 6: For all p in P and for all t in T: $m(p)\dfrac{d^2 l}{dt^2} = \sum_{q \in P} f(p,q,t)$.

The left-hand side of the equation in Axiom 6 denotes the second derivative of the operation l. The class C_N contains all the structures that satisfy the predicate N, and so C_N is the class of models of Newtonian Mechanics.

For our purposes the details of this extrinsic axiomatisation do not matter. What interests us at this point is not whether Suppes provides an adequate analysis of Newtonian Mechanics.[10] What interests us is what *kind* of analysis of Newtonian mechanics Suppes presents, because this axiomatisation exemplifies the manner in which Suppes suggests we analyse theories in general.

The first striking feature of Suppes' axioms is that they have no empirical content at all because they are couched in purely set-theoretical terms. The axioms make no references to particles, motions and forces. Indeed, the axioms make no reference to anything physical at all. This sits well with the fact that Suppes intends to define a *set-theoretical* predicate, but it does not sit well with the fact that this is supposed to be the analysis of an empirical theory. If a set-theoretical predicate is what a theory consists in, then the theory has no empirical content and it is not about anything in the real world. This cannot be. A scientific theory is about something in the world. What is the empirical content of a theory and how does it represent its subject matter?

Throughout the discussion of the axioms of Newtonian mechanics Suppes refers to the "intended interpretation" of the various sets and operations (see, for instance, 1957, 291–305, 2002, 319–323). He explains that θ is "physically interpreted" as time, and P as the particles of the system. L is interpreted as the three-dimensional physical space and l as the location operation that assigns each particle a location in that space. M is interpreted as the mass of a particle and m as the operation that assigns a mass to each particle. Finally, F is interpreted as force and f as an operation that assigns to each pair of particles a force with which they attract or repel each other. Under this interpretation, Axiom 5 is Newton's third law (the *action-reaction principle*, which says that if particle p exerts a force f on particle q, then particle q must exert a force of equal magnitude in opposite direction back on particle p), and Axiom 6 is Newton's second law (his equation of motion, which says that the acceleration a particle experiences as result of a force is proportional to the force).

This way of endowing a set-theoretical structure with empirical content is common in theoretical science, and there is nothing objectionable about it. However, it is important to note that it presupposes a *fully interpreted language* in which terms like "particle", "location" and "mass" have well-defined meanings. Suppes passes over this point in silence and says neither where this language comes from nor how it works.

Let us for the time being assume that we have such a language and need not concern ourselves with its origins or workings. Even under this assumption, questions remain about how the theory's models refer to the *specific* target systems that the theory aims to represent.[11] How, for instance, does a model of Newtonian mechanics relate to the solar system? Suppes does not discuss this issue in any detail and extracting an account of representation from his writings requires interpretative work. The effort is worth it, however, because we will be rewarded with nothing less than the leading ideas of two accounts of representation that will both play important roles in later versions of the Model-Theoretical View.

The first account, which seems to be the one that Suppes favours, is suggested by an analysis of experimental practice. As we have seen in Section 3.6, data models are constructed through a process of filtering, correction, rectification, and regimentation of the raw data that are collected in experiments. In his discussion of the relation between theory and experiment, Suppes emphasises the importance of data models. Considering an example from learning theory (1960, 19–23, 1962, 25–32), he submits that assessing a theory amounts to asking whether the data model "bears a satisfactory goodness-of-fit relation" (1962, 32) to a model in C_r. Suppes offers no account of goodness-of-fit, but given that both the theoretical model and the data model are set-theoretical structures, it is natural to assume that this is some kind of structural relationship. This squares with his remark that "in moving from the level of theory to the level of experiment we do not need to abandon formal methods of analysis" and that therefore "the distinction between pure and applied mathematics is spurious" (1962, 33). A plausible option is that data models are *embedded* in the models of the theory. The view then becomes that a theory represents its target if C_r contains a model M that is such that a data model D that has been obtained from observations on the target system can be embedded into M.[12] I call this the *Data Matching Account* of representation.

The second account of representation can be extracted from Suppes' discussion of the nature of models. Discussing the "orbital theory of the atom" he notes that physicists think of models as "more than a certain kind of set-theoretical entity" and that they envisage a model as a "concrete physical thing built on the analogy of the solar system" (2002, 21). Suppes then submits "that there is no real incompatibility in these two viewpoints", because "[t]he physical model may be simply taken to define the set of objects in the set-theoretical model" (*ibid.*; cf. 1960, 13). More generally, a "set-theoretical model of a theory will have among its parts a basic set which will consist of the objects ordinarily thought to constitute the physical model being considered, and the given primitive relations and functions may be thought of the same way" (2002, 22). So the suggestion is that we reconcile the set-theoretical and the physical view of models by taking the elements of the objects of a structure to be the material objects of interest and the relations and operations of the structure to be the physical interaction between the objects.

This proposal needs qualification. As we have seen in Section 2.6, mathematics studies abstract structures, which are structures that consist of dummy objects and purely extensionally defined relations. And this better be so. In addition to the principled arguments we have already discussed, it is a fact that many scientific models outstrip the inventory of the physical world. We can consider models of the solar system with ten or more planets (but there are only nine),[13] and models in statistical physics frequently consist of infinitely many particles (but there is only a finite number of particles in the universe). So the structures that Suppes talks about are abstract structures, and as such they cannot have among their parts physical objects like planets. However, there is claim in the vicinity of Suppes' proposal that captures the core of Suppes' idea without attributing constituents to abstract structures that they cannot have. As we have seen in Section 2.6, abstract structures contrast with concrete structures, structures in which both the objects and the relations have specified "intrinsic natures". Hence, concrete structures *do* consist of things that are the potential target systems of models, things like planets, magnets, and populations. Appealing to the dichotomy between abstract and concrete structures, Suppes' proposal can then be understood as saying that target systems are concrete structures, and that the abstract structures of a theory's models are isomorphic to the target's concrete structures (see Section 2.7 for a discussion of isomorphism).[14] A theory then represents a target system if C_τ contains a model M that that is isomorphic to the target. Derivatively, a theory represents its entire target domain if for every system in the target domain, C_τ contains a model that is isomorphic to the system.[15]

Once the relation of a theory's models and their respective targets is analysed in terms of there being an isomorphism between a model's abstract structure and a target's concrete structure, it is just a small step to realise that isomorphism is not the only option: the relation could be one of homomorphism or embedding, or indeed of any other mapping that can relate two structures. For this reason I call this the *Morphism Account* of representation.

Due to the emphasis placed on structures, Suppes' account is a brand of *structuralism*. His structuralism is schematically represented in Figure 5.1. The top half of the diagram covers what one might call the *formalism of the theory*; the bottom half contains the two different versions of how a theory represents the target systems in the theory's domain of application.[16] The remainder of this chapter is dedicated to a discussion of the formalism of a theory; and the question of how a formalism represents reality is the subject matter of Chapter 6.

5.3 The Model-Theoretical Family

Two sizeable movements grew directly out of Suppes' structuralism. The first is the "Partial Structures Programme", championed by Bueno, da Costa, French, and Ladyman. The second is what is now known as "Munich Structuralism", the programme pursued in the group around Balzer, Moulines, Sneed, and Stegmüller. Both movements qualify and further develop Suppes' approach in various ways while retaining its core ideas. We will discuss these two approaches in Section 6.7 and Chapter 7 respectively.

Another account that is closely related to Suppes' structuralism is van Fraassen's state-space version of the Model-Theoretical View. A system can be in a number of different states. What these states are depends on the nature of the system. The state of a moving particle is specified by its position and momentum, and the state of a gas in equilibrium is given by its pressure, temperature, and volume. These states can be represented by elements of a mathematical space, the

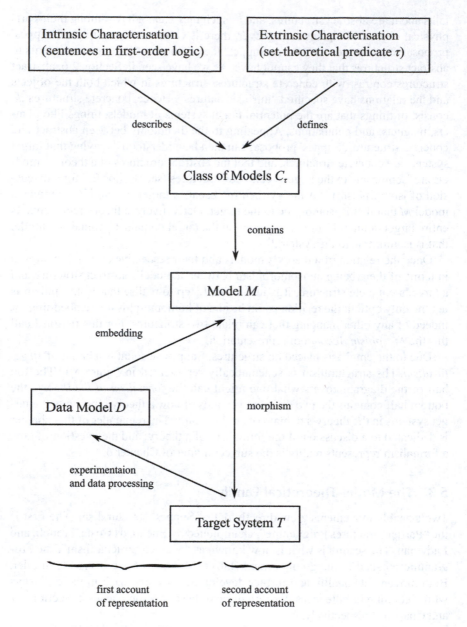

FIGURE 5.1 Suppes' structuralism.

system's *state space*. In van Fraassen's version of the Model-Theoretical View, the models that constitute a theory are the state spaces of the systems that the theory represents.[17] The states that are actually accessible to the system are constrained by laws, and these fall into two broad categories: laws of succession and laws of coexistence. Laws of succession specify which sequence of states a system is allowed to trace over time. Newton's second law is of this kind. Laws of coexistence determine which spots of state space a system can occupy. The ideal gas law (also known as the Boyle-Charles law), for instance, specifies that pressure, temperature and volume of a gas stand in a particular relation when the gas is in equilibrium.

The state space approach is a specific version of the set-theoretical approach, not an alternative to it.[18] Van Fraassen agrees with Suppes' data matching account of representation and gives it a precise formulation. A theory not only gives us a class of structures for the representation of its subject matter; it also picks out an *empirical substructure* within each model. This substructure represents those parts, areas or regions of the world that are observable to us and are therefore candidates for the "direct representation of observable phenomena" (1980, 64). The structures that result from a process of measurement are called *appearances*. Appearances can be "isomorphic to empirical substructures of that model", and a theory is *empirically adequate* iff for every appearance there is a model in the theory so that the appearance is isomorphic to the empirical substructure of the model (*ibid.*, 64–65). We discuss van Fraassen's approach later in this chapter and the next.

Approaches that are close to van Fraassen's, or explicitly build on it, have been proposed by Beatty (1980, 1981, 1987), Lloyd (1984, 1989, 1994), and Thompson (1983, 1987, 1988, 1989). Alternative, non-structuralist versions of the Model-Theoretical View have been developed by Giere and Suppe, whose views we discuss in Chapter 8.

5.4 Revolutionary Promises

The Model-Theoretical View of theories was announced as a revolution in the philosophy of science, and, as all revolutions, it was meant to break with the mistakes of the past and lead to a brighter future. What does the promised brighter future look like?

Language independence. Most of the problems that beset the Received View were in one way or another related to the fact that it offered a linguistic analysis of theories, and so it is only logical that proponents of the Model-Theoretical View emphasised that theirs was a non-linguistic analysis of theories and that this allowed them to sidestep all the problems of a linguistic analysis. The Model-Theoretical View claims to offer an approach that liberates philosophers from spurious problems with language and allows them to focus on things that really matter. But exorcising language comes at a price and we will assess whether this is a price worth paying.

Theory equivalence. As we have seen in Section 1.5, theories can be formulated in different ways, and the Received View stands accused of not being able to individuate theories correctly because it conflates theories with their descriptions. The Model-Theoretical View claims to solve this problem elegantly by associating theories with classes of models. Since the same class of models can be described in many ways, a change of description does not result in a new theory. I have previously voiced some reservation about the claim that the Received View cannot solve this problem, but, as we have also noted, being in principle able to solve a problem and having a solution in hand are two different things. So it is worth investigating the Model-Theoretical View's solution to the problem of theoretical equivalence, which is the project for Section 5.5.

Unintended models. As we have seen in Section 2.8, a formal system can have unintended models. Proponents of the Model-Theoretical View claim that this is a problem because a theory that has unintended models is unable to circumscribe its subject matter adequately. The Semantic approach claims to avoid this difficulty because it defines a theory as a class of models, which rules out unintended models right at the start. We discuss unintended models in Section 5.7.

Theory-world relation. The critique of correspondence rules (Chapter 4) and the arguments against the separability of theory and observation (Chapter 3) add up to the claim that the Received View completely misconstrues the relation between theory and observation. The Model-Theoretical View offers an entirely different analysis of theory-world relations, and this analysis is claimed to avoid these difficulties. We discuss the Model-Theoretical View's handling of the theory-world relation in Chapter 6.

Closeness to scientific practice. High on the list of things that matter in philosophy of science is an engagement with scientific practice, and the Model-Theoretical View is advertised as offering a way of thinking about theories that is close to scientific practice. This claim is based on the combination of the facts that the Model-Theoretical View assigns models a core role in the edifice of a theory and that models occupy centre stage in scientific practice. We return to the relation of the Model-Theoretical View and scientific practice in Section 12.7, after having discussed models in scientific practice.

Tools of Modern Logic. Model theory (as discussed in Section 2.6) plays an important role in modern logic, and crucial insights into the structure of formal systems are gained by also studying their models (rather than only their syntax). Considerations of completeness and soundness lie at the heart of modern logic, and they describe a relation between the syntax and the formal semantics of a theory. Questions concerning proof systems, the definability of concepts and the identity of theories are best addressed within a framework that takes both the syntax and the semantics of a system into account. By introducing models into the analysis of theories, the Model-Theoretical View makes the tools of modern logic available to philosophers of science. I take this claim to be uncontroversial, and the discussions in Sections 5.5–5.7 testify to the usefulness of modern logic in the discussion of scientific theories.

5.5   What Is a Theory?

The Model-Theoretical analysis as discussed so far contains many elements. As we have seen in Section 5.2, and as we have illustrated with the example of Newtonian mechanics, the analysis features a set-theoretical predicate, the models of the theory which form a class that is defined by the predicate, an internal characterisation of the structure in terms of first-order logic, data models, structural relations between the models of the theory and the data models, an intended interpretation of the structure, and isomorphisms between the theory's models and their target systems. Which of these elements define the entity that we refer to when we talk about a scientific theory?

There is a temptation to dismiss this question as a matter of linguistic convention because any subset of the above could be called "theory". Alas, things are not quite as simple. What gets included in the unit we call "theory" has a profound impact on how we think about the identity of theories, and whether two theories are identical is not just a matter of linguistic convention. Suppes does not discuss this issue explicitly, and he only gives us a few clues about what would define a theory. Among those clues are that he seems to adopt a notion of model that has no linguistic components (in the language of Chapter 2, his models seem to be bare structures); he only mentions intrinsic characterisations in passing; and he pays little attention to how the models of the theory are described.

Van Fraassen is more explicit that language should not be considered to be a part of a theory. In his major works on the nature of theories, van Fraassen begins his presentation of the Model-Theoretical View by introducing models as the objects that make a set of sentences true, but then stresses that the theory should be associated with the class of models and not the set of sentences that describes that class (1980, 41–44, 1989, 217–220, 2008, 309). He emphasises that we present a theory "by identifying a class of structures as its models" (1980, 44). He summarises Suppes' analysis approvingly as the view that "if the theory as such, is to be identified with anything at all – if theories are to be reified – then a theory should be identified with its class of models" (1989, 222), and he emphasises that "[t]he impact of Suppes's innovation is lost if models are defined, as in many standard logic texts, to be partially linguistic entities, each yoked to a particular syntax" (*ibid.*, 366). For this reason, "[t]he semantic view of theories makes language largely irrelevant to the subject" and the language of science "can largely be ignored" in discussions of the structure of theories (1989, 222). In the same vein he warns the reader that "[t]he main lesson of twentieth-century philosophy of science may well be this: no concept which is essentially language-dependent has any philosophical importance at all" (1980, 56).[19]

This suggests a definition of a theory that excludes linguistic elements: if τ is the theory's set-theoretical predicate, then the theory is C_τ. Or, in other words: a scientific theory *is* a class of models.[20]

In a recent paper, van Fraassen has qualified his views on language. He pointed out that "[t]he idea was not to banish language from scientific theorizing" and issued a "mea, mea culpa" for making statements about the role of language that lend themselves to misunderstandings (2014, 281). However, the contributors to the debate, proponents and critics alike, took his initial pronouncements at face value and, as a result, the anti-linguistic view has taken a firm hold in the debate in the over thirty years between the initial pronouncements and the qualifications. Explicit statements to the effect that theories are non-linguistic entities have been issued, among others, by French and Ladyman (1999, 114), Lloyd (1994, 15), Muller and van Fraassen (2008, 201), Suppe (1977, 221, 1989, 4, 82, 2000c, 105), and Thompson (1987, 87); Gaifman notes that the Model-Theoretical View is "based on the advice to ignore language and to use Bourbaki-style structures" (1984) and Earman notes that the view requires that "theories are to be construed in a way that makes them language-independent" (2005, 20). This consensus is reflected in the fact that the slogan that theories are extra-linguistic entities has also become a mantra in encyclopaedia entries and reviews of the subject matter (see, for instance, Da Costa and French 2003, 22; Lloyd 2006, 825; Suppe 2000b, 525, 1998, 344, 348). So it pays investigating the cogency of the view that theories are non-linguistic irrespective of van Fraassen's "mea culpa".

If one associates a theory with a set of models, it follows immediately that two theories are identical iff they have the same class of models.[21] The consequences of this view are radical. Since languages do not belong to the theory, statements that scientists formulate, and theorems that they prove, are not part of the theory either. To appreciate how radical this view is, consider the example of arithmetic. While arithmetic rarely is "the" theory that we are interested in, arithmetic is part of most empirical theories and it is used every time we count something. We can therefore use arithmetic to illustrate the problems that arise for a "no language" view. I choose arithmetic for the ease of presentation; the same point could be made with the formalism of theories from physics (which would, however, require a considerably more complex formal apparatus).

The *natural number structure* is defined as follows (Machover 1996, 149–150): the domain U of the structure is the set $\{0, 1, 2, ...\}$, R contains the identity relation, and O contains the operation that assigns to each number its immediate successor, the operation of addition, the operation of multiplication, and the operation of designating number zero. The structure can be described in different languages, and various propositions about the natural numbers can be formulated. Some are simple statements like "$5 + 7 = 12$"; some are general rules like $x + (y + z) = (x + y) + z$ for all numbers x, y, and z (the associative law); and some are high level claims like "there is no largest prime" or "every even integer greater than two can be expressed as the sum of two primes" (Goldbach's conjecture). Formulating such claims and proving them is the bread and butter of a working scientist. But none of this now counts as "theory". According to the Model-Theoretical View, the theory of arithmetic *is* the natural number structure, and linguistic descriptions of that structure, as well as claims about numbers formulated in a language, stand outside the theory. But a view of arithmetic according to which neither the associative law nor claims like Goldbach's conjecture are part of arithmetic would seem to be rather absurd.

An obvious response to this objection is that the Model-Theoretical View is not committed to identifying a theory *with* a family of structures. When commenting on the identity of theories, van Fraassen notes that "a theory may be identified *through* a class of models" (1995, 6, emphasis added). A person can be identified through her passport, her fingerprints, her retina, and her DNA, and yet she is not to identified with any of these. Likewise, a theory can be identified through a structure without being identical with it. This suggests a reading according to which a theory *consists* of both a language and a family of models, but only the family of structures figures in the theory's identity criteria. On such a reading, a theory is a tuple (L, C_τ), where L is a language and C_τ is the class of models of the theory, where L can, for instance, be a first-order description as envisiged in Suppes' intrinsic characterisation. Two theories are identical iff they have the same class of models: if L_1 and L_2 are different descriptions of C_τ, then the theories (L_1, C_τ) and (L_2, C_τ) are identical. This avoids the problems of a view that regards a theory as nothing more than a class of structures while at the same time not falling into the trap of having to say that one has a new theory every time the description of the structure changes.

While attractive at first sight, this position does not look plausible on closer inspection. Descriptions are not always interchangeable, and the choice of a description has a profound influence on the nature of the theory. Consider again the example of arithmetic. On the current approach, a theory is identified through a family of structures. This family is defined directly through a set-theoretical predicate and *not* through a first-order axiomatisation. So arithmetic is identified by specifying that its family of structures has exactly one element, namely the natural number structure. After this structure has been identified, it can be described and axiomatised in different ways. But these alternative descriptions contribute nothing to the identity of the theory, which only depends on the structure (which has been chosen prior to any axiomatisations being stated).

This is difficult to square with actual discussions of arithmetic. Let us begin by assuming that the kind of descriptions admitted into the theory are Suppes' intrinsic characterisations (i.e. axiomatic descriptions in a first-order logic) and let us have a look at different first-order axiomatisations of arithmetic. Machover (1996) offers a helpful discussion of different systems of arithmetic. He starts by defining what he calls "Baby Arithmetic", which is a simple system based on only four axioms (*ibid.*, 243).[22] Within Baby Arithmetic one can prove some basic truths of arithmetic like the addition and multiplication tables (the correct results of adding and multiplying numbers), but nothing more. The limitations of Baby Arithmetic are at least in part owed to the fact that it does not contain inequalities and comparative relations like *greater than*. This limitation is lifted in what Machover calls "Junior Arithmetic" (*ibid.*, 249), which contains all axioms of baby arithmetic plus three axioms dealing with equalities and comparisons. Junior Arithmetic allows for the formulation of statements like "there is no largest prime", which cannot be expressed in baby arithmetic. He then goes on to define a system of arithmetic based on nine axioms (*ibid.*, 256), and then finally formulates *Peano Arithmetic*. The essential difference between Peano Arithmetic and the other theories is that only Peano Arithmetic contains an induction scheme, roughly a scheme that allows the iterative attribution of properties to numbers (*ibid.*, 263).

On the above account, which identifies theories through a family of structures, we are forced to say that all these systems of arithmetic are the same theory, which is implausible. The theories have different expressive powers and they offer different instruments to those working with them. Is all this irrelevant to arithmetic? Machover at least does not think so, and he presents the different versions of arithmetic *as different theories*. The choice of a language, and the axioms that are formulated in the chosen language, have a profound impact on the nature of a theory, and not all theories that are based on the same family of models are identical.

A recurrent theme in discussions about theories are the limitations of first-order logic (see Section 1.4), and so one might be led to believe that these problems are an artefact of first-order logic that vanishes when we work in higher order logic. One could therefore consider relaxing Suppes' requirement that intrinsic characterisations are couched in first order logic and also admit intrinsic characterisations in second order logic. Unfortunately, this does not resolve the problem. Consider an example due to Corcoran (1980). In the context of a study of categoricity, Corcoran compares a standard second order formulation of Peano Arithmetic with a deviant system of arithmetic. He presents the axioms of the deviant theory and proves that they are consistent and categorical, their only model being the natural number structure. Let us call this system *Corcoran Arithmetic*. Second-order Peano Arithmetic is also categorical with its model also being the natural numbers. By the lights of the current version of the Model-Theoretical View, Corcoran Arithmetic and Peano Arithmetic are identical because they have the same classes of models. Yet the two systems of arithmetic turn out to be completely different. In Peano Arithmetic all the standard truths of arithmetic can be proven, for instance addition can be shown to be associative and commutative.[23] Not so in Corcoran Arithmetic, where these seemingly obvious truisms about numbers cannot be established because the sentences "$x+(y+z)=(x+y)+z$" and "$x+y=y+x$" do not follow from the axioms. But now we are committed to saying that a system of arithmetic in which the laws of associativity and commutativity are not provable is the same theory as a system in which they are. This is implausible. Associativity and commutativity are fundamental to our understanding of numbers and if two systems disagree on them, then they are two different theories.[24]

The lesson from this example generalises. Corcoran warns that we should not expect any categorical characterization of a structure to allow for the deduction of the obvious truths about this structure (1980, 204). Corcoran Arithmetic provides a vivid illustration of the general point that there is a "vast difference" between characterizing a structure and axiomatising a set of truths about it (*ibid.*). In fact, the connection between the two is weak, and a good (or even the best possible) characterisation of the structure can be a poor axiomatisation (*ibid.*). This goes right to the heart of the matter. The Model-Theoretical View has reduced the task of characterising a theory to characterising a set of structures. It thereby not only neglects the way in which we establish truths about these structures; it expressly bans such considerations. Andreas has seen this problem clearly when he observed that "the merits of the semantic account were purchased at a certain price, viz., that deductive reasoning in science dropped out of consideration" (2013, 1094). But a notion of a theory that has no place for formulating claims and running arguments is too narrow. The choice of a language is not a matter of indifference, and a theory's language must be taken into account when considering the questions of what a theory is.

The same conclusion has recently also been reached through a general discussion of theoretical equivalence. The discussion got started by Halvorson (2012), who argued that the Model-Theoretical View of theories returns the wrong verdict on when theories are equivalent: it regards theories as equivalent when they are not, and it distinguishes them when they are in fact equivalent. Halvorson's paper sparked a heated exchange on the issue, which is still ongoing.[25] While there is much that the protagonists in this exchange disagree about, the debate has reached a point of convergence: all participants, including van Fraassen, agree that language matters and should be part of a philosophical account of theories.[26] Varying Hudetz's (2019b) terminology slightly, we can say that a consensus has been reached that a liberal Model-Theoretical View is the right approach.[27] In Section 2.10 we encountered a liberal Received View, which is a version of the Received View that also incorporates models. But a view that sees a theory as a family of models with a language is indistinguishable from a view that sees a theory as a language with a family of models, and so the two liberal views are in fact the same position! In what follows I refer to this analysis of theories as the *Dual View*. The consensus then is that any reasonable analysis of a theory must be a Dual View. However, this consensus is programmatic. To say that an analysis of theories will have to integrate language and structures does not prejudge what precise form this integration takes and many options are left open. We articulate a particular version of the Dual View in Section 5.8.

5.6* Unintended Models

In their reviews of van Fraassen's (1980), Friedman (1982, 276–277), and Worrall (1984, 71) express bewilderment about the alleged superiority of the Model-Theoretical View because, they argue, a semantic and a syntactic approach are equivalent. Following van Fraassen, they take a theory to be a class of models. They then assume that this class of models is *elementary*, meaning that it contains precisely the models of some first-order theory. Worrall notes that "syntax and semantics go hand-in-hand" because "to every consistent set of first-order sentences there corresponds a non-empty set of models, and to every normal ('elementary') set of models there corresponds a consistent set of first-order sentences" (*ibid.*). Hence there is no difference between a syntactic and semantic approach and any purported superiority of the semantic approach must be illusionary.

Van Fraassen (1985, 301–302) responds that Friedman and Worrall make an illegitimate assumption when they presume that the class of models is elementary. He asks us to begin with a set M of structures that forms the theory. Assume that the structures in M contain the real numbers, which is plausible for a scientific theory. Then come up with a first-order axiomatisation A of M. Now consider the class N of all models of A. As we have seen in Section 2.9, the Löwenheim-Skolem theorem says that a set of first-order sentences that has a model of one infinite cardinality also has models of all other infinite cardinalities. Since M only incorporates the real numbers and no sets of other cardinalities, N is much larger than M. So A has *unintended models* (only the models in M are intended). In such a case A fails to offer a concise characterisation of M.[28]

Why should we regard the failure to give a concise characterisation of M as a problem? The idea seems to be that an investigation always starts with a family of models (the intended models), and then tries to offer a concise description of the models in that family. If it then turns out that the description also describes other models (which can be very different from the ones that were intended), then the description seems to miss essential features of the intended models. This is what happens in arithmetic. One starts with the natural numbers and looks for a set of axioms that pin down the structure of the natural numbers along with the essential operations of addition and multiplication. Implicit in the project of "pinning down" the natural numbers is the idea that *only* the natural numbers should satisfy the axioms, or, in other words, that the axioms exclusively describe the natural numbers. If it then turns out that a host of other structures (which are not isomorphic to the natural numbers) also satisfy the axioms, then it seems that we have failed in our attempt to pin down the numbers with the axioms.

But is this the only way of characterising an investigation? While this way of looking at things may be plausible in some cases, it does not seem to be plausible in others. Not all scientific theories are like arithmetic in that one starts with a well-circumscribed class of intended models, and then tries to find an adequate description of that class. Newtonian mechanics can be seen as providing a linguistic formulation of general principles, the most important of which is Newton's equation of motion, and one can then ask what a class of models that satisfy these principles looks like. From that point of view, there was no pre-fixed class of models, and whatever structure turns out to satisfy the axioms is a model of Newtonian mechanics. Finding these models is often a hard task, and occasionally models surface that no one would have thought were there. The discovery of chaos in classical mechanics is a case in point. Until Poincaré noticed the sensitive dependence of trajectories on initial conditions, no one would have expected chaotic models to exist.[29] Likewise, when Gödel discovered that Einstein's field equations have solutions with closed timelike curves that make time travel possible, this came as a shock because no one expected the field equations to have such solutions. So whatever the class of intended models of general relativity was when Einstein formulated the theory, Gödel spacetimes would not have been in that class. This, however, does not disqualify them as somehow "not belonging" to the general theory of relativity; it just shows that the theory has models that no one expected.[30]

In other cases, theories are specified axiomatically, and it is unclear whether they have any models at all. Axiomatic quantum field theory is a case in point. The axioms were formulated over 50 years ago by Wightman, and since then it has been a major challenge to construct models for these axioms (in fact, so much so that the discipline got its own name: "constructive quantum field theory"). The problem is unsolved to date. There are two-dimensional models, but so far there are no three-dimensional models.[31] The theory is given through its axioms and not by specifying a class of models, and it is in fact unknown how to specify that class.

Have we been misled by the example of the natural number structure? In the case of the natural numbers, a relatively straightforward description of the structure was easy to give. Using this as an intuition pump, we assumed that "specifying" a class of structures would always amount to explicit construction, and then we were struck by the observation that things do not work in this way in physics. However, we find there to be no explicit constructions in Suppes' external axiomatisation of classical mechanics in Section 5.2. The class is specified as whatever satisfies the set-theoretical predicate, and Newton's equation of motion was just one element of that predicate. In general, there is no way to specify a theory's models other than indirectly by saying that it is the class of structures that satisfies certain theoretical postulates. And these so-called "predicates" are in fact highly complex linguistic entities, which involve an entire deductive machinery (something cannot be said to satisfy Newton's equation if it is not a twice differentiable function, and to say this much requires calculus).[32]

So we have come full circle: the relevant structures are simply the things that satisfy a chosen description! Once this is acknowledged, the difference between the Model-Theoretical View and an axiomatic characterisation of a theory collapses. The axioms of the theory (for instance, Newton's equation of motion) have been packed into a unit that is referred to as a "predicate", and the theory is the set of structures that satisfies that "predicate". But this is just a roundabout way of saying that the models of the theory are exactly those structures that satisfy the axioms.[33]

Finally, the objection from unintended models vanishes when axioms are stated in higher order logic. The Löwenheim-Skolem theorem only holds in first-order logic, and in higher order logics one can characterise the models of a theory up to isomorphism.[34] As we have seen in Section 1.4, the Received View is in no way committed to first-order logic and hence can avoid the problem with unintended models by using higher order logic.

For all these reasons, the existence of unintended models does not provide an argument in support of the Model-Theoretical View.

5.7   Staying Quiet About Theories?

Let's pause and take stock. We have set out to answer the question "what is a scientific theory?". In response we have first developed a linguistic conception of theories (Part I), and then a structuralist conception of theories (this chapter). As we have seen, both conceptions run up against problems. The default reaction to this situation is to tackle these problems head on and to endeavour to come to an analysis of theories that is not open to these problems. But there is an alternative reaction. One can question the point of departure and argue that our initial question is one that we should not have asked in the first instance: by seeking an answer to the question "what is a scientific theory?" we have in fact got started on the wrong foot.

This is the stance taken by a school of thought that insists that we should take a "quietist" attitude to the nature of theories. In French's words, this means to "refrain from ontological speculation as to the nature of scientific theories and models and focus on their appropriate representation for various purposes within the philosophy of science" (French 2010, 231). So we should not aim to say what a theory *is*; this is a problem we should remain quiet about. Indeed, the discussion so far is guilty of confusing "the means of representation with that which is being represented" (*ibid.*). Philosophy of science should *represent* theories in our philosophical analyses in a way that is conducive to various purposes within the philosophy of science. On this approach, the Model-Theoretical View should not be taken to say that a family of structures *is* or *constitutes* a theory; it should be taken to say that such a family *represents* a theory.[35] As Da Costa and French put it, "on our view, theories – whatever they *are*, ontologically – are represented, from the extrinsic perspective, in terms of models or classes of models" (2003, 34). The central posit of the Model-Theoretical View is therefore not that theories are families of models, but instead that theories are best represented as families of models.[36] The same can be said of the linguistic view. Indeed, both views are representations of theories, and which representation we choose depends on the issue at stake. This does not force us to take a view on what theories *are*. Quietists insist that the problem of ontology is not one that the philosophy of science should address. The task for philosophy of science is to find the most useful way to represent theories.

A philosophical analysis of scientific theories then involves two notions of representation: the representation relation between a theory and the world, and the representation relation between our philosophical instruments (such as structures) and theories themselves. We turn to the representation relation between a theory and the world in Chapter 6. The question for the quietist is whether the structuralist representation of theories as a family of structures is an accurate or useful one. Quietists adopt a pluralist position when it comes to what they see as representational tools and emphasise that the approach "allows both linguistic and non-linguistic resources to play their appropriate role" (French 2010, 231), and potential critics are warned that quietists "should not be taken to be advocates of an unrealistically 'pure' structuralism, in the sense of either taking theories to be (with 'is' of identity) *just* structures, or, more moderately, presenting them as such" (*ibid.*, 235–236, original emphasis).[37] This means that quietists can help themselves to both structures and language when representing theories.

To see how this approach avoids the problems we have been wrestling with earlier, consider the problem of theory identity (Sections 1.6 and 5.5). From the quietist perspective, the question of theory identity has to be exorcised along with the question of ontology, with quietists insisting that we should simply remain silent about the issue. As French puts it: "in terms of what is the identity of theories given? Given the complexity and messiness of practice touched on above, my suggestion is to stop seeking answers to this question and drop the demand for identity conditions entirely" (2021, 5901). Instead, we should use the Model-Theoretical View "to develop a more nuanced approach to how we, philosophers of science, should represent, for our own purposes, the elements of practice that we are concerned with" (*ibid.*).

So the quietist insists that we should neither ask what theories are, nor when two theories are identical. If the aim is to eliminate items from our philosophical "problems list", then this is successful move. But those interested in these questions will be unmoved by these prohibitions. Whether, say, Heisenberg's matrix mechanics and Schrödinger's wave mechanics are identical theories is an important and legitimate scientific question in the field of quantum mechanics, and the question of theory identity plays an important role in current discussions in fundamental physics, most notably in superstring theory.[38] Many who are interested in these questions see them as important scientific problems in the foundations of their disciplines; they do not see them as questions that are superimposed by an exalted and ultimately dispensable philosophical agenda. Similarly, what theories are is not just a question in ontology that can be set aside without detriment to anybody except ontologists. Our analysis of theories has important implications for how we understand other issues in connection with theories, first and foremost scientific representation. Someone who sees a theory as a linguistic entity will see scientific representation as a problem for the philosophy of language; someone who sees a theory as a non-linguistic entity will analyse representation in terms of relations like isomorphism and similarity. Which way we go here matters to how we understand the relation between theories and their subject matter, and this is substantive problem in the philosophy of science and not an "introspective" problem about how we represent theories for ourselves. Finally, it remains unclear what the representation relation between our philosophical tools and (ontologically elusive) theories are. In the absence of an account of what it means for a set of philosophical tools to represent a theory to which we have no direct access, and in particular of what it means to represent a theory adequately, it is difficult to see how the claim that a certain set of tools represents a theory adequately can be evaluated or justified. For all these reasons, it remains doubtful that the problems we have encountered so far can be exorcised through the maxim of remaining quiet about them.

5.8 A Dual View

In Section 5.5, we have seen that a language is an important part of a theory. At the same time, we have seen in Sections 2.8 and 2.9 that considering the models of formal sentences is important in many ways. Furthermore, as we will see in Parts III and IV, models are best regarded as objects of sorts. So we need an understanding of theories that integrates both linguistic and non-linguistic elements. For this reason, a tenable analysis of a theory's formalism must be a *Dual View*, a view that sees a theory's formalism as constituted by linguistic and structural elements. This leaves open the question of how the marriage of language and structure works.

In a recent paper, Hudetz (2018) addresses the issue of the relation between structures and languages. He suggests that two languages are involved in specifying the formalism of a theory: an object-language and a meta-language (see Section 2.6 for a discussion of these languages).[39] The object-language is a formal language of *any* order. The selection of an object language is a pragmatic choice that depends on the aims and purposes of a theory (or the philosophical reconstruction of a theory). If the emphasis is on proving theorems, first-order logic enjoys the advantage of having a complete proof system, something which higher order logics lack. If the emphasis is on characterising structures, higher order logics have the benefit of being able to characterise models up to isomorphism because the Löwenheim-Skolem theorem does not hold in them. The object language is given a "Tarski style" formal semantics, providing an interpretation that assigns symbols of the language to parts of a structure. In fact, it is the formulation of such an interpretation that makes the language an object-language. Theorems are formulated and proofs are given in this language.

The meta-language can be any language we find convenient. It can be a formal language or an informal language like informal set-theory or "mathematical English".[40] As a meta-language it has no Tarski semantics and it talks about the structures and languages in an informal way. Meta-linguistic statements can be of different kinds. They can be statements that are directly concerned with the relevant structures ("the symbol '*r*' refers to relation ρ in the structure"); they can be descriptions of the constituents of structure ("the structures of mechanics contain a real line"); or they can refer to structures in an indirect way ("the structures of classical mechanics are the ones introduced in Goldstein's 1980 book").

These languages perform complementary functions in the specification of a formalism, which proceeds in two steps.[41] In the first step, the meta-language is used to specify the type of structures that occur in the theory, the object language of the theory, and the interpretation of the object language. These specifications provide the *background framework* of the theory. In Newtonian Mechanics, for instance, we first use the meta-language to specify the theory's vocabulary and its *framework signature*, which consists of auxiliary mathematical symbols like "$\mathbb{R}$" and "$+$", predicate symbols like "σ_p" and "σ_θ", and function symbols like "σ_f", "σ_l" and σ_m. The full language of the theory results from adding specific logical operations, quantifiers, and rules of inference to the signature.

The *framework structures* are specified as those structures that have as their domain the union of P, θ, M, L, and F with the operations f, l, m and that are such that the framework's signature symbols denote the relevant parts of the structure ("σ_P" denotes P, etc.). Axioms 1–4 of the axioms of mechanics that we have seen in Section 5.2 in fact specify the background structure.[42]

In the second step, the substantive laws of the theory are stated *in the object language*. These statements are true in some framework structures but not in others. The background structures in which these object language statements are true are the models of the theory. In the case of Newtonian mechanics, the substantive laws are (something like) Suppes' Axioms 5 and 6, and only the framework structures that satisfy these laws are models of Newtonian mechanics.

The Dual View implies that both object-language and meta-language are needed to specify a theory's models. Suppes' axioms are now seen as belonging to different languages: Axioms 1–4 are meta-language statements specifying features of the framework structures while Axioms 5 and 6 are object-language statements singling out the models of Newtonian mechanics among all framework structures.

An advantage of the Dual View is that mathematical techniques that do not belong to the theory under analysis can be packed into the background, and only the specific propositions of the theory are stated explicitly (Hudetz 2019b, 1147). Number theory and differential calculus, for instance, are not "proper" parts of Newtonian mechanics and so it would be odd to state them as part of a presentation of Newtonian mechanics. Yet they are crucial for the theory, which would not be able to operate without them. This issue is resolved by assuming that the background, which is specified through the meta-language, contains number theory and differential calculus. This ties in well with scientific practice, where theories are often defined by taking a background for granted and only stating those propositions explicitly that are an original part of the theory.

How is a theory individuated in the Dual View? The object language is clearly part of a theory and a change of the object language and the characterising formulas of a theory can lead to a different theory. Whether it does depends on one's criteria of theoretical equivalence. An advantage of the Dual View is that it can appeal to linguistic criteria like definitional equivalence, and thereby avoid the problems of a purely structural view. This resolves the issues we encountered in Section 5.5 because they give us the means to say that Corcoran Arithmetic and Peano Arithmetic are distinct theories. The more difficult question is whether the meta-language is part of the theory too. The meta-language plays an important role in specifying the theoretical background, the object-language of the theory, and the theory's structures. This might suggest that the meta-language should be included in the unit we call "the theory". There are, however, reasons not to do so. First, changing the object-language of a formalism changes the formalism. By contrast, changing the meta-language does not. For instance, whether we specify a formalism in German or in English has no bearing on the formalism. Second, the meta-language has no well-defined rules or definitions and is notoriously hard to pin down, and so it would be rather unclear *what* one would include in the theory in the first place. For these reasons, it seems better to see the meta-language as belonging to a scientific discipline, or field of research, to which the theory belongs. The analysis of the meta-language then belongs to a study of an entire discipline and not a particular theory.

This is the *broad outline* of a Dual View. As such it leaves many details unspecified, and to spell out what exactly the parts of the view are, how they hang together, and how they solve the problems of other accounts is a question for future research. But research can only be carried out fruitfully if there is a direction of travel, and I hope that this section has provided such a direction.

5.9 Conclusion

The Model-Theoretical View is to be credited with having brought models within the purview of an analysis of scientific theories. But the claim that a theory is nothing over and above a family of models is untenable, and theories are not extra-linguistic entities. Language is essential to both the specification of structures and to the formulation of the theory itself, and any workable account of the structure of a scientific theory will have to explain what roles models and languages play and how they are integrated with each other. We have seen an outline of how this could be done in Section 5.8, but there will be other options.

In all this, we must not forget that what we have discussed in this chapter is only the *formalism* of a theory. Nothing has been said so far about how this formalism acquires empirical content, and how it relates to the theory's subject matter. This is the task for the next chapter.

Before moving on, I would briefly like to mention alternative analyses of theories. So far, the space of discourse was determined by the Linguistic View (mostly in the guise of the Received View) and the Model-Theoretical View, and the discussion revolved around assessing the pros and cons of each. There are, however, other analyses of theories. In his review of accounts of scientific theories, Suppe explicitly discusses two of them in great length: the Weltanschauungen Analysis and the Sceptical Descriptive Analysis (Suppe 1977, 119–221). As its name suggests, the Weltanschauungen Analysis starts from the premise that science is practiced in concrete historical circumstances and is developed by human beings who hold beliefs and belong to societies. The analysis then focuses on the sort of worldview that is embedded in a theory, the conceptual schemes on which it is based, and the nature of the language in which it is expressed. This is an interesting and important approach, but it does not stand in competition, let alone conflict, with any of the views we have discussed so far. It is simply a different project that explores different dimensions of theories. We can discuss whether a theory is a linguistic or a non-linguistic entity and at the same time ask what kind of worldview it embodies in much the same way in which we can discuss whether the boat we see is made from wood or metal and at the same time ask what colour it has.

The Sceptical Descriptive Analysis is close to what Winther (2016, Sec. 4) calls the Pragmatic View. This view renounces rational reconstruction and aims to describe how theories are presented in the practice of science. The task of an analysis of theories is therefore to provide a historical and sociological description of how theories are presented by their users. We discussed rational reconstruction in Section 1.7, where it became clear that there is a tension between philosophical programmes that buy into rational reconstruction and ones that do not. So unlike with the Weltanschauungen Analysis, we cannot retreat to peaceful coexistence. However, as we have seen in Section 5.4, the Model-Theoretical View also has descriptive ambitions and it is advertised as providing an analysis that is in sync with scientific practice. We will turn to descriptive approaches in Chapter 12; Section 12.8 is dedicated specifically to the question of how the Model Theoretical View fares if interpreted as a descriptive account of theories.

Notes

1 However, as we noted in Chapter 1, the Received View is not committed to first-order logic.
2 See Suppes' (1957, 249–260, 2002, 30–35). Da Costa and Chuaqui (1988) provide a definition of a set-theoretical predicate in terms of Bourbaki's theory of structures.
3 See Suppes' (1967, 60–62, 2002, 5–6, 27–32). Suppes often used informal set theory, and some of his followers have seen this as the preferred method (see, for instance, Moulines and Sneed 1979, 65–66). Krause and Arenhart (2017, xii) note that this is not without its perils because informal set theory is inconsistent, and they offer a detailed discussion of various methods of formalisation.
4 Another example would be *group*; see Suppes' (1988).
5 A binary relation is reflexive if for element of $a \in U$, the relation applies to the element itself: $r(a, a)$. An example of a reflexive relation is equality on the set of numbers, because every number is equal to itself. A relation is transitive if for any three elements $a_1, a_2, a_3 \in U$ the following holds: if $r(a_1, a_2)$ and (a_2, a_3), then $r(a_1, a_3)$. A simple example of transitive relation is *taller than.*
6 Suppes (1957, 250–252) provides reasons for why axiomatisations are generally desirable.
7 The slogan is often attributed to Suppes (see, for instance, van Fraassen 1972, 309, 1987, 109). While it certainly encapsulates Suppes' view, I have not been able to trace an exact citation. The idea is that set-theory is mathematics while formal logic (which would be used in an intrinsic characterisation) belongs to meta-mathematics, the philosophical reflection on mathematics. These associations are rather unintuitive to modern readers; we return to this issue in Section 5.7. Alternative formulations of the same slogan are "set-theory rather than metamathematical methods" (Stegmüller 1979, 4) and "mathematics is for the philosophy of science, not meta-mathematics" (Muller 2011, 94). However, Lutz (2012, 88) points out that these slogans make sense only under the assumption that "meta-mathematics" is confined to first-order logic because higher order logics have no problem capturing mathematical practice.
8 Muller says that it is a "terminological howler" (2004, 716).
9 The foundational papers are McKinsey et al. (1953) and McKinsey and Suppes' (1953), and variants of these axioms can be found in Suppes' (1957, 291–305, 1968, 2002, Ch. 7). For alternative but related axiomatisations see Sneed's (1971, Ch. 6), Balzer et al. (1987, Ch. 3), and Krause and Arenhart's (2017, Ch. 5). The presentation here in

essence follows Suppes's (1957, 291–305) but uses different notation to ensure consistency with the formal conventions used in this book and omits the sixth axiom, which seems unnecessary and which is also not listed in Suppes' (1953). For an introductory discussion of these axioms, see Vorms' (2018, Sec. 3).

10 For a spirited criticism of these axioms, see Truesdell's (1984, 519–554).

11 Suppes does not use the term "target system". I use the term here as introduced in Chapter 1.

12 Suppes sometimes emphasises that the relation between models and data may not be direct and that it is instead mediated by a "hierarchy of models" (1962, 25, 31–34, 1967, 62–64, 2002, 7–8). The nature of this hierarchy, however, remains elusive in Suppes' writings. For a discussion of hierarchies of models, see Brading and Landry's (2006), Bueno's (1997, 2002), French and Ladyman's (1999), Giere's (2018), Harris' (1999), Kellen's (2019), Laymon's (1982), Leonelli's (2019), Teller's (2010), and Winsberg's (1999). The hierarchy might also be explained in terms of the notions introduced in Section 7.4.

13 Or, if one takes the recent downgrading of Pluto from a planet to a dwarf planet into account, there are in fact only eight.

14 Since isomorphic structures are often said to be the same, this could then be paraphrased as the target structure just being the structure of the model, which is probably what Suppes had in mind. However, this conflates concrete and abstract structures, and for reasons that will become clear in Section 6.5, it is important to keep them separate.

15 In fact, this option has been proposed independently by Ubbink at the same time when Suppes developed his view. Ubbink says that if one understands models as structures, then "a model represents an object or matter of fact in virtue of this structure; so an object is a model [. . .] of matters of fact if, and only if, their structures are isomorphic" (1960, 302).

16 Landry (2007) challenges the assumption that models, and their relations to their targets, must be framed and analysed within a single formal framework, set-theoretical or otherwise. Landry's point is well taken, but the question of which formal framework ought to underpin an analysis does not matter for our current question because we are not concerned with what framework exactly is chosen, but rather with how a formal framework is integrated in the wider structure of the theory.

17 See van Fraassen's (1970, 328–330, 1972, 311–318, 1980, 66–67, 1987, 109–110, 1989, 23).

18 Several commentators have pointed out that state spaces in fact are set-theoretical structures; see, for instance, Da Costa and French's (2000, 119, 2003, 22–23), Hudetz's (2019b, 1136) and Suppe's (1989, 4). Van Fraassen (1980, 43, 64–65, 1987, 109) explicitly acknowledges the Suppesian heritage of his approach and he repeatedly refers to the models of a theory as "structures" (1997, 516, 528–529, 1980, 43–45, 64–65, 1989, 224, 1995, 6); he also gives the standard definition of a structure (1989, 365). Unlike Suppes, who takes his cues from Tarski, van Fraassen refers to the work of Beth as his source of inspiration (1970, 1972). See Beth's (1949) for a brief a statement of his views.

19 These are not occasional slips, taken out of context. Statements to the same effect can also be found in van Fraassen's (1980, 64, 1991, 483, 1995, 5–6, 1997, 528–529, 2008, 309), and, writing with Muller, in their (2008, 201). In his early writings, van Fraassen included a minimal linguistic element in his characterisation of theories, namely what he called *elementary statements*. Statements of this kind specify that a certain physical magnitude has a certain value at certain time (1970, 328, 1972, 312). However, he comments that the views developed by Suppes and Beth "shed these linguistic trappings as they were developed" (1980, 67) and that his own view had evolved into a direction that had "not even a bow in the direction of syntactic description" (1989, 365).

20 Thomson-Jones (2006, 529) notes that this posit is central to the majority of variants of the Model-Theoretical View.

21 See, for instance, Lorenzano's (2013, 603), Moulines's (2002, 6), Muller's (2004, 713), and van Fraassen's (1995, 5–6).

22 To be precise, they are axiom schemes. Nothing in what follows depends on the difference between axioms and axiom schemes, and all of Suppes' so-called axioms are actually axiom schemes.

23 We have seen associativity above. Commutativity says that $x + y = y + x$ for all numbers x and y.

24 Dutilh Novaes sums up the discussion of different systems of arithmetic concisely when she says that "first-order Peano Arithmetic is non-categorical but deductively well-behaved, while second-order Peano Arithmetic is categorical but deductively ill-behaved" (2019, 2583).

25 A first reaction came from Glymour (2013) and Halvorson (2013) responded. The next reaction was from van Fraassen himself (2014). Lutz (2017) and Hudetz (2019b) find van Frassen's reply to Halvorson wanting. This initial exchange was followed by renewed debate about theoretical equivalence with contributions from Barrett (2020), Barrett and Halvorson (2016, 2017), Butterfield (2018), Coffey (2014), Dewar (2019), French (2017), Halvorson and Tsementzis (2017), Hudetz (2019a), Lutz (2017), Nguyen (2017), Nguyen et al. (2018), and Weatherall (2016a, 2016b, 2016c). For reviews of these debates, see Halvorson's (2016) and Weatherall's (2019a, 2019b). Halvorson's argument is based on the notion of definitional equivalence. For an introduction to this notion, see Rodgers' (1971). Some of these contributions work within the framework of category theory. Marquis' (2015) and Halvorson's (2019) provide elementary introductions to category theory. Landry's (2011) offers a discussion of philosophical implications of category theory, and her (2017) offers an overview of the uses of category theory in philosophy. Early uses of category theory to analyse scientific theories are Mormann's (1975) and Ibarra and Mormann's (2006). Relatedly, but independently from the debate about Halvorson's paper, Le Bihan (2012, 252–253) argues that we should subscribe to a "Modest Semantic View" according to which a class of models can only ever offer a partial definition of theories.

26 A variant of this debate focuses on the empirical equivalence of the theories rather on their "full" theoretical equivalence. Building on arguments by Boyd and Gardner, van Fraassen (2019, Sec. 4.3) argues that the Received View is unable to articulate a workable definition of empirical equivalence between theories and then claims that the Model-Theoretical View offers an elegant solution to this problem. However, Lutz (2014a) showed that van Fraassen's notion of empirical adequacy, based on embeddability of data models, can be captured in the Received View, and that the Model-Theoretical View enjoys no advantage over the Received View when it comes to analysing empirical equivalence (2014b, 2021).

27 Hudetz uses the term "liberal semantic view". This view is variously referred to as "semantic+L" (Halvorson 2013, 475), "neo-Received View" (van Fraassen 2014, 276), and a "weak version" of the Model-Theoretical View (Hendry and Psillos 2007, 137), and a view based on "labelled structures" (Lutz 2017, 330).

28 This argument is also discussed in Suppe's (2000c, 104, 2000a, 9–10) and Lloyd's (2006, 823–824).

29 For discussion of the history of the discovery of chaos, see Parker's (1998).

30 Gödel spacetimes are not an isolated case. Advanced potentials in electrodynamics and Dirac's negative energy solutions, among others, raise the same issue.

31 For a discussion of axiomatic quantum field theory, see Summers' (2016).

32 Azzouni (2014, 2997–2998) mentions a further problem. The Model-Theoretical View assumes that its language is strong enough to fix reference to only the intended models.

Azzouni argues that it is not clear that the view actually has these resources and so it is open to the problem of unintended models in the same way in which the Received View is.

33 Furthermore, notice that if all we know about the models in C_N (the class of models of Newtonian Mechanics) is that they satisfy Newton's equation and a few other constraints, then the notion of an intended model is a hollow one. In fact, it is then not even clear what an unintended model would be because by definition all models that satisfy the constraints are intended models of the theory.

34 See, for instance, Hudetz's (2019b, 1147) and Lutz's (2014c, 1478–1479).

35 See also Bueno and French's (2011, 890, 2018, 70), Bueno et al. (2002, 498), Da Costa and French's (2003, 25, 30, 33–34), French's (2000, 105), and French and Saatsi's (2006, 552). The position is further developed in French's (2010, 2017, 2020), French and Vickers' (2011), and Vickers's (2014). These discussions are couched in terms of partial structures, which we discuss in Section 6.7. It is, however, immaterial to the current question whether one analyses theories in terms of "ordinary" or partial structures.

36 French and Saatsi emphasise that theories can also be represented as a set of sentences, as in Suppes' intrinsic characterisation (2006, 553).

37 See also Da Costa et al. (2010) and Krause and Bueno's (2007).

38 For a discussion see QM, for instance, Hendry's (1999) and Muller's (1997a, 1997b), and for fundamental physics, see, for instance, Butterfield's (2018). Notice, however, that questions of theory identity not only arise in modern physics. Indeed, the same question arises in connection with different formulations of classical mechanics; see North's (2009), Curiel's (2014), and Barrett's (2015).

39 There is an exegetical question whether Suppes' distinction between extrinsic and intrinsic characterisation is in fact the distinction between meta-language and object-language. His insistence on extrinsic characterisations being couched in informal languages and serving the purpose of identifying classes of structures speaks in favour of this interpretation. His emphasis on Tarski semantics, the view that structures "satisfy" axioms in the extrinsic language, and the fact that his axioms of mechanics look like straightforward object language statements speak against this interpretation.

40 The term "mathematical English" is used in Thompson's (1987, 27) and van Fraassen's (1972, 304, 310).

41 These steps bear some similarity to the specification of a theory's potential and actual models in the Munich Structuralist programme, which we discuss in Chapter 7. The main difference is that languages are not part of the Munich Structuralist's scheme.

42 There are numerous ways of setting up the framework of Newtonian mechanics (or indeed the framework of any theory that is analysed), and the details raise important foundational questions. This brief sketch only intends to illustrate what kind of specifications occur in this process; it is not meant to prejudge what the right analysis of Newtonian Mechanics is.

References

Andreas, H. 2013. Deductive Reasoning in the Structuralist Approach. *Studia Logica* 5: 1093–1113.

Azzouni, J. 2014. A New Characterization of Scientific Theories. *Synthese* 191: 2993–3008.

Balzer, W., C.-U. Moulines, and J. D. Sneed 1987. *An Architectonic for Science: The Structuralist Program*. Dordrecht: Reidel Publishing Company.

Barrett, T. W. 2015. On the Structure of Classical Mechanics. *The British Journal for the Philosophy of Science* 66: 801–828.

Barrett, T. W. 2020. Structure and Equivalence. *Philosophy of Science* 87: 1184–1196.

Barrett, T. W. and H. Halvorson 2016. Morita Equivalence. *The Review of Symbolic Logic* 9: 556–582.

Barrett, T. W. and H. Halvorson 2017. From Geometry to Conceptual Relativity. *Erkenntnis* 82: 1043–1063.

Beatty, J. 1980. Optimal-Design Models and the Strategy of Model Building in Evolutionary Biology. *Philosophy of Science* 47: 532–561.

Beatty, J. 1981. What's Wrong with the Received View of Evolutionary Theory? In P. Asquith and R. Giere (eds.), *Philosophy of Science (Proceedings)* (Vol. 2). East Lansing: Philosophy of Science Association, pp. 397–426.

Beatty, J. 1987. On Behalf of the Semantic View. *Biology and Philosophy* 2: 17–23.

Beth, E. W. 1949. Towards an up-to-Date Philosophy of the Natural Sciences. *Methodos* 1: 178–185.

Brading, K. and E. Landry 2006. Scientific Structuralism: Presentation and Representation. *Philosophy of Science* 73: 571–581.

Bueno, O. 1997. Empirical Adequacy: A Partial Structure Approach. *Studies in the History and Philosophy of Science* 28: 585–610.

Bueno, O. and S. French 2011. How Theories Represent. *The British Journal for the Philosophy of Science* 62: 857–894.

Bueno, O. and S. French 2018. *Applying Mathematics: Immersion, Inference, Interpretation.* New York: Oxford University Press.

Bueno, O., S. French, and J. Ladyman 2002. On Representing the Relationship between the Mathematical and the Empirical. *Philosophy of Science* 69: 497–518.

Butterfield, J. 2018. On Dualities and Equivalences between Physical Theories. *arXiv:1806.01505.* https://arxiv.org/pdf/1806.01505.pdf.

Coffey, K. 2014. Theoretical Equivalence as Interpretative Equivalence. *The British Journal for the Philosophy of Science* 65: 821–844.

Corcoran, J. 1980. Categoricity. *History and Philosophy of Logic* 1: 187–207.

Curiel, E. 2014. Classical Mechanics Is Lagrangian; It Is Not Hamiltonian. *The British Journal for the Philosophy of Science* 65: 269–321.

Da Costa, N. C. A. and R. Chuaqui 1988. On Suppes' Set Theoretical Predicates. *Erkenntnis* 29: 95–112.

Da Costa, N. C. A. and S. French 2000. Models, Theories, and Structures: Thirty Years On. *Philosophy of Science (Supplement)* 67: 116–127.

Da Costa, N. C. A. and S. French 2003. *Science and Partial Truth: A Unitary Approach to Models and Scientific Reasoning.* Oxford: Oxford University Press.

Da Costa, N. C. A., D. Krause, and O. Bueno 2010. Issues in the Foundations of Science, I: Languages, Struct rues, and Models. *Manuscrito* 33: 123–141.

Dewar, N. 2019. Ramsey Equivalence. *Erkenntnis* 84: 77–99.

Dutilh Novaes, C. 2019. Axiomatizations of Arithmetic and the First-Order/Second-Order Divide. *Synthese* 196: 2583–2597.

Earman, J. 2005. The Emperor's New Theory: The Semantic/Models View of Theories. *Draft.*

French, S. 2000. The Reasonable Effectiveness of Mathematics: Partial Structures and the Application of Group Theory to Physics. *Synthese* 125: 103–120.

French, S. 2010. Keeping Quiet on the Ontology of Models. *Synthese* 172.

French, S. 2020. *There Are No Such Things as Theories.* Oxford: Oxford University Press.

French, S. 2021. Identity Conditions, Idealisations and Isomorphisms: A Defence of the Semantic Approach. *Synthese* 198: 5897–5917. https://doi.org/10.1007/s11229-017-1564-z.

French, S. and J. Ladyman 1999. Reinflating the Semantic Approach. *International Studies in the Philosophy of Science* 13: 103–121.

French, S. and J. Saatsi 2006. Realism About Structure: The Semantic View and Nonlinguistic Representations. *Philosophy of Science* 73: 548–559.

French, S. and P. Vickers 2011. Are There No Things That Are Scientific Theories? *The British Journal for the Philosophy of Science* 62: 771–804.

Friedman, M. 1982. Review of 'the Scientific Image'. *The Journal of Philosophy* 79: 274–283.

Gaifman, H. 1984. Why Language? In W. Balzer (ed.), *Reduction in Science*. Dordrecht: Reidel, pp. 319–330.

Giere, R. N. 2018. Models of Experiments. In I. Peschard and B. C. van Fraassen (eds.), *The Experimental Side of Modeling*. Minnesota: University of Minnesota Press, pp. 59–70.

Glymour, C. 2013. Equivalence and the Semantic View of Theories. *Philosophy of Science* 80: 286–297.

Halvorson, H. 2012. What Scientific Theories Could Not Be. *Philosophy of Science* 79: 183–206.

Halvorson, H. 2013. The Semantic View, If Plausible, Is Syntactic. *Philosophy of Science* 80: 475–478.

Halvorson, H. 2016. Scientific Theories. In P. Humphreys (ed.), *The Oxford Handbook of Philosophy of Science*. Oxford: Oxford University Press, pp. 585–608.

Halvorson, H. 2019. *The Logic in Philosophy of Science*. Cambridge: Cambridge University Press, pp. 402–429.

Halvorson, H. and D. Tsementzis 2017. Categories of Scientific Theories. In E. Landry (ed.), *Categories for the Working Philosopher*. Oxford: Oxford University Press, pp. 402–429.

Harris, T. 1999. A Hierarchy of Models and Electron Microscopy. In L. Magnani, N. Nersessian, and P. Thagard (eds.), *Model-Based Reasoning in Scientific Discovery*. New York: Kluwer Academic; Plenum Publishers, pp. 139–148.

Hendry, R. F. 1999. Theories and Models: The Interactive View. In R. Patan and I. Neilsan (eds.), *Visual Representations and Interpretations*. London: Springer, pp. 121–130.

Hendry, R. F. and S. Psillos 2007. How to Do Things with Theories: An Interactive View of Language and Models in Science. In J. Brzezinski, A. Klawiter, T. A. F. Kuipers, K. Lastowski, K. Paprzycka, and P. Przybysz (eds.), *The Courage of Doing Philosophy: Essays Dedicated to Lezek Nowak*. Amsterdam and New York: Rodopi, pp. 123–157.

Hudetz, L. 2018. *How to Present the Formalism of a Theory?* Manuscript.

Hudetz, L. 2019a. Definable Categorical Equivalence. *Philosophy of Science* 86: 47–75.

Hudetz, L. 2019b. The Semantic View of Theories and Higher-Order Languages. *Synthese* 196: 1131–1149.

Ibarra, A. and T. Mormann 2006. Scientific Theories as Intervening Representations. *Theoria* 21: 21–38.

Kellen, D. 2019. A Model Hierarchy for Psychological Science. *Computational Brain & Behavior* 2: 160–165. https://psyarxiv.com/yk45u/.

Krause, D. and J. R. B. Arenhart 2017. *The Logical Foundations of Scientific Theories. Languages, Structures, and Models*. New York and London: Routledge.

Krause, D. and O. Bueno 2007. Scientific Theories, Models, and the Semantic Approach. *Principia* 11: 187–201.

Landry, E. 2007. Shared Structure Need Not Be Shared Set-Structure. *Synthese* 158: 1–17.

Landry, E. 2011. How to Be a Structuralist All the Way Down. *Synthese* 179: 435–454.

Landry, E. (ed.) 2017. *Categories for the Working Philosopher*. Oxford: Oxford University Press.

Laymon, R. 1982. Scientific Realism and the Hierarchical Counterfactual Path from Data to Theory. *Proceedings of the Biennial Meeting of the Philosophy of Science Association*. East Lansing, MI: Philosophy of Science Association, (Vol. 1), pp. 107–121.

Le Bihan, S. 2012. Defending the Semantic View: What It Takes. *European Journal for Philosophy of Science* 2: 249–274.

Leonelli, S. 2019. What Distinguishes Data from Models? *European Journal for Philosophy of Science* 9: Article 22.

Lloyd, E. A. 1984. A Semantic Approach to the Structure of Population Genetics. *Philosophy of Science* 51: 242–264.

Lloyd, E. A. 1989. A Structural Approach to Defining Units of Selection. *Philosophy of Science* 56: 395–418.

Lloyd, E. A. 1994. *The Structure and Confirmation of Evolutionary Theory*. Princeton: Princeton University Press.

Lloyd, E. A. 2006. Theories. In S. Sarkar and J. Pfeifer (eds.), *The Philosophy of Science: An Encyclopedia*. New York: Routledge, pp. 822–828.

Lorenzano, P. 2013. The Semantic Conception and the Structuralist View of Theories: A Critique of Suppe's Criticisms. *Studies in History and Philosophy of Science* 44: 600–607.

Lutz, S. 2012. On a Straw Man in the Philosophy of Science: A Defence of the Received View. *HOPOS* 2: 77–120.

Lutz, S. 2014a. Empirical Adequacy in the Received View. *Philosophy of Science* 81: 1171–1183.

Lutz, S. 2014b. Generalizing Empirical Adequacy I: Multiplicity and Approximation. *Synthese* 191: 3195–3225.

Lutz, S. 2014c. What's Right with the Syntactic Approach to Theories and Models? *Erkenntnis* 79: 1475–1492.

Lutz, S. 2017. What Was the Syntax-Semantics Debate in the Philosophy of Science About? *Philosophy and Phenomenological Research* 95: 319–352.

Lutz, S. 2021. Generalizing Empirical Adequacy II: Partial Structures. *Synthese* 198: 1351–1380. https://doi.org/10.1007/s11229-019-02121-z.

Machover, M. 1996. *Set Theory, Logic and Their Limitations*. Cambridge: Cambridge University Press.

Marquis, J.-P. 2015. Category Theory. In E. N. Zalta (ed.), *The Stanford Encyclopedia of Philosophy*. https://plato.stanford.edu/archives/win2015/entries/category-theory/.

McKinsey, J. C. C., A. Sugar, and P. Suppes 1953. Axiomatic Foundations of Classical Particle Mechanics. *Journal of Rational Mechanics and Analysis* 2: 253–272.

McKinsey, J. C. C. and P. Suppes 1953. Transformations of Systems of Classical Particle Mechanics. *Journal of Rational Mechanics and Analysis* 2: 273–289.

Mormann, T. 1975. Topologische Aspekte Strukturalistischer Rekonstruktionen. *Erkenntnis* 23: 319–359.

Moulines, C.-U. 2002. Introduction: Structuralism as a Program for Modelling Theoretical Science. *Synthese* 130: 1–11.

Moulines, C.-U. and J. D. Sneed 1979. Suppe's Philosophy of Physics. In R. Bogdan (ed.), *Patrick Suppes*. Dordrecht: Reidel, pp. 59–91.

Muller, F. A. 1997a. The Equivalence Myth of Quantum Mechanics – Part I. *Studies in History and Philosophy of Modern Physics* 28: 35–61.

Muller, F. A. 1997b. The Equivalence Myth of Quantum Mechanics – Part II. *Studies in History and Philosophy of Modern Physics* 28: 219–241.

Muller, F. A. 2004. Review of Patrick Suppes' 'Representation and Invariance in Scientific Structures'. *Studies in History and Philosophy of Modern Physics* 35: 713–720.

Muller, F. A. 2011. Reflections on the Revolution at Stanford. *Synthese* 183: 87–114.

Muller, F. A. and B. C. van Fraassen 2008. How to Talk About Unobservables. *Analysis* 68: 197–205.

Nguyen, J. 2017. Scientific Representation and Theoretical Equivalence. *Philosophy of Science* 84: 982–995.

Nguyen, J., N. Teh, and L. Wells 2018. Why Surplus Structure Is Not Superfluous. *The British Journal for the Philosophy of Science* 71: 665–695.

North, J. 2009. The 'Structure' of Physics: A Case Study. *The Journal of Philosophy* 106: 57–88.

Parker, M. W. 1998. Did Poincaré Really Discover Chaos? *Studies in History and Philosophy of Modern Physics* 29: 575–588.

Rodgers, R. L. 1971. *Mathematical Logic and Formalized Theories*. Amsterdam: North Holland.

Sneed, J. D. 1971. *The Logical Structure of Mathematical Physics* (2nd revised ed.). Dordrecht: Reidel.

Stegmüller, W. 1979. *The Structuralist View of Theories: A Possible Analogue of the Bourbaki Programme in Physical Science*. New York and Berlin: Springer.

Summers, S. J. 2016. A Perspective on Constructive Quantum Field Theory. *arXiv:1203.3991*. https://arxiv.org/abs/1203.3991.

Suppe, F. 1977. The Search for Philosophical Understanding of Scientific Theories. In F. Suppe (ed.), *The Structure of Scientific Theories*. Urbana and Chicago: University of Illinois Press, pp. 3–241.

Suppe, F. 1989. *The Semantic Conception of Theories and Scientific Realism*. Urbana and Chicago: University of Illinois Press.

Suppe, F. 1998. Theories, Scientific. In E. Craig (ed.), *Routledge Encyclopedia of Philosophy* (Vol. 2008). London: Routledge, pp. 344–355.

Suppe, F. 2000a. Axiomatization. In W. H. Newton-Smith (ed.), *A Companion to the Philosophy of Science*. Oxford: Wiley-Blackwell, pp. 9–11.

Suppe, F. 2000b. Theory Identity. In W. H. Newton-Smith (ed.), *A Companion to the Philosophy of Science*. Oxford: Wiley-Blackwell, pp. 525–527.

Suppe, F. 2000c. Understanding Scientific Theories: An Assessment of Developments, 1969–1998. *Philosophy of Science* 67: 102–115.

Suppes, P. 1957. *Introduction to Logic*. New York: D. Van Nostrand Company.

Suppes, P. 1960. A Comparison of the Meaning and Uses of Models in Mathematics and the Empirical Sciences. In P. Suppes (ed.), *Studies in the Methodology and Foundations of Science: Selected Papers from 1951 to 1969*. Dordrecht: Reidel, 1969, pp. 10–23.

Suppes, P. 1962. Models of Data. In P. Suppes (ed.), *Studies in the Methodology and Foundations of Science: Selected Papers from 1951 to 1969*. Dordrecht: Dordrecht, 1969, pp. 24–35.

Suppes, P. 1967. What Is a Scientific Theory. In S. Morgenbesser (ed.), *Philosophy of Science Today*. New York: Basic Books, pp. 66–67.

Suppes, P. 1968. The Desirability of Formalization in Science. *The Journal of Philosophy* 65: 651–664.

Suppes, P. 1988. Representation Theory and the Analysis of Structure. *Philosophia Naturalis* 25: 254–268.

Suppes, P. 2002. *Representation and Invariance of Scientific Structures*. Stanford: CSLI Publications.

Teller, P. 2010. 'Saving the Phenomena' Today. *Philosophy of Science* 77: 815–826.

Thompson, P. 1983. The Structure of Evolutionary Theory: A Semantic Approach. *Studies in History and Philosophy of Science* 14: 215–229.

Thompson, P. 1987. A Defence of the Semantic Conception of Evolutionary Theory. *Biology and Philosophy* 2: 26–32.

Thompson, P. 1988. Explanation in the Semantic Conception of Theory Structure. *Philosophy of Science (Proceedings)* 2: 286–296.

Thompson, P. 1989. *The Structure of Biological Theories*. Albany: State University of New York Press.

Thomson-Jones, M. 2006. Models and the Semantic View. *Philosophy of Science* 73: 524–535.

Truesdell, C. 1984. Suppesian Stews. In C. Truesdell (ed.), *An Idiot's Fugitive Essays on Science: Methods, Criticism, Training, Circumstances*. New York and Berlin: Springer, pp. 503–579.

Ubbink, J. B. 1960. Model, Description and Knowledge. *Synthese* 12: 302–319.

van Fraassen, B. C. 1970. On the Extension of Beth's Semantics of Physical Theories. *Philosophy of Science* 37: 325–339.

van Fraassen, B. C. 1972. A Formal Approach to the Philosophy of Science. In R. G. Colodny (ed.), *Paradigms and Paradoxes*. Pittsburgh: University of Pittsburgh Press, pp. 303–366.

van Fraassen, B. C. 1980. *The Scientific Image*. Oxford: Oxford University Press.

van Fraassen, B. C. 1985. Empiricism in the Philosophy of Science. In P. M. Churchland and C. A. Hooker (eds.), *Images of Science*. Chicago: Chicago University Press, pp. 245–308.

van Fraassen, B. C. 1987. The Semantic Approach to Scientific Theories. In N. Nersessian (ed.), *The Process of Science. Contemporary Philosophical Approaches to Understanding Scientific Practice*. Dordrecht: Martinus Nijhoff, pp. 105–124.

van Fraassen, B. C. 1989. *Laws and Symmetry*. Oxford: Clarendon Press.

van Fraassen, B. C. 1991. *Quantum Mechanics*. Oxford: Clarendon Press.

van Fraassen, B. C. 1995. A Philosophical Approach to Foundations of Science. *Foundations of Science* 1: 5–9.

van Fraassen, B. C. 1997. Structure and Perspective: Philosophical Perplexity and Paradox. In M. L. Dalla Chiara (ed.), *Logic and Scientific Methods*. Dordrecht: Kluwer, pp. 511–530.

van Fraassen, B. C. 2008. *Scientific Representation: Paradoxes of Perspective*. Oxford: Oxford University Press.

van Fraassen, B. C. 2014. One or Two Gentle Remarks About Hans Halvorson's Critque of the Semantic View. *Philosophy of Science* 81: 276–283.

van Fraassen, B. C. 2019. *The Semantic Approach, after 50 Years*. Manuscript.

Vickers, P. 2014. Scientific Theory Eliminativism. *Erkenntnis* 79: 111–126.

Vorms, M. 2018. Theories and Models. In A. Barberousse, D. Bonnay, and M. Cozic (eds.), *The Philosophy of Science*. Oxford: Oxford University Press, pp. 171–224.

Weatherall, J. O. 2016a. Are Newtonian Gravitation and Geometrized Newtonian Gravitation Theoretically Equivalent? *Erkenntnis* 81: 1073–1091.

Weatherall, J. O. 2016b. Categories and the Foundations of Classical Field Theories. *arXiv:1505.07084*. https://arxiv.org/abs/1505.07084.

Weatherall, J. O. 2016c. Understanding Gauge. *Philosophy of Science* 83: 1039–1049.

Weatherall, J. O. 2019a. Part 1: Theoretical Equivalence in Physics. *Philosophy Compass* 14(5): e12592: 1–11.

Weatherall, J. O. 2019b. Part 2: Theoretical Equivalence in Physics. *Philosophy Compass* 14(5): e12591: 1–12.

Winsberg, E. 1999. The Hierarchy of Models in Simulation. In L. Magnani, N. Nersessian, and P. Thagard (eds.), *Model-Based Reasoning in Scientific Discovery*. New York: Kluwer Academic; Plenum Publishers, pp. 255–269.

Winther, R. G. 2016. The Structure of Scientific Theories. In E. N. Zalta (ed.), *The Stanford Encyclopedia of Philosophy*. https://plato.stanford.edu/archives/win2016/entries/structure-scientific-theories/.

Worrall, J. 1984. An Unreal Image. *The British Journal for the Philosophy of Science* 34: 65–80.

6

REPRESENTING WITH STRUCTURES

6.1 Introduction

In Section 5.2 we have seen that two accounts of representation emerge from Suppes' discussion of theories: the Data Matching Account and the Morphism Account. We then put these accounts aside and focused on the formalism of a theory. It is now time to return to the question of how models, understood as set-theoretical structures, represent their respective target systems. The task for this chapter is to develop and evaluate these two accounts of representation.

Before we can evaluate accounts of representation, we need to get clear on what we expect from them. To this end, we begin by formulating problems that an account of representation must answer, and we state conditions of adequacy that answers must meet (Section 6.2). We then examine the Data Matching Account and discuss the most important objection against it, the so-called loss of reality objection (Section 6.3). This calls for a reflection on the nature of a model's target. We introduce Bogen and Woodward's distinction between data and phenomena, and we conclude that models represent phenomena in Bogen and Woodward's sense (Section 6.4). We then turn to the Morphism Account and examine its most important presupposition, namely that a target system must have a structure (Section 6.5). We continue with a discussion of how the account fares with the questions and conditions that we introduced previously (Section 6.6). The so-called Partial Structures Programme offers an alternative formulation of the structuralist programme. We introduce the approach and analyse what notion of representation it offers (Section 6.7*). We end by taking stock and ask whether the claim that the Model-Theoretical View offers a better account of the model-world relation than the Received View holds water (Section 6.8).

DOI: 10.4324/9781003285106-9

6.2 Questions Concerning Scientific Representation

Before we can assess an account of representation, we need to know what questions such an account is expected to answer and what criteria answers to these questions must satisfy.[1] This groundwork is necessary because even though the issue of scientific representation has generated a sizeable literature, there seems to be little agreement on what the problem of scientific representation is. In fact, there does not seem to be anything like *the* problem of scientific representation. What we find is a cluster of different yet interrelated problems. The result of our discussion will be five *problems* that every account of scientific representation will have to answer, and five *conditions* of adequacy that these answers have to satisfy. Figure 6.1 at the end of this section provides a visual summary of all the problems and conditions. These problems and conditions will also guide our discussion of alternative accounts of representation in Chapters 8 and 9.

In the terminology of Chapter 2, the models we are looking at in this chapter are representational models. Such models represent a selected part or aspect of the world: the model's *target system*. The central question therefore is: in virtue of what is a model a representation of something else? To appreciate the thrust of the question let us first consider the analogous problem in pictorial representation, which is known as the *enigma of depiction* (Schier 1986, 1). When seeing, say, Raphael's *The School of Athens* we immediately recognise that it represents a group of ancient philosophers embroiled in thought and discussion. Why is this? Per se the painting is a plane surface covered with pigments. How can an arrangement of pigments on a surface, a welter of lines and dots, represent something beyond itself? The analogue question arises for models. Per se, the models of the Model-Theoretical View are set-theoretical structures. What turns structures into representations of something beyond themselves?[2] To probe potential answers it is helpful to give the question a precise form and formulate it in terms of necessary and sufficient conditions. The question then is: what fills the blank in the scheme "M is a scientific representation of T iff ___", where "M" stands for the model doing the representing and T for the target system? This is the *Scientific Representation Problem*.

A bust of Socrates represents Socrates, but Socrates does not represent the bust. Likewise, a scientific model represents its target, but its target does not represent the model (at least not in general). Hence, as Goodman (1976, 5) points out, representation is directed. An account of representation must provide an analysis of representation that is directed and, ideally, identify the root of this directionality. This is the *Directionality Condition*, which is our first condition of adequacy.

Models represent their targets in a way that allows scientists to generate hypotheses about the target from the model. In fact, many investigations are carried out on models rather than on reality itself, and this is done with the aim of discovering features of the things that the models stand for. A study of the Newtonian model of the solar system reveals important properties of the paths of planets (for instance, that they are ellipses). This feature distinguishes scientific representations from lexicographical representations. Studying the internal constitution of a word does not reveal anything about the object the word stands for. Investigating the expression "solar system", for instance, does not reveal anything about the motion of heavenly bodies. Reasoning about a model, by contrast, yields conclusions about its target. So the blank in the Scientific Representation Problem must be filled in a way that explains how this is possible. This gives us the second condition of adequacy: the *Surrogative Reasoning Condition*. The term "surrogative reasoning" is owed to the fact that the model serves as a surrogate when reasoning about the target.[3]

There is a question whether the Surrogative Reasoning Condition is too permissive because it is likely to be satisfied also by representations that are not, or at least not *prima facie*, scientific representations. Maps, plans, diagrams, photographs, drawings, charts, architectural models, and paper mock-ups all provide information about their subject matter and hence allow for some sort of surrogative reasoning. This raises the question of how, if at all, scientific representations differ from other kinds of representations that perform a cognitive function. Callender and Cohen (2006, 68–69) note that this is a semantic version of Popper's demarcation problem, and so we refer to it as the *Representational Demarcation Problem*. They voice scepticism about there being a solution to this problem and argue that the line between scientific and non-scientific representations is circumstantial (*ibid.*, 83), meaning that scientific representations are simply ones that are used in context that is considered scientific or ones that are developed by someone who is a scientist. A sceptical stance akin to Callender and Cohens' is implicit in all approaches that analyse scientific representation alongside other kinds of representations, for instance by drawing analogies between scientific and pictorial representation.[4]

Those who deny that there is an essential difference between scientific and other kinds of representation can follow Contessa (2007) and broaden the scope of the investigation. Instead of analysing scientific representation, they can examine the wider category of *epistemic representation*. This category contains scientific representations alongside other forms of representation that underwrite surrogative reasoning. The Scientific Representation Problem then turns into the *Epistemic Representation Problem*, which amounts to filling the blank in "*M* is an epistemic representation of *T* iff ___ ".

Not all representations are of the same kind. An Egyptian mural, a perspectival drawing, a pointillist painting, an architectural plan, and a nautical map represent their respective targets in different ways. A plurality of representational styles is not a prerogative of visual representations. Models are not all of the same kind either. Weizsäcker's liquid drop model and the quantum mechanical shell model represent the nucleus of an atom in different ways; a neural network model and an electric circuit model offer different kinds of representation of the brain; and Phillips and Newlyn's hydraulic machine represents an economy in a different manner than Hicks' equations. In other words, there are different representational styles. So the question is: what styles are there and how can they be characterised? This is the *Problem of Style*. A response to this problem does not have to take the form of a complete list of representational styles. Indeed, it is unlikely that such a list exists, and new styles will be invented as science progresses. For this reason, a response to the Problem of Style will always be open-ended, providing a description of the styles that are currently available while leaving room for new additions.

Representations can be accurate or inaccurate. The Ptolemaic model of the world is an inaccurate representation; the Copernican model is accurate. The Schrödinger model of the Hydrogen atom is accurate; the Thomson model is not. On what grounds do we make such judgments? Morrison (2008, 70) points out that this is a crucial and yet non-trivial problem, and she reminds us that it is a task for theory of representation to identify what constitutes an accurate representation. This is the *Problem of Accuracy*.[5] It is worth noting that being an accurate representation is not tantamount to being a mirror image. There is a prejudice that an accurate representation is *ipso facto* a mirror image, a copy, or an imitation of the thing it represents. This is a mistake. An accurate representation need not be a copy of the real thing. This observation lies at the heart of the satire of the cartographers who produce maps as large as the country itself only to then abandon them as useless.[6] Scientists who aim to construct accurate representations are not satirical cartographers.

This problem is closely related to the next condition of adequacy: the *Misrepresentation Condition*. If we ask what makes a representation an accurate representation, we tacitly presuppose that inaccurate representations are representations too. This is the right assumption. A medieval map of the world that lacks the Americas is a misrepresentation of the world, but it is a representation nevertheless. If M does not accurately portray T, then M is a misrepresentation but not a non-representation. An account that classifies misrepresentations as non-representations is mistaken, and an account of representation must be able to explain how misrepresentation is possible.[7]

A further condition of adequacy concerns models that have no target systems at all. Models of the ether or four-sex populations, for instance, have no target systems, and yet they are representations. An account of representation has to provide an understanding of how models that lack targets work. This is the *Targetless Models Condition*.

Many scientific models are mathematised, and their mathematical aspects are crucial to their functioning. At the heart of Newton's model of the sun-earth system lies the equation of motion for a planet moving around the sun, and this equation is critical to the cognitive function of the model. This brings us back to the time-honoured philosophical puzzle of the applicability of mathematics in the empirical sciences: how is it that mathematics can be applied to a part or aspect of the world? Phrased in terms of models, the problem is how a mathematical model can represent a material target system like a system of planets or biological organisms. The fifth and final condition of adequacy is therefore that an account of representation has to explain how mathematics is applied to the physical world. This is the *Applicability of Mathematics Condition*.[8]

When tackling the above questions, we run up against the *Problem of Carriers*. The carrier of a representation is the "thing" that does the representing, and representation can be thought of as the relation between a carrier and a target. A piece of wall covered with paint is the carrier of *The School of Athens*; a canvass

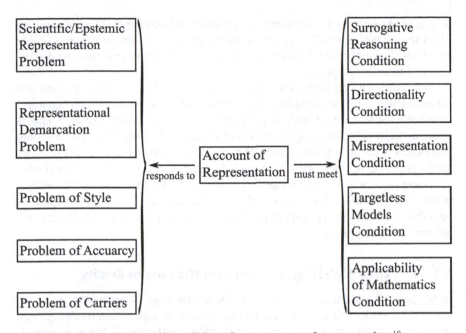

FIGURE 6.1 The problems and conditions for an account of representation.[10]

covered with pigments is the carrier of Max Ernst's *Forest and Dove*; a system of pipes filled with water is the carrier of the Phillips-Newlyn model of an economy; and so on. However, not all carriers are mannerly material objects. As Hacking (1983, 216) puts it, some models one holds in one's head rather than one's hands. The Newtonian model of the solar system, the Lotka-Volterra model of predator-prey interaction, and the quantum model of the atom are not things you can put on your laboratory table and look at. The Problem of Carriers is to get clear on our commitments and provide a list with things that we recognise – or indeed reject – as entities performing a representational function, and to give an account of what they are in cases where these entities raise questions (what exactly do we mean by something that one holds in one's head rather than one's hands?).[9]

In sum, an account of representation has to come to grips with either the Scientific Representation Problem or the Epistemic Representation Problem, take a stance on the *Representational Demarcation Problem*, address the Problem of Style, respond to the Problem *of Accuracy*, and discuss the Problem of Carriers. A satisfactory answer to these five questions has to meet five conditions of adequacy, namely the Surrogative Reasoning Condition, the Misrepresentation Condition, the Targetless Models Condition, the Directionality Condition and the Applicability of Mathematics Condition. Among these, the Scientific/Epistemic Representation Problem is the most important problem and the Surrogative Reasoning Condition is the most important condition of adequacy, which is why they are shown at the top of Figure 6.1. To frame the problem of representation in this way is not to say that the problems are separate and unrelated. What answer one gives to one problem will have implications for the answers one gives to other problems. Separating out different issues, however, helps to structure the discussion and to assess proposals.

In keeping with the topic of this book, we focus on how models represent and set aside other forms of scientific representation like images, graphs, and charts.[11] Another issue that we set aside is the realism versus antirealism issue.[12] This is because the structuralist programme is not committed to any particular position. Advocates of the structuralist notion of models and representation span the entire spectrum, ranging from empiricism (van Fraassen) to structural realism (Ladyman) and wholesale realism (Suppes). The difference between these positions lies in how they articulate the details of the structuralist view (and, in particular, in how they see models as relating to their targets); it does not lie in their basic commitment to structuralism.

6.3   The Data Matching Account and the Loss of Reality

In Section 5.2 we encountered Suppes' Data Matching Account of representation, which posits that a model represents a target through a data model, gained from observations on the target, being embedded into the model. Since an embedding is, by definition, an isomorphism to a substructure (see Section 2.7), Suppes' analysis in effect comes down to a data model being isomorphic to a substructure of a theoretical model. This is, as we noted in Section 5.3, also van Fraassen's account. In van Fraassen's version, *appearances* are the structures that result from a measurement process on the target system; so appearances are data models. A theory designates parts of a model as the model's empirical substructure, which is a candidate for the representation of an observable aspects of the target. If the appearances are isomorphic to the model's empirical substructure, then the model represents the target accurately, and an entire theory is *empirically adequate* iff for every appearance there is a model in the theory whose empirical substructure is isomorphic to the appearance.[13]

The structuralist literature does not, as we just did in the previous section, distinguish between the Scientific Representation Problem and the Problem of Accuracy, and so it is not clear whether isomorphism to a substructure is proposed as a response to the former or to the latter. At this point, we keep an open mind about this because for the arguments in Sections 6.3 to 6.5 nothing will depend on whether we interpret isomorphism as a response to the Scientific Representation Problem or the Problem of Accuracy. We will return to this issue in Section 6.6.

To appreciate how radical this account is, recall our discussion of data models in Section 3.6, where we have seen that a data model is a processed, corrected, rectified, regimented, and idealised summary of the data gained when performing measurements; our examples for data models were PSMSL's curves for the monthly and yearly average sea levels. Assume that we have a physics model of the tidal dynamics in Venice. This model would contain information about the topography of the Venetian Lagoon (including its seabed), the water masses, the motion of the moon, dominant currents in the Adriatic Sea, and a number of other relevant physical processes. The data matching account now says that the only connection between this model and the world consists in a part of the model matching a graph of the kind shown in Figure 3.3. There is no connection between the moon in the model and the real moon, or the topography of the model lagoon and the real lagoon. The only point of contact between model and target is the data model.

This is very little, and Muller objects that embedding data models in theoretical models is too little to explicate representation (2004, 716–717, 2011, 97–98). The problem Muller draws attention to is that data models, like theoretical models, *are* structures and hence an embedding simply relates one structure to another structure. This relation lives in the realm of set theory. If a theory's models represent only data models, then the theory fails to establish contact with the things in the world that the theory is supposed to be about, namely atoms, earthquakes, populations, and so on. The theory loses its grip on reality. In Muller's words:

> The best one could say is that a data structure [*D*] seems to act as simulacrum of the concrete actual being B, because [*D*] is a set-theoretical representation of the qualitative results of experiments or observations extracted from some phenomenon that necessarily involves B; the embeddability relation between data structure [*D*] and the model . . . then acts as the simulacrum of the nexus between the abstract model (structure, theory) and the concrete actual being B. But this is not good enough. We don't want simulacra. We want the real thing. Come on.
>
> *(2011, 98)*

Muller calls this the "problem of the lost beings". In the above example, B is the Venetian Lagoon with its water levels. According to Muller's objection, the Data Matching Account fails because it does not explain how a model relates to, and represents, that actual target system – the Lagoon – rather than data measured on it.

Suppes' reply to Muller's point is astonishing. He simply concedes the point and proclaims that understanding the theory-world relation has never been his concern:

> This is the view of pure mathematics I carried over to scientific structures in my 2002 book *Representation and invariance of scientific structures*. I quite agree that this book of mine, as embodying my systematic views of scientific theories, does not deal at all with the problem of how to talk about actual beings or even experiments, but I have been under no illusion that it does.
>
> *(2011, 119)*

The book Suppes refers to in this passage is the *summa* of his work, presenting in a systematic way his positions on various subject matters as he developed them since the 1950s. So this passage contains nothing less than the admission that the entire analysis of theories that he has developed over 60 years contributes nothing to understanding how a theory relates to the world! However, Suppes may have thrown in the towel a bit too quickly because, as we have seen in Section 5.2, his view of theories does contain the core ideas not only for one, but for two accounts of representation, and we have not yet discussed the second account at all. But there is a grain of truth in Suppes' admission, namely that these accounts were not developed in his work on theories and models.

Van Fraassen, by contrast, takes the problem seriously and discusses it as the "loss of reality objection" (2008, 254–261). His response to the objection is that if we take the pragmatic features of the context in which a representation is used into account, then, for an individual in that context, there is no pragmatic difference between accurately representing a physical system and accurately representing a data model extracted from it. Van Fraassen's argument for this conclusion is intricate and drawn-out, and we cannot trace its every move here.[14] At the heart of the argument lies Moore's paradox. The paradox is that for any proposition p we cannot assert sentences of the form "p and I don't believe that p". For instance, I cannot assert "Kant was born in 1724 and I don't believe that Kant was born in 1724". Speakers cannot assert such sentences because they incur a commitment to believing p when uttering the first conjunct and retracting that commitment in the second conjunct results in a pragmatic contradiction. Van Fraassen thinks that representation incurs similar commitments. A scientist cannot, on pain of pragmatic contradiction, assert that a theoretical model accurately represents the data and at the same time doubt that the theoretical model accurately represents the real system.[15]

Nguyen argues that representation differs from belief in that representation does not incur the kind of pragmatic commitments that drive Moore's paradox, and that therefore there is no contradiction in denying that the theoretical model also represents the real system. He illustrates the point with reference to one of van Fraassen's own examples, a famous caricature of Margaret Thatcher showing her as a boxer and thereby representing her as draconian and brutal. Moore's paradox is that a speaker cannot assert "Thatcher is brutal, and I don't believe that Thatcher is brutal". By contrast, a caricaturist can represent Thatcher as brutal without thereby committing herself to the belief that Thatcher really is brutal (2016, 183). The caricaturist could be politically disinterested and have no view about Thatcher at all, or privately believe she is measured and compassionate and simply draw her as brutal because that is how the newspaper that commissioned the piece wanted it. Likewise, a scientist can without contradiction assert that a theoretical model accurately represents the data and at the same time doubt that the theoretical model accurately represents the real system. This happens, for instance, when a solid state physicist uses a model with infinitely many particles to represent phase transitions in a laboratory system, which only consists of a finite number of particles. The model can get the observable features of the system (like its critical temperature) right, while misrepresenting the system as regards its particle number. Acts of representation are, pragmatically speaking, weaker than acts of assertion, and so the appeal to Moore's paradox does not dispel the loss of reality objection.[16]

Muller suggest resolving this problem by postulating that data always have to be accompanied by a "story", specifying *"how and in which scientific context the data sets are obtained"* (2011, 100, original emphasis). Data models "float in a sea of stories", and "[w]ithout such stories we cannot even begin to address the relation between theory and observation" (*ibid.*). Stories endow data with an empirical interpretation, and stories turn a bare structure into a structure connected to a particular phenomenon in the world. These stories, Muller emphasises, must be told in language that refers to "concrete actual beings" (*ibid.*), and he notes that the Model-Theoretical View "lacks the resources to tell the necessary stories: language" (*ibid.*, 101). So we're back to the same point we have already encountered in Chapter 5, namely that the Model-Theoretical View needs an interpreted language, and it is not clear where this language is supposed to come from.

6.4   Data and Phenomena

Bogen and Woodward (1988) draw a distinction between data and phenomena, and then argue that theories (or theoretical models) are about phenomena and not data.[17] Let us introduce the distinction with Bogen and Woodward's example of the melting point of lead (*ibid.*, 307–310). Scientists do not determine the melting point of lead by taking one single thermometer reading. They will have to take a series of measurements because even when the equipment is working properly there will be variation in the outcomes due to small measurement errors and uncontrollable environmental disturbances. A record of this scatter of results constitutes the *data* (the record can take any format, for instance a chart, a graph, or a list).[18] If one then assumes that individual measurements are independent and normally distributed, one can process the data to calculate the melting point of lead. Under these assumptions, the mean of all the measurements will give a good approximation of the melting point of lead, which is the *phenomenon*. However, unless we are lucky, the mean will not coincide exactly with the actual melting point of lead. The phenomenon itself is therefore not directly observable. The actual melting point of 327°C is inferred from the data and a number of statistical assumptions. Data are directly observed and publicly accessible through reports in laboratory books or other storage devices; phenomena are usually not accessible in this way and they are the outcome of an inferential process.[19]

Scientific theories, and this is the crucial point in Bogen and Woodward's argument, predict and explain phenomena and facts about phenomena, but not data. A chemical theory of molecular structure will invoke the nature of bonds and other features of the atom to explain the melting point of lead; but that theory will not explain the data that are found in particular experiments. This is because data are highly contextual in that they depend not only on the melting point of lead itself, but on a myriad of features of the experimental setup like the type of thermometer employed to carry out the measurement, the purity of the led sample studied in the experiment, the level of insulation of the experiment from the environment, and so on. None of these factors are part of the theory, and so one cannot expect the theory to account for them. In other words, data are contextual while phenomena are not. This makes data an unsuitable target for theories, which do not contain any of these peculiar local circumstances under which an observation is carried out. The function of data is evidential: data provide evidence for the existence of certain phenomena, and for the fact that phenomena possess certain features. In sum, data perform a crucial function in corroborating phenomena while phenomena are the robust and repeatable features of the world that are explained by scientific theories.

Bogen and Woodward claim that the characterisation of data and phenomena that they extract from the simple example of the melting point of lead can equally be found in cutting edge science. To underwrite this claim, they discuss an example from particle physics: the discovery of weak neutral currents (*ibid.*, 315–318). The relevant theory of elementary particles, the so-called *standard model*, posits the existence of so-called weak neutral currents. In the 1970s both the Conseil Européen pour la Recherche Nucléaire (CERN) in Geneva and the National Accelerator Laboratory (NAL) in Chicago performed experiments to empirically confirm the existence of these currents. The data gathered at CERN consisted of 290,000 bubble chamber photographs of which roughly 100 were considered to provide evidence for the existence of neutral currents. The data from NAL were very different. The experiment at NAL produced records of patterns of discharge in electronic particle detectors, and 8 out of 330 records were interpreted as supporting the existence of neutral currents. The two sets of data were completely different, and yet they were taken to provide evidence for the same phenomenon, namely weak neutral currents. Likewise, the relevant theory is about weak neutral currents, and it contains nothing that would explain the data that were gathered in the two laboratories. This is because the data are the product of contextual factors that are idiosyncratic to the particular experimental environment and that are not part of the standard model of particle physics. The theory is about neutral currents and not about their manifestations in a particular context, and the theory is supported (or confirmed) by the existence of these currents and not by the data themselves.

Phenomena do not belong to one of the traditional ontological categories (*ibid.*, 321). In fact, they fall into different established ontological categories, including objects, features, events, processes, and states of affairs, and some of them defy classification in these terms altogether. They are therefore difficult to categorise in current ontological schemes. This, however, neither detracts from the fact that they are what a theory explains, nor does it pose problems for an understanding of theories as being about phenomena.

This has direct consequences for the Data Matching Account of representation. Bogen and Woodward focus on explanation rather than representation and emphasise that theories explain phenomena and not data. However, their point about explanation is at once a point about representation because a theory can only explain X if it is about X. Therefore, theories represent phenomena, not data. If so, then phenomena and not data are the targets of models that belong to a theory. Vice versa, there is nothing in a theory to which data could be directly compared, much less do theories have parts (empirical substructures) into which these data can be embedded. Theories represent phenomena like melting points, neutral currents, space-time curvature, and electron masses. They do not represent the data that are gathered in experiments in support of these phenomena, either in their raw form or in the "processed" form of a data model.

An empiricist could try to push back against this view and argue that by postulating phenomena over and above data we leave the firm ground of observable things and started engaging in trans-empirical speculation, but science has to restrict its claims to observables and remain silent (or at least agnostic) about everything else. Therefore, so the empiricist continues, theories have to be reinterpreted somehow so that they end up accommodating data. It is doubtful that such a manoeuvre is successful. Even if one is an antirealist (as, for instance, McAllister 1997), it is phenomena that models portray and not data. The antirealist will simply see phenomena as constructions rather than as mind-independent parts of the furniture of the world. Denying the reality of phenomena will not alter the representational content of theories, which are about phenomena irrespective of whether phenomena are understood realistically or antirealistically. Regardless of whether neutral currents are real or not, it is neutral currents that are portrayed in the standard model, not bubble chamber photographs. This pulls the rug from underneath a view that analyses representation as data matching.

6.5   Target Systems and Structures

As we have seen in Section 5.2, there is another option available to the structuralist. Rather than saying that a model represents its target by having a substructure that is isomorphic to a data model, the structuralist might say that the model is isomorphic to its target system. Stated thus, this is a category mistake. Isomorphism is a relation between two structures, and a target system per se is not a structure. Hence, a target system is simply not the right kind of thing to enter into an isomorphism relation with a model.[20] When articulating Suppes' second account of representation in Section 5.2, we circumvented this problem by saying that the target system was a *concrete structure*. Since concrete structures are structures, saying that a model is isomorphic to a *concrete structure* is not a category mistake.

So the claim that a target has a concrete structure is what saves the day for the structuralist. This raises two sets of questions. The first concerns the notion of a target system being a concrete structure. We have introduced the notion of a concrete structure in Section 2.6, and we have appealed to it again in Section 5.2. On both occasions we have used the notion intuitively and without offering a philosophical analysis. The moment has now come to fill this gap and get clear on what the notion involves. This is the task for the current section, and we will see that neither structural claims, nor the claim that structures are suitably morphic, end up standing on their own because they depend on there being a substantive description of the target. The second question concerns the exact role that isomorphism plays in the analysis of representation. As noted at the beginning of Section 6.3, we have so far deliberately remained vague about this. In Section 6.6 we will explicitly address the question of what role exactly isomorphism plays in an analysis of representation.

The morphism account requires target systems to be concrete structures. This is for a good reason: an isomorphism can hold only between two structures and not between a structure and a part of the physical world per se – it would be a category mistake to say that a set-theoretical structure is isomorphic to a piece of matter. What, then, does it take for target system to be a concrete structure rather than just a "bare" thing?

A radical view denies that targets are concrete structures and insists that not only models, but also targets are abstract structures. If targets and models both are abstract structures, there is no problem in there being an isomorphism between them. Tegmark (2008) defends such a view with an argument from the objectivity of science.[21] He begins by introducing what he calls the "external reality hypothesis", the claim that "there exists an external physical reality completely independent of us humans" and then claims that this seemingly innocuous realist posit implies that the world is a mathematical structure (*ibid.*, 102). This, according to Tegmark, implies that a final "theory of everything" (which physics is supposed to reach one day) must be expressible in a way that is free from human-centric "baggage", and the only kinds of theories that can be so expressed are mathematical theories. But mathematical theories describe mathematical structures. Therefore, a theory of everything is a theory about mathematical structures, and reality fundamentally *is* a mathematical structure.

Given how we have characterised mathematical structures in Section 2.6, there is a question whether this position is meaningful at all. But let us set this worry aside for the sake of argument. The crucial premise in Tegmark's argument is that that only mathematical theories can be objective and that a complete theory of everything is therefore purely mathematical. There are reasons to doubt this claim, but the view faces more immediate problems.[22] The argument is phrased in terms of a theory of everything and the nature of the character of fundamental reality, but no currently available theory works at this level. The targets of most (if not all) current theories are *not* at a fundamental level, and when representing these targets, theories do not make reference to their fundamental structure. A population dynamic representation of a group of rabbits does not invoke the rabbits' superstring structure (or whatever else one might regard as the fundamental constituents of matter), and so the fundamental structures are not the target of that model. For Tegmark's arguments to apply at other levels, he would have to argue that the world is just a structure at all levels, but his arguments cannot do this because they crucially appeal to what happens at the *fundamental* level according to a *theory of everything*. So even if one were to buy into Tegmark's premises (and there is big "if" here), the account fails to illuminate how existing theories represent their targets because it has nothing to say about how non-fundamental theories like population dynamics represents "ordinary" objects like populations of rabbits, or even how classical mechanics represents large bodies like planets.

A different idea emerges from the philosophy of mathematics, where there is a time time-honoured position that construes mathematics as the study of structures.[23] This approach to mathematics also offers a vision of how mathematics is applied to objects in the world: mathematical structures are like properties and target systems can *instantiate* structures in much the same way in which they can instantiate other properties. Shapiro offers a clear statement of this position when he notes that on the structuralist account of mathematics,[24]

> the problem of the relationship between mathematics and reality is a special case of the problem of the instantiation of universals. Mathematics is to reality as universal is to instantiated particular. As above, the 'universal' here refers to a pattern or structure; the 'particular' refers not to an individual object, but to a system of related objects. More specifically, then, mathematics is to reality as pattern is to patterned.
>
> *(1983, 538)*

We can then say that a target system is a concrete structure iff it is a material object that instantiates a certain structure.

This answer is good as far as it goes. The question is whether it goes far enough. If one is willing to accept the notion of a material target system instantiating a structural universal as primitive, and if one is also willing to assume that scientists are able to identify such structural universals and bring them into a morphic relation to the structures of models, then we are done.

I submit, however, that we should not assume the notion of a target system instantiating a structure as primitive. The notion should be, and can be, analysed, and the analysis will provide important insights into the relation between structures and targets. At a basic level, given that a structure consists of set of objects on which relations are defined, one can say that a target system T instantiates structure S iff T consists of individuals that make up the domain of S and enter into the relations that are specified in R. Our group of women in the example in Section 2.6 illustrates this. The group consisting of Jane, Nora, and Lily instantiates the abstract structure $S = (U, R)$ with $U = (a_1, a_2, a_3)$ and R containing only the relation $r = \{(a_1, a_2), (a_2, a_3)\}$ if we take the three women to be the three elements of U and if we interpret the relation r as *mother of*. On this account, instantiation of structure amounts to interpreting the elements of an abstract structure in concrete terms.[25]

This account faces an immediate problem. The problem is one we have already encountered in Section 4.7, namely Newman's problem. The core of Newman's problem is that a collection of things can be organised so that it has any structure, subject only to the constraint that there is the right number of things. Our group of women also instantiates another structure where R contains only the relation $r' = \{(a_1, a_3), (a_3, a_1)\}$. Indeed, the group instantiates *any* relation that is definable with three objects. So a target system instantiates any structure that has the cardinality of the target! This trivialises that view since, as Collier notes, it makes finding isomorphisms "altogether too easy" because models "do not determine anything more than cardinality", and for this reason "isomorphisms leave the relation between a mathematical structure and the empirical world almost entirely open" (2002, 294).

One might be tempted to dismiss Newman's argument as logical trickery. It relies on a purely extensive understanding of relations and, so the argument goes, once the physical character of system is taken into account, the Newmanesque underdetermination of structure by the target vanishes.[26] Unfortunately this reply does not stand up to scrutiny because even when attention is restricted to genuine "physical" properties no unique structure emerges.[27] Let us illustrate this with the example of the methane molecule. Methane consists of a carbon atom and four hydrogen atoms grouped around it forming a tetrahedron. There is a covalent bond between each hydrogen atom and the carbon atom. What structure does methane instantiate? Consider the structure S_A with the domain $U = \{a, b, c, d, e\}$ and the relation $r = \{(a,b), (b,a), (a,c), (c,a), (a,d), (d,a), (a,e), (e,a)\}$. If we interpret a as the carbon, and b, c, d, and e the four hydrogen atoms, and if we further interpret the relation r as 'being connected by a covalent bond', the methane molecule instantiates S_A. Now consider the structure S_B with the domain $U' = \{a', b', c', d'\}$ and the relation $r' = \{(a', b'), (b', a'), (a', c'), (c', a'), (a', d'), (d', a'), (b', c'), (c', b'), (b', d'), (d', b'), (c', d'), (d', c')\}$. If we interpret a', b', c' and d' as covalent bonds and the relation r' as "sharing a node with", then the methane molecule instantiates S_B.

Obviously S_A and S_B are not isomorphic (their domains do not even have the same number of elements!). So by providing two different descriptions of methane – one that regards atoms as objects and the bonds as relations and another one that regards the bonds as objects and the atoms as relations – we get methane to instantiate two different non-isomorphic structures. But which is "the" true structure of methane? This question has no answer. What structure one attributes to methane depends on how the molecule is described, and there is no way to say which of the two descriptions is privileged. Furthermore, the two structures we have introduced are not the only possibilities. It takes little ingenuity to come up with further descriptions of the methane molecule that result in yet other structures.[28]

There is nothing special about the methane molecule. Any system can be described in alternative ways that lead to different and non-isomorphic structures being instantiated. But to connect a model to a target via isomorphism a particular structure has to be singled out, and so we are now faced with an identification problem. If it is not a brute fact that a system instantiates a particular structure, and if the same system can instantiate multiple structures, how are we to determine *which* of those structures is being invoked when a model is claimed to be isomorphic to the target? The methane example points to a solution. Target systems have a certain structure only under a certain description, and to identify a structure a scientist has to offer a description of the target in physical terms, with the description identifying relevant objects and relations in the target. Talk of the structure of a target make sense only when such a description is in place, and hence the attribution of a structure to a target system is always relative to a substantive – non-structural – description.[29]

The need for descriptions also arises at a different point. So far we have focused on finding the target structure that a model can be connected to through a morphism. Chakravartty (2001) argues that a language is also needed to establish the morphism itself. When operating at a formal level, one can just say that an isomorphism is a mapping that satisfies certain conditions. But what does it take for a model to enter into this mapping relation with a target? Models and targets do not "automatically" or "by themselves" enter into such a mapping relation. Chakravartty argues that this relation has to be constructed in a language:

> A model can tell us about the nature of reality only if we are willing to assert that some aspect(s) of the model has a counterpart in reality. That is, if one wishes to be a realist, some sort of explicit statement asserting a correspondence between a description of some aspect of a model and the world is inescapable. This requires the deployment of linguistic formulations, and interpreting these formulations in such a way as to understand what models are telling us about the world is the unavoidable cost of realism. . . . Theories can't tell us anything substantive about the world unless they employ a language.
>
> *(ibid., 330–331)*

In this passage Chakravartty focuses on scientific realism, but he is explicit that the point equally applies to other epistemic positions, for instance empiricism and instrumentalism (*ibid.*, 330). This is because the problem arises as soon as *any* correspondence between model and reality is asserted, even if this correspondence only concerns observables. So the problem faced by the structuralist is that even if the target has a structure, setting up a morphism between model structure and target structure requires an interpreted language in which the requisite correspondences can be expressed.

Both strands of argument in this section converge toward the point that a language is required to connect a model to its target. Without a language we can neither formulate the description that identifies the target structure, nor can we express the mapping between model and target. And let us be clear on the nature of this language: we are not talking only about a formal language. Nothing short of a fully interpreted language is capable of carrying out these tasks.

As we have seen in Section 5.5, some proponents of the Model-Theoretical View seem to defend a purist version of the view that sees theories as consisting of set-theoretical structures and *nothing else*, in particular not a fully interpreted physical language. It is hard to see how such an account could accommodate the observation that the attribution of a structure to a system and the establishment of a relevant model-target correspondence depend on a description of a target.

However, not all versions of the Model-Theoretical View are committed to this kind of austerity. Bueno and French have recently endorsed the view that targets must be described in particular ways to have a structure, and that different descriptions will lead to different structures (2011, 887). The Munich Structuralists (whom we will discuss in detail in Chapter 7) also explicitly acknowledge the need for a concrete description of the target-system, and they consider these "informal descriptions" to be "internal" to the theory (see, for instance, Balzer et al. 1987). This is a plausible move, but those endorsing this solution have to concede that there is more to representation than structures and morphisms, and that a fully interpreted physical language is an irreducible part of a theory. This does not sit well with the official line of the Model-Theoretical View that theories are "extralinguistic" entities, consisting of families of models which are strictly separated from their linguistic formulations. This line becomes untenable if, as we have argued, a theory cannot perform its most essential function – representing parts of the world and informing scientists about their features – without a language. If a language is an ineliminable part of a theory, a philosophical analysis has to explicate the nature of this language and its systematic place in the edifice of a theory. Current versions of Model-Theoretical View fail to do this.

6.6   Morphisms and Representation

Assuming that targets have structures, and assuming that models and targets can meaningfully be said to be isomorphic, how does an account based on isomorphism fare with the problems concerning representation and the conditions of adequacy on answers that we introduced in Section 6.2? Before we can discuss this question, we have to return to the question of what role exactly isomorphism plays in analysis of representation. As noted at the beginning of Section 6.3, it is unclear whether isomorphism is meant to respond to the Scientific Representation Problem or the Problem of Accuracy (and this ambiguity besets both the Data Matching Account and the Morphism Account).

Interpreted as a response to the Scientific Representation Problem, isomorphism is an obvious non-starter, and it is better interpreted as a response to the Problem of Accuracy. However, the extant literature on the topic is not clear on this so it is worth pointing out why exactly isomorphism is a non-starter. For ease of presentation we focus on the Morphism Account; the arguments are *mutatis mutandis* the same for the Data Matching Account. To ground our discussion, we first have to give a concise statement of the Morphism Account interpreted as a response to the Scientific Representation Problem. Assuming that target T instantiates structure S_T, the account says: M is a scientific representation of T iff M is isomorphic to S_T.[30]

The account does not satisfy the Directionality Condition: isomorphism is symmetrical and reflexive, but representation is not. That is, if A is isomorphic to B, then B is always also isomorphic to A; and A is always isomorphic to itself. By contrast, if A represents B, then B (usually) does not represent A. The photographs in the entry hall represent the university's Nobel laureates, but the laureates do not represent their photographs, and neither do the photographs represent themselves.[31] For these reasons, representation cannot be equated with isomorphism. As we have seen in Section 5.2, isomorphism is not the only mapping that the Morphism Account can appeal to, and so one might try to address this problem by replacing isomorphism with an alternative mapping. Suggestions include homomorphism, partial isomorphism, embeddings, and so-called $\Delta / \Psi -$ morphisms.[32] The shift from isomorphism to a more general class of morphisms can in principle solve the problem with symmetry because some of these mappings are asymmetrical. But it leaves the reflexivity problem untouched because morphisms are typically reflexive.

The account also faces a problem with the Misrepresentation Condition. A misrepresentation is one that portrays its subject as having features that it does not have. In the case of structural representation this would require that the model represent the target as having structural properties that the target fails to have (Pincock 2005, 1252). However, isomorphism requires identity of structure because the structural properties of two isomorphic objects must correspond to one another exactly (indeed, isomorphism is often taken to be a criterion for the sameness of structure). A misrepresentation therefore cannot be isomorphic to its target. However, the account at issue says that M represents T iff M is isomorphic to S_T, which implies that if M fails to be isomorphic to S_T then M does not represent T at all. This is a conflation of misrepresentation and non-representation. We can now ask again whether morphisms other than isomorphism can eschew this problem. As we will see in the next section, partial isomorphisms can accommodate misrepresentations that are effectively omissions elegantly, while it seems that they struggle with distortions. In general, one cannot rule out that morphisms can be constructed to accommodate any kind of misrepresentation, but so far no general framework is available that would cover all misrepresentations.

Morphism accounts are ill-equipped to deal with the Targetless Models Condition. A model cannot possibly be morphic to something that does not exist. If there is no ether and if there are no four-sex populations, then a model cannot be morphic to these, no matter what morphism one chooses.

Let us return to the Scientific Representation Problem. An account that says that M is a scientific representation of T iff M is isomorphic to the target structure

S_T implies that M represents *everything* that is isomorphic to it: anything with a structure that is isomorphic to M is automatically represented by M (and the same is the case for any other morphism). This is too inclusive. The problem is that the same structure can be instantiated in different target systems. Newton's law of gravity and the Coulomb's law of electrostatic attraction both have the "mathematical skeleton" of an $1/r^2$ law and so phenomena that instantiate these laws have isomorphic structures even though they are physically different. Likewise, an electric circuit with a condenser and a solenoid has the same mathematical structure as a simple pendulum.[33] As a consequence, a model that represents gravity also represents electrostatic attraction, and a model that represents an electric circuit also represents a pendulum. These examples show that the Morphism Account does not correctly identify the extension of a representation (i.e. the class of systems a model represents). Using a notion from the philosophy of mind we can give the problem a name: many structures are *multiply realisable*, meaning that different systems can have the same structure. The problem then is that an account of representation that explains representation solely in terms of morphisms will misidentify the extension of the representation whenever a structure is multiply realised.

The difficulties we have seen so far have a common root. The version of the Morphism Account discussed so far tried to explicate representation *solely* in terms of morphisms and had no place for the scientists who produce and use representations. The problems this view ran into can be avoided by assigning representing agents and their reasoning a systematic place in an account of representation. A way of doing this is to say that a model M represents a target system T iff there is an agent A who intends to use M to represent a target system T and, to this end, first offers a description D of the target that identifies S_T as the target structure and then proposes a hypothesis H stating that a suitable morphism holds between M and S_T. A suggestion along these lines has been made by Adams (1959, 259), who says that a theory represents *intended* systems, where the requisite intentionality comes from the theory's users. Van Fraassen has given this idea prominence in what he calls the "Hauptsatz" (central theorem) of a theory of representation. His Hauptsatz specifies that for something to be a representation it must be *"used, made, or taken, to represent things"* (2008, 23, original emphasis). In a similar vein, Bueno declares that "representation is an *intentional* act relating two objects" (2010, 94, original emphasis), and Bueno and French say that a model representing a target not only depends on a morphism but also on "pragmatic" factors "having to do with the use to which we put the relevant models" (2011, 885).[34]

This account resolves the above difficulties because users' intentions are directed. The act of a scientist describing an intended target and then formulating a hypothesis about the model being suitably morphic to the target is neither symmetrical nor reflexive, which solves the problem with directionality. The account asks that a hypothesis be formulated about M and S_T entering into a relevant morphism; there is no requirement that the hypothesis be true. This deals with the problem of misrepresentation. Targetless models are dealt with by saying that in such cases scientists offer a target description D and formulate a hypothesis about the system described in D, but it then turns out that D is false because the system described does not exist. This is what happened in cases of (what we now view as) scientific errors like the ether.[35] The scientist is free to pick her targets and to offer descriptions of some systems and not others, which resolves the problem that isomorphism is too inclusive.

Despite successfully resolving a number of issues, the inclusion of a user's activities and intentions in the definition of representation is Pyrrhic victory for the morphism view as far as the Scientific Representation Problem is concerned. The reason for this is that the role of isomorphism has shifted. All the heavy lifting in the above definition is done by the agent's activities (offering descriptions and formulating hypotheses), and morphisms have in fact become a somewhat idle wheel. Morphisms only appear in the content of the hypothesis that an agent formulates, but the content of that hypothesis could be anything and the resulting statement would still be a response to the Scientific Representation Problem. One could formulate hypotheses saying that M and T are similar, that M licences inferences about T, or that M denote T. Under all these hypotheses M would still end up representing T. But if being morphic is only one way among others in which a model can be related to its target in a representation, then morphisms are otiose in a reply to the Scientific Representation Problem. Morphisms have dropped out of the picture as the relation that grounds representation, and the work is done by the agent's actions.

But surely morphisms must do some work? Yes, but that work is not to bring about representation. This is where the alternative interpretation we have mentioned previously comes into play: isomorphism (or other morphisms) can be understood as a response to the Problem of Accuracy. On that interpretation, M is an *accurate* representation of T iff M is isomorphic to S_T. This is a plausible reading. M and S_T being isomorphic in effect means that they have the same structure (recall the discussion of isomorphism in Section 2.7), and this is a reasonable criterion of accuracy. Similar things can then be said about other morphisms, and one would in the end probably want to introduce different standards of accuracy associated with different morphisms: a representation can be isomorphism-accurate, embedding-accurate, and so on. So the morphism account does offer a natural response to the Problem of Accuracy.

By the same token the account also offers a response to the Problem of Style. The Problem of Style is to recognise representational styles and to analyse them. Identifying different morphisms, studying their properties, and getting clear on the relations between them can naturally be seen as contribution to understanding different kinds of representations, and a research programme focusing on morphism can be seen addressing the Problem of Style.

A view of representation that uses isomorphism as criterion of accuracy also satisfies the Applicability of Mathematics Condition. As we have seen in the previous section, structuralists construe mathematics as the study of structures and explicate the application of mathematics in terms of the instantiation of structures in physical systems. The Morphism Account can adopt this stance, which, combined with the view that target systems have structures, provides a natural explanation of how mathematics is applied in the sciences.

The view also has an obvious and convincing answer to the Surrogative Reasoning Condition, namely that the morphisms between the model and the target allow scientists to convert truths found in the model into claims about the target system, provided that the representation is accurate. If a result holds in the model and the model is isomorphic to the target, then the result also holds in the target.

Next on our list of problems is the Representational Demarcation Problem. Structuralism's stance on the demarcation problem is by and large an open question. Unlike other accounts of representation (such as the similarity account, which we will discuss in Chapter 8), morphism accounts originate in scientific contexts and have gained little traction in other areas. Exceptions are French, who claims that pictorial representation involves isomorphism (2003, 1475–1476), and Bueno, who submits that partial isomorphisms accommodate "outputs of various instruments, micrographs, templates, diagrams, and a variety of other items" (2010, 94). If so, then there is no demarcation and structuralism offers a universal account covering representations in different domains.

The straightforward answer to the Problem of Carriers is that models are set-theoretical structures. However, as we briefly noted in Section 2.6, the ontology of set-theoretical structures is discussed controversially in the philosophy of mathematics and one might say that the Problem of Carriers of models has not been solved until that question is settled. One could push back against this verdict by insisting on a division of labour, arguing that problems in the philosophy of mathematics need not trouble philosophers of science: as far as a theory of scientific representation goes, all that needs to be said in response to the problem of ontology is that models are set-theoretical structures, and what these structures themselves are is a question for the philosopher of mathematics. This is a viable response, and one that we may also want to appeal to with regard to other notions (we might insist, for instance, the intentionality is the subject matter of the philosophy of mind and can be taken for granted in theory of scientific representation).

In Section 5.7 we encountered another response to the Problem of Carriers. Quietists insist that we should not answer the question of what a theory is, and therefore we should remain quiet about what the constituents of a theory are. But insisting on silence in matters of ontology does not make any of the other issues raised in Section 6.2 go away. The quietist will still have to address these issues, but she will have to do so with an added layer of complexity. The quietist cannot discuss the question of how a model M represents target T because we have no access to M. All we have access to is a representation of M, and so the Scientific Representation Problem has to be addressed through a discussion of the representation of the representation. Whether that is a recipe for success remains to be seen.

In sum, the Morphism View is a non-starter when interpreted as response to the Scientific Representation Problem, but it offers a viable response to the Problem of Accuracy, which, in turn, gives rise to a viable response to a number of other problems and conditions.

6.7* Partial Structures

Isomorphism is an all-or-nothing matter. Either a representation is isomorphic or it is not, and if scientists have to assess whether a representation is accurate all they can say is whether it or it is not isomorphic. This binary character of isomorphism does not sit well with scientific practice, where models (and theories) often grow gradually through successive steps of improvements. The *Partial Structures Programme* (PSP) takes as its point of departure Suppes' account of theories discussed in Section 5.2 and reworks the notion of structure on which the analysis was based.[36] PSP's crucial move is to replace structures with so-called partial structures, which are intended to capture the way in which knowledge is encoded in theories and the way in which it grows in the process of research.

To introduce partial structures, we first have to define partial relations. In Section 2.6 we have seen that a relation is defined extensionally: an n-ary relation is a set of n-tuples.[37] This means that the relation holds exactly between the tuples in the set and not any other tuples. Hence, for any n-ary relation r we can sort the set of all n-tuples into two disjoint sets, a set $r^\in$ of tuples that belong to a relation and set $r^\notin$ of the tuples that do not. The crucial idea behind partial relations is to replace this dual division by a tripartite separation. Rather than separating all n-tuples into two groups we now separate n-tuples into three: n-tuples that belong to the relation, n-tuples that do not belong to the relation, and ones for which it is indeterminate whether they belong to the relation or not. Let us denote the last set by "$r^?$". Hence, a *partial relation* r is defined by the triple $(r^\in, r^\notin, r^?)$. These three sets are mutually exclusive (no n-tuple can be in more than one) and jointly exhaustive (every n-tuple must belong to one group). If $r^? = \varnothing$, where "$\varnothing$" denotes the empty set, then a partial relation is in fact an "ordinary" relation. In the context of PSP, ordinary relations of the kind we have seen so far are called *total relations*. Hence a total relation is a special case of a partial relation where $r^?$ is the empty set.

The idea behind the introduction of partial relations is to make room for situations where we have incomplete knowledge.[38] In many cases we know that a relation applies to certain objects; we also know that it does not apply to other objects; but there are a number of objects where we simply do not know whether or not the relation applies. So the three sets that define a partial relation can be given an epistemic interpretation. $r^\in$ is the set of n-tuples to which the relation applies and is known to do so; $r^\notin$ is the set of n-tuples to which the relation does not apply and is known that it does not; $r^?$ is the set of n-tuples of which it is unknown whether or not the relation applies. Under this epistemic interpretation, partial relations offer a representation of the incompleteness of our knowledge and capture the openness of scientific theories to new developments. The relations in $r^?$ suggest lines of inquiry because scientists will aim to find out whether certain objects do or do not belong to the relation. Scientific progress then amounts to gaining sufficient information to be able to a reclassification of n-tuples originally in $r^?$ as belonging to either $r^\in$ or $r^{\notin}$.

If the set R of a structure contains at least one partial relation, then the structure is a partial structure. Formally, a *partial structure* S_p is a tuple (D, R_p) where D is a domain of objects and R_p is an indexed set of partial relations on D.[39] An "ordinary" structure, i.e. one with no partial relations, is called a *total structure*. As in Suppes' account, these structures are the *models of the theory*. The difference with previous accounts is that a theory is now seen as being a family of partial rather than total structures.[40]

A *partial isomorphism* is a mapping f from a partial structure $S_p^{(1)}$ to another partial structure $S_p^{(2)}$ that is one-to-one and preserves the system of relations in the following sense. For all relations r in $R_p^{(1)}$ it is the case that $(a_1, ..., a_n)$ is in $r^\in$ iff $(f(a_1), ..., f(a_n))$ is in $s^\in$ and $(a_1, ..., a_n)$ is in $r^{\notin}$ iff $(f(a_1), ..., f(a_n))$ is in $s^{\notin}$, where s is the relation in $R_p^{(2)}$ that corresponds to r in $R_p^{(1)}$, and *vice versa*. Other morphisms between partial structures are defined in the same way.[41]

PSP assigns a systematic place to language in theorising and assumes a language L as given. This language is a formal language of the kind we encountered in Section 2.6 and it is endowed with an interpretation relating the terms of the language with elements of a partial structure. In Suppes' terms, L provides an intrinsic characterisation. A certain set of such sentences can be deemed important in certain contexts. Indeed, sentences can be so important that it is worth extending S_p to include these sentences. Adding a set of sentences to a partial structure yields a pragmatic structure.[42] Formally, a *pragmatic structure* S_{pr} is a triple (D, R_p, P), where D and R_p are as above, and P is a set of distinguished sentences in language L containing accepted statements about the domain and its relations, for instance regularities or laws that hold in the structure.

Since a pragmatic structure contains *partial* relations there may be statements that come out neither true nor false under the standard Tarskian semantics. As an example consider a partial structure with a five-object domain $D = \{a_1, ..., a_5\}$ and two 1-ary relations ρ_1 and ρ_2 defined on D. For the first relation we have $\rho_1^\in = \{a_1, ..., a_5\}$ and $\rho_1^{\notin} = \rho_1^? = \varnothing$ (so that ρ_1 is in fact a total relation). For the second relation we have $\rho_2^\in = \{a_1, a_2\}$, $\rho_2^{\notin} = \varnothing$, and $\rho_2^? = \{a_3, a_4, a_5\}$ (so that ρ_2 is proper partial relation). In other words, ρ_1 is known to apply to all elements of D while ρ_2 is only know to apply to the first two, and it is unknown whether it applies to the third, fourth and fifth element. Now consider the sentence "$\forall x (Ax \rightarrow Bx)$", where A and B are two predicate symbols, and adopt an interpretation whereby A refers to ρ_1 and B refers to ρ_2. It is then indeterminate whether this sentence is true because it is indeterminate whether the third, fourth and fifth elements belong to ρ_2.

Yet, intuitively, one can say more about this sentence than that it is indeterminate: it is known to be true of all objects for which the relevant properties are determinate, and there are no cases in which it is known to be false. To capture insights of this kind PSP introduces the notion of *pragmatic truth*. Intuitively a sentence is pragmatically true if what it says about the determinate cases is true and it says nothing false. To make this precise, PSP introduces the notion of a total structure S being Q-normal with respect to a pragmatic structure Q. A total structure S is Q-normal iff

(1) S and Q have the same domain D;
(2) All relations of S are extensions of the corresponding relations of Q;
(3) Sentences in Language L are given the same interpretation in both S and Q (that is, individual constants refer to the same element in D, etc.);
(4) All sentences p in P are true in S.

The second condition needs unpacking.[43] A total relation r is an *extension* of a partial relation ρ iff $\rho^{\in} \subseteq r^{\in}$ and $\rho^{\notin} \subseteq r^{\notin}$. In intuitive terms, r is an extension ρ iff ρ agrees with r on the cases in which the relation does apply and the cases in which it does not, and it just disagrees with r on the indeterminate cases. Take the above example and consider a total the total relation $r_2 = \{a_1,...,a_5\}$. It is obvious that r_2 is an extension of ρ_2. Now consider a slightly different partial relation $\tilde{\rho}_2$ that which is defined through $\tilde{\rho}_2^{\in} = \{a_1, a_2\}$, $\tilde{\rho}_2^{\notin} = \{a_3\}$, $\tilde{\rho}_2^{?} = \{a_4, a_5\}$. It is now no longer the case that r_2 is an extension of $\tilde{\rho}_2$ because $\tilde{\rho}_2$ disagrees with r_2 on the cases to which the relation does not apply (formally: $\tilde{\rho}_2^{\notin} \not\subseteq r_2^{\notin}$).

With the notion of Q-normality at hand, one can say that sentence p is *pragmatically true* in the pragmatic structure Q iff there is a Q-normal full structure S and p is true in S.[44] On this definition of pragmatic truth $\forall x(Ax \rightarrow Bx)$ comes out pragmatically true because there is a total structure in which r_2 contains all five elements of the domain and hence the all the objects that belong to r_1 also belong to r_2. If, for whatever reason, there was no structure in which r_2 contained all five elements, then there would be no extension in which $\forall x(Ax \rightarrow Bx)$ was true and hence it would not be pragmatically true in the above pragmatic structure.[45]

It is important to be clear that the discussion so far was couched *entirely* at a formal level, and even the so-called "pragmatic" truth is a concept that describes the relation between a formal sentence and set-theoretical partial structure. This raises the question of how the formal machinery of PSP relates to a domain of empirical inquiry. The idea in PSP is that models bear a special relation to target systems in the world and that the information in the formalism "trickles down" to the world through that relation. In their summative presentation of PSP, da Costa and French say that a sentence of the formal language "can be said to 'point' to the world by means of a model" (2003, 17). This is possible because a model "represents a portion of reality"; a model "effectively substitutes" or "partially reflects" the relevant domain of inquiry; a model is capable of "partially mirroring" the domain; and a model "has to capture some fundamental aspects of Δ [the domain of knowledge], or some 'elements of truth,' although it does not mirror Δ perfectly" (*ibid.*, 17–18, cf. 34–35).[46] So sentences that are pragmatically true in pragmatic structures also express partial truths about the world because the structures in which they are pragmatically true adequately mirror relevant aspects of the world.

The question then is how the notion of mirroring or capturing aspects of a target system can be unpacked. At this point the two options that we have discussed earlier in this chapter re-enter the scene. Both the Morphism Account and the Data Matching Account are invoked, often side-by-side. In some places da Costa and French say that "data structures" represent aspects of reality (2003, 17). In other places, the relevant relation seems to be one of isomorphism (presumably partial) between model and target, for instance when they say that the elements in the domain of the structure can correspond to elementary particles in high-energy physics and the partial relations to various relationships that hold between these particles (*ibid.*, 18).

In as far as these accounts are invoked, PSP faces all the challenges that we have discussed in previous sections. The question then is whether PSP has a solution to offer to the problems that we identified. The answer is that it does not. Relatively little is said about data models in the literature on PSP and so things still stand were we left them in Section 6.3. Regarding the Morphism Account, da Costa and French explicitly recognise the problem when they emphasise that an isomorphism cannot hold between a structure and domain of knowledge because only structures can enter into morphisms (*ibid.*, 17).[47] At the same time they candidly admit that they have no response to this problem. Appealing to Wittgenstein, they say that the way in which data structures relate to the objects of the domain "lies beyond linguistic expression" (*ibid.*, 17). In the same vein, French and Ladyman acknowledge that "there is the more profound issue of the relationship between the lower most representation in the hierarchy – the data model perhaps – and reality itself" but issue the disclaimer that "of course this is hardly something that the semantic approach alone can be expected to address" (1999, 113). Hence, one of the main problems in the structuralist approach remains unresolved also in PSP.

Morrison argues that the situation may be even worse for PSP. This is because to get the target and a model to enter into a partial isomorphism, one need not only identify a structure in the target, but additionally we must have substantive knowledge of the target because "we must have already designated or know the particular features that have empirical support, features that are then expressed formally in the model" (2007, 207). So we can connect a theory to its targets only once we have acquired substantive knowledge about the target and the theory, but this is odd, not least because theories are supposed to provide exactly that knowledge. So models end up telling us nothing that we did not already know before we connected them to their targets. Discussing the example of the pendulum model, Morrison sums up this point by observing that PSP's "'structural' reconstruction hasn't told us anything about the pendulum model that we don't already know, nor has it clarified which structural features we are entitled to call quasi-true" (*ibid.*).

How does PSP fare with respect to the other problems and conditions identified in Section 6.2? PSP has the same options as other structuralist positions when it comes to answering the Representational Demarcation Problem. PSP is also on par with other structuralist position as regards the Problem of Carriers, the Directionality Condition, the Surrogative Reasoning Condition, the Targetless Representations Condition, and the Applicability of Mathematics Condition. As regards the Problem of Style, SPS can say that representing a target through a partial isomorphism is a particular style, and the Problem of Accuracy is answered by saying that the representation is accurate if the claimed partial isomorphism holds.

The question is how far these answers reach. Proponents of PSP see the programme as a comprehensive metatheory of science that can account for all aspects of scientific theorising and modelling. Whether the programme successfully accounts for the use of models and theories in scientific practice has been the subject matter of heated debate. We turn to this debate in Section 12.8. At this point, we only have a brief look at the extent to which PSP can deal with cases where there is a mismatch between model and target. Compared to standard structuralism, PSP has added flexibility in dealing with misrepresentations, but this flexibility does not stretch far enough. Partial structures deal well with incomplete representations, because the features that are left out can be put into $r^?$, which is a clear advantage over standard structures. However, partial structures do not seem to enjoy a similar advantage when it comes to dealing with distortive representations.[48] A surface is modelled as frictionless when it in fact has friction; a planet is modelled as spherical when it is in fact pear-shaped; and a population is modelled as isolated from its environment when it in fact interacts with it in various ways. Models of this kind do not omit but rather distort their target's features. And these distortions are not accidental features that could be eliminated; they are crucial to what scientists do with the model and to how the model tells scientists something about the target. These distortions cannot be converted into omissions, and so it is unclear how partial structures would deal with them.

6.8   Conclusion

In order to assess accounts of representation, we have introduced five problems that every account of representation has to address, along with five conditions of adequacy on answers to these problems. We have used these conditions to analyse accounts that explicate representation in terms of morphisms. We found that morphisms are a non-starter when they are employed to explain why, and how, a model represents its target, but they fare relatively well when understood as analyses of accuracy. A core problem for all morphism accounts is that they have to explain how a target system can have a structure. We have investigated this problem in some detail, and the different strands of argument converge toward the conclusion that language matters. Without a physical language we can neither identify a target structure, nor can we establish the relevant correspondences between models and targets. A language is therefore an ineliminable part of a theory. The requisite language is not merely a formal language (as in Chapter 5); the language of a theory must be a fully interpreted language that allows scientists to talk about phenomena in the world. One of the primary motivations for adopting the Model-Theoretical View is that it purportedly offers an escape route from all the (real or perceived) difficulties that attach to the use of language (discussed in Chapter 3 and in Chapter 4). If that escape route is blocked – or, indeed, if it has never been available in the first place – then an important advantage that has been claimed for the Model-Theoretical View has faded away.

Notes

1 The discussion in this section is based on work I have done with James Nguyen. The problems are presented in a slightly simplified version here. For a full discussion, see Frigg and Nguyen's (2020, Ch. 1).

2 See my (2006). This question is, of course, not specific to the structuralist version of the Model-Theoretical View. The models we will encounter in later chapters are abstract objects, fictional entities, equations, and ordinary material objects. The same question arises for them.

3 The term "surrogative reasoning" is due to Swoyer (1991, 449). The point that scientific representations must allow scientists to reason about their targets has also been made, among others, by Bailer-Jones (2003, 59), Bolinska (2013, 219), Contessa (2007, 50), Frigg (2006, 51), Liu (2013, 93), Morgan and Morrison (1999, 11), Suárez (2003, 229), and Weisberg (2013, 150).

4 Among others, Elgin (2017, Ch. 12), French (2003), Frigg (2006), Hughes (1997), Suárez (2004), and van Fraassen (2008) pursue such a programme. For a reflection on the integration of discussions on scientific and artistic representation Sánchez-Dorado's (2017).

5 There is a methodological question attached to this condition: when analysing representation, should we first analyse representation *tout court* and then say what makes such a representation accurate, or should we rather begin our discussion with an analysis of accurate representations? In what follows, I pursue the former option; Bolinska (2013, 2016) and Poznic (2018) opt for the latter.

6 The satire is told by Lewis Carroll in *Sylvie and Bruno* and by Jorge Luis Borges in *On Exactitude in Science*.

7 See Contessa's (2007, 54–55), Frigg's (2002, 16–17), Suárez's (2003, 233–235), and van Fraassen's (2008, 13–15). Stich and Warfield (1994, 6–7) argue that a theory of mental representation should be able to account for misrepresentation.

8 The problem of the applicability of mathematics can be traced back at least to Plato's *Timaeus*. Its modern expression is due to Wigner, who famously remarked that "the enormous usefulness of mathematics in the natural sciences is something bordering on the mysterious and that there is no explanation for it" (1960, 2). For a survey and discussion, see Bangu's (2012) and Shapiro's (1983). Rédei (2020) points that even though mathematics and physics are in a close relationship, that relationship is not free of tensions. Saatsi (2011) notes that a representational and an explanatory use of mathematics have to be distinguished. The Applicability of Mathematics Condition requires a response to the former, but not to the latter.

9 Contessa (2010b), Frigg (2010), Godfrey-Smith (2006), (Levy 2012), Thomson-Jones (2010), Toon (2012), and Weisberg (2013, Ch. 4) have drawn attention to this problem

in different ways. In our (2020), James Nguyen and I further divide this problem into two subproblems, which we call the Problem of Ontology and the Problem of Handling. I suppress this distinction here for brevity.

10 This diagram is adapted from Figure 1.2 in Frigg and Nguyen's (2020, 19).

11 For a discussion of visual representations in science, see Perini's (2005, 2010), and Elkins' (1999).

12 See Psillos' (1999) for a discussion.

13 This account is clearly articulated in van Fraassen's (1980, 64–66). For further statements, see his (1981, 667, 1985, 271, 1989, 229, 1997, 524, 2002, 164, 2008, 246, 252–259, 309–311). Worrall (2011) distinguishes between data equivalence and empirical equivalence. Parker (2020) has recently argued that full empirical adequacy may well be too strong a requirement and that we should demand only that models meet the weaker criterion of "adequacy-for-purpose". For a discussion of van Fraassen's views on representation, see also González's (2014), Okruhlik's (2009), and Padovani's (2012).

14 Nguyen's (2016) offers an extensive discussion of the argument; see also Muller's (2009, 271–272) and Giere's (2009, 107–109).

15 Van Fraassen's argument is phrased in terms of accurate representation rather than representation simpliciter. See Nguyen's (2016, 175, 188–189) for a discussion of the impact of this point.

16 As we have seen in Section 5.2, Suppes takes theoretical models to be related to the world through a hierarchy of models. This has no bearing on the loss of reality objection. As Brading and Landry (2006, 573–575) point out, no matter how long the hierarchy is, there is always the question of how the lowest model in the hierarchy connects to reality.

17 The dichotomy between data and phenomena is further articulated in Woodward's (1989, 2000, 2010, 2011), and a similar distinction has been introduced (independently) in Teller's (2001). The dichotomy is scrutinised in Bailer-Jones' (2009, Ch. 7), Bogen's (2010), Brading's (2010), Brown's (1994, Ch. 7), Glymour's (2000), Kaiser's (1991), Lusk's (2021), McAllister's (1997, 2010), Schindler's (2007, 2011), Tal's (2011), Teller's (2010), and Votsis' (2010), as well as in the contributed papers to Woody's (2010) and Machamer's (2011). Lyon's (2016) offers a review of the state of play.

18 What Bogen and Woodward call "data" corresponds to what we called "raw data" in Section 3.6.

19 Phenomena are usually unobservable but being unobservable is not one of their defining features. Phenomena such as the Poisson spot and colour constancy in changing light are observable (Woodward 2011, 171).

20 Contessa calls this the "bridging problem" (2010a, 516).

21 One would expect ontic structural realists to subscribe to this position too. They have, however, been hesitant to do so; see, for instance, Ladyman's (1998, 113) and French's (2014, 195). For a general discussion of structural realism, see Frigg and Votsis' (2011).

22 For further discussion of Tegmark's views, see Butterfield's (2014).

23 For an introductory overview of this programme, see Hellman and Shapiro's (2019).

24 A similar position is articulated in Resnik's (1997, 204). Recent developments of this view include Bueno and Colyvan's (2011) and Pincock's (2012). For a critical discussion of Pincock's position, see Walsh et al. (2014).

25 For a more detailed discussion of this notion of abstraction, see my (2006, 55–56). For critical discussions of this argument, see Frisch's (2015, 289–294) and Portides' (2017, 43–44). Hendry (1999) discusses how structures in chemistry result from processes of abstraction.

26 Many responses to Newman in the realism debate have taken something like this route and resolved the problem by appeal to natural kinds. See Ainsworth's (2009) for a discussion of the different responses.

27 The presentation of the example follows Frigg and Nguyen's (2017, 74). An earlier version can be found in Frigg's (2006). Weisberg (2013, 90–93) makes a similar point when he draws a distinction between what he calls *phenomena* and *target systems*.

28 Sometimes structural changes are brought about through historical developments. For a long time the solar system was considered to have a structure with ten objects in its domain: the sun and nine planets. This changed in August 2006, when the International Astronomical Union stripped Pluto of its status as planet. So now the solar system has a structure with nine objects in its domain. But nothing in the solar system itself has changed – it's the same physical system! What has changed is how we describe it.

29 See Nguyen and Frigg's (2017) for details.

30 An early statement of this position can be found in Byerly's (1969, 135–138), more recent discussions can be found in Frigg's (2006, 55), Suárez's (2003, 227), and van Fraassen's (2010, 549–550). The discussion in this section builds on Frigg an Nguyen's (2020, Ch. 4). I here only discuss the use of isomorphism in the morphism account. The equivalent condition for the Data Matching account would be: M is a scientific representation of target T iff a measurement performed on T yields data model D and D is isomorphic to M's empirical substructure. *Mutatis mutandis*, this condition faces the same problems as the condition of the morphism account.

31 Goodman (1976, 5) levelled this point against the similarity account of representation, which we discuss in Chapter 8.

32 We discuss partial isomorphisms in the next section. For homomorphism, see Bartels' (2006) and Mundy's (1986), for embeddings, see Redhead's (2001), and for $\Delta / \Psi -$ morphisms, see Swoyer's (1991). For a comparison of various morphisms, see Pero and Suárez's (2016).

33 Kroes (1989) discusses the case of the pendulum in detail. Kaushal (1999) and Shive (1982) give a large number of examples of physically different systems that have the same structure.

34 Giere held a similar view in the context of the similarity account of representation. We discuss his view in Section 8.3.

35 This resolution looks less natural in cases like the four-sex population, where no one ever thought that such populations exist. However, one might say that in such cases D can be interpreted as description of a hypothetical system, and the model represents this hypothetical system.

36 The programme originates in the Brazilian school of logic and philosophy of science around Newton da Costa. The foundations for the framework were laid in Mikenberg et al. (1986). Da Costa and French's (1990) introduced the framework into the philosophy of science. A canonical statement of the programme is da Costa and French's (2003). Discussions of specific physical theories include quantum mechanics (French 2000), statistical mechanics (Bueno et al. 2002), and superconductivity (French and Ladyman 1997).

37 I follow da Costa and French's (2003) and introduce the approach in terms of sets. Nothing depends on whether the domain is a set in the strict sense of the term.

38 For a discussion, see French's (2000, 105) and Bueno's (2002, 498). Partial relations bear a close relation to Mary Hesse's classification of analogies as positive, negative, and neutral (Bueno et al. 2002, 502). We will discuss Hesse's theory of analogy in Chapter 10.

39 As noted in Section 2.6, operations are reducible to relations. For this reason, operations are not usually explicitly included in the definition of partial structures.

40 Or, for those with quietist preferences, a theory is represented as a family of partial structures.

41 For a definition of partial homomorphisms, see Bueno (2002, 503).

42 See, for instance, da Costa and French's (2003, 18).

43 See Bueno's (1999, 63–64) and da Costa and French's (2003, 18).

44 The terms "quasi-true" or "partially true" seem to be used as synonyms of "pragmatically true"; see da Costa and French's (2003, 29, 1990, 256–257), French and Ladyman's (1997, 370), and Bueno's (1999, 64).

45 Lutz (2015) argues that everything that can be said in the partial structures approach can also be expressed in standard first-order or second-order model theory, and that it therefore offers no fundamental advantage over other formalisms. This, however, leaves open the option that the relevant insights can be formulated in a simpler and more elegant way in the partial structures approach, which may therefore have practical advantages.

46 See also Bueno and French's (2011, 860).

47 In line with Suppes, PSP sees a theory as relating to the world through a cascade of models rather than through a direct mapping (Da Costa and French 2003, 28). Accordingly, Suppes' hierarchy is discussed approvingly in French and Ladyman's (1999, 112–114) and Bueno's (1997, 600–602, 1999, 66, 2002, 499–500). However, irrespective of whether a partial structure relates to reality directly or through a hierarchy of structures, the account needs an "ultimate" structure as an anchor, and the question is where this structure comes from.

48 See Contessa's (2006, 373–375). Pincock makes a related point when he argues that PSP is forced into thinking that all idealisations are in fact approximations (2005, 1255–1257). We discuss idealisations and approximations in Chapters 11 and 12. Vickers (2009) discusses the question of whether PSP can accommodate inconsistent theories.

References

Adams, E. W. 1959. The Foundations of Rigid Body Mechanics and the Derivation of Its Laws from Those of Particle Mechanics. In L. Henkin, P. Suppes, and A. Tarski (eds.), *The Axiomatic Method: With Special Reference to Geometry and Physics*. Amsterdam: North-Holland, pp. 250–265.

Ainsworth, P. 2009. Newman's Objection. *The British Journal for the Philosophy of Science* 60: 135–171.

Bailer-Jones, D. M. 2003. When Scientific Models Represent. *International Studies in the Philosophy of Science* 17: 59–74.

Bailer-Jones, D. M. 2009. *Scientific Models in Philosophy of Science*. Pittsburgh: Pittsburgh University Press.

Balzer, W., C.-U. Moulines, and J. D. Sneed 1987. *An Architectonic for Science: The Structuralist Program*. Dordrecht: Reidel Publishing Company.

Bangu, S. 2012. *The Applicability of Mathematics in Science: Indispensability and Ontology*. Basingstoke: Palgrave Macmillan.

Bartels, A. 2006. Defending the Structural Concept of Represenation. *Theoria* 21: 7–19.

Bogen, J. 2010. Noise in the World. *Philosophy of Science* 182: 778–791.

Bogen, J. and J. Woodward 1988. Saving the Phenomena. *The Philosophical Review* 97: 303–352.

Bolinska, A. 2013. Epistemic Representation, Informativeness and the Aim of Faithful Representation. *Synthese* 190: 219–234.

Bolinska, A. 2016. Successful Visual Epistemic Representation. *Studies in History and Philosophy of Science* 56: 153–160.

Brading, K. 2010. Autonomous Patterns and Scientific Realism. *Philosophy of Science* 77: 827–839.

Brading, K. and E. Landry 2006. Scientific Structuralism: Presentation and Representation. *Philosophy of Science* 73: 571–581.

Brown, J. R. 1994. *Smoke and Mirrors: How Science Reflects Reality*. London and New York: Routledge.

Bueno, O. 1997. Empirical Adequacy: A Partial Structure Approach. *Studies in the History and Philosophy of Science* 28: 585–610.

Bueno, O. 1999. What Is Structural Empiricism? Scientific Change in an Empiricist Setting. *Erkenntnis* 50: 59–85.

Bueno, O. 2010. Models and Scientific Representations. In P. D. Magnus and J. Busch (eds.), *New Waves in Philosophy of Science*. Hampshire: Palgrave MacMillan, pp. 94–111.

Bueno, O. and M. Colyvan 2011. An Inferential Conception of the Application of Mathematics. *Nous* 45: 345–374.

Bueno, O. and S. French 2011. How Theories Represent. *The British Journal for the Philosophy of Science* 62: 857–894.

Bueno, O., S. French, and J. Ladyman 2002. On Representing the Relationship between the Mathematical and the Empirical. *Philosophy of Science* 69: 452–473.

Butterfield, J. 2014. Our Mathematical Universe? A Discussion of Some Themes in Max Tegmark's Recent Book 'Our Mathematical Universe'. *arXiv:1406.4348*. https://arxiv.org/abs/1406.4348.

Byerly, H. 1969. Model-Structures and Model-Objects. *The British Journal for the Philosophy of Science* 20: 135–144.

Callender, C. and J. Cohen 2006. There Is No Special Problem About Scientific Representation. *Theoria* 55: 7–25.

Chakravartty, A. 2001. The Semantic or Model-Theoretic View of Theories and Scientific Realism. *Synthese* 127: 325–345.

Collier, J. D. 2002. Critical Notice: Paul Thompson, the Structure of Biological Theories. *Canadian Journal of Philosophy* 22: 287–298.

Contessa, G. 2006. Scientific Models, Partial Structures and the New Received View of Theories. *Studies in History and Philosophy of Science* 37: 370–377.

Contessa, G. 2007. Scientific Representation, Interpretation, and Surrogative Reasoning. *Philosophy of Science* 74: 48–68.

Contessa, G. 2010a. Empiricist Structuralism, Metaphysical Realism, and the Bridging Problem. *Analysis Reviews* 70: 514–525.

Contessa, G. 2010b. Scientific Models and Fictional Objects. *Synthese* 172: 215–229.

Da Costa, N. C. A. and S. French 1990. The Model-Theoretic Approach in the Philosophy of Science. *Philosophy of Science* 57: 248–265.

Da Costa, N. C. A. and S. French 2003. *Science and Partial Truth: A Unitary Approach to Models and Scientific Reasoning*. Oxford: Oxford University Press.

Elgin, C. Z. 2017. *True Enough*. Cambridge, MA and London: MIT Press.

Elkins, J. 1999. *The Domain of Images*. Ithaca and London: Cornell University Press.

French, S. 2000. The Reasonable Effectiveness of Mathematics: Partial Structures and the Application of Group Theory to Physics. *Synthese* 125: 103–120.

French, S. 2003. A Model-Theoretic Account of Representation (or, I Don't Know Much About Art . . . But I Know It Involves Isomorphism). *Philosophy of Science* 70: 1472–1483.

French, S. 2014. *The Structure of the World: Metaphysics and Representation*. Oxford: Oxford University Press.

French, S. and J. Ladyman 1997. Superconductivity and Structures: Revisiting the London Account. *Studies in History and Philosophy of Modern Physics* 28: 363–393.

French, S. and J. Ladyman 1999. Reinflating the Semantic Approach. *International Studies in the Philosophy of Science* 13: 103–121.

Frigg, R. 2002. Models and Representation: Why Structures Are Not Enough. *Measurement in Physics and Economics Project Discussion Paper Series, DP MEAS 25/02*.

Frigg, R. 2006. Scientific Representation and the Semantic View of Theories. *Theoria* 55: 49–65.

Frigg, R. 2010. Fiction and Scientific Representation. In R. Frigg and M. Hunter (eds.), *Beyond Mimesis and Convention: Representation in Art and Science*. Berlin and New York: Springer, pp. 97–138.

Frigg, R. and J. Nguyen 2017. Models and Representation. In L. Magnani and T. Bertolotti (eds.), *Springer Handbook of Model-Based Science*. Dordrecht, Heidelberg, London, and New York: Springer, pp. 49–102.

Frigg, R. and J. Nguyen 2020. *Modelling Nature: An Opinionated Introduction to Scientific Representation* (Synthese Library). Berlin and New York: Springer.

Frigg, R. and I. Votsis 2011. Everything You Always Wanted to Know About Structural Realism But Were Afraid to Ask. *European Journal for Philosophy of Science* 1: 227–276.

Frisch, M. 2015. Users, Structures, and Representation. *The British Journal for the Philosophy of Science* 66: 285–306.

Giere, R. N. 2009. Essay Review: Scientific Representation and Empiricist Structuralism. *Philosophy of Science* 76: 101–111.

Glymour, B. 2000. Data and Phenomena: A Distinction Reconsidered. *Erkenntnis* 52: 29–37.

Godfrey-Smith, P. 2006. The Strategy of Model-Based Science. *Biology and Philosophy* 21: 725–740.

González, W. J. 2014. On Representation and Models in Bas Van Fraassen's Approach. In W. J. González (ed.), *Bas Van Fraassen's Approach to Representation and Models in Science*. Dordrecht: Springer, pp. 3–37.

Goodman, N. 1976. *Languages of Art* (2nd ed.). Indianapolis and Cambridge: Hacket.

Hacking, I. 1983. *Representing and Intervening*. Cambridge: Cambridge University Press.

Hellman, G. and S. Shapiro 2019. *Mathematical Structuralism*. Cambridge: Cambridge University Press.

Hendry, R. F. 1999. Structure as Abstraction. *Philosophy of Science* 83: 1070–1081.

Hughes, R. I. G. 1997. Models and Representation. *Philosophy of Science* 64(Supplement): 325–336.

Kaiser, M. 1991. From Rocks to Graphs – the Shaping of Phenomena. *Synthese* 89: 111–133.

Kaushal, R. S. 1999. The Role of Structural Analogy in Physical Sciences: A Philosophical Perspective. *Indian Philosophical Quarterly* 26: 543–573.

Kroes, P. 1989. Structural Analogies between Physical Systems. *The British Journal for the Philosophy of Science* 40: 145–154.

Ladyman, J. 1998. What Is Structural Realism? *Studies in the History and Philosophy of Science* 29: 109–124.

Levy, A. 2012. Models, Fictions, and Realism: Two Packages. *Philosophy of Science* 79: 738–748.

Liu, C. 2013. Deflationism on Scientific Representation. In V. Karakostas and D. Dieks (eds.), *Epsa11 Perspectives and Foundational Problems in Philosophy of Science*. Berlin and New York: Springer, pp. 93–102.

Lusk, G. 2021. Saving the Data. *The British Journal for the Philosophy of Science* 72(1): 277–298. https://doi.org/10.1093/bjps/axy072.

Lutz, S. 2015. Partial Model Theory as Model Theory. *Ergo* 2: 563–580.

Lyon, A. 2016. Data. In P. Humphreys (ed.), *The Oxford Handbook of Philosophy of Science*. Oxford: Oxford Univeristy Press, pp. 738–758.

Machamer, P. (ed.) 2011. *Phenomena, Data and Theories* (Special Issue of Synthese 182 (1)). Berlin: Springer.

McAllister, J. W. 1997. Phenomena and Patterns in Data Sets. *Erkenntnis* 47: 217–228.

McAllister, J. W. 2010. The Ontology of Patterns in Empirical Data. *Philosophy of Science* 77: 804–814.

Mikenberg, I., N. C. A. Da Costa, and S. French 1986. Pragmatic Truth and Approximation to Truth. *Journal of Symbolic Logic* 51: 201–221.

Morgan, M. S. and M. Morrison 1999. Models as Mediating Instruments. In M. Morgan and M. Morrison (eds.), *Models as Mediators: Perspectives on Natural and Social Science*. Cambridge: Cambridge University Press, pp. 10–37.

Morrison, M. 2007. Where Have All the Theories Gone? *Philosophy of Science* 74: 195–228.

Morrison, M. 2008. Models as Representational Structures. In S. Hartmann, C. Hoefer, and L. Bovens (eds.), *Nancy Cartwright's Philosophy of Science* (Routledge Studies in the Philosophy of Science, Vol. 3). New York: Routledge, pp. 67–90.

Muller, F. A. 2004. Review of Patrick Suppes' 'Representation and Invariance in Scientific Structures'. *Studies in History and Philosophy of Modern Physics* 35: 713–720.

Muller, F. A. 2009. The Insidiously Enchanted Forrest. Esssy Review of 'Scientific Representation' by Bas. C Van Fraassen. *Studies in History and Philosophy of Modern Physics* 40: 268–272.

Muller, F. A. 2011. Reflections on the Revolution at Stanford. *Synthese* 183: 87–114.

Mundy, B. 1986. On the General Theory of Meaningful Representation. *Synthese* 67: 391–437.

Nguyen, J. 2016. On the Pragmatic Equivalence between Representing Data and Phenomena. *Philosophy of Science* 83: 171–191.

Nguyen, J. and R. Frigg 2017. Mathematics Is Not the Only Language in the Book of Nature. *Synthese* 198: 5941–5962. https://doi.org/10.1007/s11229-017-1526-5.

Okruhlik, K. 2009. Critical Notice. Bas C. Van Fraassen. Scientific Representation: Paradoxes of Perspective. Oxford: Oxford University Press 2008. *Canadian Journal of Philosophy* 39: 671–694.

Padovani, F. 2012. Bas C. Van Fraassen: Scientific Representation: Paradoxes of Perspective. *Science and Education* 21: 1199–1204.

Parker, W. 2020. Model Evaluation: An Adequacy-for-Purpose View. *Philosophy of Science* 87: 457–477.

Perini, L. 2005. The Truth in Pictures. *Philosophy of Science* 72: 262–285.

Perini, L. 2010. Scientific Representation and the Semiotics of Pictures. In P. D. Magnus and J. Busch (eds.), *New Waves in the Philosophy of Science*. New York: Macmilan, pp. 131–154.

Pero, F. and M. Suárez 2016. Varieties of Misrepresentation and Homomorphism. *European Journal for Philosophy of Science* 6: 71–90.

Pincock, C. 2005. Overextending Partial Structures: Idealization and Abstraction. *Philosophy of Science* 72: 1248–1259.

Pincock, C. 2012. *Mathematics and Scientific Representation*. Oxford: Oxford University Press.

Portides, D. 2017. Models and Theories. In L. Magnani and T. Bertolotti (eds.), *Springer Handbook of Model-Based Science*. Dordrecht and Heidelberg: Springer, pp. 25–48.

Poznic, M. 2018. Thin Versus Thick Accounts of Scientific Representation. *Synthese* 195: 3433–3451.

Psillos, S. 1999. *Scientific Realism: How Science Tracks Truth*. London: Routledge.

Rédei, M. 2020. On the Tension between Physics and Mathematics. *Journal for General Philosophy of Science* 51: 411–425.

Redhead, M. 2001. The Intelligibility of the Universe. In A. O'Hear (ed.), *Philosophy at the New Millennium*. Cambridge: Cambridge University Press, pp. 73–90.

Resnik, M. D. 1997. *Mathematics as a Science of Patterns*. Oxford: Oxford University Press.

Saatsi, J. 2011. The Enhanced Indispensability Argument: Representational Versus Explanatory Role of Mathematics in Science. *The British Journal for the Philosophy of Science* 62: 143–154.

Sánchez-Dorado, J. 2017. Methodological Lessons for the Integration of Philosophy of Science and Aesthetics. The Case of Representation. In O. Bueno, G. Darby, S. French, and D. Rickles (eds.), *Thinking About Science, Reflecting on Art*. London: Routledge, pp. 10–26.

Schier, F. 1986. *Deeper in Pictures: An Essay on Pictorial Represenation*. Cambridge: Cambridge University Press.

Schindler, S. 2007. Rehabilitating Theory: Refusal of the 'Bottom-up' Construction of Scientific Phenomena. *Studies in History and Philosophy of Science* 38: 160–184.

Schindler, S. 2011. Bogen and Woodward's Data-Phenomena Distinction, Forms of Theory-Ladenness, and the Reliability of Data. *Synthese* 182: 39–55.

Shapiro, S. 1983. Mathematics and Reality. *Philosophy of Science* 50: 523–548.

Shive, J. N. and R. L. Weber 1982. *Similarity in Pgysics*. New York: Wiley.

Stich, S. and T. Warfield (eds.) 1994. *Mental Represenation: A Reader*. Oxford: Blackwell.

Suárez, M. 2003. Scientific Representation: Against Similarity and Isomorphism. *International Studies in the Philosophy of Science* 17: 225–244.

Suárez, M. 2004. An Inferential Conception of Scientific Representation. *Philosophy of Science* 71(Supplement): 767–779.

Suppes, P. 2011. Future Development of Scientific Structures Closer to Experiments: Response to F.A. Muller. *Synthese* 183: 115–126.

Swoyer, C. 1991. Structural Representation and Surrogative Reasoning. *Synthese* 87: 449–508.

Tal, E. 2011. From Data to Phenomena and Back Again: Computer-Simulated Signatures. *Synthese* 182: 117–129.

Tegmark, M. 2008. The Mathematical Universe. *Foundations of Physics* 38: 101–150.

Teller, P. 2001. Whither Constructive Empiricism. *Philosophical Studies* 106: 123–150.

Teller, P. 2010. 'Saving the Phenomena' Today. *Philosophy of Science* 77: 815–826.

Thomson-Jones, M. 2010. Missing Systems and Face Value Practise. *Synthese* 172: 283–299.

Toon, A. 2012. *Models as Make-Believe: Imagination, Fiction and Scientific Representation*. Basingstoke: Palgrave Macmillan.

van Fraassen, B. C. 1980. *The Scientific Image*. Oxford: Oxford University Press.

van Fraassen, B. C. 1981. Theory Construction and Experiment: An Empiricist View. *Philosophy of Science (Proceedings Vol. 2)*, pp. 663–677.

van Fraassen, B. C. 1985. Empiricism in the Philosophy of Science. In P. M. Churchland and C. A. Hooker (eds.), *Images of Science*. Chicago: Chicago University Press, pp. 245–308.

van Fraassen, B. C. 1989. *Laws and Symmetry*. Oxford: Clarendon Press.

van Fraassen, B. C. 1997. Structure and Perspective: Philosophical Perplexity and Paradox. In M. L. Dalla Chiara (ed.), *Logic and Scientific Methods*. Dordrecht: Kluwer, pp. 511–530.

van Fraassen, B. C. 2002. *The Empirical Stance*. New Haven and London: Yale University Press.

van Fraassen, B. C. 2008. *Scientific Representation: Paradoxes of Perspective*. Oxford: Oxford University Press.

van Fraassen, B. C. 2010. Reply to Contessa, Ghins, and Healey. *Analysis Reviews* 70: 547–556.

Vickers, P. 2009. Can Partial Structures Accomodate Inconsistent Science. *Principia* 13: 233–250.

Votsis, I. 2010. Making Contact with Observations. In M. Suárez, M. Dorato, and M. Redei (eds.), *Epsa Philosophical Issues in the Sciences* (Vol. 2). Berlin: Springer, pp. 267–277.

Walsh, S., E. Knox, and A. Caulton 2014. Critical Review of Mathematics and Scientific Representation. *Philosophy of Science* 81: 460–469.

Weisberg, M. 2013. *Simulation and Similarity: Using Models to Understand the World*. Oxford: Oxford University Press.

Wigner, E. 1960. The Unreasonable Effectiveness of Mathematics in the Natural Sciences. *Communications on Pure and Applied Mathematics* 13: 1–14.

Woodward, J. 1989. Data and Phenomena. *Synthese* 79: 393–472.

Woodward, J. 2000. Data, Phenomena, and Reliability. *Philosophy of Science (Proceedings)* 67: 163–179.

Woodward, J. 2010. Data, Phenomena, Signal, and Noise. *Philosophy of Science* 182: 792–803.

Woodward, J. 2011. Data and Phenomena: A Restatement and Defense. *Synthese* 182: 165–179.

Woody, A. (ed.) 2010. *Syposia Papers from the Psa 2008 Program*. Chicago: Chicago University Press.

Worrall, J. 2011. Underdetermination, Realism and Empirical Equivalence. *Synthese* 180: 157–172.

7
FAMILY TIES

7.1 Introduction

The core of the Model-Theoretical View of Theories is that a theory is a family of models. So far, little has been said about what binds this family together. This makes the current formulations of the Model-Theoretical View what Halvorson calls a "flat view" of theories (2016, 600). Flat views contrast with "structured views", which are views that explicate how the models in a theory are related to each other. A structured view explicates, as it were, what the family ties between the various members of the family of models are. In this chapter we discuss the structured view of theories that is associated with *Munich Structuralism* (MS),[1] which offers a comprehensive answer to the question of how the models of a theory are related to each other.[2] We start by introducing the main tenets of MS (Section 7.2), and then articulate the notion of a theory's empirical claim (Section 7.3). MS's analysis of theories offers a new perspective on the problem of theory-ladenness, and one which is able to address some of the concerns we raised in Sections 3.4 and 3.5 (Section 7.4). We conclude by noting some of the problems that attach to MS (Section 7.5).

7.2 The Anatomy of a Theory

Taking Suppes' analysis of theories as its starting point, MS offers a refined analysis of the internal structure of the family of models that constitutes a theory, and based on that analysis sheds light on a number of issues in connection with scientific theories, notably the theory-ladenness of observation, the identity of theories, scientific explanation, idealisation and approximation, holism, reductionism, and the diachronic development of theories (both cumulative and revolutionary). In this chapter we concentrate on MS's analysis of the structure of theories and its

DOI: 10.4324/9781003285106-10

implications for the issues of the theory-ladenness of observation.[3] Throughout the discussion we illustrate the concepts and claims of MS with the example of Newtonian mechanics. This example plays a prominent role in the writings of the movement's protagonists, and it allows us to build on the discussion of Newtonian mechanics in Section 5.2.

The initial step in specifying a theory T is to get clear on what kind of structures it should contain. To this end one lists the primitive concepts of the theory (sometimes called T-concepts). In the case of Newtonian mechanics these are *particle, mass, location, time*, and *force*. There is no need to list concepts that can be defined through primitive concepts (there is no need to list velocity, for instance, because it can be defined through time and location). Then one specifies what properties these concepts have. To this end, the concepts are sorted into relations and operations, and their formal properties are specified. For instance, time is stipulated to be an interval of the real numbers, and location is said to be a function from particles and times to space. In effect this is what has happened in Section 5.2 when we said that the domain of the structure of Newtonian mechanics was the product of P, θ, M, L, and F, that the of set relations of the structure was empty, that the set of operations contained the operations l, m, and f, and that these satisfied Axioms 1–4. These posits do not say anything substantial; they just specify the *structure type* of the structures that Newtonian mechanics works with. The conditions specifying the structure type are called *frame conditions* (sometimes also *improper axioms*). The frame conditions specify the class C_T^p of *potential models* of the theory T. They are potential in the sense that they have the correct formal structure (a structure that has no particle number and no time in it could not possibly be a model of Newtonian mechanics). Whether they really are models of Newtonian mechanics will depend on the substantive laws of the theory, but these are not yet specified.

The *axioms* of T (sometimes also *proper axioms* of T) specify the substantive laws of the theory. In the case of Newtonian mechanics these are Axioms 5 and 6 in Section 5.2, namely the action-reaction principle and Newton's law of motion. Many structures in C_T^p do not satisfy these laws. The class C_T^p will contain, for instance, models that have no reaction force or ones in which the acceleration of a particle in response to the force varies with the square of its mass. The subclass of C_T^p consisting of models that satisfy the axioms of T is the class C_T^a of *actual models* of T. As a mnemonic device we introduce a diagram, show in Figure 7.1, illustrating the notions at work in MS and the relations between them.[4]

So far we have done little more than relabelling the elements in Suppes' account (notice that C_T^a is the same class as Suppes' C_τ). The first substantive innovation of MS is the notion of a concept being *theoretical with respect to theory T*, or *T-theoretical* for short. Intuitively a concept is *T-theoretical* if it is original to T and is not "imported" or "borrowed" from another theory. A concept is *T-non-theoretical* if it is not *T*-theoretical. This distinction can be seen in operation in mechanics. *Space, time*, and *particle* are concepts that Newtonian mechanics takes over from kinematics, the subfield of mechanics concerned with the description of motions *without* attributing the motion to the operation of any causes, let alone forces. Kinematics has been around before Newton. Galileo and Kepler took it as a given that objects like planets have certain positions at certain times and described the motion of an object as a trajectory, which they thought of as a continuous curve in space. Trajectories can have geometrical properties, and theorems can be formulated about them. The most prominent examples are Kepler's laws, which we encountered in Section 1.2. These laws attribute geometrical properties to a planet's trajectory without seeing the trajectories as the result of the action of forces. Even theorists like Descartes and Leibniz, who held very different views on the nature of motion than Newton, could agree on a kinematic description of, say, a planet's path. This is because kinematic notions are understood and used prior to the formulation of Newtonian mechanics, and they come to the theory "from outside". As we have seen in Section 1.2, Newton himself regarded these as notions that were "very familiar to everyone". In the current idiom, they are Newtonian-mechanics-non-theoretical. Newton's innovation was the introduction of the concepts of *force* and *mass*, and the idea to tie the change in the state of motion to the action of forces in exactly the way specified in his law of motion.[5] These concepts are original to Newtonian mechanics, which is to say that they are Newtonian-mechanics-theoretical. These concepts are now referred to as *dynamical* concepts, where dynamics is the branch of mechanics that studies how forces affect motion. So, in brief, kinematic concepts are Newtonian-mechanics-non-theoretical, while dynamical concepts are Newtonian-mechanics-theoretical.

Considerations of origin are good to boost intuition, but they do not provide an analysis (let alone definition) of the concept of T-theoreticity. The key to an analysis of T-theoreticity lies in the notion of the *applicability* of a concept. A crucial aspect of understanding a concept is to know when, where, how, and under what conditions it is applicable. For instance, we understand the concept "round" if we know to which objects it applies. Often the conditions of applicability are given in the context of a theory. In the case of "round" it is elementary geometry that tells us how to apply the concept. T-non-theoretical concepts are understood prior to T being available and so their application does not depend on T. For instance, we do not need Newtonian mechanics to describe the shape of a trajectory. T-theoretical concepts do not enjoy this independence. Their conditions of applicability are *always* given by T, and the concepts are inapplicable outside the context of T. "Force", for instance, is inapplicable without Newtonian mechanics, just as "round" is inapplicable without elementary geometry. Concepts in modern science are mostly metrical: they assign numbers to quantities. "Mass" and "force" are cases in point. We not only say that planets have mass and are acted upon by a force; we specify their exact mass as a real number and say what exactly the strength of the force is. In these cases, applying a concept also involves being able to determine its magnitude. This realisation furnishes the sought-after definition of T-theoreticity: a concept is T-theoretical iff *all* methods of determining the extension of the concept presuppose at least one law of T. If the concept has numerical magnitudes (as, for instance, *mass* and *force*), then being T-theoreticity means that on every occasion where the numerical value of the concept is determined, at least one law of T must be used.[6]

Balzer et al. (1987, 47) illustrate this with the concept *hermaphrodite*. To decide whether something is a hermaphrodite, we need a theory specifying what a hermaphrodite is. Let us assume that this is done in reproductive biology, which has a law that says $\forall x(x$ is a hermaphrodite if, and only if, x is a living being which is male and female simultaneously). Any determination of whether something is a hermaphrodite will have to appeal to this law. For this reason, the concept of a hermaphrodite is reproductive-biology-theoretical. Such a determination will also rely on being able to tell whether an object is a living being, and whether it is male or female. The concepts do not originate in our reproductive biology and are therefore reproductive-biology-non-theoretical. This simplistic example illustrates the "dual" character of applying T-theoretical concepts. On the one hand, a law of the theory is always required, and in this sense any application of a T-theoretical concept is theory-laden (namely laden with T); on the other hand, the application also depends on T-non-theoretical concepts and is therefore grounded notions outside T.

Returning to Newtonian mechanics, consider the example of the determination of the mass of an ordinary object like a suitcase. One way to do this is to take a spring balance fixed to the ceiling with a hook and fix the object whose mass one wants to determine at the bottom of the spring. Hooke's law tells us that the restoring force of a spring is $f_s = -kx$, where k is constant specific to the particular spring we use and x is the spring's elongation (how far the spring has been stretched). The law of gravity close to the surface of the earth is $f_g = gm$, where g is a constant and m is the mass of the object. Newton's second law tells us that the mass of an object times its acceleration is equal to the sum of the forces acting on it: $ma = f_s + f_g$. We are looking at a scenario in which the suitcase is at rest: $a = 0$. So Newton's equation becomes $f_s + f_g = 0$, from which it follows that $m = kx / g$. So if we measure x (how far the suitcase has moved downwards after hanging it on the hook), we get the suitcase's mass. This determination of an object's mass requires three laws of Newtonian mechanics: Newton's equation of motion (Axiom 6), Hooke's law, and the law of gravity close to the earth. To say that mass is Newtonian-mechanics-theoretical is tantamount to claiming that there is *no* determination of an object's mass that does not appeal to at least one law of Newtonian Mechanics.

Concepts do not wear their status on their sleeves. It is neither obvious, nor an a priori truth that mass is Newtonian-mechanics-theoretical. In general, when confronted with a theory in the form one encounters in textbooks or research papers, it is not clear what the theory's basic concepts are, and it is even less clear which ones are T-theoretical. The status of concepts is revealed by a systematic reconstruction of the theory in MS's terms.

Given a sorting of the parts of the structure of T into T-theoretical and T-non-theoretical, one can now construct a "reduced" version of the potential models of T by "cutting off" their T-theoretical parts. The result of this process are *partial potential models*, which form the class of potential partial models is C_T^{pp}. In formal terms, this process can be described as a *reduction function* $r: C_T^p \rightarrow C_T^{pp}$ which assigns every $m \in C_T^p$ the partial potential model $r(m)$. The model $r(m)$ is a substructure (in the sense introduce in Section 2.7) of m. In the case of Newtonian mechanics, the reduction function simply omits forces and masses from the structures. In formal terms (as introduced in Section 5.2), a partial potential model of Newtonian mechanics has a domain that is the Cartesian product of P, θ, and L (M and F have been omitted) and contains only the operation l (m and f have been omitted). Partial potential models will later play a crucial role in explaining what a theory's empirical claim is; that is, in explaining what a theory says about its subject matter. But before we can spell out how partial potential models do this, we need to introduce a few additional elements of MS.

The three classes of models we have introduced so far taken together form the *core* of T (sometimes also *mathematical* core of T): $K_T := (C_T^p, C_T^{pp}, C_T^a)$.[7] Intuitively speaking, C_T^p is a set-theoretical version of the conceptual machinery of T (because the structures in it reflect every primitive concept of T); C_T^{pp} is (as we will see below) the basis against which T is tested; and C_T^a reflects the laws of the theory.

A theory is not just a formal apparatus; it is a formal apparatus intended to represent specific aspects and parts of the world. In contrast with Suppes, who defines a theory entirely formally, MS, following a suggestion of Adams' (1959), regards the domain of application of a theory as a crucial part of the theory itself: a theory cannot be individuated solely through its formal apparatus. For this reason, the core of the theory has to be complemented with a specification of the *domain of intended applications I_T*.

In principle, the domain of intended applications of a theory is simply the class of all systems in the universe to which practitioners in the field intend to apply the theory. In the case of Newtonian Mechanics that class would contain moving planets, falling bodies, flying projectiles, oscillating swings, and so on. It is of course impossible to explicitly list all objects to which a theory is to be applied. Not only would it take too long to do so; there may also be systems that we do not yet know, or that do not yet exist, to which the theory will be applied. MS solves this problem by appeal to paradigms and similarity. In a first step, a number of paradigmatic examples are selected to be intended applications. In a second step, systems that satisfy two additional criteria are included: they are sufficiently similar to one of the paradigm examples and the theory can be expected to apply successfully to them. Neither of these steps is automatic. Examples can be moved in and out of I_T as research progresses, and what counts as similar may change in response to new insights. Newton considered light to be an instance of particle motion and hence classified it as an intended application of his mechanics. It became clear later that this was a mistake, and light was subsequently removed from the set of intended applications of Newtonian mechanics. So I_T is historically changeable and essentially dependent on the intentions of scientists working with the theory.

A further qualification is crucial. I_T contains only "structural versions" of physical systems. So if we were to make an inventory of what is in I_T, we would not find a full-fledged pendulum consisting of a copper ball hanging on a string made from twisted hemp fixed to a plaster wall with an iron nail. What we would find in I_T is a structure, which has the form of a partial potential model of T, which is deemed to "correspond" to the real pendulum. So the "pendulum" we find in I_T is in fact a structure with a domain consisting of P, T, and L, and an operation l. So contrary to what talk of "intended applications" might suggest, I_T is a class of structures and not of material things. In fact, I_T is a subclass of C_T^{pp}: $I_T \subseteq C_T^{pp}$. Intended applications are associated with partial potential models (rather than "full" potential models) because, as we will see in Section 7.3, they are the "empirical" basis against which a theory is tested, and therefore do not already contain the theory's theoretical parts.

The crucial concept is the notion of a structure "corresponding" to a physical system. A natural way to cash out this somewhat elusive notion of correspondence between a physical system and a structure is to say that the system instantiates the relevant C_T^{pp} structure. In fact, we have encountered this suggestion in Chapter 6 when we discussed the isomorphism account of representation. This account required a transition from physical systems to structures, and this transition was brought about by the idea that systems instantiate structures. Appealing to this idea, we can then say that I_T is the subset of C_T^{pp} consisting of structures that are instantiated in the physical systems to which the theory is intended to apply. This is a cogent suggestion in so far as one can make sense of the notion of a physical system instantiating a structure. MS takes this notion as an unanalysed primitive and says nothing further about it. This gap can be filled, for instance, by appealing to the options outlined in Section 6.5

Let us now have a look at the internal constitution of C_T^{pp}, which is illustrated in Figure 7.1. This class not only contains I_T; it also contains $r(C_T^a)$, the class of the partial versions of a theory's actual models. These are models that satisfy the axioms of T but whose T-theoretical part has been cut off. The theory is successfully applied to a particular system in the class of its intended applications if the intended application is also in $r(C_T^a)$. In formal terms, the successful applications of T lie in the intersection of $r(C_T^a)$ and I_T. But the classes $r(C_T^a)$ and I_T typically do not overlap perfectly. There can be models in $r(C_T^a)$ that are not in I_T. These are models that satisfy a theory's axioms but do not correspond to an intended application. At any given time, these models are a "theoretical surplus" of T. This, however, does not mean that they will never have applications. A model that is a purely theoretical option at some point may suddenly become useful in describing a new system that has been added to the class of intended applications. Vice versa, there may be systems in I_T that are not in $r(C_T^a)$. These are systems to which T is intended to apply, but that have not yet successfully been brought under the auspices of T. Scientific progress in applying a theory then consists in moving "I_T only" models into the intersection of $r(C_T^a)$ and I_T (and, indeed, in extending I_T itself to enlarge the scope of the theory).

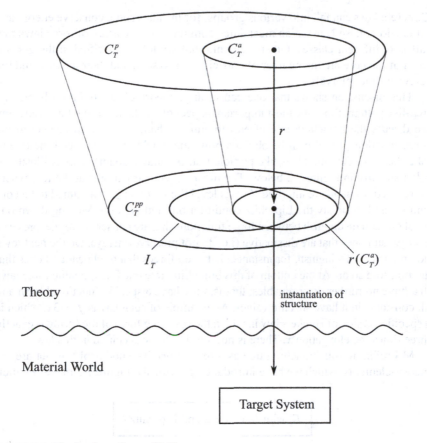

FIGURE 7.1 The basic notions of MS.

The core of a theory with its intended applications together form what MS calls a *theory-element* $E_T = (K_T, I_T)$. A crucial thing to realise at this point is that the core K_T of a theory contains many models that are determinables and not determinates because they contain a number of "free parameters". The most important one is the force function f. Axioms 5 and 6 only specify extremely abstract properties of a force function, but leave it completely open how this function actually looks. In fact all that is required is that f satisfy certain conditions for the equation of motion to be well-behaved. The standard condition is that f be continuous and satisfy the Lipschitz condition, which ensures – by the Picard-Lindelöf theorem – that Newton's equation has unique solutions (O'Regan 1997, Ch. 3).[8] But physical objects do not move according to functions whose only properties are continuity and satisfying the Lipschitz condition. Forces that act in the world are specific. Examples include Hooke's law, which we have encountered earlier in this section, and the law of gravity, which we have encountered in Section 1.2.

Concrete laws can fall into various groups, for instance some conserve energy and others do not. So Newtonian mechanics contains a whole array of force laws that fall into different classes. Other elements that are left unspecified in the general form of the core are the number of particles in a system and their masses, and the relevant time intervals.

This discussion shows that one can arrange theory elements into a branching tree-like pattern. Since the most important aspect of mechanics is the force function, we discuss the branching tree of Newtonian mechanics only with respect to the force function (it will then be obvious how one would have to extend the tree to take the other determinables like particle number into account). This is illustrated schematically in Figure 7.2 below. The most general structure is at the top, where no restrictions at all are imposed. At this level the function f is assumed to be continuous and to satisfy the Lipschitz condition but nothing else. Moving down one level one can distinguish between force functions that are conservative (i.e. preserve energy) and ones that are dissipative (i.e. do not preserve energy). On the next level down one can distinguish, for instance, between forces that are linear and ones that are not. And so on. At the bottom of this branching tree one finds specific force laws that have no further determinables; that is, they have a specific functional form and all constants in it have specific values. An example of such law is $f = 3x$, which is a specific version of Hooke's law in which the restoring force of the spring is exactly three times the elongation x. There is nothing left to be specified in this law.

MS refers to this branching tree as a *theory-net*. The nodes of this net are the theory-elements, which we have introduced previously. Figure 7.2 makes explicit

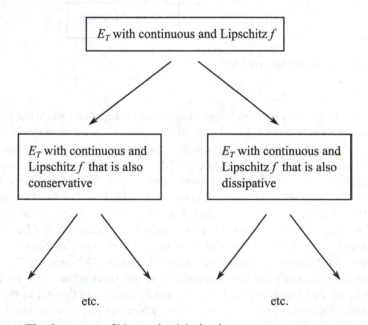

FIGURE 7.2 The theory-net of Newtonian Mechanics.

that theory elements can be located at different levels of abstraction. At the top there is the basic element from which the rest of the net derives through a process of successive "filling in" of ever more specific details. Close to the top one finds a theory-element containing all systems that preserve energy. This element corresponds to a theory of conservative dynamical systems. At the bottom one finds a theory element containing a pendulum moving under a fully specified linear restoring force (and having a particular mass and length). In all this, the theory-net is what corresponds to the intuitive notion of a complete theory. It contains not only the general structures and general laws (like Newton's equation of motion); it also contains subsidiary laws specifying specific forces, and it contains various classifications of these. The process of moving down in the branching tree is called *specialisation*, because each level adds specificity to the level above by adding further detail. For instance, a theory element with the law of gravity in it is a specialisation of the theory element that has energy-preserving forces in it because the law of gravity is energy preserving. Hence, specialisation is a fundamental relation between theory elements, and every knot further down in the net specialises the knots upstream in the net. This answers our question about the family ties between models that belong to the same theory T: the family ties consist in the specialization-relation holding between different theory elements.

Discussions about the nature of scientific theories often circle around the issue of the "structure of a theory".[9] MS has a clear answer to what the structure of a theory is: the structure of theory T (at a given time) is the branching tree that constitutes the theory-net of T. The topology of the tree gives information about how the laws of the theory are structured, and looking at branches of the tree provides information about how the different parts of a theory relate to one another.[10] In other words, the theory-net lays bare the anatomy of a theory (at a given time), just as the family tree lays bare the structure of a family.

7.3 A Theory's Empirical Claim

The analysis of the different components of a theory allows for a precise articulation of a theory's empirical content, or, in the jargon of MS, it allows for an articulation of a theory's *empirical claim* (although, as we will see in the next section, "empirical" is a bit of a misnomer).

Intuitively, a theory's empirical claim is that all systems in the theory's domain of intended applications are covered by the theory and that what the theory says about these systems is correct. The crucial question at this point is: with respect to which features of the systems does a theory have to be correct? Traditionally the answer to this question was taken to be: with respect to observations. MS revises this picture and submits that the "empirical basis" of a theory T is not defined by what is observable but by the target domain as conceptualised in terms of the theory's T-non-theoretical vocabulary. In other words, a theory is tested against an account of the target domain that is couched in terms that are used by the theory but that are not original to the theory (in the sense of being T-theoretical). In effect this means that theory is tested against an account of the target system that could have been given independently of the theory (because the application of T-non-theoretical concepts does not require any of the theory's laws). Consider again the example of Newtonian mechanics. The conceptual apparatus of the theory that is Newtonian-Mechanics-non-theoretical is the apparatus of kinematics. A kinematic description of the motion of a planet contains a specification of the planet's trajectory. This is the empirical basis against which the claims of Newtonian mechanics have to be tested. If, after specifying the masses of the sun and the planet and the gravitational attraction between them, the theoretical trajectory that is part of the model of Newtonian mechanics coincides with the trajectory that kinematics provides us with, then the theory is correct; if what follows from the equation of motion about the planet's path does not correspond to the kinetic trajectory of the planet, then the theory is wrong.

This idea can be given a general formulation in terms of the notions introduced in the last section. As we have seen, the class of intended applications is a subset of the theory's partial potential models. It is now clear why it is important that I_T contains *partial* potential models: these are the models that had their T-theoretical parts truncated and that consists only of T-non-theoretical parts. So partial potential models are the models that form the empirical basis of the theory. The notion that what the theory says with the aid of T-theoretical concepts about an intended application must be correct can then be expressed as follows: the class of *actual* models of Newtonian mechanics (i.e. the class of models that contain forces and masses which obey Newton's equation of motion and other relevant laws) contains a model that is such that if its theoretical parts are removed, then it is isomorphic to the model in I_T that corresponds to the phenomenon that we are interested in. Or put simply, there is an actual model of Newtonian mechanics that has the correct trajectory in it.

A theory is correct if this holds for all intended applications. Hence a theory's *empirical claim* is that for every intended application $i \in I_T$ there is an actual model $m \in C_T^a$ so that $r(m)$ is isomorphic to i.[11] In other words, the empirical claim of the theory is that every intended application can be embedded in one of its actual models. Referring back to Figure 7.1, we can give a geometrical interpretation of a theory's empirical claim: the part of the diagram that consists of models that are in I_T but not in $r(C_T^a)$ is empty because that set contains models that are intended applications but are not embeddable in an actual model of the theory. Or, in other words, I_T is a subset of $r(C_T^a)$. The theory's empirical claim can be true or false, depending on how the systems in I_T behave. If the empirical claim is true, then the theory is *empirically adequate*. Intuitively, if the theory is empirically adequate, the T-theoretical part of the theory accounts correctly for the behaviour of the T-non-theoretical part of the theory in *all* applications.

As we just noted, a theory's empirical claim can be wrong, and no guarantee of success is built into the theory! Indeed, this happens when predictions fail. This is chiefly for two reasons. First, the intended applications are identified, and their laws formulated, *without* using the T-theoretical machinery (one can

describe the motion of planets without any reference to Newtonian dynamics); the
T-theoretical machinery is then tested against the T-non-theoretical machinery.
Second, unlike a theory's basic concepts, which can be separated into ones that are
T-theoretical and ones that are not, its laws cannot usually be so separated. Consider Newton's equation of motion (Axiom 6 in Section 5.2). By saying how the
trajectory l of a particle changes as result of the action of a force and the particle's
mass, it establishes a connection between T-theoretical and T-non-theoretical concepts. In fact the T-theoretical concepts are used to make a claim about the T-non-
theoretical concepts. This is what makes the theoretical part open to refutation by
the empirical part. Imagine an alternative theory, Squtonian Mechanics, which is
like Newtonian mechanics except that the fundamental equation of motion says
that F is proportional to the square of the mass: $\vec{F} = m^2\vec{a}$. Squtonian Mechanics
has the same T-non-theoretical machinery as Newtonian mechanics, and it has the
same intended applications. But if one were to solve the equation of Squtonian
Mechanics in applications, it would turn out that what it says about particle trajectories is wrong. So there are no self-fulfilling predictions, and there is no circular
"self-confirmation".

7.4   Revisiting Theory-Ladenness

With these new instruments at hand, we can now return to the discussion of
theory-ladenness in Sections 3.4 and 3.5. According to MS, theory-ladenness
is ubiquitous, but not vicious. It is the nature of T-theoretical concepts that they
can be applied only by appeal to the theory itself. We cannot determine a force
or a mass without relying on Newtonian mechanics. This is a strong form of
theory-ladenness, but it is not one that is problematic. Recall that one of the main
worries in connection with theory-ladenness was that it leads to confirmatory
circularity: if the correctness of a theory's laws is presupposed in a theory's testing, then the theory must end up looking correct no matter what. It is one of the
merits of MS that it admits theory-ladenness while at the same time ruling out
"self-confirmation" of this kind. T-theoretical claims have to be tested against
T-non-theoretical claims, and, as we have seen, this test can fail. In fact, there
is no guarantee that what a theory says about its intended applications using its
T-theoretical vocabulary is correct. Theories can be wrong even if observation
is theory-laden.

The reason for this is that a theory is not a monolithic bloc that faces observation wholesale and in an "unstructured" manner. A theory has a strict separation
of T-theoretical and T-non-theoretical parts. From this point of view, one ought to
give up the notion of theory-ladenness *tout court* and instead speak of "T-theory-
ladenness", specifying which theory is involved in making a certain claim. And
the distinction between a claim that is T-theory-laden and one that is not T-theory-
laden is only a small part of a complete analysis of how (a branch of) science
faces reality. As we have seen in the last section, a theory is tested against partial
potential models. In the case of Newtonian mechanics these are kinematic models,

which are the theory's empirical structures. At this point it is important to note that being T-theoretical is a relational property. A concept can be T-theoretical with respect to one theory and T-non-theoretical with respect to another theory. For instance, kinematic concepts, which are Newtonian-mechanics-non-theoretical, are kinematics-theoretical, where kinematics is understood as descriptive theory of motion. Kinematics' concepts can be separated into kinematics-theoretical concepts and kinematics-non-theoretical concepts, and the latter can appear as the T-theoretical concepts in yet another theory. And so on. So if we look at an entire domain of science rather than just one theory, what we see is a "layer structure" with one theory built on top of another theory. Claims can be theory-laden with respect to one theory but not with respect to another, and the T-theoretical claims of every theory are tested against T-non-theoretical claims.

This contrasts with how theory-ladenness has been discussed by Hanson, Kuhn and Feyerabend (Section 3.4), who seemed to regard theory-ladenness as an all-or-nothing matter. This has turned out to be too coarse a picture. Theory-ladenness has to be relativised to particular theories, which makes many of the problems that arise in connection with theory-ladenness appear in a new light. The basis against which a theory T is tested is T-non-theoretical and therefore, by definition, not T-laden. This, of course, does not imply that this basis is not theory-laden with any number of *other* theories, but, and that is what matters, it is not laden with T. This rules out any form of self-confirmation. As we have seen in Section 3.5, Hempel and Lewis appealed to the idea that we should distinguish between new and previously understood concepts. This introduced a layering, where the order of the layers is given by historical precedence. As we have seen previously, this is problematic because not all relations between concepts are adequately captured by the temporal order in which they made their appearance on the stage of history. MS offers a systematically motivated and carefully articulated alternative to a historical account.[12]

MS makes clear progress on previous accounts, but two important questions arise: where does observation fit into this layering and what, if anything, is the bottom layer? Let us begin with observation. It is crucial to note that "empirical" as used in MS is not synonymous with "observable". As Díez points out, the T-theoretical vs. T-non-theoretical distinction and the observational vs. non observational distinction "do not coincide, neither intensionally nor extensionally" (2002, 15).[13] In fact, the T-non-theoretical part of a model need not be observable. The kinematic facts that Newtonian mechanics is tested against are trajectories of material objects like planets. But trajectories need not themselves be observable, at least not in any obvious way (the observation of the trajectories of celestial bodies sometimes requires elaborate equipment like telescopes, which also rely on theories). Or, if someone insists that trajectories are observable (recall van Fraassen's notion of observability in Section 3.3), then consider the example of pressure. It is defined as force divided by surface area, and it is not directly observable. At the same time, force, and with it pressure, are Newton-mechanics-theoretical but at the same time thermodynamics-non-theoretical, and so facts about pressure can be used to test thermodynamics. So, what constitutes the empirical basis of a theory T can itself be unobservable. For this reason, calling a theory's T-non-theoretical claims its "empirical claim" might be a bit of misnomer because "empirical" refers to something that is directly observable.[14] So it would be more appropriate to refer to the T-non-theoretical part of a theory as the theory's *testing basis*, and thereby leave it open whether this basis is also observable or "empirical".

That T-non-theoretical claims need not be observable is at once an advantage and a problem. It is an advantage because, as we have noted towards the end of Section 3.3, many advanced sciences contain no (or hardly any) concepts that are observable through our unaided senses, and observation often relies on elaborate instruments. According to MS there is nothing wrong with that because theories can relate to other theories, and contact with observation can be made somewhere further down in the layer structure of science. But this brings us to the problem: where and how does a cascade of theories make contact with observation? It is vital that such a point of contact exists. That one theory is confirmed relative to another theory is, by itself, not good enough. It would allow for there to be a collection of theories all relating to each other exactly as they should but at the same time being completely disconnected from direct experience. This is incompatible with empiricism and there must be a point at which the layer of theories makes contact with experience. Recall Feigl's schematic representation of a theory in Figure 1.1, which shows the theory as being grounded in the "soil" of observation. Even if one does not share Feigl's linguistic analysis of theories, or the idea that a theory has to make contact with observation directly, a theory about the physical world will have to make contact with experience *at some point*.

The question is where that point lies. Díez addresses this issue in his account of what he calls *observational scenes*. To introduce the idea, Díez recalls Hanson's example of Kepler and Tycho watching the dawn that we encountered in Section 3.4 (2002, 16). Hanson's line on this is that while Kepler and Tycho have the same retinal stimulation, they do not see the same thing because the state of people's retinas does not determine what they see. Díez takes issues with this verdict. He grants that, in some sense, they do not see the same thing: Tycho sees the sun move around the earth while Kepler sees the earth move around the sun. But he insists that this is not the only relevant sense of seeing something, and that there is another sense in which they do see the same thing: both see a yellow circle move upward from the line that marks the horizon. This is the observational scene that both Kepler and Tycho experience. Contra Hanson, Díez insists that this sense of seeing is not irrelevant; it is crucial for theory testing and theory choice. The observational scene is what both see, and it is what they do, and indeed must, agree on. It is the point at which theory makes contact with observation.

The Kepler and Tycho case is no exception, and observational scenes are also important in other areas. Examples of such scenes are white dots in the blue sky, grey paths in vapour, moving pins, coloured rings on computer screens, and angular displacements of a needle (2002, 34, 2006, 46). Observational scenes have two important properties. First, they are theory-independent and hence not influenced by the observer's theoretical commitments. This implies that they do not change even if observers with different theoretical perspectives and different beliefs look at them. Second, they are indisputable. As Díez puts it, observational scenes "are bio-evolutionary universals in that rational disagreement about them among bio-logically normal human being is not possible" (2006, 47, cf. 2002, 33). So observational scenes constitute the undisputable theory-free bedrock against which theories are ultimately tested. The qualification "ultimately" matters because "this bottom level is only implicit in scientific testing, for agreement on 'data' is found earlier at some higher level" (2002, 34). Díez submits that this holds true even in prominent cases of scientific controversy like the dispute between Galileo and the Aristotelians. What they disagreed about, according to Díez, is not the observational scene that was presented to them in the telescope: they agreed on what colours and shapes could be seen in the lens. What they disagreed about was the significance of this observational scene, which in MS's terms amounts to a disagreement about intended applications of a theory. Therefore, if the Aristotelians had agreed that a telescope was an instrument capable of veridical celestial observation, they would have had to agree on the astronomical claims Galileo made (2002, 34–35, 2006, 46–47).

Observational scenes play the same role in MS as protocol sentences in the Received View: they are the theory-free elements against which theories are ultimately tested. They are, however, different in important ways. Unlike protocol sentences, observational scenes are not linguistic; they do not have to be described in any particular vocabulary (or any vocabulary at all); they do not have to be the subject of beliefs; and they do not bear the justificatory burden protocol sentences did (2002, 33). But what then are observational scenes? Díez regards this as an open question and admits that beyond the negative characterisation just given, the options are wide open (*ibid.*, 34).

An important difference with protocol sentences is that theories need not (and usually do not) have a direct relation to observational scenes. The Received View demanded that there be bridge laws that connect the vocabulary of the theoretical language of a theory to the vocabulary of the observation language. MS requires no such direct relation. Newtonian dynamics is tested against kinematics. But kinematics is not an account of observational scenes. Kinematics is tested against an account of space-time positioning formulated in a certain coordinate system; this account tested against a theory that allows us to say in mathematical terms where something is; and such a theory is tested against basic pointing. The details of this would have to be worked out, and to the best of my knowledge this has not been done in the literature on MS. But it is clear that observational scenes only enter our discussion at the end where we consider how we point to things (Díez's dots in the sky), and there is a rich layer of theories above that basic layer, and no theory in that rich layer makes *direct* contact with experience.

For the sake of argument, let us assume that the structure of these layers can be worked out and that a cogent account of observational scenes can be given.

Does this solve the problem of theory-ladenness of observation? This is largely an open question, but it stands to reason that the followers of Hanson and Feyerabend would not be moved. Recall Hanson's example of the Eskimo baby seeing an X-ray tube (Section 3.4), where Hanson insists that one can see an X-ray tube only once one understands the basic concepts behind it. A similar point could be made about observational scenes. While the concepts involved here are much more basic than in the case of the X-ray tube, there are concepts involved nevertheless. To see a white spot move in the dark sky, an observer will need to possess geometrical notions like "point" and "line", and she will have to be able to apply colour predicates. Someone who does not possess basic geometrical concepts and basic colour concepts cannot make sense of the observational scene. At this point, Díez will insist that the observational scene itself is not linguistic and hence does not depend on observers having these concepts. But the Hansonians will insist that without these concepts, theories can neither be applied nor tested, and "observational scenes in themselves" are cognitively inert. So we may just have run up against the same issues yet again, albeit at a lower level.

But even if one agrees with the Hansonians (and there is an important "if" here), then the situation has changed. The fact that we are at a lower level is crucial. X-ray tubes and other scientific equipment are imbued with theory, and hence theory-ladenness is unavoidable. However, once we are at the level of white dots, the theories we are appealing to are so basic that they not only barely deserve to be called theories, but they are also largely shared and uncontroversial. Díez's point here would be that while reasonable people can disagree about the nature and properties of light, they cannot disagree about white spots on a blue background, even if, in an ultimate analysis, also this requires recourse to some sort of theory.[15]

Setting aside the particulars of Díez's account, the discussion about observational scenes highlights an important philosophical problem. MS suggest that we always test theories against other theories, and so the prospect of an infinite regress rears its head. Díez's account of observational scenes is in effect an attempt to block such a regress. As Díez notes, this amounts to defending a foundationalist position. So what we are up against is the foundationalism versus coherentism question. Balzer, Moulines, and Sneed discuss this issue at the end of their book and outline the options (1987, 411–423). Foundationalism holds that knowledge is structured like a layer cake. Every layer rests on the layer immediately below, but there is bottom layer on which everything else rests. The theory that is at the bottom of the layer structure is *basic* in the sense that it is not tested against anything else, and it is simply taken for granted. On that view, the cascade of theories ends when we "eventually reach a solid end, a bed-rock that grounds the empirical content, however indirectly" (*ibid.*, 412).[16] If there is such a bottom layer, there is a final level of theory that is not itself justified through testing it against *T*-non-theoretical claims. Coherentism rejects the claim that the edifice of science has such a layer cake structure and submits that science is rather like a web in which a certain part of the web is supported by its neighbouring parts. Theories relate to each other in loops and provide mutual support without being anchored in a foundation that is regarded as basic. According to coherentism, there is no basic theory. Balzer, Moulines, and Sneed end their discussion by noting that "coherentism shows some *a priori* advantages of a conceptual kind over foundationalism" (*ibid.*, 423) but eventually remain agnostic about the issue. The analysis of theories presented in this chapter provides an interesting angle from which the foundationalism vs. coherentism discussion as regards scientific knowledge can be revisited, but the issue eventually must be resolved somewhere else.

7.5 Conclusion

MS offers a comprehensive account of the internal structure of a theory, and it offers a new perspective on the issue of theory-ladenness. However, questions remain about how and where a theory makes contact with observation, and MS remains silent about how target systems have structures. These are important open questions. MS also faces many of the problems that other versions of the model-theoretical view of theories face, which we have discussed in Chapters 5 and 6. For instance, like other model-theoretical accounts, MS regards language as unimportant. Indeed, the description of the relevant structures does not appear at all in MS's account of theories and Suppes' intrinsic characterisations have dropped out of the picture altogether. This is no accident, and Moulines is explicit that MS regards the linguistic description of structures as unimportant:

> the choice of the particular axioms to be satisfied by the models of the class constituting a theory-element, is considered by structuralism as a relatively unimportant question (hence the label "non-statement view" which has sometimes been applied to this approach). Which axioms you take is just a matter of convenience, so long as the ones you choose allow for an exact determination of the class of models you need to represent a certain field of phenomena you are interested in.
>
> *(2002, 5)*

And he then goes on to note that alternative descriptions of the class of models that constitutes the theory are of no theoretical interest because a "theory's identity is given by M [the class of models], not by the set-theoretical predicate; the latter is just a useful tool to get that identity" (*ibid.*, 6). We have discussed this approach in Section 5.5, and we have seen that it leads to serious difficulties. Future iterations of MS will have to integrate linguistic formulations into their accounts of theories.[17]

Notes

1 Sometimes the movement is also referred to as "German structuralism" or "Metatheoretical structuralism". The members of the movement self-identify as "structuralists", but that label is too unspecific to single out the relevant group or body of work. The

qualification "Munich" is owed to the fact that several prominent exponents of the movement held chairs at the Ludwig Maximilians University of Munich, making it the epicentre of the movement. Early works in this tradition are Sneed's (1971) and Stegmüller's (1976, 1979). Balzer et al. (1987) is the foundational text that the crystalised the movement. The collections edited by Balzer and Moulines (1996) and Balzer et al. (2000) give insight into the panorama of work done in the movement. For a discussion of the aims of MS, and a defence against criticisms, see Lorenzano's (2013).

2 I would like to thank José Díez for many illuminating discussions on MS and for a long list of helpful comments on earlier drafts of this chapter.

3 The presentation of the material in this section and the next follows Balzer et al. (1987). Moulines' (2002) and (1996) offer introductions. Concise summaries of the main ideas can be found in Díez's (2002, Sec. 1) and Gähde's (2002, Sec. 2); Kuiper's (2001, Ch. 12) and Niiniluoto's (1984, Ch. 6) offer chapter-length introductions.

4 The notation in this chapter is chosen so that it is continuous with the notation used earlier in the book, in particular in Chapter 5. This notation deviates from what is common in the literature on MS, where M is used to designate the class of actual models, C_T^a, M_p is used to designate the class of potential models C_T^p, and M_{pp} is used to designate the class of partial potential models C_T^{pp} (which we introduce shortly).

5 The words "force" and "mass" have, of course, been used before Newton. But when used by other writers they did not denote the same concepts as they do in Newton. In fact, before Newton, "mass" was used as a synonym for "weight" and the difference between something somehow being heavy and something having a determinate mass can only be made in Newtonian mechanics.

6 The quantifiers are crucial. A concept is T-theoretical iff *all* determinations of a concept use a law of T. If this is not that case, then a concept is T-non-theoretical. Being T-non-theoretical is, however, compatible with there being *some* determinations of the concept that rely on a law of T; the crucial condition is that there is at least one determination that does not. For instance, distance is Newtonian-mechanics-non-theoretical because is it can be measured with rods, but it can *also* be measured using dynamical laws. The notion of T-theoreticity originates in Sneed's (1971). Its canonical formulation is due to Balzer et al. (1987, Sec. II.3). Further discussions can be found in Andreas' (2008), Balzer's (1986), Díez's (2002), and Moulines' (1985). Torretti's (1990, Secs. 3.3 and 3.4) offers a critical discussion of MS's conception of T-theoreticity.

7 MS's full definition of the core contains three other elements. *Constraints* take relations between models into account (for instance, if the same particle appears in several models of the theory); *links* specify the relations of the model of one theory to the models of related other theories; and *approximations* specify what kind of idealisations are permissible to make the theory applicable to physical systems. I set these additional elements aside because they are not essential for the discussion in this chapter.

8 Force functions that lead to equations that have no unique solutions are then dismissed as "unphysical". Norton (2008) objects and argues that that there is no reason to dismiss such force functions. For our current purposes it is immaterial how this issue is resolved.

9 For instance, Suppe's sizeable collection is entitled "The Structure of Scientific Theories". Darrigol (2008) gestures in a similar direction as MS when he emphasises that physical theories have a modular structure.

10 Formally, a theory net is "a partially ordered set of theory-elements with a basic element on the 'top', from which the rest of the theory-elements come out by a process of successive restrictions of the class of actual models (and constraints and links) and of the range of intended applications. What gives its unity to the theory-net is the basic element" (Moulines 2002, 8).

11 It is interesting to note that the empirical claim can also be expressed through the Ramsey sentence, which we introduced in Section 4.6 (Díez 2005, 89).

12 Looking back at Section 5.2, one might also want to explore the suggestion that MS's layer structure of theories is the best way to articulate Suppes' hierarchy of models.
13 See also Díez's (2014, 1421).
14 See our discussion in Chapter 3. This is seconded by the Oxford English Dictionary, which defines "empirical" as gained "by means of direct observation".
15 Whether at the "low" level of "basic" perception intersubjectivity is really forthcoming is a question that we have leave to open at this point. For a discussion of philosophical issues pertaining to perception, see, for instance, Schellenberg's (2018).
16 For further discussion of this issue in the spirit of MS, see Falguera's (2006) and Moulines' (2006). For a discussion of foundationalism and coherentism in epistemology, see Steup and Neta's (2020) and references therein; for a discussion of the metaphysical aspects of the divide, see Morganti's (2018, 2020a, 2020b).
17 Andreas (2013) offers an account that goes into that direction.

References

Adams, E. W. 1959. The Foundations of Rigid Body Mechanics and the Derivation of Its Laws from Those of Particle Mechanics. In L. Henkin, P. Suppes, and A. Tarski (eds.), *The Axiomatic Method: With Special Reference to Geometry and Physics*. Amsterdam: North-Holland, pp. 250–265.

Andreas, H. 2008. Another Solution to the Problem of Theoretical Terms. *Erkenntnis* 69: 351–333.

Andreas, H. 2013. Deductive Reasoning in the Structuralist Approach. *Studia Logica* 5: 1093–1113.

Balzer, W. 1986. Theoretical Terms: A New Perspective. *The Journal of Philosophy* 83: 71–90.

Balzer, W. and C.-U. Moulines (eds.) 1996. *The Strcturalist Theory of Science: Focal Issues, New Results*. Berlin and New York: De Gruyter.

Balzer, W., C.-U. Moulines, and J. D. Sneed 1987. *An Architectonic for Science: The Structuralist Program*. Dordrecht: Reidel Publishing Company.

Balzer, W., J. D. Sneed, and C.-U. Moulines (eds.) 2000. *Structuralist Knowledge Representation: Paradigmatic Examples*. Amsterdam: Rodopi.

Darrigol, O. 2008. The Modular Structure of Physical Theories. *Synthese* 162: 195–223.

Díez, J. A. 2002. A Program for the Individuation of Scientific Concepts. *Synthese* 130: 13–48.

Díez, J. A. 2005. The Ramsey Sentence and Theoretical Content. In M. J. Frápolli (ed.), *F.P. Ramsey: Critical Reassessments*. London and New York: Continuum Publishing Group, pp. 70–103.

Díez, J. A. 2006. Rivalry and Comparability: Looking Outside the Theories. In G. Ernst and K. G. Niebergall (eds.), *Philosophie Der Wissenschaft – Wissenschaft Der Philosophie*. Berlin: Mentis, pp. 31–50.

Díez, J. A. 2014. Scientific W-Explanation as Ampliative, Specialized Embedding: A Neo-Hempelian Account. *Erkenntnis* 79: 1413–1443.

Falguera, J. L. 2006. Foundherentist Philosophy of Science. In G. Ernst and K. G. Niebergall (eds.), *Philosophie Der Wissenschaft – Wissenschaft Der Philosophie*. Berlin: Mentis, pp. 67–86.

Gähde, U. 2002. Holism, Underdetermination, and the Dynamics of Empirical Theories. *Synthese* 130: 69–90.

Halvorson, H. 2016. Scientific Theories. In P. Humphreys (ed.), *The Oxford Handbook of Philosophy of Science*. Oxford: Oxford University Press, pp. 585–608.

Kuipers, T. A. F. 2001. Structures in Science. Heuristic Patterns Based on Cognitive Structures. An Advanced Textbook in Neo-Classical Philosophy of Science. In J. Hintikka (ed.), *Synthese Library*. Dordrecht: Springer, pp. 3–24.

Lorenzano, P. 2013. The Semantic Conception and the Structuralist View of Theories: A Critique of Suppe's Criticisms. *Studies in History and Philosophy of Science* 44: 600–607.

Morganti, M. 2018. The Structure of Physical Reality: Beyond Foundationalism. In R. Bliss and G. Priest (eds.), *Reality and Its Structure: Essays in Fundamentality*. Oxford: Oxford University Press, pp. 254–272.

Morganti, M. 2020a. Fundamentality in Metaphysics and the Philosophy of Physics. Part I: Metaphysics. *Philosophy Compass* 15(7): e12690.

Morganti, M. 2020b. Fundamentality in Metaphysics and the Philosophy of Physics. Part II: The Philosophy of Physics. *Philosophy Compass* 15(10): e12703.

Moulines, C.-U. 1985. Theoretical Terms and Bridge Principles: A Critique of Hempel's (Self-) Criticisms. *Erkenntnis* 22: 97–117.

Moulines, C.-U. 1996. Strcturalist: The Basic Ideas. In W. Balzer and C. U. Moulines (eds.), *The Strcturalist Theory of Science: Focal Issues, New Results*. Berlin and New York: De Gruyter, pp. 1–13.

Moulines, C.-U. 2002. Introduction: Structuralism as a Program for Modelling Theoretical Science. *Synthese* 130: 1–11.

Moulines, C.-U. 2006. The Role of Empirical Operations and Model Construction in the Ontological Commitments of Science. In C. Thiel (ed.), *Operations and Constructions in Scienc*. Erlangen: Erlanger Forschungen, pp. 21–39.

Niiniluoto, I. 1984. *Is Science Progressive?* (Synthese Library). Dordrecht: Springer.

Norton, J. D. 2008. The Dome: An Unexpectedly Simple Failure of Determinism. *Philosophy of Science* 75: 786–798.

O'Regan, D. 1997. *Existence Theory for Nonlinear Ordinary Differential Equations*. Dordrecht: Springer.

Schellenberg, S. 2018. *The Unity of Perception: Content, Consciousness, Evidence*. Oxford: Oxford University Press.

Sneed, J. D. 1971. *The Logical Structure of Mathematical Physics* (2nd revised ed.). Dordrecht: Reidel.

Stegmüller, W. 1976. *The Structure and Dynamics of Theories*. New York and Berlin: Springer.

Stegmüller, W. 1979. *The Structuralist View of Theories: A Possible Analogue of the Bourbaki Programme in Physical Science*. New York and Berlin: Springer.

Steup, M. and R. Neta 2020. Epistemology. In E. N. Zalta (ed.), *The Stanford Encyclopedia of Philosophy*. https://plato.stanford.edu/archives/fall2020/entries/epistemology/.

Torretti, R. 1990. *Creative Understanding: Philosophical Reflections on Physics*. Chicago: The University of Chicago Press.

8
BEYOND STRUCTURES

8.1 Introduction

The versions of the Model-Theoretical View that we have seen so far took models to be set-theoretical structures, and they articulated both a theory's representational capacity and its internal setup in structural terms. There are, however, versions of the Model-Theoretical View that do not rely on structures to articulate what models are and how they relate to their targets. These approaches are the subject matter of this chapter.

We begin by introducing Giere's view that models are abstract entities (Section 8.2) and present the Similarity Account of Representation (Section 8.3). We then discuss the Problem of Accuracy and the Problem of Style (Section 8.4), and we reflect on the Problem of Carriers and the ontology of scientific theories (Section 8.5). Next, we turn to Suppe's view that models are abstract replicas (Section 8.6), and we investigate how this account fares with the problems and conditions we previously identified for an account of representation (Section 8.7). We conclude that neither the similarity view nor the notion that models are abstract replicas provide a satisfactory answer to these problems and conditions (Section 8.8).

8.2 Models as Abstract Entities

Like other proponents of the Model-Theoretical View, Giere regards theories as families of models. However, his analysis of models and their relation to the world is different from the accounts we have seen so far. Rather than regarding models as set-theoretical structures, he regards them as "*abstract entities* having all and only those properties ascribed to them in standard texts" (1988, 78, original emphasis).[1] As an example, Giere discusses the linear oscillator (*ibid.*, 68–70), which is introduced in standard textbooks through something like the following description. Consider a mass that is located between two walls that are far enough apart so that the mass

DOI: 10.4324/9781003285106-11

can move between them. The mass can move only horizontally and is fixed to both walls with a spring. Neither the mass nor the spring are subject to any frictional forces; the spring itself is massless; the force the spring exerts on the mass is a linear function of the displacement of the mass from the midpoint; the walls are completely rigid. This is not a realistic description of a real system; it is a *theoretical definition* that introduces the abstract entity that serves as a model and which – by stipulation – has exactly those properties specified in the definition.[2] In other words, the model is an abstract entity that satisfies theoretical definition.

Giere submits that scientific textbooks are replete with definitions of this kind, and to present a theory in fact amounts to presenting theoretical definitions of the abstract entities that make up the theory's models. Next to the definition of the linear oscillator, a textbook of classical mechanics will also contain definitions of the mass point in free fall, the ideal pendulum, the damped pendulum, the two-body system, the three-body system, and so on.

Theoretical definitions are subject to an important constraint: the models must be defined so that they satisfy a theory's equations. A physical theory has over-arching equations and the theory's models have to be such that these equations come out true when applied to them. In the case of classical mechanics, models must satisfy Newton's equation of motion. This means that one interprets the equations so that they become true descriptions of the model. Giere emphasises there is nothing miraculous about this. The fact that the equations are true of the model does not have any "*epistemological* significance" because "the model is defined as something that exactly satisfies the equations" (1988, 79, original emphasis).

The laws of theory together with a class of theoretical definitions define a cluster of abstract models, but these models by themselves are not about anything in the world and have no connection to real physical systems. Yet Giere insists that models function representationally: they are "the means by which scientists represent the world" (1988, 80). For a model to become a representation, a scientist has to put forward a *theoretical hypothesis* specifying the relationship between the model and its target system. The relevant relation is similarity, and so the theoretical hypothesis states that a model is similar to its target. But unqualified similarity is too weak to ground a representation relation because anything is similar to anything else in some way.[3] A theoretical hypothesis has to assert that the model is similar to the target to in relevant *respects* and to certain *degrees* (*ibid.*, 81). So the general form of a theoretical hypothesis is that model M is similar to its designated target T in a respect that is relevant in the current theoretical context and to a degree that serves the purpose at hand.

The linear oscillator, for instance, becomes a representation of a lead block on a laboratory table if a scientist first singles out the block as the target system and then specifies that the linear oscillator is similar to the block in certain respects and to certain degrees. To do this, the scientist can point out that the block slides on a rail that is installed horizontally, thus ruling out motion in any other direction. She further takes into account that the block is connected to springs that are fixed to both opposite walls; that the springs are made from high quality steel so that the force that they exert on the block is linear to a good degree of approximation; that the internal friction of the spring can be neglected; that the mass of the springs is much smaller than the mass of the block and so the spring is almost massless compared to the block; that the rail is well greased and the density of air in the room is low so that friction between the block and its environment is small; and that the office is in a massive concrete building with walls that are completely rigid for all practical purposes. This specification is a theoretical hypothesis, and it turns the abstract linear oscillator into a representation of the lead block in the laboratory.

The choice of similarity rather than isomorphism as the relevant relation between model and target is motivated by the fact that similarity is more flexible than isomorphism. As we have noted in Section 6.7, it is unclear how isomorphism deals with distortive idealisations (like modelling a rail as frictionless or a wall as completely rigid). Giere notes that in such cases model and target in fact fail to be isomorphic, and that this failure is explicitly reported in the relevant textbooks (*ibid.*, 80–81). Similarity can accommodate such distortions naturally, which is a significant advantage.

Theoretical hypothesis can be true or false. If the similarity that is asserted in the theoretical hypothesis holds, then the hypothesis is true; if not, then it is false. To find out whether a hypothesis is true or false, the standard scientific procedures are employed: a prediction is derived from the model, an experiment is performed on the target, and the results are compared.[4] It also pays noting that Giere's models are models in both senses identified in Chapter 2: they are interpretations of a formal theory's equations (like Newton's equation of motion) and they are representations of something in the world. Giere's view on models is summarised in in Figure 8.1.[5]

What do models that belong to the same theory have in common? Discussing the example of classical mechanics, Giere notes that the models are constructed by combing Newton's equation of motion with various specific force functions such as Hooke's law, the law of gravity, and so on (*ibid.*, 82–83). Even though Giere does not refer to Munich Structuralism, what he says about the

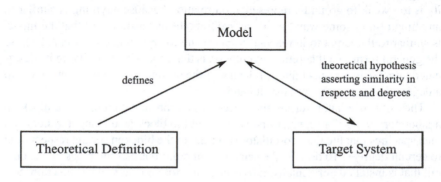

FIGURE 8.1 Giere's account of models.

internal structure of the family of models is in line with the structuralist approach, which we discussed in Chapter 7.[6] But a family of models is not sufficient to identify a theory. In addition to the models themselves, the theoretical hypotheses that tie the models to their target systems are part of the theory too. So a theory should be seen "as comprising two elements: (1) a population of models, and (2) various hypotheses linking those models with systems in the real world" (*ibid.*, 85, cf. 1997, 27).

Giere calls his position *constructive realism* to signal that his view is the realist alternative to van Fraassen's constructive empiricism. The position is constructive because models and theories are constructions of the human mind; it is realism because there are substantial similarities between models and their targets and hence models capture at least some aspects of how the world is (1988, 93).

Models are non-linguistic entities. Nevertheless, language is an integral part of Giere's account. Abstract objects are specified through theoretical definitions, which are linguistic items.[7] While theoretical definitions can be seen as standing outside a theory, theoretical hypotheses are, by Giere's own lights, a constitutive part of a theory. A theory therefore is a complex entity that involves both linguistic and non-linguistic elements. So in contrast with at least some of the structuralist approaches that we discussed in Chapter 5, Giere's approach does not attempt to exorcise language entirely.

8.3   Similarity and Representation

We now return to the questions concerning scientific representation introduced in Section 6.2 and ask how well the similarity account deals with them.[8] Analyses of representation in terms of similarity have a long history and they have been around at least since Plato's *The Republic* (Book 10). This conception of representation always had universal aspirations in that it aimed to explain the workings of representational objects as different as sculptures, paintings, and drawings.[9] Giere argues that it also covers scientific models, and, indeed, visual scientific representations like images (1996). For this reason, the similarity account gives a negative answer to the Representational Demarcation Problem.

Like isomorphism, similarity has a straightforward answer to the Surrogative Reasoning Condition because similarities between model and target can be exploited to carry over facts from the model to the target. If a model has property *P* and if the similarity between model and target is based on shared properties, then we can infer that property *P* will also be present in the target. If the similarity holds between properties themselves, we can infer that the target instantiates a property that is relevantly similar to *P*.

Giere does not discuss the Applicability of Mathematics Condition explicitly and simply assumes that models are the kind of things of which equations can be true. The assumption will also have to extend to target systems in as far as theoretical hypotheses can involve mathematical similarities. This is a sin of omission, but not a serious problem. As we have seen in Section 6.5, the application of mathematics can be grounded in the use of structure-inducing descriptions. This approach fits naturally with Giere's account, and it can be added to his view of theories without running into difficulties (for instance by including structure-inducing description in theoretical hypotheses).

To assess how well similarity fares as a response to the Scientific Representation Problem it is helpful to first discuss a simple version of a similarity account before turning to Giere's more complex account. The simple account says that a model M represents a target T iff M and T are similar. Goodman objects that this is an untenable analysis of representation because similarity is symmetric and reflexive, but representation is not (1976, 4–5).[10] If M is similar to T, then T is similar to M; but if M represents T, then T does not represent M (at least not usually). The abstract linear oscillator represents the lead block, but the lead block does not represent the abstract linear oscillator. Everything is similar to itself, but not everything represents itself. So the simple similarity account fails to meet the Directionality Condition.

Weisberg (2012, 787–789) points out that similarity need not be symmetric. A gradual notion of similarity allows one to state that something is more or less similar to something else. Using such a notion, Tversky found in empirical studies that many people think that North Korea is more similar to China than China is to North Korea. So gradual similarity can be asymmetric. This draws attention to the thorny issue of the correct definition of similarity. We turn to this problem in the next section. But even if we concede that there is an asymmetric notion of similarity, this does not solve the problem with reflexivity because even gradual similarity is reflexive.

A further problem is that similarity is too inclusive to ground representation because many objects that are similar to each other do not represent each other. Two copies of the same book are similar but they do not represent each other. This problem persists even if similarity is asymmetric. From that fact that North Korea is asymmetrically similar to China it does not follow that North Korea represents China (or *vice versa*). That similarity is too weak to ground representation has been brought home in now-classical thought experiment.[11] Imagine an ant crawling on the beach in a way that it leaves a trace that happens to be similar to Winston Churchill. Does the trace in the sand represent Churchill? Putnam (1981, 1) answers that it does not because the ant has never seen Churchill and had no intention to draw an image of him. Someone else might come to see the trace depicting Churchill, but the trace itself is no representation. This, Putnam concludes, shows that "[s]imilarity . . . to the features of Winston Churchill is not sufficient to make something represent or refer to Churchill." (*ibid.*, p. 1). There is nothing special about the trace of the ant and the lesson generalises: similarity on its own is too weak to establish representation.

Similarity is not only too weak to ground representation; it is altogether too easy to come by. As Goodman pointed out, if two things are similar when they have at least one property in common, then everything is similar to everything else because every two things have some property in common (1972, 443). If so, then everything represents everything else, which is absurd.

The Misrepresentation Condition spells further trouble for the simple similarity account. As we have seen in Section 6.2, a misrepresentation portrays its target in a way that it is not. In the context of a similarity account of representation this means that the model has properties that are not similar to the properties of the target. However, if this is the case, then the model is not similar to the target and hence not a representation at all. So the simple similarity account mistakes misrepresentation for non-representation.

Simple similarity also fails to meet the Targetless Models Condition. There are paintings representing dragons and angels, and there are models representing the ether and four-sex populations. Yet there are no dragons and angels, and (for all we know) neither the ether nor four-sex populations exists. But a representation cannot be similar to something that does not exist and hence it cannot represent it.

For these reasons, the simple similarity account is a non-starter. As we have seen in the previous section, Giere's view is more complex in that it requires that M and T be similar in relevant respects and to certain degrees, and in that a theoretical hypothesis asserts that the intended similarity obtains. Hypotheses do not affirm themselves; they are formulated and asserted by scientists who work with models. So the account tacitly appeals to model users in its analysis of representation. In more recent publications Giere has made this explicit and proposed an agent-based conception of representation. At the heart of this conception lies the notion that what should be analysed is not the notion of representation, but the "activity of *representing*" which is carried out by scientists who are "intentional agents with goals and purposes" (Giere 2004, 743, original emphasis). Analysing representation along these lines results in the "formula" for an "agent-based" account of representation: "Agents (1) intend; (2) to use model, M; (3) to represent a part of the world, W; (4) for some purpose, P", where this formula "legitimates using similarity as the basic relationship between models and the world" (Giere 2010, 269).[12] This translates into the following response to the scientific representation problem: a scientific model M represents a target system T iff there is an agent A who intends to use M to represent target system T by proposing a theoretical hypothesis H specifying a similarity (in certain respects and to certain degrees) between M and T for purpose P. I call this the *agent-based similarity account of representation*.

The agent-based account solves the problems of the simple similarity account. The problem with directionality is resolved by the agent formulating the hypothesis that designates M as the representation and T as the target, which makes representation asymmetric and irreflexive, as it should be. This move also sorts out the problem with accidental similarities like the one between the ant's trace and Churchill. M represents T only if a hypothesis has been formulated saying that M is used to represent T, which has not happened in the case of the ant's trace. The problem that similarity is too easy to get vanishes once similarity in particular respects and to particular degrees are required. The agent-based conception avoids problems with misrepresentation because hypotheses can be true as well as false, and so a misrepresentation is one that is based on a false theoretical hypothesis.

A targetless representation, finally, is one where the theoretical hypothesis is false because T does not exist (the claim that M and T are similar in a particular way is false if T does not exist).

It looks like the agent-based account establishes similarity as the concept that grounds representation. Unfortunately, this impression is delusive. It is true that the agent-based account avoids the problems of the simple similarity account, but it does so by effectively taking similarity out of the equation. What is doing the work in the resolution of the problems is the asymmetrical form of the hypothesis – that agent A intends to use M to represent T rather than T to represent M – and the fact that hypotheses can be false. That the hypothesis asserts a similarity relation is otiose. The hypothesis could specify any relation between M and T and nothing in the agent-based account's resolution of the problems with directionality, accidental similarities, misrepresentation, and targetless models would change. This is not surprising because similarity is not an essential part of the "formula" that defines the agent-based account and it is mentioned only as an afterthought. In fact, Giere himself noted that similarity is an idle wheel when it comes to establishing representation:

> How do scientists use models to represent aspects of the world? What is it about models that makes it possible to use them in this way? One way, perhaps the most important way, *but probably not the only way*, is by exploiting *similarities* between a model and that aspect of the world it is being used to represent. Note that I am not saying that the model itself represents an aspect of the world because it is similar to that aspect. There is no such representational relationship. [footnote omitted] Anything is similar to anything else in countless respects, but not anything represents anything else. It is not the model that is doing the representing; it is the scientist using the model who is doing the representing.
>
> *(2004, 747, first italicisation added)*

If similarity is not the only way in which a model can represent, then there are other model-target relations that can be used in representations; and if it is the scientist's use of the model rather than the objective model-target relation that turns a model into a representation, then similarity is superfluous in a response to the Scientific Representation Problem. So similarity must play a different role in the agent-based account. Two candidates come to mind: similarity could either play the role of a representational style, or it could furnish a normative criterion for accurate representation.

8.4 The Problems of Accuracy and Style

Interpreting similarity as a response to the Problem of Style builds on the idea that the respects in which M is said to be similar to T specify the style of the representation. If, for instance, the model and the target are claimed have a similar causal structure, we might say that the representation has the style of causal modelling; or if the model relates to the target by certain limit idealisations, then we have a limit style representation.[13]

The step towards an explication of styles must be an explicit analysis of the notion of similarity. As we have seen in the last section, the standard analysis in the philosophical literature explicates similarity in terms of shared properties: two objects are similar if they co-instantiate a property. Two trees, for instance, are similar if their leaves instantiate the same shade of green. This is a rather coarse notion of similarity that does not provide the means to capture more fine-grained similarity relations. In particular, it does not allow us to explicate degrees of similarity, as Giere's account requires. Unfortunately, Giere himself remains silent on the matter and offers no analysis of similarity.

To overcome this difficulty, one can turn to psychology where an entire body of literature is concerned with the analysis of similarity. The two most prominent accounts that have emerged in that context are the geometric account and the contrast account.[14] Geometric accounts introduce a multidimensional space of attributes and place objects in that space based on values assigned to their properties. The space is assumed to be equipped with a metric and the degree of similarity between two objects is taken to be a function of the distance between the points in the space occupied by the objects. As an example, consider colours, which can be described by three numbers corresponding to their hue, saturation, and brightness. So each colour corresponds to a point in the three-dimensional hue-saturation-brightness space and the degree of similarity between two colours is an inverse function of the distance between the two points representing the colours (the smaller the distance the higher the degree of similarity).

The drawback of this account is that it is based on the assumption that values can be assigned to all properties that are relevant to a similarity judgement, which is often unrealistic. In what space would one place China and North Korea to assess their degree of similarity? This difficulty is overcome in the contrast account, which works with a weighted comparison of properties. Weisberg (2013, Ch. 8) recently introduced this account into the philosophy of science and used it to develop what he calls the *weighted feature matching account of model world-relations*. To begin, define a set Δ of relevant properties, and let $\Delta_M \subseteq \Delta$ be the subset of properties instantiated in the model and $\Delta_T \subseteq \Delta$ the subset of properties instantiated in the target. The intersection of these two sets, $\Delta_T \cap \Delta_M$, is a set that contains all the properties that the model and the target share. The set-subtraction $\Delta_M - \Delta_T$ contains all properties in Δ that only the model (but not the target) has, and, vice versa, $\Delta_T - \Delta_M$ contains all properties in Δ that only the target (but not the model) has. Next we choose a ranking function f, which assigns a real number to every subset of Δ. A simple example of such a function is one that assigns to every set the number of its members. The degree of similarity between M and T is then defined as (*ibid.*, 144)

$$S(M,T) = \theta f(\Delta_M \cap \Delta_T) - \alpha f(\Delta_M - \Delta_T) - \beta f(\Delta_T - \Delta_M),$$

Where α, β and θ are weights. This equation provides us with "a similarity score that can be used in comparative judgments of similarity" (*ibid.*). The score is essentially determined by the difference of the weight of the properties shared by the model and target and the properties in which they differ.[15] The value of S can in principle lie between any two values, depending on the choice of the ranking function, the weights, and the set Δ.

The score S is asymmetrical whenever $\alpha \neq \beta$, which makes room for the possibility of M being similar to T to a different degree than T being similar to M (a possibility which we mentioned in the previous section). S also has a property known as *maximality*: everything is maximally similar to itself and less or equally similar to any other object. That is, $S(A,A) \geq S(A,B)$ for all objects A and B where $A \neq B$ (*ibid.*, p. 154).

To determine the similarity score in a particular situation, a number of choices have to be made to concretise the abstract notions in the definition of S. The first issue is to define the set Δ. Weisberg is explicit that there are no general rules, let alone algorithmic procedures, to determine what properties go into the set Δ, and that the choice of the elements of Δ relies on a "combination of context, conceptualization of the target, and theoretical goals of the scientist" (*ibid.*, 149). There are no general constraints on the choice of a ranking function and of weights either, and so one enjoys considerable latitude in constructing a similarity score.[16]

The weighted feature matching account offers a general framework in which similarity can be discussed and allows for the calculation of a similarity score, but it does not help with the question of style. In fact, matters of style stand outside the account, and have to be answered prior to its application. If one has a classification of properties into different stylistic categories, then these categories can be used to formulate inclusion criteria for the construction of Δ and, possibly, guide the construction of an appropriate ranking function. If, for instance, we want to construct a geometrical representation of the target and know how to identify geometrical properties, then we can include all geometrical properties that are relevant to the problem at hand in Δ and interpret S as a score for geometrical similarity; but the feature matching account offers no guidance on what geometrical properties are and on what an appropriate ranking function would be. In other words, a general theory of similarity offers no help in understanding the specific relation between a model and its target.

Those who have been critical about similarity will say that this was to be expected. Goodman quips that "[s]imilarity, ever ready to overcome philosophical problems and overcome obstacles, is a pretender, an impostor, a quack . . . professing powers that it does not possess" (1972, 437). But even those who are more sympathetic to an analysis of the model-target relation in terms of similarity have pointed out that no general characterisation of similarity was possible. In this vein Teller notes that "[t]here can be no general account of similarity, but there is also no need for a general account because the details of any case will provide the information which will establish just what should count as relevant similarity in that case." (Teller 2001, 402). So an appeal to similarity will do nothing to answer the Problem of Style.[17]

A further problem is that the weighted feature matching account is in effect an elaborate version of the co-instantiation account of similarity. It offers a significant improvement over the simple account, but it cannot overcome its basic limitation. The limitation is that it can only deal with the kind of similarity that Niiniluoto (1988, 272–274) calls partial identity, but not with the kind of similarity that he calls likeness. M and T stand in that relation of *partial identity* iff both instantiate properties $P_1,...,P_n$ (M and T are then partially identical with respect to $P_1,...,P_n$). M and T are similar in the sense of *likeness* iff M instantiates properties $P_1,...,P_n$ and T instantiates properties $Q_1,...,Q_n$ and the two sets of properties are such that P_i is similar to Q_i for all $i=1,...,n$. In other words, in the case of likeness the similarity is located at the level of properties themselves. If flowers have identical colours, they are similar in the sense of partial identity; if they instantiate different colours that resemble each other (say scarlet and crimson), then the flowers are similar in the sense of likeness.

Parker notes that Weisberg's account – like all co-instantiation accounts – is designed to deal with partial identities but has no systematic place for likeness (2015, 273). The problem is that in the case of likeness, model and target have no co-instantiated properties; therefore $\Delta_T \cap \Delta_M$ is always empty, and so the similarity score does not indicate how similar the model and the target are. Parker suggests solving this problem by introducing "imprecise" properties. For each pair of P_i and Q_i one has to introduce a property R_i such that an object that instantiates R_i automatically also instantiates P_i and Q_i. If properties have numerical values (which is the case if the property is a physical magnitude), this can be done, for instance, by introducing intervals around precise values. The property R_i would then be something like "having a value in the interval $[x-\varepsilon, x+\varepsilon]$", where x is the value we are interested in and ε is a tolerance threshold. Weisberg accepts this and says that he is pursuing a programme that aims to explicate all similarities in terms of shared properties (2015, 302). But imprecise properties have to be part of Δ from the outset. This means that standards for two properties to be similar have to be put into the account from the outside. So an important decision regarding whether or not M and T are similar is in effect put in by hand.

Could $S(M,T)$ be understood as a measure for the accuracy of a model, the idea being that the higher the value of $S(M,T)$ the more accurate the model? Such an interpretation of $S(M,T)$ is supported by the fact that Weisberg sees $S(M,T)$ as providing "standards of fidelity" (2013, 147). Due to maximality, $S(M,T)$ assumes its highest value when M is a perfect replica of T, and the score drops when M and T share fewer properties. This suggests that $S(M,T)$ can plausibly be interpreted as a measure of accuracy, and hence would provide a response to the Problem of Accuracy. It pays bearing in mind, however, that this score operates against the background of the choice of a particular set Δ (which includes the choice of imprecise properties to capture likenesses), the choice of a ranking function and the choice of weights. These are substantial assumptions, and what verdict one reaches about accuracy crucially depends on them.

8.5 Problem of Carriers and the Ontology of Theories

The remaining problem on our list is the Problem of Carriers. The account of similarity we discussed in the last section requires that models instantiate properties and explicates similarity in terms of co-instantiation. Some models are ordinary material objects. Watson and Crick's model of DNA is a contraption of metal plates (Schindler 2008); the Army Corps of Engineers' model of the San Francisco Bay is a basin filled with water, shaped like the original Bay, and equipped with pumps to simulate tidal flows (Weisberg 2013, Ch. 1); ball and stick models of molecules are made from metal or wood (Toon 2011); and model organisms in biology are animals like worms and mice (Ankeny and Leonelli 2020). From an ontological point of view, these models are commonplace material objects and as such similarity is no problem for them – or at least they do not give rise to ontological questions over and above the questions that one can ask about every other material object.

But many models are not of this kind. Newton's model of the sun-earth system (Section 1.2) or a model featuring a single-species population reproducing at a fixed rate in isolation from its environment (the logistic growth model) are not material objects. They are what Hacking aptly described as "something you hold in your head rather than your hands" (1983, 216). Thomson-Jones (2012, 762) calls such models "nonconcrete models". For reasons that will become clear in Section 14.5, I prefer the term *non-material models*. The question then is what kind of objects non-material models are. As we have seen in Section 8.2, Giere regards models as abstract entities.[18] The problem with this answer is that it is too unspecific. Herfel notes that "Giere is not crystal clear about his ontology of models" and adds: "[d]oes he want to posit the existence of an abstract realm of where abstract entities exist? Is there some immaterial substance from which the SHO [simple harmonic oscillator] is made? Giere never really says" (1995, 70–71). The root of the problem is that the class of abstract objects is rather large: it comprises numbers and other mathematical object, classes, propositions, concepts, the letter "B", and literary works like Dostoyevsky's "Crime and Punishment". Hale (1988, 86–87) lists no less than twelve different characterisations of abstract objects. Which of these, if any, captures the group of abstract objects to which models are supposed belong? Giere dismisses this problem as one that philosophers of science can safely set aside as irrelevant because he doubts that "a deeper understanding of imaginative processes and of the objects produced by these process" is required "to get on with the job of investigating the functions of models in science" (2009, 250).

While it may be true that philosophers of science need not engage with metaphysical issues for metaphysic's sake, they should offer an analysis of their subject matter that is sufficiently specific not to leave essential problems unanswered. Identifying models with abstract entities falls short of that goal. Thomson-Jones argues that there is an "internal inconsistency" in Giere's account because no abstract object can have the properties that a theoretical description ascribes to them (2010, 291). The problem is that being abstract implies having no spatiotemporal existence. But an entity that has no spatiotemporal existence cannot have the properties ascribed to the linear oscillator. Discussing the example of the simple pendulum (another of Giere's examples of an abstract entity used as a model), Thomson-Jones points out that "no object which has, for example, a length, and behaves in the way the simple pendulum is said to behave in descriptions of it – moving through space over time in a particular way – can be non-spatiotemporal" (*ibid.*). For this reason, "we cannot say both that there are no simple pendula in the world around us and that there exists an object which has, in the straightforward way of having properties, the properties mentioned in descriptions of the simple pendulum" (*ibid.*).

This problem hits right at the heart of the account. If similarity is explained in terms of co-instantiation of properties and if models cannot possibly instantiate the kinds of properties that the model would want to attribute to the target (such as being located at certain place at a certain time), then the account of models on offer fails to explain essential characteristics of modelling.[19]

An alternative is to regard models as being akin to the objects and places of literary fiction. The linear oscillator would then be the same kind of object as Sherlock Holmes or Middle Earth. Occasionally Giere seems to be sympathetic to this view, for instance when he observes that "ontologically, scientific models and works of fiction are on a par" (2009, 249). However, he then immediately comes out strongly against such an analysis of models. We discuss this view, which has become known as the "fiction view of models", in detail in Sections 14.5 and 14.6, where we also examine Giere's arguments against it.

A further issue concerns the properties of models. As we have seen, Giere insists that models are abstract entities "having *all and only* those properties ascribed to them in standard texts" (1988, 78, emphasis added). Since models are defined by theoretical definitions, presumably this is tantamount to saying that models have all and only those properties ascribed to them by their theoretical definitions. If so, this cannot be quite right. Models are used in a context of investigation and scientists often make a tremendous effort to find out whether or not a model has a certain property. It took Poincaré years to find out that the three-body system was dynamically unstable, and the fact that the two-dimensional Ising model exhibits phase transitions was a Nobel Prize winning discovery. But if models have all and only the properties ascribed to them in their theoretical definitions, this fact of modelling remains a mystery. To find our whether a model has a certain property, scientists would simply have to check whether the property is mentioned in the theoretical definition. If it is mentioned, then the model has the property; if not, then not. This is not how research is done. Models must have properties other than the ones that the theoretical definition explicitly attributes to them. In fact, these "surplus" properties are what makes models interesting as objects of investigation: models are of interest in a process of investigation exactly because they have properties that are not expressly written into their specification right at the outset. In addition to the properties attributed to the model in the theoretical definition, the model must also have properties that are suitably connected to those properties. The question is what "suitably connected" means. The problem can be formulated as one of truth conditions. Assume P is property that is not mentioned in the theoretical definition of model M (like, for instance, dynamical instability, which is not mentioned in the definition of the three-body problem). Under what conditions is the statement "Model M has property P" true?

The discussion so far was concerned with the ontology of models. Let us now turn to the ontology of theories. As we have seen in Section 8.2, a theory consists of a family of models *and* various theoretical hypotheses connecting the models to real-world target systems. As Hendry and Psillos note (2007, 134), there is an ironic historical parallel between the Received View and Giere's version of the Model-Theoretical View. In the Received View there was "free-floating" theoretical calculus that needed to be connected to reality with correspondence rules. In Giere's account there is family of "free-floating" models that need to be anchored to their targets with theoretical hypotheses. While different in detail, "theoretical hypotheses do play the same role in the strong nonlinguistic view as did the correspondence rules in the strong linguistic view" (*ibid.*, 136): they give empirical content to a theoretical apparatus that is otherwise disconnected from reality. The Syntactic View was in for much criticism for its language dependence because, so the argument went, every change in a correspondence rule also amounts to a change of the theory (see Section 1.6). In as far as this is a problem for the Syntactic View it is also a problem for Giere's version of the Model-Theoretical View. The Received View's manoeuvres to avoid the problem are of course also available to the Model-Theoretical View, but it is important to note that the shift from one view to other has in no way eliminated difficulties with language dependence.

The theoretical apparatus of a theory is the family of models. But these are abstract entities and what one reads in a textbook (or research paper) are descriptions of these abstract entities. Giere is explicit about the fact that a consequence of this view is that "what one finds in the textbooks is not literally the theory itself, but statements defining the models that are part of the theory" (1988, 85). Hendry and Psillos denounce this as a "category mistake" and argue that "[t]he theory itself is inseparable from the statements that in any particular instance express it, and if it is not to be found where they are, we do not know where else to find it" (2007, 133). In a similar vein, both Toon (2012, 250–251) and Savage (1998, 10–11) note that Giere's account of how models are introduced and used is at odds with his emphasis on understanding scientific representation as something non-linguistic. So the problem of the relation between language and theory remains unresolved in Giere's account.

8.6 Models as Abstract Replicas

According to Suppe, a model is an *abstract replica* of a *phenomenon* (or a *phenomenal system*).[20] Phenomena can be either observable or unobservable and they are in effect what we previously called target systems. To avoid confusion with other senses of "phenomenon" (which we encountered in Sections 5.3 and 6.4), I will keep referring to the parts of the world that models are about as target systems when discussing Suppe's account. Three features are constitutive of being an abstract replica: being the result of a process of abstraction and idealisation, having states specified in terms of defining parameters, and counterfactual truth conditions.

A process of abstraction strips away properties that are deemed irrelevant to the problem at hand. If, for instance, we're interested in how an object moves through space, we focus on its position, mass, and velocity, and we can disregard its colour, temperature, chemical composition, history of production, and legal status of ownership. The parameters that are singled out as pertinent are the *defining parameters* of the abstract replica. These parameters are typically not studied as they occur in nature but rather under idealised conditions, for instance by assuming that surfaces are frictionless, bodies are spherical, springs are massless, and objects are isolated from the influence of their environment. These are idealising assumptions. Hence, models are "highly abstract and idealized replicas of phenomena" (1989, 65, cf. 82–83, 94–96).[21] A set of simultaneous values of the defining parameters of the abstract replica is a possible state of the replica. At any particular instant of time the system can be in exactly one state (1989, 83). All states taken together form the system's state space (as we have seen in Section 5.3).

The laws that are in operation in a certain situation decide which trajectories through state space are allowed and which are ruled out. What laws are in force in a physical replica? As we have seen earlier, Giere solves this problem by stipulating that models must satisfy certain laws by definition. Suppe opts for a different strategy and proposes a counterfactual account. Abstract replicas portray their targets *as if* their behaviour depended only on a few selected variables that change under the influence of idealised factors: the replica behaves exactly as the target "*would have* behaved *had* the idealized conditions been met" (1989, 65, original emphasis).[22] For this reason Suppe calls his position *quasi-realism* (1989, 101).[23]

In keeping with the spirit of the Model-Theoretical View, Suppe understands theories as "suitably connected families of models" (2000, 105), i.e. as a families of abstract replicas. The question now is how to analyse "suitably connected". Unfortunately, Suppe offers little advice on this matter. However, an account of what binds the models of the theory together seems to emerge from his discussion of the "empirical truth" of a theory. Intuitively, a theory is empirically true if what it says about its intended applications is correct.

The first step in the analysis of empirical truth is the introduction of the class of "causally possible physical systems". Every theory has a scope, and it aims to describe systems within its scope. The scope of mechanics, for instance, is the motion of all masses under the influence of forces. We have encountered this idea in the last chapter, where the intended scope of a theory turned out to be an essential aspect of Munich Structuralism's analysis of a theory. The scope of a theory obviously includes all actual systems of the requisite kind: the solar system, satellites shot into orbit, the stone falling from the tower, etc. Suppe points out, however, that the scope of a theory is wider than that because it also includes systems that are not actual but, if they were, would fall within the scope of the theory. It may so happen that the history of the universe is such that a 287-body system never came into existence, but if there was one, it would be covered by classical mechanics. The set of all systems, actual and possible, to which a theory is applicable is the class of *causally possible physical systems* (1989, 67–68, 83–84).[24] Through the steps of abstraction and idealisation previously described, each of these systems corresponds to an abstract replica that is a model of the system. Let us call this class of models C_P, the class of all *causally possible abstract replicas*.

Next let us construct the class C_L of all nomologically possible abstract replicas.[25] This class is constructed by first considering "all (logically) possible states of all (logically) possible physical systems for the theory" and then restrict the class so that it includes only the models that satisfy the "laws of the theory" (1974, 48–49, 1989, 84–85). Like van Fraassen (in Section 5.3) Suppe distinguishes between laws of succession and laws of coexistence. The former say which state transitions are allowed as time evolves (for instance, when a planet revolves around the sun); the latter specify what states system can occupy in an equilibrium situation (for instance, in the ideal gas law). Suppe does not discuss the construction of this class in any detail, but it seems safe to think of it as essentially the same as the construction of the structuralist theory-net in Section 7.2. The class C_L is what we find at the bottom of the theory-net's branching tree.

We are now in a position to give a definition of empirical truth: a theory is empirically true iff $C_P = C_L$ (1974, 48–49, 53–54, 1989, 84–85, 96–99). In effect, this condition says that the class of the models of the theory is identical with the class of models that are abstracted from target systems.[26]

This brings us back to the question of what makes a family of models "suitably connected". Taking our cue from the construction of C_L, we can say that a family of models is suitably connected if its models are applications of the basic law(s) of the theory, or, using the language of Munich Structuralism, if they are nodes in a theory-net that is defined by the laws of the theory.[27]

Suppe is one of the main proponents of the view that theories are "extralinguistic entities". We can now see how this claim is borne out in Suppe's own account. The theory is the suitably connected family of models.[28] These are described using a language, but they should not be confused with the sentences of such language. Indeed, what we read in a textbook or research paper is a *formulation of a theory*. A formulation of theory is "a collection of propositions which are true of the theory", where the "propositions constituting a theory formulation are of

some language, known as the *theory formulation language*" and the language is
sufficiently rich to be able to express laws (1989, 87–90).[29] There is freedom of
choice in this language and the class of models can be described in different ways
(1977, 222, 1989, 82).

8.7   Abstract Replicas and Representation

How does Suppe's account deal with our questions concerning scientific representation in Section 6.2? Let us begin with the Problem of Carriers. Frisch rightly
observes that Suppe's abstract replicas are closely related to Giere's theoretical
models (Frisch 1998, 6). The two differ in their genesis: Giere's abstract entities
are individuated by a theoretical definition while Suppe's abstract replicas derive
from a target system through a process of abstraction and idealisation. But from
an ontological point of view the two are identical: they are abstract objects. So
Suppe's account faces the same questions as Giere's concerning the nature of
these objects. There is one aspect, however, in which Suppe's account enjoys
an advantage. As we have seen previously, Giere's account does not offer truth
conditions for statements about models involving properties that are not part of
the definition of the system. Suppe offers an answer in terms of counterfactuals:
the statement "Model M has property P" is true iff the target of M would have P
if the idealised conditions were met. But this counterfactual is meaningful only if
both the model and the target are the kind of things that can at least in principle
have property P, which gets us right back to Thomson-Jones' point that abstract
objects do not have physical properties.

Suppe regards a theory as a suitably connected family of models, and hence
Hendry and Psillos's worries about Giere's account reoccur. Their second worry
reappears unaltered: if all we ever get in scientific publications are theory formulations, where and when do we find the theory itself? The first point arises in a slightly
different way. Suppe's account does not consider theoretical hypotheses to be a part
of a theory, and for him the connection between theory and reality is not linguistic.
That is why a theory is an extralinguistic entity. This, Hendry and Psillos argue, has
the consequence that on Suppe's account a theory by itself is not about anything:
"theories *qua* families of abstract entities are free-floaters" (2007, 136, original italics). In fact Suppe faces a dilemma. Either the connection between models and
their target is not part of the theory and as a result theories lack empirical content;
or models are anchored in the world through statements like Giere's theoretical
hypotheses, but then the theory is no longer an extralinguistic entity and all the
problems with formulations reoccur. Hendry and Psillos recommend endorsing the
second horn of the dilemma and regard statements as part of the theory.

Suppe does not explicitly discuss scientific representation and so one can only
speculate what he would say about the Scientific Representation Problem. Given
how much emphasis Suppe puts on replicas, he might say that M represents T iff
M is a replica of T, where being a replica is explained in terms of M bearing certain specific idealisation and abstraction relations to T. Let us assume (plausibly)

that idealisation and abstraction are asymmetric and irreflexive relations and hence the replica account does not run up against problems with logical properties and the Directionality Condition. The other problems of the simple similarity account, however, reappear. Like similarity, idealisation is too week to pick out the model's target; it mistakes misrepresentation for non-representation; and it violates the Targetless Models Condition. One might try to fix these problems by following Hendry and Psillos' advice to introduce theoretical hypotheses, but, as with the move from a simple to an agent-based similarity account, one would do so at the expense of making idealisation and abstraction redundant in an answer to the Scientific Representation Problem. Occasionally Suppe emphasises theoretical models' relation to models of data (see, for instance, 2000, 112). This could be interpreted as Suppe subscribing to the Data Matching Account. However, as we have seen in Section 6.3, this account is a blind alley. So it remains an open question what the abstract replica account's response to the Scientific Representation Problem is.

Idealisation and abstraction can plausibly be understood as representational styles, but we have only a dim idea of what they are until a full analysis of these notions is provided. This also affects the understanding of standards of accuracy and surrogative reasoning. An account of idealisation could shed light on these, but until such an account is actually stated this remains a promissory note. Suppe does not explicitly discuss the application of mathematics, but, like Giere, Suppe could adopt the account in Section 6.5. The answer to the Representational Demarcation Problem is wide open. It again depends on how idealisation and abstraction are defined. Portides adopts a broad reading of these concepts and introduces them with the work of Picasso (2018). On such a reading, replication would account for representation beyond science. But on a more restrictive reading this may well not be the case.

8.8 Conclusion

In this chapter we have seen versions of the Model-Theoretical View of theories that are not based on the notion that models are structures. The similarity account of representation is almost as old as (our records of) Western philosophy, but it is brought sharply into focus when put into service in the context of scientific theories. We have seen what challenges the view faces and what it would take to address them. The abstract replica account is more recent, but faces challenges of the same kind as the similarity view. As in Chapters 5 and 6, we have come to the conclusion that language plays an essential role in many aspects of models and theories, and an attempt to exorcise language, and view theories as extralinguistic entities, fails.

Notes

1 The main sources for Giere's account of models and theories are his (1985, 1988, Chs. 3 and 4, 1997, Ch. 2, 1999, Chs. 7 and 9). Giere distinguishes between *models* and *theoretical models*. The latter are subspecies of the former, and the models discussed in

this chapter are theoretical models. Theoretical models contrast with scale models such as the double helix model of DNA, which are material objects. Such material objects are models but not theoretical models (1985, 90–95, 1997, 11–18, 21–22). We discuss material models in Section 13.4 and here follow Giere's own convention (1988, 79) to use "model" as shorthand for "theoretical model" when the context is clear.

2 The term "theoretical definition" is due to van Fraassen (1985, 289).

3 For a discussion of the point that everything is similar to everything else, see Goodman's (1972).

4 Giere discusses theory testing and the role of models in experiments in some detail in his (1988, Ch. 7, 1997, 27–46).

5 This figure is adapted from Giere's (1988, 83).

6 An alternative approach is developed in Giere's (1994), where he employs the resources of cognitive psychology to analyse the structure of scientific theories and applies these insights to classical mechanics.

7 Giere also recognises "visual modes of presentation for both theory and data", for instance through "pictures and diagrams" (1999, 118).

8 Section 8.3 and Section 8.4, as well as the first half of Section 8.5 are based on Frigg and Nguyen's (2017, 57–66, 2020, Ch. 3)

9 For a recent discussions of similarity in visual representation, see Abell's (2009) and Lopes' (2004). In aesthetics the term "resemblance" seems to be more common than "similarity", but there does not seem to be substantive difference between the two.

10 Similar problems arise with transitivity. See Frigg's (2002, 11–12) and Suárez's (2003, 232–233).

11 The canonical formulation is due to Putnam (1981, 1–3); Black (1973, 104) tells a similar story.

12 In fact, this conception of scientific representation was proposed over half century ago by Apostel, who wrote: "[l]et then $R(S, P, M, T)$ indicate the main variables of the modelling relationship. The subject S takes, in view of the purpose P, the entity M as a model for the prototype T" (Apostel 1961, 4). Mäki (2011) suggested an extension of Giere's view by adding two further components: the agent uses the model to address an audience E and adds a commentary C. For a discussion of Mäki's account, see Reiss' (2014). For further discussions of what constitutes a representational action, see Boesch's (2019a, 2019b).

13 We discuss these idealisations in Chapter 12.

14 Geometrical accounts are associated with Shepard's (1980), contrast accounts with Tversky's (1977). See Decock and Douven's (2011) for a review.

15 This account can therefore be seen as a quantitative version of Hesse's theory of positive and negative analogy, which we discuss in Chapter 10.

16 Weisberg's is a notion of overall similarity between model and target. It can, however, be adapted to provide similarity score for certain respects by restricting the properties that are included in Δ to properties that pertain to a certain respect. For a general discussion of overall similarity, see Morreau's (2010). For further discussions of Weisberg's account, see Boesch's (2021), Fang's (2017), Khosrowi's (2020), and Odenbaugh's (2015, 2018)

17 A discussion of styles might proceed along similar lines as a classification of analogies. See Section 10.3 for discussion.

18 See also Giere's (1988, 78, 1999, 5, 50, 2001, 1060, 2004, 747, 2010, 270).

19 Teller (2001, 399) offers a variant of the abstract object view which sees models as (something like) a bundle of properties. However, as Thomson-Jones points out (2010, 294–295), this view runs up against similar problems as Giere's original suggestion.

20 The main source of Suppe's account of models and theories is his (1989, Part II). His views are also discussed in his (1972a, 1972b, 1974, 1979, 2000). For Suppe's use of "phenomenon", see specifically his (1989, 93–99). Suppe refers to abstract replicas

as "physical systems". As we will see, Suppe's models are abstract object much like Giere's. Calling models "physical systems" is therefore misleading. I avoid this terminology and refer to models as "abstract replicas", which is in line with Suppe's own terminology (see, for instance, 1974, 48, 52, 1977, 224, 1989, 67, 94).

21 We discuss abstraction and idealisation in more detail in Chapter 11.

22 See also Suppe's (1972b, 12, 1974, 47–48, 1989, 82–83, 94–95, 2000, 106).

23 In Suppe's words, "*[q]uasi-realism* consists in ontological commitment to all variables that could be detected and the claim that empirically true theories provide counterfactual characterizations how systems *would* behave *were* they isolated from influences not taken into explicit account by the theory" (2000, 107, original emphasis).

24 See also Suppe's (1972b, 14, 1974, 48–49).

25 Suppe calls this the class of "theory-induced physical systems". Since the notion of theory is what is being analysed in the current context and since it is really the laws of the theory that do the heavy lifting in defining this class, the term "nomologically possible" seems to be more suitable.

26 This raises the question of how we test whether a theory is empirically true. Suppe discusses this issue in detail in Chapter 4 of his (1989).

27 Munich Structuralism's ideas are complementary to Suppe's, even though Suppe is critical of that position (see, for instance, 1989, 19–20). Diederich rightly points out that Suppe misunderstands structuralism and that his account would benefit from the inclusion of some structuralist notions (1994, 425).

28 This view can be extrapolated from his (1989, 82–84, 1998, 348, 2000, 111–112). This extrapolation seems to be justified and in line with Suppe's overall approach, even though, as Forge notes, it is "a little difficult to find a completely clear statement to the effect" that "theories are sets of physical systems" (1991, 608).

29 See also Suppe's (1974, 50–51). However, a theory formulation must consist of sentences and not propositions. Propositions are abstract objects that are expressed by sentences and so cannot be the items a reader finds in textbook, and they are not formulated in any particular language.

References

Abell, C. 2009. Canny Resemblance. *The Philosophical Review* 118: 183–223.

Ankeny, R. A. and S. Leonelli 2020. *Model Organisms*. Cambridge: Cambridge University Press.

Apostel, L. 1961. Towards the Formal Study of Models in the Non-Formal Sciences. In H. Freudenthal (ed.), *The Concept and the Role of the Model in Mathematics and Natural and Social Sciences*. Dordrecht: Reidel, pp. 1–37.

Black, M. 1973. How Do Pictures Represent? In E. Gombrich, J. Hochberg, and M. Black (eds.), *Art, Perception, and Reality*. Baltimore and London: Johns Hopkins University Press, pp. 95–130.

Boesch, B. 2019a. The Means-End Account of Scientific, Representational Actions. *Synthese* 196: 2305–2322.

Boesch, B. 2019b. Resolving and Understanding Differences between Agent-Based Accounts of Scientific Representation. *Journal for General Philosophy of Science* 50: 195–213.

Boesch, B. 2021. Scientific Representation and Dissimilarity. *Synthese* 198: 5495–5513.

Decock, L. and I. Douven 2011. Similarity after Goodman. *Review of Philosophy and Psychology* 2: 61–75.

Diederich, W. 1994. The Semantic Conception of Theories and Scientific Realism Byfrederick Suppe. *Erkenntnis* 41: 421–426.

Fang, W. 2017. Holistic Modeling: An Objection Toweisberg's Weighted Feature-Matching Account. *Synthese* 194: 1743–1764.

Forge, J. 1991. The Semantic Conception of Theories and Scientific Realism by Frederick Suppe. *Isis* 82: 607–608.

Frigg, R. 2002. Models and Representation: Why Structures Are Not Enough. *Measurement in Physics and Economics Project Discussion Paper Series, DP MEAS 25/02.*

Frigg, R. and J. Nguyen 2017. Models and Representation. In L. Magnani and T. Bertolotti (eds.), *Springer Handbook of Model-Based Science*. Dordrecht, Heidelberg, London, and New York: Springer, pp. 49–102.

Frigg, R. and J. Nguyen 2020. *Modelling Nature: An Opinionated Introduction to Scientific Representation* (Synthese Library). Berlin and New York: Springer.

Frisch, M. 1998. *Theories, Models, and Explanation*. PhD Dissertation, University of California, Berkely.

Giere, R. N. 1985. Constructive Realism. In P. M. Churchland and C. A. Hooker (eds.), *Images of Science: Essays on Realism and Empiricism with a Reply from Bas C. Van Fraassen*. Chicago and London: Chicago University Press, pp. 75–98.

Giere, R. N. 1988. *Explaining Science: A Cognitive Approach*. Chicago: Chicago University Press.

Giere, R. N. 1994. The Cognitive Structure of Scientific Theories. *Philosophy of Science* 61: 276–296.

Giere, R. N. 1996. Visual Models and Scientific Judgement. In B. S. Baigrie (ed.), *Picturing Knowledge: Historical and Philosophical Problems Concerning the Use of Art in Science*. Toronto: University of Toronto Press, pp. 269–302.

Giere, R. N. 1997. *Understanding Scientific Reasoning* (4th ed.). Orlando, FL: Harcourt Brace.

Giere, R. N. 1999. *Science without Laws*. Chicago: University of Chicago Press.

Giere, R. N. 2001. The Nature and Function of Models. *Behavioral and Brain Sciences* 24: 1060.

Giere, R. N. 2004. How Models Are Used to Represent Reality. *Philosophy of Science* 71: 742–752.

Giere, R. N. 2009. Why Scientific Models Should Not Be Regarded as Works of Fiction. In M. Suárez (ed.), *Fictions in Science: Philosophical Essays on Modelling and Idealization*. London: Routledge, pp. 248–258.

Giere, R. N. 2010. An Agent-Based Conception of Models and Scientific Representation. *Synthese* 172: 269–281.

Goodman, N. 1972. Seven Strictures on Similarity. In N. Goodman (ed.), *Problems and Projects*. Indianapolis and New York: Bobbs-Merrill, pp. 437–446.

Goodman, N. 1976. *Languages of Art* (2nd ed.). Indianapolis and Cambridge: Hacket.

Hacking, I. 1983. *Representing and Intervening*. Cambridge: Cambridge University Press.

Hale, S. 1988. Spacetime and the Abstract/Concrete Distinction. *Philosophical Studies* 53: 85–102.

Hendry, R. F. and S. Psillos 2007. How to Do Things with Theories: An Interactive View of Language and Models in Science. In J. Brzezinski, A. Klawiter, T. A. F. Kuipers, K. Łastowski, K. Paprzycka, and P. Przybysz (eds.), *The Courage of Doing Philosophy: Essays Dedicated to Lezek Nowak*. Amsterdam and New York: Rodopi, pp. 123–157.

Herfel, W. E. 1995. Nonlinear Dynamical Models as Concrete Construction. In W. E. Herfel, W. Krajewski, I. Niiniluoto, and R. Wojcicki (eds.), *Theories and Models in Scientific Processes* (Poznań Studies in the Philosophy of Science and the Humanities 44). Amsterdam: Rodopi, pp. 69–84.

Khosrowi, D. 2020. Getting Serious About Shared Features. *The British Journal for the Philosophy of Science* 71: 523–546.

Lopes, D. 2004. *Understanding Pictures*. Oxford: Oxford University Press.

Mäki, U. 2011. Models and the Locus of Their Truth. *Synthese* 180: 47–63.

Morreau, M. 2010. It Simply Does Not Add Up: The Trouble with Overall Similarity. *The Journal of Philosophy* 107: 469–490.

Niiniluoto, I. 1988. Analogy and Similarity in Scientific Reasoning. In D. H. Helman (ed.), *Analogical Reasoning: Perspectives of Artificial Intelligence, Cognitive Science, and Philosophy*. Dordrecht: Kluwer, pp. 271–298.

Odenbaugh, J. 2015. Semblance or Similarity? Reflections on Simulation and Similarity. *Biology and Philosophy* 30: 277–291.

Odenbaugh, J. 2018. Models, Models, Models: A Deflationary View. *Synthese* 198: 1–16. https://doi.org/10.1007/s11229-017-1665-8.

Parker, W. S. 2015. Getting (Even More) Serious About Similarity. *Biology and Philosophy* 30: 267–276.

Portides, D. 2018. Idealization and Abstraction in Scientific Modeling. *Synthese* 198: 5873–5895.

Putnam, H. 1981. *Reason, Truth, and History*. Cambridge: Cambridge University Press.

Reiss, J. 2014. Models, Representation, and Economic Practice. In U. Gähde, S. Hartmann, and J. H. Wolf (eds.), *Models, Simulations, and the Reduction of Complexity*. Hamburg: De Gruyter, pp. 107–116.

Savage, C. W. 1998. *The Semantic (Mis)Concdeption of Theories*. http://citeseerx.ist.psu.edu/viewdoc/download?doi=10.1.1.14.6280&rep=rep1&type=pdf.

Schindler, S. 2008. Model, Theory and Evidence in the Discovery of the DNA Structure. *The British Journal for the Philosophy of Science* 59: 619–658.

Shepard, R. N. 1980. Multidimensional Scaling, Tree-Fitting, and Clustering *Science* 210: 390–398.

Suárez, M. 2003. Scientific Representation: Against Similarity and Isomorphism. *International Studies in the Philosophy of Science* 17: 225–244.

Suppe, F. 1972a. Theories, Their Formulations, and the Operational Imperative. *Synthese* 25: 129–164.

Suppe, F. 1972b. What's Wrong with the Received View on the Structure of Scientific Theories? *Philosophy of Science* 39: 1–19.

Suppe, F. 1974. Theories and Phenomena. In W. Leinfellner and E. Köhler (eds.), *Developments in the Methodology of Social Science*. Dordrecht: Reidel, pp. 45–91.

Suppe, F. 1977. The Search for Philosophical Understanding of Scientific Theories. In F. Suppe (ed.), *The Structure of Scientific Theories*. Urbana and Chicago: University of Illinois Press, pp. 3–241.

Suppe, F. 1979. Theory Structure. In P. D. Asquith and H. E. J. Kyburg (eds.), *Current Research in Philosophy of Science: Proceedings of the P.S.A. Critical Research Problems Conference*. East Lansing: Philosophy of Science Association, pp. 317–338.

Suppe, F. 1989. *The Semantic Conception of Theories and Scientific Realism*. Urbana and Chicago: University of Illinois Press.

Suppe, F. 1998. Theories, Scientific. In E. Craig (ed.), *Routledge Encyclopedia of Philosophy* (Vol. 2008). London: Routledge, pp. 344–355.

Suppe, F. 2000. Understanding Scientific Theories: An Assessment of Developments, 1969–1998. *Philosophy of Science* 67: 102–115.

Teller, P. 2001. Twilight of the Perfect Model Model. *Erkenntnis* 55: 393–415.

Thomson-Jones, M. 2010. Missing Systems and Face Value Practise. *Synthese* 172: 283–299.

Thomson-Jones, M. 2012. Modeling without Mathematics. *Philosophy of Science* 79: 761–772.

Toon, A. 2011. Playing with Molecules. *Studies in History and Philosophy of Science* 42: 580–589.

Toon, A. 2012. Similarity and Scientific Representation. *International Studies in the Philosophy of Science* 26: 241–257.

Tversky, A. 1977. Features of Similarity. *Psychological Review* 84: 327–352.

van Fraassen, B. C. 1985. Empiricism in the Philosophy of Science. In P. M. Churchland and C. A. Hooker (eds.), *Images of Science*. Chicago: Chicago University Press, pp. 245–308.

Weisberg, M. 2012. Getting Serious About Similarity. *Philosophy of Science* 79: 785–794.

Weisberg, M. 2013. *Simulation and Similarity: Using Models to Understand the World.* Oxford: Oxford University Press.

Weisberg, M. 2015. Biology and Philosophy Symposium on Simulation and Similarity: Using Models to Understand the World: Response to Critics. *Biology and Philosophy* 30: 299–310.

PART III

9

RECONSIDERING REPRESENTATION

9.1 Introduction

Models represent their respective target systems. But what does it mean for a model to represent its target? In Section 6.2 we introduced this problem, articulated specific questions that an account of scientific representation must answer, and formulated conditions of adequacy for answers. We then discussed how the structuralist account and the similarity account address these questions and conditions. As we have seen, both accounts face a number of difficulties. Over the last two decades, several alternative accounts have been proposed that promise to overcome these difficulties. The aim of this chapter is to introduce, discuss, and evaluate these accounts.[1] We begin with a position dubbed General Griceanism, which casts doubt on the entire endeavour of analysing scientific representation (Section 9.2). After having dispelled the Gricean challenge, we turn to a position that self-identifies as "direct representation" (Section 9.3). We then discuss a family of proposals that sails under the flag of "inferentialism" (Section 9.4). An altogether different approach emphasises that models represent their targets *as* thus and so and therefore analyses scientific representation in terms of representation-as (Section 9.5). We end by noting that while representation is important, not all models function representationally (Section 9.6).

9.2 Chasing Rainbows?

Attempts to address the various questions associated with scientific representation are in vain if the argument in a paper by Callender and Cohen (2006) is correct. They submit that "there is no special problem about scientific representation" (*ibid.*, 67) and that "isomorphism, similarity, and inference generation are all idle wheels in the representational machinery" (*ibid.*, 78). Those who are after a theory of scientific representation are chasing rainbows.[2]

DOI: 10.4324/9781003285106-13

This verdict is motivated by a position Callender and Cohen call *General Griceanism*.[3] The core of General Griceanism is the reductive claim that there is one privileged class of representations, and all other representations derive their representational status from their relation to this privileged class (*ibid.*, 70). The privileged class of core representations are mental states (*ibid.*, 73). The representational power of other representations such as linguistic utterances and pictures is then reduced to the representational power of the specific mental states that a subject has when engaging with these representations. For the General Gricean, the analysis of a representation therefore is a two-stage process. She first "explains the representational powers of derivative representations in terms of those of fundamental representations" and then "offers some other story to explain representation for the fundamental bearers of content" (*ibid.*, 73). Since the fundamental bearers of content are mental states, the core challenge for the General Gricean is to formulate an account of how mental states are about something in the world. This is the problem of mental representation, which is one of the core concerns in the philosophy of mind.[4]

Like language and pictures, scientific representation is a derivative type of representation, and therefore "the varied representational vehicles used in scientific settings (models, equations, toothpick constructions, drawings, etc.) represent their targets (the behavior of ideal gases, quantum state evolutions, bridges) by virtue of the mental states of their makers/users" (*ibid.*, 75). So how does this reduction of the representational capacity of scientific representations to mental representations work? Callender and Cohen offer an answer in terms of stipulation:

> Can the salt shaker on the dinner table represent Madagascar? Of course it can, so long as you stipulate that the former represents the latter. . . . Can your left hand represent the Platonic form of beauty? Of course, so long as you stipulate that the former represents the latter. . . . On the story we are telling, then, virtually anything can be stipulated to be a representational vehicle for the representation of virtually anything . . . the representational powers of mental states are so wide-ranging that they can bring about other representational relations between arbitrary relata by dint of mere stipulation. The upshot is that, once one has paid the admittedly hefty one-time fee of supplying a metaphysics of representation for mental states, further instances of representation become extremely cheap.
>
> *(ibid., 73–74)*

So General Griceanism's response to the Scientific Representation Problem is that something becomes a scientific representation by "stipulative fiat" (*ibid.*, 75): a scientific model *M* represents a target system *T* iff a model user stipulates that *M* represents *T*.

This makes scientific representations cheap to come by: take any object and declare it to be a model of your intended target. Why, then, do scientists spend time constructing and studying models? Callender and Cohen do not deny that some models are useful while others are not, and they would agree that saltshakers and left hands are useless. Yet they insist that "the questions about the utility of these representational vehicles are questions about the pragmatics of things that are representational vehicles, not questions about their representational status *per se*" (*ibid.*, 75), where "vehicle" denotes what we previously called the carrier of a representation (Section 6.2).

To assess the merits of this take on representation we start by enquiring into the relationship between General Griceanism and stipulative fiat. Even though Callender and Cohen mention the two in the same breath, they are actually separate doctrines. As Toon points out (2010a, 77–78, 2012b, 244), General Griceanism requires that *some* account be given of how non-fundamental representations relate to mental states, but the position is not committed to that account being of any particular kind, much less to it being stipulative fiat. So one can be a proponent of General Griceanism without being a proponent of stipulative fiat. Scientific representation can, in principle, be reduced to mental representation in many different ways. In fact, the more developed versions of both the morphism account and the similarity account of scientific representation (as well as other accounts that we encounter later in this chapter) are consonant with a General Gricean outlook in that they see an agent's intentions as a constitutive ingredient of an account of scientific representation. Agents designate intended targets, choose objects to be used as models, formulate hypotheses concerning the relation between models and targets, and evaluate these with respect to certain goals, purposes, and standards of accuracy. These actions are the result of an agent's mental activities. The relevant mental activities are just more complex than merely stipulating that M represents T and leaving it at that. Yet, the Gricean can still argue that the primary task of a theory of fundamental representation is to identify the mental states that correspond to these activities. It is then simply a question of one's research interests whether one sees an analysis of the mental states or the scrutiny of, say, similarity claims as the more pertinent problem.

This said, how does stipulative fiat fare as an account of scientific representation? Callender and Cohen support stipulative fiat by noting that anything can represent anything else (*ibid.*, 73). This is correct. Objects that function representationally do not belong to a particular category of things.[5] Anything from an assembly of toothpicks to a second order differential equation can, in principle, be a scientific representation. But that anything can, in principle, be a scientific representation does not imply that a mere act of stipulation is sufficient to turn anything into an actual scientific representation. The most obvious problem of stipulative fiat is that it violates the Surrogative Reasoning Condition. As a number of commentators have noticed,[6] one can stipulate that the saltshaker represents Madagascar or that the espresso machine represents the Big Bang, but these representations are cognitively inert because the account makes no provision for claims about Madagascar or the Big Bang to be extracted from reasoning about the carriers of the representation. Bare stipulation does not ground surrogative reasoning. As we have seen, the ability to use a model to reason about its target is a crucial, and indeed defining, feature of scientific representation, and an account of scientific representation must be able to explain how this is done. Stipulative fiat is therefore untenable as an account of scientific representation.

9.3 Direct Representation

We encountered different notions of models in the previous chapters. In Chapter 2 we distinguished between logical and representational models; in Chapter 5 we saw that some authors take models to be set-theoretical entities; and in Chapter 8 we encountered the views that models are abstract entities or abstract replicas. We now add a further notion to the list, namely that models are sets of assumptions about their target systems. Achinstein articulates this view as follows:

> The term "model" is frequently used by the scientist in the expression "model of an x" to refer to a set of assumptions or postulates describing certain physical objects, or phenomena, of type x. . . . Thus, e.g., when the physicist speaks of the Bohr model of the hydrogen atom he is generally referring to Bohr's assumptions about the properties of hydrogen atoms (or to the hydrogen atom as described by such assumptions).
>
> *(1964, 330)*

He then encapsulates this view in the slogan that a "model consists of a set of *assumptions* about some object or system" (1965, 103, cf. 1968, 212). This notion is closely connected to scientific practice, where models are often introduced with locutions like "consider" and "assume". A physicist introducing the Newtonian model of the solar system might thus say "assume that planets are perfect spheres and . . .". By making these assumptions, the physicist introduces the model.

The view is not particular to Achinstein, and it also appears in the writings of other philosophers. Bailer-Jones says that "[a] model is an interpretative description of a phenomenon that facilitates access to that phenomenon" (2002, 108). Hartmann notes that a model is "a set of assumptions about some object or system" (1999, 327). Cartwright likens models to "prepared descriptions" presenting the target as if it had the properties specified in the description (1983, 134). Nowak says that models are "sets of statements" about the target (1998, 42), which is a view shared by Nowakowa (2000, 10). And, finally, Thomson-Jones (2012, 762) and Leplin (1980, 274) associate a model with a set of "propositions" about the target system.[7]

This view of models does not itself offer an account of representation, but it opens the door for an approach to the problem that has become known as *Direct Representation*. The theories of representation that we encountered so far regard models as objects of sorts and construed representation-as a relation between the model-object and the target. This ties in with a widely shared understanding of models as independent objects. In fact Weisberg sees the construction of an object that is put into a relation with a target as the defining feature of modelling that distinguishes it from other forms of scientific investigation (2007, 209–210). If so, then model-representation is "indirect" representation: a modeller does not describe the target directly but introduces a secondary system, the model, to represent the target.

This view has met with opposition from Toon and Levy, who (independently) propose a competing "direct" account of representation.[8] Their view does not recognise models as independent entities and instead sees models as special kind of description. Model descriptions are direct in that the referent of a model description is not a model system that is distinct from the target, but the target itself. Hence Levy submits that models provide an "imaginative description of real things" (2012, 741), and Toon emphasises that there are no model systems, understood as objects of which model descriptions are literally true (Toon 2012a, 43–44).

This approach is a natural continuation of the earlier view that models are assumptions, but it also moves beyond that view in an important way. Both Toon and Levy offer an account of what it means to make an assumption about a system, and in doing so they transform the "assumptions view" into a theory of scientific representation. Both views draw on Walton's (1990) account of fiction, at the heart of which lies the notion of a *game of make-believe*. A simple example of such a game is what children do when they play games like "spot the bear". In this game a group of children walks through a forest and they agree that whoever sees a stump is to *imagine* a bear. In the context of the game, stumps function as *props* and the rule that one has to imagine a bear when seeing a stump is a *principle of generation*. The props together with the principles of generation define a game of make-believe by prescribing what is to be imagined. A proposition that is so mandated to be imagined is *true in the game*. The set of propositions that are true in the game need not coincide with the set of propositions actually imagined by the participants. Someone playing the game may mistake a molehill for a stump (and hence imagine a bear where she should not); or there could be a stump hidden behind a tree which does therefore not trigger any imaginings (and yet the proposition that there is a bear behind the tree is true in the game).

There is a vast variety of different games of make-believe, and they use different props and different rules of generation. In an important kind of game, the props are the texts of literary fiction. Toon offers the example of the H. G. Wells' *The War of the Worlds* (2012a, 39). The words and sentences we read are the props, which, together with the rules of the English language and the genre-conventions of the literary category to which the work belongs, mandate the reader to imagine certain things. Readers of *The War of the Worlds* are, for instance, prescribed to imagine that St Paul's Cathedral was attacked by aliens and now has a gaping hole in the western side of its dome.

In Walton's terminology something is a *representation* if it is a prop in a game of make-believe. The stumps in the children's game are representations, and so is the text of *The War of the Worlds*. Something is the *object of a representation* if the representation prescribes participants in the game to imagine something about the object. In Wells' novel St Paul's Cathedral is the object of the representation.

The crucial move now is to say that the descriptions that articulate assumptions about the target perform the same function as the text of literary fictions: they are props in a game of make believe. This makes them representations in Walton's sense, and the target is the object of the representation because the description mandates imaginings about the target. Newton's model is the description that Newton offered in *Principia*. Like the text of *The War of the Worlds*, it prescribes readers to imagine about the object of the representation, the sun-earth system, that that the sun and the earth are both perfect spheres that gravitationally interact with each other and nothing else. Hence, models are pieces of text that prescribe imaginings about a target system in much the same way in which novels prescribe imaginings about objects like St Paul's Cathedral.[9] Hence, models are not object that represent their targets by bearing a particular relation (like isomorphism or similarity) to them, but by being descriptions that serve as props in a game of make-believe that prescribe imaginings about the target system. We call this view *Direct Representation*. So Direct Representation offers the following response to the Scientific Representation Problem: A scientific model M represents a target system T iff M is a text which functions as prop in game of make-believe (Levy 2015, 791; Toon 2012a, 62).

An obvious advantage of Direct Representation is that the Problem of Carriers has practically disappeared. There is no model object and so there is no question about what this object is, and the problems concerning the nature of models that plagued in particular the similarity view disappear. Both Levy (2012, 744–747, 2015, 780–790) and Toon (2012a, 41–45) see this as a major advantage of their accounts. The view meets the Directionality Condition because the model prescribes imaginings about the target, but not vice versa. There is no requirement that imaginings make true claims about the target (there is no hole in the dome of St Paul's Cathedral), and so the account has no problem with misrepresentation. Given that the view originates in aesthetics and takes its cues from an analysis of literary fiction, it is natural to assume that Direct Representation gives a negative answer to the Representational Demarcation Problem. Neither Toon nor Levy address the question of the application of mathematics, and so this remains as an open question for Direct Representation.

It is unclear, however, how Direct Representation meets the Surrogative Reasoning Condition. By itself, imagining that the target has certain properties tells us nothing about how truths about the model provide claims about the target. Imagining the sun and the earth as gravitationally interacting perfect spheres tells us nothing about which, if any, claims about perfect spheres are also true of the real sun and earth. As formulated so far, Direct Representation lacks a mechanism of transfer that allows model users to carry over insights gained in the model to the target. Toon touches on this problem briefly and responds that the transfer of representational content is effected by principles of generation:

> Principles of generation often link properties of models to properties of the system they represent in a rather direct way. If the model has a certain property then we are to imagine that system does too. If the model is accurate, then the model and the system will be similar in this respect.
>
> *(2012a, 68–69)*

This involves an extension of Walton's notion of a principle of generation. In its original formulation, a game of make-believe mandates imaginings about something; it does not ask us to turn these imaginings into claims about the target. Wells' readers are supposed to imagine that there is a hole in the dome of St Paul's Cathedral; the novel does not tell anybody to form the hypothesis that there really is such a hole. The country bumpkin who jumps on the stage to save the heroine fails to understand how a game of make-believe works. But even if we assume that a suitable extension of the notion of a principle of generation can be formulated, serious problems remain. If the mechanism of transfer is property identity, then the notion of modelling provided is too narrow. Models mostly portray targets as having properties that they do not have, and so an account of representation based on property identity fails to explain how such models work. Toon mentions that not all models work in this way (*ibid.*, 69), but gives no further indication about how to deal with such cases.

Levy (2015, 792–796) addresses the Surrogative Reasoning Condition through an appeal to Yablo's (2014) account of partial truth. A sentence is partially true if part of the sentence is true. In more detail, a sentence is partially true "if it is true when evaluated only relative to a subset of the circumstances that make up its subject matter – the subset corresponding to the relevant content-part" (Levy 2015, 792). Consider a sentence describing the solar system that states how many planets there are, gives an account of the internal constitution of planets, and specifies their relative positions. Assume that this sentence is uttered in a context in which we are interested in the number of planets. The relevant subset of the circumstances that make up the sentence's subject matter then is the number of planets. The sentence is partially true if what it says about the number of planets is true. Levy submits that this account also works for some cases of modelling. He offers the example of the ideal gas. The ideal gas model contains all kind of assumptions, for instance that particles do not interact and that the gas is perfectly isolated from the environment. If used in a context in which we are only interested in the relation between pressure p, volume V, and temperature T, the subject matter of the model is the ideal gas law (which says that these quantities are related by the equation $pV = kT$, where k is a constant), and all other features can be bracketed. The model is then partially true if this law is true. This works for some models, but as Levy himself notes (*ibid.*, 794), there are cases of modelling that resist a treatment along these lines. Such cases are typically ones that involve limit idealisations, for instance when the particle number in a system is assumed to tend toward infinity (see Section 12.3). Such models require a different treatment, and no account of that treatment has been given.

Levy's solution shares with Toon's an emphasis on identity. Both accounts in fact say that a certain feature of the model is ascribed to the target; they differ in how they identify that feature. Toon's account assumes that it is singled out in a generalised rule of generation; Levy's account appeals to a subject matter and partial truth. This implies a stance on style and accuracy: the style is identity-representation and a model is accurate if the target indeed possesses the property that it is said to share with the model.

Direct Representation submits that models prescribe imaginings about target systems, which is the move that allows Direct Representation to eliminate ontologically problematic model systems. However, as we have previously seen, not all models have targets. Models of the ether or other discredited entities have no targets. But not all targetless models are the fallout of error. Models of four-sex populations and the architectural model of a planned but not yet realised building were designed in the full knowledge of the absence of a target. Toon addresses this issue by noting that only some models are like *The War of the Worlds*, which has an object. Others are like *Dracula*, which belongs to a group of works that "do not represent any actual, concrete object but are instead about fictional characters" (2012a, 54). But what do they represent then? *Dracula*, Toon submits, is about a fictional character, and so are targetless models. Four sex-populations and unrealised buildings are fictional characters like Dracula and Hamlet, and the respective models represent these fictional characters. This, however, brings back all the problems with fictional entities that the direct view was meant to avoid, and so at least in the case of targetless models, Direct Representation enjoys no ontological advantage over accounts of indirect representation like the isomorphism view and the similarity view. Toon acknowledges this and thinks that it is a problem one can live with.

Levy is less sanguine about accepting fictional characters and offers a radical solution to the problem of targetless models: there are no such models! This suggestion has two prongs. The first is a generalisation of the notion of target (Levy 2015, 796–797). Appealing to Godfrey-Smith's notion of "hub-and-spoke" cases, he allows for families of models where only some of them have targets (which makes them the hub models), while the models without a target are connected to the hub models through conceptual links (spokes). Four-sex population models, for instance, could be seen as being the spoke models of two-sex population models which have targets. This allows Levy to regard hub-and-spoke cases as direct representations of "generalized targets" (*ibid.*, 796). A four-sex model, for instance, is then a direct representation of something like "population growth in general" (*ibid.*, 796). If a targetless model turns out to have no spoke to a model with a target, it has to be stripped of its (supposed) status of being a model. Levy mentions purported models like the Game of Life, which, on closer inspection, turn out to be just "bits of mathematics" that are not models (*ibid.*, 797). This eliminates the necessity of introducing fictional characters as the targets of models that fail to represent a real-world system.

The hub-and-spoke metaphor and the only loosely defined notion of a generalised target are insufficient to dissolve the problem of targetless models. The key innovation of Direct Representation is to excise model systems and redefine modelling as the prescription to imagine something about the *actual* target. If a model has no target this cannot be done, then the fact that the model has conceptual links to other models does not change this. Notions like "population growth in general" do not single out concrete things that can serve as the object of an act of pretence, and even if one were to generalise the notion of an object so that the imagination can be about generalisations of that kind, they raise the same ontological worries as Toon's fictional characters. One cannot at once reap the ontological benefits of viewing modelling as imagining something about a concrete object, while at the same time allowing for targets that are not concrete objects.

9.4 Inferentialism

As we have seen in Section 6.2, an adequate analysis of scientific representation must meet the Directionality Condition and the Surrogative Reasoning Condition. That is, it must account for the facts that representation is asymmetric and that models allow scientist to generate hypotheses about the target. Suárez's *Inferential Conception of Scientific Representation* (*Inferential Conception*, for short) offers an account of scientific representation directly in term of these two features: "*A* represents *B* only if (i) the representational force of *A* points towards *B*, and (ii) *A* allows competent and informed agents to draw specific inferences regarding *B*" (2004, 773).

The conception owes its name to the fact that it places the practice of drawing inferences at the heart of an analysis of representation. Models are identified neither by their material constitution nor by the relations they bear to other things; they are characterised functionally as things that serve as "inferential prostheses" or "instruments for surrogative reasoning" (de Donato Rodriguez and Zamora Bonilla 2009, 101). Suárez's Inferential Conception offers conditions on representation *tout court* and does *not* differentiate between scientific and non-scientific representation, and hence gives a negative answer to the Representational Demarcation Problem. This is in keeping with the spirit of Suárez's discussion, in which he often draws on analogies between representation in art and science.[10] Since there is no requirement that the inferences drawn must be correct, the account has no problem with misrepresentation. A representation is accurate to the extent that the inferences drawn from the model are true of the target. No assumptions are made about what sort of object *A* is supposed to be other than that it somehow has to ground inferences, and so the Problem of Carriers is set aside. Since *A* can be a mathematical entity, the account makes room for mathematical representations. Users can draw inferences about non-existent targets, which addresses the Targetless Models Condition. Although Suárez is not concerned with representational styles, different styles could be accounted for in terms of agents drawing different kinds of inferences, for instance deductive, analogical, and abductive inferences.

We start facing difficulties when we ask what the Inferential Conception's response to the Scientific Representation Problem is. Responding to this problem amounts to filling the blank in the biconditional "*M* is a scientific representation of *T* if and only if ___". However, Suárez's condition specifies that *A* represents *B* "only if", not "if and only if". So the Inferential Conception offers necessary but not sufficient conditions for *A* to represent *B*. This is deliberate because Suárez explicitly rejects the search for necessary and sufficient conditions and submits that "necessary conditions will certainly be good enough" (2004, 771).[11] This amounts to rejecting the Scientific Representation Problem *per se*, which Suárez would not accept as a problem that an account of scientific representation should solve.

The reason for this is that he argues that one should adopt a "deflationary" attitude toward scientific representation (2004, 770). Being a deflationist has two aspects, and the first is precisely to reject necessary conditions (we turn to the second aspect shortly). Deflationism, according to Suárez, "entails abandoning the aim of a substantive theory to seek universal necessary and sufficient conditions that are met in each and every concrete real instance of scientific representation", which is the right move because "[r]epresentation is not the kind of notion that requires, or admits, such conditions" (*ibid.*, 771). It remains unclear, however, why an analysis of representation neither allows nor needs sufficient conditions. Indeed, a position that recognises only necessary conditions is in the awkward position that it can never say that something actually is a representation. That is, based on the Inferential Conception's criterion we are never in a position to assert that a given model (or graph, or diagram, or painting, or . . .) represents, or indeed that mankind has ever produced anything that qualifies as a representation.

The second aspect of a deflationary attitude is that one should not seek "deeper features to representation other than its surface features" (2004, 771) and, as Suárez and Solé put it, instead turn "platitudes into the defining conditions for the concept" (2006, 40). The above conditions embody this programme. The first condition, that the representational force of *A* point towards *B*, is designed to ensure that *A* and *B* enter into a representational relationship and Suárez emphasises that representational force is "necessary for any kind of representation" (2004, 776). But explaining representation in terms of representational force would seem to shed little light on the nature of representation as long as no analysis of representational force is provided. However, Suárez insists that any attempt to further analyse representational force, for instance in terms of denotation, would violate the imperative of deflationism (2015, 41).

The Inferential Conception's second condition, that *A* allow competent and informed agents to draw specific inferences regarding *B*, is just the Surrogative Reasoning Condition, now taken as a necessary condition for representation. This condition, however, makes no attempt to elucidate how inferences are generated and what it is about a representation that allows an agent to draw inferences. Contessa voices dissatisfaction with this state of affairs and complains that on the Inferential Conception an agent's ability to draw inferences from a model has to be accepted as a "brute fact", which "makes the connection between epistemic representation and valid surrogative reasoning needlessly obscure and the performance of valid surrogative inferences an activity as mysterious and unfathomable as soothsaying or divination" (2007, 61).

The Inferential Conception's deflationary analysis leaves us with only necessary conditions for representation, and these are formulated in terms of an inexplicable notion of representational force and of an unanalysable capacity to ground inferences. This is very little. So the crucial question is: why accept deflationism? Suárez (2015) mounts a defence of the deflationist stance on representation by drawing an analogy with deflationist theories of truth. This approach faces two challenges. First, a defence of deflationism concerning representation by appeal to deflationism concerning truth is at best as strong as the case for deflationism concerning truth. Deflationary theories of truth, however, do not command universal support,[12] and those who favour alternative conceptions of truth will find attempts to muster support for a deflationary approach to representation through Suárez's analogy wanting. Second, even those who are supportive of deflationary theories of truth may wonder how robust the analogy between truth and representation is. The analogy is based on the premise that what is good for truth is good for representation, but Suárez offers little by way of explicit argument in support of this analogy.

Contessa is not swayed by the virtues of deflationism and sets out to reinflate the Inferential Conception. His "interpretational account" is intended to be a "substantial account" which formulates conditions that explain how inferences are drawn (2007, 48). The core concept in Contessa's account is that of an "interpretation", which also holds the key to Contessa's answer to the Scientific Representation Problem: M is a scientific representation of T "if and only if the user adopts an interpretation of M in terms of T" (*ibid.*, 57). Interpreting a model in terms of the target proceeds in three steps. In the first step the user identifies a set of pertinent objects in the model, along with properties and relations that the objects instantiate. In the second step the user does the same for the target. In the third step the user takes M to denote T, takes every object in the model to designate a unique object in the target, and pairs up every property and relation in the model with a property or relation of the same arity in the target. In fact, interpreting M in terms of T is formally equivalent to setting up an isomorphism between M and T. The difference between the interpretational account and the isomorphism account is that Contessa does not require models to be set-theoretical structures, and that the relevant objects and relations can be fully interpreted (and not merely extensionally specified).

If M is an interpretation of T in Contessa's sense, the interpretation relation can be exploited to transfer findings from the model to the target. In this way, the interpretational account offers a clear-cut solution to the Scientific Representation

Problem that meets the Surrogative Reasoning Condition, but does so in a non-deflationary way. It also offers an obvious response to the Directionality Condition and it inherits from the Inferential Conception the rejection of the Representational Demarcation Problem. Since the interpretational account shares with the structuralist account an emphasis on relations and one-to-one model-target correspondence, it can appeal to the same account of the applicability of mathematics as the structuralist. The interpretational account places few restrictions on what can be a model other than requiring that it consist of objects with relations. If a model is mathematical, this leads to an ontology of structures (Section 2.6); if models are non-mathematical, then the questions we encountered with the similarity account reoccur (Section 8.5). Due to the close relation between Contessa's notion of an interpretation and isomorphism, the interpretational account can be seen as offering "isomorophism style" representations and adopt the same standards of accuracy. This is a viable answer, but, as noted in Section 6.6, it is doubtful that it covers the entire spectrum of representations.

Things get more involved when we turn to the issues of misrepresentation and targetless models. Contessa explains misrepresentation in terms of there being model objects that have no correspondents in the target, and vice versa (2007, 59). As Shech (2015, 3473–3478) notes, this account faces a problem with models that misrepresent not because they include too little, but because they distort. A model that portrays a slippery surface as frictionless omits nothing but deforms an important property of the surface. Contessa anticipates this objection and responds with an appeal to the corrective abilities of users, who are able to use a model successfully despite shortcomings (2007, 60). This may well be true, but it is unclear how this ability fits into the interpretational account, which assigns no systematic place to practitioners' corrective competences.[13]

Ducheyne formulates a variant of the interpretational account that deals with the problem of distortive idealisations in a different way. The account retains the idea of there being a one-to-one correspondence of elements and relations in the model and in the target, but allows for relations in the target to be approximations of the corresponding relations in the model (2012, 83–86). Ducheyne calls this the *pragmatic limiting case account* of representation. So a model can represent a target if model relations are limiting cases (or approximations) of the pertinent target relations. This points in the right direction. The problem with this account is a lack of specificity. Ducheyne operates at an abstract level and does not further analyse the notion of a relation holding approximately in the target relative to a certain purpose. Unless a specific notion of approximation is provided, it remains unclear how exactly models relate to targets. This has consequences for the misrepresentation problem. The account is designed to deal with misrepresentation, but it remains unclear whether every misrepresentation is a case of approximation. For instance, is Thomson's "plum pudding model" of the atom an approximation of the atom as we understand it today? If not, then it seems we have to say that it is not a representation at all, which is counterintuitive. If it is, then one would like to know what notion of approximation is at work and what sort of inferences it warrants.

Contessa and Ducheyne address the problems of the Inferential Conception by specifying inference-generating mechanisms that are conceptually prior to the practice of drawing inferences. Inferentialist purists resist such amendments and insist that the issues within inferentialism will have to be resolved in terms of inferences themselves. De Donato Rodriguez and Zamora Bonilla (2009) develop an inferentialist conception of models. Building on Brandom's inferentialism in philosophy of language, they outline an account of modelling in terms of the practice of drawing inferences. Their focus is on idealisation, credibility, and the process of model building rather than on representation, and they are not concerned with the problems of the Inferential Conception of Scientific Representation. It would, however, be interesting to see how the issues of the Inferential Conception could be resolved from such a point of view.

9.5 Representation-As and the DEKI Account

Images often represent their subject *as* thus and so. A caricature portrays Churchill as a bulldog; a painting shows Nelson Mandela as a prisoner; and a photograph shows Marianela Nuñez as a swan. Hughes notes that this familiar aspect of visual representations is also characteristic of scientific representations, which often represent their targets as such-and-such. The wave theory of light represents light as a wave motion, and a theory of matter can represent a plasma either as a classical system or as a quantum system (1997, 331). The observation extends to models. Maxwell's model represents the ether as a mechanical system; the Philips-Newlyn model represents the economy as a hydraulic system; and Weizsäcker's model represents the nucleus as a drop of liquid.

Hughes formulates what he calls the *DDI account* of scientific representation, where "DDI" is the acronym for "denotation, demonstration and interpretation".[14] Taking his cue from Goodman's theory of artistic representation, Hughes identifies *denotation* as the first core ingredient of scientific representation: a theory denotes its subject matter and a model denotes its target (1997, 330). If theories or models represent particulars (a cosmological model may represent the big bang), then the denotation relation between model and target is like the relation between a proper name and its bearer. If theories or models represent types, then the relation is like that between a predicate and the elements in its extension.

The second element is *demonstration*. Hughes notes that a model is a "secondary subject that has, so to speak, a life of its own", and that a "representation has an internal dynamic whose effects we can examine" (*ibid.*, 331). This is the place in his account where representation-as resides. The choice of the secondary subject determines the kind of the representation. If the secondary subject is a system of waves and if the system denotes light, then the model represents light as a wave. Because the model is a system with an internal dynamic of its own, its behaviour can be studied and various results about the model can be demonstrated. Hughes discusses the example of waves passing through two nearby slits, where it can be demonstrated that this leads to the waves exhibiting an interference pattern.

The third and final step is *interpretation*. Demonstrations in the model are about the model itself and *per se* imply nothing about the target. Effects found in the wave system are about waves, not light. An act of interpretation is required to make model-results relevant to the target (1997, 332–333). The model user has to interpret results concerning waves so that they become results (or at least hypotheses) about light. By interpreting, say, an interference pattern found in water waves as pertaining to light, the modeller infers that light, when directed at two nearby slits, will also show an interference pattern. This effect is then confirmed in experiments.

Unfortunately, Hughes says little about what it means to interpret a model-result in terms of the target. So one either has to retreat to an intuitive understanding of interpretation, or import a notion of interpretation from elsewhere into Hughes' account. A candidate would be Contessa's notion of interpretation, but there is no textual evidence that Hughes would have had anything like Contessa's notion in mind. Hughes offers a favourable discussion of Giere's version of the Model-Theoretical View of theories which sees models as connecting to their targets through theoretical hypotheses (1998, 121). This might suggest that Hughes sees models as relating to targets through theoretical hypotheses that express similarity claims. If so, then Hughes' account becomes indistinguishable from Giere's.

Hughes is explicit that he does not intend the DDI account to offer individually necessary and jointly sufficient conditions for scientific representation (1997, 339) and that he intends to keep the account "designedly skeletal" (*ibid.*, 335). This means that the DDI account does not offer an answer to the Scientific Representation Problem. It remains unclear what exactly Hughes' motivation for this is. He states that he wants to put forward the "modest suggestion that, if we examine a theoretical model with these three activities in mind, we shall achieve some insight into the kind of representation that it provides" (*ibid.*, 339) and notes that the account needs to be "supplemented on a case-by-case basis" (*ibid.*, 335). However, context dependence does not *ipso facto* undermine the status of conditions as necessary and sufficient. Denotation, demonstration and interpretation could be interpreted as abstract conditions, and a specific account would have to be given on every occasion of how denotation is established, of how demonstrations are performed, and of how results are interpreted. Thus understood, context-sensitivity would be compatible with these conditions being necessary and sufficient, and the account could be taken to offer a response to the Scientific Representation Problem.

An alternative is to interpret Hughes' account as a diachronic analysis of the *process* of modelling: we first stipulate that the model stands for the target, then establish relevant results in the model, and finally transfer these to the target through an interpretation. As far as it goes, this seems correct, but thus understood the account does not explain how representation works.

This problem is remedied in Goodman and Elgin's account of *representation-as*.[15] In their analysis, the grammar of "representation-as" is that an object X (a picture, a model, . . .) represents a subject T (a person, a target system, . . .) as being thus or so (Z).

To explain how this relationship is established, we need to introduce three notions of Goodman and Elgin's theory of symbols – *representation of*, *Z-representation*, and *exemplification* – in terms of which *representation-as* will be defined.

Goodman submits that "[d]enotation is the core of representation" (1976, 5). For X to be a representation of T, X must denote T. Bohr's model, Schrödinger's model, the drawing on the white board, the English word "hydrogen atom", and the chemical symbol "H" all denote hydrogen atoms and are therefore representations *of* the hydrogen atom. The crucial qualification is "of". The "of" is what distinguishes a denotation-based notion of representation from other notions of representation.

This raises the question of how to understand items that seem to be representations without being representations *of* something because the items they seemingly represent do not exist. Pictures showing unicorns or mermaids, maps of Atlantis or Westeros, Gaudí's drawings of the hotel he was going to build in New York, and scientific models of the ether are of this kind. They are not representations of anything because the things they are seemingly about do not exist, and something that does not exist cannot be denoted. And yet there is a clear sense in which these pictures, drawings and models are not just gobbledygook. Goodman and Elgin account for this intuition by introducing the distinction between a representation of a Z and a Z-representation. A Z-representation is a representation that portrays a Z, even if the Z-does not exist. Gaudí's drawings are hotel-representations even though there is no hotel they are a representation of (his New York hotel has never been built). A map of Atlantis is an island-representation even though there is no island called Atlantis. And so on.

We have introduced Z-representations in response to the problem of representations that lack a target. But Z-representations are not limited to such cases. They are not just an emergency exit for semanticists when they are faced with targetless but seemingly meaningful representations. Representations that have a target can be Z-representations. A painting of the Colosseum is a Roman-theatre-representation, and it is at once a representation of a Roman theatre. Examples like these might engender the view that if a Z-representation has a target, then it must be a representation of a Z. Goodman points out that this is not so: "the denotation of a picture no more determines its kind than the kind of picture determines the denotation. Not every man-picture represents a man, and conversely not every picture that represents a man is a man-picture" (Goodman 1976, 26). A statue of Justitia is a blindfolded-women-representation while it is a representation of justice, and the smiling house that the insurance company uses as a cover for its contracts is a house-representation but it denotes customer satisfaction. From the fact that something is a Z-representation nothing follows about what it is a representation of. Some Z-representations are representations of Zs; some Z-representations are representations of things that are not Zs; and some Z-representations are not representations of anything at all. Vice versa, not every representation of Z has to be a Z-representation. The word "hydrogen atom" is a representation of hydrogen, and yet it is not a hydrogen-representation; in fact it is not a Z-representation at all.

Let us finally introduce the notion of *exemplification*. Something *exemplifies* a property if it at once instantiates the property and refers to it. To instantiate a property without referring to it is merely to possess the property, while referring to the property without instantiating it is to represent the property in a way other than by exemplification (Goodman 1976, 53).[16] Familiar examples of representation by exemplification are samples: the olive we try on the market before buying a whole glass exemplifies the flavour of the particular kind of olives we're looking at, and the fabric swatch we are shown in the tailor's shop exemplifies the make, texture, and colour of the fabric from which the suit will be made.

Instantiation is a necessary but not a sufficient condition for exemplification. An olive or a fabric swatch have any number of properties but they do not exemplify all of them. The olive does not exemplify the property of having been filled into the glass by an Italian, and the fabric does not exemplify the property of being in a shop in Maoming Road. Exemplification is selective, and which properties are selected depends on context. In the tailor's shop, the swatch exemplifies a certain quality of wool; if used in a geometry class the same piece of fabric can exemplify rectangularity.

With these ingredients in place, we are now in a position to define representation-as. A first stab at the topic would be to say that X represents T as Z if X is a Z-representation and denotes T. In effect this is a slightly generalised version of Hughes' definition of representation-as. Hughes thought that a model represents its target as such-and-such if the model is a such-and-such and denotes the target: a model represents light as a wave if the model is a wave system and denotes light. It is now a small step to replace the requirement that the model is a such-and-such by the condition that it is a such-and-such-representation. However, as we have seen above, this account fails to explain how the model is informative about the target. This problem receives an elegant solution in Elgin's account:

> [X] does not merely denote [T] and happen to be a [Z]-representation. Rather in being a [Z]-representation, [X] exemplifies certain properties and imputes those properties or related ones to [T]. .... The properties exemplified in the [Z]-representation thus serve as a bridge that connects [X] to [T].'
>
> *(Elgin 2010, 10)*

The crucial idea here is that Z-representations exemplify properties associated with Z's and then impute these to the target. The caricature showing Churchill as bulldog instantiates certain properties one associates with bulldogs such as being menacing, persevering and relentless,[17] and imputes these to Churchill. In doing so, the caricature represents him as menacing, persevering and relentless. Representation does not imply truth. The subject T may or may not have the properties that the representation imputes to it. The representation generates a claim about T, and that claim can be true or false.

Putting the different elements together and rephrasing the points in terms of models and targets yields an answer to the Scientific Representation Problem: M is a scientific representation of T iff M represents T as Z, where M represents T as

Z iff (i) M denotes T, (ii) M is a Z-representation exemplifying properties $P_1,...,P_n$, and (iii) $P_1,...,P_n$, or related properties, are imputed to T. The first condition can be extended to include denotation between parts of the model and parts of the target. On this account, the Newtonian model is a planetary-system-representation that denotes our solar system (and there is part-part denotation in that the large sphere denotes the sun and the small sphere denotes the earth), that exemplifies certain properties (for instance that planets move in stable elliptical orbits), and imputes these to the sun and the earth. In doing so the Newtonian model represents the sun and the earth as a planetary system.

This account is on the right track, but the three conditions need to be further developed for it to become a full-fledged account of scientific representation. The first condition raises questions of detail: how is denotation characterised and how is it established? It seems that models often borrow denotation from the linguistic descriptions that accompany them, and so the denotation of models is in effect reduced to the denotation of terms. As such the problem is one for the philosophy of language, which we set aside here.[18]

The second condition requires M to be a Z-representation. What makes something a Z-representation? In the case of visual representations this is a much-discussed question. So-called *perceptual accounts* say that X portrays a certain subject Z if an observer with normal visual capabilities would see a Z in X when seeing X under normal conditions.[19] On that account, Constable's *Salisbury Cathedral from the Meadows* is a cathedral-representation because when looking at the canvass under normal conditions (the lights are switched on, etc.) a normal onlooker (someone who is not blind, etc.) will see a cathedral in the canvass. Elgin takes a different route and explains Z-representation in terms of *genres*. On this view a picture portrays, say, a griffin because it belongs to the genre of animal pictures and some animal pictures denote animals (2010, 1–2).

Neither of these accounts is helpful in the context of scientific models. The perceptual account is an obvious non-starter because most models are not perceptual objects that can meaningfully be classified by how they appear when looked at under normal circumstances. Unlike paintings and other visual representations, scientific models do also not seem to belong to genres, at least not in an obvious way. The Newtonian model consists of two imaginary perfect spheres; the Schelling model represents social segregation with a checkerboard; Boltzmann appealed to billiard balls to represent molecules; the Phillips-Newlyn model employs a system of pipes and reservoirs to represent an economy; the worm Caenorhabditis elegans is used as a model organism to study cell division. But perfect spheres, checkerboards, billiard balls, pipes, and worms do not belong to genres in the way in which paintings like Constable's *Salisbury Cathedral from the Meadows* do. And neither do the mathematical structures that are used in scientific theories and models. Matrices, curvilinear geometries, and Hilbert spaces have been studied as mathematical objects in their own right long before they became important in the empirical sciences, and they can be used as representations of very different systems.[20]

To solve this problem, one can ground Z-representation in an agent's practices.[21] Let O be the object that is used as a model: the spheres, the checkerboard, the worm, etc. The question now is: what makes O a Z-representation? An appeal to O's intrinsic features does not help. There is nothing about being a checkerboard or a worm that makes them, respectively, a social-segregation-representation and cell-division-representation. In fact, most items of that kind are not representations at all; they are just checkerboards and worms. These objects turn into representations when they are used *as such* by an agent. The question then becomes: what does it mean for an agent to use an object as a representation? The suggestion is that this requires an act of *interpretation* whereby we interpret certain properties of the object in terms of properties of the target domain.[22] When using the Philipps-Newlyn machine as an economy representation we interpret certain water-flow properties as economy properties: we interpret an amount of water as an amount of money and we interpret the reservoir in the middle of the machine as the central bank.[23]

A more formal characterisation of an interpretation is as follows. The model object O has a host of properties. Let us call these O-properties. These are the properties the object has *qua* object. A checkerboard has checkerboard properties like *consisting of squares*, and a hydraulic system as hydraulic properties like having a flow of five litres per minute through a certain pipe. Among the many O-properties some are selected as relevant. These form a set $\Omega = \{O_1, ..., O_n\}$. If the object is intended to be used as a Z-representation, then a set $Z = \{Z_1, ..., Z_n\}$ of relevant Z-properties is chosen. An *interpretation* is bijective function $I : \Omega \to Z$; i.e., a function that assigns to each member of Ω a unique member of Z so that no member of Z is left out and so that the character of the properties is respected.

The last condition needs unpacking. A property like *being a reservoir* is a qualitative property: it is an all-or-nothing property in that an object either does or does not have it. By contrast, a property like *having a flow of x litre per minute* is a quantitative property that can assume different values. I respecting the properties' character means that qualitative O-properties are mapped onto qualitative Z-properties; and quantitative O-properties are mapped onto quantitative Z-properties while at the same time providing a scaling function specifying how the quantities of an O-property transform into quantities of the corresponding Z-property. If, for instance, the flow of water through a certain point is mapped onto the flow of money though the treasury, then I provides a scaling function saying, for instance, that a litre of water corresponds to a million of the model currency. To make explicit that the interpretation connects O-properties to Z-properties we refer to it as an O-Z-interpretation.

We can now define a Z-representation: A Z-representation is a pair (O, I) where O is an object with O-properties and I is an O-Z-interpretation. Loosely speaking one can say that O is a Z-representation (for instance, we can say that the Philipps-Newlyn machine is an economy representation), but it must be understood that this makes sense only against the background of an interpretation I. A model, then, is just a Z-representation whose object O has been chosen by a scientist or a scientific community to serve as the carrier of a Z-representation in a certain scientific context. Thus defined, a model need not have a target because, as we have seen, a Z-representation need not be a representation of a Z (or, indeed, anything else).

In Elgin's account, if M represents T as Z, M exemplifies certain properties and imputes "those properties or related ones" to T. The observation that a representation need not impute exactly the same properties to the target that it exemplifies is important: few, if any, models portray their target systems as having properties that are identical to the properties of the model. The problem is that reference to "related" properties is too unspecific because any property can be related to any other property in some way. For this reason it is preferable to build an explicit specification of the relation between model properties and the properties that will be imputed to the target into the account. Let $P_1,...,P_m$ be the Z-properties exemplified by the model,[24] and let $Q_1,...,Q_j$ be the properties that the model aims to impute to the target. The representation must then come with *key K* specifying how the Ps are converted into Qs. Adapting notation from algebra somewhat loosely, one can write $K(\{P_1,...,P_m\}) = \{Q_1,...,Q_j\}$. The posit that a representation imputes related properties to the target then has to be replaced by the clause that M exemplifies $P_1,...,P_m$ and imputes properties $Q_1,...,Q_j$ to the target where the Ps and the Qs are connected by a key K. In principle there are no restrictions on keys. K can be the identity function, but usually it is not. In some cases K will contain idealisations and approximations, or some suitable analogical relationship. We will discuss these in the next three chapters.

Drawing these elements together yields the DEKI account of representation-as (where the acronym derives from its central features: denotation, exemplification, keying-up and imputation). Let $M = (O,I)$ be a model, where O is an object used by a scientist (or scientific community) as the carrier of the representation and I is an O-Z-interpretation. M represents T as Z iff all of the following hold: (i) M denotes T (and in some cases parts of M denote parts of T); (ii) M exemplifies Z-properties $P_1,...,P_m$; (iii) M comes with key K associating the set of properties $\{P_1,...,P_m\}$ with a set of properties $\{Q_1,...,Q_j\}$; (iv) M imputes at least one of the properties in the set $\{Q_1,...,Q_j\}$ to T. DEKI's response to the Scientific Representation Problem then is: M is a scientific representation of T iff M represents T as Z.

Language has played an important role throughout. The interpretation is formulated in a language, and before one can even formulate an interpretation, one must conceptualise the carrier in a certain way, which is done in a language too. If the carrier in question is a material object, this does not raise any particular issues. Things get a bit more involved when we deal with non-material models because this gets us into all the issues that we have encountered in previous chapters. Let us set these issues aside for now and simply assume that we're describing an object of sorts, even when the model is non-material. This could be a set-theoretical structure (as in Section 6.2), or an abstract object (as in Section 8.5) or fictional entity (as we will see in Section 14.6). What matters at this point is not what the carrier is, but only that there is a carrier (whatever it may be ontologically speaking). The description we use to introduce the model consists of three parts. The first part describes the carrier X with a description D_X; we call this the *carrier description*.

In our example it would be a description of the two-body system (something like "there are two spheres such that . . ."). So D_X is couched entirely in a language consisting of terms referring to O-properties. The second part describes the interpretation with a description D_I, which is written in language that contains both terms referring to O-properties and terms referring to Z-properties; we call this the *interpretation description*. In our example it would be a statement of the connection between two-body properties and planetary-system properties (something like "the large sphere corresponds to the sun"). Finally, the third part of the description, D_B describes relevant modelling assumptions and background knowledge; we call this the *background description*. Such an assumption might concern, for instance, the dynamical laws that one takes to be operational in the model (something like "the two spheres move according to Newton's second law of motion") and the properties that such dynamical laws have. D_X, D_I, and D_B taken together form the *model description* D_M. Finally, in the context of modelling one often uses a description D_T to identify the target. This description is in principle independent from the model description because the target has to be identified independently of the model. Astronomers, for instance, use a target-idetifying description to pick out a planet as the target of a model. This description does not have to be rich, or even informative in any way. It just has to identify the target. We now have all parts of the DEKI account in place, and the account is illustrated in Figure 9.1.[25]

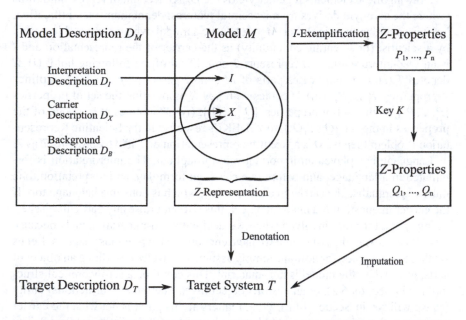

FIGURE 9.1 The DEKI account of representation. The two concentric circles symbolise the fact that X becomes a Z-representation when it is "embellished" in an interpretation.

DEKI has no problem with targetless models because models are Z-representations, which need not be representations of a Z (or indeed anything at all). So a model can be an ether-representation without being a representation of the ether. The notion of representation in DEKI is asymmetric and irreflexive due to (i) and (iv), which take care of the Directionality Condition. Surrogative reasoning takes place when scientists study what properties a model exemplifies and use the key to convert them into properties that are imputed to the target. DEKI allows for misrepresentation because it is possible that the target does not possess the properties that the model imputes to it. Representational style has several dimensions. First, scientists can choose different objects as the basis of a representation, and so one can speak of a "pipe system model" or a "checkerboard model". Second, the kind of interpretation used has an impact on the style of a representation, for instance through the choice of relevant properties and scaling functions. Third, different keys instigate different styles. Some keys are based on idealisations, others on analogies, and yet others on conventional associations, which results in the model representing the target in different ways. Standards of accuracy enter both in the definition of keys (a key can associate a precisely defined Q with a given P, or a Q that has some leeway for instance by allowing for a range of values), and in the criteria used when judging whether claims of the form "target T has property Q" are true. Like other accounts we have encountered so far, DEKI gives a negative answer to the Representational Demarcation Problem and submits that there is no significant difference between scientific representations and other kinds of representation.

Many parts of DEKI are abstract and they need to be concretised to get the full picture. In particular, proponents of DEKI will have to provide analyses of keys that are used in certain modelling endeavours. Another important issue is the problem of carriers. The account builds on the notion of a model instantiating properties. That is relatively straightforward when the model is a material object. The claim that the Philipps-Newlyn machine instantiates the property of having five litres of water in the central tank is no more problematic than any other property ascription. If the model is not a material object, then things are not so simple. What does it mean to say that the model-planets in Newton's model instantiate the property of moving in stable elliptical orbits? At this point DEKI faces the same difficulties as the similarity view. One way to respond to these difficulties is to view models as fictional objects; we discuss this proposal, along with other options, in Chapter 14. Similar comments apply to the application of mathematics condition. While DEKI makes room for a number of ways to think about the problem, it does not embody a particular solution and such a solution has to be added to DEKI using resources external to the account.

9.6 Conclusion

We have discussed various accounts of representation, each with its pros and cons. We made this effort because representation is important. This, however, is not to say that representation is the only aspect of models that matters, nor that all models function representationally. The question we have discussed in this chapter is a conditional one: if models represent, then how do they do so? This makes room for models to perform functions other than representation. But before turning to other functions of models, we continue our discussion of representation by looking at analogies (Chapter 10) and idealisations (Chapters 11 and 12).

Not all models representations; conversely, not all representations are models. The point is obvious when we look beyond science, where we find paintings, statues, and so on. But even within the confines of science various types of images, graphs, diagrams, drawings, etc. perform representational functions without being models.[26] This raises the question of how these representations work, and, in particular, of whether they represent in the same way as models do. Can the same account of representation that explains how models relate to their targets be applied to, say, diagrams? Different accounts of representation will give different answers. What all accounts share is that they must address the issue.

Notes

1 This chapter is largely based on Frigg and Nguyen's (2017a, Secs. 2, 5, 6, 7, 2020, Chs. 2, 5, 6, 7, 8).

2 A more fundamental threat might come from the pragmatist doctrine of anti-representationalism. Broadly construed, representationalism is the view that there is a relation between an epistemic device and the subject matter that the device deals with that involves veridicality, copying, and a causal relation to success (Godfrey-Smith 2020, 153). Many pragmatists reject representationalism. In this vein, Price argues for a naturalism without representationalism (Price 2011). However, as Godfrey-Smith notes, things can be representations in various senses and not all of them necessarily fall prey of the pragmatist criticisms. So the project to formulate an account of representation is not a non-starter, even from pragmatist point of view (*ibid.*).

3 This position is further developed in Ruyant's (2021).

4 See, for instance, Pitt's (2018) for a discussion.

5 This point has also been made by authors who are not signed up to the Gricean programme. See, for instance, Frigg's (2010, 99), Frisch's (2014, 3028), Giere's (2010, 269), Suárez's (2004, 773), Swoyer's (1991, 452), Teller's (2001, 397), and Wartofsky's (1979, xx).

6 See, for instance, Boesch's (2017, 972), Gelfert's (2016, 33), and Morrison's (2015, 127).

7 These authors are concerned with different kinds of models and so some add qualifications. Achinstein discusses "theoretical" models; Hartmann focuses on "phenomenological" models; and Leplin analyses "developmental" models. These differences are immaterial in the current context. We discuss different kinds of models in Part IV of the book.

8 See Levy's (2012, 2015) and Toon's (2010a, 2010b, 2012a).

9 Toon also offers an account of material models, which he treats as being analogous to statues. A statue of Napoleon on horseback is a prop in a game of make-believe, and so are material models like ball-and-stick models of molecules (2012a, 37). We discuss material models in Chapter 14.

10 Suárez's views on representation are discussed in his (1999, 2003, 2004, 2009, 2013, 2015), Suárez and Solé's (2006), and Pero and Suárez's (2016). There is a question about

how inferentialism about scientific representation relates to the broader programme of inferentialism in the philosophy of language (Brandom 1994). For a discussion of this point, see, for instance, De Donato and Zamora Bonilla's (2009), Kuorikoski and Lehtinen's (2009), and Nguyen and Frigg's (2022, Ch. 3). For a discussion of Suárez's use of conditionals, see Poznic's (2016). For further discussions of inferentialism, see McCullough-Benner's (2020).

11 Suárez and Solé give a formulation with a biconditional, but they immediately add that they "are not suggesting to replace the original" (cited in the first paragraph of this section) and that it is only "one case in a large family of interesting possibilities" (2006, 41).

12 Künne's (2003) offers a survey of different theories of truth.

13 This problem finds an elegant solution in Díez's (2020) *Ensemble-Plus-Standing-For* account of representation.

14 The account is developed in his (1997, 2010, Ch. 5). There is no unanimity about the classification of the DDI account. The current presentation highlights the notion of representation as in Hughes's account; Suárez regards it as variant of inferentialism (2004, 770). For a discussion of the account, see Gelfert's (2011).

15 Their account is developed in Goodman's (1976, Chs. 1–2) and Elgin's (1983, Ch. 8, 1996, Ch. 6, 2010, 2017, Ch. 12).

16 Properties are understood in the widest possible sense, including relations and higher order properties.

17 Note that instantiation here is *metaphorical exemplification*. A painting can literally instantiate greyness; it can metaphorically instantiate sadness (Elgin 1983, 81, Goodman 1976, 50–52).

18 See Lycan's (2008) for an introduction to the common theories of denotation.

19 For a discussion of pictures, and in particular perceptual accounts, see Lopes' (2004).

20 We discuss the use of the same mathematical formalism to represent different, and different kinds of, target systems in Section 10.3.

21 In the remainder of this section I discuss the view of scientific representation that James Nguyen and I have developed in our (2016, 2017b, 2018, 2020, Chs. 8 and 9).

22 Notice that this notion of interpretation is different from Contessa's.

23 For a more extensive discussion of this machine, see Frigg and Nguyen's (2020, Ch. 8) and the references therein.

24 A painting does not literally instantiate sadness, and a model does not literally instantiate Z-properties whenever $Z \neq O$. The Philipps-Newlyn machine literally instantiates water flows but not flows of capital. This problem can be solved by saying that a model *instantiates a Z-property P under an interpretation I* iff the model instantiates an O-property B such that B is mapped onto P under I (Frigg and Nguyen 2018, 215).

25 This figure is adapted from Frigg and Nguyen's (2020, 177). There is a question whether the description should be considered part of the model. For a discussion of this issue, see Salis' (2021) and Salis et al. (2020).

26 For a discussion of visual representation in science, see, for instance, Elkins' (1999, 2007) and Perini's (2005, 2010).

References

Achinstein, P. 1964. Models, Analogies, and Theories. *Philosophy of Science* 31: 328–350.

Achinstein, P. 1965. Theoretical Models. *The British Journal for the Philosophy of Science* 16: 102–120.

Achinstein, P. 1968. *Concepts of Science: A Philosophical Analysis*. Baltimore: Johns Hopkins Press.

Bailer-Jones, D. M. 2002. Models, Metaphors, and Analogies. In P. Machamer and M. Silberstein (eds.), *The Blackwell Guide to Philosophy of Science*. Oxford: Blackwell, pp. 108–127.

Boesch, B. 2017. There Is a Special Problem of Scientific Representation. *Philosophy of Science* 84: 970–981.

Brandom, R. B. 1994. *Making It Explcit: Reasoning, Representing and Discursive Commitment*. Cambridge, MA: Harvard University Press.

Callender, C. and J. Cohen 2006. There Is No Special Problem About Scientific Representation. *Theoria* 55: 7–25.

Cartwright, N. 1983. *How the Laws of Physics Lie*. Oxford: Oxford University Press.

Contessa, G. 2007. Scientific Representation, Interpretation, and Surrogative Reasoning. *Philosophy of Science* 74: 48–68.

de Donato Rodriguez, X. and J. Zamora Bonilla 2009. Credibility, Idealisation, and Model Building: An Inferential Approach. *Erkenntnis* 70: 101–118.

Díez, J. A. 2020. An Ensemble-Plus-Standing-for Account of Scientific Representation: No Need for (Unnecessary) Abstract Objects. In C. Martínez-Vidal and J. L. Falguera (eds.), *Abstract Objects: For and Against*. Cham: Springer, pp. 133–149.

Ducheyne, S. 2012. Scientific Representations as Limiting Cases. *Erkenntnis* 76: 73–89.

Elgin, C. Z. 1983. *With Reference to Reference*. Indianapolis and Cambridge: Hackett Publishing Company.

Elgin, C. Z. 1996. *Considered Judgment*. Princeton: Princeton University Press.

Elgin, C. Z. 2010. Telling Instances. In R. Frigg and M. C. Hunter (eds.), *Beyond Mimesis and Convention: Representation in Art and Science*. Berlin and New York: Springer, pp. 1–17.

Elgin, C. Z. 2017. *True Enough*. Cambridge, MA and London: MIT Press.

Elkins, J. 1999. *The Domain of Images*. Ithaca and London: Cornell University Press.

Elkins, J. (ed.) 2007. *Visual Practices Across the University*. Berlin: Wilhelm Fink.

Frigg, R. 2010. Fiction and Scientific Representation. In R. Frigg and M. Hunter (eds.), *Beyond Mimesis and Convention: Representation in Art and Science*. Berlin and New York: Springer, pp. 97–138.

Frigg, R. and J. Nguyen 2016. The Fiction View of Models Reloaded. *The Monist* 99: 225–242.

Frigg, R. and J. Nguyen 2017a. Models and Representation. In L. Magnani and T. Bertolotti (eds.), *Springer Handbook of Model-Based Science*. Dordrecht, Heidelberg, London, and New York: Springer, pp. 49–102.

Frigg, R. and J. Nguyen 2017b. Scientific Representation Is Representation-As. In H.-K. Chao and J. Reiss (eds.), *Philosophy of Science in Practice: Nancy Cartwright and the Nature of Scientific Reasoning* (Synthese Library). Dordrecht, Heidelberg, London, and New York: Springer, pp. 149–179.

Frigg, R. and J. Nguyen 2018. The Turn of the Valve: Representing with Material Models. *European Journal for Philosophy of Science* 8: 205–224.

Frigg, R. and J. Nguyen 2020. *Modelling Nature: An Opinionated Introduction to Scientific Representation* (Synthese Library). Berlin and New York: Springer.

Frisch, M. 2014. Models and Scientific Representations Or: Who Is Afraid of Inconsistency? *Synthese* 191: 3027–3040.

Gelfert, A. 2011. Mathematical Formalisms in Scientific Practice: From Denotation to Model-Based Representation. *Studies in History and Philosophy of Science* 42: 272–286.

Gelfert, A. 2016. *How to Do Science with Models: A Philosophical Primer*. Cham: Springer.

Giere, R. N. 2010. An Agent-Based Conception of Models and Scientific Representation. *Synthese* 172: 269–281.

Godfrey-Smith, P. 2020. Dewey and Anti-Representationalism. In S. Fesmire (ed.), *The Oxford Handbook of Dewey*. Oxford: Oxford University Press, pp. 151–172.

Goodman, N. 1976. *Languages of Art* (2nd ed.). Indianapolis and Cambridge: Hacket.

Hartmann, S. 1999. Models and Stories in Hadron Physics. In M. Morgan and M. Morrison (eds.), *Models as Mediators: Perspectives on Natural and Social Science*. Cambridge: Cambridge University Press, pp. 326–346.

Hughes, R. I. G. 1997. Models and Representation. *Philosophy of Science* 64(Supplement): 325–336.

Hughes, R. I. G. 1998. Laws of Nature, Laws of Physics, and the Representational Account of Theories. *ProtoSociology* 12: 113–143.

Hughes, R. I. G. 2010. *The Theoretical Practises of Physics: Philosophical Essays*. Oxford: Oxford Univeristy Press.

Künne, W. 2003. *Conceptions of Truth*. Oxford: Clarendon Press.

Kuorikoski, J. and A. Lehtinen 2009. Incredible Worlds, Credible Results. *Erkenntnis* 70: 119–131.

Leplin, J. 1980. The Role of Models in Theory Construction. In T. Nickles (ed.), *Scientific Discovery, Logic, and Rationality*. Dordrecht: Reidel, pp. 267–283.

Levy, A. 2012. Models, Fictions, and Realism: Two Packages. *Philosophy of Science* 79: 738–748.

Levy, A. 2015. Modeling without Models. *Philosophical Studies* 152: 781–798.

Lopes, D. 2004. *Understanding Pictures*. Oxford: Oxford University Press.

Lycan, W. G. 2008. *Philosophy of Language: A Contemporary Introduction* (2nd ed.). New York and London: Routledge.

McCullough-Benner, C. 2020. Representing the World with Inconsistent Mathematics. *The British Journal for Philosophy of Science* 71: 1331–1358.

Morrison, M. 2015. *Reconstructing Reality: Models, Mathematics, and Simulations*. New York: Oxford University Press.

Nguyen, J. and R. Frigg 2022. *Scientific Representation*. Cambridge: Cambridge University Press.

Nowakowa, I. and L. Nowak 1998. Model(S) and Experiment(S) as Homogeneous Families of Notions. In N. Shanks (ed.), *Idealization IX: Idealization in Contemporary Physics* (Poznań Studies in the Philosophy of the Sciences and the Humanities 63). Amsterdam: Rodopi, pp. 35–50.

Nowakowa, I. and L. Nowak 2000. Introduction. Science as a Caricature of Reality. In I. Nowakowa and L. Nowak (eds.), *Idealization X: The Richness of Idealization* (Poznań Studies in the Philosophy of the Sciences and the Humanities 69). Amsterdam: Rodopi, pp. 9–14.

Perini, L. 2005. The Truth in Pictures. *Philosophy of Science* 72: 262–285.

Perini, L. 2010. Scientific Representation and the Semiotics of Pictures. In P. D. Magnus and J. Busch (eds.), *New Waves in the Philosophy of Science*. New York: Macmilan, pp. 131–154.

Pero, F. and M. Suárez 2016. Varieties of Misrepresentation and Homomorphism. *European Journal for Philosophy of Science* 6: 71–90.

Pitt, D. 2018. Mental Representation. In E. N. Zalta (ed.), *The Stanford Encyclopedia of Philosophy*. https://plato.stanford.edu/archives/win2018/entries/mental-representation/.

Poznic, M. 2016. Representation and Similarity: Suárez on Necessary and Sufficient Conditions of Scientific Representation. *Journal for General Philosophy of Science* 47: 331–347.

Price, H. 2011. *Naturalism without Mirrors*. Oxford: Oxford University Press.

Ruyant, Q. 2021. True Griceanism: Filling the Gaps in Callender and Cohen's Account of Scientific Representation. *Philosophy of Science* 88: 533–553.

Salis, F. 2021. The New Fiction View of Models. *The British Journal for the Philosophy of Science* 72: 717–742. https://doi.org/10.1093/bjps/axz015.

Salis, F., R. Frigg, and J. Nguyen 2020. Models and Denotation. In C. Martínez-Vidal and J. L. Falguera (eds.), *Abstract Objects: For and Against*. Cham: Springer, pp. 197–219.

Shech, E. 2015. Scientific Misrepresentation and Guides to Ontology: The Need for Representational Code and Contents. *Synthese* 192: 3463–3485.

Suárez, M. 1999. Theories, Models, and Representations. In L. Magnani, N. Nersessian, and P. Thagard (eds.), *Model-Based Reasoning in Scientific Discovery*. Dordrecht: Kluwer, pp. 75–83.

Suárez, M. 2003. Scientific Representation: Against Similarity and Isomorphism. *International Studies in the Philosophy of Science* 17: 225–244.

Suárez, M. 2004. An Inferential Conception of Scientific Representation. *Philosophy of Science* 71(Supplement): 767–779.

Suárez, M. 2009. Scientific Fiction as Rules of Inference. In M. Suárez (ed.), *Fictions in Science: Philosophical Essays on Modelling and Idealization*. London and New York: Routledge, pp. 158–178.

Suárez, M. 2013. Fictions, Conditionals, and Stellar Astrophysics. *International Studies in the Philosophy of Science* 27: 235–252.

Suárez, M. 2015. Deflationary Representation, Inference, and Practice. *Studies in History and Philosophy of Science* 49: 36–47.

Suárez, M. and A. Solé 2006. On the Analogy between Cognitive Representation and Truth. *Theoria* 55: 39–48.

Swoyer, C. 1991. Structural Representation and Surrogative Reasoning. *Synthese* 87: 449–508.

Teller, P. 2001. Twilight of the Perfect Model Model. *Erkenntnis* 55: 393–415.

Thomson-Jones, M. 2012. Modeling without Mathematics. *Philosophy of Science* 79: 761–772.

Toon, A. 2010a. Models as Make-Believe. In R. Frigg and M. Hunter (eds.), *Beyond Mimesis and Convention: Representation in Art and Science*. Berlin: Springer, pp. 71–96.

Toon, A. 2010b. The Ontology of Theoretical Modelling: Models as Make-Believe. *Synthese* 172: 301–315.

Toon, A. 2012a. *Models as Make-Believe: Imagination, Fiction and Scientific Representation*. Basingstoke: Palgrave Macmillan.

Toon, A. 2012b. Similarity and Scientific Representation. *International Studies in the Philosophy of Science* 26: 241–257.

Walton, K. L. 1990. *Mimesis as Make-Believe: On the Foundations of the Representational Arts*. Cambridge, MA: Harvard University Press.

Wartofsky, M. W. 1979. *Models: Representation and the Scientific Understanding*. Dordrecht: Reidel.

Weisberg, M. 2007. Who Is a Modeler? *The British Journal for the Philosophy of Science* 58: 207–233.

Yablo, S. 2014. *Aboutness*. Princeton: Princeton University Press.

10

ANALOGY

10.1 Introduction

An important way of coming to grips with something unknown is to draw a parallel to something known. In his quest to understand the behaviour of light, Huygens compared light to waves of sound and water; Boltzmann studied the behaviour of a gas by likening molecules to hard balls; Maxwell drew on similarities between field lines and the motion of an incompressible fluid through a pipe in order to formulate the equations of electrodynamics; Gamow and von Weizsäcker studied nuclear energy by treating a nucleus as a drop of water; and Fisher treated a population in the same fashion as an ideal gas.[1] In all these cases scientists drew an *analogy* between the domain they were investigating and something they were already familiar with.

Analogies play a role in almost every domain of intellectual activity. They feature prominently, for instance, in jurisprudence, rhetoric, politics, philosophy, pedagogy, and of course science. In this chapter we focus on the use of analogies in the context of scientific modelling and the construction of scientific theories. We begin by offering a general characterisation of analogies and analogical inferences (Section 10.2), and we distinguish different kinds of analogies (Section 10.3). We then turn to different uses of analogies in science and discuss first analogical models (Section 10.4), and then the heuristic use of analogies in theory construction (Section 10.5). Analogies are often mentioned in one breath with metaphors and models, which raises the question of how they are related (Section 10.6). We end by noting that there are interesting connections between representation and analogy (Section 10.7).

10.2 Circumscribing Analogies

An *analogy* is a relation between two objects that is based on a similarity between them, and we *draw an analogy* if we compare the two things based on them being similar in certain respects.[2] But "analogy" is not merely a synonym for

DOI: 10.4324/9781003285106-14

"similarity". There are two additional conditions.[3] The first condition is that the two items must be of a different type. The comparison between a nucleus and a drop of water is an analogy because it focuses on similarities between objects of different kinds. The observations that the son is like the father or that the Palace of Schönbrunn is like the Palace of Versailles are not analogies; they are straightforward comparisons of two things of the same kind. A change in size does not count as a change in type: that the model railway looks like the real thing is a scale relation and not an analogy. The second condition is particularly important in science and says that there must be an epistemic asymmetry between the two items: one item of the analogy is well understood while the other is new and unexplored. The analogy between water waves and light waves was cognitively relevant because when it was proposed, scientists knew a lot about water waves but little about light waves.

Let us now introduce some terminology to aid our discussion. As we have seen, an analogy is a relation between two items based on similarity under certain conditions. If there is such a relation between two items, we call it an *analogical relation*. It is common to refer to the first item as the *source* and to the second as the *target*.[4] From now on, let S stands for the source and T for the target. In the above example, the billiard balls are S and the gas is T. Let us also adopt the convention that by "analogy" we mean the *relation* between S and T, and that the relata of the analogy – S and T – are called "analogues".[5]

Similarity can be understood in two different ways, and the difference matters to an understanding of analogies. A common analysis of the claim that S is similar to T takes the claim to mean that S and T share certain properties $P_1,...,P_n$ (that is, that both S and T instantiate $P_1,...,P_n$). As we have seen in Section 8.4, Niiniluoto (1988, 272–274) calls this kind of similarity *partial identity*, and so it is natural to say that two items that are so related are *partial-identity-similar*. An analogy can be based on a partial identity, in which case it is a *partial-identity-analogy*. Partial identity contrasts with what Niiniluoto calls *likeness* (*ibid.*). Likeness operates at the level of properties. The objects S and T are similar in the sense of likeness if S and T instantiate properties that are similar. In more detail, S and T stand in the relation of likeness iff S instantiates properties $P_1,...,P_n$ and T instantiates properties $Q_1,...,Q_n$ and it is the case that P_1 is similar to Q_1, P_2 is similar to Q_2, and so on. In this case we will say that S and T are *likeness-similar*, and that an analogy based on a likeness is a *likeness-analogy*.[6] As an example consider a London bus and a traditional English telephone box. The two are partial-identity-similar with respect to colour if they instantiate exactly the same red; they are likeness-similar if they instantiate different tones of red which are, however, similar to each other. Sometimes it does not matter whether a similarity is based on partial identity or likeness. We say that S and T *agree* on a property P if either they both instantiate P (partial-identity-similarity) or if S instantiates P and T instantiates Q, where P and Q are similar (likeness-similarity).

The properties concerned can be either monadic properties or relations (i.e. polyadic properties). The analogy between the London bus and the phone box concerns the monadic property redness. If S and T are complex entities consisting of parts that enter in certain relationships, the analogy can also be based on one of these relationships. Hesse mentions the example of an analogy between a family and a society that is based on the notion that the father is to the child what the state is to the citizen (1963, 69). The idea here is that the relation a father bears to his children is the same as (or is similar to) the relation that a state bears to its citizens: it is a relationship of responsibility for maintenance, welfare, and care. The relation can also hold between a part and the whole system. When we say that the prime minister is to the government what the chief executive officer is to the company, we point out a similarity in the position of two individuals in the entire group.

The special case of an analogy based on a relation is *proportion*.[7] When we say that the height of the Parthenon (A) is to the length of its columns (B) as the length of Monalisa's upper body (C) to the length of her torso (D), we say that the proportion of these two pairs of numbers are the same. In mathematical terms this means that the quotient A/B is equal to the quotient C/D. In our example the numerical value of the quotients is the so-called golden ratio, approximately 1.61803.

Hesse (1963) sorts the properties of S and T into three groups, which she calls the positive, negative, and neutral analogy.[8] The properties on which S and T are known to agree constitute the *positive analogy*. The properties on which S and T are known to disagree constitute the *negative analogy*. The properties about which it is unknown whether or not S and T agree on them constitute the *neutral analogy*. The categories of positive, negative, and neutral analogy are mutually exclusive (every property can belong only to one of the three) and jointly exhaustive (every property must belong to one of the three). As an illustration, consider the earth and the moon (Hesse 1963, 64–65). Both are large, solid, opaque, and spherical bodies, that spin around their own axis and receive light from the sun. These properties constitute the positive analogy. They differ in size, and the moon has neither an atmosphere nor surface water. This is the negative analogy. There are open questions about the geological composition of the lunar surface and the moon's inner constitution, for instance whether it has an earth-like core. This is the neutral analogy.

This tripartite division is an *epistemic* division, and the qualification "known" in the definition of positive and negative analogy matters. While this is obvious in the case of the neutral analogy, it is important that the positive and negative analogies are sets of properties on which S and T are known to agree or disagree. The set of properties on which S and T agree or disagree can be (and usually is) much larger than the set of properties on which they are *known* to agree or disagree.[9]

The dividing line between these three classes can shift when research progresses (Hesse 2000, 300): properties in the neutral analogy will cross a boundary and become part of either the positive or the negative analogy. In fact, neutral analogies are the points where research is carried out and where knowledge grows. In the above example of the earth and the moon, the question of whether the moon has an earth-like core has recently been answered affirmatively, and having an earth-like core has been moved from the neutral to the positive analogy.

Analogical reasoning is a kind of reasoning that, in one way or another, relies on analogies. If we aim to establish a conclusion by appeal to an analogy, we offer an *analogical argument* (or we draw an *analogical inference*). Peirce describes the basic pattern of an analogical argument as

> the inference that a not very large collection of objects which agree in various respects may very likely agree in another respect. For instance, the earth and Mars agree in so many respects that it seems not unlikely they may agree in being inhabited.
>
> *(Hartshorne and Weiss 1931–1935, CP 1.69)*

So the basic form of reasoning at work here is to infer from the premise that S and T agree on certain properties to the conclusion that S and T will also agree on other properties.[10] Let us spell this out in some more detail. If the argument is based on a *partial-identity-analogy*, then the argument is:

Premise 1: S and T both instantiate properties $P_1 \ldots P_n$.
Premise 2: S has property P_{n+1}.
Conclusion: T has property P_{n+1}.

If the argument is based on a *likeness-analogy*, then the argument is:

Premise 1: S instantiates properties $P_1 \ldots P_n$; T instantiates properties $Q_1 \ldots Q_n$; P_1 is similar to $Q_1, \ldots, P_n$ is similar to Q_n.
Premise 2: S has property P_{n+1}.
Conclusion: T has property Q_{n+1}, where Q_{n+1} is similar to P_{n+1}.

Analogical arguments are not deductively valid. It is possible that the premises are true while the conclusion is false. In fact, analogical arguments only support their conclusion with varying degrees of strength and never confer certainty on them. This gives raise to the *justification problem*: under what conditions is an analogical inference justified and what degree of strength does it confer on the conclusion?

An answer to this question will depend on many factors: the kinds of objects that the source and the target are, the kinds of properties that we are concerned with, and the context in which the argument is made. An extensive discussion of the justification problem can be found in Bartha's (2010). Our focus in this chapter is on analogies themselves, not on analogical reasoning, and so we will not pursue issues of justification further.

10.3 Different Kinds of Analogies

Analogies are based on similarities. But it is a commonplace that everything is similar to everything else in one way or another (Goodman 1972). Analogies can do work only if similarity is constrained and certain respects are specified as the relevant ones. So the challenge is to classify analogies and give an account of those kinds of analogies that are relevant in scientific contexts. In this section we discuss a number of specific kinds of analogies that have been introduced in the literature. However, a specification of different kinds of analogies is an open-ended quest. An analogy can, in principle, be based on any similarity and there is no complete list of relevant similarities. So what follows is the initial segment of an open list.

A prominent distinction is the one between material and formal analogy. The *locus classicus* for the distinction is Hesse's work on models and analogies, which also provides the most extensive discussion of the distinction.[11] She characterises the distinction as follows:

> In a formal analogy there may be no similarity between the individuals and predicates of two models of the same formal system other than their relation of isomorphism. But in a replica model there are also what might be called material similarities between the parent system and its replica. The wings of an aircraft and its replica, for example, may have similar shape and hardness and may be made of the same material although they differ in at least one respect, size. Where two systems exhibit such similarities, which are not – or not simply – similarities by virtue of being logical models of the same formal system, we shall say they have material analogy.
>
> *(1967, 355)*

In a nutshell, the idea is that there is a formal analogy between S and T if the two share formal properties, and that there is a material analogy if they have non-formal properties in common. The above analogy between the earth and the moon is a material analogy because it concerns material attributes such as shape, size, and geological constitution. Analogies of this kind contrast with the analogy between a swinging pendulum and an oscillating electric circuit. The pendulum is a metal bob hanging from the ceiling on a rope; the electric circuit consists of a solenoid and a condenser connected to each other by copper wires. The communalities between these two systems do not lie in shared material properties. What these systems have in common is that they are correctly described by the same mathematical equation.

Let us pay closer attention to the notion of formal analogy. A look at Hesse's writings reveals different characterisations. Formal analogy is variously para-phrased as an "analogy of structure" (1967, 355, 2000, 299), as being based on "isomorphism" (1967, 355), as having analogues that are "logical models of the same formal system" (1967, 355), as being based on a "one-to-one correspondence between different interpretations of the same formal theory" (1963, 75), and as a relation in which "the same formal axiomatic and deductive relations connect individuals and predicates of both [S and T]" (1967, 355). These characterisations are typically mentioned in one breath, often in the same sentence.[12] There is no attempt to distinguish between them, and Hesse seems to think of them as alternative ways of describing the same concept. This is too hasty. In fact, two different types of formal analogy emerge from the above. For want of better names I call them structural analogy and symbolic analogy. Both are formal analogies, but they are not equivalent.

As we have seen in Section 2.7, isomorphism is a relation between two structures. If the relation between S and T is described as one of isomorphism, the claim must be that S and T instantiate structures S_S and S_T respectively, and that S_S and S_T are isomorphic. Thus understood, the analogy is based on a shared structure and for this reason I call this type of analogy *structural analogy*. Since an isomorphism involves a one-to-one mapping, accounts of formal analogy describing them as being based on a one-to-one correspondence of elements can be interpreted as being descriptions of a structural analogy too.[13]

There is a *symbolic analogy* between S and T if both are logical models of the same formal calculus (in the sense introduced in Section 2.2). This is tantamount to saying that for S and T to stand in a symbolic analogy, the equation describing the behaviour of S and the equation describing the behaviour of T must have that same mathematical form, and they only differ in how the terms in the equation are interpreted. In fact, we have already encountered this kind of analogy in Section 2.3, where we have seen that logical empiricists regarded models as alternative logical models for the theory's formalism. In the current idiom this is tantamount to saying that they thought that models and targets stood the relation of symbolic analogy. Examples of symbolic analogies in science are legion. We will encounter a number of them in Section 10.5. As a quick example, think of the analogy between mechanical, acoustical, electrical, optical, and thermal waves, which is based on them all having the same mathematical backbone – namely a wave equation.[14]

Structural analogy and symbolic analogy are related, but they are not equivalent. In fact, there are symbolic analogies that are not structural analogies, and vice versa. As we have seen in Section 2.9, the same formal system can have models of different cardinalities. These models are symbolically analogous because they are interpretations of the same formalism. Yet, given that they have different cardinalities, they are (trivially) non-isomorphic and therefore fail to be structurally analogous. The converse happens in the case we encountered in Section 5.5, where we have two different formal systems – Peano Arithmetic and Corcoran Arithmetic – that nevertheless describe the same structure. So if S is described by Peano Arithmetic and T is described by Corcoran Arithmetic, then S and T are structurally analogous without also being symbolically analogous.

Let us now turn to the material analogy. Hesse characterises material analogies as ones that "may be said to exist between two objects in virtue of their common properties" (1963, 64) and as "pre-theoretic analogies between observables" (1963, 75). Both characterisations are misleading because the former is too broad, and latter is too restrictive. As we have seen above, any partial-identity-analogy is based on shared properties, but there is no assumption that shared properties be material in any sense. Indeed, structural analogies are a prime example of analogies that are based on shared properties (namely shared structures). As regards the second definition, material analogies neither have to be pre-theoretical nor be restricted to observables. The most fitting characterisation of a material analogy is that it is an analogy which is based on S and T being similar with regard to material properties. This definition is of course vacuous unless it is supplemented with a specification of what makes a property material. Material properties are mainly defined negatively: they are not formal properties. But beyond that very little can be said about them at a general level. However, the problem that this poses should not be overstated. When looking at specific cases it is often relatively clear what material properties are, and so decisions can be made on a case-by-case basis.

As we have seen above, analogies can be based on similarities between monadic properties as well as between relations. These relations can be of different kinds. If the relation we select is a functional relation, then we have *functional analogy*. The gill of a fish is like the lung of a quadruped in that both perform the function of providing the organism with oxygen (Achinstein 1968, 206; Hesse 1963, 68–69), and the clutch of a car is like the switch of an electric circuit in that they both allow one to interrupt the transmission of power to a system (Sarlemijn and Kroes 1988, 240). If the extant relations in S and T are causal, then we have a *causal analogy* (Hesse 1963, 65, 86–88). Computer malware and biological viruses are analogous in that they cause damage to the system into which they enter. There are many difficult questions about the nature of causation and the difference between functional and causal relations (why is the relation between the switch and the flow of power functional rather than causal?). Important as they are, both functional and causal relations stand outside a theory of analogy, and analogies are classified as functional or causal against the background of an account of functional and causal relations.

If the parts (or aspects) of a system are governed by the same laws, then we have what Sarlemijn and Kroes call an *anamorphy* (1988, 238). For instance, a traditional light bulb and an infrared heater are based on the same physical principle (namely Planck's law of radiation). It is worth noting that an anamorphy does not imply a formal analogy. The same general principles, if applied in different settings, can result in different equations (and different structures). For instance, the equation of motion governing a pendulum is different from the equation of motion governing the movement of a planet even though they are both instances of Newton's law of motion.

Properties can be located at different levels of abstraction. Darden (1982, 149–151) discusses what she calls an analogy from *shared abstraction*, which she attributes to Genesereth. The idea behind this kind of analogy is that some situations can share a common abstraction. Her example is the analogy between the organisation chart of a corporation and the taxonomy of animals in biology. Although they are dissimilar at the level of basic properties, they share a common abstract property, namely that of being a hierarchy. Darden is quick to add that "abstractions are not merely Hesse's formal analogies, since Genesereth's abstractions may have more semantic content than an uninterpreted formalism"

(Darden 1982, 151). So the analogy is based on shared general but still material properties.

Finally, analogies can be distinguished by looking at the origin of the source. In some analogies the source is a pre-existing object that is relatively well understood even before it is used in an analogy. Morgan (1997, 305) calls such cases *ready made analogies* and offers the example of Fisher's use of the familiar mechanical balance as an analogy for the aggregate exchanges in the American economy. Ready made analogies contrast with what she calls *designed analogies* (*ibid.*). In such cases, the source is built deliberately and with the declared aim to be used as an analogy. Her example is Fisher's hydraulic model of a monetary system, which is a hydraulic system that was built with the express purpose of modelling monetary processes.

There are no doubt other dimensions along which analogies can be classified, and other types of analogies that can be identified. But rather than continuing this classificatory endeavour, we now turn to a discussion of the roles analogies play in science. Among these two stand out: the role analogies play in analysing the model-target relationship, and the heuristic roles analogies play in the construction of new theories.[15] We discuss them in Sections 10.4 and 10.5 respectively.

10.4 Analogue Models

So far, we left it open what S and T are. A first important way of adding specificity to the general discussion of analogies is to take S to refer to a scientific model and T to the model's target system. This yields a picture whereby a model stands in an analogical relation to its target system. Such a model is called an *analogue model* (Achinstein 1968, 210; Black 1962b, 222–223). This approach occupies a prominent place in Hesse's discussion of analogies. She argued that the "most obvious property of a satisfactory model is that it exhibits an analogy with the phenomenon to be explained" (Hesse 1961, 22), and encapsulated this view in the slogan that "a model is an analogue" (Hesse 2000, 299).[16] Others followed suit. Harré (1988, 120–123) and Horgan (1994, 600–603) emphasised the importance of analogies in the understanding of how models relate to their targets. Psillos (1995, 112–113) submits that the choice of modelling assumptions is guided by "substantive similarities" between model and target and labels this an "analogical approach to model construction". Discussing Fisher's monetary models, Morgan (1999, 365–366) appeals to analogies when explaining how learning from models takes place. And Gilboa et al. (2014) argue that economic models relate to their targets through analogies.

Examples of analogue models are not difficult to come by. The billiard ball model of a gas and the liquid drop model of a nucleus, which we mentioned in the introduction, are cases in point. A classic example of an analogue model is the so-called Phillips-Newlyn machine, a system of pipes and reservoirs which features a flow of water generated by a pump.[17] The machine is an analogue model of an economy. In his original paper about the machine, Philipps explains that "the production flow of a commodity is represented by the flow of water into a tank" (1950, 284), and that there is a price scale that is chosen such that "one cubic inch of water is made equivalent to one hundred tons of the commodity" (*ibid.*, 285). So the properties that the machine and an economy share are quantities of a flow. If there is a cubic inch of water in a certain reservoir, this corresponds to there being a hundred tons of, say, wheat in the central storage facility. Knowing how the quantity of water in the reservoir informs the model user about the amount of wheat that is held in reserve. So when using the Phillips-Newlyn machine as a model of an economy we do exactly what Hesse thought was constitutive of an analogical model, namely "to assert correspondences" between model and target (1961, 22).

Analogical models of this sort are not remnants of the past. Cosmologists study properties of black holes by using so-called dumb holes as analogue models. A dumb hole is a setup where a fluid flows faster than the speed of sound and in this way traps phonons (sound understood as a small vibratory disturbance in the liquid). Physicists are interested in these systems because in such environments phonons show behaviour that is similar to the behaviour of light in gravitational black holes. In particular they are interested in a "sonic version" of Hawking radiation. Since gravitational black holes cannot be studied experimentally, they use dumb holes as a convenient analogue model.[18] And dumb holes are not just a serendipitous find; similar analogue models are employed in other cases, for instance when a Bose-Einstein condensate is used as an analogue for the universe as a whole (Mattingly and Warwick 2009) and when bouncing oil droplets are studied as analogue representations of quantum phenomena (Evans and Thébault 2020).

These examples also help illustrate why the distinction (in Section 10.2) between partial identity and likeness matters. If the relation between model and target is taken to be a partial-identity-analogy, then the properties of the target have to be strictly identical to the ones of the model. While this could happen, it certainly would be an exceptional occurrence because models rarely, if ever, have exactly the same properties as their targets. In the above examples, wheat reserves are not volumes of water, and the properties of phonons are not, in general, identical to properties of light. Allowing for analogies to be based on likeness (rather than partial identity) makes room for there being certain discrepancies, which will almost invariably occur in practice.

What is the relation between analogy and representation? How one answers this question depends both on one's account of representation and on one's take on similarity. Analogy naturally fits into the similarity account of representation. As we have seen in Section 8.3, the Similarity Account explains representation in terms of there being a similarity between model and target, and since an analogy is grounded in a similarity, M representing T *ipso facto* implies that there is an analogy between M and T. This would seem to be what Hesse has in mind when she says that "[t]he relation between model and the thing modeled can be said generally to be a relation of analogy" (1967, 355). So on the similarity account of representation, there being an analogy between M and T is tantamount M representing T. The Morphism Account will restrict allowable analogies to formal structural analogies, which, as we have seen, are based on the source and the target being isomorphic.[19] The other accounts of representation can also accommodate analogies, but they will generally not commit to the representation relation always being one of analogy. According to Direct Representation, scientists represent a target by imagining certain things about it in a game of make-believe. This can involve imagining properties that are similar to properties of the target, but there is no requirement that this be so. There is nothing to stop a scientist imagining an atom as being large enough to fill a room. Likewise, inferentialists can welcome analogies as the "engine" that drives inferences, but they are not committed to the claim that all representations are of this kind and they can recognise alternative means of drawing inferences. In the DEKI account analogies figure as keys, which connect model-properties to target-properties. DEKI can welcome analogies as providing one kind of keys, but it can recognise other kinds of keys and does not have to limit model-world relations to analogical relations.

10.5 Heuristic Analogies

A second important way of adding specificity to the general discussion of analogies is to take *both* S and T to refer to a scientific theory or model. We then say that one theory is analogous to another theory, or that one model is analogous to another model. The theories or models can both belong to the same domain (for instance when we draw an analogy between two branches of physics) or they can pertain to different domains (for instance when we draw an analogy between physics and economics). The motivation to draw such analogies is their heuristic power. By looking at something we understand, and by then pointing out similarities to an unfamiliar (or less familiar) domain, we can get important clues about that domain and thereby use the analogy as a tool for theory (or model) construction. This heuristic function of analogies has been widely acknowledged. Nagel observes that the "apprehension of even vague similarities between the old and the new are often starting points for important advances in knowledge" (1961, 108); and Darden and Rada point out that "[t]he key idea in the use of analogies in theory construction is to use knowledge from some other domain as a source of ideas to construct the theory in the target area" (1988, 344).[20]

Scientists were often excited about the heuristic power of analogies. Kepler enthusiastically proclaimed: "I cherish more than anything else the analogies, my trustworthy masters. They know all the secrets of Nature" (quoted in Gentner 1982, 106). Maxwell acknowledges: "It is by the use of analogies of this kind [Thomson's analogy between heat conduction and attractive forces] that I have attempted to bring before the mind, in a convenient and manageable form, those mathematical ideas which are necessary to the study of the phenomena of electricity" (Maxwell 1855/1965, 157). More recently, Oppenheimer professed that "analogy is indeed an indispensable and inevitable tool for scientific progress" (1956, 129) and Pólya notes that "analogy pervades all our thinking, our everyday speech and our trivial conclusions as well as artistic ways of expression and the highest scientific achievements" (quoted in Lichter 1995, 285).

Maxwell's discussion of the electric field is a perfect illustration of the heuristic use of analogies.[21] The problem he is grappling with is to give an exact mathematical description of the electric field, and he begins by looking at the phenomenon of electrostatic attraction. When a small electric charge is brought into the vicinity of a charged object, it experiences a force of a certain strength pointing in a certain direction. Faraday described the force experienced by the particle with the concept of *line of force*, which, in Maxwell's words, is such that "this curve will indicate the direction of that force for every point through which it passes" (Maxwell 1855/1965, 158). What is missing from Faraday's account is a mathematical description of these lines and a quantitative expression of the magnitude and direction of the force acting on the particle. To provide such a description Maxwell invokes the method of analogy. He is explicit about his choice and explains: "By a physical analogy I mean that partial similarity between the laws of one science and those of another which makes each of them illustrate the other" (*ibid.*, 156). The first of the two sciences, the target domain, is electrostatics. The crucial question is what other science to choose because this science has to be such that it can bring before the mind the mathematical ideas that are essential to the study of the electricity.

Maxwell's ingenious idea was to take hydrodynamics as the source domain and think of the lines of force as tubes filled with an incompressible liquid. Talking about Faraday's lines, Maxwell says:

> If we consider these curves not as mere lines, but as fine tubes of variable section carrying an incompressible fluid, then, since the velocity of the fluid is inversely as the section of the tube, we may make the velocity vary according to any given law, by regulating the section of the tube, and in this way we might represent the intensity of the force as well as its direction by the motion of the fluid in these tubes. This method of representing the intensity of a force by the velocity of an imaginary fluid in a tube is applicable to any conceivable system of forces.
>
> *(*ibid., *158–159)*

So Maxwell analogises the direction of the flow of the fluid with the direction of the force and the velocity of the fluid with the strength of the force. They are also analogous in that both a flow and a field originate in a source, and later he also compares the pressure of the liquid to the potential of the electric field (*ibid.*, 175–177). Equipped with this analogy Maxwell sets himself the task

> first to describe a method by which the motion of such a fluid can be clearly conceived; secondly to trace the consequences of assuming certain

conditions of motion, and to point out the application of the method to some of the less complicated phenomena of electricity, magnetism, and galvanism.

(ibid., 158–159)

This is what he does. He first works out how the source domain operates and derives an equation for the flow of a liquid through a pipe. He then uses his correspondences and carries the fluid results over to the electric field. So Maxwell arrived at a mathematical description of the electric field by studying the flow of a liquid through a pipe!

Maxwell's case of the electric field is no exception. Analogical thinking has played an important role in many scientific developments.[22] Galileo drew an analogy between observations on a ship and the earth to establish (what we would now call) the law of inertia. To develop a theory of light, Huygens drew an analogy between water waves, sound waves and light. Fourier constructed a theory of heat conduction based on an analogy between heat and the flow of a liquid. Maxwell and Boltzmann set out to understand the dynamical behaviour of a gas by drawing an analogy between gas molecules and billiard balls. Rutherford explained the structure of atoms in analogy with the solar system. Maxwell likened the luminiferous ether to a mechanical system of rotating cells.

The importance of analogies is not restricted to historical cases, and analogies keep playing a role in contemporary science. Yukawa's theory of nuclear forces is based on an analogy between electrical and nuclear forces (Oppenheimer 1956, 132). Currie and Weiss used an analogy between fluids and magnets (Hughes 1999, 137–138). The nuclear shell model is based on the analogy between the atomic nucleus and extra-nuclear electron shells (Achinstein 1968, 204). The dynamics of polymers is studied by drawing an analogy between polymers and a chain of beads connected by springs (Doi and Edwards 1986, 14–16). Analogical reasoning turns out to play an essential role in ecology (Colyvan and Ginzburg 2006); it is an important aspect of synthetic biology (Knuuttila and Loettgers 2014); and it constitutes the methodological backbone of econophysics, which aims to apply techniques from statistical physics to economic systems (Bradley and Thébault 2019; Thébault et al. 2018).[23] It also pays noting that the importance of analogy is not restricted to "fundamental" science either. Shelley (1999) draws attention to the use of analogies in archaeology and Sarlemijn (1987) in engineering.

What makes an analogy heuristically useful? Gentner (1982, 113–118) offers four dimensions along which analogies can be evaluated. *Base specificity* is the degree to which the source of the analogy is understood. The more we know about the source, the better the analogy because a well-understood source domain adds specificity to the properties and relations that are carried over to the target. *Clarity* is the precision with which the similarity relations between the source and the target are defined. As already noted, everything is similar to everything else in one way or another and hence an analogy is heuristically useful only if the relevant similarity relations are precisely circumscribed. *Richness* is the number of source features that are set into a relation with the target. An analogy can be clear but frugal if only a few source properties are related to target properties. The larger the number of connections between the source and the target, the richer the analogy. *Systematicity* is the degree to which the source properties that figure in the analogy are connected to one another. An analogy that is based on a motley collection of unrelated properties is unsystematic. If the relevant properties in the source belong to a mutually constraining conceptual scheme, or even theory, the analogy is systematic. Systematicity is important because it allows for the derivation of predictions about the source properties, and these predictions are candidates for being carried over the target.

Maxwell's analogy between a fluid and the electric field scores well in all four dimensions. Maxwell could rely on the powerful theory of fluid dynamics when working out the properties of the flow of water through pipes. His analogy has base specificity because the properties of the fluid are clearly defined and described by exact equations. The analogy is clear because Maxwell specified exactly which aspect of the flow corresponds to which aspect of the electric field. The analogy is rich because it connects many fluid properties to field properties. Finally, the analogy has systematicity because the overarching theory of hydrodynamics sets the different properties of the liquid in relation to one another, and each property is constrained by the other properties.

An important feature of heuristic analogies is that they circumvent the justification problem. It is a defining feature of a *heuristic* analogy that it does not draw the conclusion that the target has a certain property; it merely suggests that it might have it and whether it really does must be checked independently. Oppenheimer is explicit:

> This is not to say that analogy is the criterion of truth. One can never establish that a theory is right by saying that it is like some other theory that is right. The criterion of truth . . . must come from experience.
>
> *(1956, 129)*

Once the analogical transfer of properties from the source to the target has taken place, the new theory offers a representation of the phenomena, and it has to be tested directly against the phenomena. The new theory (or model) is successful only if it passes this test, and the theory's analogical origin contributes nothing to its confirmation. In this sense, heuristic analogies are like Wittgenstein's ladder that one can throw away once one has reached the higher ground.

This point is important because analogies can also be misleading. Analogies can fail to meet Gentner's criteria, for instance when they are unspecific or are based only on loosely characterised similarities that do not constrain the transfer from source to target in a systematic way. Examples of unproductive analogies are the analogy between chemical bonds and interpersonal attraction (Gentner 1982, 113), and animistic accounts of physical events (Nagel 1961, 108). But not all misleading analogies must be completely wrong. Errors can also be made when a neutral analogy is (as it turns out) wrongly reclassified as a positive rather than as a negative analogy. This happened, famously, when 19th century physicists took the analogy between mechanical systems and the ether seriously and attributed a certain material constitution to the ether. However, Maxwell had already warned against hasty conclusions. He emphasised that "[t]he other analogy, between light and the vibrations of an elastic medium, extends much farther, but, though its importance and fruitfulness cannot be over-estimated, we must recollect that it is founded only on a resemblance in form between the laws of light and those of vibrations", and he noticed that by "stripping it of its physical dress and reducing it to a theory of 'transverse alternations', we might obtain a system of truth strictly founded on observation" (Maxwell 1855/1965, 156). In this passage he effectively foreshadowed later developments, which saw the formal aspect of the analogy (Maxwell's equations) confirmed but dismissed the ether altogether.

Finally, it is worth noting that the distinction between an analogue model and heuristic analogy is not always sharp. While the two are conceptually distinct, it is sometimes difficult to classify particular cases clearly as either an analogical model or a heuristic analogy. Analysing Kelvin's discussion of the ether in his Baltimore lectures, Achinstein (1964, 334) points out that it is not always clear whether Kelvin proposes a mechanical model of the ether (which bears an analogical relation to the ether) or whether Kelvin merely considers an elastic solid as an aid for the formulation of equations (in the same way in which Maxwell considered water flowing through pipes). Achinstein adds that this is not the fault of philosophical analysis; rather such cases "simply reflect ambiguity on the part of the scientist himself" (*ibid.*). In fact, asking whether it is one or the other can be the beginning of a productive engagement with particular scientific analogy.

10.6 Analogies, Metaphors, and Models

"Analogy", "metaphor", and "model" are often mentioned in the same breath, suggesting that there is a close connection between them. In this section we discuss what this connection is and how the relation between the three should be understood.

Let us begin with analogy and metaphor. Is there such a connection, and if so, what is it? Some regard "analogy" and "metaphor" as synonyms that can be used interchangeably.[24] Others see metaphors as a special kind of analogy.[25] And yet others have suggested that analogy and metaphor are distinct but closely related. In this vein, Aristotle observes that a metaphor is "the application of an alien name by transference . . . or by analogy" (1902, 1457b). This understanding of the term lives on in standard encyclopaedia definitions of metaphor. The Merriam Webster dictionary, for instance, defines a metaphor as "a figure of speech in which a word or phrase literally denoting one kind of object or idea is used in place of another to suggest a likeness or analogy between them" (2017). Others describe a metaphor as a "poetically or rhetorically ambitious use of words" (Hills 2016) or a "figure of speech" (Leatherdale 1974, 91) without reference to analogy.

Views that take metaphors and analogies to be the same thing, or take one to be a subset of the other, offer an easy and straightforward answer to the question of how analogies and metaphors relate. However, as the short review in the last paragraph shows, views that equate metaphors and analogies are by no means universally accepted. In fact, many authors identify metaphors as linguistic objects, as "names", "figures of speech", or a certain "use of words". Thus understood, metaphors are clearly distinct from analogies. An analogy is a specific kind of resemblance between two objects, the analogues, and neither the analogues nor the analogy itself are linguistic: they are objects and relations. The connection between metaphors and analogies starts coming into sight when we notice that many metaphors bring two things that are spoken about in relation to one another by likening or comparing them. When Shakespeare's Romeo says "Juliet is the sun" or when an enlightenment physicist says "the universe is a clockwork" they utter metaphors, and these metaphors liken two objects to one another. Romeo expresses the view that Juliet is like the sun, and the enlightenment physicist submits that the universe is like a clockwork. Since analogy is based on similarity, or likeness, the observation that a metaphor expresses a likeness is then tantamount to saying that a metaphor expresses an analogy.

This is the core idea of an approach that has become known as *comparativism*. One of the earliest articulations of comparativism can be found in Aristotle's *Poetics* (cited at the beginning of this section); a recent elaboration is Fogelin's (2011). A *simile* is a phrase comparing two objects, where the phrase is often marked syntactically by the use of the words "like" or "as". The leading idea of comparativism is that metaphors are elliptical similes: we get from the simile to the metaphor by omitting the word "like", and from the metaphor to the simile by adding it. In this vein, the Roman rhetorician Quintilian defined a metaphor as a "shortened comparison" (quoted in Groddeck 1995, 255). "Juliet is like the sun" and "the universe is like a clockwork" are the similes corresponding to the above-mentioned metaphors; and Maxwell's analogy between the flow of a fluid and the electric field can be encapsulated in the metaphor "the electric field is a fluid". Comparisons are based on similarities, and these can be seen as constituting an analogical relation. Hence, metaphors that can be translated into similes can be seen as expressing analogies, and as being true in virtue of the relevant analogy holding.

Comparativism is not universally accepted and alternative accounts of metaphor have been put forward.[26] But the core insight of comparativism is correct: metaphors and analogies are neither identical, nor are metaphors special kinds of analogies. Analogies are specific similarity relations between two objects; metaphors are certain linguistic structures. Different accounts of metaphor will analyse the relation between metaphors and analogies in different ways, but any such account will have to keep the two separate.

Similar remarks apply to the relation between models and metaphors. Like analogies, models are often mentioned in the same breath as metaphors. For instance, Bhushan and Rosenfeld say that "[i]n chemistry essentially all models are metaphorical models" (1995, 578). How are we to make sense of claims that identify models and metaphors given that we consider metaphors to be linguistic expressions and models to be objects of sorts? The answer follows naturally from what we have said about analogy. A model can stand in an analogical relation with its target, and an analogy can be expressed in a metaphor. Hence, derivatively one can express the relation of a model to its target in a metaphor. This happens, for instance, if we say that "molecules are billiard balls" and thereby describe the analogical relation between the model and its target in a metaphor. One can then paraphrase the model as a *metaphorical model*. This is in line with Bailer-Jones' use of the term when she says that a metaphorical model is one in which "a transfer from one domain to another has taken place" (Bailer-Jones 2009, 118). As long as it is understood that this is an elliptic way of describing the relation between a model and its target there is no harm in this way of speaking. The view becomes problematic if the "are" in the slogan "models are metaphors" is taken to express identity. Metaphors and analogies are not identical, and neither are metaphors and models.

10.7 Conclusion

Analogies play an important part both in how models relate to their targets and in the heuristics of theory construction, historically and in contemporary science. Analogies are based on similarities, and different kinds of similarities give rise to different kinds of analogies. An important distinction is between formal and material analogies, but other distinctions can be drawn. There are interesting connections between representation and analogy, but how exactly this relation is understood depends on which account of representation one adopts.

Notes

1 The analogy between light and waves, and the billiard ball model are discussed in Hesse's (1963). Gyenis (2017) discusses the checkered history of the "elastic sphere model", as the billiard ball model is also called. Maxwell's field lines are discussed below in Section 10.5. For a discussion of the liquid-drop model, see Portides' (2005); for Fisher's analogy, see Morrison's (1997).

2 There is widespread agreement on a characterisation of analogies in terms of similarity. See, for instance, Achinstein's (1968, 205), Bartha's (2010, 1), Cat's (2021), Copi and Cohen's (1998, 472), Davies's (1988, 227), Gentner's (1982, 108), Harré's (2004, 76), Hesse's (2000, 299), Russell's (1988, 251), Saha's (1988, 41), and Sarlemijn and Kroes's (1988, 238).

3 For the first condition, see Achinstein's (1964, 332, 1968, 207), Black's (1962b, 222), Gentner's (1982, 108), Harré's (1988, 122), and Saha's (1988, 41–42). For the second constraint, see Gentner's (1982, 108), Harré's (1988, 122), and Hesse's (1961, 21–23).

4 See, for instance, Bartha's (2010, viii), Johnson's (1988, 25), Psillos's (1995, 113), and Russell's (1988, 251). Other terminologies include "base" and "target" (Kedar-Cabelli 1988, 66; Gentner 1982, 108), "analogue set" and "new domain" (Carloye 1971, 562), and "projected theory" and "accepted theory" (Hesse 1963, 106).

5 See Bunge's (1969, 17), Leatherdale's (1974, 2) and Mellor's (1968, 283). Sometimes "analogy" is used as a synonym of "analogue", and hence is used to refer to S and T. This ambiguity should be avoided, and I reserve the term "analogy" for the relation itself. Another ambiguity concerns the issue of whether "analogy" refers to the collective of all (relevant) similarity relations between S and T or to an individual relation (that is somehow singled out). I adopt the former as my default option and speak of an "analogy in a certain respect" to pick out a particular relation.

6 The distinction between likeness and partial identity is implicit in Hesse's discussion (see, for instance, 1963, 66–67, 2000, 300), but she does not discuss it explicitly and the point remains underexplored. A complete account of likeness-analogy would require an analysis of what it means for one property to be similar to another property. Such an analysis will depend on the properties at hand, and it will have to be provided in the context of specific applications.

7 Historically this is the archetypal analogy. Indeed, the Greek work "ἀναλογία" (analogia) means proportion.

8 The notions of positive and negative analogy originate in Keynes' (1921, Ch. XIX). The negative analogy is sometimes also called "disanalogy" (Copi and Cohen 1998, 480). In some places Hesse portrays this tripartite distinction as one that pertains only to the material analogy (2000, 299–300); sometimes she explicitly says that it is a general distinction for all analogies (1967, 355). Setting exegetic matters aside, there is no reason to restrict the triad to material analogies, and I will use it as a classification that pertains to all analogies.

9 Hesse's presentation of this triad wavers between an epistemic and an ontic reading. Following Keynes' (1921, Ch. XIX), she sometimes frames the distinction ontologically and says that the positive analogy consists of "the set of similarities" and the negative analogy of "the set of differences" (1967, 355), and she then speaks of the "known positive analogy" and the "known negative analogy" to refer to features that are known to belong to the set of shared features or the set of differences (Hesse 1963, 10–11). Other times she frames the distinction epistemically: "Let us call those properties we know belong to billiard balls and not to molecules the *negative analogy* of the model. Motion and impact, on the other hand, are just the properties of billiard balls that we do want to ascribe to molecules in our model, and these we can call the *positive analogy*" (*ibid.*, 9). Since the notion of the neutral analogy is intrinsically epistemic, an epistemic reading of the entire triad is more coherent. The epistemic reading is endorsed in Bartha's (2010, 14), and I adopt this reading in what follows.

10 While different authors offer different analyses of the exact logical form of an analogical inference, there is widespread agreement on the leading idea (as sketched here). See, for instance, Agassi's (1964, 352), Bartha's (2010, 13), Copi and Cohen's (1998, 473), Davies' (1988, 228–229), Hesse's (1963, 80–81, 1988, 319), Kedar-Cabelli's (1988, 65), Niiniluoto's (1988, 272–274), Russell's (1988, 251), and Sarlemijn and Kroes's (1988, 246).

11 The distinction between material and formal analogy begins to emerge in Hesse's (1952) and (1953), but without being articulated clearly. The distinction is fully developed in her (1963), and became widely known through her (1967). Around the same time other authors have gestured at the same distinction. Achinstein (1964, 338–342) distinguishes between "physical analogies" and "formal analogies"; Bunge (1969, 17) distinguishes between systems that are "substantially analogous" and "formally analogous"; Hempel speaks of "syntactic isomorphism" (1965, 436); and Nagel introduces a distinction between "substantive analogies" and "formal analogies"(1961, 110). Later authors have also referred to the distinction as the one between "material analogy" and "mathematical analogy" (Kroes 1989, 147) and between "substantive analogy" and "non-substantive analogy" (Psillos 1995, 112). Nappo (2021) argues for a broadening of Hesse's notion of material analogy.

12 Similar characterisations have also been offered by a number of other authors. A characterisation of analogy in terms of isomorphism and/or sameness of equations can be found in Abrantes' (1999, 256), Achinstein's (1968, 207), Black's (1962b, 222–223), Darden's (1982, 151), Gentner et al. (1988, 172), Johnson's (1988, 25), Kaushal's (1999, 545), Kroes' (1989, 147–150), Oppenheimer's (1956, 129), Rickart's (1995, 23–27), and Sarlemijn and Kroes' (1988, 241). Gentner (1982) sees analogies as grounded in "structure mappings", which are in effect isomorphisms. Typically, authors who use both characterisations follow Hesse in not distinguishing between them.

13 Analogies based on "structure" are also mentioned in Achinstein's (1968, 206–207). The notion of a structural analogy as defined here can easily be generalised by replacing isomorphism with another morphism. Bunge (1969, 17) suggests that an analogy can be grounded in a homomorphism, and Rickart in effect defines analogies in terms of embeddings when he submits that two analogue structures "contain substructures that are isomorphic" (1995, 23).

14 Extensive collections of examples of symbolic analogies from physics and engineering can be found in Kaushal's (1999) and in Shive and Weber's (1982). Symbolic analogies are closely related to what Schlimm (2008) calls the "axiomatic approach to analogies", which is based on source and target being given a common linguistic description in terms of axioms.

15 Other uses of analogies are, for instance, in confirmation theory (Achinstein 1963; Agassi 1964; Dardashti et al. 2019; Hesse 1964; Niiniluoto 1988), concept formation (Hesse 1988), explanation (Bailer-Jones 2009, Ch. 3), and understanding (Nagel 1961, Ch. 6).

16 See also Hesse's (1953, 201, 1964, 319, 1967, 355, 2000, 305).

17 For discussion of the machine, see Barr's (2000) and Morgan's (2012, Ch. 5).

18 For a discussion of this case, see Crowther, Linnemann and Wüthrich's (2021), Dardashti et al. (2017), and Unruh's (2018).

19 As noted previously, this can be extended to other kinds of morphisms.

20 See also Achinstein's (1963, 207, 1968, 244), Gentner's (1982, 108), Hesse's (1988, 318), McMullin's (1968, 389), and Niiniluoto's (1988, 276). Holyoak and Thagard (1995) discuss the role analogies play in creative thought in science and beyond. For a discussion of analogy in theory-construction, see Ippoliti's (2018).

21 The source is Maxell's 1855 paper "On Faraday's Lines of Force" (1855/1965, 155–229). This case is generally acknowledged as a paradigmatic example of a heuristic use of analogy; see, for instance, Achinstein's (1964, 333), Cat's (2001, 411), Darrigol's (2016), and Nagel's (1961, 109). For further discussion of Maxwell's use of analogies, see Achinstein's (1991), Hesse's (1974, Ch. 11), Kargon's (1969), Nersessian's (1984), Psillos's (1995), and Turner's (1955). Chalmers disagrees and argues that "[m]uch of Maxwell's case is independent of his model" (1986, 422).

22 A discussion of at least one, and often several, of the examples to follow can be found in Achinstein's (1964, 1968, Ch. 7), Gentner's (1982), Hesse's (1963), Leatherdale's (1974, Ch. 1), Nagel's (1961, Ch. 6), Oppenheimer's (1956), Ruse's (1973), and Sterrett's (1998). For an in-depth discussion of the analogy between light and sound, see Darrigol's (2010a, 2010b).

23 For critical discussion of the transfer of models from physics to socio-economic systems, see Knuuttila and Loettgers' (2016), and for a discussion of the difficulties with using models from physics in biology, see Rowbottom's (2011).

24 See, for instance, Gentner's (1982), Hesse's (1988), and Johnson's (1988).

25 See, for instance, Del Re's (2000, 12) and Kroes' (1989, 145).

26 See Hills' (2016) and Lycan's (2008, Ch. 4) for general surveys of accounts of metaphors, and Cat's (2006) and Montuschi's (2000) for metaphors in science. An influential criticism of comparativism is Black's (1962a); Harré's (2004, Ch. 8) is a rejoinder to Black.

References

Abrantes, P. 1999. Analogical Reasoning and Modeling in the Sciences. *Foundations of Science* 4: 237–270.

Achinstein, P. 1963. Variety and Analogy in Confirmation Theory. *Philosophy of Science* 30: 207–221.

Achinstein, P. 1964. Models, Analogies, and Theories. *Philosophy of Science* 31: 328–350.

Achinstein, P. 1968. *Concepts of Science: A Philosophical Analysis*. Baltimore: Johns Hopkins Press.

Achinstein, P. 1991. Maxwell's Analogies and Kinetic Theory. In *Particles and Waves: Historical Essays in the Philosophy of Science*. Oxford and New York: Oxford University Press, pp. 207–232.

Agassi, J. 1964. Analogies as Generalizations. *Philosophy of Science* 31: 351–356.

Aristotle 1902. *Poetics*. London: McMillan.

Bailer-Jones, D. M. 2009. *Scientific Models in Philosophy of Science*. Pittsburgh: Pittsburgh University Press.

Barr, N. 2000. The History of the Phillips Machine. In R. Leeson (ed.), *A. W. H. Phillips: Collected Works in Contemporary Perspective*. Cambridge: Cambridge University Press, pp. 89–114.

Bartha, P. F. A. 2010. *By Parallel Reasoning: The Construction and Evaluation of Analogical Arguments*. Oxford and New York: Oxford University Press.

Bhushan, N. and S. Rosenfeld 1995. Metaphorical Models in Chemistry. *Journal of Chemical Education* 72: 578–582.

Black, M. 1962a. Metaphor. In *Models and Metaphors: Studies in Language and Philosophy*. Ithaca and New York: Cornell University Press, pp. 25–47.

Black, M. 1962b. Models and Archetypes. In *Models and Metaphors: Studies in Language and Philosophy*. Ithaca and New York: Cornell University Press, pp. 219–243.

Bradley, S. and K. P. Y. Thébault 2019. Models on the Move: Migration and Imperialism. *Studies in History and Philosophy of Science* 77: 81–92.

Bunge, M. 1969. Analogy, Simulation, Representation. *Revue Internationale de Philosophie* 87: 16–33.

Carloye, J. C. 1971. An Interpretation of Scientific Models Involving Analogies. *Philosophy of Science* 38: 562–569.

Cat, J. 2001. On Understanding: Maxwell on the Methods of Illustration and Scientific Metaphor. *Studies in History and Philosophy of Science* 32: 295–441.

Cat, J. 2006. Scientific Metaphors. In S. Sarkar and J. Pfeifer (eds.), *The Philosophy of Science: An Ecyclopedia*. New York: Tayolr & Francis, pp. 737–740.

Cat, J. 2021. Synthesis and Similarity in Science: Analogy in the Application of Mathematics and Application of Mathematics to Analogy. Forthcoming in S. Wuppuluri and A. C. Grayling (eds.), *Words and Worlds: Use and Abuse of Analogies and Metaphors with Sciences and Humanities*. Cham: Springer.

Chalmers, A. F. 1986. The Heuristic Role of Maxwell's Mechanical Model of Electromagnetic Phenomena. *Studies in History and Philosophy of Science* 17: 415–427.

Colyvan, M. and L. R. Ginzburg 2006. Analogical Thinking in Ecology: Looking Beyond Disciplinary Boundaries. *The Quarterly Review of Biology* 85: 171–182.

Copi, I. M. and C. Cohen 1998. *Introduction to Logic* (10th ed.). Upper Saddle River: Prentice Hall.

Crowther, K., N. S. Linnemann, and C. Wüthrich 2021. What We Cannot Learn from Analogue Experiments. *Synthese*: 3701–3726.

Dardashti, R., S. Hartmann, K. P. Y. Thébault, and E. Winsberg 2019. Hawking Radiation and Analogue Experiments: A Bayesian Analysis. *Studies in History and Philosophy of Modern Physics* 67: 1–11.

Dardashti, R., K. P. Y. Thébault, and E. Winsberg 2017. Confirmation Via Analogue Simulation: What Dumb Holes Could Tell Us About Gravity. *The British Journal for the Philosophy of Science* 68: 55–89.

Darden, L. 1982. Artificial Intelligence and Philosophy of Science: Reasoning by Analogy in Theory Construction. *PSA: Proceedings of the Biennial Meeting of the Philosophy of Science Association 1982* (Vol. 2), pp. 147–165.

Darden, L. and R. Rada 1988. Hypothesis Formation Using Part-Whole Interrelations. In D. H. Helman (ed.), *Analogical Reasoning: Perspectives of Artificial Intelligence, Cognitive Science, and Philosophy*. Dordrecht: Kluwer, pp. 341–375.

Darrigol, O. 2010a. The Analogy between Light and Sound in the History of Optics from the Ancient Greeks to Isaac Newton. Part 1. *Centaurus* 52: 117–155.

Darrigol, O. 2010b. The Analogy between Light and Sound in the History of Optics from the Ancient Greeks to Isaac Newton. Part 2. *Centaurus* 52: 206–257.

Darrigol, O. 2016. Models, Structure, and Generality in Clerk Maxwell's Theory of Electromagnetism. In K. Chemla, R. Chorlay, and D. Rabouin (eds.), *The Oxford Handbook of Generality in Mathematics and the Sciences*. Oxford: Oxford University Press, pp. 345–356.

Davies, T. R. 1988. Determination, Uniformity, and Relevance: Normative Criteria for Generalization and Reasoning by Analogy. In D. H. Helman (ed.), *Analogical Reasoning: Perspectives of Artificial Intelligence, Cognitive Science, and Philosophy*. Dordrecht: Kluwer, pp. 227–250.

Del Re, G. 2000. Models and Analogies in Science. *Hyle* 6: 5–15.

Doi, M. and S. F. Edwards 1986. *The Theory of Polymer Dynamics*. Oxford: Clarendon Press.

Evans, P. W. and K. P. Y. Thébault 2020. What Can Bouncing Oil Droplets Tell Us About Quantum Mechanics? *European Journal for Philosophy of Science* 10: Article 39.

Fogelin, R. 2011. *Figuratively Speaking* (2nd ed.). Oxford: Oxford University Press.

Gentner, D. 1982. Are Scientific Analogies Metaphors? In D. S. Miall (ed.), *Metaphor: Problems and Perspectives*. Brighton: Harvester Press, pp. 106–132.

Gentner, D., B. Falkenhainer, and J. Skorstad 1988. Viewing Metaphor as Analogy. In D. H. Helman (ed.), *Analogical Reasoning: Perspectives of Artificial Intelligence, Cognitive Science, and Philosophy*. Dordrecht: Kluwer, pp. 171–177.

Gilboa, I., A. Postlewaite, L. Samuelson, and D. Schmeidler 2014. Economic Models as Analogies. *The Economic Journal* 124: 513–533.

Goodman, N. 1972. Seven Strictures on Similarity. In N. Goodman (ed.), *Problems and Projects*. Indianapolis and New York: Bobbs-Merrill, pp. 437–446.

Groddeck, W. 1995. *Reden Über Rhetorik. Zu Einer Stilistik Des Lesens*. Basel: Stroemfeld.

Gyenis, B. 2017. Maxwell and the Normal Distribution: A Colored Story of Probability, Independence, and Tendency Toward Equilibrium. *Studies in History and Philosophy of Modern Physics* 57: 53–65.

Harré, R. 1988. Where Models and Analogies Really Count. *International Studies in the Philosophy of Science* 2: 118–133.

Harré, R. 2004. *Modeling: Gateway to the Unknown*. Amsterdam: Elsevier.

Hartshorne, C. and P. Weiss (eds.) 1931–1935. *Collected Papers of Charles Sanders Peirce* (Vols. I–VI). Cambridge, MA: Harvard University Press.

Hempel, C. G. 1965. *Aspects of Scientific Explanation and Other Essays in the Philosophy of Science*. New York: Free Press.

Hesse, M. B. 1952. Operational Definition and Analogy in Physical Theories. *The British Journal for the Philosophy of Science* 2: 281–294.

Hesse, M. B. 1953. Models in Physics. *The British Journal for the Philosophy of Science* 4: 198–214.

Hesse, M. B. 1961. *Forces and Fields: The Concept of Action at a Distance in the History of Physics*. London and Edinburgh: Thomas Nelson and Sons.

Hesse, M. B. 1963. *Models and Analogies in Science*. London: Sheed and Ward.

Hesse, M. B. 1964. Analogy and Confirmation Theory. *Philosophy of Science* 31: 319–327.

Hesse, M. B. 1967. Models and Analogy in Science. In P. Edwards (ed.), *Encyclopedia of Philosophy*. New York: Macmillan, pp. 354–359.

Hesse, M. B. 1974. *The Structure of Scientific Inference*. London: Macmillan.

Hesse, M. B. 1988. Theories, Family Resemblances and Analogy. In D. H. Helman (ed.), *Analogical Reasoning: Perspectives of Artificial Intelligence, Cognitive Science, and Philosophy*. Dordrecht: Kluwer, pp. 317–340.

Hesse, M. B. 2000. Models and Analogies. In W. H. Newton-Smith (ed.), *A Companion to the Philosophy of Science*. Oxford: Blackwell, pp. 299–307.

Hills, D. 2016. Metaphor. In E. N. Zalta (ed.), *The Stanford Encyclopedia of Philosophy*. https://plato.stanford.edu/archives/fall2016/entries/metaphor/.

Holyoak, K. and P. Thagard 1995. *Mental Leaps: Analogy in Creative Thought*. Cambridge, MA: Bradford.

Horgan, J. 1994. Icon and Bild: A Note on the Analogical Structure of Models – the Role of Models in Experiment and Theory. *The British Journal for the Philosophy of Science* 45: 599–604.

Hughes, R. I. G. 1999. The Ising Model, Computer Simulation, and Universal Physics. In M. Morgan and M. Morrison (eds.), *Models as Mediators*. Cambridge: Cambridge University Press, pp. 97–145.

Ippoliti, E. 2018. Building Theories: The Heuristic Way. In D. Danks and E. Ippoliti (eds.), *Building Theories: Heuristics and Hypotheses in Sciences*. Cham: Springer, pp. 3–20.

Johnson, M. 1988. Some Constraints on Embodied Analogical Understanding. In D. H. Helman (ed.), *Analogical Reasoning: Perspectives of Artificial Intelligence, Cognitive Science, and Philosophy*. Dordrecht: Kluwer, pp. 25–40.

Kargon, R. 1969. Model and Analogy in Victorian Science: Maxwell's Critique of the French Physicists. *Journal of the History of Ideas* 30: 423–436.

Kaushal, R. S. 1999. The Role of Structural Analogy in Physical Sciences: A Philosophical Perspective. *Indian Philosophical Quarterly* 26: 543–573.

Kedar-Cabelli, S. 1988. Analogy – From a Unified Perspective. In D. H. Helman (ed.), *Analogical Reasoning: Perspectives of Artificial Intelligence, Cognitive Science, and Philosophy*. Dordrecht: Kluwer, pp. 65–103.

Keynes, J. M. 1921. *A Treatise on Probability*. London: McMillan & Co.

Knuuttila, T. and A. Loettgers 2014. Varieties of Noise: Analogical Reasoning in Synthetic Biology. *Studies in History and Philosophy of Science* 68: 76–88.

Knuuttila, T. and A. Loettgers 2016. Model Templates within and between Disciplines: From Magnets to Gases – and Socio-Economic Systems. *European Journal for Philosophy of Science* 6: 377–400.

Kroes, P. 1989. Structural Analogies between Physical Systems. *The British Journal for the Philosophy of Science* 40: 145–154.

Leatherdale, W. H. 1974. *The Role of Analogy, Model and Metaphor in Science*. Amsterdam: North Holland Publishing Company.

Lichter, T. 1995. Bill Clinton Is the First Lady of the USA: Making and Unmaking Analogies. *Synthese* 104: 285–297.

Lycan, W. G. 2008. *Philosophy of Language: A Contemporary Introduction* (2nd ed.). New York and London: Routledge.

Mattingly, J. and W. Warwick 2009. Projectible Predicates in Analogue and Simulated Systems. *Synthese* 169: 465–482.

Maxwell, J. C. 1855. On Faraday's Lines of Force. In W. D. Niven (ed.), *The Scientific Papers of James Clerk Maxwell*. New York: Dover Publications, 1965, pp. 155–229.

McMullin, E. 1968. What Do Physical Models Tell Us? In B. van Rootselaar and J. F. Staal (eds.), *Logic, Methodology and Science III*. Amsterdam: North Holland, pp. 385–396.

Mellor, D. H. 1968. Models and Analogies in Science: Duhem Versus Campbell? *Isis* 59: 282–290.

Merriam-Webster 2017. *Metaphor*. www.merriam-webster.com/dictionary/metaphor (accessed 26 March 2017).

Montuschi, E. 2000. Metaphor in Science. In W. H. Newton-Smith (ed.), *A Companion to the Philosophy of Science*. Malden and Oxford: Blackwell, pp. 277–282.

Morgan, M. S. 1997. The Technology of Analogical Models: Irving Fisher's Monetary Worlds. *Philosophy of Science* 64(Supplement): 304–314.

Morgan, M. S. 1999. Learning from Models. In M. S. Morgan and M. Morrison (eds.), *Models as Mediators: Perspectives on Natural and Social Science*. Cambridge: Cambridge University Press, pp. 347–388.

Morgan, M. S. 2012. *The World in the Model: How Economists Work and Think*. Cambridge: Cambridge University Press.

Morrison, M. 1997. Physical Models and Biological Contexts. *Philosophy of Science* 64(Supplement): 315–324.

Nagel, E. 1961. *The Structure of Science*. London: Routledge and Keagan Paul.

Nappo, F. 2021. Close Encounters with Scientific Analogies of the Third Kind. *European Journal for Philosophy of Science* 11: Article 82.

Nersessian, N. 1984. Aether/Or: The Creation of Scientific Concepts. *Studies in History and Philosphy of Science* 15: 175–212.

Niiniluoto, I. 1988. Analogy and Similarity in Scientific Reasoning. In D. H. Helman (ed.), *Analogical Reasoning: Perspectives of Artificial Intelligence, Cognitive Science, and Philosophy*. Dordrecht: Kluwer, pp. 271–298.

Oppenheimer, R. 1956. Analogy in Science. *American Psychologist* 11: 127–135.

Phillips, A. W. 1950. Mechanical Models in Economic Dynamics. *Economica* 17: 283–305.

Portides, D. 2005. Scientific Models and the Semantic View of Theories. *Philosophy of Science* 72(Supplement): 1287–1298.

Psillos, S. 1995. The Cognitive Interplay between Theories and Models: The Case of 19th Century Physics. In W. E. Herfel, W. Krajewski, I. Niiniluoto, and R. Wojcicki (eds.), *Theories and Models in Scientific Processes* (Poznań Studies in the Philosophy of Science and the Humanities 44). Amsterdam and Atlanta, GA: Rodopi, pp. 105–133.

Rickart, C. E. 1995. *Structuralism and Structure: A Mathematical Perspective*. Singapore: World Scientific.

Rowbottom, D. P. 2011. Approximations, Idealizations and 'Experiments' at the Physics – Biology Interface. *Studies in History and Philosophy of Biological and Biomedical Sciences* 42: 145–154.

Ruse, M. 1973. The Nature of Scientific Models: Formal V Material Analogy. *Philosophy of the Social Sciences* 3: 63–80.

Russell, S. 1988. Analogy by Similarity. In D. H. Helman (ed.), *Analogical Reasoning: Perspectives of Artificial Intelligence, Cognitive Science, and Philosophy*. Dordrecht: Kluwer, pp. 251–269.

Saha, P. K. 1988. Metaphorical Style as Message. In D. H. Helman (ed.), *Analogical Reasoning: Perspectives of Artificial Intelligence, Cognitive Science, and Philosophy*. Dordrecht: Kluwer, pp. 41–61.

Sarlemijn, A. 1987. Analogy Analysis and Transistor Research. *Methodology and Science* 20: 40–61.

Sarlemijn, A. and P. A. Kroes 1988. Technological Analogies and Their Logical Nature. In P. T. Durbin (ed.), *Technology and Contemporary Life*. Dordrecht: Reidel, pp. 237–255.

Schlimm, D. 2008. Two Ways of Analogy: Extending the Study of Analogies to Mathematical Domains. *Philosophy of Science* 75: 178–200.

Shelley, C. 1999. Multiple Analogies in Archaeology. *Philosophy of Science* 66: 579–605.

Shive, J. N. and R. L. Weber 1982. *Similarity in Pgysics*. New York: Wiley.

Sterrett, S. G. 1998. Sounds Like Light: Einstein's Special Theory of Relativity and Mach's Work in Acoustics and Aerodynamics. *Studies in History and Philosophy of Science Part B: Studies in History and Philosophy of Modern Physics* 29: 1–35.

Thébault, K. P. Y., S. Bradley, and A. Reutlinger 2018. Modelling Inequality. *The British Journal for the Philosophy of Science* 69: 691–718.

Turner, J. 1955. Maxwell on the Method of Physical Analogy. *The British Journal for the Philosophy of Science* 6: 226–238.

Unruh, W. G. 2018. Map and Territory in Physics: The Role of an Analogy in Black Hole Physics. In S. Wuppuluri and F. A. Doria (eds.), *The Map and the Territory: Exploring the Foundations of Science, Thought and Reality*. Cham: Springer, pp. 233–243.

11

ABSTRACTION, APPROXIMATION, IDEALISATION

11.1 Introduction

Representational models represent their target systems. But, as we have seen in previous chapters, models are not mirror images of their targets. Most, if not all, scientific models provide a simplified and distorted rendering of their target system. This truism is sometimes summed up in the slogan that all models are wrong.[1] Models involving frictionless planes, infinitely many particles, isolated populations, and omniscient agents are cases in point. But what exactly does it mean to say that models are simplified and distorted, or, indeed, wrong, and why do scientists study such models? To answer this question, we must have a closer look at *how* models are wrong. Models are not just wrong *tout court*; they are wrong in ways that are advantageous in the context of scientific research. To pinpoint what these ways are, both philosophers and scientists regularly appeal to the notions of idealisation, approximation, and abstraction. Models are qualified as being idealised representations of their targets; as being approximations of the truth; and as being based on abstractions of the real thing. The aim of this chapter is to get clear on what these notions are, on how they are related to each other, and on how they help advancing scientific investigation.

We begin our discussion with a mechanical model of a swing. This example, which will accompany us throughout this chapter and the next, illustrates idealisation, approximation, and abstraction, and it boosts our intuitions before we delve into an analysis (Section 11.2). The first task is to demarcate the concepts. We discuss how idealisation is different from abstraction (Section 11.3) and how idealisation is different from approximation (Section 11.4). We then analyse approximation (Section 11.5), and we reflect on the possibility of defining idealisation, which leads us to the conclusion that there is no unified definition of idealisation (Section 11.6). Our analysis will therefore have to proceed in a piecemeal manner. This is the project for Chapter 12, in which we discuss two prevalent types of idealisation, namely limit idealisations and factor exclusions in detail. We discuss

DOI: 10.4324/9781003285106-15

abstraction, approximation and idealisation as they occur in the context of models. This is a choice of convenience and the same points can be made about idealisations in laws and theories (Section 11.7).

11.2 Getting Started

There is a swing in the schoolyard. The teacher has a knack for physics and decides to calculate how fast the children move when they are on the swing and where they are located at different instants of time. To this end, she constructs a model of the swing. The model is based on two sets of assumptions. First, she sets aside properties of the swing she deems irrelevant: that the frame is made of pine wood, that the ropes attach to the axle with metal hooks, that the seat is blue, that the swing is located on the south side of the school building, that the swing has been donated to the school by the neighbourhood association, that there was a stock market crash exactly a year before the installation of the swing, and so on. Second, she makes assumptions about the mechanical aspects of the swing: that the motion is confined to a plane, that the ropes holding the seat are linear rigid rods, that the ropes and the seat are massless, and that the mass m of a child on the swing is concentrated in one point. She also assumes that the only force acting on a child is linear gravity pulling downwards with $F = mg$, where g is the gravitational constant, which she assumes to be 9.81 m/s². In doing so she sets aside all other forces such as air resistance, mechanical friction, buoyancy (the upward force due to the presence of air), and the Coriolis force (the force due the rotation of the earth). These assumptions define the model-swing.

The teacher then chooses spherical coordinates to describe the situation: r is the distance between the mass and the axle, and θ is the angle of deflection (the deviation of the rope from the vertical). With this in place, she turns to Newtonian mechanics. She regards forces as vectors, and using some simple trigonometry she finds that the restoring force acting on the swing (i.e. the force pulling the swing back to the vertical position) is $F = mg\sin(\theta)$. Newton's equation of motion, $\vec{F} = m\vec{a}$, says that the force acting on an object is equal to the product of the object's mass and the acceleration that an object experiences as a result of the force (see Section 1.2). Applying this general equation to her model yields the equation of motion of the model-swing:

$$\frac{d^2\theta}{dt^2} = -\frac{g}{l}\sin(\theta), \tag{11.1}$$

where the left-hand side of the equation denotes the second derivative of the angle with respect to time, and l is the distance of the centre of mass of the child from the axle. The solution to this equation will provide both the angular velocity and the angle as a function of time, which answers the teacher's question about a child's speed and position. The equation is of course the so-called ideal pendulum equation. The general solution to this equation is given in terms of so-called elliptical functions.[2] These functions are, however, difficult to handle and hard to use in generating predictions. But the teacher figures that she only needs to consider small angles because a child cannot move the swing too far away from the vertical. So she makes the assumption that $\sin(\theta) = \theta$, which is approximately correct for angles of up to about $\pi/8$ (the teacher measurs angles in radians). With this assumption the equation becomes

$$\frac{d^2\theta}{dt^2} = -\frac{g}{l}\theta. \tag{11.2}$$

The general solution for this equation is $\theta(t) = A\cos(\omega t) + B\sin(\omega t)$, where $\omega = \sqrt{g/l}$ is the frequency of the oscillation and A and B are real numbers that depend on where the child starts swinging (i.e. the initial condition). If we assume that the swing is in the vertical position at time $t = 0$ and that the speed they get (for instance due to the teacher pushing them) is such that it gets them to a maximum angle of $\pi/8$, then we have $A = 0$ and $B = \pi/8$. This solution is shown in Figure 11.1a.

This little anecdote illustrates the three concepts that are the focus of this chapter and the next. The first set of assumptions, which set aside properties of the swing that are deemed irrelevant, are abstractions. The second set

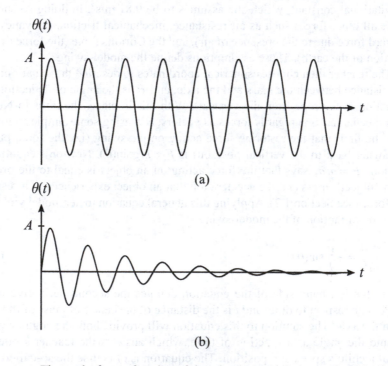

FIGURE 11.1 The angle θ as a function of time for the pendulum equation (a) without air resistance and (b) with air resistance.

of assumptions, which concern the mechanical aspects of the swing, are idealisations. The final assumption, $\sin(\theta) = \theta$, is an approximation. *In nuce*, the idea is that abstractions set aside properties that are irrelevant to the problem at hand; idealisations intentionally distort relevant properties; and approximations replace a mathematical expression by other, more tractable and yet sufficiently close, expression. Derivatively, we can speak of an *idealised model* when the model involves an idealisation, of an *abstract model* when the model involves abstractions, and of an *approximate model* when the model's mathematical form involves an approximation. Articulating the tripartite distinction between abstraction, idealisation, and approximation, and giving detail to each notion, is our task in this chapter.

A word of caution about terminology is in order. Going over the literature on the subject one finds the terms "idealisation", "abstraction", and "approximation" used with different, and sometimes conflicting, meanings. Analysing these notions and understanding the relations between them requires regimentation and restriction, and the result of the analysis will not conform with everybody's understanding of these notions. Hence, deviating from some usages of the terms will be unavoidable. I will alert readers when this happens.

11.3   Abstraction and Idealisation

Our introductory example suggests that the difference between abstraction and idealisation is one between omission and distortion. The model does not contain information about the material constitution of the frame, the colour of the seat, or the circumstantial factors in the acquisition of the swing. These have been stripped away when constructing the model, and so the omission of these factors in the model is an *abstraction*.[3] Mechanical properties, by contrast, are distorted rather than omitted. The children experience air resistance when they move (even though the resistance is weak). The ropes are not massless linear rods; they have mass (even though their mass is small compared to other masses in the system) and they wobble when the swing moves (albeit in a way that keeps them relatively straight on average). The axle is not frictionless; there is some resistance in its motion (even though it is relatively small). And so on. Abstracted properties are omitted while idealised properties are misrepresented.

Jones (2005, 174–175) and Godfrey-Smith (2009, 47) suggest an analysis of the distinction between abstraction and idealisation in terms of truth. An abstraction remains silent about features or aspects of the system: it ignores details, and it sets aside certain traits of the target system. But in doing so it does not say anything false, and it still offers a literally true description. The description is incomplete but not false.[4] An idealisation, by contrast, treats the target as having properties that it does not have and therefore asserts a falsehood. There is a deliberate discrepancy between the properties in the idealisation and the properties in the target system, and any claim that the idealised properties are the properties of the target is false.

This analysis faces the challenge that both idealisations and abstractions can be described as omitting something. The model of the swing omits colour and air resistance. On the face of it, remaining silent about colour does not seem to be different from remaining silent about air resistance. Both are omissions and neither seems to introduce an obvious falsehood into the description. If so, then the distinction between abstraction and idealisation is ill-defined. Ducheyne takes this observation to its logical conclusion and submits that "idealization is a subset of abstraction" (2007, 10).

Yet there is something intuitively wrong about collapsing the distinction between abstraction and idealisation. Jones' observation that when a model that omits a factor like friction it omits that factor in a way that involves misrepresenting the target in a certain *respect* (2005, 175–176, 183) points to a solution.[5] Friction is a force and omitting friction amounts to misrepresenting the forces in the system. But forces are a crucial aspect of the model, and the model does represent forces (it says that the force acting on the swing is gravity). Omitting friction therefore amounts to misrepresenting the system in a respect that is represented in the model, which is why omitting friction is not an abstraction. The omission of the fact that the seat is blue, by contrast, is an abstraction because the model is completely silent about colours, and omitting the blueness of the seat therefore is no misrepresentation. If the model specified that the rope was white and if that assumption played a role in the use of the model (for instance because white ropes reflect sunlight and hence do not expand in sunny weather conditions), then omitting the blueness of the seat would be an idealisation and not an abstraction. Omissions are abstractions only if they are "wholesale".

This raises the question of what counts as a respect and of what it means to pertain to a certain respect. The key to an answer lies in the realisation that this is a version of the issue of the relation between the specific and the general, and a number of answers are available. One option would be to say that respects are determinables and the specific properties that are replaced by others are determinates; another option is to explain respects in terms of the relation of grounding; and yet another option is to appeal to a ladder of abstraction.[6] For the purpose of a discussion of idealisation we do not need to resolve this issue (or take sides), and we can operate with an intuitive understanding of what respects are. Examples to boost intuitions are readily at hand. Mechanical models represent forces but not colour, temperature, or social factors; micro-economic models represent agents' preferences but not their body weights, nationalities, and religious beliefs; and so on.

Even in the absence of a deeper analysis of the relation between respects and the factors that we subsume under them, an important point emerges from these examples, namely that the theoretical context in which a model stands plays a crucial role in selecting relevant respects. Background theories carve up the world in certain ways and classify factors. It is Newtonian mechanics that tells us to focus on forces and to neglect colour; and if our mechanical model of the swing was used in a context that did not classify buoyancy as a force, its omission would not be regarded as an idealisation. Hence what counts as an idealisation is to a large extent dependent on the theoretical backdrop against which the model is formulated.[7]

In sum, an abstraction is the wholesale omission of a property, meaning that the property is omitted *and* that it does not fall under a respect that is represented in the model. An idealisation is the distortion of a property that falls under a respect that is represented in the model. For this reason, abstractions offer a literally true (albeit incomplete) representation of the target, while idealisations assert, if understood literally, falsehoods.[8]

11.4   Approximation and Idealisation

In common parlance, an approximation is anything that is relevantly similar to something else without being exactly the same. The airport announces that the flight is approximately half an hour late; the new colour of the door is approximately the same as the old one; the account of events in the investigator's report is a good approximation of what really happened; and that the reconstruction of Lindbergh's aeroplane in the museum is a good approximation of the original. This liberal usage of the term extends to scientific contexts, where almost any likeness can be paraphrased as an approximation. Theoretical calculations can approximate empirical values; models can be good approximations of their targets; and the old theory approximates the new one in a certain regime. In this broad usage "approximation" is largely congruent with "idealisation", and there is no clearly identifiable difference between the two.

Thus construed, "approximation" is not a useful concept: in so far as "approximation" is a synonym of "idealisation", our analysis can concentrate on the latter. There is however, a more precise meaning of the term that emerges from discussions in philosophy of science, and this meaning is what we are interested in. Rueger and Sharp point out that the "traditional sense of approximation is one of *quantitative* closeness" (1998, 204, original emphasis); Ramsey observes that approximations become important when scientists are "confronted with computational difficulties caused by analytically intractable equations" (1992, 154); Liu says that approximation "is a relation of relative closeness defined on a set which forms a strict or partial ordering" (Liu 1999, 230); and Portides submits that "the prevailing mode of approximation in science is mathematical" (2007, 705). Approximation, on this reading, is a notion pertaining to closeness in the realm of *mathematical* reasoning. I follow this usage and take approximations to operate exclusively at the level of mathematics.[9]

Consider two mathematical objects A and M.[10] Saying that A is an approximation of M then expresses the fact that A is close enough to M for it to serve as a stand-in or substitute for M in a certain context. What "close enough" means depends of course not only on the context, but also on the nature of the mathematical objects themselves. We impose no restrictions on the kind of mathematical objects that are able to play a part in approximations. The most common ones are numbers, functions, solutions to equations, and equations themselves, and we will discuss these in Section 11.5. In contrast with an approximation, idealisation does not concern the relation between two mathematical objects; it concerns the relation between a model and its target system. What this relation is, or whether there is a general characterisation of it at all, is the question we address in Section 11.6, as well as in Chapter 12. It is, however, clear from the outset that an idealisation need not be mathematical; nor does it have to be defined in terms of closeness. Indeed, as we will see, in some cases there are significant differences between idealised models and their targets.

How clear-cut is the distinction between approximation and idealisation? At least some idealisations have a mathematical expression that one could describe as an approximation. The idealisation that there is no Coriolis force removes a term from the equation of motion and makes it easier to solve. The effect of that term is known to be small and therefore the solutions of the idealised equation are close to the solutions of the full equation. So one could say that the simpler equation is an approximation of the full equation and conclude that approximation and idealisation coincide after all.

This objection prompts an important qualification. Approximations operate *solely* at the mathematical level, while idealisations *must have* a physical interpretation (or more generally, an interpretation in terms of the subject matter of the discipline that the model belongs to).[11] When saying that the axel has no friction and that the swing faces no air resistance, the teacher proposes a model that has physical properties that differ from the target's, and statements like "the frequency is $\omega = \sqrt{g/l}$" are statements about that model. The assumption $\sin(\theta) = \theta$, by contrast, involves no reference to a model. It merely says that for small enough angles, the value of the sine of the angle is close to the value of the angle itself. This is a purely mathematical statement and it can meaningfully be made without reference to a swing, or in fact without reference to anything non-mathematical. Indeed, approximations are often studied as part of pure mathematics and they do not require applications in the empirical sciences to be meaningful.

In some cases, the interpretation of a given distortion as either an idealisation or an approximation is relatively clear. In population models, the size of a population is often described by continuous variables. The use of such variables has no physical interpretation since it makes no sense to say there are 37.19 rabbits in the population. The continuous values are an approximation of the actual values, which are integers. Reinterpreting this distortion as an idealisation would involve the introduction of fractional rabbits as model entities, which is incoherent (or would at least require significant adjustments in our understanding of biological organisms). Conversely, not all idealisations lead to approximations. First, idealisations may introduce distortions that are so significant that the mathematical expression of the model in no way approximates the mathematical description of the unidealised situation. This happens, for instance, in our introductory example. Including friction into the mathematical description of the situation leads to an equation whose solutions "shrink" to a line (which is the mathematical manifestation of the fact that the swing will coming to standstill after a while); the idealised equation's solution is a sine function. But a sine function is not an approximation of a line. This is illustrated in Figure 11.1b[12] Second, it may not always be the case that the relevant factor of an idealisation has a well-defined mathematical expression, and in the absence of there being such an expression the question whether the model with the factor approximates the model without the factor becomes meaningless. The logistic model of population growth, for instance, assumes that the population is isolated from the rest of the ecosystem. But it is unclear what equation, if any, would describe a complete ecosystem, and so the question whether the logistic growth equation approximates the growth equation that one would get if the population was embedded in an entire ecosystem is ill-defined.[13]

Classifying a given distortion as either an idealisation or an approximation may not be straightforward; nor is there always a single correct answer. Some distortions can legitimately be understood either as idealisations or as approximations. But legitimacy is not indifference. How we analyse a given distortion has important consequences for our understanding of a model because idealisations and approximations have different epistemic, methodological, and metaphysical implications. In Section 12.3 we will encounter cases where the classification of certain distortions as either idealisations or as approximations is at the heart of heated controversies.

Let us briefly compare our account to an alternative proposal due to Norton. This proposal distinguishes between approximation and idealisation by saying that an "*approximation* is an inexact description of a target system" while an "*idealization* is a real or fictitious system, distinct from the target system, some of whose properties provide an inexact description of some aspects of the target system" (2012, 209, original emphasis). For this reason, approximations are "propositional" (*ibid.*, 207) and the difference between approximations and idealisations is referential: "only idealizations introduce reference to a novel system" (*ibid.*, 209).

While this way of drawing the line between approximation and idealisation is in many ways congenial to the position we have developed in this section (in particular in regarding idealisations as pertaining to a model), there are differences between them. First, as we have seen, approximations need not describe a target (inexactly or otherwise) because approximations operate at a mathematical level. One might push back against this and say that Norton's approach does not presuppose that the target be a system in the real world; it can regard the mathematical object M as the target of an idealisation. If so, harmony is restored, but the required broadening of the term "target system" would seem to be somewhat counterintuitive. Second, a view that regards approximation as based on a closeness relation between two mathematical objects does not line up neatly with a view that sees approximation as propositional. Third, in our proposal, the difference between idealisation and approximation is not referential because approximations also involve two objects, objects A and M; they are just of a different kind than the two objects involved in idealisations. Fourth, at least on some accounts of models there is no model object. As we have seen in Section 9.3, the

Direct View says that models – including idealised models – are just imaginative descriptions of their target. At least on such a view of models, models operate like Norton's approximations.

Having disentangled idealisation, approximation and abstraction, we now have to analyse these concepts in more detail. The challenges that this involves are uneven. Abstraction, although inevitable in modelling, is a simple concept and no analysis beyond what has already been said in Section 11.3 is needed. There are of course important questions in every scientific field about how much abstraction is appropriate and which properties can be safely abstracted, but these are scientific questions concerning a discipline's subject matter rather than philosophical questions about the notion of abstraction per se. Approximation and idealisation are less easily dealt with. We discuss approximations in the next section, and idealisation in the section after the next.

11.5 Understanding Approximation

As we have seen, a mathematical object A is an approximation of a mathematical object M iff A is close enough to M for A to serve as a stand-in for M in a certain context. The condition that the two objects are close requires that we have a way to quantify distances, and so the first question we have to address is how distances are measured. There is no one-size-fits-all answer to this question because different mathematical objects require different notions of closeness. We now zoom in on some of the most common mathematical objects – numbers, functions, solutions to equations, and equations themselves – and discuss how the distance between them could be understood. This is for the purpose of illustration and should not be understood as describing the only (or the only legitimate) ways of dealing with distances. Distances can be described using other methods.

Numbers are ubiquitous in science. They occur as outcomes of measurements, and as values of physical quantities, parameters, and constants of nature. The specification of a value can be more or less precise, and we can assess the closeness by using a metric to measure the distance between the actual value and the real value.[14] In principle there are infinitely many metrics to choose from. The most intuitive is the arithmetic distance: the difference between the value we use and the true value. The true speed of light is 299,792,458 m/s. If we use the value 300,000,000 m/s in a calculation, the arithmetic distance between the value used and the true value is 207,542 m/s, which is sufficiently small in many (but not all) applications. Sometimes the true value is unknown and all we are given is an interval around a certain value. We may be told, for instance, that London had 594±5mm of rain in 2015, which means that the rainfall was somewhere in the interval [589mm, 599mm]. Laymon suggests that when considering intervals, we are dealing with a special kind of approximation, namely a species of "vagueness or permissiveness" (1987, 198).[15] The interval can be said to approximate the actual value, and the narrower the interval the closer the approximation.

Functions are frequently approximated by other functions. We have encountered such an approximation in our introductory example when we used $\sin(\alpha) = \alpha$ for small values of α. Writing this as an equality is actually misleading and it is more accurate to write $\sin(\alpha) \approx \alpha$, where "$\approx$" designates an approximation relation. The formula $\sin(\alpha) \approx \alpha$ then expresses the fact that the sine is close to the identity function $f(\alpha) = \alpha$ as long as the angle remains small. This can be seen in the plot of the two functions in Figure 11.2:

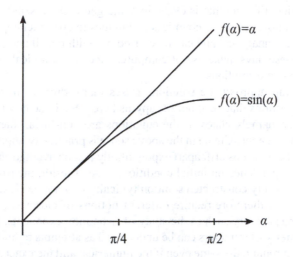

FIGURE 11.2 Approximation of $\sin(\alpha) \approx \alpha$.

The graph also shows clearly that the approximation is valid only for small values of α and it that starts breaking down when α comes close to $\pi/4$; in fact the approximation is good for values of α of up to about $\pi/8$. This is typical for approximations of functions: they are valid in a certain range and fail outside that range. The approximation can be justified by appeal to what is known as a Taylor series expansion. Many functions can be written as a sum of simpler functions. For the sine function this expansion is:

$$\sin(\alpha) = \alpha - \frac{\alpha^3}{3!} + \frac{\alpha^5}{5!} - \ldots$$

For small values of α the values of $\alpha^3, \alpha^5, \ldots$ are so small that they are negligible and hence $\sin(\alpha) \approx \alpha$ for small α. Another well-known example of an approximation of this kind is Stirling's formula, $n! \approx \sqrt{2\pi n} \, (n/e)^n$, which approximates factorials with exponential functions. Approximation relations of this kind are studied extensively in applied as well as in pure mathematics, and much effort goes into the proofs of relevant approximation theorems because not all approximations are as easy to justify as $\sin(\alpha) \approx \alpha$. [16]

Sometimes functions appear as solutions of differential equations. Newton's equation of motion, Maxwell's equations of the electromagnetic field, and many other equations in physics (and indeed other sciences) are differential equations and the solutions to these equations are functions satisfying the equations. Unfortunately, differential equations are often difficult to solve. While there are powerful general theorems asserting the existence of solutions under certain conditions, most of the time we are unable to specify these solutions explicitly. In such cases we may look for approximate solutions. An approximate solution is a function that we can identify and that is close, in some geometrical sense, to the true yet unknown solution. There are countless techniques to construct approximate solutions. Some are analytical and can be carried out with pencil and paper, but most techniques these days make use of computers and let numerical algorithms construct approximate solutions.

Constructing approximate solutions raises many difficult mathematical and numerical questions that need not occupy us here. One issue deserves brief mention, however, namely chaos. If the equations are non-linear, then constructing solutions that are approximate in the above sense is practically impossible because nearby initial conditions drift apart exponentially fast on average, an effect known as sensitive dependence on initial conditions.[17] As a result, the true solution and the computationally constructed solution typically will not be close to each other. Chaotic systems therefore require different notions of closeness, and important aspects of chaos theory such as the study of Lyapunov exponents, power spectra, and the geometry of attractors can be understood as attempts to find aspects of the dynamics that remain the same even if the numerical and the exact solutions differ (Rueger and Sharp 1998, 205).

Rather than look for approximate solutions to exact equations, one can try to look for exact solutions to approximate equations (Redhead 1980, 150). This is what happened in our introductory example. When faced with equation (11.1), which is difficult to handle, we used an approximation for the right-hand side of the equation which led to equation (11.2), for which exact solutions are readily available. So we have approximated one equation with another equation. While this works well in some cases, approximating equations is fraught with difficulties. Typically, one is not interested in approximate equations per se and approximate equations are treated as a means to constructing approximate solutions. The strategy, in other words, is to solve an approximate equation exactly in order to get an approximate solution to the exact equation. Under what circumstances does this strategy work? The critical issue here is what is known as *structural stability*. Roughly speaking, an equation is structurally stable if a small change in the equation only results in a small change in the solution. So the strategy works only if the equation is structurally stable. Some equations are structurally stable and approximate solutions can be constructed by solving approximate equations. But unfortunately many equations are not structurally stable, and so the strategy of studying approximate equations faces limitations.[18]

Once it is has been decided what the objects are and how the distance between them is assessed, we are faced with the issue of how close A has to be to M for A to be able to serve as a stand-in for M in a certain context. In brief: how close is close enough? The adoption of a certain threshold is a pragmatic choice that depends on the specifics of the situation, the computational complexity of the problem, and the nature of the question at stake. In some contexts an error of 10% is an excellent approximation while in others a deviation of 1% is a dramatic failure. The standard view of approximation is that once a consideration of all contextual factors has resulted in the choice of a threshold, the matter has been brought to a close and nothing more needs to be said.[19]

Ramsey (1992) argues that this is too quick, and he submits that being within a certain threshold is only a necessary but not a sufficient condition for something to be a good approximation. The issue is that, on its own, the nearness of results tells us nothing about their reliability, and the nearness could, for all we know, be a mere coincidence. To be scientifically valuable, Ramsey submits, an approximation must also satisfy the following criteria: (1) it has to be controllable; (2) we must be able to rule out that its effect is cancelled out by other factors; and (3) it must be justifiable (*ibid.*, 158). The above example with the sine curve illustrates the first two points. We know exactly which terms we omit and we can estimate the error. If we end up working in a regime where α is not sufficiently close to $\sin(\alpha)$ we can change the approximation, for instance by also including the second term of the Taylor expansion and approximating $\sin(\alpha)$ by $\alpha - \alpha^3/3!$. The interference of other factors can be ruled out by observing that *all* that is needed to get $\sin(\alpha)$ close to α is the cancellation of higher order terms in the Taylor expansion. These two criteria jointly ensure that the closeness of the approximation is not a fortuitous coincidence. To illustrate the third point, consider a case where a continuous curve is fitted to a finite set of points. The function typically has free parameters and the values for these may be chosen such that the curve comes to lie close to the points. How good such an approximation is depends on what motivates the choice of values. We judge an approximation differently if the values are chosen based on theoretical principles than if the function ends up being close to the points only because the parameters have been estimated statistically to do exactly that. This aspect is particularly important when approximating a function that has many free parameters and there is a serious worry that closeness can be achieved too easily (the problem known as "overfitting").[20]

What we have seen in this section is that there is no one-size-fits-all account of approximation. What counts as close depends on the kinds of mathematical objects one is interested in, and what counts as close enough depends on the context and on how much one requires by way of controllability and justification. Yet, the abstract characterisation of approximation (which we have stated at the beginning of the section) provides guidance in filling in the details in every case by focusing attention on the issues that matter.

11.6 Defining Idealisation?

So far we have characterised idealisation as a model-target relation that is such that if model-features were asserted to be present in the target, the assertion would be false. But not every assertion of a falsehood is an idealisation. Saying that the string is a linear rod is an idealisation; saying that it is a cube made from jelly is not. Being false if taken literally is a necessary but in no way sufficient condition for being an idealisation. This raises the question whether the analysis can be improved to also give sufficient conditions.

Rudner offers an analysis of idealisation in terms of uninstantiated properties. He submits that "the outstanding characteristic of idealizations is that they literally describe nothing – there is no entity, process, or state of affairs to which the idealisation stands in a designatory or descriptive relation" (1966, 57), and he offers an analysis of this notion in terms of existential statements being false. Let Q be a predicate (falling under a respect represented in the model). The corresponding existential statement, $\exists o(Qo)$, says that there is an object in the world that instantiates the property that predicate Q denotes. The predicate Q then describes an idealised situation if the existential statement is false (*ibid.*, 58). There are no frictionless swings in the world and, on Rudner's view, this is what makes the predicate *frictionless swing* an idealisation.

Unfortunately, not being applicable to a real-world object is too weak to offer a sufficient condition for being an idealisation.[21] The predicates *Being a Jedi* and *Beethoven's Tenth Symphony* produce false existential statements, but they are not idealisations of anything (even if suitable respects are chosen). The mistake in Rudner's suggestion is that it tries to characterise idealisations without reference to the target system. The crucial aspect of idealisations is not that they are false, but that they bear a special relation to their target system. A description may even change its status depending on what the target is. Having no air resistance is an idealisation of the swing; it is simply nonsense when asserted of the axioms of arithmetic. The challenge is to identify the relevant relation between model and target.

Barr introduces the notion of a state variable, a variable describing a system's condition. His examples are the *friction acting on a body o*, the *buoyancy of air acting on a body o*, and *deflecting magnetic forces acting on a body o* (1971, 263). The statement $f(o) = y$ asserts that the state variable f assumes value y for object o. An idealisation is the statement $f(o) = y$, where its constituents are such that they satisfy the following condition: $f(o) = y$ is false, but there is a value y' such that $f(o) = y'$ is true.[22]

However, as we have seen above, mere falsity is not sufficient to define idealisation. If the swing is so rusty that the axle hardly moves at all, the friction being zero is no idealisation. Likewise, a model in which molecules have the weight of elephants is hardly an idealisation of a hydrogen gas. Yet both satisfy Barr's condition.

Schwartz (1978, 596) thinks that Barr (at least tacitly) holds a stronger view: idealisations are not merely assigning a wrong value to a variable; they assign a value which, albeit strictly speaking false, makes the statement $f(o) = y$ approximately true in the sense that y and y' are sufficiently close. So the defining feature of idealisations is approximate truth.[23]

Unfortunately approximate truth and idealisation do not line up neatly. It is approximately true that there is no buoyancy and that the Coriolis force is zero. But not all approximate truths are idealisations. A measurement may conclude that The London Eye is 134.8 m high even though the true height is 135 m. Such a measurement result is approximately true, but it is not an idealisation.[24] Likewise, the statement that flying from London to Barcelona takes 2 hours is approximately true without being an idealisation. Vice versa, not all idealisations are approximately true. Some models are so highly idealised that their assumptions are not approximately true. The Lotka-Volterra model assumes that all fish in the Adriatic Sea are either predators or prey and that these two groups interact with each other according to a simple law; and when studying the exchange of goods, economists consider situations in which there are only two goods, two perfectly rational agents, no restrictions on available information, no transaction costs, no money, and dealings are done instantaneously. These assumptions are not approximately true, but they can be understood as idealisations. Hence, the connection between idealisation and approximate truth is tenuous at best, and trying to analyse one in terms of the other seems to be a dead end.

While these considerations do not afford a proof that there is no unified sufficient condition for something to be an idealisation, they make plain that no obvious candidate is available and suggest that a programme aiming at unearthing such a condition is likely to end in failure. But this does not mean that we must throw in the towel. An analysis can be piecemeal in the sense that one can identify different kinds of idealisations and offer sufficient conditions for something to be an idealisation of a particular kind. This raises the question of what kinds of idealisations there are. McMullin (1985) distinguishes six, Weisberg (2007) identifies three, Pemberton (2005) recognises two, and Nowakowa and Nowak (2000) find five. It is a commonplace that there are many ways of slicing up a cake, and so it is unsurprising that different authors offer different classifications. In the next chapter I discuss two kinds of idealisations, which I call *limit idealisations* and *factor exclusions*. Roughly, a limit idealisation pushes a property to an extreme, for instance when friction is assumed to be zero, or if the number of particles in a system is assumed to be infinite. In a factor exclusion, factors like particle collisions in a mechanical model or mutations in a genetic model are omitted altogether. There is no claim that this is an exhaustive list, and other kinds of idealisations could be added. However, these two notions cover a large range of idealisations, and an analysis of these two types goes a long way to understanding the idealisations one encounters in different scientific contexts.

Finally, even if there is no unified general definition of idealisation, we must still get clear on what kind of notion an idealisation is. Specifically, the issue is whether idealisation is an ontic or an epistemic notion.[25] An ontic view of idealisation holds that whether something is an idealisation depends on how the target system is *irrespective* of what the scientists building a model know about it. An epistemic view of idealisation holds that whether something is an idealisation depends on what scientist think and believe. Jones defends an ontic view. After introducing falsity as a necessary (but not sufficient) condition on something being an idealisation, he notes that "what matters . . . is whether, in the relevant respect, the model represents the system as being the way it is; the issue is not whether the model represents the system as being the way *we take it to be*" (2005, 183, original emphasis). In other words, whether a model is an idealisation of its target depends on the target's mind-independent features, not on what modelers happen to know or believe about it. As a consequence it is possible to discover that a model is an idealisation, or, vice versa, that it is not (*ibid.*). Lind, by contrast, supports an epistemic view when he insist that a definition of idealisation "is related to beliefs, not to how things really are" and therefore an "assumption is an idealization if the scientist that makes it believes that it is false, even though this belief eventually may turn out to be mistaken" (1993, 494).

As we have seen at the beginning, one of the key motivations for introducing idealisations is to make difficult problems tractable. This might suggest that idealisation is an epistemic concept. However, this is the wrong conclusion to draw; idealisation is an ontic concept. To see why, consider the example of a climate model. Until the late 1990s, models of the global climate represented processes in the atmosphere, the oceans, and on land surfaces, but they ignored vegetation.[26] We said that abstractions ignore details without saying anything false, while idealisations assert falsehoods. Is the omission of vegetation an abstraction or an idealisation? The answer is: it depends. If the vegetation has no influence on any of the processes represented in the model, then it is an abstraction. If it does have an influence on at least one process, then it is an idealisation. It so happens that the latter is the case: vegetation has an influence on carbon concentrations in the atmosphere, and carbon concentrations in the atmosphere have an influence on global temperatures. These temperatures are represented in the model, and so leaving out vegetation is like leaving out friction rather than like leaving out colour in our introductory example with the swing. For this reason it is an idealisation and not an abstraction. And the crucial point is: it is an idealisation because of how the earth is, not because of what we believe about the earth. If the earth happened to be such that vegetation had no influence on temperatures, then the omission of vegetation would be an abstraction. This shows that idealisation is an ontic concept.

11.7 Conclusion

We have introduced the notions of abstraction, approximation and idealisation, and we have drawn boundaries between them. We have given accounts of abstraction and approximation. This leaves idealisation, to which we turn to in the next chapter. It remains to be noted that I have discussed these notions as they occur in the context of models. This was a choice of convenience. The same points can be made about any part or aspect of science that is recognised as being representational, the most common examples being laws and theories. Galileo's law of inertia, Kepler's laws of planetary motion, and the ideal gas law all involve some kind of idealisation or approximation, and the same can be said of the theories in which these laws occur. This poses no problem because what we have said about idealisation, abstraction, and approximation equally applies to laws and theories.[27]

Notes

1 The slogan is often attributed to Box's (1976), but many other authors have made similar points. For a discussion, see Section 14.2. In keeping with the topic of the book, I focus on representational models. However, as Colyvan (2013) notes, idealisations also occur in normative disciplines like logic, epistemology, and decision theory.

2 For a discussion of the mathematical aspects of this equation, see Thorn (2012, Ch. 4).

3 The term "abstraction" derives from the Latin "abstrahere", which means to pull away, to drag away, and to remove. Although we note that the term "abstract model" is used with a different meaning in the context of a discussion of the ontology of models (see Section 8.5).

4 For further discussions of this notion of abstraction, see Levy's (2018), Levy and Bechtel's (2013), Love and Nathan's (2015), Tee's (2020), Portides's (2005), and Woods and Rosales' (2010). Framing the distinction in this way implies regarding abstraction as a relation between the model and its target. Chakravartty (2001), Portides (2018), and Leonelli (2008) criticised this perspective for overlooking the *process* by which abstractions are produced, and suggested that abstraction should better be analysed as an epistemic *activity*. This contrast is reminiscent of the debate between accounts of representation that see representation as relation into which model and target enter and accounts that see it as an activity. It remains, however, unclear whether these options really are mutually exclusive; more plausibly, they can be seen as complementary (Frigg and Nguyen 2020, 93–95).

5 Nicholas Jones (2008, 4–5) gestures at a similar solution (note that the author cited in the main text is Martin Jones) when he responds to Ducheyne (2007) that his arguments equivocates on properties: what is omitted in an idealisation are not physical parameters (for instance temperature) but physical magnitudes (for instance the temperature being 304.5°K); abstractions omit parameters.

6 See Wilson's (2017), Bliss and Trogdon's (2016), and Cartwright's (1999, Ch. 3), respectively, for discussions of these three options.

7 For a discussion of how models relate to theories, see Chapter 13.

8 I note that this use of "abstraction" conflicts with Cartwright's (1989, Ch. 5), who understands abstraction as the isolation of an individual factor which is then studied in isolation. Rather than asking what influence, say, air resistance has on the behaviour of the swing (which is the business of idealistion), an abstraction asks what air resistance *per se* does when studied in isolation and removed from all concrete circumstances. Humphreys (1995, 157) refers to this as "Aristotelian abstraction". One might then ask: what is an abstract claim about? Cartwright's answer is: capacities. Capacities are tendencies, or dispositions, to produce characteristic results. As such they are a part of the real world. Hence, on Cartwright's view, abstract propositions describe capacities. For a discussion of capacities, see, for instance, her (1988, 1989). For further discussions of capacities, see Hüttemann's (2014), Psillos'(2008), and Reiss' (2008, 2016, 2018).

9 This characterisation is in agreement with Laymon's (1990, 520–521, 1991, 171–172) and Ramsey's (2006, 25), as well as with Torretti's (1990, 139–142) analysis of approximation in terms of what he calls a "uniformity" on a set. Niiniluoto (1986, 267–268) comes close to this characterisation when he explicates approximation as being close in a metric state space.

10 I take the term "mathematical object" to refer broadly to the things studied by mathematicians, whatever these things are. Platonic connotations of "object" are unintended and should be bracketed.

11 Norton (2012, 208–211) and Ramsey (2006, 24) in essence draw the line in this way, even though they frame the distinction somewhat differently.

12 The case of damped oscillation is discussed in more detail in Section 12.3.

13 For a discussion of the logistic equation, see Argyris et al. (1994, Ch. 3).

14 Ramsey (1992, 155) points out that it is common to define approximation in terms of a metric. For the purposes of this section an intuitive understanding of the notion of a metric is sufficient. For a rigorous mathematical definition, see Mendelson's (1962, Ch. 2).

15 Laymon offers a formalization of this idea based on the notion of Scott domains. Ben-Menahem (1988, 170–172) offers a user-friendly summary of the approach.

16 Luke (1975) discusses approximations of a large class of functions, including binomial functions, gamma functions, and Bessel functions.

17 Rueger and Sharp (1998) discuss the consequences of chaos for approximations. Peter Smith (1998) and Leonard A. Smith (2007) offer introductions to chaos for non-experts. Werndl (2009) offers a rigorous definition of chaos.

18 Rueger and Sharp (1998, 208–211) offer an accessible introduction to structural stability. For a discussion of the effects that structural instability can have on our ability to construct approximate solutions, see Frigg et al. (2014), and with a special focus on scales, see Baldissera Pacchetti's (2021). Fletcher (2020) and Schmidt (2017) discuss Duhem's "principle of stability".

19 This view is articulated, for instance, in Balzer et al. (1987, 347).

20 Forster and Sober (1994) discuss the general problem of overfitting. Jebeile and Barberousse (2016) discuss the problem of overfitting in the context of climate models. Hendry (1998) and Woody (2000) discuss approximations in quantum chemistry.

21 Rudner's characterisation is embedded in a syntactic analysis of idealisation statements, and it suffers from a number of difficulties having to do with the logical form of these statements. For a discussion of these difficulties, see Barr's (1971, 1974).

22 A significant part of Barr's discussion is concerned with the syntax of idealisation statements. For a critical discussion of Barr's conditions, see Schwartz's (1978).

23 The use of the word "approximate" in this context is unfortunate as it does not line up with the discussion of approximation in the last section. I keep the term "approximate truth" because it of its intuitive appeal. Those wishing to preserve terminological purity can replace it with "truthlikeness" or "verisimilitude". For a discussion of this concept, see Oddie's (2016).

24 Similar examples can be found in Schwartz's (1978, 598) and Jones' (2005, 186).

25 In fact, the same question can be asked about abstraction and approximation.

26 For an introductory discussion of climate models and their history, see Maslin's (2004, Ch. 5).

27 For a discussion of idealised laws, see, for instance, Hempel's (1965, 344–345) and Liu's (1999).

References

Argyris, J., G. Faust, and M. Haase 1994. *An Exploration of Chaos: An Introduction for Natural Scientists and Engineers*. Amsterdam: Elsevier.

Baldissera Pacchetti, M. 2021. Structural Uncertainty through the Lens of Model Building. *Synthese* 198: 10377–10393.

Balzer, W., C.-U. Moulines, and J. D. Sneed 1987. *An Architectonic for Science: The Structuralist Program*. Dordrecht: Reidel Publishing Company.

Barr, W. F. 1971. A Syntactic and Semantic Analysis of Idealizations in Science. *Philosophy of Science* 38: 258–272.

Barr, W. F. 1974. A Pragmatic Analysis of Idealization in Physics. *Philosophy of Science* 41: 48–64.

Ben-Menahem, Y. 1988. Models of Science: Fictions or Idealizations. *Science in Context* 2: 163–175.

Bliss, R. and K. Trogdon 2016. Metaphysical Grounding. In E. N. Zalta (ed.), *The Stanford Encyclopedia of Philosophy*. https://plato.stanford.edu/archives/win2016/entries/grounding/.

Box, G. E. P. 1976. Science and Statistics. *Journal of the American Statistical Association* 71: 791–799.

Cartwright, N. 1988. Capacities and Abstractions. In P. Kitcher and S. Salmon (eds.), *Scientific Explanation*. Minneapolis: University of Minnesota Press, pp. 349–356.

Cartwright, N. 1989. *Nature's Capacities and Their Measurement*. Oxford: Oxford University Press.

Cartwright, N. 1999. *The Dappled World: A Study of the Boundaries of Science*. Cambridge: Cambridge University Press.

Chakravartty, A. 2001. The Semantic or Model-Theoretic View of Theories and Scientific Realism. *Synthese* 127: 325–345.

Colyvan, M. 2013. Idealisations in Normative Models. *Synthese* 190: 1337–1350.

Ducheyne, S. 2007. Abstraction Vs. Idealization. *The Reasoner* 1: 9–10.

Fletcher, S. C. 2020. The Principle of Stability. *Philosopher's Imprint* 20: 1–22.

Forster, M. R. and E. Sober 1994. How to Tell When Simpler, More Unified, or Less Ad Hoc Theories Will Provide More Accurate Predictions. *The British Journal for the Philosophy of Science* 45: 1–35.

Frigg, R., S. Bradley, H. Du, and L. A. Smith 2014. The Adventures of Laplace's Demon and His Apprentices. *Philosophy of Science* 81: 31–59.

Frigg, R. and J. Nguyen 2020. *Modelling Nature: An Opinionated Introduction to Scientific Representation* (Synthese Library). Berlin and New York: Springer.

Godfrey-Smith, P. 2009. Abstractions, Idealizations, and Evolutionary Biology. In A. Barberousse, M. Morange, and T. Pradeu (eds.), *Mapping the Future of Biology: Evolving Concepts and Theories. Boston Studies in the Philosophy and History of Science* (Vol. 266). Dordrecht: Springer, pp. 47–56.

Hempel, C. G. 1965. *Aspects of Scientific Explanation and Other Essays in the Philosophy of Science*. New York: Free Press.

Hendry, R. F. 1998. Models and Approximations in Quantum Chemistry. In N. Shanks (ed.), *Idealization IX: Idealization in Contemporary Physics* (Poznań Studies in the Philosophy of the Sciences and the Humanities 63). Amsterdam: Rodopi, pp. 123–142.

Humphreys, P. 1995. Abstract and Concrete. *Philosophy and Phenomenological Research* LV: 157–161.

Hüttemann, A. 2014. Ceteris Paribus Laws in Physics. *Erkenntnis* 79: 1715–1728.

Jebeile, J. and A. Barberousse 2016. Empirical Agreement in Model Validation. *Studies in History and Philosophy of Science*: 168–174.

Jones, M. 2005. Idealization and Abstraction: A Framework. In M. Jones and N. Cartwright (eds.), *Idealization XII: Correcting the Model-Idealization and Abstraction in the Sciences* (Poznań Studies in the Philosophy of the Sciences and the Humanities 86). Amsterdam: Rodopi, pp. 173–217.

Jones, N. 2008. Is All Abstracting Idealizing? *The Reasoner* 2: 4–5.

Laymon, R. 1987. Using Scott Domains to Explicate the Notions of Approximation and Idealised Data. *Philosophy of Science* 54: 194–221.

Laymon, R. 1990. Computer Simulations, Idealizations and Approximations. *Proceedings of the Biennial Meeting of the Philosophy of Science Association*. East Lansing, MI: Philosophy of Science Association, (Vol. 2), pp. 519–534.

Laymon, R. 1991. Thought Experiments by Stevin, Mach and Gouy: Thought Experiments as Ideal Limits and as Semantic Domains. In T. Horowitz and G. J. Massey (eds.), *Thought Experiments in Science and Philosophy*. Savage, MD: Rowman and Littlefield, pp. 167–191.

Leonelli, S. 2008. Performing Abstraction: Two Ways of Modellingarabidopsis Thaliana. *Biology and Philosophy* 23: 509–528.

Levy, A. 2018. Idealization and Abstraction: Refining the Distinction. *Synthese* 198: 5855–5872. https://doi.org/10.1007/s11229-018-1721-z.

Levy, A. and W. Bechtel 2013. Abstraction and the Organization of Mechanisms. *Philosophy of Science* 80: 241–261.

Lind, H. 1993. A Note on Fundamental Theory and Idealizations in Economics and Physics. *The British Journal for the Philosophy of Science* 44: 493–503.

Liu, C. 1999. Approximation, Idealization, and Laws of Nature. *Synthese* 118: 229–256.

Love, A. C. and M. J. Nathan 2015. The Idealization of Causation in Mechanistic Explanation. *Philosophy of Science* 82: 761–774.

Luke, Y. L. 1975. *Mathematical Functions and Their Approximations*. New York, San Francisco, and London: Academic Press.

Maslin, M. 2004. *Global Warming a Very Short Introduction*. Oxford: Oxford University Press.

McMullin, E. 1985. Galilean Idealization. *Studies in the History and Philosophy of Science* 16: 247–273.

Mendelson, B. 1962. *Introduction to Topology*. Boston: Allyn and Bacon.

Niiniluoto, I. 1986. Theories, Approximations, and Idealizations. In R. Barcan Marcus, G. J. W. Dorn, and P. Weingartner (eds.), *Logic, Methodology and Philosophy of Science VII: Proceedings of the Seventh International Congress of Logic, Methodology and Philosophy of Science, Salzburg, 1983*. Amsterdam, New York, Oxford, and Tokyo: Elsevier Science Publishers B.V., pp. 255–289.

Norton, J. D. 2012. Approximation and Idealization: Why the Difference Matters. *Philosophy of Science* 79: 207–232.

Nowakowa, I. and L. Nowak 2000. On Multiplicity of Idealization. In I. Nowakowa and L. Nowak (eds.), *Idealization X: The Richness of Idealization* (Poznań Studies in the Philosophy of the Sciences and the Humanities 69). Amsterdam: Rodopi, pp. 213–232.

Oddie, G. 2016. Truthlikeness. In E. N. Zalta (ed.), *The Stanford Encyclopedia of Philosophy*. https://plato.stanford.edu/archives/win2016/entries/truthlikeness/.

Pemberton, J. 2005. Why Idealized Models in Economics Have Limited Use. In M. R. Jones and N. Cartwright (eds.), *Correcting the Model: Idealization and Abstraction in the Sciences* (Poznań Studies in the Philosophy of the Sciences and the Humanities 86). Amsterdam: Rodopi, pp. 35–46.

Portides, D. 2005. A Theory of Scientific Model Construction: The Conceptual Process of Abstraction and Concretisation. *Foundations of Science* 10: 67–88.

Portides, D. 2007. The Relation between Idealisation and Approximation in Scientific Model Construction. *Science & Education* 16: 699–724.

Portides, D. 2018. Idealization and Abstraction in Scientific Modeling. *Synthese* 198: 5873–5895. https://doi.org/10.1007/s11229-018-01919-7.

Psillos, S. 2008. Cartwright's Realist Toil: From Entities to Capacities. In S. Hartmann, C. Hoefer, and L. Bovens (eds.), *Nancy Cartwright's Philosophy of Science*. London: Routledge, pp. 167–194.

Ramsey, J. L. 1992. Towards an Expanded Epistemology for Approximations. *Proceedings of the Biennial Meeting of the Philosophy of Science Association* 1: 154–164.

Ramsey, J. L. 2006. Approximation. In S. Sarkar and J. Pfeifer (eds.), *The Philosophy of Science: An Encyclopedia*. New York: Routledge, pp. 24–27.

Redhead, M. 1980. Models in Physics. *The British Journal for the Philosophy of Science* 31: 145–163.

Reiss, J. 2008. Social Capacities. In S. Hartmann, C. Hoefer, and L. Bovens (eds.), *Nancy Cartwright's Philosophy of Science*. London: Routledge, pp. 265–288.

Reiss, J. 2016. Are There Social Scientific Laws? In L. McIntyre and A. Rosenberg (eds.), *The Routledge Companion to Philosophy of Social Science*. New York: Routledge, pp. 295–309.

Reiss, J. 2018. Thought Experiments and Idealisations. In M. Stuart, Y. Fehige, and J. Brown (eds.), *The Routledge Companion to Thought Experiments*. London: Routledge, pp. 469–483.

Rudner, R. S. 1966. *Philosophy of Social Science*. Eaglewood Cliffs: Prentice Hall.

Rueger, A. and D. Sharp 1998. Idealization and Stability: A Perspective from Nonlinear Dynamics. In N. Shanks (ed.), *Idealization IX: Idealization in Contemporary Physics* (Poznań Studies in the Philosophy of the Sciences and the Humanities 63). Amsterdam: Rodopi, pp. 201–216.

Schmidt, J. C. 2017. Science in an Unstable World. On Pierre Duhem's Challenge to the Methodology of Exact Sciences. In W. Pietsch, J. Wernecke, and M. Ott (eds.), *Berechenbarkeit Der Welt? Philosophie Und Wissenschaft Im Zeitalter Von Big Data*. Wiesbaden: Springer, pp. 403–434.

Schwartz, R. J. 1978. Idealizations and Approximations in Physics. *Philosophy of Science* 45: 595–603.

Smith, L. A. 2007. *Chaos: A Very Short Introduction*. Oxford: Oxford University Press.

Smith, P. 1998. *Explaining Chaos*. Cambridge: Cambridge University Press.

Tee, S.-H. 2020. Abstraction as an Autonomous Process in Scientific Modeling. *Philosophia* 48: 789–801.

Thorn, C. B. 2012. *Classical Mechanics*. www.phys.ufl.edu/~thorn/homepage/cmlectures.pdf.

Torretti, R. 1990. *Creative Understanding: Philosophical Reflections on Physics*. Chicago: The University of Chicago Press.

Weisberg, M. 2007. Three Kinds of Idealization. *The Journal of Philosophy* 104: 639–659.

Werndl, C. 2009. What Are the New Implications of Chaos for Unpredictability? *The British Journal for the Philosophy of Science* 60: 195–220.

Wilson, J. 2017. Determinables and Determinates. In E. N. Zalta (ed.), *The Stanford Encyclopedia of Philosophy*. https://plato.stanford.edu/archives/spr2017/entries/determinate-determinables/.

Woods, J. and A. Rosales 2010. Virtuous Distortion. Abstraction and Idealization in Model-Based Science. In L. Magnani, W. Carnielli, and C. Pizzi (eds.), *Model-Based Reasoning in Science and Technology*. Berlin and Heidelberg: Springer, pp. 3–30.

Woody, A. 2000. Putting Quantum Mechanics to Work in Chemistry: The Power of Diagrammatic Representation. *Philosophy of Science* 67: 612–627.

12

LIMIT IDEALISATIONS AND FACTOR EXCLUSIONS

12.1 Introduction

In this chapter we analyse two specific types of idealisation, namely limit idealisations and factor exclusions. Limit idealisations push a certain property to an extreme, for instance when the friction in a system is assumed to be zero; a factor exclusion amounts to omitting a certain factor entirely, for instance when a model omits the collision of particles. While there is no claim that these are the only kinds of idealisation, the two cover a large range of cases, and they go a long way to understanding the idealisations we encounter in different scientific contexts. Factor exclusions also serve as a springboard for a discussion of Galilean and minimalist idealisations. Comprehending these kinds of idealisation is crucial both for understanding how "distorted" models relate to their targets and how surrogative reasoning with them works. Beyond that, a discussion of idealisations also helps us understand the aims and purposes of "distorted" models. Some distortions have a purely practical goal: they make something intractable tractable. But not all distortions are just expedients. Some idealisations provide explanations and foster understanding. To see how they do so, we have to distinguish between different kinds of idealisations and explain how they work.

To pave the way for a discussion of limit idealisation, we begin by introducing limits and reviewing some of their important properties (Section 12.2). We then turn to a discussion of limit idealisations. We present a definition and examine how surrogative reasoning with limits works (Section 12.3). We then leave limits behind and discuss factor exclusions (Section 12.4). Excluded properties can later be reintroduced into a model, which leads to the inclusion scheme. The inclusion scheme can be interpreted in at least two different ways, leading to Galilean idealisations and minimalist idealisations (Section 12.5). There is no claim that the notions discussed in this chapter comprehensively cover all idealisations, and there is scope for further discussions (Section 12.6).

DOI: 10.4324/9781003285106-16

12.2 A Primer on Limits

An important kind of idealisation pushes a certain property to the extreme. I call such idealisations *limit idealisations* because the mathematical formulation of pushing a property to an extreme involves taking a limit. This happens in our introductory example in the previous chapter when the child on the swing is assumed to move without air resistance and the axle is assumed to be friction-less, even though we know that the child does experience air resistance and that the axle is far from frictionless. It also happens when we describe the moon as a perfect sphere even though in reality it has a bumpy surface. In cases like these, the values of parameters describing features of objects – air resistance, friction, roughness of a surface – are assumed to be zero even though their values are not zero in the target. But not all limit idealisations involve assuming that a value is zero; assuming that a value is infinite is equally important. This happens, for instance, when we assume that the number of particles in a gas is infinite or that the volume of a large system is infinite.

To understand limit idealisations, we first have to understand the mathematical notion of a limit. Consider a function $f(x)$ that takes real numbers as inputs and maps them onto other real numbers.[1] A simple example of such a function is $f(x) = x^2$, which maps every real number x onto its square. We can now consider how the values of $f(x)$ change when we let x tend to a particular limit value c. In our introductory example this value was zero, but nothing in the notion of a limit depends on this and we can ask for any number c how the function behaves when x tends toward c. We write "$x \rightarrow c$" to express that we are interested in studying what happens when x tends toward c. The value toward which $f(x)$ tends when x tends toward c is $\lim_{x \rightarrow c} f(x)$. To simplify notation we define $F_c := \lim_{x \rightarrow c} f(x)$ and refer to F_c as the *limit value* of the function $f(x)$ as $x \rightarrow c$. Such limits are called *finite limits* (because c is a finite number). It is crucial not to conflate F_c with $f(c)$, the value of the function at c, which we refer to as the *value at the limit*. We discuss the difference between the two in more detail shortly.

With this notation in place, we need a definition of $\lim_{x \rightarrow c} f(x)$. The standard definition, which goes back to 19th Century mathematician Karl Weierstrass, says that F_c is the limit of $f(x)$ as $x \rightarrow c$ iff for every real number $\varepsilon > 0$ there exits another real number $\delta > 0$ such that: for all x, if $0 < |x - c| < \delta$, then $|f(x) - F_c| < \varepsilon$.[2] This condition says that you can choose an upper bound ε to the difference between $f(x)$ and F_c completely freely as long as it is not zero, and for *any* such choice there must be a number δ such that if x is less then δ away from c, then the difference between $f(x)$ and F_c is smaller than ε. If it turns out that for a certain choice of ε there is no δ that meets this condition, then the limit does not exist. Or, more intuitively, the existence of a limit means that we can keep $f(x)$ arbitrarily close to F_c by keeping x sufficiently close to c. This is illustrated in Figure 12.1a. It shows a function for which it is the case that no matter what ε we choose, there is always a δ

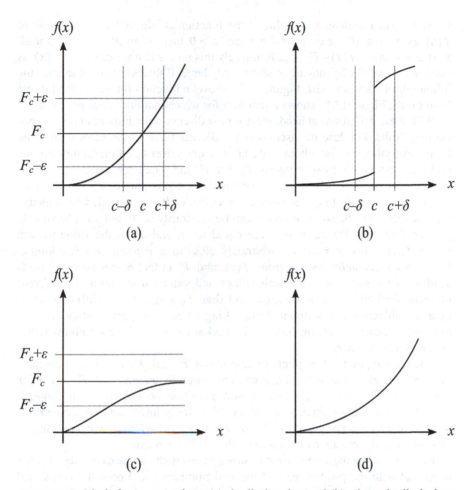

FIGURE 12.1 Limit for $x \to c$ where (a) the limit exists and (b) where the limit does not exist. Limit for $x \to \infty$ where (c) the limit exists and (d) where the limit does not exist.

that will keep $f(x)$ close to F_c. This is not the case for the function shown in Figure 12.1b because for every ε that is smaller than the "jump" that the function makes at $x = c$ there is no value F_c such that $|f(x) - F_c| < \varepsilon$ for all x, no matter how close to c we get.

As we have seen at the beginning of this section, not all limits let the value of a variable tend toward a finite value c; some have the variable tend toward infinity. In this case, the above notation and the definition of a limit need to be adapted slightly. We write "$x \to \infty$" to express that x tends toward infinity, where "∞" denotes infinity. We define $F_\infty := \lim_{x \to \infty} f(x)$ as the limit value of the function as $x \to \infty$. We call this an infinite limit. Taking certain mathematical liberties, we write $f(\infty)$ to denote the value of the function at infinity.[3] F_∞ is the limit of $f(x)$ as $x \to \infty$ iff for every real number $\varepsilon > 0$ there is an x' such that: for all x, if $x > x'$ then $| f(x) - F_\infty | < \varepsilon$. Intuitively this means that we can keep $f(x)$ as close F_∞ as we like by making x sufficiently large. If this is not possible, then the infinite limit does not exist. Figure 12.1c shows a function for which the infinite limit exists; Figure 12.1d shows a function for which that limit does not exist.

With these definitions at hand, we can now discuss some important points concerning limits. For ease of discussion we discuss these in the context of finite limits; everything we say about finite limits carries over to infinite limits *mutatis mutandis*, essentially by substituting F_∞ for F_c and $f(\infty)$ for $f(c)$.

The first point is that, as we have mentioned previously, F_c must not be confused with $f(c)$. In our definition we consider $0 < | x - c | < \delta$, which means that the difference between x and c can be arbitrarily small but must be strictly greater than zero. Hence x is *never* equal to c, and F_c is the value toward which $f(x)$ tends as x comes arbitrarily close to c *without ever reaching c*. So F_c is conceptually distinct from $f(c)$, and F_c in fact places no restrictions at all on what happens at c. Limit values and values at the limit are different mathematical objects. That said, the fact that $f(c)$ and F_c are different mathematical objects does not stop us from asking whether, in a given situation, they assume the same values. Indeed, much in what follows will depend on whether or not this is the case.

The second point is that freely talking about F_c and $f(c)$, and even comparing their values, might suggest that one can naturally assume that F_c and $f(c)$ always exist. This is not so. In fact, F_c and $f(c)$ may not exist at all. In "benign" cases both exist. But existence cannot be taken for granted and, worse, the existence of the two is not even correlated: F_c may exist without $f(c)$ existing or vice versa, and there are cases where neither of the two exists.

Let us illustrate these somewhat abstract points with simple examples of functions that map the positive part of the real numbers ($\mathbb{R}^+$) onto the entire real numbers ($\mathbb{R}$). To begin with, consider the function $f(x) = 1 + x^2$, which is shown in Figure 12.2a. Now take the limit $x \to 0$ (hence $c = 0$). We have $f(0) = 1$ and it is obvious that $F_0 = 1$. So the limit value and value at the limit both exist and coincide. But not all functions are so well-behaved. Consider a function, shown in Figure 12.2b, that assumes value 1 everywhere except at zero, where it assumes value 2. In this case, the limit of the function for $x \to 0$ is 1 (that is, $F_0 = 1$), and yet the value of the function at 0 is 2 (that is, $f(0) = 2$). So the limit value and the value of the limit both exist but are different. Next, consider the limit of the function $f(x) = x \sin(1/x)$ for $x \to 0$, which is shown in Figure 12.2c. One finds $F_0 = 0$, yet $f(x)$ does not exist at $x = 0$ because division by zero is not a meaningful mathematical operation. Next, we construct a function by the following rule: $f(x) = 1$ if x is rational (that is, if x can be written as the quotient of two integers) and $f(x) = -1$ otherwise. This function is illustrated in Figure 12.2d. It is a consequence of an important theorem in number theory that any interval always contains rational numbers. From this it follows that $f(x)$ will keep

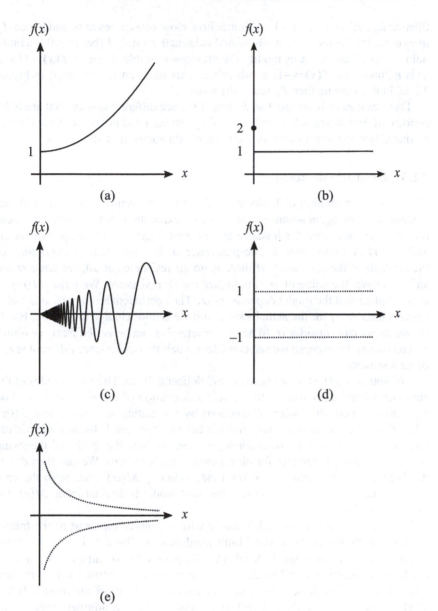

FIGURE 12.2 Five functions illustrating different situations with regard to the existence and non-existence of F_c and its relation to $f(c)$. The dots in figures (d) and (e) symbolise values taken on rational and irrational numbers respectively.

fluctuating between 1 and −1 no matter how close one comes to 0, and hence F_0 does not exist. Yet there is a well-defined value at 0, namely 1 (because 0 is a rational number). Finally, let us modify the previous example slightly: $f(x) = 1/x$ if x is rational and $f(x) = -1/x$ otherwise. This function is illustrated in Figure 12.2e. In this case neither F_0 nor $f(0)$ exist.

These examples illustrate that F_c and $f(c)$ are different objects that are independent of each other. When both exist, they can but need not coincide; and it can be that either one or the other, or indeed both, do not exist at all.

12.3   Limit Idealisations

With this understanding of limits at hand, let us now return to models and idealisations. Think again about our introductory example with the swing and focus on only one parameter, for instance air resistance. Let us call this parameter α, and let $M(\alpha)$ be the model. The parameter α is a quantitative expression of the strength of the resistance. If there is no air resistance at all, we have $\alpha = 0$ and the higher the value of α, the higher the air resistance. We write $M(\alpha)$ to make explicit that the model depends on α. The coefficient has a particular value (greater than zero) for the actual swing, and we cannot change that value. But *in the model* we can consider α to be a parameter that can be varied freely (within a certain range). In doing so we can consider models that experience different levels of air resistance.

The notation $M(\alpha)$ is suggestive, and deliberately so. The leading idea of the approach we are discussing is to connect a discussion of models that depend on a parameter to our discussion of functions by associating α with x and $M(\alpha)$ with $f(x)$. We can then ask how models behave if α tends toward a particular limit value c (or to ∞). For example, we can ask how the model of the swing behaves when the parameter for air resistance tends to zero. We can then define the *limit model* M_c through the limit $M_c := \lim_{\alpha \to c} M(\alpha)$ and, as in the case of pure mathematics, emphasise that the limit model is distinct from $M(c)$, the *model at the limit*.

This an important move which, as we will see, lies at the heart of the framework in which we can understand limit idealisations. There is, however, a complication that we must tackle head on. The parameter α and the variable x are both real numbers, and so there is no problem associating them with each other. The association becomes more tenuous at the level of the model. While $f(x)$ is also a real number, $M(\alpha)$ is a model and not a number. This has an unwelcome consequence. When defining the limit, we appeal to the difference between $f(x)$ and F_c through the condition $|f(x) - F_c| < \varepsilon$. This condition is well-defined because both $f(x)$ and F_c are numbers. This condition would translate into $|M(\alpha) - M_c| < \varepsilon$ under our association. However, the expression $|M(\alpha) - M_c| < \varepsilon$ is undefined because no notion of a difference between $M(\alpha)$ and M_c has been introduced. When numbers are mapped onto models rather than onto other numbers, we can no longer appeal to the familiar concept of the difference between two numbers to define the limit, and we have to introduce an alternative notion of difference that applies to models.

What notion of difference one chooses will depend on what one takes models to be, an issue which we discuss in Chapter 14. In some cases, models can be associated with (or at least be seen as expressed through) functions, in which case one can appeal to a notion of difference on a function space. In other cases, models may be mathematical objects of a different kind, or they may not be mathematical at all. There does not seem to be an overarching framework that accommodates all model types and equips models with a universally applicable notion of distance. This is not a problem per se because in every context we are free to choose a notion of distance that is appropriate to the case at hand. However, we have to be mindful of the issue and make sure that in each case we say what notion of distance we operate with before discussing limits. Unsurprisingly, the choice of a distance has been a matter of controversy in important applications, and, as we will see, choices can have far-reaching consequences for issues like reduction and emergence.

An important (but by no means the only) way to articulate a workable notion of distance is to focus on a particular property P and ask whether the model retains this property when we take the limit. Using standard logical notation we write $P(M(\alpha))$ to say that model $M(\alpha)$ has a property P, and we introduce the abbreviation $P(\alpha) := P(M(\alpha))$ for notational ease. One can then study how $P(\alpha)$ changes as $\alpha \to c$. If P is a property that has a magnitude attached to it, one can compare the values of the magnitudes, which, in fact, brings the model case back to the functions which we started off with. We will see an example of a limit involving a property P shortly.

It is then natural to ask three questions. First, does the *limit property* P_c, where $P_c := \lim_{\alpha \to c} P(\alpha)$, exist? Second, does $P(c)$, the *property at the limit*, exist? Third, if both P_c and $P(c)$ exist, do they coincide?

If we consider a model $M(\alpha)$, pick a particular property P of $M(\alpha)$, and study what happens as $\alpha \to c$, then I say that we deal with a *P-limit*. Understanding such a limit involves understanding both the limits of $M(\alpha)$ and $P(\alpha)$, and, crucially, their interplay. Let us begin by classifying such limits. If $M(\alpha)$ has no limit (i.e. if M_c does not exist), then the P-limit does not exist. If $M(\alpha)$ has a limit but $P(\alpha)$ does not (i.e. if M_c exists but P_c does not), then the P-limit does not exist either. If both limits exist (i.e. if M_c and P_c exist), then the P-limit exists. P-limits can be classified as either regular or singular. A P-limit is *regular* iff it satisfies one of the following conditions (Butterfield 2011, 1076):[4]

(R1) There is no model at the limit (i.e. $M(c)$ does not exist) and a fortiori there is no property at the limit (i.e. $P(c)$ does not exist).

(R2) There is a model at the limit (i.e. $M(c)$ exists); there is a property at the limit (i.e. $P(c)$ exists), and $P_c = P(c)$.

It is worth pointing out that this definition is relative to certain a property $P(\alpha)$ and so it would be more accurate to say that a model that satisfies one of the above conditions is *P-regular*. We suppress this qualification to keep language simple, but it is important to keep the point in mind because it can happen that the limit for the same model $M(\alpha)$ is regular for property $P(\alpha)$ and not regular for another property $Q(\alpha)$.

(R1) is the trivial case because nothing can "go wrong" if there is no model at the limit – the limit is regular by default, as it were. The interesting case is (R2). Let us now think about what happens when (R2) fails. We say that property P is the *correct* property if the claim "the real-world target has property P" is true. We can then say that a P-limit is *singular* iff, $M(c)$ and $P(c)$ exist, $P_c \neq P(c)$, and $P(c)$ rather than P_c is correct (*ibid.*, 1077). In other words, if a P-limit is singular, then the property of the model at the limit is different from the properties of the model away from the limit, and it is the property at the limit that is the correct one.

The last clause is added for the following reason. The real target is not represented accurately by the model at the limit; it is accurately represented by a model somewhere "on the way to the limit". For instance, the real target will always have some air resistance; and, if we consider infinite limits, the there is no gas with an infinite number of particles. If we assume that the limit exists and the model that accurately represents the target is close to the limit, then that model (and with it the target) has a property that is close to P_c. So a property that is close to P_c is the correct property. By the same token, if the target system is "somewhere on the way to the limit", then it need not be represented accurately by $M(c)$ and so $P(c)$ need not be the correct property. This cautionary point becomes moot if the limit is regular because in that case we have $P_c = P(c)$, and the correct property being close to P_c is the same as the correct property being close to $P(c)$. This changes if the limit is singular. In the singular case, P_c and $P(c)$ are different and so if a property close to P_c is correct, then a property close to $P(c)$ cannot also be correct, and so we can simply set aside $P(c)$ as irrelevant for an understanding of the target. Or so the reasoning goes. If it then turns out that $P(c)$ rather than P_c (or property close to it) is correct, then something very strange has happened: the model that one would expect to be the accurate representation of the target (for instance, the model with the correct particle number) is not actually correct, and the model that one would think *cannot* be an accurate representation (for instance because it features an infinity of particles) actually turns out to be correct. For this reason, physicist Michael Berry describes singular limits as ones that "involve concepts that are qualitatively very different" from the ones used to describe the system away from the limit (Berry 2002, 10). Both singular and regular limits are important in many contexts and we will now look at each in turn, starting with regular limits.

The swing with air resistance provides an example of a regular limit. As previously discussed, let $M(\alpha)$ be the model of the swing and α the parameter for air resistance. Furthermore, let us assume that we are interested only in what happens over an initial segment of time beginning at $t = 0$ and ending at $t = t_e$, where the subscript "e" stands for "end". When considering a sequence of swings

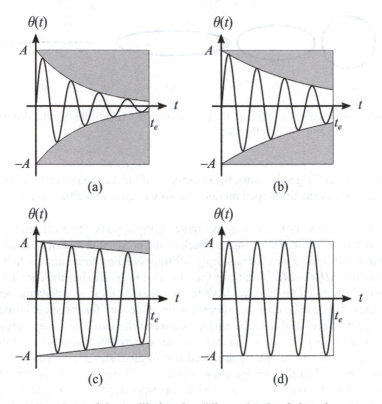

FIGURE 12.3 Envelope of the oscillation for different levels of air resistance, ranging from high (a) to zero (d).

with decreasing air resistance, we are interested in the swing's amplitude. The amplitude of the swing is the deviation of the rope from the vertical at the turning point, and it can be measured numerically. The deviation will decrease with time if the swing is left to its own, an effect known as "dampening". An *envelope* of the oscillation is a line through all turning points on the same side. So there are two envelopes for our swing: one for the turning points on the left and one for the turning points on the right (assuming that that child swings from left to right and back). The two envelops together encode all amplitudes over time. This is shown in Figure 12.3, where the envelopes are the curves going through the "tips" of the oscillating curves. Let the shape of envelope of the oscillation be the property $P(\alpha)$ that we are interested in. For the sake of illustration, let us assume that other damping forces (like air resistance) are zero. We can then take the limit for $\alpha \to 0$. This is illustrated in Figures 12.3a – 12.3c, which show oscillations and their envelopes of models for decreasing values of air resistance. Figure 12.4d shows oscillation of the model for $\alpha = 0$, which is the model

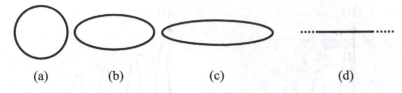

(a)　　　　　(b)　　　　　(c)　　　　　(d)

FIGURE 12.4 Singular limit, where the dotted lines in (d) indicate that the line extends to infinity on both sides.

at the limit. As the graphs show, the envelopes of the damped model tend towards the envelope of the undamped model, and so we have $P_0 = P(0)$ and the limit is regular.[5]

In telling the story in this way, we have tacitly appealed to a certain notion of two lines being close. This brings us back to the problem mentioned earlier: lines are not numbers and we cannot simply subtract one line from another line to get a value for $M(\alpha) - M_0$, which can then be said to be smaller than ε. To speak meaningfully about the limit we have to introduce a notion of a distance between two lines. This can be done in different ways. One can, for instance, introduce a "surface distance" and take the surface between the two lines as a measure for how far apart they are; or one can take the maximum difference between the two curves over the interval $[0, t_e]$ as a measure of the distance between the curves; or one can consider the average distance; or . . . . There are many options. Let us work with the "surface distance", which corresponds to the grey surface in Figures 12.3a – 12.3c. As the figures indicate, this surface tends toward zero when $\alpha \to 0$. So the choice of the surface distance puts the narrative in the previous paragraph on a firm footing.[6]

The fact that a limit is regular can be exploited to learn about the target from the model at the limit. The teacher can study $M(0)$ and find that it has property $P(0)$: the envelope consisting of two horizontal straight lines. This expresses the fact that the amplitude does not decrease. If the α is close to zero, the fact that the limit is regular implies that $P(\alpha)$ is close to to $P(0)$, meaning that the envelope is close to a horizontal straight line. We see this in Figure 12.3c.

For this reason, regular limits are informative. They allow us to study the model at the limit and carry over conclusions from *that* model to the models away from the limit. To see how such limits are informative, recall our earlier characterisation of a limit. Since the limits are regular, we know that $M_c = M(c)$ and $P_c = P(c)$. This implies we can keep $M(\alpha)$ arbitrarily close to $M(c)$ and $P(\alpha)$ arbitrarily close to $P(c)$ by keeping α sufficiently close to c. So if $M(c)$ has property $P(c)$ we know that a model close to $M(c)$ has a property close to $P(c)$, which allows us to extrapolate from $P(c)$ to properties $P(\alpha)$ for $\alpha \neq c$ and rest assured that to the extent that α is close to c, anything we discover about $M(c)$ and $P(c)$ is close to true claims about $M(\alpha)$ and $P(\alpha)$. In other words, one can study the *model at the limit* to discover properties of the *model close to the limit*.

This is particularly obvious if the limit can be articulated mathematically in terms of the standard ε and δ definition. However, actual numbers for δ and ε are rarely forthcoming in scientific practice. Scientists make informal judgments about how slippery the axle has to be to be "close enough" to the regular limit, and judgments often depend on contextual factors: what is close enough for one application is not nearly close enough for another. That said, there is no harm in making informal judgements and in the hands of seasoned practitioners such idealisations can be used fruitfully even without exact estimations of δ and ε.[7]

This kind of reasoning breaks down if the limit is singular. If $P_c \neq P(c)$, then even models that are very close to the limit do not have properties that are close to the property of the model at the limit, and hence the above inference fails. A simple example, adapted from Redhead (2001, 86–87), illustrates the point. Assume you have a rubber cylinder. Its profile is a sphere. Now apply a downward force to the cylinder such that the circular profile turns into an ellipse. Assume that the deformation is such that the semi-axes of the ellipse assume values α for the vertical semi-axis and $1/\alpha$ for the horizontal semi-axis. Increasing the force will increase the deformation of the ellipse, which is reflected in α getting smaller. This is illustrated in Figures 12.4a to 12.4c, which show a sequence of profiles of the rubber cylinder under increasing downward force. So the different $M(\alpha)$ are ellipses with semi-axes of length α and $1/\alpha$. The property P we are interested in is the surface area of the ellipse, and we readily find that $P(\alpha) = \pi$ for all $\alpha > 0$.[8] We can now ask what happens to the profile and the area in the limit for $\alpha \to 0$. Since $P(\alpha) = \pi$ for all $\alpha > 0$ we have $P_0 = \pi$. Yet at $\alpha = 0$ the object $M(\alpha)$ is a line: it is infinitely extended and one-dimensional (its "thickness" is literally zero). This is illustrated in Figure 12.4d. But the surface of a line is zero and so we have $P(0) = 0$ at the limit. Hence, $P(0) \neq P_0$.

This simple example illustrates Berry's point that a singular limit involves concepts that are qualitatively very different. The model at the limit is a one-dimensional object while models away from the limit are two-dimensional, and these objects require different concepts to describe them adequately. It also illustrates the epistemic and methodological differences between singular and regular limits. As we have seen, if a limit is regular, we can study the object at the limit and draw valid inferences about the object close to the limit. This strategy fails if the limit is singular. Studying a line will not reveal anything about an ellipse, no matter how squeezed the ellipse is. Investigating the properties of the model at the limit gives no information about the properties of the models "on the way to the limit" unless the limit is regular, no matter how close to the limit a model is.

Science is rife with singular limits. Prominent examples are the so-called classical limit of quantum mechanics, the low velocity limit of special relativity, and the Newtonian limit of general relativity, all of which recover classical Newtonian mechanics in one way or other. Further examples are the thermodynamic limit of statistical mechanics (which recovers classical thermodynamics) and the low-wavelength limit of wave optics (which recovers ray optics). All these limits are singular in that qualitatively different behaviour appears at the limit. In the classical limit, for instance, an indeterministic theory becomes deterministic. The details of these limits are complicated, and their correct formulation is subtle and often a matter of controversy. The issues that arise go deep into the foundations of the respective disciplines, and a discussion of these is beyond the scope of this book. However, to illustrate the kind of issues that arise when considering such limits, and to explain how these issues relate to the conceptual apparatus introduced in this section, we now have a brief look at the thermodynamic limit in the context of a study of phase transitions, which will also illustrate how broader philosophical issues depend on the nature of limits.

Phase transitions are a familiar phenomenon: if we cool water below zero, it transitions from the liquid phase to the solid phase (it becomes ice), and if we heat it above 100°C it transitions from the liquid phase to the gaseous phase (it becomes vapour). The theoretical description of these transitions in statistical mechanics involves what is known as a thermodynamic limit: letting the number of particles in the model tend towards infinity while at the same time letting the volume of the model tend to infinity so that the particle density stays constant. In this context α is the particle number, $M(\alpha)$ is model with α particles in it, and the relevant limit is $\alpha \to \infty$. Taking this limit is crucial because in statistical mechanics a phase transition is commonly associated with the free energy function of a model being non-analytic (in intuitive terms this means the derivative of the function becomes discontinuous, i.e. it looks something like the function in Figure 12.1b). The analyticity of the free energy function is the property $P(\alpha)$ we are interested in. The function depends on α and it is a mathematical fact that for *any* finite α the function is analytic, and a non-analyticity *only* occurs for an infinite model. So we are in a situation where the limit $\alpha \to \infty$ is singular because models on the way to the limit are all analytical and the non-analyticity only occurs at the limit. In fact, the situation is like in Redhead's example with the ellipse where a sudden change takes place at the limit. Because the non-analyticity of the free energy function is crucial, statistical mechanics considers models with infinitely many particles and sets $\alpha = \infty$.

The correct understanding of the thermodynamic limit is the subject matter of a spirited debate. Some argue that the fact that a non-analyticity occurs only at the limit has to be taken seriously and submit that thermodynamics only applies to systems that are "idealized to be actually infinite" and that this "idealization is necessary" (Ruelle 2004, 2). But since real systems are never infinite (and yet phenomena of interest occur only at the limit), the conclusion is drawn that phenomena of interest are *emergent* phenomena that are irreducible to the underling micro-theory (Batterman 2002). In other words, a limit being singular is used to support a view of macro-properties and macro-laws as emergent. Others push back against this view and argue that no actual infinity is needed and that therefore limiting behaviour is neither emergent not indicative of a failure of reduction. Norton (2012) reaches this conclusion by demoting the limit to a mere approximation, understood as a purely mathematical operation (see Section 11.4).

The functions of real finite systems are analytical, but they have to be such that they can be approximated by the kind of non-analytical functions that result from an infinite system in something like the way in which $\sin(\alpha)$ can be approximated by α. That such an approximation is possible, argues Norton, is all that is required for a phase transition to take place. The non-analytic functions have pragmatic value but should not be taken seriously, either metaphysically or methodologically. Butterfield (2011) also argues against the conclusion that phase transition can only occur in an actually infinite system, but rather than appealing to approximations, he argues that there is "emergence before the limit" and that such emergence is compatible with reductionism because it does not require actual infinities.[9]

This is not the place to adjudicate between these positions. The point that matters here is that far-reaching views about reduction and emergence depend on how limit idealisations are understood, and a discussion of these doctrines will have to pay careful attention to the issues we have discussed in this section.

12.4   Factor Exclusions

Rather than distorting a certain property by pushing it to an extreme, one can omit properties altogether. As we have seen in Section 11.3, omitting properties that do not fall under a respect that is represented in the model is an abstraction, and models involving only abstractions provide truthful yet incomplete representations of the target. We now turn to the question of how we should understand situations in which we leave out properties that *do* fall under a respect that is represented in the model. What is the epistemic import of models that are idealised in this way? To answer this question, we now introduce a general schema to describe first the exclusion, and then the successive reintegration, of properties into a model. For reasons that will become clear soon, we call this the *inclusion scheme*.[10] We then discuss different uses and interpretations of this scheme.

Let R be a predicate specifying a certain type of system. R could, for instance, be "is a swing", "is a hydrogen atom", "is a population of fish", or "is an open economy". The variable o refers to an object in the world and " $R(o)$" means that object o is an R. Returning to the example in Section 11.2, if o refers to the big toy in the schoolyard and R is assumed to be "is a swing", then $R(o)$ says that the big toy in the schoolyard is a swing. Let $f_1,...,f_n$ be factors that contribute to a certain aspect of the phenomenon under study (where n is a natural number), and let us assume that this aspect is represented in the model. In our example, the aspect is the force acting on the swing and the factors are the various contributions to the total force (air resistance, friction, buoyancy, and so on).[11] We write " $f_i(o) = 0$ " to indicate that i^{th} factor is taken to be absent in object o. In our example, $f_1(o) = 0$ means that the swing has no air resistance. We denote by Q a quantity of the object o that we wish to determine, for instance the amplitude of the swing at a given time t. Finally, let $v_1,...,v_m$ be physical magnitudes (other than Q) that characterise the system (where m is a natural number). In our example $v_1(o)$ could be the initial amplitude of the swing at time $t = 0$, $v_2(o)$ could be the mass of the swing, $v_3(o)$ could be the length of the rope of the swing.

With this in place, consider the following statement:

(I0) For all o: if $R(o)$ & $f_1(o) = 0$ & ... & $f_n(o) = 0$, then $Q(o) = g_0[v_1(o), ..., v_m(o)]$

We call this statement "I0" to indicate that it describes an idealisation (hence "I") and that *none* of the factors $f_1, ..., f_n$ have been included (hence "0"). The statement says for all objects o that are R, it is the case that if all factors are zero, then quantity Q is given by the function g_0 which only depends on the physical magnitudes v_i. The function g_0 results from a study of the model. In our example, this statement says that for any swing, if and there is no air resistance, no friction, no buoyancy, no . . ., then the amplitude of the swing is given by function $g_0 = v_1(o)$, meaning that the amplitude stays constant at the initial level of $v_1(o)$ for all times and does not depend on any other factors.

The antecedent of this conditional defines a model, namely one in which all factors $f_1, ..., f_n$ are absent. The target of the model is an object o, and so the model represents o as not having $f_1, ..., f_n$. The consequent of the conditional states that a certain result holds true in the model, namely that the quantity Q is given by function g_0.

I say that the factors $f_1, ..., f_n$ have been *excluded* in such a model and refer to the kind of idealisation that leads to (I0) as a *factor exclusion*. However, terminology varies. Cartwright (1989), Krajewski (1977), and Niiniluoto (1986) refer to the exclusion of factors as "idealisation"; Nowak (1980) calls it both "idealisation" and "abstraction" and often seems to use the terms interchangeably; Laymon (1995) dubs it "subtraction"; and Mäki (1994) refers to it as "isolation". Ultimately, nothing depends on the choice of words, but I would like to avoid referring to exclusion as "abstraction" because this would contradict the use of the term in Section 11.3 (because in general excluding factors introduces a falsehood into the model).

After excluding all factors, one can ask what happens when the exclusions are reversed one by one. It is natural to refer to the process of putting excluded factors back into the model as *inclusion*. Terminology again varies. Nowak (1980) calls this process "concretisation"; Krajewski (1977) refers to it as "factualisation"; Laymon (1995) labels it "addition"; Mäki (1994) refers to it as "de-isolation"; and occasionally it is also referred to simply as "de-idealisation" (McMullin 1985). Including the first factor, f_1, into the model leads to

(I1) For all o: if $R(o)$ & $f_1(o) = c_1$ & $f_2(o) = 0$ & . . . & $f_n(o) = 0$, then
      $Q(o) = g_1[v_1(o), ..., v_m(o), f_1(o)]$,

where $c_1 \neq 0$ is the value of factor f_1 in o. We call this statement "I1" to indicate that it is an idealisation that includes the first factor. In our example this means that we no longer assume air resistance to be absent in the swing, and that the air resistance is assumed to have the specific value c_1. Again, one can see that the antecedent of this conditional defines a model, now one in which f_1 is no longer absent, and the consequent states that Q is given by different function g_1. It is crucial that if the first factor is no longer omitted, then the functional dependence of Q on the other variables can change, which is taken care of by replacing function g_0 by function g_1. Note that the resulting function g_1 will now, in general, depend on the included factor $f_1(o)$. In our example, if air resistance is no longer excluded, then g_1 will depend on the level of air restance.[12]

One can now repeat this procedure in a cascade-like manner, including one factor after the other. After having included k factors we have:

(Ik)　For all o: if $R(o)$ & $f_1(o) = c_1$ & $\ldots$ & $f_k(o) = c_k$ & $f_{k+1}(o) = 0$ & $\ldots$ &
　　　$f_n(o) = 0$, then $Q(o) = g_k[v_1(o), ..., v_m(o), f_1(o), ..., f_k(o)]$.

One can continue including factors until all omitted factors have been put back into the equation.[13] The result of this is:

(In)　For all o: if $R(o)$ & $f_1(o) = c_1$ & $\ldots$ & $f_n(o) = c_n$, then
　　　$Q(o) = g_n[v_1(o), ..., v_m(o), f_1(o), ..., f_n(o)]$.

We call the sequence (I0) $\ldots$ (In) the *inclusion scheme*.[14] For ease of notation, in the remainder of the chapter we let "$C_k(o)$" stand for the condition $f_1(o) = c_1$ & $\ldots$ & $f_k(o) = c_k$ & $f_{k+1}(o) = 0$ & $\ldots$ & $f_n(o) = 0$, and we omit the argument of the function for $Q(o)$ and just write g_k, thereby taking it as understood that g_k is a function of $v_1(o), ..., v_m(o), f_1(o), ..., f_k(o)$, and, possibly, other parameters such as time. With these notational conventions the above conditions can be rewritten as:

(Ik)　For all o : if $R(o)$ & $C_k(o)$, then $Q(o) = g_k$.

Let us add a few qualifications about to the inclusion scheme. First, it is important that the inclusion scheme concerns real properties. In excluding factors, we start from a completely realistic description of the system and then strip away factors. This process is not a matter of changing or distorting properties, and when excluded factors are included again, they have to be put back into the scheme as they are in reality.

Second, in formulating the inclusion scheme it is assumed that we know which factors have been excluded and that we know, at least in principle, how to put them back into the model. This amounts to saying that we consider what has been called a *controlled idealisation* (Sklar 1993, 258). In a controlled idealisation one knows which factors are left out. One can estimate in what ways and to what degree the result thus reached will diverge from the behaviour of the actual target, and there is the possibility to include the omitted factors again in a more advanced version of the model. This is exactly what happens if we move downward in the inclusion scheme. But not all idealisations are controlled. In some cases we simply may not know how the model differs from the target. Such idealisations are *uncontrolled* idealisations. As an example of an model that is constructed through an uncontrolled idealisation, Morgan and Morrison (1999, 28) offer the liquid drop model of the nucleus, which is not constructed by mentally stripping away factors from the actual nucleus and hence cannot be improved by putting the excluded factors back into the model. For this reason, Nowak makes the assumption that for every property Q there is a *complete* space of factors $f_1, ..., f_n$ influencing the property. Completeness means that (In), which includes all factors that have an influence on Q, is a literally true and complete description of the actual target. If the list of factors is incomplete – i.e. if there are factors influencing Q that do not appear in the list of factors in the inclusion scheme – then Nowak says that we are dealing with a *semi-idealisation* and not an idealisation (Nowak 1992, 31–32).

Third, an important question concerns the nature of the functions $g_k(o)$. The exact form of the functions depends on the problem at hand, but a general condition emerges from Krajewski's discussions of the van der Waals equation and of Ohm's law (1977, 326–327): if one lets factor f_k tend toward zero, then g_k has to tend toward g_{k-1}, and this has to hold true for all $k = 1, ..., n$. Intuitively this requirement says that if we remove the kth factor, and thereby in effect reverse the kth inclusion, then we get back to where the kth inclusion started, namely (Ik-1), the next lower level in the scheme. Niiniluoto (1986, 277) calls this the *principle of correspondence*. Our simple example satisfies this principle because one can show that if one writes down the trajectory of a pendulum with air resistance (which is (I1)) and then lets the strength of the air resistance tend towards zero, one recovers the equation of the undamped oscillation (see Section 12.3, and in particular Figure 12.3).

Fourth, the above formulation of (Ik) has the form "for all o: if ... then ...". This is how the conditionals are formulated in the literature.[15] This makes it look as if (Ik) were material conditionals. That, however, cannot be right. In most cases, the antecedent of the conditional, $R(o)$ & $C_k(o)$, will be false (in the real world there are no swings that move without air resistance!), and so the conditional itself will end up being trivially true. This is off the mark because there is a clear sense in which (Ik) can be false even if the relevant antecedent is not instantiated. A response to this problem is to say that the conditional in (Ik) is actually a *counterfactual conditional* (Niiniluoto 1986, 277). Stated more accurately, (Ik) then says that "for all o: if $R(o)$ & $C_k(o)$ were the case, then it would be the case that $Q(o) = g_k$". (Ik) is then no longer trivially true whenever $C_k(o)$ is false. The truth conditions of this conditional are nowadays stated in term of possible worlds. Let a "C_k-world" be a possible world in which all objects o that are R also satisfy condition C_k. A C_1-world in our example is a world in which all swings are subject only to gravity and air resistance. According to the standard semantics for counterfactuals, (Ik) is true iff in the C_k-world that is closest to the actual world it is true that $Q(o) = g_k$ (Lewis 1973). This move is plausible, but it comes at a cost. Not only do we have to buy into the entire framework of possible worlds;

we also face the epistemic problem of how we come to know whether (Ik) is true. Modal epistemology is a difficult matter and there is a question of how the truth of a claim like (Ik) is established.[16]

With these clarifications made, let us finally reflect on the relation between factor exclusion and limit idealisation. As we have seen, limit idealisations push a property to the extreme, while exclusions eliminate them entirely. Many idealisations are clearly categorisable as either one or the other. Whenever properties of the entire system like spatial extension and the number of constituent particles are concerned, we are dealing with limits. If we idealise a gas as having an infinity of particles or condenser plates as being infinitely extended, it makes little sense to describe these idealisations as the exclusion of the factor "particle-finiteness" or the exclusion of the factor of "extension-finiteness". They are idealisations that involve taking a limit rather than excluding factors. Vice versa, if we idealise the particles in the gas as being such that they cannot collide or a population as developing in isolation, then we cannot re-describe this as involving a limiting process. Either particles can collide or they cannot, and either a population develops in isolation or it does not. These are cases of factors – collisions and the environment – being excluded.

It is, however, immediately clear that there is an overlap between the two ways of thinking about idealisation whenever quantities can vary continuously and we can take a limit for the quantity going to zero. One can let the strengths of a factor tend towards zero and see the eventual disappearance of that factor as a limit idealisation; or one can exclude the factor directly and see the idealisation as an exclusion. Our example of air resistance is a case in point. We can think of it as a quantity that can tend towards zero (which is what we have done in Section 12.3) or we can think of it as factor that can be omitted (which is what we have done in this section).

In this case it should not matter which way one looks at the situation: A model that simply excludes a factor and one that has it but takes it to the limit value zero must give the same result. Karjewski and Niiniluoto's principle of correspondence guarantees that this is the case. If we impose this principle as a condition on the inclusion scheme, then it does not matter which way one looks at such idealisations. This leads to the question of when the scheme satisfies the principle, and our discussion in the previous section gives us an answer: it does if the limit is regular. The condition that g_k tend toward g_{k-1} as f_k tends towards zero is in fact a restatement of the condition that the limit be regular because g_{k-1} is in effect g_k at the limit for $f_k = 0$. If one adheres to the principle of correspondence, then the inclusion scheme cannot be used if one of the limits $f_k \rightarrow 0$ is singular. So understanding limit idealisation is important also for understanding how to handle exclusions and inclusions.

Let us briefly return to our above examples of factor exclusions that are not limit idealisations: particle collision and environmental isolation. One might respond that these examples do not hold water because these exclusions can be recast as limits. A gas without particle interaction can be seen as a limiting case of gas with interactions when one takes the limit of the cross section toward zero, and an isolated population can be seen a limiting case of a population that does interact with its environment when we take the strength of the interaction to zero. And, so the argument goes, the same move can be made for every exclusion. It is an open question whether every case of an idealisation that prima facie looks like an exclusion can eventually be recast as limit idealisation, but, for the sake of argument, let us assume that this is so. What are the consequences? Has the inclusion scheme become obsolete? It would seem not. Even if such an "ultimate reduction" were possible, it remains the case that in practice many idealisations are treated as factors that are removed and added, and even if one thinks of removal and addition as limits, we need to have a complete list of all f_k and g_k to know what limits to take. Indeed, thinking about factors in terms of limits presupposes that we know (In) and then take the relevant parameters to zero in order to get to (Ik), but this is an unrealistic way of thinking about a model which is often constructed by adding factors to a simple model like $(I0)$. So even if one thinks of exclusions as limits, the inclusion scheme has significant heuristic value.

12.5   Galilean and Minimalist Idealisations

The inclusion scheme provides us with a framework in which we can discuss two important kinds of idealisation, namely Galilean idealisation and minimalist idealisation.

To make a complicated problem tractable, scientists can introduce deliberate simplifications. When studying the motion of falling objects, Galileo considered situations in which "impeding" factors like friction and air resistance were excluded, and when calculating the orbit of a satellite scientists focus, at least in the first instance, on the gravitational force exerted by the earth on the satellite and neglect other forces such as the gravitational pull of the sun and the moon. Because idealisations of this kind played an important role in Galileo's scientific thinking, they are now often referred to as "Galilean Idealisations".[17]

Galilean idealisations have three defining characteristics. First, situations are often so complicated that a realistic model of them would be unmanageable. As Weisberg puts it, "Galilean idealization is the practice of introducing distortions into theories with the goal of simplifying theories in order to make them computationally tractable" (2007, 640). For instance, it would be very difficult, if not impossible, to construct a model of a satellite that includes literally all factors and then solve its equations. Galilean idealisations serve the practical goal of simplifying a complicated situation so that that the resulting model is manageable. Second, the idealisation is meant to provide useable information about the target. In McMullin's words, the purpose of a Galilean idealisation is not "simply to escape from the intractable irregularity of the real world into the intelligible order of Form"; rather it is to "make *use* of this order in an attempt to grasp the real world from which the idealization takes its origin" (1985, 248, original emphasis).

Third, Galilean idealisations can ultimately be "de-idealised" by removing simplifying assumptions. This is closely tied to scientific progress. As new techniques to deal with complicated equations – such as powerful computers – become available, scientists can put factors back into the model that they have initially omitted. In doing so, they remove distortions and make the model more realistic. In principle this process of "re-inclusion" can be continued until all factors are back in the model, which is then a completely realistic representation. For this reason, as Elliott-Graves and Weisberg put it, the "characteristic feature of Galilean idealization is that the distortions are supposed to be temporary, at least in principle" (2014, 177).

The inclusion scheme in the previous section allows us to give a precise formulation of Galilean idealisation and its three defining characteristics. In fact, (I0) is a Galilean idealisation! It has the first feature because g_0 is usually tractable and, if plugged into an equation, leads to a tractable equation. In our example with the swing (I0) describes a model in which the only force acting on the swing is linear gravity and all other factors like air resistance and friction are excluded. The equation of this model is easily solved, as we have seen in Section 11.2. (I0) also has the third feature in an obvious way. By marking the beginning of the inclusion scheme, (I0) can obviously be de-idealised until the perfectly realistic model described by (In) is reached.

The second feature requires more work. What exactly is it that (I0), or any (Ik) for $k < n$, tells us about the actual target system? Answering this question requires understanding what happens if only a few inclusion steps are carried out and if the model stops short of reaching (In). Nowak in effect addresses this question by claiming that results converge to the true value as one moves down the scheme, and the further down one gets the closer one comes to the truth (Nowak 1992, 12; cf. Nowakowa and Nowak 1998, 37).[18] Formally, this means that for all $k < n$ there is a threshold ε_k so that the value of $Q(x)$ given by (Ik) is not more than ε_k away from the true value. The fact that the results converge as one moves down the scheme means that $\varepsilon_k \le \varepsilon_l$ when $k > l$ for all k and l. It is important to note, however, that this does not happen automatically, as it were. Whether Nowak's condition is satisfied depends on the situation at hand. So one can say that meeting Nowak's condition is necessary for an idealisation to be a Galilean idealisation. The swing is a case that fits the mould of Nowak's scheme. Nelson and Olsson (1986) offer an in-depth treatment of the system and go to great length to include a host of factors that have initially been left out. At every step their results get more precise, as the doctrine of convergence suggests.

In cases that meet Nowak's condition, one can sometimes also achieve a rapprochement of model and target by designing carefully controlled experiments.[19] The idea is intuitive: rather than including certain factors in the model, which may be complicated, one can contrive a target so that the factors are absent. For instance, rather than correcting for air resistance, we could let the real swing move in a vacuum. In such a situation, including air resistance would not only be unnecessary, it would actually be a mistake. In this way, the inclusion scheme then serves as a guide to the construction of controlled laboratory experiments that are closer to idealised models than targets "in the wild".

Galilean idealisations are such that de-idealisation is always possible, at least in principle, and initially excluded factors can, and wherever feasible should, be included in the model.[20] There are approaches to idealisation that disagree with this methodological prescription and insist that in many cases the successive inclusion of formerly excluded factors is undesirable, even if it was feasible. Weisberg calls such idealisations *minimalist idealisations*, and the models that are the product of such idealisations are *minimalist models* or, simply, *minimal models* (2007, 642).[21] The defining feature of a minimalist idealisation is that it produces a model that includes only the core factors that give rise to a phenomenon and excludes everything else. So contra Galilean idealisation, minimalist idealisation counsels against de-idealisation and insists that factors that are not essential to the production of the phenomenon under investigation must be, and must remain, excluded. This basic idea has been formulated and justified in different ways by different authors, and we will now have look at some of these formulations.

A minimalist idealisation is appropriate if the exclusions are what Musgrave calls *negligibility assumptions*. Excluding a factor is a negligibility assumption if "some factor [. . .] which might be expected to affect [the] phenomenon actually has no effect upon it" (Musgrave 1981, 378). Assume this factor is f_{k+1}. Then including f_{k+1} will not change the functional dependence of Q on the factors and so one trivially has $g_k = g_{k+1}$. If this is the case for all factors with an index greater than k, then there is simply no need to include any of them and g_k will give truthful results.

Strevens articulates this idea in the context of causal explanation.[22] The starting point of an investigation, according to Strevens, is a causal model of the phenomenon. This model can include all kind of causal factors. Initially the only requirement is that the causal models are strong enough to entail the phenomenon. The task then is to pare down the model to the essentials and get rid of all causal factors that are unnecessary. The criterion for being necessary is being a so-called *difference-maker*. A factor is a difference maker for a phenomenon if the phenomenon would not occur without the factor. Strevens provides the example of the death of Rasputin (2008, 88). The gravitational pull of Mars had an influence on the trajectory of the bullets that killed him (maybe one of the bullets hit Rasputin's body one picometer further to the left than it would without it). But this influence made no difference: the bullet would have killed Rasputin even if Mars did not interact with objects on earth. For this reason, the interaction of Mars with terrestrial objects is not a difference-maker. On Strevens' so-called kairetic account, we provide an explanation of a phenomenon if we construct a model that contains *only* difference-makers. An explanatory model has to be paired down to the essentials; if the model contains causal irrelevancies – factors that do not make a difference – it does not explain. This conflicts with Galilean idealisation because the factors that have been excluded in the production of the explanatory model cannot be included again without destroying the explanatory force of the model – indeed, it is precisely the exclusion of these factors that makes the model explanatory. In terms of the inclusion scheme this means that if factors $f_1, ..., f_k$ are the difference makers, then no other factors must be included in the model, even if this was both possible and feasible.

Batterman and Rice do not appeal to causation in their account of minimalist explanation, and they also do not presuppose that a model can be decomposed into various causal factors that can be included or excluded individually.[23] Instead, Batterman and Rice take minimal models to be highly simplified models that disregard much of the details in the target system and that are known to be inaccurate in a great many ways. We are then invited to focus on the large-scale macroscopic behaviour of these models rather than on their micro-structure, as this is what matters to their use. For example, the so-called Lattice Gas Automaton (LGA) model of a gas omits a myriad of details about molecules in a real gas and radically misrepresents their motion and the way in which they collide; and yet it reproduces the correct pattern of how a gas flows around a barrier and of how the velocity of particles at one point in space depends on the velocity of particles at other points in space (2014, 358–361). But that the LGA model exhibits the correct macro pattern of how a gas behaves might still be a lucky coincidence. To show that this is not the case one now has to broaden the investigation and look at an entire class of models rather than only the model one started with. This class has to be so broad that it contains both the original model and a truthful representation of the target. The crucial step now is to show that the relevant macro patterns are *universal* in this class in the sense that all models in this class show the same macro patterns irrespective of their details. In other words, we have to show that the details that are either distorted or excluded make no difference to the macro-behaviour that we are interested in.[24] Once this is done, one is justified in using the minimal model to explain the behaviour of the real system because it is in the same universality class as the true model of the real system. To show that such a class exists and that the relevant models are in it is no easy feat, and it is achieved with a complicated mathematical technique called the *renormalisation group* (*ibid.*, 361–364). The details of this technique are beyond the scope of our discussion; what matters is that renormalisation offers the "backstory" about why, and how, a radically simplified model can be used to explain the properties of its target system.[25]

In sum, minimalist idealisations differ from Galilean idealisations in two ways. First, the aim of a minimalist idealisations is not pragmatic (i.e. to produce a tractable model); the aim of a minimalist idealisations is to explain. Second, minimal models cannot be de-idealised without thereby destroying the model's explanatory function: explanation is antithetical to de-idealisation. In this sense, minimal idealisations are ineliminable.

The discussion in this section has put a spotlight on the question "why idealise?", and we have seen that there is no unitary answer to this question. Idealisations simplify situations, and with simplification comes tractability. Idealised models are an expedient for epistemically limited beings. They provide results in situations that one is unable to tackle in their full complexity and they yield predictions where faithful descriptions remain silent. Galilean idealisation sees these pragmatic virtues as central in justifying the use of idealisation, and the focus on tractability is shared also by approaches that are not committed to the Galilean programme.[26] But the potential purposes of idealisation are not exhausted by pragmatic considerations. As we have seen, minimalist idealisations are seen as desirable due to their explanatory power. But minimalist idealisations are not the only kind of idealisation that can explain. Batterman (2009) argues that many limit idealisations (which we have discussed in Section 12.3) are explanatorily ineliminable and that explanations cannot be obtained through more complete and non-idealised models. Other authors regard all idealisations as explanatory. Bokulich (2009, 2011) reasons that the idealisations in a model uncover explanatory patterns of counterfactual dependence. Hindriks (2013) argues that idealised models play an explanatory role when scientists start relaxing some of its unrealistic assumptions and in doing so provide causal explanations of why the model regularities fail to obtain in the target system. Graham Kennedy (2012) submits that idealisations explain because they generate comparisons which help uncover causal mechanisms. Jebeile and Graham Kennedy (2016) see idealisations as crucial to the identification of explanatory components in a model. Weirich (2011) argues models are explanatory if there is an isomorphism between model-features and certain target-features. Finally, Gallegos Ordorica (2016) argues that not only idealisations, but also abstractions (as discussed in Section 11.3) explain.

Recent debates have also emphasised the role idealisations play in scientific understanding. Elgin (2004, 2017) argues that the fact that idealisations, if interpreted literally, are falsehoods, does not make them dispensable expedients. On the contrary, they are "felicitous falsehoods" (2017, 1) and understanding is non-factive. Scientific understanding involves "an epistemic commitment to a comprehensive, systematically linked body of information that is grounded in fact, is duly responsive to reasons or evidence, and enables nontrivial inference, argument, and perhaps action regarding the topic the information pertains to" (*ibid.*, 44). Idealisations, Elgin argues, play an important, and, crucially, ineliminable, role in gaining understanding in this sense because they make an essential contribution to the construction of a comprehensive and systematically linked body of information.[27] In a similar vein, Potochnik (2017) argues that scientific understanding is often furthered by sacrificing truth and accuracy. She notes that recognising simple patterns is cognitively valuable and that idealisations aid scientists in the pursuit of simple patterns, which is why idealisations, even though they are falsehoods, promote understanding. Khalifa (2017) agrees that idealisations provide understanding, but he prefers to see them as quasi-factive rather than non-factive, which requires at least approximate truth. De Regt (2017) locates understanding in intelligible theories that are both empirically adequate and internally consistent, and such theories often involve idealisations. Differences notwithstanding,[28] these authors agree that idealisation contributes to understanding, and that it does so in an ineliminable way: removing idealisations would annihilate understanding.

12.6   Conclusion

We have introduced and analysed two different types of idealisations, namely limit idealisations and factor exclusions, and we discussed the relationship between them. The scheme introduced to analyse factor exclusions has also proven to be a fruitful tool for understanding Galilean idealisations and minimal idealisations. There is no claim that these cover all idealisations in science, and there is scope for further discussions.

Notes

1   For ease of presentation, and to keep the discussion intuitive, we only discuss the case of real valued functions. Limits can of course be studied for other functions, and indeed in other contexts such as number sequences and function sequences. These are discussed in any introduction to calculus, for instance Spivak's (1994). Their philosophical relevance in the context of limit idealisation is discussed in Nguyen and Frigg's (2020).

2   This is the standard definition of a limit that can be found in every textbook on calculus; see, for instance, Spivak's (1994, 96).

3   Taking liberties is necessary because ∞ is not, strictly speaking, a number. In the current context, we can set this problem aside and consider the function to be defined on $\mathbb{R} \cup \infty$, where "$\mathbb{R}$" denotes the real numbers (Butterfield 2011, 1075).

4   Butterfield uses the term "non-singular". I use "regular" and "non-singular" interchangeably. Regular limits are closely related to what Laymon (1991, 167) calls *ideal limits*, which require that the closer the system comes to the limit, the closer the system's behaviour must come to the behaviour of the system at the limit.

5   Mathematically, the argument is as follows. Considering air resistance amounts to adding the term $-\alpha \, d\theta / dt$ to the right-hand side of Equation 11.2, where α is the parameter for air resistance. The solutions to this equation show that the envelopes of $M(\alpha)$ are $P(\alpha) = \pm A e^{-(k\alpha)t}$, where k is a constant that depends on the specifics of system (see, for instance, Young and Freedman 2000, Ch. 13). It is then obvious that $\lim_{\alpha \to 0} \pm A e^{-t(k\alpha)} = \pm A$ for all $t \in [0, t_e]$.

6   Further to the previous endnote, the calculations are as follows. The surface of the grey area is given by $2A \int_0^{t_e} [1 - e^{-(k\alpha)t}] dt$. Using the fact that the integral of e^{ct} is e^{ct} / c for all $c \neq 0$, calculating the definite integral for the given upper and lower bounds, and expanding the resulting expression into a Taylor series, we find that the integral is equal to $2AO(\alpha)$, where $O(\alpha)$ is polynomial in α containing only terms of order α or higher. This implies that $\lim_{\alpha \to 0} O(\alpha) = 0$ and hence the surface of the grey area tends towards zero when $\alpha \to 0$.

7   The question of how we learn from limit idealisations is discussed in greater detail in Nguyen and Frigg's (2020).

8   The surface of an ellipse is π times the product of the two semi-axes, hence $P(\alpha) = \pi\alpha(1/\alpha) = \pi$.

9   For a survey of, and an introduction to, infinite limits in physics, see Shech's (2018). Belot (2005) offers critical comments on Batterman's discussion; Batterman (2005) replies to them. For further discussions of this issue, see Bangu's (2009), Butterfield's (2014), Knox's (2016), Palacios' (2019), and Strevens (2019). Bokulich (2008) discusses the transition from quantum to classic mechanics. Pincock (2014) reflects on the ontological commitments incurred by infinite idealisations and their implications for the realism debate.

10   The canonical source for the scheme is Nowak's (1980, Part III). Earlier treatments have been given in Nowak's (1972, 536–538) and Krajewski's (1977, 333–336). Statements

of the scheme can be found in Nowak's (1992, 10–14, 2000, 110–128), and Nowakowa and Nowak's (1998, 36–37), as well as in Cartwright's (1989, Ch. 5, 202–206), Laymon's (1995), and Niiniluoto's (1986, 275–284). Kuokannen and Tuomivaara (1992) analyse the scheme from the structuralist point of view that we introduced in Chapter 7.

11 Not all factors are the same. Nowak (1992, 30, 30–31) and Mäki (1994, 150–159) draw a number of distinctions that contribute to a classification of factors. Grüne-Yanoff (2011) argues against Mäki's claim that isolation is a common method in model-building.

12 It follows directly from what has been said in endnote 5 that for our pendulum the function is $g_1 = \pm A e^{-(k\alpha)t}$.

13 An interesting question concerns the issue of whether g_k can be written as a sum of contributions of each individual factor f_i for $i = 1,...,k$. For a discussion of this issue, see Laymon's (1995).

14 Nowak (1992, 12) refers to (In) as the "final concretisation" and to each (Ik) as an "idealisation statement". Some factors are more significant than others. Nowak calls the most important factors "principal factors" and the others "secondary factors" (Nowak 1992, 11). The notion of significance has to be adopted as primitive and all attempts to define it suffer from "severe drawbacks" (*ibid.*). The set of factors ordered by the antisymmetric and transitive relation *more significant than* is the *essential structure* of Q (Nowak 2000, 111).

15 See, for instance, Nowak's (1972) and (1991).

16 See, for instance, Williamson's (2005) for a discussion of this issue.

17 The first example is discussed in McMullin's (1985, 266) and the second in Elliott-Graves and Weisberg's (2014, 177). I here follow Weisberg's (2007, 640–642) and Elliott-Graves and Weisberg's (*ibid.*) characterisation of Galilean idealisations. The term "Galilean Idealisation" entered the current debate through McMullin's paper. As described by McMullin, Galilean idealisation encompasses what I call exclusion (1985, 258). But at the same time McMullin also includes other aspects like the mathematisation of nature in his discussion, which I have covered in Chapter 6. For a discussion of Galilean idealisation in the context of thought experiments, see Reiss' (2018).

18 Nowakowa and Nowak use the term "approximation" and say that (Ik) becomes a good approximation of (In) (2000, 10). I use "convergence" in order to avoid conflict with the notion of approximation developed in Section 11.4.

19 See, for instance, Cartwright's (1989, 186–187), Laymon's (1995, 355–356), and Weisberg's (2007, 641).

20 In practice things may be less straightforward. See Knuuttila and Morgan's (2019) for a discussion of difficulties faced by de-idealisation.

21 As far as I can see, Weisberg uses "minimalist model" and "minimal model" interchangeably. We will encounter a use of "minimal model" that contradicts Weisberg's in Section 16.3.

22 See in particular Chapters 3 and 8 of Strevens' (2008). For a discussion of his account, see Levy's (2012) and Nola's (2011). For a discussion of the use of difference-makers for predictions, see Strevens' (2021).

23 Indeed, Rice (2019) argues that such a decomposition is typically impossible.

24 It is worth noting that there are far reaching similarities between an approach to models based on universality and robustness reasoning, which we discuss in Section 15.3.

25 For a general discussion of renormalisation, see Butterfield and Bouatta's (2015); for a discussion of the explanatory function of renormalization, see Reutlinger's (2017).

26 See, for instance, Gale's (1998, 165), Jones' (2005, 187), Laymon's (1990, 520), Norton's (2012, 209), and Rueger's (1998, 201).

27 For a discussion of Elgin's account, see, for instance, Baumberger and Brun's (2017), Frigg and Nguyen's (2021), and Lawler's (2021). For further discussions of how simplified models provide understanding, see Illari's (2019).

28 For a comparison of the different positions, see Potochnik's (2020).

References

Bangu, S. 2009. Understanding Thermodynamic Singularities: Phase Transitions, Data, and Phenomena. *Philosophy of Science* 76: 488–505.

Batterman, R. W. 2002. *The Devil in the Details: Asymptotic Reasoning in Explanation, Reduction, and Emergence*. Oxford: Oxford University Press.

Batterman, R. W. 2005. Response to Belot's 'Whose Devil? Which Details?'. *Philosophy of Science* 72: 154–163.

Batterman, R. W. 2009. Idealization and Modeling. *Synthese* 169: 427–446.

Batterman, R. W. and C. C. Rice 2014. Minimal Model Explanations. *Philosophy of Science* 81: 349–376.

Baumberger, C. and G. Brun 2017. Dimensions of Objectual Understanding. In S. Grimm, C. Baumberger, and S. Ammon (eds.), *Explaining Understanding: New Perspectives from Epistemology and Philosophy of Science*. New York: Routledge, pp. 165–189.

Belot, G. 2005. Whose Devil? Which Details? *Philosophy of Science* 72: 128–153.

Berry, M. 2002. Singular Limits. *Physics Today* 55: 10–11.

Bokulich, A. 2008. *Reexamining the Quantum-Classical Relation: Beyond Reductionism and Pluralism*. Cambridge: Cambridge University Press.

Bokulich, A. 2009. Explanatory Fictions. In M. Suárez (ed.), *Fictions in Science: Philosophical Essays on Modelling and Idealization*. London and New York: Routledge, pp. 91–109.

Bokulich, A. 2011. How Scientific Models Can Explain. *Synthese* 180: 33–45.

Butterfield, J. 2011. Less Is Different: Emergence and Reduction Reconciled. *Foundations of Physics* 41: 1065–1135.

Butterfield, J. 2014. Reduction, Emergence and Renormalisation. *The Journal of Philosophy* 111: 5–49.

Butterfield, J. and N. Bouatta 2015. Renormalization for Philosophers. In T. Bigaj and C. Wüthrich (eds.), *Metaphysics in Contemporary Physics* (Poznań Studies in the Philosophy of the Sciences and the Humanities 104). Amsterdam: Rodopi pp. 437–485.

Cartwright, N. 1989. *Nature's Capacities and Their Measurement*. Oxford: Oxford University Press.

de Regt, H. W. 2017. *Understanding Scientic Understanding*. Oxford: Oxford University Press.

Elgin, C. Z. 2004. True Enough. *Philosophical Issues* 14: 113–131.

Elgin, C. Z. 2017. *True Enough*. Cambridge, MA and London: MIT Press.

Elliott-Graves, A. and M. Weisberg 2014. Idealization. *Philosophy Compass* 9: 176–185.

Frigg, R. and J. Nguyen 2021. Mirrors without Warnings. *Synthese* 198: 2427–2447.

Gale, G. 1998. Idealization in Cosmology: A Case Study. In N. Shanks (ed.), *Idealization IX: Idealization in Contemporary Physics. Poznań Studies in the Philosophy of the Sciences and the Humanities* (Vol. 63). Amsterdam: Rodopi, pp. 165–182.

Gallegos Ordorica, S. A. 2016. The Explanatory Role of Abstraction Processes in Models: The Case of Aggregations. *Studies in History and Philosophy of Science* 56: 161–167.

Graham Kennedy, A. 2012. A Non Representationalist View of Model Explanation. *Studies in History and Philosophy of Science* 43: 326–332.

Grüne-Yanoff, T. 2011. Isolation Is Not Characteristic of Models. *Erkenntnis* 25: 119–137.

Hindriks, F. 2013. Explanation, Understanding, and Unrealistic Models. *Studies in History and Philosophy of Science* 44: 523–531.

Illari, P. 2019. Mechanisms, Models and Laws in Understanding Supernovae. *Journal for General Philosophy of Science* 50: 63–84.

Jebeile, J. and A. Graham Kennedy 2016. Explaining with Models: The Role of Idealizations. *International Studies in the Philosophy of Science* 29: 383–392.

Jones, M. 2005. Idealization and Abstraction: A Framework. In M. Jones and N. Cartwright (eds.), *Idealization XII: Correcting the Model-Idealization and Abstraction in the Sciences* (Poznań Studies in the Philosophy of the Sciences and the Humanities 86). Amsterdam: Rodopi, pp. 173–217.

Khalifa, K. 2017. *Understanding, Explanation, and Scientific Knowledge*. Cambridge: Cambridge University Press.

Knox, E. 2016. Abstraction and Its Limits: Finding Space for Novel Explanation. *Nous* 50: 41–60.

Knuuttila, T. and M. S. Morgan 2019. Deidealization: No Easy Reversals. *Philosophy of Science* 68: 641–661.

Krajewski, W. 1977. Idealization and Factualization in Science. *Erkenntnis* 11: 323–339.

Kuokannen, M. and T. Tuomivaara 1992. On the Structure of Idealizations. In J. Brzezinski and L. Nowak (eds.), *Idealization III: Approximation and Truth* (Poznań Studies in the Philosophy of the Sciences and the Humanities 25). Amsterdam: Rodopi, pp. 67–102.

Lawler, I. 2021. Scientific Understanding and Felicitous Legitimate Falsehoods. *Synthese* 198: 6859–6887.

Laymon, R. 1990. Computer Simulations, Idealizations and Approximations. *Proceedings of the Biennial Meeting of the Philosophy of Science Association* (Vol. 2), pp. 519–534.

Laymon, R. 1991. Thought Experiments by Stevin, Mach and Gouy: Thought Experiments as Ideal Limits and as Semantic Domains. In T. Horowitz and G. J. Massey (eds.), *Thought Experiments in Science and Philosophy*. Savage, MD: Rowman and Littlefield, pp. 167–191.

Laymon, R. 1995. Experimentation and the Legitimacy of Idealization. *Philosophical Studies* 77: 353–375.

Levy, A. 2012. Makes a Difference. Review of Michael Strevens' Depth: An Account of Scientific Explanation. Harvard University Press, Cambridge, Ma, 2008. *Biology and Philosophy* 26: 459–467.

Lewis, D. K. 1973. *Counterfactuals*. Oxford: Blackwell.

Mäki, U. 1994. Isolation, Idealization and Truth in Economics. In B. Hamminga and N. B. De Marchi (eds.), *Idealization VI: Idealization in Economics* (Poznań Studies in the Philosophy of the Sciences and the Humanities 38). Amsterdam: Rodopi, pp. 147–168.

McMullin, E. 1985. Galilean Idealization. *Studies in the History and Philosophy of Science* 16: 247–273.

Morgan, M. S. and M. Morrison 1999. Models as Mediating Instruments. In M. Morgan and M. Morrison (eds.), *Models as Mediators: Perspectives on Natural and Social Science*. Cambridge: Cambridge University Press, pp. 10–37.

Musgrave, A. 1981. Unreal Assumptions' in Economic Theory: The F-Twist Untwisted. *Kyklos* 34: 377–387.

Nelson, R. A. and M. G. Olsson 1986. The Pendulum – Rich Physics from a Simple System. *American Journal of Physics* 54: 112–121.

Nguyen, J. and R. Frigg 2020. Unlocking Limits. *Argumenta* 6: 31–45.

Niiniluoto, I. 1986. Theories, Approximations, and Idealizations. In R. Barcan Marcus, G. J. W. Dorn, and P. Weingartner (eds.), *Logic, Methodology and Philosophy of Science VII: Proceedings of the Seventh International Congress of Logic, Methodology and Philosophy of Science, Salzburg, 1983*. Amsterdam, New York, Oxford, and Tokyo: Elsevier Science Publishers B.V., pp. 255–289.

Nola, R. 2011. Michael Strevens: Depth: An Account of Scientific Explanation. *Science and Education* 20: 201–206.

Norton, J. D. 2012. Approximation and Idealization: Why the Difference Matters. *Philosophy of Science* 79: 207–232.

Nowak, L. 1972. Laws of Science, Theories, Measurement: (Comments on Ernest Nagel's the Structure of Science). *Philosophy of Science* 39: 533–548.

Nowak, L. 1980. *The Structure of Idealization: Towards a Systematic Interpretation of the Marxian Idea of Science*. Dordrecht: Reidel.

Nowak, L. 1991. The Method of Relevant Variables and Idealization. In E. Eells and T. Maruszewski (eds.), *Probability and Rationality: Studies on L. Jonathan Cohen's Philosophy of Science* (Poznań Studies in the Philosophy of the Sciences and the Humanities 21). Amsterdam: Rodopi, pp. 41–63.

Nowak, L. 1992. The Idealization Approach to Science: A Survey. In J. Brzezinski and L. Nowak (eds.), *Idealization III: Approximation and Truth* (Poznań Studies in the Philosophy of the Sciences and the Humanities 25). Amsterdam: Rodopi, pp. 9–63.

Nowak, L. 2000. The Idealizaton Approach to Science: A New Survey. In I. Nowakowa and L. Nowak (eds.), *Idealization X: The Richness of Idealization* (Poznań Studies in the Philosophy of the Sciences and the Humanities 69). Amsterdam: Rodopi, pp. 109–184.

Nowakowa, I. and L. Nowak 1998. Model(S) and Experiment(S) as Homogeneous Families of Notions. In N. Shanks (ed.), *Idealization IX: Idealization in Contemporary Physics* (Poznań Studies in the Philosophy of the Sciences and the Humanities 63). Amsterdam: Rodopi, pp. 35–50.

Nowakowa, I. and L. Nowak 2000. Introduction. Science as a Caricature of Reality. In I. Nowakowa and L. Nowak (eds.), *Idealization X: The Richness of Idealization* (Poznań Studies in the Philosophy of the Sciences and the Humanities 69). Amsterdam: Rodopi, pp. 9–14.

Palacios, P. 2019. Phase Transitions: A Challenge for Intertheoretic Reduction? *Philosophy of Science* 86: 612–640.

Pincock, C. 2014. How to Avoid Inconsistent Idealizations. *Synthese* 191: 2957–2972.

Potochnik, A. 2017. *Idealization and the Aims of Science*. Chicago: The University of Chicago Press.

Potochnik, A. 2020. Idealization and Many Aims. *Philosophy of Science* 87: 933–943.

Redhead, M. 2001. The Intelligibility of the Universe. In A. O'Hear (ed.), *Philosophy at the New Millennium*. Cambridge: Cambridge University Press, pp. 73–90.

Reiss, J. 2018. Thought Experiments and Idealisations. In M. Stuart, Y. Fehige, and J. Brown (eds.), *The Routledge Companion to Thought Experiments*. London: Routledge, pp. 469–483.

Reutlinger, A. 2017. Do Renormalization Group Explanations Conform to the Commonality Strategy? *Journal for General Philosophy of Science* 48: 143–150.

Rice, C. 2019. Models Don't Decompose That Way: A Holistic View of Idealized Models. *The British Journal for the Philosophy of Science* 70: 179–208.

Rueger, A. and D. Sharp 1998. Idealization and Stability: A Perspective from Nonlinear Dynamics. In N. Shanks (ed.), *Idealization IX: Idealization in Contemporary Physics* (Poznań Studies in the Philosophy of the Sciences and the Humanities 63). Amsterdam: Rodopi, pp. 201–216.

Ruelle, D. 2004. *Thermodynamic Formalism: The Mathematical Structures of Classical Equilibrium Statistical Mechanics*. Cambridge: Cambridge University Press.

Shech, E. 2018. Infinite Idealizations in Physics. *Philosophy Compass* 13: e12514.

Sklar, L. 1993. Idealization and Explanation: A Case Study from Statistical Mechanics. *Midwest Studies in Philosophy* 18: 258–270.

Spivak, M. 1994. *Calculus* (3rd ed.). Houston: Publish or Perish.

Strevens, M. 2008. *Depth: An Account of Scientific Explanation*. Cambridge, MA: Harvard University Press.

Strevens, M. 2019. The Structure of Asymptotic Idealization. *Synthese* 196: 1713–1731.

Strevens, M. 2021. Permissible Idealizations for the Purpose of Prediction. *Studies in History and Philosophy of Science*: 92–100.

Weirich, P. 2011. The Explanatory Power of Models and Simulations: A Philosophical Exploration. *Simulation & Gaming* 42: 155–176.

Weisberg, M. 2007. Three Kinds of Idealization. *The Journal of Philosophy* 104: 639–659.

Williamson, T. 2005. Armchair Philosophy, Metaphysical Modality, and Counterfactual Thinking. *Proceedings of the Aristotelian Society* 105: 1–23.

Young, H. D. and R. Freedman 2000. *University Physics with Modern Physics* (10th ed.). San Francisco and Reading, MA: Addison Wesley.

PART IV

PART-IV

13

CHALLENGING SUBORDINATION

13.1 Introduction

In the Received View models are alternative interpretations of a formalism; in the Model-Theoretical View they are the building blocks of a theory. Despite their differences, both views regard models as subordinate to theories and as playing no role in science outside the context of a theory. This vision of models as being subordinate to theories has been challenged. Philosophers have argued that models enjoy various degrees of independence from theory; that models function autonomously in many contexts; and that models occupy centre stage in the fabric of science. The task for this chapter is to discuss these arguments.

In what way are models independent from theories, how do they function autonomously, and what roles do they play in scientific research? A meta-philosophical consensus has emerged among those contributing to this discussion that these questions are best answered by paying close attention to scientific practice. A philosophical analysis of the function and purpose of models must be informed by the way in which science operates "in the wild". As a result, investigations of models frequently take the form of case studies: a particular model or scientific project is studied in detail, and lessons are extracted from it.[1]

On the one hand, this method ensures that philosophical theorising retains ground traction because claims about models are both informed and constrained by scientific practice. On the other hand, the focus on detailed case studies inevitably introduces a degree of heterogeneity into philosophical accounts. As attention has been focused on detailed analyses of particular cases, the student of the literature on models finds a plethora of case studies. Some of the cases provide a springboard for claims of a certain scope; but they rarely lead to overarching generalisations. Hence, a focus on the practice of modelling has gone hand in hand with a tendency towards a more particularist style of doing philosophy, which prioritises scientific detail over grand philosophical design.

DOI: 10.4324/9781003285106-18

The heterogeneity of the subject matter and the particularist approach to the philosophical engagement with it are reflected in the structure of this chapter. Rather than introducing and scrutinising general accounts of modelling, it discusses different cases that are representative of certain kinds of models. Such a discussion remains incomplete by necessity. Alternative cases could have been chosen, and other points could have been emphasised. Nevertheless, I hope that the discussion below provides a representative sample that acquaints the reader with some of the main strands of argument.

I use the issue of the independence of models from theories as the ordering principle for the chapter, discussing models in descending order of independence from theory. We start by looking at models that are constructed without the aid of a theoretical framework and that therefore end up being wholly independent from theory (Section 13.2). An interesting class of models serves the purpose of exploring properties of a theory by providing simplified renderings of a theory's features (Section 13.3). In some cases, models live in a symbiotic relation with theories, adding specifics about which the theory remains silent (Section 13.4). Some have claimed that the reliance of theories on models is even stronger because theories require interpretative models in order to relate to real-world targets (Section 13.5), or that models play the role of mediators between theories and the world (Section 13.6). After discussing different construals of how models relate to theories, we return to the Model-Theoretical View's claim (introduced in Section 5.4) that it offers an account of models and theories that is aligned with scientific practice. We will see that this claim comes under pressure from the kinds of cases we have discussed in this chapter, and that it has been actively disputed (Section 13.7). In the practice of science, it is often difficult to draw the line between models and theories, and we discuss how, and where, such a line could be drawn (Section 13.8). These considerations cast doubt on the Model-Theoretical View's claim that it offers a universal view of scientific modelling (Section 13.9).

13.2   Independent Models

The most radical departure from a theory-centric analysis of models is the realisation that there are models that are completely independent from any theory. An example of such a model is what is now known as the Lotka-Volterra model.[2] Umberto D'Ancona did market statistics of the Adriatic fisheries around the time of the First World War. He noted that there was an increase in the proportion of predacious species among the fish that were offered on the market compared to pre-war levels. This struck him as odd given that fishing had almost come a halt during the war. He brought this problem to the attention of his father-in-law, renowned mathematical physicist Vito Volterra, because he knew that Volterra had an interest in mathematical ecology. A few years passed before Volterra started working on this problem in earnest, but by 1926 Volterra had published his findings in Italian, and a summary of his results appeared in an article in *Nature* (Volterra 1926).

Volterra conceptualised the problem as a population-level phenomenon with a population of predators interacting with a population of prey. The populations are described solely in terms of their sizes, and no biological facts about the animals that constitute the populations are taken into account beyond the obvious truism that predators eat prey and not *vice versa*. Let N_1 be the number of prey and N_2 the number of predators. Volterra then asked how these numbers change over time. The change in these numbers is due both to intrinsic birth and death in the populations, as well as to the interaction between the two. The general form of the interaction can therefore be expressed as follows (Kingsland 1985, 109–100):

Change in N_1 per unit of time = Natural increase in N_1 per unit of time minus decrease in N_1 per unit of time due to destruction of prey by predators

Change in N_2 per unit of time = Increase in N_2 per unit of time due to ingestion of prey by predators minus decrease of N_2 due to deaths of predators per unit of time.

These "verbal equalities" can be turned into proper mathematical equations by replacing the natural numbers N_1 and N_2 by continuous quantities V (for the quantity of prey) and P (for the quantity of predator), and by choosing specific functions for the population growth and the interactions between the populations. The simplest choice is to assume that each population grows linearly and that the interaction between the populations (predators eating prey and growing as result) is proportional to the product of the two densities. Inputting these formal choices into the above equalities leads to the so-called Lotka-Volterra equations, two coupled non-linear differential equations (Weisberg and Reisman 2008, 111):

$$\dot{V} = rV - (aV)P$$
$$\dot{P} = b(aV)P - mP,$$
(13.1)

where r is the birth rate of the prey population; m is the death rate of the predator population; and a and b are linear response parameters. The dot on V and P indicate the first derivative with respect to time. Intuitively, $\dot{V}$ is the rate of change of V, and ditto for $\dot{P}$. So the first equation says that the rate of change of V is equal to V itself multiplied by the growth rate r minus the product of the sizes of the predicator and prey populations multiplied by the response parameter a. These equations are called the "Lotka-Volterra equations" rather than the "Volterra equations" because the American mathematician, statistician, and biophysicist Alfred Lotka (1925) derived the same equations simultaneously but independently of Volterra.

An analysis of the equations shows that the interaction between the two populations gives rise to periodic oscillations in both populations. As one would expect, the oscillations are out of phase, meaning that the population sizes don't reach their maxima and minima at the same time. The prey population reaches a maximum when there are relatively few predators, and when the predator population reaches a peak, the population of prey is greatly diminished. Volterra also showed that the populations have the following feature: "If we try to destroy individuals of both species uniformly and proportionately to their number, the average number of individuals of the *eaten* species grows and the average number of the eating species diminishes" (1926, 558). In other words, a general biocide (the uniform reduction of all species) will increase the relative size of the prey population. This result is now known as the *Volterra Property* (Weisberg and Reisman 2008, 113). This provides the answer to D'Ancona's question. Fishing reduces both species uniformly and hence increases the proportion of prey. When the fisheries closed, this "uniform destruction" stopped, and as a result the predator population grew.

Even though Volterra notes that Darwin had made an observation similar to his own (1926, 559), neither Darwinian evolutionary theory nor any other biological theory is at work in the model. Indeed, the model has been constructed without a theoretical framework; it does not instantiate theoretical principles; and hence the model is completely theory-independent. The model was constructed based on a fisherman's working knowledge of the marine life, augmented with mathematical techniques. This is not surprising given that Volterra was a professor of mathematical physics with no prior experience of fisheries. In the terminology of Section 2.2, the model is a representational model. It represents its target system, the fish population in the Adriatic Sea, and successfully captures some of its key features. It is not a logical model because it does not make formal sentences of a theory true.

The Lotka-Volterra model is not an isolated instance. The Schelling model of social segregation (Schelling 1978), the Fibonacci model of population growth (Bacaër 2011, Ch. 1), the logistic model of population growth (May 1976), the Akerlof model of the market for used cars (Akerlof 1970), and complexity models for the behaviour of sand piles (Bak 1997) are "theory-free" in the same way. Models of this kind are sometimes characterised as bottom-up models. A model is *bottom-up* if the process of model construction departs from basic features of the target and from what we know about the unfolding of events in the domain of interest, while not relying on general theories. Bottom-up models contrast with top-down models. A model is *top-down* if the process of model construction starts with a theoretical framework, and the model is built by working the way down from the theory to the phenomena. The Newtonian model of planetary motion that we encountered in Section 1.2 is an example of a top-down model. The process of model construction starts with Newton's general equation of motion and the laws of gravity, and then various steps are made to apply these general principles to the phenomenon of interest.[3]

A special case of models that are independent of theory are models that are built with the express aim of aiding the construction of a theory. We have encountered such a case in Section 10.5, where we discussed Maxwell's use of a system of hypothetical tubes filled with an incompressible fluid in the development of his electromagnetic field equations. The tubes can be seen as constituting a model, and by Maxwell's own lights the tubes provided a "physical analogy" of the electromagnetic field. Maxwell then used this model to develop the equations of his general theory of electromagnetism.

This function of models has been recognised in the philosophical literature. Leplin emphasises the importance of models in the construction of theories and calls models that are constructed with this purpose in mind *developmental models* (1980, 274). A developmental model "opens several lines of research toward the development" of a theory (*ibid.*, 278). The importance of models in the development of theories has also been emphasised by other authors. Cushing notes that "[a]n important tool in this process of theory construction is the use of models" (1982b, 32), and illustrates this with a detailed case study from high-energy physics (see also Cushing 1982a). Hartmann observes that "[a]s a major tool for theory construction, scientists use models" (1995b, 49), which "are – historically and systematically – precursors of a theory" (1995a, 35, my translation), and he illustrates this with how quantum chromodynamics, the fundamental theory of strong interactions, has been constructed "by means of a hierarchy of consecutive *Developmental Models*" (1995b, 59). Wimsatt sees "false models as a means to truer theories", and discusses their role in the context of evolutionary biology (1987, see in particular 28–32; cf. Wimsatt 2007, Ch. 6). Emch dedicates two long papers to the study of "models and dynamics of theory-building in physics" (2007a, 2007b).

13.3 Models to Explore Theories

Models can also be used to explore features of theories. An obvious way in which this can happen is when a model is a logical model of a theory. As we have seen in Section 2.2, a logical model is a set of objects, along with their properties and relations, that make a formal sentence true if the terms of the sentence are interpreted as referring to them. In Section 2.4 we have seen that proponents of the Received View located the value of models in their ability to provide intuitive access to a possibly complicated and confusing formal theory. In a model we can see how the axioms play out in a particular setting and what kind of behaviours they dictate. This is why students often look at examples when studying a theory. Those taking an introductory course to classical mechanics, for instance, will learn the theory mainly through simple logical models of the theory like the harmonic oscillator and the sun-earth system. By going through simple examples the student learns how the theory works and what features it has.

But models can be more than just pedagogical tools for students; they can provide genuine insight into the structure of a theory. A case in point is the discovery of chaos with the three-body model. For a long time it was thought that Newtonian mechanics was dynamically stable, meaning that a small variation in the initial condition of system would result in a small variation of the path of the system. If, for example, the position of the earth relative to the sun had been slightly different in the moment in which the solar system came into being, then the path of the earth would also be only slightly different. This commonly held belief was shattered at the beginning of the 20th century when Poincaré discovered that Newtonian systems can display what is now known as *sensitive dependence on initial conditions*, which is often taken to be the defining feature of chaos.[4] As we have seen in Section 1.2, the sun-earth model is based on the idealising assumption the earth *only* interacts with the sun. This is an extremely strong assumption because we know that the earth in fact interacts gravitationally with every mass in the universe. Poincaré worried about this idealisation and asked how the motion of the earth would change if this assumption was relaxed. To answer this question, he considered the model that marks the smallest possible departure from the original model, namely a model in which the earth also interacts with the moon. Because this model has three bodies in it – sun, earth, and moon – calculating the trajectories of the three objects when they interact with each other is known as the *three-body problem*. In performing calculations on this model, Poincaré realised that even small changes in initial conditions can lead to significant changes in the objects' trajectories. In other words, the model displayed sensitive dependence on initial conditions. This was a significant discovery in its own right, but beyond that it taught physicists that Newtonian mechanics is not dynamically stable: the structure of the theory is such that it allows for sensitive dependence on initial conditions. Once the discovery was made, other systems with the same property were found, and important parts of what is now known as *chaos theory* are dedicated to the study of such systems.

Once we know that Newtonian models can exhibit sensitive dependence on initial conditions, one can ask how the dynamic of such systems looks like. The equations of motion of systems like the three-body model do not have analytical solutions and so one cannot simply write down the functions that solve the equations and study their properties; and even if one could write down the solutions, they would be objects in high-dimensional mathematical spaces that are hard to trace and impossible to visualise. So other means to understand the behaviour of such systems have to be found, and models play a crucial role in that process too.

Abstract considerations about the qualitative behaviour of solutions in chaotic systems show that there is a mechanism that has been dubbed *stretching and folding*. Sensitive dependence on initial conditions means that nearby initial conditions drift away from each other, which amounts to stretching the area where they lie. The motion of chaotic systems is such that the system's movement is confined to a restricted part of the state space. This means that the stretching can't continue forever, and the stretched bits must be folded back onto themselves. This is illustrated schematically in Figure 13.1. We start with the line segment between A and B at time t_1. In the period between t_1 and t_2 this segment is stretched to the line segment between A and C. At t_2 stretching comes to an end and a folding process begins that continues until t_3. In that process the line segment is folded back onto itself. And then the entire process of stretching and folding begins again from the start.

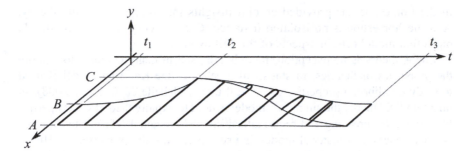

FIGURE 13.1 Stretching and folding.

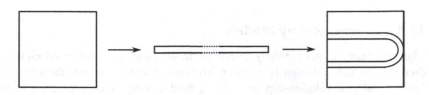

FIGURE 13.2 The horseshoe map. The dots indicate that the strip is longer than can be shown in the graph.

In practice, it is impossible to trace this stretching and folding in the full state space the three-body model. To obtain an idea of the complexity of the dynamic exhibiting stretching and folding, Smale proposed to study a model of the flow. The model is a simple two-dimensional map which is now known as the horseshoe map (Tabor 1989, 200–202). The map consists of a sequence of stretching and folding operations, which are illustrated in Figure 13.2. The map begins by stretching a rectangle horizontally while squeezing it vertically, which turns the rectangle into a strip. This models what happens between t_1 and t_2. The map then folds the strip over in the shape of horseshoe, which models what happens between t_2 and t_3. The same map can then be applied iteratively to the result of the first application. The map "mimics" the stretching and folding motion of the full Newtonian dynamic, but without having any of its mathematical complexities. In this way the horseshoe map provides a model of an important aspect of the full dynamic of Newtonian theory.

The horseshoe map has a number of interesting and important features (Ott 1993, 108–114). An *invariant set* is a set of states that does not change under the dynamic of a model – it is as if the set was not "affected" by the changes that the dynamic brings with it. One can show that the so-called Cantor set is an invariant set of the horseshoe. This is interesting because the Cantor set is a fractal, and so we learn from the model that chaotic dynamical systems can have invariant sets that are fractals. Furthermore, it can be shown that the set of points on periodic orbits in the invariant set is dense. So the simple model of the horseshoe has provided crucial insights into properties of the theory. And the horseshoe is no isolated instance. Chaos theory is rife with simple maps that model certain aspects of the full dynamic.[5]

Chaos theory is no exception; models are used in many contexts to explore the properties of theories. In statistical mechanics the Kac ring model is used to study equilibrium properties of the full theory (Jebeile 2020; Lavis 2008). In quantum field theory the simple φ^4 model is used to explore theoretical properties like symmetry breaking and renormalisability (Hartmann 1995b). The Phillips-Newlyn machine, a material model, is used to explore the properties of Hicks' formalisation of Keynes' theory (Barr 2000; Morgan and Boumans 2004). And the dome model is used to understand causality and determinism in Newtonian mechanics (Norton 2003, 2008).

13.4 Complementary Models

Theories may be incompletely specified in one way or another. Models can then step in and add what is missing. The model and the theory thereby enter into a symbiotic relationship in which a model complements the theory. The nature of this "completion" depends on the specifics of the case, and there is no one-size-fits-all characterisation. Redhead (1980, 147) mentions the case of axiomatic quantum field theory. The theory is an attempt to offer a mathematically rigorous formulation of quantised fields. In its most common formulation, the theory is based on the so-called Wightman Axioms, which were formulated by Arthur Wightman in the 1950s. Roughly, the axioms say things like that fields must be invariant under the transformations of Einstein's theory of special relativity, and that fields can be expressed as sums of operators acting on the vacuum state. The details of this need not occupy us here.[6] What matters is that the theory's axioms only impose certain general constraints on fields. The theory does not provide an account of what fields there are and of how they interact. The specification of a particular field is left open in the theory. The specifics of particular fields and their interactions are given by models. In doing so, the model provides missing details and enriches the theory. This is not an easy task because it turns out that identifying models that satisfy the axioms of the theory is rather difficult.

There are different ways in which a theory can be incompletely specified. Apostel identifies one of these ways when he notes that there are cases where "a qualitative theory is known for a field and the model introduces quantitative precision" (1961, 2). As an example, consider the so-called *quantity theory of money* in monetary economics.[7] Somewhat ironically, the "quantity theory" is purely qualitative and essentially says that the price of goods in an economy is determined by the amount of money that is in circulation in the economy. This law leaves open what the level of prices is and how they vary as a function of money supply. To answer these quantitative questions, Fisher constructed a model that is now known as *Fisher's equation of exchange*. The model considers an economy that can be characterised by four quantities: the amount M of money in circulation in the economy, the transaction velocity V of money, the level of prices P, and the volume of trade Y. All these are variables with precise numerical values that can, in principle, be measured empirically. The equation of exchange says $MV = PY$. If velocity and volume are constant, the equation says that $P = cM$, where c is a constant. So if the amount of money increases by ΔM, then prices go up by $c\Delta M$. In this way Fisher's model gives quantitative specificity to the qualitative law of the theory.

Harré noted that models can complement theories by providing mechanisms for processes left unspecified in the theory but that are nevertheless responsible for bringing about the observed phenomena (1970, Ch. 2, 2004, Ch. 1). In some cases the model mechanism is known; in other cases it is hypothesised. The notion of a mechanism is broad, and Harré emphasised that it is not restricted to "anything specifically mechanical": a "[c]lockwork is a mechanism, Faraday's strained space is a mechanism, electron quantum jumps is a mechanism, and so on" (2004, 4). As an example, take Boltzmann's justification of the Second Law of Thermodynamics through the collision of molecules.[8] To illustrate this law, consider a gas that is confined to the left half of a container. Now pull out rapidly the dividing wall between the left half and the right half of the container. Immediately after the removal of the dividing wall the gas is in a non-equilibrium state. It leaves this state quickly by dispersing until it fills the container evenly. At this point the system will have reached a new equilibrium state, as predicted by the Second Law. However, the Second Law is completely silent about why the gas behaves in this way and about why the spreading takes place in the first instance. In a paper published in 1872, Boltzmann introduced a mechanical model to underpin the Second Law. He assumed that a gas consisted of molecules that can be modelled as hard balls. The balls collide with each other, and the collisions are elastic (meaning that energy and momentum are preserved). Based on a number of modelling assumptions, most importantly the infamous *Stosszahlansatz*,[9] Boltzmann argued that it was the mechanical interaction of the balls in collisions that pushed the gas towards equilibrium. In this way, Boltzmann's mechanical model provides the causal mechanism that underpins the Second Law.

On some occasions, models can step in when theories are too complex to handle. This can happen, for instance, when the equations of the theory are mathematically intractable. In such cases one can find a model that approximates the theory. As Redhead noted, this can be done in two ways (1980, 150–152): either one finds approximate solutions to exact equations or one finds an approximate equation that one can solve exactly. We have discussed these options in Section 11.5. If one finds either an approximate solution or an approximate equation, these can be seen as approximate models of the theory. But models can step in also when the relation between the model and the theory is not a clearly defined mathematical approximation. Hartmann (1999) discusses the case of quark confinement in elementary particle physics.[10] The nucleus of atoms is made up of nucleons: protons and neutrons. Nucleons themselves are made up of quarks. How do quarks interact to form a stable nucleon? The general theory covering the behaviour of quarks is quantum chromo dynamics. Unfortunately, the theory is too complicated to apply to protons. Computer simulations suggest that at low energies so-called quark confinement occurs, and quarks come together to form nucleons. This, however, leaves the nature of this confinement unexplained and poorly understood, with a number of different kinds of confinement possible and the theory unable to adjudicate between them. To fill this gap physicists constructed a phenomenological model, now known as the MIT Bag Model, which takes the main known features of the theory into account and fills the missing details with postulated configurations. According to the model, nucleons consist of three massive quarks that move freely in a rigid sphere of radius R, where the sphere guarantees that the quarks remain confined within the nucleon. This assumption is motivated by the basic theory, but it does not deductively follow from it. The model then allows for the calculation of the radius R and the total energy of the particle. In this way the model yields results where the theory is silent, and it fills a gap that the theory left open.

13.5 Applying Theories Through Models

Cartwright argues that models not only aid the application of theories that are somehow incomplete; she submits that models are always involved when a theory with an overarching mathematical structure is applied to a target system. The main theories in physics fall into this category: classical mechanics, quantum mechanics, electrodynamics, etc. In fact, applying such theories involves two notions of models: interpretative models and representative models. We now look at each and then see how they work together in the application of a theory to a target system.

Let us begin with interpretative models. Overarching mathematical theories like classical mechanics appear to provide general descriptions of a wide range of objects that fall within their scope. However, on closer inspection it turns out that these theories do not apply to the world directly. The reason for this is that they employ abstract terms, i.e. terms that apply to a target system only if a description couched in more concrete terms also applies to the target. Cartwright offers the following two conditions for a concept to be abstract relative to another concept:

> First, a concept that is abstract relative to another more concrete set of descriptions never applies unless one of the more concrete descriptions also applies. These are the descriptions that can be used to "fit out" the abstract description on any given occasion. Second, satisfying the associated concrete description that applies on a particular occasion is what satisfying the abstract description consists in on that occasion.

(1999a, 39)

She offers the example of "work".[11] Having responded to email, having revised a section of a paper, and having attended a meeting is what my having done work this morning consists of. If I tell a friend over lunch what I have done and he responds "well, you've responded to email, revised a section, and attended a meeting, but when did you work?", he either does not understand the concept of work, or, more likely, pulls a joke on me.

Cartwright submits that important concepts that appear in mathematised theories like Newtonian mechanics are abstract in the same way as "work". As we have seen in Section 1.2, Newton's law links force to mass and acceleration. The concept *force* is abstract in that it applies only if some more concrete concept also applies. There is no such thing as "nothing but a force" acting on a body. There being a force between two bodies on a particular occasion consists in them gravitationally attracting with each other, or electrostatically repelling each other, or . . . . These more concrete claims fit out the abstract claim of there being a force. Force therefore is an abstract property and "Newton's law tells that whatever has this property has another, namely having a mass and an acceleration which, when multiplied together, give the . . . numerical value, F" (1999a, 43). Force, therefore, has no independent existence; it exists only in its more specific forms like gravity, electrostatics, and so on. In this way "force" is like "work". Specifying what concrete claims fit out abstract claims amounts to specifying an *interpretative model*.[12] An interpretative model then consists of the "actors" that fit out the abstract claims of the theory.

Now turn to representative models. Cartwright regards representative models as ones that are built to "represent real arrangements and affairs that take place in the world" (1999a, 180). Thus, at a basic level, representative models are what we have previously called "representational models" (Section 2.2), namely models that represent a real-world target system. What is special about Cartwright's notion of a representative model is the role that it plays in the application of a theory.

To see what that role is, let us have a look at Cartwright's analysis of the process of theory entry. This process proceeds in two stages (1983, 133–134). In the first stage we begin by writing down everything that we know about the system. This "unprepared description" contains any information that might be relevant in whatever form: theoretical principles to be used, engineering specifications of the materials, information about the environment, potential idealisations, useful approximation schemes, and so on. In the second stage of theory entry the unprepared description is turned into a "prepared description", which presents the phenomenon in a way that makes it amenable to theoretical treatment because the "most apparent need is to write down a description to which the theory matches an equation" (*ibid.*, 133). In coming up with a prepared description, we also "dictate equations, boundary conditions, and approximations" (*ibid.*, 134), which are then subjected to a full formal treatment with the aim of finding solutions to the equations.

The result of this process is a highly idealised description of the target, and this description in fact specifies a *representative model*. This model has two crucial features. The first is that it is a highly idealised. Going through the two stages involves twisting and distorting the properties of the target in many ways and the result of this process is in no way a mirror image of the target. Indeed, Cartwright notes that "it is not essential that the models accurately describe everything that actually happens; and in general it will not be possible for them to do so" (1983, 140).[13] Second, all these distortions notwithstanding, the model still is a representation of the target. Cartwright says relatively little about what this amounts to and merely urges "a few cautions about thinking of representations too much on the analogy of structural isomorphism" and suggests that, tentatively, we can "make do with a loose notion of resemblance" (1999a, 192–193). At this point in the argument this is not a problem; everything that has been said about representation in previous chapters can, in principle, be used to understand how representative models represent their targets.

What is important is that on this view the principles of the theory do not apply to the real world. They apply to the "highly fictionalized objects" (1983, 136) in the representative model.[14] So one has to distort reality to force it into the corset of the theory: "our prepared descriptions lie" because "in general we will have to distort the true picture of what happens if we want to fit it into the highly constrained structures of our mathematical theories" (ibid., 139).

We are now in position to see how the two notions of an interpretative model and a representative model work together in the application of a theory to a real-world target. To apply a theory scientists must construct a model. This model must be such that it is, at once, an interpretative model of the general theory at hand (which means that it is couched in terms of concepts that fit out the abstract concepts of the theory) and a representative model of the target system (which means that it stands in a loose resemblance relation to the target).

Cartwright illustrates her case with complex examples from quantum theory, but her view can also be illustrated with our simple example of the Newton's treatment of the planets from Section 1.2. The construction of the model will start by gathering all known facts about planets in an unprepared description: they are material objects with a roundish shape; they are subject to gravity; they move periodically; the distance between them is large compared to their own size; they spin around their own axis, and so on. The prepared description describes planets as perfect spheres with a homogenous mass distribution because this allows us to pretend that the entire planet is a point mass located at the sphere's centre, which is what the theory can deal with effectively. Because many-body systems are known to be hard to tackle mathematically, the prepared description identifies the sun and one planet as the unit to be described and declares them isolated not only from the rest of the solar system, but indeed from the rest of the universe, which allows us to assume that the planet and the sun only interact gravitationally with each other and nothing else. To further reduce the number of variables, the description portrays the sun as being fixed and the planet as revolving around the sun.

This model is at once a representative model of the target system and an interpretative model of Newtonian mechanics. With this in place we can solve

Newton's equation for the solar system and find as its solutions Kepler's well-known ellipses. But, and that's Cartwright's point, Newtonian mechanics has not been applied directly to the solar system; it has been applied to the idealised system of two perfect homogenous spheres that interact gravitationally with each another and nothing else, whereby one sphere is fixed so that the other moves around it. Real planets are neither spherical nor is their mass distribution homogeneous; they gravitationally interact with the entire universe and not only the sun; the sun is not fixed and the sun and the planet move around their common centre of mass; etc. This is why theoretical laws only apply to "highly idealized fictional objects and processes, more akin to artful theatrical distortions than to true descriptions of things in the world" (1983, 128).

Cartwright presents this analysis of modelling as part of an anti-realist view of theories. Theories do not apply to real target systems, and they do not govern their behaviour. Instead, theories apply to the stylised objects of the model, and theories can be true of models but they are not true of the real world (1983, 128–129, 1999a, 4–5, 180).[15] If models are "corrected" to make them more realistic, this takes them away from the theories (1999b, 251). So there is a trade-off between constructing a model that conforms to the theory and one that conforms to the target.

Realists see theories as providing true (or at least approximately) true descriptions of the world, which is antithetical to Cartwright's vision of theories governing only stylised objects in fictional models. Where do realists and Cartwright part ways? Let us begin by looking at interpretative models. Cartwright portrays realists as looking for a "single concrete way in which all the cases that fall under the same predicate resemble each other" (1999a, 36). So realists would have to look for a single unifying feature that binds all instances of, say, "force" together. Realists would, in other words, have to look for something like the essence of force, or "forceness", and then say that forceness is what Newtonian mechanics is about.

While there may be realists who think about abstract theoretical terms along those lines, it seems that realists are not committed to understanding terms like force in this way. Assume Joe says, "I was unable to work yesterday due to illness". Jill believes Joe and takes him to make a true statement about the state of the world yesterday, which makes her a realist about Joe's statement. The statement contains two abstract terms, namely "work" and "illness". Is Jill committed to taking of this a statement as being about some single unifying nature of all instances of "work" and "illness"? It seems not. Jill can agree with Cartwright that these are abstract terms that need fitting out: Joe's being ill yesterday may have consisted in having a flue with fever and the work he could not do was revising their joint paper. And yet she can believe that Joe's statement is a true description of matters of fact. Morrison in effect draws this conclusion when she defends a view that "ascribes a representational function to theories" even though the concepts in theories are abstract, (2007, 217).

It is with representative models where the conflict really comes to a head. Cartwright argues that theories only apply to stylized and simplified objects in models, and not to real things. Realists oppose this view and argue that the fact that theories are applied to stylised models is due to *in practice* limitation and not due to *in principle* restrictions.[16] Realists view models of the kind Cartwright describes as expedients. They agree that target systems in the world are too complex for us to be able to apply a theory to them, and this is why we construct simplified models. These practical limitations should, however, not be conflated with it being in principle impossible to apply the theory to the target; nor should they be taken to show either that the theory is fundamentally inapplicable or that the theory is false when applied to the target. Newton applied his mechanics to spherical spinning tops because this yielded tractable equations, and these were vindicated by the fact that their solutions closely track planets' actual trajectories. But in principle one could write down Newton's equation for pear-shaped planets that are subject to many forces and for a sun that is not fixed in space. Contra Cartwright, realists insist that the theory provides an equation for such a situation, and that the solutions will be true of how the actual system behaves. That the solution is too complex for us to find and study is our limitation, not the theory's. Whether one sides with Cartwright or with the realist depends on other philosophical commitments, most notably on how one assesses the scope of theories.

13.6 Models as Mediators

The relation between models and theories can be more complicated and disorderly than in the cases we have discussed so far. The contributors to a programmatic collection of essays edited by Morgan and Morrison (1999b) rally around the idea of "models as mediators", and so I call the vision of modelling that emerges from this project the *Models as Mediators View*. This view sees models as instruments that mediate between theories and the world, while remaining independent from both. Models are therefore, as Morgan and Morrison put it, "autonomous agents" in the practice of science, which allows them to function as "instruments of investigation" (1999a, 10).[17] The autonomy of models has four dimensions: construction, functioning, representing, and learning (*ibid.*, 10–12). Let us look at each of these in turn.

The first and most important dimension is independence in construction. Morgan and Morrison observe that "model construction is carried out in a way which is to a large extent independent of theory" (1999a, 13), and Morrison locates models as being "between physics and the physical world" (1998, 65). This is because "theory does not provide us with an algorithm from which the model is constructed and by which all modelling decisions are determined" (Morgan and Morrison 1999a, 16). In her contribution to the collection Cartwright portrays the Model-Theoretical View as having a "vending machine" approach to model construction:

> The theory is a vending machine: you feed it input in certain prescribed forms for the desired output; it gurgitates for a while; then it drops out the sought-for representation, plonk, on the tray, fully formed, as Athena from

the brain of Zeus. This image of the relation of theory to the models we use to represent the world is hard to fit with what we know of how science works. Producing a model of a new phenomenon such as superconductivity is an incredibly difficult and creative activity.

(1999b, 247)

The "vending machine view" of theories is wrong on at least two counts. First, it wrongly assumes that all ingredients that are needed for the construction of a model are already contained in the theory. Discussing quantum models of superconductivity, Cartwright notes that theories leave out much of what is needed to produce a model capable of generating an empirical prediction. While theories contain general principles, they contain no information either about the real materials from which a superconductor is built, or about the various approximation schemes and the mathematical techniques needed to handle them; and they do not tell us how to construct the Hamiltonian of a particular material (1999b, 264).[18] So not only do theories not provide algorithms for the construction of models; they are in fact only one item on a long list of ingredients that are needed to build a model. By gathering all these ingredients, models bring otherwise detached theories to bear on concrete physical situations. It is in this sense that the models mediate between theories and the world.

The second count on which the "vending machine view" is wrong is that models are rarely applications of just one theory. The internal setup of a model is often a complicated conglomerate of elements from different theories. Cartwright illustrates this point with the Ginsburg-Landau model of superconductivity (1999b, 244–245). The starting point for the study of superconductivity was classical electrodynamics; quantum mechanics was then used to construct a "macroscopic model" in which superconductivity is described as a quantum state; this led to an equation for the supercurrent that unites electrodynamic and quantum mechanical elements; finally thermodynamics was used to find the model's equilibrium properties. So what delivers the results is not the stringent application of one theory, but the principles of different theories when put together in a symbiotic entirety.

Cartwright's quantum model of superconductivity is no exception. Suárez (1999) discusses the London brothers' classical model of superconductivity and argues that the model equations that describe superconductivity were not derivable from electromagnetic theory. Instead, the equations were the result of a new conception of superconductivity that resulted from the model, which was motivated by the phenomena themselves rather than by theory (we return to this case in the next section). As we have seen in Section 13.4, Hartmann (1999) looks at a model of quark confinement and points out that an understanding of confinement follows from an empirically driven model rather than from high-level theory because the theory is inapplicable to the problem at hand. Boumans (1999) looks at models of the business cycle and argues that not only can these models not be derived from theory; the theories do not even determine their form. Rather, the model is the result of a messy process of skilful integration of certain empirical findings, elements of a mathematical formalism, and eclectic bits of theory.

The second dimension of autonomy is functioning: models can perform many functions without relying on theories. One of these functions is to aid in theory construction (Morgan and Morrison 1999a, 18). We encountered developmental models in Section 13.2. They are models that serve as tools in the construction of a new theory, and they can do so only if they are independent from theory. Models can also be used as a means to explore properties and implications of a theory that is already in place (*ibid.*, 19). We have seen such cases in Section 13.3. Models furthermore play important roles in some measurement processes (*ibid.*, 21). Morgan (1999) discusses the case of Irving Fisher's accounting-balance model and points out that the model plays an important role in measuring various economic quantities. Finally, models can serve as a means for policy intervention (Morgan and Morrison 1999a, 24). Central banks use economic models to inform monetary policy decisions, for instance whether to change the base rate. There is no one model that is applicable in all situation and central banks typically use a plurality of models, often aided by expert opinions. This list is not exhaustive, and no list will ever be. Models are ubiquitous in almost all areas of science and their uses will differ from context to context. The points mentioned here illustrate without being exhaustive.

Representation is the third dimension of autonomy. Morgan and Morrison point out that the "critical difference between a simple tool, and a tool of investigation is that the latter involves some form of representation: models typically represent either some aspect of the world, or some aspect of our theories about the world, or both at once" (1999a, 11). They emphasise that representing does not presuppose that there is "a kind of mirroring of a phenomenon, system or theory by a model". This is consonant with what we have said about representation in previous discussions (in Chapters 2, 6, 8, and 9), where we have seen that representing is in no way tantamount to producing a copy, or effigy, of the target.

The final dimension of autonomy is learning. Morgan and Morrison point out that we learn from models and argue that this happens in two places: in building the model and in manipulating it (1999a, 11–12). As we have seen earlier in this section, there are no general rules or algorithms for model building and hence insights gained into what fits together and how during the process of construction are invaluable sources for learning about the model (*ibid.*, 30–31). Morrison illustrates this with a case from hydrodynamics (1999).[19] The fluid had to be conceptualised as consisting of two layers, and a number of simplifications and approximations had to be devised to describe the situation formally. Many important insights into the model were gained in this process of interpretation, conceptualisation, and integration of different elements into a coherent whole. The second place to learn about the model is when we manipulate it. Morgan (1999) notes that Fisher did not find out about the properties of his monetary models by contemplating them, but by manipulating them to show how the various parts of the model work together to produce certain results.[20]

In sum, models are the result of a cooperative effort among different theories, empirical knowledge, information about the specific make-up of the target system, mathematical techniques and approximation schemes, and often an element of guesswork.

13.7 The Model-Theoretical View and Scientific Practice

The thrust of the arguments Sections 13.2 to 13.6 is that the Model-Theoretical View misconstrues how models operate in scientific practice. The point was made implicitly in Sections 13.2 to 13.4, where we have discussed models that enjoy degrees of freedom from theories that seem to be incompatible with the Model-Theoretical View's understanding of models; the point is made explicitly in Section 13.6 where proponents of the Models as Mediators View argued that models are not anything like what the Model-Theoretical View says they are. [21]

This negative verdict stands in stark contrast with the Model-Theoretical View's self-assessment as an account of theories that is schooled on scientific practice and that offers an analysis of theories that captures how theories and models are used by scientists. In this vein, van Fraassen sees "as the main virtue of the semantic approach its naturalness and closeness to scientific practice" (1985, 302) (recall that proponents of the Model-Theoretical View refer to it as the "semantic view" or the "semantic approach"), and French and Ladyman submit that their partial structures approach offers "a unitary perspective on the various sorts of models used in the sciences – 'iconic', 'analogue', 'theoretical' or whatever" (1997, 370), and, more generally, claim that the Model-Theoretical view offers "the possibility of incorporating the various senses of the word 'model', as used in scientific practice, within a single, unitary account" (1999, 106). And the Model-Theoretical approach is not only recommended by those interested in mathematical physics. Thompson submits that "[t]he most significant advantage of the semantic account is that it quite naturally corresponds to the ways in which biologists expound, employ and explore the theory" (1983, 227). Lloyd recommends the adoption of the Model-Theoretical View because "models themselves are the primary theoretical tools used by evolutionary biologists", who "often present their theories in term of models, and they often draw conclusions using these models" (1994, 9). [22]

So the battle lines are drawn. The Model-Theoretical View claims that it offers an account of theories and models that is in sync with scientific practice, and the proponents of the Models as Mediators View deny that this is the case. To defend their claim, advocates of the Model-Theoretical View can pursue two strategies. First, they can reassess the examples on which the claim that models are independent from theory are based and argue that, on closer inspection, the cases in question turn out to be in line with the Model-Theoretical View. Second, they can question the scope of the claims and argue that core cases of the Models as Mediators View are the exception rather than the rule, and that they are not representative of how large parts of science works. Let us discuss these strategies in turn.

A full implementation of the first strategy would require going through all the examples we have seen in this chapter (and indeed many others) and explaining how, first impressions notwithstanding, they fit into the Model-Theoretical View. Such a task is beyond the scope of this chapter, and, historically, the debate has also been more narrowly focused. Rather than going through a vast array of models, the debate has centred around a particular model, namely the classical model of superconductivity. Superconducting materials exhibit two crucial behaviours. When cooled below a certain critical temperature (which usually is not far above zero degrees Kelvin), their electric resistance suddenly drops to almost zero (which is what earns the materials the name "superconductor") and all magnetic fluxes are suddenly expelled from the conductor (which is known as the Meissner effect). This case has been discussed by Cartwright et al. (1995), who used it to illustrate the failings of the Model-Theoretical View in accounting for how models work in practice.[23] A key ingredient in their argument is that the crucial equations of the model, which account for the properties of superconducting materials, were not actually consequences of electromagnetic theory: neither could the equations be derived from theory, nor could they be construed as some kind of approximation to the theory that can be arrived at by introducing correction factors or idealisations. To construct their model, the London brothers abandoned the equations that follow from the theory and postulated a new equation of superconductivity that was motivated by the phenomena rather than by the theory. For this reason, the new equation, which forms the core of what is now known as the London model, must look ad hoc from the point of view of the fundamental theory (*ibid.*, 147–148). This supports the view that models are independent from theory, which means that the Model-Theoretical View is incompatible with scientific practice.

French and Ladyman (1997) respond to this argument and aim to show that it fails to establish its conclusion. To this end they re-analyse the London model from the perspective of the Model-Theoretical View of theories and aim to show that, *pace* Cartwright and co-workers, the case fits neatly into the Model-Theoretical View.[24] They see the introduction of new equations not as a departure from the theory, but as the result of a fundamental re-interpretation of the phenomenon that is, however, still located within the broad context of Maxwell's equations, which are the crucial driver of the derivation of the model's equations.

The details of this case and their correct interpretation have become the subject matter of a heated debate.[25] As is often the case in controversies of this kind, neither of the two sides conceded and the debate has reached a stalemate. Persisting disagreements notwithstanding, some conclusions can be drawn. According to the Model-Theoretical View, to apply a theory means that one of its models has to be used to represent a target system. Whether this has happened in the London case depends on how the Sematic View is articulated. If one assumes with Munich Structuralism (see Chapter 7) that the models of a theory belong to a theory net defined by a narrow set of theoretical principles, then the London model of superconductivity is not an application of a theory. It has been one of Cartwright, Shomar, and Suárez's main points that the model does not follow

from electromagnetic theory, and French and Ladyman agree when they acknowledge that models "may not be, in certain cases, logically derivable from theories"
(*ibid.*, 374). Coming up with a model for superconductivity did not amount to
simply going through the family of models making up electromagnetic theory
and picking the right one for the case at hand – the theory simply contained no
such model. A tailor-made model had to be constructed, which involved going
against the grain of the theory at least in certain respects. French and Ladyman
agree with that, but they prefer to see this as a process of theory change rather
than as the construction of an autonomous model. This, however, presupposes a
"flat" view of theories because it requires the possibility to add a model to the
family of models that constitutes a theory that does not satisfy the fundamental
equations of the theory. In the terms of Section 7.2, the resulting model does not
belong to the theory net of electromagnetic theory and can be seen as being part
of electromagnetic theory only if the requirement that models satisfy theoretical
constraints is dropped.[26]

Even if the London model could be brought back under the auspices of the
Model-Theoretical View, this would only be one case among many. To drive
home the point that the Model-Theoretical View offers a universal account of
scientific theories that is fully in line with scientific practice, proponents of the
view would also have to show that the other models discussed in the Models as
Mediators View can be recast in the same matter. There is no proof that this cannot be done. But it has not been done, and in the light of the examples we have
discussed in this chapter, it would seem unlikely that such an undertaking would
be crowned with success.

This brings us to the second strategy, to question whether the examples used
by the opponents of the Model-Theoretical View are representative and therefore
suitable to cast doubts on the view. The proponents of the Models as Mediators
View claim that the independence of models from theory that they describe is the
norm. Morgan and Morrison note that the examples they discuss in support of
their claim "are not the exception but the rule" (1999a, 15). Cartwright, Shomar,
and Suárez reject what they call the "theory-driven view" because "*it is rarely the
case that models of the phenomena are arrived at as de-idealisations of theoretical models*" (1995, 142, original emphasis). Proponents of the Model-Theoretical
View could disagree and argue that the kind of cases discussed in the Models as
Mediators View are cherry-picked exceptions rather than the norm, and that the
notion of models at work in the Model-Theoretical View captures at least the bulk
of the cases in science.[27]

Counting cases and judging some as typical is notoriously difficult and I am
not aware of any statistics on this matter. But even if it was true that the majority
of models were as envisaged by the Model-Theoretical View, the mere fact that
there are exceptions – and, what is more, that there are entire fields like superconductivity and climate science that seem to be based wholly on exceptional models[28] – calls into question the claim that the Model-Theoretical View is universal
modulo a few negligible exceptions.

Suppe argues this objection is a red herring because the view never held universalist aspirations. He argues that it has never been the Model-Theoretical View's claim that it "encompasses, explains, and accommodates *all* scientific models", and he accuses Cartwright, Shomar and Suárez of shooting at a straw man (2000, 113, original emphasis). He also takes issue with Morgan and Morrison's claim that the Model-Theoretical View undercuts models' autonomy. He says that "[m]any models are developed independent of theories. Models often are advanced where theory is insignificant (much of experimental chemistry is like this). So what?" (*ibid.*). He regards Morgan and Morrison's points (discussed in Section 13.6) as "valid observations" (*ibid.*) and takes it as a given that not every legitimate scientific model must qualify as a component of a theory. For this reason, the Model-Theoretical View cannot be invalidated by noting that there are models that are independent from theory (*ibid.*).

Proponents of the Models as Mediators View may welcome Suppe's conciliatory approach. It is, however, less clear whether his fellow proponents of the Model-Theoretical View are willing to follow. As we have seen at the beginning of this section, the Model-Theoretical View is advertised as the approach that corresponds to the ways in which scientists expound, employ, and explore theories and the approach that encompasses all models that scientists use. These claims are incompatible with Suppes conciliatory minimalism, which in effect admits that the Model-Theoretical View has only limited scope.

13.8 Separating Models From Theories

The Models as Mediators View submits that models mediate between theory and the world. Something can mediate between two things only if it is clearly distinct and independent from both. While models are clearly distinct from the world, i.e. their targets, it is much less clear where the boundaries between models and theories lie. Indeed, in the cases discussed in Sections 13.5 and 13.6 models and theories got so entangled that it is sometimes unclear where the line between the two should be drawn.

This problem not only besets philosophical analysis; it also arises in scientific practice. Bailer-Jones interviewed a group of nine physicists about their understanding of models and their relation to theories. She reports that the following views were expressed:[29]

1) There is no real difference between model and theory.
2) Models turn into theories once they are better and better confirmed.
3) Models contain necessary simplifications and deliberate omissions, while theories are the best we can do in terms of accuracy.
4) Theories are more general than models. Modeling becomes a case of applying general theories to specific cases.

(2002, 293)

The first suggestion is too radical to do justice to many aspects of practice, where a distinction between models and theories is clearly made. The second view has already been discussed in the Introduction, where we found it irrelevant for our current concerns. The third proposal is up to something (which we discuss in Section 14.2), but it ultimately does not hold water. It is true that models involve idealisations and omissions of all kind, but so do theories. Newtonian mechanics, for instance, deals with point masses that move in a Euclidean space, and it omits most properties of the objects in its target domain (it omits, for instance, colour, temperature, and chemical constitution of its targets), but that does not seem to strip Newtonian mechanics of its status as a theory.

The fourth suggestion is closely aligned with a view that has emerged in the literature on models. In the wake of the debates we have reviewed in this chapter, models have become the focal point of attention and the emphasis has shifted so far away from theories that Morrison detects the need of a "redress of the imbalance" (2007, 195). She asks "where have all the theories gone" and then sets out to articulate how theories are different from models. Morrison points out that models contain a great deal of "excess" structure like approximation methods, mathematical techniques, and highly stylised descriptions of certain parts of the target, and she notes that one would not want to count these as part of a theory (*ibid.*, 197). This can be avoided if "theory" is reserved for a "theoretical core", which contains the constitutive assumptions of the theory. In the case of Newtonian mechanics, the core consists of the three laws of motion and the law of universal gravitation (*ibid.*, 197), in the case of classical electrodynamics of Maxwell's equations, in the case of relativistic quantum mechanics of the Dirac equation (*ibid.*, 205), and in the case of quantum mechanics of the Schrödinger equation (*ibid.*, 214). The core of theory constrains the behaviour of objects that fall within the scope of the theory, and it plays a crucial role in the construction of models. Models concretise the abstract laws of the theory and put them to use by adding additional elements that are specific to the situation. In this way theories assist the construction of models without determining the way in which they are built. Models are specific in that they are adapted to a particular situation and a particular problem, while the theories on which they are based contain the general principles of wide scope. Theories are only one ingredient of a model, which usually contains contextual factors and case-specific information. In brief, models are local and specific; theories are overarching and general.[30]

The problem with the "theoretical core" view of theories as presented by Morrison is that the notion of a theoretical core is introduced through examples – Newton's laws of motion, Maxwell's equations, and so on – and is then not further analysed. Morrison seems to regard this as an advantage when she observes that "nothing about this way of identifying theories requires that they be formalized or axiomatized" (2007, 205). However, this pragmatism must seem unsatisfactory to those who have contributed to the development of the two grand views of theories and who will feel that we have now come full circle. Neither the Received View nor the Model-Theoretical View would disagree that what makes a theory a theory is a theoretical core. The question they are concerned with is how this notion can be analysed and what kind of objects theoretical principles are. This question is left open. Formulating a nuts-and-bolts account of scientific theories that is compatible with a conception of models as autonomous agents is challenge that has yet to be met.

13.9 Conclusion

We have discussed a number of different relationships between models and theories that can be found in the practice of science. These range from complete independence to total dependence, and many things in-between. Many of these cases do not seem to sit well with the Model-Theoretical View of theories and therefore cast doubt on the view's claim that it offers a universal view of modelling that is in line with scientific practice.

Notes

1 Currie's (2015) offers a meta-philosophical discussion of the use of case studies.
2 Kingsland's (1985, Ch. 5) gives a historical account of the development of the model with a special focus on the relation between Lotka and Volterra. Hirsch et al. (2004, Ch. 11) and Hofbauer and Sigmund's (1998, Part 1) offer mathematically rigorous discussions of the model. Colyvan and Ginzburg's (2003), Gelfert's (2016, Sec. 3.4), Knuuttila and Loetgers's (2017), Levy and Currie's (2015, Sec. 3), Nguyen's (2020), Räz's (2017), Weisberg's (2013), and Weisberg and Reisman's (2008) provide philosophical discussions of the model. We will return to this model in Section 15.3.
3 The terms "bottom-up" and "top-down" are used in different ways in different contexts. For a discussion of some of these ways, see Dennett's (1995), Dieks' (2009), and Koperski's (1998).
4 For basic introductions to chaos and discussions of its philosophical ramifications, see Kellert's (1993), Leonard A. Smith's (2007), and Peter Smith's (1998). Argyris et al. (1994), and Tabor's (1989) offer advanced discussions. Parker (1998) discusses the question whether it was really Poincaré who discovered chaos.
5 For instance, the dynamics of KAM type systems near a hyperbolic fixed point can be modeled by the baker's transformation. For a discussion, see Berkovitz et al. (2006, 680–687).
6 For a discussion of quantum field theory, see Ruetsche's (2011).
7 Apostel does not provide an example. I am grateful to Julian Reiss for suggesting the quantity theory of money to me. The theory was introduced in Fisher's (1911). For a discussion of the theory, see Humphrey's (1974).
8 Harré's own example of a mechanical model complementing theories is Darwin's use of natural selection, which, according to Harré, was not part of Darwin's theory and was provided by a model built on the analogy with domestic selection in breeding (2004, 16–17). For a discussion of Boltzmann's mechanical model, see Uffink's (2007, 932–974), and for a discussion of the second law, see Uffink's (2001). For a review of various attempts to provide a mechanical underpinning of thermal phenomena, see Frigg's (2008), Sklar's (1993), and Uffink's (2007). Machamer et al. (2000) provides the background for many contemporary discussions of mechanisms. For surveys and further discussions of mechanisms, see the contributions to Glennan and Illari's (2017).
9 Roughly, the Stosszahlansatz says that the number of collisions in a certain volume of space during a certain time between two particles with certain initial velocities v_1 and v_2 is proportional to the product of the numbers of particles with these velocities in the volume (Uffink 2007, 949).

10 See also his (1995b, 1997).

11 For further discussions of Cartwright's notion of abstraction, see her (1991, 1999a, Ch. 3, 2010) and Cartwright and Mendell's (1984). Humphreys (1995) and Le Poidevin (1991) critically engage with her position. The above is a definition of the relation "more abstract than". However, sometimes Cartwright speaks of abstract and concrete properties as if being abstract and being concrete were absolute properties (see, for instance, Cartwright 1983, 8–10). In this manner of speaking, the claim is that the concepts of high-level theory are abstract while the claims of phenomenological models are concrete, and that the former need the latter to apply to target systems.

12 Interpretative models are intimately related to "bridge principles", which tell us what concrete form abstract concepts can take, and which in effect lay out interpretative models (1999b, 243, 256).

13 See also her (1997) and (1999a, Chs. 1–3).

14 This development was foreshadowed by Hutten who notes that "[t]he model is, then, not an application of the theory: rather, we apply the theory with its help" (1954, 289) and Groenewold, who introduced the notion of a "substitute model", which is based on "conscious theoretical approximations" and serves "as an intermediate stage between an observed phenomenon and the more fundamental theory by which it should actually be treated" (1961, 99).

15 Giere's (1999) vision of a "science without laws" pulls in the same direction and agrees with Cartwright that general laws like Newton's equation of motion are not descriptions of real systems and instead characterise the behaviour of models. For a discussion, see Cat's (2005).

16 For arguments along those lines, see Hoefer's (2003, 1408–1412) and Smith's (2001, 464–475). For further discussions of Cartwright's argument concerning the scope of laws, see Sklar's (2003), Teller's (2004) and the contributions to Hartmann et al. (2008). Related themes also recur in later in Section 13.8.

17 The "models as mediators" programme is the contemporary *locus classicus* for the view that models are autonomous units of scientific investigation. Early pronouncements of a model-centric understanding of science are Deutsch's (1948, 1951), Hesse's (1953), Hutten's (1954), and Rosenblueth and Wiener's (1945). Hesse (1963) locates the origin of a model-centric perspective on science in Campbell's (1920), which she contrasts with Duhem's (1906) theory-centric approach. Mellor questions this attribution and argues that Campbell's and Duhem's views on models and theories "conflict hardly at all" (1968, 282). For a brief history of the discussion of models in philosophy of science, see Bailer-Jones' (1999).

18 The Hamiltonian is essentially the energy function of the system, which determines how a system evolves over time.

19 For another discussion hydrodynamics, see Heidelberger's (2006).

20 McCoy and Massimi interpret this list of dimensions of independence to be directed and see Morgan and Morrison as moving "from the construction of models to their autonomy to their function as tools of learning" (McCoy and Massimi 2018, 100) and then offer examples of modelling projects where this order is reversed. They note that this is a complementary and not a competing point of view (*ibid.*, 101).

21 Doubts concerning the naturalistic credentials of the Model-Theoretical View have recently also been voiced in other corners. Halvorson notes that "that the set-theoretic approach requires translating scientific theories out of their natural idiom and into the philosopher's preferred foundational language" (2016, 599), a worry that is shared by many of the contributors to the recent discussion about theoretical equivalence (see Section 5.5). Discussing models of the nucleus, Portides concludes that the Model-Theoretical View "does not adequately account for the relation between theory and scientific models" (2005, 1297). Sloep and Steen, examining the claim that the Model-Theoretical View is faithful to the practice of evolutionary biology,

cast the verdict that the Model-Theoretical View "falls short of making it the best candidate for philosophical analysis of biological theories" (1987, 1).

22 Similar views are expressed in Da Costa and French's (1990, Sec. 4, 2000, Sec. 5, 2003, Ch. 3), French's (2000, Sec. 2), Liu's (1997, 154), and van Fraassen's (1989, 224). To further support the claim that the Model-Theoretical View has a seamless connection to scientific practice, its proponents also refer to the large number of theories from different fields that have been reconstructed in terms of the Model-Theoretical View (see, for instance, Lloyd 2006, 825). Examples include classical mechanics (see Section 5.2), quantum mechanics (French and Ladyman 1998; van Fraassen 1991), statistical mechanics (Emch and Liu 2002), evolutionary theory (Beatty 1981; Lloyd 1994; Sintonen 1991; Thompson 1987), population genetics (Lloyd 1984), ecology (Castle 2001), and sex and gender (Crasnow 2001).

23 Suárez and Pero have recently given a different spin to this debate. Rather than renouncing the semantic view on grounds that it misconstrues the historic and pragmatic factors, they announce the programme of "liberating the semantic conception from the shackles of structuralism" (2019, 348) and propose what they call the "representational semantic conception" which regards a theory as a family of representational models, where representation is explained in deflationary terms (see Section 9.4).

24 To be precise, they work within the Partial Structures Programme, which we have discussed in Section 6.7.

25 The following are contributions to this debate: Bueno et al. (2002, 2012), French and Ladyman's (1998, 1999), Morrison's (2008), Suárez's (1999, 2005), and Suárez and Cartwright's (2008).

26 Furthermore, Suárez and Cartwright (2008, 73–76) argue that French and Ladyman's assurances notwithstanding, partial structures cannot capture the relations between the relevant models.

27 This point has been made to me in conversation on many occasions, but I have been unable to locate it in print.

28 Modern climate science aims to construct models that integrate as much of known science as possible. This knowledge comes from diverse theories, including mechanics, fluid dynamics, electrodynamics, quantum theory, chemistry, and biology. Models aim to integrate elements from all the different fields so that they end up forming an operable entirety. Models of this kind do not belong to family of models that form a theory in anything like the way in which the models of General Relativity form a theory; in fact, they don't belong to any particular theoretical framework at all. See Maslin's (2004) for a brief introduction to climate models; McGuffie and Henderson-Sellers' (2005) provides an in-depth presentation of different kinds of climate models. Bokulich and Oreskes' (2017) discusses modelling in geophysics from a philosophical perspective.

29 A similar diversity of opinions is documented in Emch's (2007a, 559–562) and Hartmann's (1995a, 34). Gibbard and Varian say that "[t]he theory of the firm . . . is a model" (1978, 667), which shows how difficult practitioners find it to draw the distinction.

30 Morrison reaffirms these points in her (2016, 380–387). A similar separation of model and theory has also been suggested in Hartmann's (1995a, 34), McMullin's (1968, 389), Morgan and Morrison's (1999, 12), and Weinert's (1999, 307).

References

Akerlof, G. A. 1970. The Market for 'Lemons': Quality Uncertainty and the Market Mechanism. *Quarterly Journal of Economics* 84: 488–500.

Apostel, L. 1961. Towards the Formal Study of Models in the Non-Formal Sciences. In H. Freudenthal (ed.), *The Concept and the Role of the Model in Mathematics and Natural and Social Sciences*. Dordrecht: Reidel, pp. 1–37.

Argyris, J., G. Faust, and M. Haase 1994. *An Exploration of Chaos: An Introduction for Natural Scientists and Engineers*. Amsterdam: Elsevier.

Bacaër, N. 2011. *A Short History of Mathematical Population Dynamics*. London: Springer.

Bailer-Jones, D. M. 1999. Tracing the Development of Models in the Philosophy of Science. In L. Magnani, N. J. Nersessian, and P. Thagard (eds.), *Model-Based Reasoning in Scientific Discovery*. New York: Kluwer Academic; Plenum Publishers, pp. 23–40.

Bailer-Jones, D. M. 2002. Scientists' Thoughts on Scientific Models. *Perspectives on Science* 10: 275–301.

Bak, P. 1997. *How Nature Works: The Science of Self-Organised Criticality*. Oxford: Oxford University Press.

Barr, N. 2000. The History of the Phillips Machine. In R. Leeson (ed.), *A. W. H. Phillips: Collected Works in Contemporary Perspective*. Cambridge: Cambridge University Press, pp. 89–114.

Beatty, J. 1981. What's Wrong with the Received View of Evolutionary Theory? In P. Asquith and R. Giere (eds.), *Philosophy of Science (Proceedings)* (Vol. 2). East Lansing: Philosophy of Science Association, pp. 397–426.

Berkovitz, J., R. Frigg, and F. Kronz 2006. The Ergodic Hierarchy, Randomness and Chaos. *Studies in History and Philosophy of Modern Physics* 37: 661–691.

Bokulich, A. and N. Oreskes 2017. Models in Geosciences. In L. Magnani and T. Bertolotti (eds.), *Springer Handbook of Model-Based Science*. Dordrecht, Heidelberg, London, and New York: Springer, pp. 891–911.

Boumans, M. 1999. Built-in Justification. In M. S. Morgan and M. Morrison (eds.), *Models as Mediators: Perspectives on Natural and Social Science*. Cambridge: Cambridge University Press, pp. 66–96.

Bueno, O., S. French, and J. Ladyman 2002. On Representing the Relationship between the Mathematical and the Empirical. *Philosophy of Science* 69: 452–473.

Bueno, O., S. French, and J. Ladyman 2012. Models and Structures: Phenomenological and Partial. *Studies in History and Philosophy of Modern Physics* 43: 43–46.

Campbell, N. R. 1920. *Physics: The Elements*. Cambridge: Cambridge University Press (Reprinted as *Foundations of Science*. New York: Dover, 1957).

Cartwright, N. 1983. *How the Laws of Physics Lie*. Oxford: Oxford University Press.

Cartwright, N. 1991. Fables and Model. *Proceedings of the Aristotelian Society. Supplementary Volue* 65: 55–68.

Cartwright, N. 1997. Models: The Blueprints for Laws. *Philosophy of Science* 64: 292–303.

Cartwright, N. 1999a. *The Dappled World: A Study of the Boundaries of Science*. Cambridge: Cambridge University Press.

Cartwright, N. 1999b. Models and the Limits of Theory: Quantum Hamiltonians and the Bcs Models of Superconductivity. In M. Morgan and M. Morrison (eds.), *Models as Mediators: Perspectives on Natural and Social Science*. Cambridge: Cambridge University Press, pp. 241–281.

Cartwright, N. 2010. Models: Parables V Fables. In R. Frigg and M. C. Hunter (eds.), *Beyond Mimesis and Convention: Representation in Art and Science*. Berlin and New York: Springer, pp. 19–32.

Cartwright, N. and H. Mendell 1984. What Makes Physics' Objects Abstract? In J. Cushing, C. F. Delaney, and G. M. Gutting (eds.), *Science and Reality*. Notre Dame: University of Notre Dame Press, pp. 134–152.

Cartwright, N., T. Shomar, and M. Suárez 1995. The Tool-Box of Science: Tools for the Building of Models with a Superconductivity Example. In W. E. Herfel, W. Krajewski,

I. Niiniluoto, and R. Wojcicki (eds.), *Theories and Models in Scientific Processes* (Poznań Studies in the Philosophy of Science and the Humanities 44). Amsterdam: Rodopi, pp. 137–149.

Castle, D. G. A. 2001. A Semantic View of Ecological Theories. *Dialectica* 55: 51–65.

Cat, J. 2005. Modeling Cracks and Cracking Models: Structures, Mechanisms, Boundary Conditions, Constraints, Inconsistencies and the Proper Domains of Natural Laws. *Synthese* 146: 447–487.

Colyvan, M. and L. R. Ginzburg 2003. The Galilean Turn in Population Ecology. *Biology and Philosophy* 18: 401–414.

Crasnow, S. L. 2001. Models and Reality: When Science Tackles Sex. *Hypatia* 16: 138–148.

Currie, A. 2015. Philosophy of Science and the Curse of the Case Study. In C. Daly (ed.), *The Palgrave Handbook of Philosophical Methods*. Houndsmills and New York: Palgrave Macmillan, pp. 553–572.

Cushing, J. T. 1982a. Models and Methodologies in Current Theoretical High-Energy Physics. *Synthese* 50: 5–101.

Cushing, J. T. 1982b. Models, High-Energy Theoretical Physics and Realism. *Proceedings of the Biennial Meeting of the Philosophy of Science Association 1982* (Vol. 2), pp. 31–56.

Da Costa, N. C. A. and S. French 1990. The Model-Theoretic Approach in the Philosophy of Science. *Philosophy of Science* 57: 248–265.

Da Costa, N. C. A. and S. French 2000. Models, Theories, and Structures: Thirty Years On. *Philosophy of Science* 67(Supplement): 116–127.

Da Costa, N. C. A. and S. French 2003. *Science and Partial Truth: A Unitary Approach to Models and Scientific Reasoning*. Oxford: Oxford University Press.

Dennett, D. C. 1995. Cognitive Science as Reverse Engineering: Several Meanings of 'Top-Down' and 'Bottom-Up'. In D. Prawitz, B. Skyrms, and D. Westerstahl (eds.), *Logic, Methodology and Philosophy of Science IX*. Amsterdam: North Holland, pp. 680–689.

Deutsch, K. W. 1948. Some Notes on Research on the Role of Models in the Natural and Social Sciences. *Synthese* 7: 506–533.

Deutsch, K. W. 1951. Mechanism, Organism, and Society: Some Models in Natural and Social Science. *Philosophy of Science* 18: 230–252.

Dieks, D. 2009. Understanding in Physics: Bottom-up Versus Top-Down. In H. W. de Regt, S. Leonelli, and K. Eigner (eds.), *Scientific Understanding, Philosophical Perspectives*. Pittsburgh: University of Pittsburgh Press, pp. 230–248.

Duhem, P. 1906. *La Théorie Physique, Son Objet Et Sa Structure* (2nd ed.). Paris, 1914 (Engl. trans. by Philip P. Wiener: *The aim and Structure of Physical Theory*. Princeton, 1954).

Emch, G. G. 2007a. Models and the Dynamics of Theory-Building in Physics. Part I – Modeling Strategies. *Studies in History and Philosophy of Modern Physics* 38: 558–585.

Emch, G. G. 2007b. Models and the Dynamics of Theory-Building in Physics. Part II – Case Studies. *Studies in History and Philosophy of Modern Physics* 38: 683–723.

Emch, G. G. and C. Liu 2002. *The Logic of Thermostatistical Physics*. Berlin: Springer.

Fisher, I. 1911. *The Purchasing Power of Money: Its Determination and Relation to Credit and Crisis*. New York: Macmillan.

French, S. 2000. The Reasonable Effectiveness of Mathematics: Partial Structures and the Application of Group Theory to Physics. *Synthese* 125: 103–120.

French, S. and J. Ladyman 1997. Superconductivity and Structures: Revisiting the London Account. *Studies in History and Philosophy of Modern Physics* 28: 363–393.

French, S. and J. Ladyman 1998. Semantic Perspective on Idealisation in Quantum Mechanics. In N. Shanks (ed.), *Idealization IX: Idealisation in Contemporary Physics. Posnan Studies in the Philosophy of the Sciences and the Humanities* (Vol. 63). Amsterdam: Rodopi, pp. 51–73.

French, S. and J. Ladyman 1999. Reinflating the Semantic Approach. *International Studies in the Philosophy of Science* 13: 103–121.

Frigg, R. 2008. A Field Guide to Recent Work on the Foundations of Statistical Mechanics. In D. Rickles (ed.), *The Ashgate Companion to Contemporary Philosophy of Physics*. London: Ashgate, pp. 99–196.

Gelfert, A. 2016. *How to Do Science with Models: A Philosophical Primer*. Cham: Springer.

Gibbard, A. and H. R. Varian 1978. Economic Models. *The Journal of Philosophy* 75: 664–677.

Giere, R. N. 1999. *Science without Laws*. Chicago: University of Chicago Press.

Glennan, S. and P. Illari (eds.) 2017. *The Routledge Handbook of Mechanisms and Mechanical Philosophy*. London: Routledge.

Groenewold, H. J. 1961. The Model in Physics. In H. Freudenthal (ed.), *The Concept and the Role of the Model in Mathematics and Natural and Social Sciences*. Dordrecht: Reidel, pp. 98–103.

Halvorson, H. 2016. Scientific Theories. In P. Humphreys (ed.), *The Oxford Handbook of Philosophy of Science*. Oxford: Oxford University Press, pp. 585–608.

Harré, R. 1970. *The Principles of Scientific Thinking*. Chicago: The University of Chicago Press.

Harré, R. 2004. *Modeling: Gateway to the Unknown*. Amsterdam: Elsevier.

Hartmann, S. 1995a. Modelle Und Forschungsdynamik: Strategien Der Zeitgenössischen Physik. *Praxis der Naturwissenschaften – Physik* 44: 33–41.

Hartmann, S. 1995b. Models as a Tool for Theory Construction: Some Strategies of Preliminary Physics. In W. E. Herfel, W. Krajewski, I. Niiniluoto, and R. Wojcicki (eds.), *Theories and Models in Scientific Processes* (Poznań Studies in the Philosophy of Science and the Humanities 44). Amsterdam: Rodopi, pp. 49–67.

Hartmann, S. 1997. Modelling and the Aims of Science. In P. Weingartner, G. Schurz, and G. Dorn (eds.), *The Role of Pragmatics in Contemporary Philosophy: Contributions of the Austrian Ludwig Wittgenstein Society*. Wien und Kirchberg: Digi-Buch, pp. 380–385.

Hartmann, S. 1999. Models and Stories in Hadron Physics. In M. Morgan and M. Morrison (eds.), *Models as Mediators: Perspectives on Natural and Social Science*. Cambridge: Cambridge University Press, pp. 326–346.

Hartmann, S., C. Hoefer, and L. Bovens (eds.) 2008. *Nancy Cartwright's Philosophy of Science*. New York: Routledge.

Heidelberger, M. 2006. Applying Models in Fluid Dynamics. *International Studies in the Philosophy of Science* 20: 49–67.

Hesse, M. B. 1953. Models in Physics. *The British Journal for the Philosophy of Science* 4: 198–214.

Hesse, M. B. 1963. *Models and Analogies in Science*. London: Sheed and Ward.

Hirsch, M. W., S. Smale, and R. L. Devaney 2004. *Differential Equations, Dynamical Systems, and an Introduction to Chaos* (2nd ed.). San Diego: Elsevier.

Hoefer, C. 2003. For Fundamentalism. *Philosophy of Science* 70: 1401–1412.

Hofbauer, J. and K. Sigmund 1998. *Evolutionary Games and Population Dynamics*. Cambridge: Cambridge University Press.

Humphrey, T. M. 1974. The Quantity Theory of Money: Its Historical Evolution and Role in Policy Debates. *Economic Review*: 2–19.

Humphreys, P. 1995. Abstract and Concrete. *Philosophy and Phenomenological Research* LV: 157–161.

Hutten, E. H. 1954. The Rôle of Models in Physics. *The British Journal for the Philosophy of Science* 4: 284–301.

Jebeile, J. 2020. The Kac Ring or the Art of Making Idealisations. *Foundations of Physics* 50: 1152–1170.

Kellert, S. 1993. *In the Wake of Chaos*. Chicago: Chicago University Press.

Kingsland, S. E. 1985. *Modelling Nature: Episodes in the History of Population Ecology*. Chicago: University of Chicago Press.

Knuuttila, T. and A. Loettgers 2017. Modelling as Indirect Representation? The Lotka – Volterra Model Revisited. *The British Journal for the Philosophy of Science* 68: 1007–1036.

Koperski, J. 1998. Models, Confirmation, and Chaos. *Philosophy of Science* 65: 624–648.

Lavis, D. A. 2008. Boltzmann, Gibbs, and the Concept of Equilibrium. *Philosophy of Science* 75: 682–696.

Leplin, J. 1980. The Role of Models in Theory Construction. In T. Nickles (ed.), *Scientific Discovery, Logic, and Rationality*. Dordrecht: Reidel, pp. 267–283.

Le Poidevin, R. 1991. Abstraction and Explanation in Physics. *Proceedings of the Aristotelian Society. Supplementary Volue* 65: 69–82.

Levy, A. and A. Currie 2015. Model Organisms Are Not (Theoretical) Models. *The British Journal for the Philosophy of Science* 66: 327–348.

Liu, C. 1997. Models and Theories I: The Semantic View Revisited. *International Studies in the Philosophy of Science* 11: 147–164.

Lloyd, E. A. 1984. A Semantic Approach to the Structure of Population Genetics. *Philosophy of Science* 51: 242–264.

Lloyd, E. A. 1994. *The Structure and Confirmation of Evolutionary Theory*. Princeton: Princeton University Press.

Lloyd, E. A. 2006. Theories. In S. Sarkar and J. Pfeifer (eds.), *The Philosophy of Science: An Encyclopedia*. New York: Routledge, pp. 822–828.

Lotka, A. J. 1925. *Elements of Physical Biology*. Baltimore: Williams & Wilkins Company.

Machamer, P., L. Darden, and C. F. Craver 2000. Thinking About Mechanisms. *Philosophy of Science* 67: 1–25.

Maslin, M. 2004. *Global Warming a Very Short Introduction*. Oxford: Oxford University Press.

May, R. 1976. A Simple Mathematical Equation with Very Complicated Dynamics. *Nature* 261: 459–469.

McCoy, C. D. and M. Massimi 2018. Simplified Models: A Different Perspective on Models as Mediators. *European Journal for the Philoxophy of Science* 8: 99–123.

McGuffie, K. and A. Henderson-Sellers 2005. *A Climate Modelling Primer* (3rd ed.). New York: Wiley.

McMullin, E. 1968. What Do Physical Models Tell Us? In B. van Rootselaar and J. F. Staal (eds.), *Logic, Methodology and Science III*. Amsterdam: North Holland, pp. 385–396.

Mellor, D. H. 1968. Models and Analogies in Science: Duhem Versus Campbell? *Isis* 59: 282–290.

Morgan, M. S. 1999. Learning from Models. In M. S. Morgan and M. Morrison (eds.), *Models as Mediators: Perspectives on Natural and Social Science*. Cambridge: Cambridge University Press, pp. 347–388.

Morgan, M. S. and M. Boumans 2004. The Secrets Hidden by Two-Dimensionality: The Economy as a Hydraulic Machine. In D. S. Chadarevian and N. Hopwood (eds.), *Model: The Third Dimension of Science*. Stanford: Stanford University Press, pp. 369–401.

Morgan, M. S. and M. Morrison 1999a. Models as Mediating Instruments. In M. Morgan and M. Morrison (eds.), *Models as Mediators: Perspectives on Natural and Social Science*. Cambridge: Cambridge University Press, pp. 10–37.

Morgan, M. S. and M. Morrison (eds.) 1999b. *Models as Mediators: Perspectives on Natural and Social Science*. Cambridge: Cambridge University Press.

Morrison, M. 1998. Modelling Nature: Between Physics and the Physical World. *Philosophia Naturalis* 35: 65–85.

Morrison, M. 1999. Models as Autonomous Agents. In M. S. Morgan and M. Morrison (eds.), *Models as Mediators*. Cambridge: Cambridge University Press, pp. 38–65.

Morrison, M. 2007. Where Have All the Theories Gone? *Philosophy of Science* 74: 195–228.

Morrison, M. 2008. Models as Representational Structures. In S. Hartmann, C. Hoefer, and L. Bovens (eds.), *Nancy Cartwright's Philosophy of Science* (Routledge Studies in the Philosophy of Science, Vol. 3). New York: Routledge, pp. 67–90.

Morrison, M. 2016. Models and Theories. In P. Humphreys (ed.), *The Oxford Handbook of Philosophy of Science*. Oxford: Oxford University Press, pp. 378–396.

Nguyen, J. 2020. It's Not a Game: Accurate Representation with Toy Models. *The British Journal for the Philosophy of Science* 71: 1013–1041.

Norton, J. D. 2003. Causation as Folk Science. *Philosopher's Imprint* 3: 1–22.

Norton, J. D. 2008. The Dome: An Unexpectedly Simple Failure of Determinism. *Philosophy of Science* 75: 786–798.

Ott, E. 1993. *Chaos in Dynamical Systems*. Cambridge: Cambridge University Press.

Parker, M. W. 1998. Did Poincaré Really Discover Chaos? *Studies in History and Philosophy of Modern Physics* 29: 575–588.

Portides, D. 2005. Scientific Models and the Semantic View of Theories. *Philosophy of Science* 72(Supplement): 1287–1298.

Räz, T. 2017. The Volterra Principle Generalized. *Philosophy of Science* 84: 737–760.

Redhead, M. 1980. Models in Physics. *The British Journal for the Philosophy of Science* 31: 145–163.

Rosenblueth, A. and N. Wiener 1945. The Role of Models in Science. *Philosophy of Science* 12: 316–321.

Ruetsche, L. 2011. *Interpreting Quantum Theories*. Oxford: Oxford University Press.

Schelling, T. C. 1978. *Micromotives and Macrobehavior*. New York: Norton.

Sintonen, M. 1991. How Evolutionary Theory Faces the Reality. *Sythese* 89: 163–183.

Sklar, L. 1993. *Physics and Chance: Philosophical Issues in the Foundations of Statistical Mechanics*. Cambridge: Cambridge University Press.

Sklar, L. 2003. Dappled Theories in a Uniform World. *Philosophy ofScience* 70: 424–441.

Sloep, P. and W. van der Steen 1987. The Nature of Evolutionary Theory: The Semantic Challenge. *Biology and Philosophy* 2: 1–15.

Smith, L. A. 2007. *Chaos: A Very Short Introduction*. Oxford: Oxford University Press.

Smith, P. 1998. *Explaining Chaos*. Cambridge: Cambridge University Press.

Smith, S. R. 2001. Models and the Unity of Classical Physics: Nancy Cartwright's Dappled World. *Philosophy of Science* 68: 456–475.

Suárez, M. 1999. The Role of Models in the Application of Scientific Theories: Epistemological Implications. In M. S. Morgan and M. Morrison (eds.), *Models as Mediators:*

Perspectives on Natural and Social Science. Cambridge: Cambridge University Press, pp. 168–195.

Suárez, M. 2005. The Semantic View, Empirical Adequacy, and Application. *Crítica* 37: 29–63.

Suárez, M. and N. Cartwright 2008. Theories: Tools Versus Models. *Studies in History and Philosophy of Modern Physics* 39: 62–81.

Suárez, M. and F. Pero 2019. The Representational Semantic Conception. *Philosophy of Science* 86: 344–365.

Suppe, F. 2000. Understanding Scientific Theories: An Assessment of Developments, 1969–1998. *Philosophy of Science* 67: 102–115.

Tabor, M. 1989. *Chaos and Integrability in Nonlinear Dynamics: An Introduction*. New York: Wiley.

Teller, P. 2004. How We Dapple the World. *Philosophy of Science* 71: 425–447.

Thompson, P. 1983. The Structure of Evolutionary Theory: A Semantic Approach. *Studies in History and Philosophy of Science* 14: 215–229.

Thompson, P. 1987. A Defence of the Semantic Conception of Evolutionary Theory. *Biology and Philosophy* 2: 26–32.

Uffink, J. 2001. Bluff Your Way in the Second Law of Thermodynamics. *Studis in History and Philosophy of Modern Physics* 32: 305–394.

Uffink, J. 2007. Compendium of the Foundations of Classical Statistical Physics. In J. Butterfield and J. Earman (eds.), *Philosophy of Physics*. Amsterdam: North Holland, pp. 923–1047.

van Fraassen, B. C. 1985. Empiricism in the Philosophy of Science. In P. M. Churchland and C. A. Hooker (eds.), *Images of Science*. Chicago: Chicago University Press, pp. 245–308.

van Fraassen, B. C. 1989. *Laws and Symmetry*. Oxford: Clarendon Press.

van Fraassen, B. C. 1991. *Quantum Mechanics*. Oxford: Clarendon Press.

Volterra, V. 1926. Fluctuations in the Abundance of a Species Considered Mathematically. *Nature* 118: 558–560.

Weinert, F. 1999. Theories, Models and Constraints. *Studies in History and Philosophy of Science* 30: 303–333.

Weisberg, M. 2013. *Simulation and Similarity: Using Models to Understand the World*. Oxford: Oxford University Press.

Weisberg, M. and K. Reisman 2008. The Robust Volterra Principle. *Philosophy of Science* 75: 106–131.

Wimsatt, W. C. 1987. False Models as Means to Truer Theories. In M. H. Nitecki and A. Hoffman (eds.), *Neutral Models in Biology*. New York and Oxford: Oxford University Press, pp. 23–55.

Wimsatt, W. C. 2007. *Re-Engineering Philosophy for Limited Beings: Piecewise Approximations of Reality*. Cambridge, MA: Harvard University Press.

14

WHAT ARE MODELS?

14.1 Introduction

What are models? After several chapters discussing various aspects of models, this is a natural question to ask. But the question is ambiguous. A first reading takes the question to ask for a functional characterisation of models, specifying what purposes models serve. On this reading the question is "what role, or roles, do models play in science?". A second reading takes the question to ask for an ontological characterisation of models, specifying what sort of objects models are. On that reading the question is "what kind, or kinds, of objects are models?". To illustrate the contrast between these two readings, consider the analogous question "what is a hammer?". If we understand that question functionally, we can answer that it is an object that is used to drive a nail into a piece of wood. If we understand the question ontologically, we can respond that it is a flat-ended medium-size piece of metal mounted to a wooden stick.

Both readings of the question are legitimate, and they are in fact not independent of each other.[1] If the hammer were made from jelly, it would not be able to drive a nail into wood; and if the function of a hammer were to provide electrical insulation, then it would not be made from metal. Obvious connections notwithstanding, it is helpful to discuss these questions separately.

Some expectation management about the results of a discussion of these questions is in order. Both the functional and the ontological question can be understood as asking for *definitions*. This is setting the bar too high. Our little hammer example shows the difficulties one is up against when asking for definitions. The doctor's hammer is used to test deep tendon reflexes and is made from rubber, and the floor layer's hammer is made from soft plastic and serves the purpose of positioning floorboards so that the thongs and the groves interlock properly. An account of hammers that defines them as metal and wood objects that drive nails into wood misses cases like the doctor's hammer and the floor layer's hammer. If

DOI: 10.4324/9781003285106-19

we revise our definition so that it includes these other hammers too, then it will not take long to come up with another kind of hammer that is not covered by the previous definitions. This game can be continued *ad infinitum*, or certainly longer than our interest in the issue remains alive. There is, however, no need to keep going until a definition is reached. Even if the end point of our analysis falls short of being a definition, the discussion will have shed light on the nature of models and found characterisations of some of their important aspects. This is the project for this chapter.

We begin with a discussion of functional characterisations of models, and we examine views that see models as objects that function representationally. This characterisation is at once too narrow and too wide, even if attention is restricted to specific kinds of representation (Section 14.2). Turning to ontological characterisations of models, we reflect on what one would expect from such a characterisation and formulate five questions that every account of the ontology of models must answer (Section 14.3). Some models are material objects. They are things like ship-shaped wood blocks, systems of water pipes, and particular biological organisms. We consider what determines the choice of such objects as models and what is required to use them as models (Section 14.4). There are at least eight prima facie candidates for an ontology of non-material models: set-theoretical structures, abstract objects, descriptions, mathematical objects, equations, computational structures, fictional objects, and artefacts. We introduce these proposals and discuss their relation to each other, concluding that upon closer analysis they can be reduced to two: mathematical models and fictional models (Section 14.5). Unless a worked-out account of fictional models is formulated, the appeal to fiction remains little more than a promissory note. We meet this challenge by formulating an account of fictional models based on Walton's pretence theory and we show how this account integrates with the DEKI account of representation (Section 14.6). Finally, we summarise what has been achieved and draw some conclusions (Section 14.7).

14.2 Functional Characterisations of Models

The most common functional characterisation of models is in terms of representation: models are things that represent. This definition is popular with scientists and philosophers alike. In his encyclopaedia entry on models, Boltzmann says that a model is a "tangible representation" which "denotes a thing, whether actually existing or only mentally conceived of" (1911/1974, 213).[2] Physicist Nancy Dise defines a model as "a representation of the system that you study" (cited in Bailer-Jones 2002b, 297). In the philosophical literature on models Hughes observes that "[t]he characteristic – perhaps the only characteristic – that all theoretical models have in common is that they provide representations of parts of the world" (1997, 325); Portides notes that "a model is meant to represent something else" (2008, 385); Barberousse and Ludwig submit "that all scientific models have some properties in common: All of them are representations, in the sense that they stand for something else" (2009, 57).[3] And even reference works for the general public define models in representational terms. The online version of the *Encyclopaedia Britannica* states that "scientific modelling" is "the generation of a physical, conceptual, or mathematical representation of a real phenomenon" and the learning website study.com defines a model as "a representation of a particular phenomenon in the world".[4]

It is true that many models are representations of a target system, and we have discussed how models represent in Chapters 6, 8 and 9. It is, however, obvious that models cannot be *defined* through representation because there are representations that are not models and, vice versa, models that are not representations. The first point is obvious: paintings, drawings, photographs, statues, maps, diagrams, charts, and written texts are representations without also being models. The second point is brought into focus by Downes' remark that "the role of models in science is by no means exhausted by representation" (2011, 760). In Section 2.2 we saw that logical models are things that make all sentences of a theory true but without thereby also being representations of a target system. In the previous chapter we encountered developmental models, whose task it is to open alternative lines of research and help develop new theories (Section 13.2). Furthermore, Bokulich (2009) and Graham Kennedy (2012) discuss models that successfully explain certain phenomena, but, so they argue, without also providing representations of a target system.[5] Finally, Schlimm discusses the use of models in psychology and points out that in certain contexts models serve the purpose of establishing the viability of a hypothesis and that this does not require these models to be representations.[6] This goes to show that there are models whose purpose is not to represent something beyond themselves. Hence, neither are all representations models, nor are all models representations. This undercuts attempts to define models in terms of representation.

Could we rescue a definition of models as representations by refining the notion of representation that is invoked? Rather than representation *tout court*, a definition of models could refer to some specific kind of representation. A number of possible ways of restricting representation in the context of models have been proposed. The most popular restriction is representational deficiency: models represent their targets in ways that are inaccurate and incomplete. Box famously observes that "all models are wrong" (1976, 792), and Morrison submits that "one of the defining features of a model is that it contains a certain degree of representational inaccuracy" and that something "is a model because it fails to accurately represent its target system" (2016, 389).[7] This does not help. While it is true that models often represent their targets in a simplified and distorted manner, this is in no way specific to models and hence does not serve as *definition* of a model. Hans Holbein the Younger's portrait of Anne of Cleves was such a poor likeness of its subject that Henry VIII, who agreed to marry her only on the basis of having seen the portrait, wanted to call the wedding off when he finally saw the real woman. Lady Spencer-Churchill destroyed Graham Sutherland's painting of her husband, Sir Winston Churchill, because, in her view, it showed him as a disgraced down-and-out drunk rather than as a distinguished statesman. A map of the world neglects a myriad of details, and a road map gives a distorted picture of the topography of a territory. And so on. Furthermore, misrepresentations of this kind not only occur in visual representations: scientific *theories* can also misrepresent. Thermodynamics assumes many processes to be quasistatic (i.e. to happen infinitely slowly) even though real processes happen in finite time, and fluid dynamics assumes matter to be continuous even though it is not.

One might try to save the argument by emphasising that models *always* misrepresent their targets while other representations do this only occasionally. This argument is difficult to assess without stringent standards of misrepresentation, but at least when operating at an intuitive level this claim does not come out looking very plausible. Portraits and maps typically misrepresent their targets in one way or another, and there is nothing stopping models from providing accurate representations, at least if representation is restricted to certain respects. But irrespective of how this point is resolved, the view that models provide simplified or distorted representations still faces the second problem of the view that models are representations, namely that models can perform functions other than representing a target. Replacing representation with inaccurate representation leaves this fact unaltered.

In a paper entitled "Who is a Modeler?" Weisberg suggest a different way of restricting representation (2007). Models, on his view, offer what he calls "indirect representations". Models are objects that are distinct from their targets, and they are often (but not always) deliberately constructed for the purpose of being model-objects. Once a model object is available, this object becomes the focus of study and large parts of an investigation are carried out on the model rather than on the target system itself. This is possible because the model represents the target, which allows scientists to carry over findings from the model to the target. Analysing the model therefore amounts to analysing the target, albeit in an indirect way. This is why models offer indirect representations.

Weisberg's characterisation of modelling as indirect representation is valid,[8] but it is not sufficiently strong to demarcate models from other forms of representation. Paintings, photographs, statues, and even maps are also indirect representations: they present users with secondary objects that they study to eventually draw conclusions about the target. And, as in the case of inaccurate representation, the fact remains that some models perform functions other than representation.

The conclusion is that neither representation *tout court* nor inaccurate or indirect representation offer a general functional definition of models. This is not a proof that there is no functional definition of models. There could, in principle, be a different functional definition, one not couched in terms of representation, that captures all these activities under one large umbrella. However, the variety of models we encounter in scientific practice makes such a project look rather hopeless.[9]

14.3 Ontological Characterisations of Models

Let us now turn to the second reading of "what are models?". According to this reading, the question asks for an ontological characterisation of models: what sort of objects are models? Posing the question in this way bears the risk of getting trapped in a fallacy. The fallacy is that the question could be understood as presupposing that models belong to a distinct ontological category, and that the problem at hand was to give an account of that category. One would then have to sort the constituents of the world into things that are models and things that are not, and offer an ontological account of things that are models.

This is the wrong approach to the question. As Harré reminded us, "nothing is a model as such" (1988, 122). This is because "[a]n object, real or imagined, is not a model in itself. But it functions as a model when it is viewed as being in certain relationships to other things. So the classification of models is ultimately a classification of the ways things and processes can function as models" (2004, 6, cf. 1970, 40). Musicians are not a special category of humans; they are humans who play music. In Section 9.2 we have seen a parallel point concerning representation. Representations are not a particular category of things; representations are objects that function representationally. Anything from an assembly of glasses on the table to a fictional character, and from a second order equation to a dream can function as a model.[10] A programme that aims to identify a special category of things that are models (or representations) gets started on the wrong foot.

Have we dug ourselves into a hole? In the previous section we concluded that models cannot be defined functionally, and now we say that they cannot be defined ontologically and should instead be defined functionally. Fortunately, there is a way out of this predicament. The project of an ontological characterisation of models does not have to be understood as the quest for an analysis of models as a distinct ontological category. The project can be understood in different manner. Contessa points the way:

> even if, from an ontological point of view, scientific models may be a heterogeneous assortment and the best general characterization the one can give of them is a functional characterization, it does not follow that it is impossible to develop an account of the ontology of scientific models. Even if not all scientific models belong to a single ontological "kind", they might nonetheless belong to a few such kinds and we might be able to formulate accounts of what each of these kinds of models are. In other words, the heterogeneity of models certainly makes the task of formulating an account of their ontology more difficult, but it does not exempt the philosopher of science from that task. Nor does it follow that the questions concerning the ontology of scientific are any less pressing. To the contrary, even if models are characterised purely functionally, it is difficult to understand how a certain object can perform the relevant function, if we have no idea of what that object is.
>
> *(2010, 216)*

The project is to see what sort of things scientist use as models, and then give an analysis of them. The project has two parts. The first part is the descriptive project of narrowing down what kind of things scientists de facto recognise as models. The second part is to give an analysis of these objects. The project could be refined by writing the specific functional characterisation used to characterise models explicitly into the question and ask: given functional characterisation X of models, what kind of things do scientists de facto recognise as performing function X and how can these objects be characterised ontologically? The X could be, for instance, a representational characterisation or an explanatory characterisation. There is an interesting question whether different functional characterisations give rise to very different lists of objects that scientists recognise as models. Do they, say, use one kind of object to explain and another kind of object to represent? As far as I can see, this is not the case, but I formulate this as a conjecture. I will work with a representational characterisation in what follows, and it remains an open question whether the conclusions we reach would be different had we chosen a different functional characterisation.

Why do philosophers of science have to get involved in this? The first part of the project seems to be largely a sociological matter that can be left to science studies, and the second part seems to be a problem for metaphysicians. So there would seem to be a division of labour, and philosophers of science would seem to be able to pass on these problems to adjacent disciplines without detriment. There are good reasons for philosophers of science not to do this. As regards the first part, what sort of objects scientists use as models has important repercussions for how models perform relevant functions such as representation, and for scientific method more generally.[11] As we will see later, these issues are of philosophical interest and so the question of what kind of objects are used as models is not "just sociology". As regards the latter, the question could indeed be left to metaphysicians if the objects that are de facto used as models were well understood and did not leave any questions open, at least insofar as these questions have a bearing on an understanding of the model's function. If, for instance, model objects were sufficiently well understood to account for how they represent, then the case could be laid to rest as far as philosophy of science is concerned. As we shall see below, this is not always the case. While it is true that some kinds of objects that are used as models are sufficiently well understood for the purposes of philosophy of science and remaining questions can safely be left to metaphysicians, this is not the case for other kinds of objects.

What does it mean to "understand" an object? Much can be said about objects, and so we have to make a selection of questions we deem relevant in the context of modelling. To add specificity to the discussion, we will focus on the understanding required for a theory of representation. But the list of questions would be very similar, if not identical, if we focused on another functional characterisation instead. The following are the issues that we have to deal with if we aim to comprehend the objects that can function representationally (Frigg 2010c, 256–257):

(1) *Identity conditions*. In different contexts, models can be presented in different ways. Different material objects can be used, and different verbal descriptions can be employed to specify the model.[12] In some cases models can also be specified through means other than verbal descriptions, for instance through graphs or drawings. Circumstantial differences notwithstanding, scientists may deal with the same model. It is important to know when we are dealing with the same model and when we are not, and so we need identity conditions to tell us when models are identical.

(2) *Property attribution*. In the discussion of representation in Chapters 6, 8, and 9 we have seen that property attribution to models is crucial in many accounts of representation. The similarity account, for instance, says that both the model and the target have properties, and that model properties are similar to target properties. What does it mean for an object to have a property? As we have seen in Section 8.5, this question becomes particularly vexing when models are not physical objects. In the context of Newton's model of planetary motion, what sense can we make of, say, the claim that the large sphere is heavier than the small sphere given that abstract objects have no mass at all?

(3) *Comparative statements*. Comparing a model and its target is essential to many aspects of modelling. We customarily say things like "real agents do not behave like the agents in the model" and "the surface of the real sun is unlike the surface of the model sun". How are we to analyse such statements? While they may be relatively easy if the model is a material object, they are not straightforward when the model is not something that you can put on your laboratory table. How can we make comparative claims about the real sun and the model sun when the model sun does not exist? Likewise, how are we to analyse statements that compare features of two model systems with each other when the model systems do not exist?

(4) *Truth in models*. There is right and wrong in a discourse about models. It is true that a planet in Newton's model moves in an elliptical orbit; it is false that it moves in a square orbit. On what basis are claims about a model qualified as true or false, in particular if the claims concern issues about which the original specification of the model remains silent? We need an account of truth in models, which, first, explains what it means for a claim about a model system to be true or false and which, second, draws the line between true and false statements at the right place.

(5) *Learning about models*. Truths about a model should not be concealed from us forever. We must be able to investigate models and find out about them. How do we find out about what is true in a model and how do we justify our claims? That is, what is the epistemology of models?

Before discussing how to answer these questions for the objects that scientists choose to use as models, it is worth having at least a brief look at how such a choice is made. In principle scientists enjoy complete freedom in the choice of an object as a model. As we noted at the beginning of this section, anything can be chosen to be a model. This does not mean, however, that de facto anything is so chosen. The choice of objects as models is constrained by a number of factors that are closely connected to the functions models are expected to perform. The first factor is that if one is interested in using a model as a representation, then objects have to be suitable to be plugged into one's favourite account of representation. An object that cannot enter into a morphism relation is not a suitable model object for someone who subscribes to a structuralist conception of representation. The second factor is that a model must exhibit a specific behaviour of interest that can be examined in a process of investigation. As Hughes puts it, a model has "a life of its own": it is an object with "an internal dynamic whose effects we can examine" (1997, 331). Morgen submits that models are "small objects" that "have a stand-alone, autonomous, quality", which is because *models function both as objects to enquire into and as objects to enquire with*" (2012, 31, original emphasis). We enquire with a model if we take the model to represent something; we enquire into the model if we study the model itself. But studying the model itself is worthwhile only if there is something to study. Objects that are too inert to exhibit interesting behaviour or too obstinate to grant us insight into their inner workings are useless as models. One way of investigating the model is to manipulate the model. Morgan and Morrison emphasise this point when they write that "models are manipulated to teach us things about themselves" and that "when we manipulate the model . . . we learn, in the first instance, about the model world" (1999, 33). For these reasons, scientists will choose as models objects that have interesting features in their own right. But this choice is pragmatic: it is dictated by what scientists intend to do with the model. It's not dictated by some imperative of ontology that models are objects of a certain kind.

14.4   Material Models

Some models are material objects. If a material object is used as a model, I call it a *material model*.[13] In broadest terms, a material model is a material object that functions as a model according to some functional characterisation of models. If one characterises models representationally, then a material model is a material object that represents. The attraction of using such objects as models is obvious. As we have seen at the end of the previous section, models ought to be objects that have an internal dynamic and stand-alone qualities; they ought to be objects one can enquire into; and ideally one ought to be able to study the model by manipulating it. These desiderata are readily met by material objects, which have properties of their own that one can study, at least in principle, by intervening on them.

Material objects belong to the sort of objects where the above-mentioned division of labour is workable. Material models, *as objects*, do not raise questions over and above those that arise with all material objects. Questions (1)–(5) in the previous section can be asked about all material objects, and the answer one would give in the case of objects that are models is no different from the answers one would give about objects that are not. These questions are of course serious: the identity conditions for objects, the nature of properties, the semantics of statements, the nature of truth, and how we learn about material objects around us are all live research topics in metaphysics, philosophy of language, and epistemology. We do, however, have enough of a grasp of these issues to proceed with a study of models without first having to delve into these fields. And, more importantly, whatever we end up saying about models should not depend on any particular philosophical view on these issues. A philosophical analysis of, say, truth should be able to make sense of our pre-philosophical use of the word "truth" when we say things like "it is true that the pendulum oscillates back and forth three times per second". A study of models can operate at this pre-philosophical level and appeal to philosophical analyses of these concepts only when problems arise.

There is, however, a qualification to be added concerning the fifth challenge. When using models, we are not confined to "everyday epistemology"; instead, we can appeal to the rich resources of the scientific methodology of experiments. This is because using material models can be interpreted as performing an experiment. As Rosenblueth and Wiener note, "[a] material model may enable the carrying out of experiments under more favourable conditions than would be available in the original system" (1945, 317).[14] Indeed, the ability to perform experiments may serve as selection criterion for material models: "if the material model does not suggest any experiments whose results could not have been easily anticipated . . . then the material model is superfluous" (*ibid.*, 318).

Material models can be classified in different ways, but classification schemes fall into two broad families. Classifications in the first family focus on the character of the model object itself when they classify material models. Various organisms, both animals like the worm *Caenorhabditis elegans* and like the plant *Arabidopsis thaliana*, are classified as *model organisms* because they are themselves organisms and are used as models for other organisms (Ankeny and Leonelli 2011).[15] So called *robot models* are robots that are used as models for something else. Biorobotics researcher Barbara Webb constructs robots that share certain cognitive mechanisms with insects and uses the robots as models for insects in order to study their behaviour, for instance in navigation and learning (Webb 2001, 2009); in other contexts robots are used to model neurological disorders (Pronin et al. 2021). We classify models as *fluid models* when the salient feature of the model system is the flow of a liquid. Among the models in this category we find so-called "dumb holes", fluid systems that mimic gravity and that are used as models of black holes (Dardashti et al. 2017); a large basin, filled with water and equipped with pumps, that is proffered as model of the San Francisco Bay's water system (Weisberg 2013); and Bill Phillips and Walter Newlyn's reservoir and pipe machine that functions as an economy model (Barr 2000; Morgan and Boumans 2004).

Classifications in the second family focus on the relation that the model system has to its target system. Some material models are *analogical material models* because they relate to their target through an analogy. We have seen examples of such models in Section 10.4, and some of the models mentioned in the previous paragraph, for instance dumb holes, are also analogical models. Further examples of models of this kind are electrical circuits that are studied as models of brain function (Sterratt et al. 2011); the *camera obscura* when studied as a model of the human eye (Wade and Finger 2001); and metal cylinders filled with hardened magma that are studied as models for exploding volcanoes (Spieler et al. 2004).

The most important kind of model in the second family are *scale models*. As the name suggests, a scale model is one in which "the relation between the material model and the original system may be no more than a change of scale" (Rosenblueth and Wiener 1945, 317).[16] The replica of Tower Bridge in the museum of architecture and the model of a ship in the window of a travel agent are typical examples. But not all scale models are miniatures. The larger-than-life-size replica of a flee in the natural history museum and the ball-and-stick model of a water molecule in the chemistry class are scale models that are larger than their targets.[17]

Even though the idea of a model that shrinks or magnifies certain features of a target seems to be intuitively clear, the notion of a "change of scale" needs to be qualified in several ways. This is the plan for the remainder of this section. The standard dimensions of scaling are the three spatial dimensions: we construct the scale model of Tower Bridge by shrinking its length, width, and depth by, say, factor 100, which is the model's scaling factor. The model is then commonly referred to as a 1:100 model. This is a special case of a scale model because in principle one could have different scale factors in different dimensions. One could, for instance, shrink the bridge's width by factor 100, its height by factor 200, and its depth by factor 300. This would result in a model that would appear "squeezed", but that would still be a scale model. The specification of the parameters that are scaled and their scale factors are crucial because the scaling factors for different parameters stand in complicated relations to one another. Assume that you're interested in the Bridge's volume rather than in its extension in the three spatial dimensions (for instance because you want to estimate the bridge's weight before you plan a reinforcement of its pillars). You know that the model is 1:100 and you managed to measure the volume of the model. If you then think that the volume of the real bridge is just 100 times the volume of the model (just like the length of the real bridge is 100 times the length of the model), then you are making a fundamental mistake. Some elementary geometry shows that the volume scales with 100^3, and so the volume of the real bridge is a million times the volume of the model.

The example of the relation between length and volume is no exception: most parameters do not scale with the same scale factor as a model's extension in the three spatial dimensions. Unfortunately, not all cases are as simple as the relation between length and volume. Naval engineering provides a vivid illustration of the complexities involved in scaling. The engineers of a shipyard want to know what resistance the ship will experience when it moves with 15 knots. Measuring the resistance when the ship is at sea is difficult, or, if the ship is only at planning stage, impossible. So they build a model and determine the ship's resistance using the model. The engineers build, say, a 1:500 replica, which has exactly the shape of the original ship. They then drag the model through a water tank and measure the resistance it experiences when it moves with 15 knots. What does this tell them about the resistance of the real ship? There is no easy answer to this question. As in the case of volume, one cannot simply multiply the resistance of the model with the model's scale to obtain the real ship's resistance. But unlike in the case of volume, elementary geometry does not help. The model's and the real ship's resistances stand in a complicated scaling relation. Determining the nature of that relation is a formidable problem, and a solution often only emerges as a result of a thoroughgoing study of the situation.[18] Similar problems arise when scale models of cars are used to determine the air resistance of real cars, or when models of buildings are used to test their static properties.

A classic kind of scale models are ball-and-stick models in chemistry.[19] The models consist of balls of different sizes and sometimes different colours, which are taken to represent elements such as carbon, hydrogen, and oxygen. The balls have holes into which rods can be inserted. The rods can be used to connect different balls, and in this way represent chemical bonds between atoms. By sticking together different balls, the student of chemistry can construct representations of different molecules, for instance H_2O. The holes are in certain positions and the sticks have certain shapes. This puts constraints on how the balls and the sticks can be put together, and not every combination is possible. The balls and the sticks are designed so that the constraints on combining balls with sticks represent the constraints on combining elements through chemical bonds. Hence, by manipulating balls and sticks and figuring out which balls can be combined through rods and how, the balls and the sticks can be used to find out which elements can be joined to form molecules.

While standard ball-and-stick models of simple molecules are now predominantly used in the classroom to teach students elementary chemistry, similar models have played crucial roles in important discoveries. Laszlo reports that while in bed with a flu, Linus Pauling played around with paper models of chemical elements and in doing so discovered the alpha helix component of protein structure (2000, 92). And Pauling was not the only chemist to use material models. When studying the structure of DNA, James Watson and Francis Crick devised different sets of cardboard and metal pieces that could be combined in different ways.[20] Different pieces represented different chemical elements and the way they could be combined embodied what was known about structural chemistry at the time. The double helix structure of DNA was eventually discovered by figuring out how these pieces could be combined under given constraints. Material models also played a crucial role in the discovery of the structure of myoglobin, a globular protein that is found in many animal cells. To study the structure of myoglobin, biochemist John Kendrew constructed a material model of myoglobin that is now often referred to as the "sausage model". The model consists of a series of vertical supporting rods (looking a bit like a bed of nails with very long nails) that served as a support for a plasticine sausage, which could be stuck on the rods in different ways. On the basis of this model Kendrew could establish that myoglobin folded to form a flat disk with the extension of about 43Å × 35Å × 23Å, where "Å" denotes the unit Ångström, which is a unit of length equal to 10^{-10} m.[21]

14.5 Non-Material Models

Not all models are material objects. The Newtonian model of the solar system, the Lotka-Volterra model of predator and prey interaction, and Smale's horse-shoe model of streching and folding are not material objects. In Hacking's words, they are "something you hold in your head rather than your hands" (1983, 216). In Section 8.5 we called such models *non-material models*.[22]

But classifying a model as non-material is about as informative as saying that an animal is a non-elephant. In Section 6.2 we introduced the Problem of Carriers, which involves providing a list of the things that we recognise as models and giving an account of what these things are. A number of model-types have been introduced in the literature that can be seen as providing a response to the Problem of Carriers: earlier in the book we have already encountered set-theoretical structures (Section 5.2), abstract objects (Section 8.5), and descriptions (Section 9.3), and further candidates include mathematical models, equations, computational models, fictional objects, and artefacts. So there are at least eight candidates for things that are used as non-material models. The task for this section is to introduce the types of models that we have not already discussed and to examine how they relate to one another.[23]

We are now faced with the question of what the relevance of these categories is for understanding non-material models. There is no doubt that scientists encounter models in all these guises in their practical work. This, however, does not *ipso facto* mean that they are independent ontological categories, and there is the possibility that some items on the list are either indistinguishable from, or just notational variants of, each other. Someone might now reply that the ontological question "fundamentally, how many kinds of models are there?" is not a question worth asking because the aim of a theory of models is to understand scientific practice rather than to contribute to fundamental ontology. This objection points in the right direction, but it misconstrues the aim of the investigation. It's not a fundamental ontology of models that we are after; the project is to identify different model types. To that end we have to understand what kinds of non-material objects are used as models.

As a first pass at the problem, it is helpful to divide non-material models into two broad categories: formal models and non-formal models. Formal models are ones that are studied in formal disciplines like mathematics, logic, and computer science;[24] non-formal models are ones that do not fit that mould. Among the items on our list in the previous paragraph, mathematical models, set-theoretical structures, equations, and computational models are formal models; fictional models, artefacts, and descriptions are non-formal models; abstract objects can fall into either category depending on what kind of abstract objects one focuses on.

We now discuss formal models, beginning with mathematical models. Thomson-Jones provides a minimal characterisation of mathematical models. He calls "a model a mathematical model when standard presentations of it in scientific contexts employ mathematical tools" (2012, 761).[25] On this definition, being a mathematical model is a general category that subsumes other formal models. Set-theoretical structures, which we discussed in Section 5.2, are presented using the tools of set-theory, which a branch of mathematics, and hence set-theoretical structures count as mathematical models on Thomson-Jones' definition. As we have seen in Section 8.5, abstract objects are a broad and heterogenous class containing objects as varied as number two and Dante's Inferno. Some of these, for instance numbers, are the kind of things that can be formal models. In as far as abstract objects are the sort of things that can be formal models, they are also mathematical models. Numbers are presented using the tools of arithmetic, which is a branch of mathematics, and so on.

Next on our list are equations. Physicist Andrew Fowler says that "[u]sually, a *mathematical* model takes the form of a set of equations describing a number of variables"(1997, 3); Contessa notes that "[w]hen talking about the logistic growth model in population biology, for example, scientists usually seem to be referring to an equation" (2010, 217); and Pincock speaks of an "equation model" (2007, 961). So, equations are formal models. However, it is obvious that equations are also mathematical models because they are presented using mathematical tools.

So what we have found so far is that set-theoretical structures, abstract objects like numbers, and equations are all mathematical models. One might say that this is merely a trivial classificatory point that says nothing about what these objects really are. Thomson-Jones would agree, and he in fact emphasises that "to classify a model as mathematical in the current sense is not to say anything about what sort of object it is" (2012, 761). For those interested in the ontology of mathematics this is an unsatisfactory state of affairs. However, for our purposes it is sufficient. The current answer comes down to saying mathematical models are whatever mathematics regards as its subject matter, and that's good enough for an account of scientific models. At this point philosophers of science can hand the problem over to philosophers of mathematics. In fact, the various things that have been labelled as mathematical models neatly correspond to different positions in the philosophy of mathematics – abstract objects to Platonism, set-theoretical structures to structuralism, and equations to formalism – and the question of which of these, ultimately, are the objects of mathematics is a question for philosophers of mathematics.[26]

What we have not yet talked about are computational models, and that is where things get interesting. Weisberg puts forward a classification of models in which mathematical models and computational models are distinct (2013, Ch. 2). On this view, computational models differ from mathematical models and cannot be subsumed under mathematical models in the way equations, structures, and abstract objects can.[27] Weisberg does not give a general definition of computational model and instead introduces the notion with the example of Schelling's model of social segregation (Schelling 1978).[28] The model is a so-called agent-based model. It consists of a checkerboard where each square on the board can be either blue, red, or left blank. The board represents a city and two colours represent agents of different types. If a square is either blue or red, it means that the place is occupied by an agent of the blue or the red type; if a square is blank, the location is unoccupied. The actors in this model have a preference to live with other actors of the same kind (i.e. the blue actors prefer to live near blue actors, and the red actors prefer to live near red actors). The preference comes in different strengths, and the strength is measured by the percentage of other actors of the other type that an actor is willing to tolerate as neighbours. If the percentage is above a certain threshold, then the actors moves to a location that meets their requirements. The dynamics of this model can be conveniently implemented on a computer and the effects can be shown visually. Simulations then show that already small preferences to live with agents of the same kind can lead to large-scale segregation.

This example shows that computational models typically consist of algorithms or procedures that can be implemented on digital computers. The question now is: are such algorithms so different from mathematical models that they should be seen as forming a separate category? O'Connor and Weatherall examine Weisberg's distinction between mathematical and computational models and argue that the difference between the two is superficial and crumbles under analysis (2016, 620–622). They discuss the example of replicator dynamics, one of the principal tools in evolutionary game theory and population dynamics to describe how a population evolves over time, and they point out that the dynamics can equally well be characterised using either continuous or discrete time. If one works with continuous time, the equation describing the dynamics is a continuous differential equation, which, by Weisberg's lights, is a mathematical model. If, however, one works with discrete time (by considering populations as changing in discrete time steps), one gets an algorithm that Weisberg's classification regards as a computational model. Hence, depending on the pragmatic decision to work with continuous or discrete time, one gets two different kinds of models. Yet both models describe the same dynamics.

The similarities between the two run even deeper. O'Connor and Weatherall point out that the continuous model can be derived from the discrete model via a limiting process when the size of the time step approaches zero, and that both give provably similar results for the evolution of a population (*ibid.*, 621). And derivation can, and often does, also proceed in the other direction, from continuous to discrete. Models like the Schelling model are an obvious fit for computers because the "moving rule" of the model naturally has the form of a computer algorithm. But not all computational models are constructed in this way. In many cases scientists will first write down a continuous differential equation and then apply a so-called discretisation scheme to it to turn a continuous equation into a discrete equation that can be studied on a computer. The reason for this is that it is often difficult, or impossible, to solve differential equations and to derive relevant results analytically. Scientists then resort to computers, which allow them to get answers to questions that otherwise remain intractable. But if continuous and discrete equations can be derived from one another, can describe the same dynamics, can represent the same processes, and can provide approximations of each other, then it would seem unnatural to say that they are different kinds of models. Rather, it would seem that they are alternative version of the same model. In this vein, Giere notes that a "computer simulation is just a fancy way of investigating the mathematical features of an abstract model characterized by a set of equations" (Giere 2001, 1060). For this reason, computational models are also mathematical models and the class of formal models in fact coincides with the class of mathematical models.

The candidate list for non-formal models includes fictional objects, abstract objects (of the non-formal kind), artefacts and descriptions. Let us begin with fictional objects. As we have seen in Section 1.2, the Newtonian model of the solar system consist of homogenous perfect spheres in empty space that attract each other gravitationally. When Maxwell studied the electromagnetic field, he used a model consisting of an imaginary incompressible fluid, and he set himself the task of studying the flow of this fluid (see Section 10.5). And when Aharonov and Bohm studied the effect that now bears their name, they investigated a "fictional system characterized by features that, though physically possible, are not realized in the actual world" (Earman 2019, 1991). Hence, none of these objects exist in the physical world, and if the corresponding model description was understood as a description of a real system it would be false.

The examples in the previous paragraph are not isolated cases. As Thomson-Jones (2010) points out, scientists habitually consider systems that do not exist in the physical world as models of their targets. This is embedded in what he calls the "face value practice" (*ibid.*, 285): the practice of talking and thinking about these models *as if* they were real. This motivates the view that models are on par with the objects of literary fiction. Godfrey-Smith summarises the idea as follows:

> I take at face value the fact that modelers often *take* themselves to be describing imaginary biological populations, imaginary neural networks, or imaginary economies. . . . Although these imagined entities are puzzling, I suggest that at least much of the time they might be treated as similar to something that we are all familiar with, the imagined objects of literary fiction. Here I have in mind entities like Sherlock Holmes' London, and Tolkien's Middle Earth. . . . the model systems of science often work similarly to these familiar fictions.
>
> *(2006, 735)*

The idea that models are akin to the places and characters in literary fiction has become known as the "fiction view of models".[29] The word "fiction" is used in two different senses: fiction as infidelity and fiction as imagination.[30] When used in the first sense, "fiction" means something that deviates from reality. A claim can be called a "fiction" to express that it is false, for instance when we say that the prime minister's account of events was a fiction; or an object can be qualified as a "fiction" to convey that it does not exist, for instance when we sarcastically say that the new MRI scanners of the National Health Service are a fiction. When used in the second sense, "fiction" is applied to a text and indicates that the text belongs to a particular genre, namely literary fiction. The events and characters in such a work are to be imagined; that's the defining feature of the genre. Rife prejudice notwithstanding, falsity is not a requisite for that. The reader of Tolstoy's *War and Peace* reads much about Napoleon, and she is mandated, by the novel, to imagine Napoleon doing various things, and yet Napoleon is not a fiction in the first sense. Being a fiction in the second sense is compatible with truth, but, of course, neither implies nor presupposes truth. *War and Peace* also mandates us to imagine things about Pierre Bezukhov even though there neither is nor ever was a Pierre Bezukhov.

This shows that our two uses of fiction are not mutually exclusive. Many places and characters that appear in literary fiction, and are to be imagined when reading a work of fiction, indeed do not exist and hence are fictions also in the first sense. But not all are. From the fact that something appears in a work fiction (in the second sense) one must not infer it also is a fiction in the first sense. Pierre Bezukhov and Napoleon both appear in *War and Peace*, but only the former is a fiction the first sense.

These points are pertinent in the current context because it is the second and not the first sense of "fiction" that is at work in the fiction view of models. When a model is qualified as fiction, this is not meant to convey that everything in the model is false. What the qualification conveys is that models prescribe certain things to be imagined while remaining *noncommittal* about whether or not the entities or processes in the model exist, or whether claims that emerge from the model are true or false. So the fiction view of models is not committed to the claim that everything that appears in a model is false. Just as a novel can contain characters that exist and ones that do not, and make claims that are true and claims that are false, a model, understood as fiction, can contain things that exist and things that do not, and make claims that are true and claims that are false. The question of which of a model's elements exist and which of its claims are true depends on how the model represents, and this is in no way prejudged by the fact that a model is a fiction.

How one sees the relation between the fiction view and an account of models that takes them to be abstract objects depends on one's analysis of fiction. The nature of fictional objects has been discussed extensively in aesthetics and metaphysics, and there is a plethora of positions to choose from. A review of these positions is beyond the scope of this book, but it is worth briefly sketching a few options.[31] *Fictional realists* insist that, first appearances notwithstanding, there *are* fictional entities like Sherlock Holmes and Tolkien's Middle-earth. They just do not have physical being, but physical being is not the only way of being. So when scientists talk about perfectly spherical planets and incompressible fluids, they talk about real things, and when they investigate a model they discover properties of these things. The pioneer of fictional realism was Meinong (1904), who thought that in addition to ordinary physical objects that exist, "*there are* – in an ontologically committed sense – things that do not exist" (Friend 2007, 141). This position has become known as *Meinongianism*. More recently, Thomasson (1999) developed a position according to which fictional entities are neither Meinogian objects nor possibilia, but what she calls *abstract artefacts*. On this account, fictional characters are abstract objects, but not of a Platonic kind; these characters are artefacts because they are brought into existence by a creative act of a writer just like a vase is brought into existence through the creative act of the potter. Thomasson (2020) and Thomson-Jones (2020) have recently adapted this approach to scientific modelling and argue that models are abstract artefacts in this sense. On this approach, the objects of fiction are at the same time abstract objects, and so the fiction view of models and the view that models are abstract objects coincide.

Fictional antirealists disagree and insist that there are no such things as fictional entities and the "as if" in the face value practice must be taken seriously. Talk of fictional entities ought not to be taken literally, and reference to fictional entities is only apparent and can be paraphrased away. We will discuss an antirealist view of fiction in some detail in the next section. For now, we just note that on fictional antirealism, models are not abstract objects. Indeed, a fictional antirealist will take abstract objects off the list of things that function as models because abstract objects (or at least the kind of abstract objects that could be non-formal models) do not exist.

As we have seen at the beginning of Section 9.3, some authors view models as descriptions. Knuuttila developed this view into a position that she calls the "artifactual account". The core of this account is "to consider the actual representational means with which a model is constructed and through which it is manipulated as irreducible parts of the model" (2021a, 5087). The account gets its name from the fact that these "representational means" – descriptions, mathematical formulas, diagrams, three dimensional contraptions, and so on (*ibid.*, 3) – are "purposefully created artifacts" (*ibid.*, 3) and that these artefacts are "irreducible parts of any representational vehicle, such as a model" (*ibid.*, 12).[32] Knuuttila's artefactualism emphasises the primacy of the model-descriptions, and it often does so by drawing a contrast with fiction. The dichotomy between fiction and artefacts is presented as being grounded in the fictional view's "separation of the imagined-object from the so-called model descriptions" and the fact that, as a consequence, the fiction view has must regard "imagined (i.e., fictional) entities" as "the locus of scientific representation" (*ibid.*, 3).

There are two readings of this position. On a strong reading, the "representational means" – model descriptions, and so on – literally *are* models. That is, the model is nothing over and above the description or the diagram that model users see printed on page, and these material objects are the representational units of science. Knuuttila seems to reach this conclusion when, at the end of the paper, she sums up her view by saying that "[e]xternal artifacts, and not imagined-objects, provide the actual locus of scientific representation even in the case of fictional modelling" (*ibid.*, 19). If so, then the artefactual account becomes indistinguishable from Direct Representation, which regards descriptions as models. If so, then the account faces all the problems of Direct Representation, which we discussed in Section 9.3.

However, Knuuttila's posit that model descriptions and the like are "parts" of models can be seen as suggesting that she would favour a weaker interpretation, whereby model descriptions (and other material artefacts) do not exhaust a model, and whereby a model is a complex entity that also has other parts. She seems to come close to such a position when she says that the artefactual account could "complement" the fiction view (*ibid.*, 11). This leaves open the questions, first, in what way the fiction view would have to be complemented to begin with and, second, wherein this complementation consists. As we will see in the next section, different versions of the fiction view have given different accounts of the relation between model descriptions and models, and indeed of the role that model descriptions play in an account of modelling, but no version of the fiction view has banished model descriptions from an account of modelling. Hence, the need for complementation may be a bit less acute than Knuuttila suggests it is.

In sum, then, the class of non-formal models coincides with the class of fictional models.

Let us recap. We started by distinguishing between two broad families of models: formal models and non-formal models. We considered various proposed kinds of models that are seen as falling within these families, and our discussion led us to the conclusion that the family of formal models consists of mathematical models and the family of non-formal models consists of fictional models. The obvious next question, then, is how these two relate to each other. Our analysis so far suggests that the two kinds of models often go hand in hand. On the one hand, mathematical models seem to need fictional models to relate to something non-mathematical. In Section 6.5 we have seen that mathematical models (analysed as structures) on their own do not represent and that they need to be supplemented with descriptions to relate to a target. In special cases these physical descriptions can be straightforward descriptions of a target system. However, as soon as the mathematics involved goes beyond arithmetic, the descriptions needed are rarely, if ever, straightforward descriptions of target. In the case of the Newtonian model, planets have to be rendered as perfect spheres with homogenous mass distributions, which is not an accurate description of any planet. Such descriptions are best understood as being descriptions of a fictional model, which then relates in some yet to be specified sense to the target.

On the other hand, fictional models are rarely useful in isolation.[33] Little insight is gained by pondering an imaginary box full of billiard balls divorced from any mathematical formalism. The billiard ball model of a gas is a useful instrument for scientific investigation because it provides an entry ticket for a mathematical description of gases, and it is that mathematical description that delivers the crucial results. Indeed, the billiard ball model is best understood as an interpretative model of the kind we encountered in Section 13.5: billiard balls that move without friction, that collide elastically, and that interact with other objects only upon impact provide the highly idealised object to which the formalism of mechanics can be applied.

Hence, models are composite objects that consist of fictional and mathematical parts. The question is how exactly these parts are analysed and how they integrate. There are many options, and how one responds to these challenges depends on one's other philosophical commitments, in particular on how one analyses representation. In the next section I will present my own favourite account of models to illustrate what such an answer might look like.

14.6   Models and Pretence

In this section, we develop a particular version of the fiction view of models, say how it integrates with mathematical models, and indicate how it deals with representation. The view we will be focusing on analyses models in terms of pretence theory, which we encountered in Section 9.3, and then ties models to the DEKI account of representation that we discussed in Section 9.5. There are alternative ways of developing the fiction view of models.[34] The discussion in this section is a "proof of concept" for the fiction view of models, and it adds specificity to the vague claims that we made at the end of the previous section.

The discussion in this section also serves to address a nagging worry that some readers may have had when going through the previous section. The worry is that the places and characters in literary fiction are beset with as many philosophical puzzles as models themselves, and a sizeable philosophical literature tries to come to terms with these puzzles.[35] So why is the fiction view of models not just explaining *obscurum per obscurius*? This is a serious challenge, and proponents of the fiction view have to make it plausible that likening models to fiction has philosophical value. This is the project for this section.

Before spelling out what philosophical work exactly the fiction view is expected to do, and before explaining how it gets this work done, it is worth articulating the motivations for the fiction view in more detail. In the last section we have seen that scientists seem appeal to fictions when they ponder things like spherical planets and imaginary fluids. But why is this a good thing to do and why would one build a philosophical account of models on it? I can see four reasons for this.

The first reason is that fiction is a genre that gives the author creative freedom. Fictions can contain characters and places that do not exist, and there is often nothing in the world of which the text of a novel is a true description. To come back to Godfrey-Smith's examples, Sherlock Holmes is not a real person and Middle-earth is not a real place. Readers are of course fully aware of this, and do not mistake the sentences of novel for a direct description of something in the actual world. The same happens in scientific modelling. When reasoning with perfect spheres and imaginary fluids, scientists do not talk about, or describe, real physical systems. The objects of enquiry are imaginary in the same way in which the objects of literary fiction are, and they are chosen because they are convenient in their respective contexts.

The second reason to ponder the parallel between models and fiction emerges from guarding against a frequent misconception. As noted previously, saying that fictions can contain characters and places that do not exist is not tantamount to saying that models, or indeed literary fictions, are plain falsities. The fiction view neither says nor implies that scientific models are nothing but untrue fabrications which contain no factually correct information about their targets. Fiction, either scientific or literary, is not defined through falsity. Historical fictions like Tolstoy's *War and Peace* contain many true elements, and the fact that a government report is at variance with fact in a number of places does not make it fiction. What makes a text fictional is not its falsity (or a particular ratio of false to true claims), but the attitude that the reader is expected to adopt toward it.[36] Readers of a novel are invited to imagine the events and characters described. They are expressly not meant to take the sentences they read as reports of fact, let alone as false reports of fact. Imagination is, as it were, neutral with respect to truth. Nevertheless, literature often provides insight into something. When reading, we may engage in comparisons between the situations in the fiction and situations we have encountered in real life, and thereby learn about the world by reading fiction. Again, this has parallels in the context of modelling, where we learn from models about the world. Once we think about models as fictions, this parallel becomes salient and urges us to think about how the "knowledge transfer" from a fictional scenario to the real world takes place. At least in the context of science this transfer involves taking the fiction to be a representation of the target system. The point that matters for now is that the fiction view is not committed to the nihilist position that scientific models are falsities without connection to realty.[37]

The third reason is that fiction comes equipped with a notion of "internal truth" that is of interest also in the context of models. It is true in Hemingway's *The Old Man and the Sea* that Santiago is a Cuban fisherman and that he went fishing by himself. It is also true in the story that Santiago has a heart and a liver, and that he does not have a degree in Japanese literature. Only the first two claims are explicitly stated in the story; the others are inferred indirectly. That something is not stated explicitly does not make it arbitrary. Whether or not claims about a story's content are correct is determined by the text without being part of its explicit content. Likewise, model descriptions usually only specify a handful of essential properties, but it is understood that the model has properties other than the ones mentioned in the model description. In fact, models are interesting exactly because more is true in them than what the model description specifies explicitly. This is what makes them interesting as objects of study. It is, for instance, true in the Newtonian model that the model-planets move in stable elliptical orbits, but this is not part of the explicit content of the model's original description. Philosophers of science have to understand what it means for a claim to be true in a model, and keep an eye on how "truth in fiction" can be heuristically useful when tackling this problem.

The fourth reason follows on from the third and concerns the epistemology of claims about what is true in a story. A story not only has content that goes beyond what is explicitly stated; we also have the means to find out what this "extra content" is. Indeed, it is an integral part of our response to fiction that we supplement the explicit content and "fill the gaps" in the plot where the text remains silent. The same goes for models. Finding out what is true in a model beyond what is explicitly specified in the relevant description is a crucial aspect of scientists' engagement with a model, and the bulk of the research that goes into exploring a model usually goes into finding out whether or not certain claims about the model are true. For this reason, an articulation of an epistemology of models may well benefit from insights gained into how we learn about fiction.

This list of communalities between scientific modelling and literary fiction is neither complete nor should it be understood as suggesting that there are no differences between the two. The purpose of this list is just to make it plausible that thinking about models as fictions is at least a plausible point of departure.

After having found a point of departure, we need to define the purpose of the journey. This purpose is to address the challenges that we formulated in Section 14.3: formulate identity conditions for models, understand property attribution, analyse comparative statements, provide an account of truth in models, and explain how we learn about models. Responses to these challenges should satisfy two requirements. The first is that they must be able to account for how models are employed in scientific practice. A philosophical theory of models that makes a mystery of how scientists use models in the practice of their work is useless, and hence answers to the above questions must be compatible with, and indeed account for, how scientists work with models. The second requirement belongs to the realm of philosophy: that we must have a clear notion of the ontological commitments that we incur in our answers and must be able to justify them, if necessary.

The contention of the current approach is that Walton's (1990) pretence theory (PT) offers convincing responses to all five challenges. We have already discussed the basic ideas of PT in Section 9.3. We here briefly recapitulate a few important points and expand on aspects that are crucial in the current context. We can do so because PT is in no way tied to Direct Representation. Walton originally formulated the account as a contribution to aesthetics, and different uses of it outside that context are possible. The fiction view as discussed in this section makes a rather different use of it than Direct Representation.

PT's point of departure is the capacity of humans to imagine things. Sometimes we imagine something without a particular reason. But there are cases in which our imagining something is prompted by the presence of a particular object. If so, this object is a *prop*. An object becomes a prop due to the imposition of a *principle of generation*, prescribing what is to be imagined in response to the presence of the object. If someone imagines something due to the presence of a prop they are engaged in a *game of make-believe*. Someone who is involved such a game is *pretending*. So "pretence" is just a shorthand way of describing participation in such a game and has nothing to do with deception. Some principles of generation are *ad hoc*, for instance when a group of children spontaneously imposes the principle that stumps are bears and play the game "catch the bear". Other principles are publicly agreed on and hence (relatively) stable. Games based on public principles are "authorised"; games involving *ad hoc* principles are "unauthorised".

The kinds of props that are used in games of make-believe can vary widely, ranging from novels to movies, from paintings to plays, and from music to children's games. In the present context we focus on the case where the prop is a text. Works of literary fiction are, on the current account, props as they prompt the reader to imagine certain things. By doing so a fiction generates its own game of make-believe. When reading *The Old Man and the Sea* the text mandates the reader to imagine a Cuban fisherman named Santiago and that Santiago went fishing by himself. By doing so, the text functions as a prop.

Props generate fictional truths by virtue of their features and principles of generation. Fictional truths can be generated directly or indirectly; directly generated truths are *primary* and indirectly generated truths are *implied*. The intuitive idea is that primary truths follow immediately from the prop, while implied ones result from the application of some rules of inference. One can then call the principles of generation that generate primary truths *principles of direct generation* and those that generate implied truths *principles of indirect generation*. The reader of *The Old Man and the Sea* is told that Santiago is a Cuban fisherman who has gone 84 days without catching a fish. These are primary truths that the reader is mandated to imagine because they are explicitly stated in the text. The reader should also imagine that Santiago was involved in an epic struggle, that he was determined and relentless, and that he has a heart and a liver. None of this is explicitly stated in the story. These are inferred truths, which readers deduces from the text given their background knowledge about human psychology and anatomy.

PT has the resources to flesh out the idea that models are like the characters and places of literary fiction and to respond to the five challenges about models. Models are usually presented to us by way of descriptions, which we earlier called "model descriptions". These descriptions should be understood as props in games of make-believe. This squares with the practice of modelling where model-descriptions often begin with "consider", "assume", or "imagine", which make it explicit that the descriptions to follow are not intended to be descriptions of real-world objects but should be understood as a prescription to imagine particular situations. Although it is often understood that the situations are such that they do not occur anywhere in reality, this is *not* a prerequisite in PT. We will come back to this point shortly.

Where does mathematics fit into this picture? The key realisation is that mathematics can be part of both the model description and of the principles of generation. Mathematical aspects are typically not prominent in literary fiction, but many novels contain basic arithmetic (for instance because money is used in the plot) and geometry (for instance because geographical and topographical aspects of a territory play a role). There is no prerequisite in PT that a prop be "maths free".

This fact can be exploited in modelling, where mathematical descriptions can be integral parts of the original model description and the principles of generation. Thus, the language in which the model is described, and in which inferences are generated from the primary truths, can already involve mathematical concepts. This happens, for instance, in the model description of Newton's model when we specify that model planets are perfect spheres and that they attract each other with a $1/r^2$ force. It happens again when we specify the principles of generation. The crucial principle of generation is Newton's equation of motion, which governs the motion of the planets and is used to find that it is true in the model that planets move in elliptical orbits.[38] The mathematics that is part of the model description can then be seen as describing a mathematical model. So, on this view, a mathematical model can be part of a fictional model, and PT provides an extended view of fiction that sees model as consisting of formal and non-formal parts.

Let us now turn to our five challenges, beginning with truth in fiction (the fourth challenge in our list). Statements like "Santiago is Cuban fisherman" are made within the fiction. Such statements are not meant to be believed; they are meant to be imagined. Although some statements are true in the fiction as well as true *tout court* ("Cuba is in the Caribbean" is true and true in Hemingway's story), we often qualify false statements as true in the fiction ("Santiago is a fisherman" is true in the fiction but false because there is no Santiago) and true statements as false in the fiction ("Cuba is governed by communist regime" is true but false in the story whose plot takes place before the revolution). So truth and truth in fiction are not only distinct notions; they are also not coextensive. Walton goes as far as saying that truth in fiction is not a species of truth at all (1990, 41).[39] I see no harm in using the moniker "truth in fiction" and I use the shorthand "$T_w(p)$" for "it is true in work w that p", where p is a placeholder for an statement.

We can now define $T_w(p)$. Let the w-game of make-believe be the game of make-believe based on work w, and similarly for "w-prop" and "w-principles of generation". Then, p is true in w iff p is to be imagined in the w-game of make-believe (1990, 39), or, in more detail: $T_w(p)$ iff the w-prop together with the w-principles of generation prescribes p to be imagined. Nothing in this definition depends on w being a work of literature, and so this definition equally applies to scientific contexts. We can take the w to be Newton's work on planetary motion. The description of the Newtonian model (which we have seen in Section 1.2) is a w-prop and the scientific principles taken to be in operation in this context, including Newton's equation of motion, are the w-principles of generation. The statement "model-planets move in elliptical orbits" is then true in the Newtonian game of make-believe because the w-prop together with the w-principles of generation prescribes participants to imagine model-planets as moving in elliptical orbits.

This analysis of truth in fiction alleviates two worries. The first worry concerns the alleged subjectivity of imaginings. Imagination, one might argue, is a private activity and everybody's imagination is different. Therefore, an understanding of models as imaginings makes them subjective because every person imagines something different. This is not so. PT regards imaginings in an authorised game of make-believe as sanctioned by the prop and the principles of generation, both of which are publicly shared by a relevant community. If someone plays a game of make-believe, their imaginings are governed by intersubjective principles and these principles force everybody involved in the game to have the same imaginings. Furthermore, for a proposition to be fictional in work w it is not necessary that it is actually imagined by anyone: fictional propositions are ones for which there is a prescription to the effect that they *have to be imagined*, and whether such a proposition is actually imagined by anybody is an altogether different matter. Props, via the principles of generation, make propositions true in a fiction independently of people's *actual* imaginings, and for this reason there can be fictional truths that no one knows of.

The other worry concerns the point mentioned in the second motivation earlier on, namely that the fiction view regards models as falsities. As we have just seen, being true and being true in the fiction are different and uncorrelated concepts. A statement can be fictional while at the same time also being true ("Cuba is in the Caribbean"). Therefore, an understanding of models as fiction does *not* force the absurd view on us, that all models must be regarded as false. The view simply leaves the question of truth open, and this is how it should be. Models are often introduced as a suggestion worth considering, and their exact relation to reality is worked out once the model is understood. This is particularly obvious in elementary particle physics, where a particular scenario is often put forward simply as a suggestion worth exploring and only later, when all the details of the model are worked out, the question is asked whether the particles in the model actually exist. We are neither committed to regarding these particles as non-existent simply because they appear in a model nor should we accept them as real because of some foot-stomping insistence that "science deals with reality!". The question whether the particles exist is answered experimentally, usually at a large research facility like CERN.

This take on truth in fiction also provides us with an answer to the question about the epistemology of models: we investigate a model by finding out what follows from the primary truths of the model and the principles of indirect generation, where these principles will include general principles and laws of nature that are taken to be in operation in the context in which the model is used. For instance, we derive that the planets move in elliptical orbits from the basic assumptions of the Newtonian model and the laws of classical mechanics. This is explained naturally in terms of pretence theory. What is explicitly stated in a model-description are the primary truths of the model, and what follows from them via laws or general principles are the implied truths.

To formulate identity conditions, we first introduce the notion of a "fictional world" or "world of a fiction": the world of work w is the set of all propositions that are true in w. It is then natural to say that two models are identical iff the worlds of the two models are identical. Note that this condition does not say that models are identical if the model descriptions have the same content. In fact, two models with the same model descriptions (the same prop) *can* be different because different principles of generation are assumed to be in operation. This is the case, for instance, when what might look like "the same model" is treated first in the context of classical physics and then in the context of quantum mechanics. A common model description of a model of a hydrogen atom says that the model consists of an electron and a proton, and that the two attract each other with a Coulomb force. If we assume that the laws of classical mechanics serve as the principles of generation in the model, we get the Bohr model and it is true in the Bohr model that electrons move in precisely defined trajectories. If we assume that the laws of quantum mechanics serve as the principles of generation in the model, we get the Schrödinger model of the atom and it is false in that model that electrons move in precisely defined trajectories. Regarding these as different models despite being based on the same model-description is the right verdict.

The attribution of a property P to a model is explained as it being true in the world of the model that the model has P. To say that the model-planet moves in an elliptical orbit is like saying that Santiago is a fisherman. Both claims follow from a prop together with principles of generation. In other words, saying that a hypothetical entity possesses certain properties involves nothing over and above saying that within a certain game of make-believe we are mandated to imagine the entity as having these properties. For this reason, there is nothing mysterious about ascribing concrete properties (like flowing regularly) to nonexistent things, nor is it a category mistake to do so.

Comparisons are more involved. The problem is that comparing a model either with another model or with a real-world object involves elements that are not part of the authorised game of make-believe, and hence are not covered by it. How to best overcome this problem is a matter of controversy, and different suggestions have been made. Walton's suggestion is that we devise an unauthorised game of make-believe to make such comparisons, one that contains the constituents of both models, or of the model and the real object, and then carry out comparisons within that extended game of make-believe. I recommend that we run with this suggestion.

We now see how PT responds to the five challenges concerning models that we formulated in Section 14.3. But some readers may be left wondering: where is *the* model? The proposed account has a large number of moving parts, and it is not obvious which of them, if any, should be called "the model". Different versions of the fiction view give different answers, which also leads to different ontological commitments. In the original formulation of the view in my (2010c) I took models to be the imaginings that scientists have when they are involved in the game of make-believe. This is a firmly antirealist view according to which models do not exist: they are figments of the imagination. As we have seen in the previous section, Knuuttila argues that model descriptions ought to be part of the model. Salis (2021) makes similar point and submits that a model should be regarded as a complex object composed of a model description together with the model description's content (generated jointly by the principles of direct and indirect generation). On this view models exists, at least insofar as texts and their content exist.

If our aim is to understand the internal workings of models, not much depends on how this issue is resolved. It becomes relevant mostly when the fiction view is combined with a theory of representation. As we have seen in Chapter 9, many accounts of representation involve the notion that models denote their target systems. Denotation is a dyadic relation between certain symbols and certain objects. But relations can obtain only between two things that exist. Hence an antirealist view of models undercuts the possibility of models denoting targets and antirealists will have to resort to the notion that models have pretend denotation rather than "real" denotation. If one insists on real denotation, then the model has to exist and Salis' version of the fiction view makes this possible.[40]

How does the PT version of the fiction view of models fare as regards our two requirements? I submit that it scores high for being able to account for how models are employed in scientific practice. Specifying basic assumptions and studying their consequences when combined with general principles like laws of nature seems to be exactly what scientists do when they investigate a model. What ontological commitments are incurred depends on which version of the fiction view is adopted. As we have just seen, the original version of the view incurs no commitments, while Salis' version is committed to the existence of texts and their content. What matters is that the account can avoid an expedition into Meinong's jungle because at no point in the argument is the account forced to introduce fictional or abstract entities into its ontology. This, of course, does not mean that the expedition must be avoided. Fictional realists who see virtue in the introduction of such entities into the fiction view are free to do so (as we have seen in the previous section); the observation at this point is only that introducing such entities is not forced on us by the internal requirements of the view, and that is a good thing.

What we have discussed so far concerns the internal structure of a model. The question now is: how does such a model represent a target system? In principle the fiction view of models as developed so far can be combined with any account of representation we have discussed in Chapters 6, 8, and 9, except for Direct Representation, which renounces a commitment to model systems altogether. My own favourite is the DEKI account (Section 9.5) and I will now briefly sketch how the fiction view integrates into that account. To begin with, recall the main tenets of the DEKI account. We consider an Agent A, and the agent chooses an object and turns it into a Z-representation by adopting an interpretation. The model M is the package of the object together with the interpretation that turns it into a Z-representation. Model M is a scientific representation of T iff M represents T as Z. M represents T as Z iff the following four conditions are satisfied: (i) M denotes T (and, possibly, parts of M denote parts of T); (ii) M is a Z-representation exemplifying certain Z-properties; (iii) M comes with a key K specifying how the Z-properties exemplified in the model translates into other properties, and (iv) M imputes at least one of these other properties to T.

The formulation of the account speaks of an "object". If the model is a material model, then this is to be taken literally because it is a physical object that figures in the account. The cue to realising how the DEKI machinery applies to non-material models is that nothing depends on the object being material and the object referred to in the definition of DEKI can equally well be an "imagined object" of the kind introduced in PT.[41] In other words, the core idea is to simply put a fictional object in the place of the material object in the statement of the account. The relevant "objects" in the Newtonian model are the two perfect spheres. They have no physical existence: they are imagined, and that is enough. We can interpret them as the sun and the earth in our imagination, and they can have all kinds of properties in the sense explicated in response to the second challenge. And neither the key nor the act of imputation depend on whether the model is material or imagined. Once this is realised, we see that the entire DEKI machinery applies to models almost unaltered.

The "almost" concerns the nature of model descriptions. As presented in Section 9.5 (and as summarised in Figure 9.1) the description D_X is a plain description of a material object. This is now reinterpreted as a model description serving as a prop in a game of make believe that mandates the scientist to imagine the content of the description. This change is seamless and can be effected by using indicative words like "assume" or "consider" at the beginning of the description. There is, however, a second change which, while still unproblematic, is less trivial. Models are object that exhibit a certain behaviour. If the model is a material model, its behaviour is generated by the material objects itself. The object simply behaves as it does, and scientists find out about this behaviour through all the usual means of observation and experimentation in the arsenal of scientific method. If the model is a non-material model, the internal dynamic of the model is not the result of some material mechanism, but rather of the principles of generation. The model is taken to operate against the background of certain principles of generation and it is these principles that generate the internal behaviour. In the Newtonian model, for instance, the motion of the planet is the result of the application of Newton's equation of motion, which is a principle of generation in this context, and scientists explore the behaviour of a fictional model by finding out what follows from the basic model assumptions stated in the model description and the principles of generation. The upshot is that when carrying over DEKI from material to non-material models, the model description D_X is the prop, and D_B, the background description, which must now be seen as containing the principles of generation. Thus interpreted, DEKI, as incapsulated in Figure 9.1, provides an account of how fictional models represent. Hence, taken together, the DEKI account and the fiction view provide a complete account of what models are and of how they represent.[42]

14.7   Conclusion

We have seen that the question "what is a model?" can be understood in two ways: functionally and ontologically. We have discussed answers to both questions. Our conclusion is that, at least so far, no complete and conclusive functional characterisation of models is available. To discuss the ontology of models one first has to distinguish between material models and non-material models. The former's ontology is clear, at least insofar as the ontology of material objects is clear. The more difficult question concerns the ontology of non-material models. We have considered a number of options and eventually proffered a version of the fiction view of models that incorporates mathematical models as a plausible candidate. There are, however, other options and it will be interesting to explore these in future research.

Notes

1 This ecumenism is not universally shared. Emch submits that "[a] deeper understanding of models is sought in considering what models do, rather what they are" (2007, 558), and Apostel favours a functional characterisation of models on grounds that "we cannot hope to give one unique structural definition for models" and that we should therefore focus on "the function of models" (1961, 36). As we will see in Section 14.3, there are good reasons why we cannot simply set aside questions of ontology.

2 The entry was originally published in the 10th edition of the *Encyclopaedia Britannica* in 1902; I here quote from the 11th edition published in 1911. For further discussions of Boltzmann's approach to models and modelling, see Cercignani's (2006, Ch. 10) and de Regt's (1999).

3 Further characterisations of models in term of representation can be found in Bailer-Jones' (2000, 51), Giere's (2001, 1060), Frey's (1961, 89), Koperski's (2006, 1), Morgan and Morrison's (1999, 5), Teller's (2001, 397), and Weisberg's (2007, 209–210). Bushkovitch (1974) presents three definitions of models, all of which appeal to representation in one way or another. A characterisation of models in broadly representational terms is also given in Harré's (2004, 5), which circumscribes models in terms of similarity; in Apostel's (1961, 36) and Kroes' (1989, 153), which characterise models as devices that allow for information transfer from the model to the target; in Achinstein's (1964, 331, 1968, 212), which says that models are a set of assumptions about a target; and in Bailer-Jones' (2002a, 108), which posits that models are descriptions of their targets. Downes, finally, notes that "[t]here is almost complete consensus among philosophers of science working on models on only one idea: models are representations or models represent" (2021, 52).

4 Both quotes were retrieved on 26 January 2019. On the same day, eight of the ten results on the first page of a Google search for "what is a scientific model?" explicated the term "model" in explicitly representational terms.

5 The claim that models explain and that they do so independently of their representational capacities is not universally accepted. Schindler (2014) deems Bokulich's account unworkable. Alexandrova (2008) argues that a model explains if the target materially realises the model's hypothesis, which means that the model represents at least aspects of the target accurately; and Alexandrova and Northcott (2013) argue that economic models do not explain at all. See Reiss' (2012b, 2012a, 2013, Ch. 7) for a general discussion of models in economics; see Lawler and Sullivan's (2021) for a discussion different accounts of how models explain.

6 Further examples of non-representational uses of models are discussed in Knuuttila's (2011), Magnani's (1999), and Peschard's (2011).

7 The same view is expressed in Achinstein's (1968, 215), Harré's (1960, 103), Hutten's (1954, 286), Nowakowa and Nowak's (1998, 35), and Stachowiak's (1973, 132), as well by physicists Lambourne (quoted in Bailer-Jones 2002b, 283) and Young and Freedman (2000, 3). Saatsi (2011) qualifies the view by adding that even though models misrepresent, they typically do so only partially.

8 Proponents of Direct Representation, which we discussed in Section 9.3, would disagree with this characterisation of modelling. Liu gestures at a similar distinction when he contrasts "purely symbolic" models with ones that are "epistemic vehicles" (2015a, 41, 2015b, 287).

9 O'Connor and Weatherall reach a similar conclusion when they discuss Weisberg's account of models. They object to his project of a uniform characterisation of models and note that "[t]he term 'modeling,' much like the term 'science,' picks out a set of practices that do not constitute any sort of natural category" (2016, 614). Bailer-Jones' (1999), Gelfert's (2017, 8–12), and Leatherdale's (1974) provide reviews of the characterisations of models that have been offered by various authors.

10 We will discuss material objects, fictional characters, and equations below. For dreams, see Windt and Noreika's (2011).

11 Ducheyne makes a similar point when he notes that "if we accept that models are functional entities . . . it should come as no surprise that when we deal with scientific models ontologically, we cannot remain silent on how such models function as carriers of scientific knowledge" (2008, 120).

12 Indeed, as Vorms points out (2011, 2012), models are often presented under different "formats", which can involve the use of a different conceptual apparatus as well as a different mathematical formalism. The format of a model matters in practice because much of what scientists do with a model in the process of research depends on how the model is presented.

13 Alternative labels are "concrete model" (Thomson-Jones 2012, 761; Weisberg 2013, 24) and "physical model" (O'Connor and Weatherall 2016, 615).

14 See also Achinstein's (1968, 211) and Groenewold's (1961, 98). For this reason, Wilde and Williamson refer to material models as "experimental models" (2016, 272).

15 There is a growing literature on model organisms. See, for instance, Ankeny's (2001), Atanasova's (2015), Bechtel's (2009, 2014), Leonelli's (2016), Love and Trevisano' (2013), and Weber's (2014). For a discussion of how model organisms represent, see Ankeny and Leonelli's (2020); and for a discussion of the parallels with models in physics, see Rowbottom's (2009).

16 See also Black's (1962, 219–220) and Hutten's (1954, 285).

17 See, for instance, Black's (1962, 219–221), Groenewold's (1961, 98), and Weinert's (1999, 314). Black explicitly classifies scale models as icons (*ibid.*, 221).

18 For a discussion of scaling relations, see Nguyen and Frigg's (2022, Ch. 4), Pincock's (2019), and Sterrett's (2002, 2006, 2017, 2021). For a discussion of ship models, see Leggett's (2013).

19 For a discussion of ball-and-stick models, see Toon's (2011) and Laszlo's (2000). The history of these models is documented in Meinel's (2004).

20 For a detailed history of the discovery of DNA, see Olby's (1974). Watson's (1998) gives a personal account of events.

21 For an account of the discovery of the structure myoglobin, see de Chadarevian's (2004).

22 They are also referred to as "nonconcrete" models (Thomson-Jones 2012, 762), "abstract" models (Weisberg 2004, 1073), and "formal or intellectual" models (Rosenblueth and Wiener 1945, 317).

23 Antoniou (2021) prefers to dissolve the problem by arguing that what models are, ontologically speaking, is either an internal theoretical question or an external question concerning the appropriate language of science. For reasons discussed in the Section 14.3, I am less sanguine about just setting aside this issue.

24 In this vein, Hesse says that a formal model "is the expression of the form or structure of physical entities and processes, without any semantic content referring to specific objects or properties" (Hesse 2000, 299).

25 Bunge gives essentially the same definition when he says that if a theoretical model "is couched in exact (mathematical) terms, it is often called a *mathematical model*" (1973, 97, original emphasis), and so does Black when he notes that in a mathematical model "[t]he original field is thought of as 'projected' upon the abstract domain of sets, functions, and the like that is the subject matter of the correlated mathematical theory" (1962, 223). Sometimes attempts are made to specify in more detail what a mathematical model consists in. Altschul and Biser, for instance, mention fundamental notions like space-time coincidence as components of mathematical models (1948, 12). However, mathematical models can operate at different levels and involve different bits of mathematics, and so it seems doubtful that a general specification of components can be given.

26 See, for instance, Shapiro's (2000) for an introduction to the different positions.

27 This ties in with the exceptionalism of Humphreys (2002, 2004) and Winsberg (2010), who claim that computer simulations are a scientific method unlike any other. For a critical discussion of this exceptionalism, see Frigg and Reiss' (2009).

28 A computational implementation of the model can be found on http://nifty.stanford. edu/2014/mccown-schelling-model-segregation/.

29 The view that models are fictions has a long pedigree, stretching back to the beginning of the 20th century. For a list of references, see my (2010a, 101). Liu (2016) calls the position "new fictionalism". See Levy's (2020) for a critical discussion of the analogy between models and the imagined objects of literary fiction.

30 For a discussion of these two senses, see Frigg's (2010b) and Frigg and Nguyen's (2020, Ch. 6). For further discussions of the notion of imagination that is at work in scientific contexts, see, for instance, McLoone's (2019), Meynell's (2014), Murphy's (2020), Nersessian's (2007), Salis' (2020a, 2020b), Salis and Frigg's (2020), Stuart's (2017, 2020), and Toon's (2017).

31 For surveys, see Crittenden's (1991), Friend's (2007), Kroon and Voltolini's (2018), and Salis' (2013). Contessa (2016) provides an analysis of influential arguments concerning the ontology of fiction.

32 Note that Knuuttila's notion of an artefact differs from Thomassons's. The artefacts Thomasson is talking about are abstract objects; the artefacts Knuuttila considers are material objects like diagrams and descriptions (cf. Knuuttila 2005, 2011). For a discussion of artefactualism in economic modelling, see Knuuttila's (2021b) and Morgan's (2014).

33 This is not to say that there are no "purely fictional" models. Downes' cell models are examples of fictional models that are not mathematised (1992, 145). But many (in fact, probably most) fictional models are used in tandem with a mathematical description.

34 The presentation of the fiction view in this section draws on my (2021). The view discussed in this section is originally articulated in my (2010a, 2010c, 2010b) and later developed in Salis and Frigg's (2020), Frigg and Nguyen's (2016, 2020, Chs. 6 and 9), and Salis, Frigg and Nguyen's (2020). Alternative ways of articulating the analogy between models and fiction can be found in Barberousse and Ludwig's (2009), Contessa's (2010), Godfrey-Smith's (2009), and Salis' (2016, 2021), as well as in several contributions to Levy and Godfrey-Smith's (2020).

35 For reviews, see the references in endnote 31.

36 This is an important point in Walton's (1990). For a discussion of the epistemology of this approach to fiction, see Poznic's (2016).

37 For an extensive discussion of this point, see Frigg and Nguyen's (2020, Ch. 6, 2021).

38 The use of mathematics in the fiction view of models is discussed in more detail in Frigg and Nguyen's (2020, Secs. 4.5, 9.1–9.2). For an alternative take on the applicability of mathematics in pretence theory, see Leng's (2010).

39 Those sceptical of the notion of "truth in fiction" introduce the notion of a statement being "fictional". For a discussion, see Frigg's (2010c, 261–262).

40 For an extensive discussion of the issue of denotation, see Salis et al. (2020).

41 For a detailed discussion of how DEKI applies in the context of non-material models, see Frigg and Nguyen's (2016, 2020, Sec. 9.1).
42 This account is not universally loved, and it has been confronted with a number of criticisms. A detailed discussion of these criticisms can be found Frigg and Nguyen's (2021).

References

Achinstein, P. 1964. Models, Analogies, and Theories. *Philosophy of Science* 31: 328–350.
Achinstein, P. 1968. *Concepts of Science: A Philosophical Analysis*. Baltimore: Johns Hopkins Press.
Alexandrova, A. 2008. Making Models Count. *Philosophy of Science* 75: 383–404.
Alexandrova, A. and R. Northcott 2013. It's Just a Feeling: Why Economic Models Do Not Explain. *Journal of Economic Methodology* 20: 262–267.
Altschul, E. and E. Biser 1948. The Validity of Unique Mathematical Models in Science. *Philosophy of Science* 15: 11–24.
Ankeny, R. A. 2001. Model Organisms as Models: Understanding the 'Lingua Franca' of the Human Genome Project. *Philosophy of Science* 68(Supplement): 251–261.
Ankeny, R. A. and S. Leonelli 2011. What's So Special About Model Organisms. *Studies in History and Philosophy of Science* 42: 313–323.
Ankeny, R. A. and S. Leonelli 2020. *Model Organisms*. Cambridge: Cambridge University Press.
Antoniou, A. 2021. A Pragmatic Approach to the Ontology Ofmodels. *Synthese* 199: 6645–6664.
Apostel, L. 1961. Towards the Formal Study of Models in the Non-Formal Sciences. In H. Freudenthal (ed.), *The Concept and the Role of the Model in Mathematics and Natural and Social Sciences*. Dordrecht: Reidel, pp. 1–37.
Atanasova, N. A. 2015. Validating Animal Models. *Theoria* 30: 163–181.
Bailer-Jones, D. M. 1999. Tracing the Development of Models in the Philosophy of Science. In L. Magnani, N. J. Nersessian, and P. Thagard (eds.), *Model-Based Reasoning in Scientific Discovery*. New York: Kluwer Academic; Plenum Publishers, pp. 23–40.
Bailer-Jones, D. M. 2000. Modelling Extended Extragalactic Radio Sources. *Studies in History and Philosophy of Modern Physics* 31: 49–74.
Bailer-Jones, D. M. 2002a. Models, Metaphors, and Analogies. In P. Machamer and M. Silberstein (eds.), *The Blackwell Guide to Philosophy of Science*. Oxford: Blackwell, pp. 108–127.
Bailer-Jones, D. M. 2002b. Scientists' Thoughts on Scientific Models. *Perspectives on Science* 10: 275–301.
Barberousse, A. and P. Ludwig 2009. Models as Fictions. In M. Suárez (ed.), *Fictions in Science: Philosophical Essays in Modeling and Idealizations*. London: Routledge, pp. 56–73.
Barr, N. 2000. The History of the Phillips Machine. In R. Leeson (ed.), *A. W. H. Phillips: Collected Works in Contemporary Perspective*. Cambridge: Cambridge University Press, pp. 89–114.
Bechtel, W. 2009. Some Virtues of Modeling with Both Hands. *Adaptive Behavior* 17: 293–295.
Bechtel, W. 2014. Cognitive Biology: Surprising Model Organisms for Cognitive Science. *Proceedings of the Annual Meeting of the Cognitive Science Society* 36: 158–163.

Black, M. 1962. Models and Archetypes. In *Models and Metaphors: Studies in Language and Philosophy*. Ithaca and New York: Cornell University Press, pp. 219–243.

Bokulich, A. 2009. Explanatory Fictions. In M. Suárez (ed.), *Fictions in Science: Philosophical Essays on Modelling and Idealization*. London and New York: Routledge, pp. 91–109.

Boltzmann, L. 1911. Model. In B. McGuinness (ed.), *Theoretical Physics and Philosophical Problems: Selected Writing*. Dordrecht and Boston: Reidel, 1974, pp. 213–220.

Box, G. E. P. 1976. Science and Statistics. *Journal of the American Statistical Association* 71: 791–799.

Bunge, M. 1973. *Method, Model, and Matter*. Dordrecht: Reidel.

Bushkovitch, A. V. 1974. Models, Theories, and Kant. *Philosophy of Science* 41: 86–88.

Cercignani, C. 2006. *Ludwig Boltzmann: The Man Who Trusted Atoms*. Oxford: Oxford University Press.

Contessa, G. 2010. Scientific Models and Fictional Objects. *Synthese* 172: 215–229.

Contessa, G. 2016. It Ain't Easy: Fictionalism, Deflationism, and Easy Arguments in Ontology. *Mind* 125: 763–773.

Crittenden, C. 1991. *Unreality: The Metaphysics of Fictional Objects*. Ithaca and London: Cornell University Press.

Dardashti, R., K. P. Y. Thébault, and E. Winsberg 2017. Confirmation Via Analogue Simulation: What Dumb Holes Could Tell Us About Gravity. *The British Journal for the Philosophy of Science* 68: 55–89.

de Chadarevian, S. 2004. Models and the Making of Molecular Biology. In S. de Chadarevian and N. Hopwood (eds.), *Models: The Third Dimension of Science*. Stanford: Stanford University Press, pp. 339–368.

de Regt, H. W. 1999. Ludwig Boltzmann's 'Bildtheorie' and Scientific Understanding. *Synthese* 119: 113–134.

Downes, S. M. 1992. The Importance of Models in Theorizing: A Deflationary Semantic View. *Proceedings of the Biennial Meeting of the Philosophy of Science Association 1992*. East Lansing, MI: Philosophy of Science Association, (Vol. 1), pp. 142–153.

Downes, S. M. 2011. Scientific Models. *Philosophy Compass* 6: 757–764.

Downes, S. M. 2021. *Models and Modeling in the Sciences: A Philosophical Introduction*. New York and London: Routledge.

Ducheyne, S. 2008. Towards an Ontology of Scientific Models. *Metaphysica* 9: 119–127.

Earman, J. 2019. The Role of Idealizations in the Aharonov – Bohm Effect. *Synthese* 196: 1991–2019.

Emch, G. G. 2007. Models and the Dynamics of Theory-Building in Physics. Part I – Modeling Strategies. *Studies in History and Philosophy of Modern Physics* 38: 558–585.

Fowler, A. C. 1997. *Mathematical Models in the Applied Sciences* (Cambridge Texts in Applied Mathematics). Cambridge: Cambridge University Press.

Frey, G. 1961. Symbolische Und Ikonische Modelle. In H. Freudenthal (ed.), *The Concept and the Role of the Model in Mathematics and Natural and Social Sciences*. Dordrecht: Reidel, pp. 89–97.

Friend, S. 2007. Fictional Characters. *Philosophy Compass* 2: 141–156.

Frigg, R. 2010a. Fiction and Scientific Representation. In R. Frigg and M. Hunter (eds.), *Beyond Mimesis and Convention: Representation in Art and Science*. Berlin and New York: Springer, pp. 97–138.

Frigg, R. 2010b. Fiction in Science. In J. Woods (ed.), *Fictions and Models: New Essays*. Munich: Philiosophia Verlag, pp. 247–287.

Frigg, R. 2010c. Models and Fiction. *Synthese* 172: 251–268.

Frigg, R. 2021. Scientific Modelling and Make-Believe. In S. Sedivy (ed.), *Art, Representation, and Make-Believe: Essays on the Philosophy of Kendall L. Walton*. London: Routledge, pp. 367–383.

Frigg, R. and J. Nguyen 2016. The Fiction View of Models Reloaded. *The Monist* 99: 225–242.

Frigg, R. and J. Nguyen 2020. *Modelling Nature: An Opinionated Introduction to Scientific Representation* (Synthese Library). Berlin and New York: Springer.

Frigg, R. and J. Nguyen 2021. Seven Myths About the Fiction View of Models. In A. Cassini, and J. Redmond (eds.), *Idealizations in Science: Fictional and Artifactual Approaches*. Berlin and New York: Springer, pp. 133–157.

Frigg, R. and J. Reiss 2009. The Philosophy of Simulation: Hot New Issues or Same Old Stew? *Synthese* 169: 593–613.

Gelfert, A. 2017. The Ontology of Models. In L. Magnani and T. Bertolotti (eds.), *Springer Handbook of Model-Based Science*. Dordrecht, Heidelberg, London, and New York: Springer, pp. 5–23.

Giere, R. N. 2001. The Nature and Function of Models. *Behavioral and Brain Sciences* 24: 1060.

Godfrey-Smith, P. 2006. The Strategy of Model-Based Science. *Biology and Philosophy* 21: 725–740.

Godfrey-Smith, P. 2009. Abstractions, Idealizations, and Evolutionary Biology. In A. Barberousse, M. Morange, and T. Pradeu (eds.), *Mapping the Future of Biology: Evolving Concepts and Theories. Boston Studies in the Philosophy and History of Science* (Vol. 266). Dordrecht: Springer, pp. 47–56.

Godfrey-Smith, P. 2020. Models, Fictions and Conditions. In A. Levy and P. Godfrey-Smith (eds.), *The Scientific Imagination: Philosophical and Psychological Perspectives*. Cambridge: Cambridge University Press, pp. 154–177.

Graham Kennedy, A. 2012. A Non Representationalist View of Model Explanation. *Studies in History and Philosophy of Science* 43: 326–332.

Groenewold, H. J. 1961. The Model in Physics. In H. Freudenthal (ed.), *The Concept and the Role of the Model in Mathematics and Natural and Social Sciences*. Dordrecht: Reidel, pp. 98–103.

Hacking, I. 1983. *Representing and Intervening*. Cambridge: Cambridge University Press.

Harré, R. 1960. Metaphor, Model and Mechanism. *Proceedings of the Aristotelian Society* 60: 101–122.

Harré, R. 1970. *The Principles of Scientific Thinking*. Chicago: The University of Chicago Press.

Harré, R. 1988. Where Models and Analogies Really Count. *International Studies in the Philosophy of Science* 2: 118–133.

Harré, R. 2004. *Modeling: Gateway to the Unknown*. Amsterdam: Elsevier.

Hesse, M. B. 2000. Models and Analogies. In W. H. Newton-Smith (ed.), *A Companion to the Philosophy of Science*. Oxford: Blackwell, pp. 299–307.

Hughes, R. I. G. 1997. Models and Representation. *Philosophy of Science* 64(Supplement): 325–336.

Humphreys, P. 2002. Computational Models. *Philosophy of Science* 69.

Humphreys, P. 2004. *Extending Ourselves: Computational Science, Empiricism, and Scientific Method*. Oxford: Oxford University Press.

Hutten, E. H. 1954. The Rôle of Models in Physics. *The British Journal for the Philosophy of Science* 4: 284–301.

Knuuttila, T. 2005. *Models as Epistemic Artefacts: Toward a Non-Representationalist Account of Scientific Representation* (Department of Philosophy). Helsinki: University of Helsinki.

Knuuttila, T. 2011. Modelling and Representing: An Artefactual Approach to Model-Based Representation. *Studies in History and Philosophy of Science* 42: 262–271.

Knuuttila, T. 2021a. Imagination Extended and Embedded: Artifactual Versus Fictional Accounts of Models. *Synthese* 198: 5077–5097.

Knuuttila, T. 2021b. Epistemic Artifacts and the Modal Dimension of Modeling. *European Journal for Philosophy of Science* 11: Article 65.

Koperski, J. 2006. Models. *Internet Encyclopedia of Philosophy*. https://iep.utm.edu/models/.

Kroes, P. 1989. Structural Analogies between Physical Systems. *The British Journal for the Philosophy of Science* 40: 145–154.

Kroon, F. W. and A. Voltolini 2018. Fictional Entities. In E. N. Zalta (ed.), *The Stanford Encyclopedia of Philosophy*. https://plato.stanford.edu/archives/win2018/entries/fictional-entities/.

Laszlo, P. 2000. Playing with Molecular Models. *Hyle* 6: 85–97.

Lawler, I. and E. Sullivan 2021. Model Explanation Versus Model-Induced Explanation. *Foundations of Science* 26: 1049–1074.

Leatherdale, W. H. 1974. *The Role of Analogy, Model and Metaphor in Science*. Amsterdam: North Holland Publishing Company.

Leggett, D. 2013. Replication, Re-Placing and Naval Science in Comparative Context, C. 1868–1904. *The British Journal for the History of Science* 46: 1–21.

Leng, M. 2010. *Mathematics and Reality*. Oxford: Oxford University Press.

Leonelli, S. 2016. *Data- Centric Biology: A Philosophical Study*. Chicago and London: University of Chicago Press.

Levy, A. 2020. Models and Fictions: Not So Similar after All? *Philosophy of Science* 87: 819–828.

Liu, C. 2015a. Re-Inflating the Conception of Scientific Representation. *International Studies in the Philosophy of Science* 29: 41–59.

Liu, C. 2015b. Symbolic Versus Modelistic Elements in Scientific Modeling. *Theoria* 30: 287–300.

Liu, C. 2016. Against the New Fictionalism: A Hybrid View of Scientific Models. *International Studies in the Philosophy of Science* 30: 39–54.

Love, A. C. and M. Travisano 2013. Microbes Modeling Ontogeny. *Biology and Philosophy* 828: 161–188.

Magnani, L. 1999. Model-Based Creative Abduction. In L. Magnani, N. Nersessian, and P. Thagard (eds.), *Model-Based Reasoning in Scientific Discovery*. New York: Kluwer Academic; Plenum Publishers, pp. 219–238.

McLoone, B. 2019. Thumper the Infinitesimal Rabbit: A Fictionalist Perspective on Some "Unimaginable" Model Systems in Biology. *Philosophy of Science* 86(4): 662–671.

Meinel, C. 2004. Molecules and Croquet Balls. In S. de Chadarevian and N. Hopwood (eds.), *Models: The Third Dimension*. Stanford: Stanford University Press, pp. 242–275.

Meinong, A. 1904. Über Gegenstandtheorie. In A. Meinong (ed.), *Untersuchungen Zur Gegenstandtheorie Und Psychologie*. Leipzig: Barth, pp. 1–50.

Meynell, L. 2014. Imagination and Insight: A New Acount of the Content of Thought Experiments. *Synthese* 191: 4149–4168.

Morgan, M. S. 2012. *The World in the Model: How Economists Work and Think*. Cambridge: Cambridge University Press.

Morgan, M. S. 2014. What If? Models, Fact and Fiction in Economics. *Journal of the British Academy* 2: 231–268.

Morgan, M. S. and M. Boumans 2004. The Secrets Hidden by Two-Dimensionality: The Economy as a Hydraulic Machine. In D. S. Chadarevian and N. Hopwood (eds.), *Model: The Third Dimension of Science*. Stanford: Stanford University Press, pp. 369–401.

Morgan, M. S. and M. Morrison 1999. Models as Mediating Instruments. In M. Morgan and M. Morrison (eds.), *Models as Mediators: Perspectives on Natural and Social Science*. Cambridge: Cambridge University Press, pp. 10–37.

Morrison, M. 2016. Models and Theories. In P. Humphreys (ed.), *The Oxford Handbook of Philosophy of Science*. Oxford: Oxford University Press, pp. 378–396.

Murphy, A. 2020. *Thought Experiments and the Scientific Imagination*. PhD Thesis, University of Leeds.

Nersessian, N. 2007. Thought Experimenting as Mental Modeling: Empiricism without Logic. *Croatian Journal of Philosophy* 7: 125–154.

Nguyen, J. and R. Frigg 2022. *Scientific Representation*. Cambridge: Cambridge University Press.

Nowakowa, I. and L. Nowak 1998. Model(S) and Experiment(S) as Homogeneous Families of Notions. In N. Shanks (ed.), *Idealization IX: Idealization in Contemporary Physics* (Poznań Studies in the Philosophy of the Sciences and the Humanities 63). Amsterdam: Rodopi, pp. 35–50.

O'Connor, C. and J. O. Weatherall 2016. Black Holes, Black-Scholes, and Prairie Voles: An Essay Review of Simulation and Similarity, by Michael Weisberg. *Philosophy of Science* 83: 613–626.

Olby, R. 1974. *The Path to the Double Helix: The Discovery of DNA*. Seattle: University of Washington Press.

Peschard, I. 2011. Making Sense of Modeling: Beyond Representation. *European Journal for Philosophy of Science* 1: 335–352.

Pincock, C. 2007. Mathematical Idealization. *Philosophy of Science* 74: 957–967.

Pincock, C. 2019. Concrete Scale Models, Essential Idealization and Causal Explanation. *The British Journal for the Philosophy of Science*. https://doi.org/10.1093/bjps/axz019.

Portides, D. 2008. Models. In S. Psillos and M. Curd (eds.), *The Routledge Companion to Philosophy of Science*. Abingdon: Rouldedge, pp. 385–395.

Poznic, M. 2016. Make-Believe and Model-Based Representation in Science: The Epistemology of Frigg's and Toon's Fictionalist Views of Modeling. *Theorema* 35: 201–218. https://doi.org/10.1007/s10838-015-9307-7.

Pronin, S., L. Wellacott, J. Pimentel, R. C. Moioli, and P. A. Vargas 2021. Neurorobotic Models of Neurological Disorders: A Mini Review. *Frontiers in Neurorobotics* 15: 634045. https://doi.org/10.3389/fnbot.2021.634045.

Reiss, J. 2012a. The Explanation Paradox. *Journal of Economic Methodology* 19: 43–62.

Reiss, J. 2012b. Idealization and the Aims of Economics: Three Cheers for Instrumentalism. *Economics and Philosophy*: 363–383.

Reiss, J. 2013. *Philosophy of Economics: A Contemporary Introduction*. New York and London: Routledge.

Rosenblueth, A. and N. Wiener 1945. The Role of Models in Science. *Philosophy of Science* 12: 316–321.

Rowbottom, D. P. 2009. Models in Biology and Physics: What's the Difference? *Foundations of Science* 14: 281–294.

Saatsi, J. 2011. Idealized Models as Inferentially Veridical Representations. In P. Humphreys and C. Imbert (eds.), *Models, Simulations, and Representations*. New York: Routledge, pp. 234–249.

Salis, F. 2013. Fictional Entities. *Online Companion to Problems in Analytical Philosophy.* http://compendioemlinha.letras.ulisboa.pt.

Salis, F. 2016. The Nature of Model-World Comparisons. *The Monist* 99: 243–259.

Salis, F. 2021. The New Fiction View of Models. *The British Journal for the Philosophy of Science* 72(3): 717–742. https://doi.org/10.1093/bjps/axz015.

Salis, F. 2020a. Of Predators and Prey: Imagination in Scientific Modeling. In K. Moser and A. C. Sukla (eds.), *Imagination and Art: Explorations in Contemporary Theory*. Leiden and Boston: Brill Rodopi, pp. 451–474.

Salis, F. 2020b. Scientific Discovery through Fictionally Modelling Reality. *Topoi* 39: 927–937.

Salis, F. and R. Frigg 2020. Capturing the Scientific Imagination. In P. Godfrey-Smith and A. Levy (eds.), *The Scientific Imagination: Philosophical and Psychological Perspectives*. Oxford: Oxford University Press, pp. 17–50.

Salis, F., R. Frigg, and J. Nguyen 2020. Models and Denotation. In C. Martínez-Vidal and J. L. Falguera (eds.), *Abstract Objects: For and Against*. Cham: Springer, pp. 197–219.

Schelling, T. C. 1978. *Micromotives and Macrobehavior*. New York: Norton.

Schindler, S. 2014. Explanatory Fictions – for Real? *Synthese* 191: 1741–1755.

Shapiro, S. 2000. *Thinking About Mathematics*. Oxford: Oxford University Press.

Spieler, O., D. B. Dingwell, and M. Alidibirov 2004. Magma Fragmentation Speed: An Experimental Determination. *Journal of Volcanology and Geothermal Research* 129: 109–123.

Stachowiak, H. 1973. *Allgemeine Modelltheorie*. Vienna and New York: Springer.

Sterratt, D., B. Graham, A. Gilles, and D. Willshaw 2011. *Principles of Computational Modelling in Neuroscience*. Cambridge: Cambridge University Press.

Sterrett, S. G. 2002. Physical Models and Fundamental Laws: Using One Piece of the World to Tell About Another. *Mind and Society* 3: 51–66.

Sterrett, S. G. 2006. Models of Machines and Models of Phenomena. *International Studies in the Philosophy of Science* 20: 69–80.

Sterrett, S. G. 2017. Experimentation on Analogue Models. In L. Magnani and T. Bertolotti (eds.), *Springer Handbook of Model-Based Science*. Dordrecht, Heidelberg, London, and New York: Springer, pp. 857–878.

Sterrett, S. G. 2021. Scale Modeling. In D. Michelfelder and N. Doorn (eds.), *Routledge Handbook of Philosophy of Engineering*. London: Routledge, pp. 394–408.

Stuart, M. T. 2017. Imagination: A Sine Qua Non of Science. *Croatian Journal of Philosophy* 17: 9–32.

Stuart, M. T. 2020. The Productive Anarchy of Scientific Imagination. *Philosophy of Science* 87: 968–978.

Teller, P. 2001. Twilight of the Perfect Model Model. *Erkenntnis* 55: 393–415.

Thomasson, A. L. 1999. *Fiction and Metaphysics*. New York: Cambridge University Press.

Thomasson, A. L. 2020. If Models Were Fictions, Then What Would They Be? In A. Levy and P. Godfrey-Smith (eds.), *The Scientific Imagination: Philosophical and Psychological Perspectives*. New York: Oxford University Press, pp. 51–74.

Thomson-Jones, M. 2010. Missing Systems and Face Value Practise. *Synthese* 172: 283–299.

Thomson-Jones, M. 2012. Modeling without Mathematics. *Philosophy of Science* 79: 761–772.

Thomson-Jones, M. 2020. Realism About Missing Systems. In A. Levy and P. Godfrey-Smith (eds.), *The Scientific Imagination: Philosophical and Psychological Perspectives*. New York: Oxford University Press, pp. 75–101.

Toon, A. 2011. Playing with Molecules. *Studies in History and Philosophy of Science* 42: 580–589.

Toon, A. 2017. Imagination in Scientific Modeling. In A. Kind (ed.), *The Routldege Handbook of Philosophy of Imagination*. London and New York Routledge, pp. 451–462.

Vorms, M. 2011. Representing with Imaginary Models: Formats Matter. *Studies in History and Philosophy of Science* 42: 287–295.

Vorms, M. 2012. Formats of Representation in Scientific Theorising. In P. Humphreys and C. Imbert (eds.), *Models, Simulations, and Representations*. New York: Routledge, pp. 250–273.

Wade, N. and S. Finger 2001. The Eye as an Optical Instrument: From Camera Obscura to Helmholtz'sperspective. *Perception* 30: 1157–1177.

Walton, K. L. 1990. *Mimesis as Make-Believe: On the Foundations of the Representational Arts*. Cambridge, MA: Harvard University Press.

Watson, J. D. 1998. *The Double Helix: Personal Account of the Discovery of the Structure of DNA*. New York: Scribner.

Webb, B. 2001. Can Robots Make Good Models of Biological Behaviour? With Peer Commentary. *Behavioral and Brain Sciences* 24: 1033–1050.

Webb, B. 2009. Animals Versus Animats: Or Why Not Model the Real Iguana? *Adaptive Behavior* 17: 269–286.

Weber, M. 2014. Experimental Modeling in Biology: In Vivo Representation and Stand-Ins as Modeling Strategies. *Philosophy of Science* 81: 756–769.

Weinert, F. 1999. Theories, Models and Constraints. *Studies in History and Philosophy of Science* 30: 303–333.

Weisberg, M. 2004. Qualitative Theory and Chemical Explanation. *Philosophy of Science* 71: 1071–1081.

Weisberg, M. 2007. Who Is a Modeler? *The British Journal for the Philosophy of Science* 58: 207–233.

Weisberg, M. 2013. *Simulation and Similarity: Using Models to Understand the World*. Oxford: Oxford University Press.

Wilde, M. and J. Williamson 2016. Models in Medicine. In M. Solomon, J. R. Simon, and H. Kincaid (eds.), *The Routledge Companion to Philosophy of Medicine*. Abingdon: Routledge, pp. 271–284.

Windt, J. M. and V. Noreika 2011. How to Integrate Dreaming into a General Theory of Consciousness – A Critical Review of Existing Positions and Suggestions for Future Research. *Consciousness and Cognition* 20: 1091–1107.

Winsberg, E. 2010. *Science in the Age of Computer Simulation*. Chicago: University of Chicago Press.

Young, H. D. and R. Freedman 2000. *University Physics with Modern Physics* (10th ed.). San Francisco and Reading, MA: Addison Wesley.

15

TAMING ABUNDANCE

15.1   Introduction

In many contexts, the scientific community produces multiple different, and
sometimes conflicting, models of the same target system. What drives the construction of multiple models, and what strategies are there to cope with the
resulting abundance? We begin by introducing the problem and by trying to
understand why, and how, an abundance of models of the same target emerges
(Section 15.2). We then turn to Robustness Analysis, a method to try to extract
veridical conclusions from model ensembles (Section 15.3). Perspectivism offers
an alternative approach which sees different models as embodying different perspectives on the same target (Section 15.4). In some situations, there is significant latitude in model construction and scientists disagree over the appropriate
way of modelling the target. These are situations of severe scientific uncertainty,
and there is a question about how such situations can be managed (Section 15.5).
We conclude that multi-model situations raise issues that are not yet fully understood (Section 15.6).

15.2   One Target, Multiple Models

It is a common occurrence in many scientific contexts that there are multiple models of the same target. Morrison discusses models in nuclear physics and points
out that there are more than thirty *different* models of the nucleus, each based
on different assumptions and offering different insights (2011, 346–351).[1] She
sorts nuclear models into three groups: microscopic models, collective models,
and mixed models. In the first group we find models like the shell model, which
represents the nucleus as consisting of individual particles that exhibit a shell structure similar to the structure we find in the electrons of the atom. In the second

DOI: 10.4324/9781003285106-20

group we find models like the liquid drop model, which represents the nucleus as a single object that behaves like a liquid drop. The third group contains models that have both microscopic and collective elements. The liquid-drop-plus-shell-correction-model, for instance, is, as its name suggests, a liquid drop model that has been amended by building certain elements of the shell model into it. Nuclear physics is no exception, and we find that similar multi-models situations arise, for instance, in hydrodynamics (Morrison 2011), population biology (Weisberg 2006b), systems biology (Green 2013), quantum chemistry (Accorinti 2019), climate science (Betz 2009),[2] and catastrophe modelling (Roussos et al. 2021b).[3]

What is the reason for this proliferation of models? From afar it sometimes looks like things "just happen this way". Scientists grapple with a problem, often in situations where they have only partial knowledge of the target domain, and they try out different ideas and approaches, which, eventually, result in a multiplicity of models. This impression is not wrong, but it omits the role of theoretical virtues. If model multiplicity was *only* the result of incomplete knowledge and insufficient understanding, one would expect the number of models to go down as science progresses. While models do get discarded as knowledge grows, this does not typically reduce the number of models significantly. The multiplicity of models remains, and often no one model can be singled out as the "true" or "best" model that makes all other models otiose. This multiplicity can be attributed to the fact that models embody different theoretical virtues and that these virtues often compete with each other. Scope, precision, specificity, accuracy, generality, completeness, simplicity, transparency, graspability, tractability, providing understanding, being explanatory, and being predictively successful are virtues that scientists may appreciate in models, and yet no model can embody all of them at once. Levins draws attention to the problem of competing virtues and singled out generality, realism, and precision as the three key virtues that stand in conflict with each other:

> The multiplicity of models is imposed by the contradictory demands of a complex, heterogeneous nature and a mind that can only cope with few variables at a time; by the contradictory desiderata of generality, realism, and precision; by the need to understand and also to control; even by the opposing esthetic standards which emphasize the stark simplicity and power of a general theorem as against the richness and the diversity of living nature. These conflicts are irreconcilable. Therefore, the alternative approaches even of contending schools are part of a larger mixed strategy. But the conflict is about method, not nature, for the individual models, while they are essential for understanding reality, should not be confused with that reality itself.
>
> *(1966, 431)*

So the conflict between key desiderata is irresolvable, and hence it is not possible to maximise all desiderata simultaneously. For this reason, there is a trade-off between conflicting desiderata, and the multiplicity of models is a result of different scientists, or different schools of thought, trading these desiderata off against each other in different ways.[4]

Levins' analysis has sparked a debate about the values involved in model-construction, and about the exact nature of the trade-off.[5] Many interesting questions arise about the use, and indeed legitimacy, of values, and about how they are balanced against each other. However, details aside, the idea that there are different desiderata in play when constructing models and that there are trade-offs between them seems to be indisputable. So the question then is not how to eliminate the multiplicity of models, but rather how to manage it. On the face of it, having a multiplicity of models engenders confusion. Which model should we use in a given situation and what do we do when models give conflicting results? The remainder of this chapter discusses different approaches to this problem.

Which route one takes depends at least in part of the nature of the situation and the models involved. In some cases, incompatible models represent different parts of the same system and hence are not actually incompatible with each other. Morrison (2011, 343–346) discusses the case of hydrodynamical models of turbulent flows and points out that seemingly incompatible models actually represent different parts or aspects of the same system which can be modelled in isolation. These models are therefore *complementary* in a way that is similar to how maps in an atlas are complementary. Taken together, these models offer a better and more comprehensive understanding of the target than any individual model in isolation would be able to provide.

Not all multi-model situations are like this. The nuclear models mentioned at the beginning of this section are not complementary in this way. As Morrison points out, they are models of the same target, and they just represent it differently and say different things about it. For instance, one model says that nucleons are approximately independent, while another model says that they are strongly coupled. In such cases "atlas-like" complementarity provides no exit route. Nuclear models are not special in this respect. The other examples mentioned at the beginning of this section also fail to be complementary, and many of the models end up being inconsistent with each other.[6]

There are at least three reactions to this situation, which can be seen as marking an increasingly more significant departure from a situation in which one expects to have one correct model. The first is Robustness Analysis, where the goal is to find a common denominator in the diverse models. The second is perspectivism, which sees different models as embodying different and equally legitimate perspectives on the same target. Phenomena have different characteristics when observed from different points of view, and a plurality of models is just a manifestation of a plurality of perspectives. If different models cannot reasonably be interpreted as being an embodiment of different perspectives, then we are in the territory of severe uncertainty and the challenge is to somehow manage this uncertainty. At this point modelling makes contact with decision theory, and models have to be understood as providing inputs into decision algorithms that are designed to deal with uncertainty. We will discuss these approaches in the remainder of this chapter.

15.3 Robustness Analysis

In Section 13.2 we encountered the Lotka-Volterra model, which studies the interdependence of a predator and a prey population and finds that the sizes of both populations oscillate. The model also shows that the populations have what is now known as the *Volterra Property*: a general biocide will increase the relative size of the prey population. This conformed with D'Ancona's observations, which initially prompted Volterra's investigation into predator-prey systems. But what exactly is the status of the model? The model is not only about the species in the Adriatic Sea that D'Ancona observed; it is about predator-prey systems in general. Does the model warrant the claim that all predator-prey systems have the Volterra Property? Furthermore, the presence of the Volterra Property in the model is a consequence of the specific mechanism of predator-prey interaction on which the model is based. Does this warrant the claim that this mechanism is also present in real predator-prey systems?

If the Lotka-Volterra model was an accurate representation of predator-prey systems in all respects, the answer to these questions would be "yes, obviously". But the model is not an accurate representation. Indeed, it is far from accurate. The model is based on number of serious idealisations and simplifications. It assumes, for instance, that population growth is linear, that the interaction between the populations is proportional to the product of the two densities, and that there are no environmental factors (other than predation) that limit the growth of prey. These assumptions are not true in actual predator-prey systems. Given this, the answer to the above questions cannot be "yes, obviously". Robustness Analysis (RA) aims to show that the answer still is "yes", albeit no longer "obviously".[7]

The basic idea of RA is to examine several different models of the same target system. All models can be idealised and simplified, but they should be based on *different* idealisations and simplifications. The analysis then looks for communalities between these different models. If there is a result on which all models agree, this is a robust result. The analysis concludes that the robust result is real in that we have good reasons to believe that it is present in the target system. Levins encapsulated this idea in his memorable phrase that "our truth is the intersection of independent lies" (1966, 423), where the "lies" are the idealised and simplified models and the "truth" is the robust result. The project for this section is to articulate this idea and to probe its validity.

Weisberg (2006b) illustrates the workings of RA with the Lotka-Volterra model, and Weisberg and Reisman (2008) discuss the different models involved in an analysis of predator-prey systems in considerable detail. We begin our discussion of RA by following their narrative.[8] The initial step in every RA consists in considering alternative models of the same target. Weisberg and Reisman consider three different families of alternative models. The first, which marks the smallest departure from the original model, contains models that have the same equations as the original Lotka-Volterra model but in which the parameters assume different values (*ibid.*, 115–116). More formally, in Section 13.2 we have seen that the Lotka-Volterra model is defined by Equations 13.1. These equations have four parameters in them: the birth rate of the prey *r*, the death rate of predators *m*, and two linear response parameters *a* and *b*. In an initial discussion of the model, these parameters are assumed to have specific values. This assumption is now given up and one studies how the model behaves if the values of the parameters are varied over a plausible range of values. Weisberg and Reisman study how the model behaves under this kind of variation and come to the conclusion that the key properties of the Lotka-Volterra model, in particular the Volterra Property, are robust, meaning that they are stable under the variation of parameter values. In other words, the Volterra Property obtains no matter what the values of the parameters are (within the range under consideration).

The second family of models introduces variations to the mathematical form of the equations. Weisberg and Reisman consider a particular variation to the model structure, which they call *density dependence* (*ibid.*, 116–121). In the original model there is no environmental factor that limits the growth of the prey population: in the absence of predators there is no bound to population growth. This is obviously unrealistic because the availability of food and living space will put a natural limit on the growth of the population. This can be taken into account by building a carrying capacity of the environment into the equations, which limits the growth of the prey population even in the absence of predators. Mathematically this amounts to replacing rV in the first equation (of Equations 13.1) by $r(1 - V/K)V$, where K is the carrying capacity of the system. Thus, the first equation changes from $\dot{V} = rV - (aV)P$ to $\dot{V} = r(1 - V/K)V - (aV)P$. The new model is considerably more complicated to analyse, but it turns out that even this new and more complex model still exhibits the Volterra Property. This is in no way a trivial result, because other properties of the original model, such as the presence of undampened oscillations, are destroyed by the addition of the new term. So the Volterra Property turns out to be robust under this variation while undampened oscillations are not.

After varying parameter values and the structure of the equations, one can push the analysis further by also varying basic modelling assumptions. The models we discussed so far dealt with the problem at the level of aggregates and conceptualised the target as consisting of two populations interacting with each other. Individual animals are invisible from this perspective. *Individual based models* leave this "aggregate perspective" behind and represent individual organisms and their behaviours. The model includes variables for each individual in the population, and it makes assumptions about how these individuals behave, interact, and develop over time. Weisberg and Reisman (*ibid.*, 121–129) formulate and study such a model and they find that as long as the model is such that different species coexist (as is the case in the original model), even the individual based model has the Volterra Property.

The conclusion of this exercise is that the Volterra Property is robust across a large class of models. It is therefore a *robust property*. But identifying a robust property is only the first step of RA. The second step consists in identifying a feature that all models have in common and that is responsible for bringing about the robust property. That is, RA now aims to identify a structure shared by all models. Weisberg calls this the *common structure* (2006b, 737).[9] A careful look at all the models shows that this common structure is what is known as *negative coupling*: "increasing the abundance of predators decreases the abundance of prey and increasing the abundance of prey increases the abundance of predators" (Weisberg and Reisman 2008, 114).

The third and final step of RA is the formulation of a *robust theorem*, which links the common structure to the robust property. The robust theorem says that under certain conditions, the common structure brings about, or gives rise to, the robust property (Weisberg 2006b, 737–738). In the case of the predator-prey system under investigation, the robust theorem says that, under certain conditions, negative coupling brings about the Volterra Property. This result is also referred to as the *Volterra Principle* (*ibid.*).[10] This principle has great significance because it shows that measures that lead to general biocide (like the application of pesticides) will favour prey over predators, which is an important factor to bear in mind in many ecological interventions.

The conditions mentioned in the robust theorem are the most difficult part of RA to pin down. Weisberg and Reisman issue the assurance that "robustness analysis has shown that the principle is highly general and will hold under a wide variety of conditions" (2008, 129–130), but then they say little about what the conditions are and how they can be identified. Obviously, one can just go through the models considered in the first step and say that the conditions in the robust theorem are just the assumptions of the models. But that would result in a rather narrow set of conditions. In our example we have only looked at parameter variation, the introduction of density dependence and a particular individual based dynamic. A theorem that says that negative coupling gives rise to the Volterra Property *exactly if* the conditions of one of these models are satisfied is of limited use because these conditions are rarely, if ever, instantiated (look back at the conditions we introduced when deriving the model in Section 13.2!). Indeed, that the models are idealised and do not offer realistic representations is the starting point of RA; if the models, or one of the models, could be interpreted as a truthful representation of the target, then RA would be unnecessary. So the conditions in the robust theorem have to be broader than that for the principle to be useful; they have to be, in some sense, a generalisation of the properties of the models that have been studied. It remains, however, unclear how to pin down the relevant conditions. But let us set this problem aside for now.

It is a crucial aspect of RA that it aims to reach conclusions about the target system and not only about the models themselves. As we have seen previously, Levins says that the *truth* is the intersection of independent lies. Weisberg notes that what RA is ultimately interested in are "properties of real-world phenomena, not mathematical structures" and that this is why the next move in RA "involves interpreting the mathematical structures as descriptions of empirical phenomena" (2006b, 738). Likewise, Eronen interprets RA as a method to justify ontological commitments (2015, 3962), and Schupbach emphasises that the Volterra Principle, which we take to be established through RA, is a "biological claim, not to be confused with claims about the mathematical representations of biological systems" (2015, 306). As we will see shortly, the claim that RA yields conclusions about the real world is contentious, and several authors either endeavoured to add nuance to it or rejected it altogether.

Before turning to criticisms, let us summarise the general structure of RA. To do so it is useful to introduce the notion of a model ensemble. A *model ensemble* Ω is a collection of models. The collection can be finite or infinite (either countably or uncountably), and its members can be specified in any way that is convenient in a given situation. For instance, the models considered by Weisberg and Reisman in their discussion of predator-prey systems can be seen as forming an ensemble. As we will see shortly, there are different kinds of model ensembles, which has implications for how their properties are studied. However, these differences are immaterial for an abstract statement of RA.

We are now in a position to give a general statement of RA, which we abstract from our discussion of the Lotka-Volterra model. The general statement consists of three steps. The three steps are the ones we encountered in Weisberg and Reisman's discussion: the discovery of the robust property, the identification of the common structure, and the formulation of a robust theorem. Each step consists of a premise and a conclusion. The premise states a result about the model ensemble; the conclusion asserts that the same result also holds in the target. In other words, the inferential step from the premise to the conclusion amounts to carrying over a result from the model ensemble to the target system. In practice, these steps are often not neatly separated, but a conceptual analysis of RA must clearly distinguish between statements that concern the model ensemble and statements that concern the target system.

Assume we have a model ensemble Ω consisting of models that represent target system T. RA then involves the following:

Step 1 – Robust property
    Premise 1 – *Ensemble-Robust-Property*: All models in Ω have property R. This property is called the "robust property".
    Conclusion 1 – *Target-Robust-Property*: T has R.
Step 2 – Common structure
    Premise 2 – *Ensemble-Common-Structure*: All models in Ω have structure S. This structure is called the "common structure".
    Conclusion 2 – *Target-Common-Structure*: T has structure S.
Step 3 – Robust Theorem
    Premise 3 – *Model-Robustness-Theorem*: In all models in Ω it is the case that under conditions C, S brings about R. This proposition is called the "robust theorem".[11]
    Conclusion 3 – *Target-Robustness-Theorem*: Under conditions C, S brings about R in T.

As noted, this formulation of RA intentionally emphasises the fact that every step consists of a premise that concerns the models in the ensemble, and a conclusion about the target system itself.[12]

The discussion of the Volterra Principle might suggest that RA departs from one model, and that other models are constructed in an attempt to vindicate the results of the initial model. Sometimes this is indeed how RA proceeds. However, there is nothing intrinsic to RA that would require this way of proceeding. The analysis could, and sometimes does, proceed in the opposite way, starting from a model ensemble. In the case of global climate models, for instance, scientists do not first construct one model, and then add further models in order to show that the results of the first model are robust. The scientific process is such that different modelling groups construct climate models (more or less) independently, and when it turns out that these models are different, then a search for robust conditions can be seen as way to deal with this diversity of models.

RA has broad appeal and its use is not confined to ecology. To mention just a few: Plutynski (2006) applies RA to models in population genetics; Guala and Salanti (2002), Kuorikoski et al. (2010), and Thoma (2012) discuss RA in the context of economic modelling; Lloyd (2010) analyses climate models in terms of RA;[13] Gueguen (2020) investigates RA in the context of cosmology; Sprenger (2012) considers RA in the context of environmental risk analysis; and Eronen (2015) advocates RA as a philosophical instrument in the debate over scientific realism.

Due to their structure, each step of RA raises two questions. The first question concerns the premise of the argument. The premise makes a claim about the model ensemble and we have to get clear on how we establish this claim, or, if establishing the claim is beyond our grasp, on what can be said in its support. The second question concerns the conclusion. The arguments are obviously not deductively valid. That a certain claim is true in a model ensemble does not imply, as matter of logic, that the claim is also true in the target: it is possible for the conclusion to be false even if the premise is true. Hence, the transfer of model ensemble results to the target stands in need of justification. Rather than going through the steps from top to bottom we first discuss all premises, and then turn to the conclusions.

To get clear on what Premise 1 involves, it is helpful to distinguish two kinds of model ensembles.[14] As we have seen, the Lotka-Volterra model depends on the four parameters r, m, a, and b. This is a common occurrence as models in other domains also depend on parameters. One can construct a model ensemble by taking the equations of the model and specifying that all the parameters in the model are varied over a certain range. A model ensemble thus constructed is referred to as a *perturbed parameter ensemble*.[15] Studying such an ensemble gives information about how sensitively the outputs of a model depend on the parameters, and the ensemble can therefore be used to explore the impact of parametric uncertainty on relevant outcomes. By contrast, a so-called *multi-model ensemble* consists of several different models: models that differ in their substantive modelling assumptions and their mathematical structure, rather than only in their parameter values.[16] The two-model ensemble consisting of the original Lotka-Volterra model and the "amended" model with the added term to reflect density dependence is a simple example of a multi-model ensemble. Ensembles of this kind can be used to investigate how the relevant model outcomes are impacted by uncertainty about the model structure. These ensemble types are of course not mutually exclusive, and one can have an ensemble that both contains different models and varies their parameter values.

The two kinds of model ensembles are explored through different techniques. Studying a perturbed parameter ensemble requires us to vary the parameters in the model and check whether, and if so how, the desired results change. This is simple in theory, but it is often difficult to do in practice. The number of parameters may be large, and equations may not be solvable analytically. In such cases scientists have to resort to computer simulations and run multiple versions of the same model, where each version incorporates a different set of parameter values. But no amount of simulation can explore the full range of parameter values, and there are always gaps. These gaps are particularly significant if models are large and computationally costly to explore. Contemporary climate models, for instance, have hundreds of parameters and yet the available computational infrastructure allows scientists to make only a comparatively small number of runs, which results in large parts of the parameter space remaining unexplored.[17] Understanding how changes in model parameters affect the model result of interest in the face of difficulties like these has turned into a scientific discipline in its own right, namely *sensitivity analysis*.[18]

Things get even more complex when we turn to multi-model ensembles. The purpose of such ensembles is to evaluate whether a result is robust under structural changes to the model. This involves changing the substantial modelling assumptions and the mathematical structure of the model. Such stability is required because if a model is idealised and it turns out that a result vanishes when idealisations are removed or changed, then the result is not epistemically significant.[19] Making good on this intuition is a challenging task. Unlike in perturbed parameter ensembles, where the problem is to establish results about a well-defined ensemble, the problem now is how to define the ensemble to begin with. In our example, Weisberg and Reiman considered a small multi-model ensemble consisting of three models and then studied each model individually. But what justifies this choice? Why these three models? Why not an ensemble of four, or five models, or an ensemble with a larger, or even infinite, number of models?

This question is of course deeply intertwined with the inference that transfer model-results to the target. From a purely formal point of view one can study any ensemble, and it may well be that any ensemble is as good as any other. However, if one wants to later base conclusions about the target system on this study, the models in the ensemble have to be "informative" of the target. In an ideal world, this would mean that the ensemble would contain all plausible models of the target. However, it is usually not only unclear what this means; even if we knew what "plausible" meant, it would in general remain unclear how to actually construct such an ensemble. It is simply not known what the class of all plausible models of a predator-prey system looks like. A second-best option might be to say that the ensemble need not contain every plausible model and that it is sufficient to have an ensemble that provides a good sample of the set of all plausible models (in much the same way in which a relatively small set of people can be a sample of the entire population of a country). However, if it is hard to say what the class of plausible models is, it is also hard to say what a representative sample of that class looks like. In practice, scientists often simply group together all the available models and consider them to form an ensemble. However, as Parker points out, models thus constructed are "ensembles of opportunity" and as such "they are not designed to systemically sample or bound uncertainties but rather are more like a collection of best guesses" (2013, 216).[20] So how to construct, and explore, a representative multi-model ensemble is by and large an open question.[21]

Let us now turn to Premise 2, the identification of the common structure. Establishing this premise relies on the fact that every model M_i in the ensemble can be decomposed into a core and a set of idealisations: $M_i = S \& I_i$, where i is an index that ranges over all the models in the ensemble. The crucial aspect here is that while idealisations are particular to each model (hence the index for the idealisations), the structure S must be common to all models. Rice calls this the "decompositional strategy" and argues that it is a dead end: "many of our best scientific models cannot be decomposed in the ways required by the decompositional strategy" (Rice 2019, 180). This is because the contributions of S to a model's output cannot be isolated from the contributions of the I_i because the two are inextricably intertwined with the model and collaborate to produce the model's output. The idealisations are introduced to render the basic mathematical frameworks applicable, and they often distort difference-making features. Hence, there is no such thing as the contribution of the idealisation that can be isolated from the result of the core (*ibid.*, 189–195).

This is a serious worry and those who wish to perform an RA on a given ensemble will have to argue that the models at stake do not face the issue Rice describes. Even if this is possible and decomposition is not an in-principle limitation, there are practical obstacles. Few ensembles will consist of models whose structure naturally decomposes into a core and idealisations, and different models may even be formulated in different mathematical frameworks. It is then a challenge to find a core structure that they all have in common. Weisberg and Reisman's ensemble is a case in point. The models use different formalisms and isolating negative coupling as the common structure involved much more than just watching out for shared elements in the mathematical formulations of the models. Weisberg recognises this difficulty and notes that "[s]uch cases are much harder to describe in general, relying as they do on the theorist's ability to judge relevantly similar structures" (2006b, 738). Even if one has faith in theorists' ability to do so, certain cases may present insurmountable obstacles. Justus discusses the case of climate models and points out that these large computational structures are opaque, and that the sheer number and complexity of equations involved undercuts any attempt to duplicate the kind of analysis that Weisberg and Reisman were able to carry out on the relatively simple models of the predator-prey system (2012, 802–803). So there are question marks about the identification of a common structure both in-principle and in-practice when complex model ensembles are at issue.

As we have already noted when discussing the Volterra Principle, the formulation of the relevant conditions of the robust theorem, which is the core of Premise 3, is a formidable problem. The problem is linked to the problems we have seen concerning the construction of multi-model ensembles. If we knew what models were in the ensemble and how to characterise them, and if we could show that in all these models S brings about R, then we would probably have at least some idea about what goes into C. But since the ensemble membership remains elusive, it is unsurprising that formulating the relevant criteria remains a hard nut to crack.

Let us now turn to the conclusions, which transfer findings about the model ensemble to the target system. Unlike the three premises, which each raise different issues, the three conclusions raise the same issues and so we can discuss them together. To facilitate the discussion, I refer to the facts that the models have R and S, and that the robust theorem (which says that S brings about R under conditions C) holds true in them, as "model results". As noted, the arguments in the three steps are not deductively valid, and so there is a question of what justifies the inference from the premise (that a result holds in a model ensemble) to the conclusion (that the same result holds in the real-world target system).

In some cases this may be a question that can be settled by empirical test, thereby in effect making the argument in Step 1 unnecessary. In the predator-prey case, for instance, D'Ancona's observations provide evidence for the presence of R in the fish system of the Adriatic Sea. How strong this evidence is depends on what one takes the scope of the analysis to be. If attention is restricted to the Adriatic Sea, then the evidence is strong; if one takes the scope of the model to be predator-prey systems in general, further evidence is needed. However, this is nothing special: we are faced with a case of a hypothesis being tested against data, and the case at hand does not raise issues that go beyond the usual questions that arise in connection with confirming theories against observations.

However, as Weisberg himself notes (2006b, 739), RA is often used in cases where empirical tests are not feasible and RA is supposed to stand in for empirical tests by providing reasons to believe that R, S, and the robust theorem connecting S and R, hold in the target. If, for instance, a RA is carried out with climate models to establish a claim about the climate in the year 2050 (for instance that the "business as usual" emission pathway leads to an increase in global mean temperature of more than 2 degrees by 2050), then this claim is, at the moment, not empirically testable and RA is used precisely to provide evidence for it; in fact, the claim may not be testable ever because the emission pathway may change and the pathway used in the models is not the pathway that the real world has taken.

How RA can establish the truth of a claim about the target is, at least prima facie, puzzling. Talking about econometric models, Cartwright formulates the worry thus:

> Now here is the reasoning I do not understand: "Econometrician X used a linear form, Y a log linear, Z something else; and the results are the same anyway. Since the results are so robust, there must be some truth in them." But . . . we know that at the very best one and only one of these assumptions can be right. We may look at thirty functional forms, but if God's function is number thirty-one, the first thirty do not teach us anything. . . . I agree that it is a coincidence that they all find the same results. But I do not see what reason we have to assume that the correct explanation for the coincidence is that each of the instruments, despite its flaws, is nevertheless reading the outcome correctly.
>
> *(1991, 154)*

Orzack and Sober share this bewilderment and suggest getting to the bottom of the matter in a piecemeal manner. To this end, they distinguish three cases and argue that the cases are either unrealistic or fail to support the conclusion (1993, 538). The first case is one in which "we know that one of a set of models [Ω] is true, but we do not know which" (*ibid.*).[22] Under this assumption, RA successfully establishes that the model result is true: a result is robust if all models in Ω agree on the result, and if Ω contains the true model, then all models agree on the truth, and therefore the robust result is true. Unfortunately, this scenario is unrealistic. First, it is far from obvious why a true model should be part of Ω to begin with given that models typically involve simplifications and omissions. Second, even if we were lucky enough to have an ensemble that contained the true model, we would rarely, if ever, be in the situation to know this to be the case. One might say that we would be in such a fortunate situation if we knew that Ω was a *complete* ensemble in that it contains all plausible models of *T*. That's correct, but we typically do not have such ensembles. If an ensemble is not complete in this sense, we would have to know *somehow* that the true model is in it, but it remains unclear how we could come to know this; and if we could simply pinpoint the true model, then we would not need RA to begin with. So the first option is sound in principle but irrelevant in practice.

Orzack and Sober's second option is that Ω is known not to contain the true model: each model in Ω is false. In this case RA seems unsound because "[i]f we know that each of the models is false (each is a 'lie'), then it is unclear why the fact that *R* is implied by all of them is evidence that *R* is true" (*ibid.*, 538). Their third option is that it is unknown whether Ω contains the true model. Orzack and Sober conclude RA is unhelpful in this case too because "[i]f we do not know that one of the models is true, then it is again unclear why a joint prediction should be regarded as true" (*ibid.*, 538–539). Hence, RA tells us something about the models, but it does not inform us about the real-world systems that the models represent.

In his reply to Orzack and Sober, Levins insists that the "logical structure of the argument is quite different from Orzack and Sober's representation of it" (1993, 553). Levins submits that we should start with an ensemble of models that have the structure $M_i = S \& I_i$ for all i. Furthermore, the model components have to satisfy the following requirements: the set of the I_i is such that the model ensemble "exhausts all the admissible alternatives" (*ibid.*) and S is deemed plausible prior to RA. Observations will play a role in assessing whether these conditions are met: "[o]bservation enters first in the choice of the core model and the selection of plausible variable parts, and later in the testing of the predictions that follow from the core model" (*ibid.*, 554). So Ω is not just any ensemble; it is an ensemble consisting of models with empirical credentials. This, Levins submits, changes the argument completely because robust conclusions drawn from *such* an ensemble *do* lend credibility to robust claims: "robustness as understood here is a valid strategy for separating conclusions that depend on the common biological core of a model from the simplifications, distortions and omissions introduced to facilitate the analysis, and for arriving at the implications of partial truths" (*ibid.*).[23]

Let us look closer at what is going on here. Orzack and Sober argue that a conclusion being robust in an ensemble of models that are all false does not lend support to the claim that the conclusion is true of the target. Levins in effect replies that this, even if true, is beside the point because we have to consider an ensemble consisting of models with observational credentials, and under that condition a result being robust does support the claim that it is true of the target. Why would this be? It is possible in principle that even models that have empirical credentials agree on a feature that does not obtain in the target. What allows us to discard this possibility?

The key to the answer would seem to lie in the notion that the models in the ensemble are independent. As we have seen previously, Levins insists that the truth is the intersection of *independent* lies. This opens the door to a well-known argument in the philosophy of science: the argument from the *variety of evidence*. The argument has a long history and has been articulated differently at different points in time, but the basic intuition is simple: if a number of different strands of evidence point to the same conclusion, then this conclusion must be true, or at least our degree of belief in it should be higher in the light of the evidence than it was before the evidence became available. Perrin famously relied on this kind of reasoning when he concluded that atoms must exist because thirteen different methods of observation lead to that conclusion.[24] We also rely on this sort of reasoning when we assert that a physical quantity has a particular value v because several measurements have been made with different measurement instruments and all have resulted in the same value. Kuorikoski, Lehtinen, and Marchionni rely on this kind of reasoning when they motivate robustness reasoning by saying that "[i]t would be a remarkable coincidence if separate and independent forms of determination yielded the same conclusion if the conclusion did not correspond to something real" (2010, 544).[25]

This, however, does not seem to help Levins. Even though he says that models ought to be independent, Orzack and Sober point out that Levins' method for determining a robust prediction not only fails to guarantee that models are independent; on the contrary, it "guarantees that the models under consideration are *not* independent" (1993, 540, original emphasis). The reason for this is that Levins urges us to carry out the RA with an ensemble of models that are all based on the *same* core, which introduces a dependence among models. This dependence can be problematic because it can introduce a systematic bias into models. Parker discusses this issue in the case of climate models and reaches a sober conclusion:

> When today's climate models agree that an interesting hypothesis about future climate change is true, it cannot be inferred . . . that the hypothesis is likely to be true or that scientists' confidence in the hypothesis should be significantly increased or that a claim to have evidence for the hypothesis is now more secure.
>
> *(2011, 579)*

This is because these models have the same technological limitations that are rooted in today's computational infrastructure, and because they are based on the same understanding of the climate system, which means that they inevitably have some common errors.[26] Or, if we study a mechanical system and construct an ensemble that is based on the Newtonian laws of motion, these models may have all kind of stable results that are, however, false because the models fail to take the effects described in quantum mechanics and relativity theory into account. The postulate that we should construct Ω by taking a core and adding different idealisations to it undermines independence and can lead to systematic biases.

This puts the spotlight on independence. The crucial question for RA is: what kind of independence must the models in Ω have to put the conclusions in RA on a firm footing? Recent discussions about RA have focused on this question. Kuorikoski et al. (2010, 544) argued that the models in an ensemble satisfy independence conditions similar to those satisfied by different measurement instruments and that this justifies RA. Odenbaugh and Alexandrova (2011) disagree. They argue that models in an ensemble do not meet the required independence conditions; RA therefore does not have the power to establish conclusions and is best regarded as a method of discovery rather than confirmation. Kuorikoski et al. (2012) respond to this criticism and argue that once certain points are clarified, their original argument stands. Kuorikoski and Marchionni (2016) provide further arguments for the conclusion that the independence condition grounds the confirmatory added value of a variety of evidence.[27] Harris (2021c) identifies problems with the approach that go deeper than the criticisms of Odenbaugh and Alexandrova, arguing that the independence conditions fail as a matter of principle and not just as a matter of practice.

In sum, RA is a method, which, despite its intuitive appeal, has to date not found a canonical formulation that would alleviate concerns about its conclusions in actual cases.

15.4   Perspectivism

Objects look different when we view them from different standpoints. The mountain looks different when seen from the north and when seen from the south, and the tower looks different when seen from one side of the river and when seen from the other side. What we perceive depends on our point of view. The core premise of *perspectivism* is that this observation holds true beyond the realm of visual experience.[28] Ever since Kant declared that objects must conform to our cognition rather than vice versa, philosophers have endeavoured to articulate the idea that objects are not simply given to us "as they are", and that the way in which we perceive, conceptualise, know, and understand them depends on who we are – on our point of view. This basic idea plays an important role in a number of fields and disciplines. To mention just a few: the founding fathers of the sociology of knowledge saw cognition as being tied to a particular location in a social system; standpoint epistemology systematically develops the idea that all knowledge is bound to a point of view; and perspectival history aims to describe events as they appear to differently positioned actors.[29] Similar developments have shaped views in contemporary epistemology, philosophy of language, philosophy of time, causation, and theories of representation.[30]

Giere articulated a perspectival vision in the philosophy of science. On his view, perspectives are defined through theories.[31] Writing about overarching theoretical principles, Giere says that

> the grand principles objectivists cite as universal laws of nature are better understood as defining highly generalized models that characterize a theoretical perspective. Thus, Newton's laws characterize the classical mechanical perspective; Maxwell's laws characterize the classical electromagnetic perspective; the Schrödinger Equation characterizes a quantum mechanical perspective; the principles of natural selection characterize an evolutionary perspective, and so on.
>
> *(2006, 14–15)*

The perspectives that are defined through theoretical principles "trickle down" to models in a straightforward manner. As we have seen in Chapter 8, Giere views theories as collections of models. But these collections are not random collections of models; the models that belong to a theory are constructed using the theory's theoretical principles. A Newtonian model, for instance, is an abstract object that has been constructed in accordance with the principles of Newtonian mechanics, most notably Newton's equation of motion, and which therefore satisfies these principles. The function of theoretical principles, on this view, "is to act as general templates for the construction of more specific models" (2006, 62). This construction has two aspects. The first aspect is "interpretation", where the "principles of Newtonian mechanics, for example, help to interpret the terms force and mass within a Newtonian perspective by showing their relationships with the terms position, velocity, and acceleration" (*ibid.*). The second aspect is "identification", where specific things in the world are set into a correspondence relation with elements of a model (*ibid.*).

Models embody the theoretical principles that are constitutive of a theory, and thereby inherit the perspectives that these principles define. To say that a model is a "Newtonian model" is tantamount to saying that it is a model that is constructed from a Newtonian perspective and that it represents its target system (if any) from a Newtonian point of view. Such a representation can be true, but its truth is relative to a perspective. Absolute truth is thus replaced by "truth within a perspective" (*ibid.*, 81), and full-blown realism becomes "perspectival realism" (*ibid.*, 88). Perspectivism goes all the way down, as it were. It not only makes the (relatively trivial) claim that the same thing can look different from different perspectives; it makes the more radical claim that from different perspectives the same target has different characteristics and different claims are true of it. For this reason, the assumption that there is only one correct model, namely the model that captures *the* true nature of the target, must be given up. The target has one set of features from one perspective and another set of features from another perspective.[32] For instance, an object can move in a well-defined trajectory at any time from the classical mechanics perspective while not having a well-defined position at any time from quantum mechanics perspective.

At first blush, it looks like this solves the problem of multiple models in Section 15.2. Different models embody different perspectives, and when seen from different perspectives the same target can have different properties. So the fact that we have a set of different and seemingly conflicting models of the same target is not indicative of there being a problem of inconsistency; it is merely indicative of there being different scientific perspectives, each of which comes with its own perspectival truths.

This account of models seems to work well when models are concerned with different parts or aspects of a target system. If we have, say, two earth models where one represents the dynamics of tectonic plates while the other represents oceanic currents, then one can naturally speak of different perspectives and of there being no conflict between them. As we have seen previously, Morrison discusses the example of fluid dynamics where different models are used to represent distinct aspects of the fluid rather than representing the same structures in different ways. Rueger discusses the case of models that are different approximations to the same unified theory. Such models, even though they are incompatible on the face of it, capture different aspects of the same underlying theory (2005). As both Morrison and Rueger note, perspectivism is plausible in such cases because there is no real conflict between perspectival models and the models operate in a complementary manner.[33]

There is, however, a question whether perspectivism retains this plausibility if we look at cases of genuine contradiction, cases where different models say different things about the same part or aspect of the target. Morrison refers to the case of nuclear models (Section 15.2) and notes that

> it isn't clear how perspectivism can help us solve the problem of interpreting the information that inconsistent models provide. We know the nucleus is a quantum phenomenon yet we use classical models to represent fission. Despite the success of the model no one is prepared to claim that there is any sense in which the liquid drop model could be an accurate representation of the nucleus. So adopting a particular perspective doesn't help in these contexts. In other words, it doesn't help us to say that from the classical perspective the nucleus behaves like a liquid drop if we know that the particles inside the nucleus are quantum mechanical.
>
> *(2011, 343)*

She continues to point out that perspectivism forces us to say that "the nucleus has no nature in itself and we can only answer questions about it once a particular perspective is specified" (2015, 160). Giere seems to endorse this conclusion and submits that this is what allows the position to avoid "silly relativism" and salvage realism in the face of different perspectives (2006, 13). Morrison argues that such a reconciliation of conflicting models does not stand up to scrutiny. Even though there can be different models of the same thing, "it shouldn't follow from this that we can have contradictory accounts of how a system is constituted", which is something Giere's perspectivism allows for (2015, 160). Perspectivism is ultimately incompatible with realism and it is committed to a "nontrivial version of instrumentalism" (*ibid.*). For this reason, Morrison concludes, "despite the appearance of success, perspectivism is of no help in resolving the problem of conflicting models" (*ibid.*, 161).

The question of whether, and if so how, perspectivism can be reconciled with realism has attracted considerable attention in the recent literature on scientific realism.[34] However, our main concern at this point is not whether perspectivism is compatible with realism; our question is whether it offers a cogent response, realist or otherwise, to the multiple models problem. And there are at least three doubts about this irrespective of how the realism issue is resolved. The first doubt concerns the relation between perspectives and practical questions. Evidence-based policy bases its decision on scientific knowledge. But which knowledge? The policy questions themselves usually do not pertain to any particular perspective. If, say, the Environment Agency wants to know in what areas flooding is likely to become a problem in the next twenty years, this question does not belong to any particular scientific perspective. If the agency is then told that there are three models pertaining to three different theoretical perspectives, and that these models make contradictory predictions, then which model should the agency base its decisions on? One is tempted to reply that it should use the model that is closest to the facts, but that goes against the grain of perspectivism which sees facts about the target as being determined by a perspective.

The second doubt is that not all contradictory models fit the perspectivist mould. The over thirty nuclear models on Morrison's list are not all constructed from different perspectives. In fact, as we have seen, she sorts them into three groups – microscopic models, collective models, and mixed models – and so there are at most three perspectives (and possibly only two because the third is a crossover of the other two). Some models are simply incompatible with each other, and this incompatibility cannot be explained away by saying that they embody different perspectives and therefore capture different perspectival facts of the target. And nuclear models are no special case. Take the example of climate models. Dozens of global climate models are developed and run by national modelling centres like the UK Met Office and the Beijing Climate Center. Many of these models participate in the so-called Coupled Model Intercomparison Project (CMIP), which defines a set of standardised tasks that are then run on each model and the results are compared. Phase 5 of this project provided the modelling data for many of the IPCC's results in the Fifth Assessment Report (Stocker et al. 2013). The models disagree with each other in important ways, providing different values for crucial climate variables like global mean temperature and climate sensitivity, as well as exhibiting different internal variability. While the models in CMIP produce different projections and use different modelling and computational techniques, they work within the same broad theoretical framework. Hence, an attempt to attribute disagreements between these models to a difference in perspectives of the kind that characterises the difference between, say, a quantum model and classical model of the same system would come out looking rather unnatural.

The third doubt is that it is often not clear what perspective a model embodies. As we have seen in Section 13.7, models often integrate elements from different theories. Climate models are again a case in point. These models are designed to integrate as much current knowledge as possible, which comes from diverse theories including mechanics, fluid dynamics, electrodynamics, quantum theory, chemistry, and biology. If one follows Giere and sees a perspective as defined by overarching theoretical principles like Newton's equation or Schrödinger's equation, then it is not clear what perspective a model like a climate model, which integrates elements from several different fields, embodies. The problem becomes even more pressing when one looks at models like the ones we discussed in Sections 13.2–13.4, which are largely independent from theories and do not embody any overarching principle.

To avoid difficulties like these, Massimi urges a reconceptualisation of perspectivism.[35] Rather than, like Giere, individuating perspectives through theories, she sees a perspective as defined through the practice of science:

> A scientific perspective . . . is the actual – historically and intellectually situated – scientific practice of a real scientific community at a given historical time. Scientific practice should here be understood to include: (i) the

body of scientific knowledge claims advanced by the scientific community at the time; (ii) the experimental, theoretical, and technological resources available to the scientific community at the time to reliably make those scientific knowledge claims; and (iii) second-order (methodological-epistemic) claims that can justify the scientific knowledge claims advanced. Metaphysical, philosophical, religious beliefs that might have been present at the time in the community do not count as part of a scientific perspective. For they cannot explain how the community comes to reliably make or justify those scientific knowledge claims.

(2018c, 152)

Models fall under (ii) of this account of a perspective. Different models can then be regarded as perspectival not because they are constructed using different theoretical principles, but because they pertain to different historically situated scientific practices.

The second important difference with Giere's account is that Massimi does not see the main purpose of perspectival models as providing truthful representations of their targets informing us about what *actually* happens. She sees the main purpose of these models as providing *modal* information about the target: information about what is possible. On this view, models still have representational content and they are still about a target. But rather than standing "in any mapping relation to worldly-states-of-affairs", their use is geared toward "exploring and ruling out the space of possibilities in domains that are still very much open-ended for scientific discovery" (2018b, 338).[36] Hence, "perspectival models are an exercise in . . . physically conceiving something about the target system so as to deliver modal knowledge about what might be *possible* about the target system" (*ibid.*, 339, original emphasis).

Massimi illustrates her notion of perspectival modelling with number of examples. In her (2018b, Sec. 5) she investigates models in elementary particle physics,[37] and in her (2022) she offers extensive discussions of nuclear models, climate models, and developmental contingency models for dyslexia. Her discussion of elementary particles focuses on two examples of research carried out at CERN: the exploration of the so-called Minimal Super-Symmetric Model (MSSM) in the ATLAS experiment and the study of simplified supersymmetric models in the CMS experiment. Let us have a look at Massimi's account of the former. Super-symmetric theories postulate that the particles of the standard models have super-symmetric "partner particles", so-called "sparticles", thus pairing quarks with "squarks", leptons with "sleptons", and so on. Given the current evidence, these particles are hypothetical. The experimental search for these particles is complicated by the fact that the model that features these particles has 19 parameters for physical quantities like the masses of the hypothetical "sparticles", and each parameter can assume a range of different values. Finding evidence for the existence of particular particles would involve comprehensively scanning the parameter space of the model and comparing each point in it with ATLAS data. This is impossible to do with available computational resources. To circumvent the problem, the project randomly chose 310,327 points in the parameter space and investigated these points. Each point is referred to as a "model point" because each point in effect stands for a particular version of the supersymmetrical model, namely the version in which the parameters assume the particular value specified by that point in parameter space. These models form what in Section 15.3 we called a perturbed parameter ensemble. Massimi refers to the models in this ensemble as "perspectival models" (2018b, 353), arguing that each of them offers a perspective on sparticles. Through a large-scale computation, physicists then determine the properties of each model, in particular the spectra of the particles. The result of this exercise is a set of possible spectra. In this way, perspectival models are an "exercise in modeling physically conceivable states for supersymmetric particles" and they serve "as a guide to what might be objectively possible in nature" (*ibid.*).[38]

This notion of perspective raises two questions. The first question is whether it offers a cogent account of how models are perspectival. To answer this question let us slightly simplify the above definition and say that a perspective P is a quintuple (C, K, E, M, S): a community C with scientific knowledge K, experimental techniques E, a set of models M, and second-order principles S. Let us now assume that we have two perspectives $P_1 = (C_1, K_1, E_1, M_1, S_1)$ and $P_2 = (C_2, K_2, E_2, M_2, S_2)$, and let us assume that the constituents are genuinely different, i.e. $C_1 \neq C_2$, and so on. In this case, it would seem to be natural to say that models in M_1 and in M_2 are perspectival because they are different models that belong to different perspectives. But what if both perspectives use the same set of models (i.e. $M_1 = M_2$)? This is a scenario in which there are different communities with different experimental techniques, but they all use the same set of models. In such a case it would seem that there is nothing perspectival about the models *themselves* because even though they are used by different communities, they are intrinsically the same. Models don't become perspectival by association, as it were.

This raises the question whether Massimi's examples are of the first kind $(M_1 \neq M_2)$ or the second kind $(M_1 = M_2)$. Massimi's cases are complex, and a final verdict must be reached through a more detailed investigation than we can provide here. However, it would seem that there is at least a prima facie case for thinking that some of her cases are of the second rather than the first kind. Consider the above MSSM case. There is only one model, defined by one set of theoretical assumption and one set of equations, and the 310,327 calculations were different only in parameter values. But different parameter values do not make different models. So even if it was the case that this model was used by different communities with K, E, and S, why would this make the model itself perspectival?

The same problem arises in the climate case. There are different communities that use different experimental techniques. One community works with tree rings, another with ice cores, and yet another with corrals. But the CMIP models are shared between them (in as far as these communities are interested in models at all); that is, it is not the case that the "tree ring community" uses one global climate model and the "ice core community" uses another global climate model.

So in what sense are the CMIP models perspectival? It would seem that these models transcend different perspectives because they are not tied to any one of them. One might respond that to require that models themselves must embody a perspective to be perspectival is too rigorous a requirement. Models, one might argue, are perspectival simply because they are a part of science, and science as whole is a perspectival endeavour. If, for the sake of argument, one grants that science as a whole is perspectival, then that could be true.[39] There is a worry, though, that this is not a substantial sense of being perspectival.

The second question concerns the relation between perspectivism and modal knowledge. Massimi presents these as two sides of the same coin. But are they really inseparable? It would seem not. In fact, there are a number of approaches to models that see models as providing knowledge about possibilities without being committed to any kind of perspectivism. Stainforth and et al. (2007) argue that climate models give us information about what is possible. More specifically, they argue that the spread of a suitably designed ensemble of climate model simulations presents the range of outcomes that cannot be ruled out, and they call the bounds of this set of results the "nondiscountable climate change envelope". Likewise, Katzav (2014) argues that climate models should not be seen as making predictions of actual happenings; rather, models ought to be used to show that certain scenarios are real possibilities. But neither Stainforth nor Katzav connect these claims to a perspectivist philosophy of science. It would seem, then, that one can see models as providers of modal knowledge without also seeing them as being perspectival.[40]

Setting perspectivism aside and focusing on modality, there is a further issue whether a perturbed parameter ensemble (or, indeed, a multi-model ensemble) can really serve as a guide to what is objectively possible in nature. These models are constructed against a certain theoretical background and they make certain assumptions. Betz (2015) argues that the outputs of climate models cannot be interpreted in any straightforward manner as giving possibilities because their assumptions are known to be false. Elementary particle models may be in a slightly better position here because the assumptions are at least not known to be false, but they are not empirically confirmed either, at least insofar as the assumptions go beyond the so-called standard model (as is the case for super-symmetrical models). But what reasons are there to believe that models that are based on false or unconfirmed assumptions provide information about true possibilities in nature? Why do they not merely tell us what is within the purview of current theories, where we always have to countenance the possibility that these theories turn out to be wrong? This is an open question.

15.5 Managing Severe Uncertainty

The existence of multiple models may be the result of there being latitude in model construction, which is not sufficiently constrained by either data or theory; or it may be the result of systematic disagreement among scientists over the nature of the system and the appropriate way of modelling it. These are situations of scientific uncertainty. The uncertainty concerns both the model structure and the values of parameters in the model, and the existence of a model ensemble can be seen as an expression of this uncertainty. The uncertainty is severe if it is impossible to reduce the uncertainty given the current state of knowledge. Models that are constructed under severe uncertainty will often not agree with each other and produce a range of different outcomes. The resulting model ensemble therefore does not produce robust results, which rules out RA as a suitable method for dealing with such an ensemble. At the same time, as we have seen in the previous section, the models in such an ensemble may not be sufficiently different to understand them as offering alternative perspectival representations.

How should we think about severe uncertainty and how should we make decisions in the face of it? Uncertainty is a concept that is poorly understood, and so the aim of this section is to make clear what the problems are rather than to introduce and assess solutions.[41] I will do so with the example of the IPCC's projections for global mean temperature.

The IPCC's Fifth Assessment Report (Stocker et al. 2013) contains projections of the global mean temperature by 2100, which are accompanied by an assessment about their uncertainty.[42] For instance, the report projects that there will be a rise in global mean temperature of 2.67°C–4.87°C by the late twentieth century under the so-called RCP8.5 scenario, which assumes a "possible future" in which greenhouse gas emissions continue to rise unabated. The IPCC qualifies this projection as being "likely". This qualification uses the IPCC's standardised language that quantifies uncertainty in a projection using likelihood intervals, where an outcome is "virtually certain" if its probability is greater than 99%, "very likely" if its probability is greater than 90%, "likely" if its probability is greater than 66%, and "more likely than not" if its probability is greater than 50%. That this projection is qualified as "likely" therefore means that, according to the projection, the probability for the rise of global mean temperature in the real world (assuming that the RCP8.5 scenario turns out to be true) to be within the 2.67°C–4.87°C range is somewhere between 66%–100%.

The 2.67°C–4.87°C range results from an analysis of the models in the Phase 5 of the Coupled Model Intercomparison Project (CMIP5), which we encountered in the previous section. The models in the ensemble were all run under the RCP8.5 scenario, and they produced a result for the projected temperature change by 2100. These results were not in agreement with each other, and so no robust result emerged from the ensemble. The IPCC reacted to this situation by using the model outputs to determine parameters of a Gaussian probability distribution. Specifically, they calculated the mean and the variance of the model outputs, and plugged these into a Gaussian distribution. The 2.67°C–4.87°C range turns out to be the interval that symmetrically spans 90% of that distribution. Based on the model ensemble, there is therefore a 90% probability that the increase in the mean global temperature of the real world (assuming the emissions follow the RCP8.5 scenario) lies within the 2.67°C–4.87°C range.

In the IPCC terminology of the last paragraph, this would mean that the range is "very likely". But we said that the IPCC qualifies the result as "likely", not "very likely". Where does this difference come from? The IPCC authors note that even though the models in the CMIP5 ensemble are state of the art models, there are uncertainties about the models and the models share systematic biases (Knutti et al. 2010): they face the same computational constraints, they use the same set of limited parametrisations, and they are all calibrated to reproduce aspects of the 20th century climate which may be less relevant for 21st century developments. For these reasons, the IPCC authors decided to downgrade the model-ensemble-derived "very likely" uncertainty quantification for the range 2.67°C–4.87°C to "likely". This means that while there is a higher than 90% probability that a model run will result in an increase in global mean temperature between 2.67°C and 4.87°C, the authors judge the probability for this to happen in the real world to be only higher than 66%. This amounts to saying that there is an up to 24% probability that the actual rise in global mean temperature (for the RCP8.5 scenario) will be outside the 2.67°C–4.87°C range. This is a clear indication that the IPCC authors recognise the uncertainty that attaches to models and regard it as essential to make adjustments to model results when translating them into real-world results.

The change of the probability range from greater than 90% to greater than 66% is the outcome of an informal process of expert judgment, consisting mainly in discussions between authors during the extended writing and review process of the report. This is important because it highlights that the IPCC's own results and methods imply the assertation that there are uncertainties about model outputs and that these should be assessed and quantified through expert opinions.

Before discussing some of the details of the IPCC's handling of the models, it is worth noting that this case is neither an exception nor a particularly problematic case. In fact, global mean temperature is widely regarded as one of the most reliable variables, and one would expect much higher degrees of uncertainty for the local-scale variables that are of interest to climate adaptation planners. The problem is also not specific to climate. Model ensembles are used in many areas of science and engineering such as natural catastrophe modelling, toxicology, public health, and nuclear safety. In all these domains, issues similar to the ones we have seen in our example arise when the outputs of multiple models have to be distilled into results that form the basis of decision-making.

Two aspects of the example deserve a closer look. The first is the use of model outputs as the basis for the construction of a probability distribution. In effect, the method fits a Gaussian distribution to a finite number of model outputs. This presupposes that individual model results can be regarded as exchangeable sources of information (in the sense that there is no reason to trust one ensemble member more than any other). There are questions about the validity of this assumption. First, as we have noted previously, climate models are not independent because they share assumptions and computer code, and model ensembles like CMIP5 are "ensembles of opportunity" that are not designed to systematically explore all relevant possibilities (and it is therefore conceivable that there are substantial classes of models that produce entirely different results). Second, the assumption to give equal weight to each model may not be justifiable, and several climate physicists have urged giving up "model democracy" and its "one-model-one-vote" approach at least in some cases (for a discussion see Knutti 2010).

The second aspect that requires scrutiny is the use of an informal process of expert judgment to adjust model-ensemble-derived probabilities. The IPCC authors ought to be commended on the forthrightness with which they acknowledge the presence of uncertainty and the fact that they take it into account through a process of expert judgment. Yet, this approach suffers from the drawback that neither the process, nor the principles that guide the process, are transparent, and that it therefore remains unclear why one result rather than another result has been reached and how the final result is justified. Why downgrade to "likely" rather than to "more likely than not"? The point here is not that expert judgment should be avoided altogether; it cannot be avoided. The point is that a structured process would be preferable to an unstructured process. This realisation connects model ensembles with so-called *structured expert elicitation*, a family of methods designed to incorporate expert knowledge into uncertainty management. The method of structured expert elicitation was originally used in defence planning and aerospace engineering, and has spread from there to other domains. There are a variety of methods and approaches, which differ in how to use experts and in how to process their opinions. This is not the place to review and discuss these methods.[43] The point here is merely that such methods are needed, and that that they deserve to be discussed in the context of model ensembles.

Multi-model situations often arise in contexts in which the problem has a decision aspect. We are interested in the rise in global mean temperature not only because we want to understand the physics of the atmosphere; we are interested in it also (or even primarily) because we have to act on climate change. The same holds true for problems in other fields like natural catastrophe modelling and public health modelling. This motivates viewing such problems as decision problems: how do we, or should we, make decisions under uncertainty? This is a question that has attracted considerable attention in the field of decision theory.[44] So far the discussions about model ensembles and decision-making under uncertainty have taken place in largely disjointed academic communities, and the interaction between the two fields has been limited. Bringing these fields into fruitful collaboration with each other will open promising avenues for future research, and widen our understanding of how we can, and should, act in situations in which models disagree.

15.6 Conclusion

The sober conclusion at the end of this chapter can only be that multi-model situations raise issues that are not yet fully understood and that the methods and approaches that have been devised to deal with them have not yet reached a stage of maturity. Important questions remain, and these will have to be addressed in future research.

Notes

1 For further discussions of nuclear models, see Morrison's (1998, 74–76, 2000, 47–52) and Portides' (2005, 2006, 2011).

2 In 2020 there were 89 models from 35 modelling groups submitted to Phase 6 of the Coupled Model Intercomparison Project, the modelling project on which many of the IPCC's projections are based.

3 Early acknowledgments of the existence of multiple models in the philosophy of science literature can be found in Achinstein's (1968, 215) and Hutten's (1954, 298).

4 Mitchell (2002) sees multiple models as a manifestation of pluralism in science. Veit (2020) goes a step further and argues that multiple models are necessary for an adequate analysis of almost any phenomenon.

5 For a discussion of Levins's analysis, and the trade-off between theoretical virtues more generally, see Gelfert's (2013, 2016, Ch. 3), Levins' (1993, 550), Matthewson's (2011), Matthewson and Weisberg's (2009), Odenbaugh's (2003, 2006), Orzack's (2005), Orzack and Sober's (1993), Weisberg's (2006a), and Yoshida's (2020). For a discussion of Levin's attitude to modelling, see Winther's (2006). Grüne-Yanoff and Marchionni (2018) discuss an account, due to Rodrik, which has it that the existence of multiple models of the same target is acceptable as long as each model is the best model for a particular purpose. Veit (2021) critically responds to Grüne-Yanoff and Marchionni.

6 For a general discussion of inconsistency and inconsistent models, see also Frisch's (2005) and Rice's (2020b).

7 I would like to thank Margherita Harris for many helpful discussions on RA, and for comments on an earlier version of this section.

8 For further discussions, see Weisberg's (2006a, 2013, Ch. 9). Räz's (2017) provides a generalisation of Weisberg and Reisman's results. The idea of studying robustness in the context of models goes back to Levins' (1966), and the term "robustness analysis" has been coined by Wimsatt (1981) in his reconstruction of Levins' methodology. The basic idea of robustness has a long history. Stegenga (2009) reports that "robustness" was first used as a methodological concept by statistician George Box in 1953. For a discussion and classifications of different kinds of robustness, see Houkes and Vaesen's (2012), Raerinne's (2013), and Woodward's (2006). Lisciandra (2017) emphasises that RA differs from de-idealisation, even though the two notions are sometimes conflated. The claim that an approach based on multiple models is superior can be seen a special case of "methodological triangulation", the view that using multiple methods simultaneously is advantageous because if these methods produce the same results, then these results are confirmed more strongly than they would be based on only one method (Heesen et al. 2019). The term "robustness analysis" also frequently appears in the context of operational research, where it, however, designates a different method than the one we discuss here (see, for instance, Wong and Rosenhead 2000).

9 At this point, the term "structure" is used in its ordinary language meaning, and not in the technical sense discussed in Chapter 2.

10 Weisberg refers to these conditions as *ceteris paribus* conditions (*ibid.*). I prefer to avoid reference to ceteris paribus clauses because these clauses have a long and troublesome history in the context of laws of nature, and it would seem preferable to keep these issues separate. For a discussion of ceteris paribus laws, see Reutlinger et al. (2015).

11 I here set aside the difficult issue of what exactly "bring about" means. In most cases it will be a causal connection of sorts, which would, however, require further analysis. For an introduction to different options, see, for instance, Reiss' (2017).

12 In some cases, the focus may be more restricted and scientists are only interested in parts of the entire scheme. This happens, for instance if the aim is to establish only that a certain property is robust without also attributing it to a common structure. In this case, only Step 1 is carried out. In other cases, scientists may carry out Step 1 and Step 3 and then infer from these that S is present both in the models and in the target (i.e. the result of Step 2) via some form of inference to the best explanation (IBE). For a general discussion of IBE, see Lipton's (2004); for a discussion IBE in the context of RA, see Odenbaugh's (2011).

13 Indeed, the discussion of RA in the context of climate models has become a subfield of its own. For further discussions, see, for instance, Carrier and Lenhard's (2019), Knutti and Sedláček's (2013), Lloyd's (2009, 2015), Odenbaugh's (2018), Parker's (2011, 2013, 2018), Pirtle et al. (2010), and Vezér's (2016).

14 For introductory discussions of model ensembles, see Frigg et al. (2015b) and Parker's (2013).

15 In the context of climate science such ensembles are also referred to as *perturbed physics ensembles* (Parker 2013, 215). I prefer the more neutral label *perturbed parameter ensemble*. First, the neutral label also applies to models in disciplines other than physics (in the Lotka-Volterra model, there is no physics to perturb). Second, while some parameters represent physical magnitudes (such as the viscosity of water), others are effective summaries of processes like cloud coverage that are not explicitly resolved in the model and so changing parameter values perturbs the model and not the physics.

16 Multi-model ensembles can, in principle encompass models that involve both changes in the functional relation between variables and changes in the kind of variables used. The former is used to study what Weisberg and Reisman (2008, 116) call "structural robustness", which is involved, for instance, when different kinds of density dependences are tested. The latter is to test what they (*ibid.*, 120) call "representational robustness", which is involved, for instance, when population-level variables are replaced by individual variables.

17 For instance, in the exploration of HadCM3, a global climate model on which the UK's official climate policies were based until recently, has 100s of parameters (leading to billions of combinations of values) and yet the results communicated to policy makers were based on less then 300 model runs, only 17 of which were runs of the full model. For a discussion of this case, see Frigg et al. (2015a).

18 Philosophical discussions of sensitivity analysis can be found in Bokulich and Oreskes' (2017, Sec. 41.6) and Raerinne's (2013, Sec. 2); its place in the broader edifice of RA is discussed in Justus' (2012, 801) and Weisberg and Reisman's (2008, 115). For a technical discussion, see Saltelli et al. (2004).

19 Fletcher (2020) traces this demand back to Duhem and Maxwell and then discusses topological notions of stability in dynamical systems. For further discussions of that kind of stability, see Frigg et al. (2014).

20 A prominent example of such an ensemble is the CMIP5 ensemble, a collection of around 20 different global climate models that have been used to reach some of the core results of the IPCC's 5th Assessment report (Stocker et al. 2013). We will briefly return to this case in Section 15.4. For a discussion of the problems that are faced by this model ensemble, see Thompson et al. (2016).

21 I note that the renormalisation group techniques that we mentioned in connection with minimal models in Section 12.5 can also be seen as providing robust results across a class of models. Indeed, Batterman and Rice occasionally paraphrase renormalisation as establishing the "robustness" of certain behaviours (see, for instance, 2014, 364, 371), and Rice argues that idealisations are justified by showing that models belong to a certain universality class (see, for instance, 2020a, 829). However, renormalisation does not seem to be discussed much in the context of RA.

22 By a model being "true" they mean that the model represents *T* accurately in the relevant respects.

23 Weisberg makes a related suggestion according to which models have "low-level confirmation", which is "what allows robust theorems to make claims about real-world phenomena" (2006b). Harris (2021a, Ch. 3) discusses this argument and concludes that it fails to provide a successful justification of the conclusions. For an elaboration of the view that the conclusions of RA can be put on a firm basis by insisting that models are confirmed independently, see Lehtinen's (2016, 2018).

24 For a discussion Perrin's argument, see Salmon's (1984, Ch. 8).

25 Schupbach's account of robustness (2015, 2018) also builds on this observation. Harris (2021b) analyses this account and reaches the conclusion that it eventually runs into similar problems as previous accounts.

26 This has been widely acknowledged; see, for instance, Knutti et al. (2010). Bishop and Abramowitz (2013) and Jun et al. (2008b, 2008a) have demonstrated and discussed the lack of model independence. For further discussion of model comparison in the context of climate models, see Bokulich and Oreskes' (2017).

27 Lisciandra and Korbmacher propose an approach that sees RA as being about "*information* not *confirmation*" and emphasise that the goal of RA should be seen as the formulation of an account of "how mutually inconsistent models can coherently *say* something about a shared target system, not an account of whether what they say is true, confirmed, or the like" (2021, 187, original emphasis). This solves the above problems at the cost of declaring them irrelevant.

28 Perspectivism is also known as *perspectivalism*. The terms are usually used interchangeably (Massimi and McCoy 2020a, 1).

29 The *locus classicus* for Kant's so-called Copernican turn is the preface to the second edition of the *Critique of Pure Reason*. For the sociology of knowledge, see, for instance, Mannheim's (1954); for standpoint epistemology, see, for instance, Harding's (1986); and for perspectival history see, for instance, Rossi's (2015).

30 For a discussion of representation, see, for instance, Moore's (1997); for a brief discussion of epistemology, philosophy of language, philosophy of time, and causation, see Massimi and McCoy's (2020a) and references therein. For a general introduction to perspectivism, see Massimi's (2017).

31 A second aspect of Giere's scientific perspectivism are "instrumental perspectives" (*ibid.*, 63). He notes that human perception is perspectival and adds "that the instruments that now dominate scientific observation are similarly perspectival seems almost equally indisputable. They are designed to interact selectively with the world in ways determined by human purposes" (*ibid.*, 93). In this chapter we focus on the theory aspect of his perspectivism.

32 Mitchell further argues that if, as Giere says, "representational models are both partial and perspectival, then in order to acquire knowledge of natural systems, science must employ a plurality of models, methods, and representations" (Mitchell 2020, 178).

33 Pincock (2011) discusses how models that represent different aspects of a phenomenon can still support a modest form of scientific realism.

34 See, for instance, the contributions to Massimi and McCoy's (2020b) and to Massimi's (2020), as well as Brown's (2009), Chakravartty's (2010, 2017, Ch. 6), Giere's (2009), Massimi's (2012, 2018a, 2019a), Rueger's (2014, 2016), Ruyant's (2020), Saatsi's (2016), and Teller's (2018b, 2018a).

35 For an extensive discussion, see her (2022). Her notion of a perspective is discussed in her (2018c), and for a discussion of models, see her (2018b, 2019b).

36 Perspectival models are therefore at once exploratory models. We will return to exploratory models in Section 16.6.

37 See also her (2019b, Sec. 3); the case is also discussed in McCoy and Massimi's (2018).

38 The notion of possibility invoked here is an epistemic notion. To say that a certain sparticle "might be objectively possible in nature" is to say that, given our current knowledge, it is conceivable that there really is such a sparticle. More generally, state X of the world is a possibility if, given current knowledge, we cannot rule out that the world really is in state X. In other words, we cannot discard X as the real state given what we know.

39 There is, however, also a worry that we are committing a fallacy of composition here. We commit this fallacy when we wrongly attribute properties of an aggregate to its parts, or vice versa (Copi et al. 2016, 149). Water is wet but water molecules are not, and each musician of an orchestra plays an instrument but the orchestra as a whole does not. What reasons are there to think that the inference from science as whole being perspectival to models being perspectival is not an instance of the fallacy of composition?

40 For a survey of modal modelling, see Sjölin Wirling and Grüne-Yanoff's (2021).

41 For introductory surveys, see Frigg et al. (2015b) and references therein.

42 The discussion of the IPCC projections and structured expert elicitation in this section follows Thompson et al. (2016). For general discussions of uncertainty, see Smith and Stern's (2011), Spiegelhalter and Riesch's (2011), and Wit et al. (2012).

43 For reviews of different approaches and discussions of applications, see Goossens et al. (2008) and Martini and Boumans' (2014).

44 For an introductory survey, see Bradley and Steele's (2015). A worked out proposal of how to make decisions under uncertainty with hurricane models is discussed in Roussos et al. (2021b, 2021a).

References

Accorinti, H. L. 2019. Incompatible Models in Chemistry: The Case of Electronegativity. *Foundations of Chemistry* 21: 71–81.

Achinstein, P. 1968. *Concepts of Science: A Philosophical Analysis*. Baltimore: Johns Hopkins Press.

Batterman, R. W. and C. C. Rice 2014. Minimal Model Explanations. *Philosophy of Science* 81: 349–376.

Betz, G. 2009. Underdetermination, Model-Ensembles and Surprises: On the Epistemology of Scenario-Analysis in Climatology. *Journal for General Philosophy of Science* 40: 3–21.

Betz, G. 2015. Are Climate Models Credible Worlds? Prospects and Limitations of Possibilistic Climate Prediction. *European Journal for Philosophy of Science* 5: 191–215.

Bishop, C. H. and G. Abramowitz 2013. Climate Model Ependence and the Replicate Earth Paradigm. *Climate Dynamics* 41: 885–900.

Bokulich, A. and N. Oreskes 2017. Models in Geosciences. In L. Magnani and T. Bertolotti (eds.), *Springer Handbook of Model-Based Science*. Dordrecht, Heidelberg, London, and New York: Springer, pp. 891–911.

Bradley, R. and K. Steele 2015. Making Climate Decisions. *Philosophy Compass* 10: 799–810.

Brown, M. J. 2009. Scientific Perspectivism: Behind the Stage Door. *Studies in History and Philosophy of Science* 40: 213–220.

Carrier, M. and J. Lenhard 2019. Climate Models: How to Assess Their Reliability. *International Studies in the Philosophy of Science* 32: 81–100.

Cartwright, N. 1991. Replicability, Reproducibility, and Robustness: Comments on Harry Collins. *History of Political Economy* 23: 143–155.

Chakravartty, A. 2010. Perspectivism, Inconsistent Models, and Contrastive Explanation. *Studies in History and Philosophy of Science* 41: 405–412.

Chakravartty, A. 2017. *Scientific Ontology: Integrating Naturalized Metaphysics and Voluntarist Epistemology*. Oxford: Oxford University Press.

Copi, I. M., C. Cohen, and K. McMahon 2016. *Introduction to Logic* (14th ed.). Harlow: Pearson.

Eronen, M. I. 2015. Robustness and Reality. *Synthese* 192: 3961–3977.

Fletcher, S. C. 2020. The Principle of Stability. *Philosopher's Imprint* 20: 1–22.

Frigg, R., S. Bradley, H. Du, and L. A. Smith 2014. The Adventures of Laplace's Demon and His Apprentices. *Philosophy of Science* 81: 31–59.

Frigg, R., L. A. Smith, and D. A. Stainforth 2015a. An Assessment of the Foundational Assumptions in High-Resolution Climate Projections: The Case of Ukcp09. *Synthese* 192: 3979–4008.

Frigg, R., E. Thompson, and C. Werndl 2015b. Philosophy of Climate Science Part II: Modelling Climate Change. *Philosophy Compass* 10: 965–977.

Frisch, M. 2005. *Inconsistency, Asymmetry, and Non-Locality: A Philosophical Investigation of Classical Electrodynamics*. Oxford: Oxford University Press.

Gelfert, A. 2013. Strategies of Model-Building in Condensed Matter Physics: Trade-Offs as a Demarcation Criterion between Physics and Biology? *Synthese* 190: 253–272.

Gelfert, A. 2016. *How to Do Science with Models: A Philosophical Primer*. Cham: Springer.

Giere, R. N. 2006. *Scientific Perspectivism*. Chicago and London: University of Chicago Press.

Giere, R. N. 2009. Scientific Perspectivism: Behind the Stage Door. *Studies in History and Philosophy of Science* 40: 221–223.

Goossens, L. H. J., R. M. Cooke, A. R. Hale, and L. Rodić-Wiersma 2008. Fifteen Years of Expert Judgement at Tudelft. *Safety Science* 46: 234–244.

Green, S. 2013. When One Model Is Not Enough: Combining Epistemic Tools in Systems Biology. *Studies in History and Philosophy of Biological and Biomedical Science*: 170–180.

Grüne-Yanoff, T. and C. Marchionni 2018. Modeling Model Selection in Model Pluralism. *Journal of Economic Methodology* 25: 265–275.

Guala, F. and A. Salanti 2002. On the Robustness of Economic Models. *Quaderni di ricerca del Dipartimento di Scienze Economiche "Hyman P. Minsky"* 8: 1–24.

Gueguen, M. 2020. On Robustness in Cosmological Simulations. *Philosophy of Science* 87: 1197–1208.

Harding, S. 1986. *The Science Question in Ferminism*. Ithaca and London: Cornell University Press.

Harris, M. 2021a. *Conceptualizing Uncertainty: The Ipcc, Model Robustness and Theweight of Evidence*. PhD Thesis, London School of Economics.

Harris, M. 2021b. *Schupbach's Account of Robustness*. Manuscript.

Harris, M. 2021c. Ambiguous Artefacts: On the Epistemic Value of Robustness Analysis. *Synthese* 199: 14577–14597.

Heesen, R., L. K. Bright, and A. Zucker 2019. Vindicating Methodological Triangulation. *Synthese* 196: 3067–3081.

Houkes, W. and K. Vaesen 2012. Robust! Handle with Care. *Philosophy of Science* 79: 345–364.

Hutten, E. H. 1954. The Rôle of Models in Physics. *The British Journal for the Philosophy of Science* 4: 284–301.

Jun, M. Y., R. Knutti, and D. W. Nychka 2008a. Local Eigenvalue Analysis of Cmip3 Climate Model Errors. *Tellus A: Dynamic Meteorology and Oceanography* 60: 992–1000.

Jun, M. Y., R. Knutti, and D. W. Nychka 2008b. Spatial Analysis to Quantify Numerical Model Bias and Dependence: How Many Climate Models Are There? *Journal of the American Statistical Association* 103: 934–947.

Justus, J. 2012. The Elusive Basis of Inferential Robustness. *Philosophy of Science* 79: 795–807.

Katzav, J. 2014. The Epistemology of Climate Models and Some of Its Implications for Climate Science and the Philosophy of Science. *Studies in History and Philosophy of Modern Physics* 46: 228–238.

Knutti, R. 2010. The End of Model Democracy? *Climate Change* 102: 395–404.

Knutti, R., R. Furrer, C. Tebaldi, J. Cermak, and G. A. Meehl 2010. Challenges in Combining Projections from Multiple Climate Models. *Journal of Climate* 23: 2739–2758.

Knutti, R. and J. Sedláček 2013. Robustness and Uncertainties in the New Cmip5 Climate Model Projections. *Nature Climate Change* 3: 369–373.

Kuorikoski, J., A. Lehtinen, and C. Marchionni 2010. Economic Modelling as Robustness Analysis. *The British Journal for the Philosophy of Science* 61: 541–567.

Kuorikoski, J., A. Lehtinen, and C. Marchionni 2012. Robustness Analysis Disclaimer: Please Read the Manual before Use! *Biology and Philosophy* 27: 891–902.

Kuorikoski, J. and C. Marchionni 2016. Evidential Diversity and the Triangulation of Phenomena. *Philosophy of Science* 83: 227–247.

Lehtinen, A. 2016. Allocating Confirmation with Derivational Robustness. *Philosophical Studies* 173: 2487–2509.

Lehtinen, A. 2018. Derivational Robustness and Indirect Confirmation. *Erkenntnis* 83: 2487–2509.

Levins, R. 1966. The Strategy of Model Building in Population Biology. *American Scientist* 54: 421–431.

Levins, R. 1993. A Response to Orzack and Sober: Formal Analysis and the Fluidity of Science. *The Quarterly Review of Biology* 68: 547–555.

Lipton, P. 2004. *Inference to the Best Explanation* (2nd ed.). London: Routledge.

Lisciandra, C. 2017. Robustness Analysis and Tractability in Modeling. *European Journal for Philosophy of Science* 7: 79–95.

Lisciandra, C. and J. Korbmacher 2021. Multiple Models, One Explanation. *Journal of Economic Methodology* 28: 186–206.

Lloyd, E. A. 2009. Varieties of Support and Confirmation of Climate Models. *Proceedings of the Aristotelian Society Supplementary Volume*: 213–232.

Lloyd, E. A. 2010. Confirmation and Robustness of Climate Models. *Philosophy of Science* 77: 971–984.

Lloyd, E. A. 2015. Model Robustness as a Confirmatory Virtue: The Case of Climate Science. *Studies in History and Philosophy of Science* 49: 58–68.

Mannheim, K. 1954. *Ideology and Utopia*. New York: Harcourt, Brace & Co.

Martini, C. and M. Boumans (eds.) 2014. *Experts and Consensus in Social Science*. NewYork: Springer.

Massimi, M. 2012. Scientific Perspectivism and Its Foes. *Philosophica* 84: 25–52.

Massimi, M. 2017. Perspectivism. In J. Saatsi (ed.), *The Routledge Handbook of Scientific Realism*. London and New York: Routledge, pp. 164–175.

Massimi, M. 2018a. Four Kinds of Perspectival Truth. *Philosophy and Phenomenological Research* 96: 342–359.

Massimi, M. 2018b. Perspectival Modeling. *Philosophy of Science* 85: 335–359.

Massimi, M. 2018c. A Perspectivalist Better Best System Account of Lawhood. In W. Ott and L. Patton (eds.), *Laws of Nature*. Oxford: Oxford University Press, pp. 139–157.

Massimi, M. 2019a. Realism, Perspectivism, and Disagreement in Science. *Synthese* 198: 6115–6141. https://doi.org/10.1007/s11229-019-02500-6.

Massimi, M. 2019b. Two Kinds of Exploratory Models. *Philosophy of Science* 86: 869–881.

Massimi, M. (ed.) 2020. Perspectivism in Science: Metaphysical and Epistemological Reflections. *Topical Collection of European Journal for Philosophy of Science* 10.

Massimi, M. 2022. *Perspectival Realism*. New York: Oxford University Press.

Massimi, M. and C. D. McCoy 2020a. Introduction. In M. Massimi and C. D. McCoy (eds.), *Understanding Perspectivism*. New York: Routledge, pp. 1–9.

Massimi, M. and C. D. McCoy (eds.) 2020b. *Understanding Perspectivism*. New York: Routledge.

Matthewson, J. 2011. Trade-Offs in Model-Building: A More Target-Oriented Approach. *Studies in History and Philosophy of Science* 42: 324–333.

Matthewson, J. and M. Weisberg 2009. The Structure of Tradeoffs in Model Building. *Synthese* 170: 169–190.

McCoy, C. D. and M. Massimi 2018. Simplified Models: A Different Perspective on Models as Mediators. *European Journal for the Philoxophy of Science* 8: 99–123.

Mitchell, S. D. 2002. Integrative Pluralism. *Biology and Philosophy* 17: 55–70.

Mitchell, S. D. 2020. Perspectives, Representation, and Integration. In M. Massimi and C. D. McCoy (eds.), *Understanding Perspectivism*. New York: Routledge, pp. 178–193.

Moore, A. W. 1997. *Points of View*. Oxford: Clarendon Press.

Morrison, M. 1998. Modelling Nature: Between Physics and the Physical World. *Philosophia Naturalis* 35: 65–85.

Morrison, M. 2000. *Unifying Scientific Theories*. Cambridge: Cambridge University Press.

Morrison, M. 2011. One Phenomenon, Many Models: Inconsistency and Complementarity. *Studies in History and Philosophy of Science* 42: 342–353.

Morrison, M. 2015. *Reconstructing Reality: Models, Mathematics, and Simulations*. New York: Oxford University Press.

Odenbaugh, J. 2003. Complex Systems, Trade-Offs, and Theoretical Population Biology: Richard Levin's 'Strategy of Model Building in Population Biology' Revisited. *Philosophy of Science* 70: 1496–1507.

Odenbaugh, J. 2006. The Strategy of 'the Strategy of Model Building in Population Biology'. *Biology and Philosophy* 21: 607–621.

Odenbaugh, J. 2011. True Lies: Realism, Robustness, and Models. *Philosophy of Science* 78: 177–188.

Odenbaugh, J. 2018. Building Trust, Removing Doubt? Robustness Analysis and Climate Modeling. In E. A. Lloyd and E. Winsberg (eds.), *Climate Modelling: Philosophical and Conceptual Issues*. Cham: Palgrave Macmillan, pp. 297–321.

Odenbaugh, J. and A. Alexandrova 2011. Buyer Beware: Robustness Analyses in Economics and Biology. *Biology and Philosophy* 26: 757–771.

Orzack, S. H. 2005. What, If Anything, Is 'the Strategy of Model Building in Population Biology?' A Comment on Levins (1966) and Odenbaugh (2003). *Philosophy of Science* 72: 479–485.

Orzack, S. H. and E. Sober 1993. A Critical Assessment of Levins's the Strategy of Model Building in Population Biology (1966). *The Quarterly Review of Biology* 68: 533–546.

Parker, W. S. 2011. When Climate Models Agree: The Significance of Robust Model Predictions. *Philosophy of Science* 78: 579–600.

Parker, W. S. 2013. Ensemble Modeling, Uncertainty and Robust Predictions. *Wiley Interdisciplinary Reviews: Climate Change* 4: 213–223.

Parker, W. S. 2018. The Significance of Robust Climate Projections. In E. A. Lloyd and E. Winsberg (eds.), *Climate Modelling: Philosophical and Conceptual Issues*. Cham: Palgrave Macmillan, pp. 273–296.

Pincock, C. 2011. Modeling Reality. *Synthese* 180: 19–32.

Pirtle, Z., R. Meyer, and A. Hamilton 2010. What Does It Mean When Climate Models Agree? A Case for Assessing Independence among General Circulation Models. *Environmental Science and Policy* 13: 351–361.

Plutynski, A. 2006. Strategies of Model Building in Population Genetics. *Philosophy of Science* 73: 755–764.

Portides, D. 2005. Scientific Models and the Semantic View of Theories. *Philosophy of Science* 72(Supplement): 1287–1298.

Portides, D. 2006. The Evolutionary History of Models as Representational Agents. In L. Magnani (ed.), *Model-Based Reasoning in Science and Engineering, Texts in Logic* (Vol. 2). London: College Publications, pp. 87–106.

Portides, D. 2011. Seeking Representations of Phenomena: Phenomenological Models. *Studies in History and Philosophy of Science* 42: 334–341.

Raerinne, J. 2013. Robustness and Sensitivity of Biological Models. *Philosophical Studies* 166: 285–303.

Räz, T. 2017. The Volterra Principle Generalized. *Philosophy of Science* 84: 737–760.

Reiss, J. 2017. *Causation, Evidence, and Inference*. London and New York: Routledge.

Reutlinger, A., G. Schurz, and A. Hüttemann 2015. Ceteris Paribus Laws. In E. N. Zalta (ed.), *The Stanford Encyclopedia of Philosophy*. http://plato.stanford.edu/archives/fall2015/entries/ceteris-paribus.

Rice, C. 2019. Models Don't Decompose That Way: A Holistic View of Idealized Models. *The British Journal for the Philosophy of Science* 70: 179–208.

Rice, C. 2020a. Universality and Modeling Limiting Behaviors. *Philosophy of Science* 87: 829–840.

Rice, C. 2020b. Universality and the Problem of Inconsistent Models. In M. Massimi and C. D. McCoy (eds.), *Understanding Perspectivism*. New York: Routledge, pp. 85–109.

Rossi, B. 2015. *From Slavery to Aid: Politics, Labour, and Ecology in the Nigerien Sahel, 1800–2000*. Cambridge: Cambridge University Press.

Roussos, J., R. Bradley, and R. Frigg 2021a. Environmental Decision-Making under Uncertainty. In W. J. González (ed.), *Current Trends in Philosophy of Science: A Prospective for the Near Future* (Synthese Library). Cham: Springer, pp. TBA.

Roussos, J., R. Bradley, and R. Frigg 2021b. Making Confident Decisions with Model Ensembles *Philosophy of Science* 88: 439–460.

Rueger, A. 2005. Perspectival Models and Theory Unification. *The British Journal for the Philosophy of Science* 56: 579–594.

Rueger, A. 2014. Idealized and Perspectival Representations: Some Reasons for Making a Distinction. *Synthese* 191: 1831–1845.

Rueger, A. 2016. Perspectival Realism and Incompatible Models. *Axiomathes* 26: 401–410.

Ruyant, Q. 2020. Perspectival Realism and Norms of Scientific Representation. *European Journal for Philosophy of Science* 10: Article 20.

Saatsi, J. 2016. Models, Idealisations, and Realism. In E. Ippoliti, F. Sterpetti, and T. Nickles (eds.), *Models and Inferences in Science*. Cham: Springer, pp. 173–189.

Salmon, W. C. 1984. *Scientific Explanation and the Causal Structure of the World*. Princeton, NJ: Princeton University Press.

Saltelli, A., S. Tarantola, F. Campolongo, and M. Ratto 2004. *Sensitivity Analysis in Practice: A Guide to Assessing Scientific Models*. Chichester: John Wiley & Sons Ltd.

Schupbach, J. N. 2015. Robustness, Diversity of Evidence, and Probabilistic Independence. In U. Mäki, I. Votsis, S. Ruphy, and G. Schurz (eds.), *Recent Developments in the Philosophy of Science: Epsa13 Helsinki*. Cham: Springer, pp. 305–318.

Schupbach, J. N. 2018. Robustness Analysis as Explanatory Reasoning. *The British Journal for the Philosophy of Science* 69: 275–300.

Sjölin Wirling, Y. and T. Grüne-Yanoff 2021. The Epistemology of Modal Modeling. *Philosophy Compass* e12775: 1–11.

Smith, L. A. and N. Stern 2011. Uncertainty in Science and Its Role in Climate Policy. *Philosophical Transactions of the Royal Society A* 369: 1–24.

Spiegelhalter, D. J. and H. Riesch 2011. Don't Know, Can't Know: Embracing Deeper Uncertainties When Analysing Risks. *Philosophical Transactions of the Royal Society A* 369: 4730–4750.

Sprenger, J. 2012. Environmental Risk Analysis: Robustness Is Essential for Precaution. *Philosophy of Science* 79: 881–892.

Stainforth, D. A., T. E. Downing, R. Washington, A. Lopez, and M. New 2007. Issues in the Interpretation of Climate Model Ensembles to Inform Decisions. *Philosophical Transactions of the Royal Society A* 365: 2163–2177.

Stegenga, J. 2009. Robustness, Discordance, Andrelevance. *Philosophy of Science* 76: 650–661.

Stocker, T. F., D. Qin, G.-K. Plattner, M. M. B. Tignor, S. K. Allen, J. Boschung, et al. (eds.) 2013. *Climate Change 2013. The Physical Science Basis. Working Group I Contribution to the Fifth Assessment Report of the Intergovernmental Panel on Climate Change*. Cambridge: Cambridge University Press.

Teller, P. 2018a. Making Worlds with Symbols. *Synthese*: 1–22. https://doi.org/10.1007/s11229-018-1811-y.

Teller, P. 2018b. Referential and Perspectival Realism. *Spontaneous Generations* 9: 151–164.

Thoma, J. 2012. *On the Robustness of Economic Models*. Master Thesis in Philosophy and Economics, University of Rotterdam. www.google.com/url?sa=t&rct=j&q=&esrc=s&source=web&cd=&ved=2ahUKEwiEodOX_NjxAhWX_7sIHSunBt4QFjABegQIBBAD&url=https%3A%2F%2Fthesis.eur.nl%2Fpub%2F11440%2FMA-thesis%2520Thoma.pdf&usg=AOvVaw0_VmkLXyXXRI-vQ0Yrif1U.

Thompson, E., R. Frigg, and C. Helgeson 2016. Expert Judgment for Climate Change Adaptation. *Philosophy of Science* 83: 1110–1121.

Veit, W. 2020. Model Pluralism. *Philosophy of the Social Sciences* 50: 91–114. https://doi.org/10.1080/1350178X.2021.1898660.

Veit, W. 2021. Model Diversity and the Embarrassment of Riches. *Journal of Economic Methodology* 28(3): 291–303. https://doi.org/10.1080/1350178X.2021.1898660.

Vezér, M. A. 2016. Computer Models and the Evidence of Anthropogenic Climate Change: An Epistemology of Variety-of-Evidence Inferences and Robustness Analysis. *Studies in History and Philosophy of Science* 56: 95–102.

Weisberg, M. 2006a. Forty Years of 'the Strategy': Levins on Model Building and Idealization. *Biology and Philosophy* 21: 623–645.

Weisberg, M. 2006b. Robustness Analysis. *Philosophy of Science* 73: 730–742.

Weisberg, M. 2013. *Simulation and Similarity: Using Models to Understand the World.* Oxford: Oxford University Press.

Weisberg, M. and K. Reisman 2008. The Robust Volterra Principle. *Philosophy of Science* 75: 106–131.

Wimsatt, W. C. 1981. Robustness, Reliability, and Overdetermination. In M. B. Brewer and B. E. Collins (eds.), *Scientific Inquiry and the Social Sciences: A Volume in Honor of Donald T. Campbell.* San Francisco: Lexington Books, pp. 123–162.

Winther, R. G. 2006. On the Dangers of Making Scientific Models Ontologically Independent: Taking Richard Levins' Warnings Seriously. *Biology and Philosophy* 21: 703–724.

Wit, E., E. van den Heuvel, and J.-W. Romeijn 2012. 'All Models Are Wrong . . . ': An Introduction to Model Uncertainty. *Statistica Neerlandica* 66: 217–236.

Wong, H.-Y. and J. Rosenhead 2000. A Rigorous Definition of Robustness Analysis. *The Journal of the Operational Research Society* 51: 176–182.

Woodward, J. 2006. Some Varieties of Robustness. *Journal of Economic Methodology* 13: 219–240.

Yoshida, Y. 2020. Multiple-Models Juxtaposition and Trade-Offs among Modeling Desiderata. *Philosophy of Science* 88: 103–123.

16

THE MODEL MUDDLE

16.1 Introduction

Since philosophers of science started studying models in earnest in the 1950s, the discussion has seen the introduction of a large number of different types of models. A recent count returned over 120 different model types. This proliferation of model types is disorientating and perplexing, and it creates the impression that no one without a degree in "model studies" will be able to navigate the literature on models without harm and injury.[1] The aim of this chapter is to impose some order on what seems to be an amorphous and confusing multiplicity of model types. To this end, we introduce each model type (and make explicit when a type has several alternative characterisations); we explain how different model types relate to one another; and we sort the different types into broad groups. This will make the collection of models easier to understand and handle.

We begin this chapter by describing how model types have proliferated and by taking stock of what model types there are (Section 16.2). To order and understand this multiplicity of models, we sort model types into four groups. Model types in the first group distinguish different ways in which models can relate to their targets (Section 16.3). Model types in the second group differentiate between different kinds of model objects, i.e. different carriers (Section 16.4). Model types in the third group qualify different processes of model construction and different ways in which models can relate to theory (Section 16.5). Model types in the fourth group capture different uses and functions of models in the practice of science (Section 16.6). We conclude by expressing the hope that the considerations in this chapter make the existence of a multiplicity of different model types less bewildering (Section 16.7).

DOI: 10.4324/9781003285106-21

16.2 Model Types

In an essay originally written in 1966, Wartofsky lamented finding himself in a "model muddle", where the "symptom of the muddle is the proliferation of strange and unrelated entities which come to be called models" (1979, 1). In the over fifty years since Wartofsky's diagnosis, things have only got worse: the list of things that have come to be called "models" has grown further, and a large number of different model types have been introduced. Wartofsky's own way out of the muddle was to propose "a typology of models", which involves arranging them "hierarchically with respect to the degree of existential commitment which each type suggest" (*ibid.*, 2). This is a natural reaction for someone who focuses on the scientific realism debate. However, we are not, at least not primarily, concerned with scientific realism and so we will be taking a different route. Our focus is the functioning of models in the scientific process broadly construed, and so we will group different models together under umbrellas that connect to notions that we have encountered earlier in the book.

Before reflecting more carefully on what this amounts to, let us get clear on the nature and the extent of the model muddle. This is best done by compiling a list of different model types that one encounters in the literature on models. To compile such a list, we need ground rules. The list is intended to contain model types that pertain to the philosophical and conceptual issues that we have been dealing with in this book, such as "analogue model", "theoretical model", and "phenomenological model". To this end we must exclude six other ways of characterising models. First, we exclude characterisations that specify a model's target system. "Atomic model", for instance, will not go on the list because an atomic model is a model of an atom and hence the label specifies the model's target system. The exclusion extends to generalised targets like causal relations or mechanisms, which is why "causal model" and "mechanistic model" are not on the list. Second, disciplinary qualifications, or the specification of an approach, are excluded. This rules out labels like "mechanical model", "econometric model", "functionalist model", and "behaviourist model". Third, we exclude labels like "Bohr model" or "Ising model" that feature the names of the models' progenitors. Fourth, we exclude names like "cellular automaton model" and "Bayesian model", which refer to particular modelling techniques, as well as names like "many-body model", "lattice model", and "agent-based model" which specify the model's internal constitution. Fifth, we exclude notions like "traditional model", "current model", "complex model", "simple model", and "enriched model" because qualifications like "traditional" and "current" are so generic that they could be attached almost anything, and labels like "traditional model" therefore fail to single out a clearly identifiable model type. Finally, we exclude proper names of positions that contain the word model such as "covering law model" and "unificationist model" because they do not refer to models in the sense that we are interested in here (recall the qualifications in the Introduction).

Those who hoped that these restrictions are sufficiently severe to make the list relatively manageable will be disappointed. In alphabetical order, the model types we have to deal with are the following:[2]

abstract model	horizontal model
adequate model	hybrid model
analogue model	hypothetical model
animal model	iconic model
approximate model	ideal model
archaic model	idealised model
behaviour model	imaginary model
black-box model	independent model
bottom-up model	in silico model
caricature model	in vitro model
complementary model	in vivo model
computational model	inconsistent model
conceptual model	instrumental model
concrete model	intellectual model
coupled model	interpretive model
data analysis model	junk model
data model	kairetic model
descriptive model	limit model
developmental model	local model
didactic model	logical model
digital model	matching model
discriminative model	material model
distorted model	mathematical model
empirical model	mediating model
equation model	megamorph model
experimental model	metamodel
explanatory model	metaphorical model
exploratory model	metriomorph model
fantasy model	micromorph model
fictional model	minimal model
floating model	minimalist model
formal model	neutral model
functional model	nonconcrete model
fundamental model	non-material model
generative model	nonlinear model
global model	null model
glocal model	numerical model
graphical model	observational model
grey-box model	open model
heuristic model	optimality model
homeomorph model	paramorph model

perspectival model	substitute model
phenomenal model	support model
phenomenological model	symbolic model
plant model	targetless model
post hoc model	teleiomorph model
probing model	theoretical model
prosthetic model	tinkertoy model
qualitative model	top-down model
quantitative model	toy model
reanalysis model	true model
representational model	unrealistic model
representative model	verbal model
robust model	visual model
scale model	working model
sentential model	white-box model
simulation model	whole system model
statistical model	xenodiagnostic model
structural model	yang model
study model	zombie model

Even though this list contains well over one hundred, entries, it has no claim to completeness. Inevitably, I will have overlooked something and new model types emerge as the discussion continues. But no further additions are needed to demonstrate that talk of a model muddle is no exaggeration.

The project for this chapter is to get clear on what these models do and on how they are related to one another. This involves two tasks. The first task is to provide a characterisation of each of the model types in our list. This requires uneven amounts of work. Some model types have been discussed extensively earlier in the book and there is no need to repeat what has been said already. In these cases, I only add a brief reminder of what the type is and refer the reader back to the relevant section of the book. Other model types make their first appearance in this chapter. Some of them are self-explanatory and can be dealt with quickly; others raise substantive issues and require a more extensive discussion. So the reader will find accounts of uneven length of the different model types, which is owed to the aims of avoiding duplication and filling gaps.

The second task is to understand the topography of the landscape of model types. This involves identifying groups of model types; understanding to which group individual types belong; and getting clear on how different types are related. To impose some structure on the diversity of model types, I will order them into four groups:

(1) Model types pertaining to model-target relations.
(2) Model types pertaining to carriers.

(3) Model types pertaining to the process of model construction and to models' relation to theory.

(4) Model types pertaining to the uses and functions of models in the scientific process.

In the remainder of this chapter, I discuss these four groups of models.[3]

16.3   Model-Target Relations

Let us begin with types that pertain to the model-target relation. As we have seen in Chapters 6, 8, and 9, many models are representations of something beyond themselves. A model that represents a target system is a *representational model*.[4] Sometimes representational models are also referred to as *descriptive models*. This is how Gibbard and Varian use the term when they say that "[d]escriptive models attempt to describe, *in some sense*, economic reality" (1978, 665, original emphasis). The restriction to economic reality is inessential and is owed to the fact that economic models are the subject matter of Gibbard and Varian's paper. The qualification "in some sense", however, is important because it emphasises that idealised and distorted models are also descriptive. Hesse, by contrast, has a more restrictive notion of descriptive models when she says that models "may be called descriptive models" if they are intended "as a factual description" and exhibit "a positive analogy and no negative analogy in all respects hitherto tested" (1961, 27). This is tantamount to saying that descriptive models are accurate representations, as far as we can tell. The label "descriptive" is, however, problematic because it suggests that models are verbal descriptions, and, as we have seen, this is controversial (Chapters 9 and 14). The more neutral term "representational model" avoids (seemingly) taking sides in this debate. Representational models often represent their target from a certain point of view or perspective. A model that represents in this way is a *perspectival model* (see Section 15.4).

If a model does not represent a target system, then it is a *targetless model* (Section 6.2). If it is not yet known whether the system that the model purports to represent exists, then we have a *hypothetical model*. Massimi discusses the practice of hypothetical modelling and illustrates it with models for supersymmetric particles which have a "hypothetical target" because supersymmetric particles "have been hypothesized but not yet discovered as of today" (2019, 870). A model can be targetless for a number of reasons. Gibbard and Varian say that a targetless model is an *ideal model* if it is "concerned with the description of some ideal case", which is, however, not realised in the real world (1978, 665). Hansen calls a model that has "no consistent application to actual phenomena" a *fantasy model* and offers the example of Maxwell's model of the propagation of electromagnetic waves (1982, 53). Previously we have seen that a model can be a Z-representation without also being a representation of a Z, or, indeed, of any other object (Section 9.5). A Z-representation that is not a representation of anything is also a targetless model.

Models can relate to their target systems in different ways. Pincock calls a model that perfectly parallels "all the physical features of the physical situation" that it represents a *matching model* (2007, 962). An *analogue model* stands in an analogical relation to its target (Section 10.4). A *metaphorical model* is an analogue model that comes with a verbal description that expresses the analogy in a metaphor (Section 10.6). An *approximate model* is a model that approximates its target, and an *idealised model* is a model that provides an idealisation of its target (Section 11.2). If the idealisation is a limit idealisation (Section 11.5), then the idealised model is a *limit model*. If a model abstracts away specific features from the concrete situation, then it is an *abstract model* (Section 11.2), although we note that the term "abstract model" is used with a different meaning in the context of the discussion of the ontology of models (Section 8.5). When understood literally, models that abstract, approximate, and idealise end up being unrealistic. For this reason, Mäki speaks of an *unrealistic model* when the model's assumption are at variance with the target (2009, 68). Hesse speaks of an *archaic model* when the model is "deliberately used for practical purposes" while it is "know to be false" (1961, 26). The reason for calling such a model "archaic" is that it has been developed in the context of a theory that is now considered outdated and false. This happens, for instance, when heat is modelled as a fluid. This model is still useful, but it originates in the caloric theory of heat which is now regarded as false (Hesse 1967, 355).

Some models are at once unrealistic and simple. In their discussion of models in economics, Gibbard and Varian say that such models are "caricatures" (1978, 665), and so one can call them *caricature models*. The assumptions of such a model "are chosen not to approximate reality, but to exaggerate or isolate some feature of reality", and by calling a model a caricature "we mean not only that the approximation is rough and simple, but that the degree of approximation is not an important consideration in the design of the model" (*ibid.*, 673). Caricature models emphasise by distortion and isolate by exaggeration, and in doing so highlight a particular feature without aiming to represent it with any degree of accuracy. But how can models help scientists understand a situation if the models' assumptions are radically false when applied to their intended target system? Gibbard and Varian hint at two possibilities. The first possibility is that a model is robust in that its main results do not depend on the false assumptions (*ibid.*, 674). We discussed *robust models* Section 15.3. The second possibility is that one can try to domesticate a caricature model by understanding it as an "approximation", even though the degree of approximation was deemed unimportant in the construction of the model. In the case of approximations, "the investigator sets an aspiration level for the accuracy of the conclusions" and if the model is a caricature "that just means that the aspiration level is low, so that various extremely simple models achieve it" (*ibid.*, 676).

Closely related to caricatures are *toy models*. Reutlinger, Hangleiter, and Hartmann characterise them as models that are "strongly idealised" and "extremely simple", but which nevertheless "refer to a target phenomenon" (2018, 1070).

On this account, toy models and caricature models coincide because both are strongly idealised and simple while still representing a target (caricatures are caricatures *of* something!). Examples of models that are frequently classified as toy models are the Ising model in statistical mechanics, the Lotka-Volterra model of predator-prey interaction, the Schelling model of social segregation (*ibid.*, 1070), and Ackerlof's "market for lemons" model (Nguyen 2020, 1014), as well the Kac ring model, the Ehrenfest urn model, the baker's transformation and the Arnold cat map (Luczak 2017, 1).[5] Reutlinger, Hangleiter, and Hartmann note that toy models do not offer accurate representations, do not explain, and do not provide predictions; toy models serve another goal, namely providing understanding (*ibid.*, 1071).[6] Nguyen analyses how we can learn about targets from toy models and notes that this only appears problematic if one associates accurate representation with similarity. However, representation need not, and indeed should not, be committed to a model and a target being similar, and once this is realised, toy models can be regarded as accurate representations of their target systems in much the same way in which more complex models can be accurate representations of their targets (2020, 1013–1014). Luczak disagrees with the third clause of the above characterisation and submits that "toy models do not perform a representational function" and insists that "they do not represent anything" (2017, 1).[7] Rather than being strongly idealised renderings of a target, toy models have heuristic value in that they help scientists understand certain formal techniques like renormalisation, shed light on certain theoretical concepts, and probe the consistency of assumptions. Thus characterised, toy models are more like exploratory models (which we discuss later) than caricature models.

Another closely related kind of models are *minimal models* (also referred to as *minimalist models*). As we have seen in Section 12.5, minimal models are ones that only include factors that are difference-makers (i.e. factors without which the phenomenon in question would not have come about). Batterman and Rice discuss these models in detail and note that "[p]erhaps *the* remarkable feature of minimal models is that they are thoroughgoing caricatures of real systems" (2014, 349–350, original emphasis). This subsumes minimal models under caricature models.[8]

This, however, is not the only characterisation of minimal models that one finds in the literature. A different characterisation of minimal models has emerged in the literature on economic models. Grüne-Yanoff characterises minimal models as models that "are assumed to lack any similarity, isomorphism or resemblance relation to the world, to be unconstrained by natural laws or structural identity, and not to isolate any real factors" (2009, 83), and he thereby also locates them in the family of caricature models. But unlike Batterman and Rice, Grüne-Yanoff sees minimal models as having no target system and therefore as not being in need of any account of how they relate to parts or aspects of the real world (which makes renormalisation superfluous, even if it were possible in the context of economic models). Yet, minimal models can still be used to learn about the world. But rather than instructing us about universal features of targets, the purpose of minimal models, Grüne-Yanoff argues, is to establish necessity or impossibility hypotheses. To do so, the model "(1) present a relevant possibility that (2) contradicts an impossibility hypothesis that is held with sufficiently high confidence by the potential learners" (*ibid.*, 97).[9]

Even though the notion of an *iconic model* makes regular appearances in discussions of models, it is surprisingly difficult to find a clear characterisation, and different authors seem to frame the notion in different ways. Among the meanings of "icon" that are listed in the Oxford English Dictionary, three are relevant for our discussion. The first characterises an icon as a "realistic representation or description in writing"; the second as an "image, figure, or representation; a portrait; a picture, 'cut', or illustration in a book"; the third as an "image in the solid; a monumental figure; a statue". In line with the first characterisation, Grobler notes that we should take scientific realists to be committed to the claim that models "are attempted iconic models of the reality under investigation" (1995, 38). On this analysis, iconic models are truthful representations. There remains, however, a significant question of what this amounts to (see Chapter 9 for a discussion). In line with the second characterisation, Frey stresses an iconic model "should have a visual and picturesque relation to the represented object" (1961, 94, my translation), and Harré says that an "iconic model is a 'picture' of a possible mechanism for producing phenomena" (1970, 54, cf. 2004, 14, 30). Given what we have said about models so far, it is, however, rather unclear what it would mean for a model to be a picture of a target, and the fact that Harré puts "picture" into scare quotes would seem to be a recognition of this problem.

The third characterisation is the most influential. In his theory of signs, Peirce defines an icon as "a sign by likeness" (Hartshorne and Weiss 1931–1935, CP 2.255). Ambrosio expands on this and notes that for Peirce, the "distinctive feature of iconic representations is that they exhibit aspects or qualities of the objects they stand for" (2014, 256). Black, explicitly referring to Peirce, says that an icon should be understood as "literally embodying the features of interest in the original" (1962, 221), and Harré describes iconic models as models that "are related to their subjects and to their sources by relations of similarity and difference in material properties" (1988, 120, cf. 2004, 78). This, Harré notes, is tantamount to saying that something is an iconic model if it "can be seen as standing in a certain analogical relation" to its target (*ibid.*, 122). On this construal, iconic models are analogical models. Similarity is most naturally understood as the sharing of properties (Section 8.4), and this, in turn, most naturally happens between two material objects. For this reason, many iconic models are material models, which is why "it is often possible to build them in the laboratory or the engineering workshop, and to experiment on them directly" (*ibid.*, 120). However, Harré acknowledges the existence of non-material iconic models when he says that some models "are not realizable in metal or wood" (*ibid.*, 120).[10]

In Section 14.4 we have seen that *scale models* are models that relate to their targets through a change of scale: they are replicas of object in a different size.

This makes scale models a kind of iconic models (Black 1962, 221). As we have seen, some scale models shrink their targets, others magnify them. Harré calls an enlarged scale model a *megamorph model* and a scale model that is contracted a *micromorph model* (1970, 38–39). If different scales are used for different aspects or parts of the model (as in our example where we scaled the bridge's width by factor 100, its height by factor 200, and its depth by factor 300), then we have a *distorted model* (*ibid.*, 210). The purpose of a scale model is to show in manageable size what would otherwise be too small to see or too large to handle. The intuition is that a scale model is a naturalistic replica of the target, which is Achinstein's reason to call scale models *true models* (1968, 209). If a scale model omits certain features of interest and hence offers only a partial representation of the target, then Achinstein speaks of an *adequate model* (*ibid.*, 209–210). Presumably the label is owed to fact that the model is adequate in those respects that it actually represents.

Scale models are instances of what Harré calls *homeomorph models*, models that are such that "the subject of the model is also the source of the model". An example is a toy car, because "a toy car is a model for which source and subject are identical, the toy being modelled on a car, and being a model of the very same car" (1970, 38–39). Homeomorph models contrast with *paramorph models*, which are such that the model system and the target system are drawn from different domains. This happens, for instance, with mechanical models of the ether, which are drawn from mechanics even though the ether itself is not a mechanical object (*ibid.*, 38–39, 43–44). For this reason, analogical models are also paramorph models. Homeomorph models that are "in some respect or respects, an improvement on their subjects" are *teleiomorph* models (*ibid.*, 41). They can "improve" their subject for instance through idealisations. A special kind of homeomorph models are *metriomorph models*. Their target is a class of objects rather than a single item, and they represent the class by metrically reflecting its properties. A typical example of such a model is the average family (*ibid.*, 43).

The term "phenomenological model" is used in two distinct senses, one of which is pertinent here (we will discuss the other in the next section).[11] In this first sense, a *phenomenological model* is one that only represents observable properties of its target system and refrains from postulating hidden mechanisms or unobservable entities. A phenomenological model is of instrumental value in that it generates predictions, but it does not give insight into the nature of the target system.[12] Thus described, phenomenological models coincide with Craver's *phenomenal models*, which "describe the function relating a mechanism's inputs to its outputs" (2010, 841) and with Bunge's *behaviour models*, which "will satisfy the requirements of empiricist philosophies (positivism, pragmatism, operationalism, phenomenalism) as well as of conventionalism since, without going much beyond the data, it enables one to condense the latter and even to predict the evolution of the system" (1973, 102–103). However, phenomenological models are not identical with models of a phenomenon, where phenomenon is understood as in Section 6.4. As we have seen, "phenomenon" is understood as an umbrella term covering all relatively stable and general features of the world, which can be observable as well as unobservable.

A *global model* is a model whose conditions of application are not restricted to a particular domain and therefore hold universally; a *local model* is a model whose assumption are restricted to certain domain; and a *glocal model* is a model that connects a local and a global model (Ohsawa et al. 2017, 1016, 1023). A *whole system model* is a model that represents the whole target system in its entirety, mostly in the context of archaeology (Wylie 2017, 991, 996). A *fundamental model* portrays entities and laws that are taken to be fundamental in a given domain. As Hesse notes, a "model will be fundamental only in relation to a particular historical situation, for example Democritan atoms, Newtonian attractive and repulsive particles, classical electrodynamics, and quantum electrodynamics, are fundamental relative to their historical context." (Hesse 1961, 28). In the context of cognitive science, a *discriminative model* "represent the dependence of unobserved target variables on observed variables", while a *generative model* offers "a principled account of top-down effects" (Williams 2021, 5–6) (we will encounter an alternative meaning of "generative model" in Section 16.5). In evolutionary biology and in ecology a *neutral model* is one without selection (Wimsatt 1987, 25).

A *data model* is a processed, corrected, rectified, and regimented summary of the data we gain from immediate observation; a *statistical model* is a mathematical representation of the observed data (Section 3.6); a data model is also an *observational model* "in the sense that, once data is collected, it is analyzed using the tools of probability theory and statistics" (Russo 2017, 955). Data models need not be mathematical; they can, in principle take any form (they can, for instance, be graphs or images). In the context of descriptive statistics, statistical models, data models, and observational models are the same. In the context of statistical hypothesis testing, the null hypothesis is the default position, or commonly accepted view, that researcher aim to test, and potentially nullify (hence the name "null hypothesis"). If this hypothesis takes the form of a model, then that model can be called the *null model*. As Kovaka (2020) points out with reference to models of mate choice in biology, there can be substantive questions about which model should be chosen as the null model. Still in statistics, an *instrumental model* is an auxiliary hypothesis that is needed to test the main hypothesis (Dhaene et al. 1998). This use of the term is counterintuitive to philosophers. The term "instrumentalism" refers to an antirealist position and so one would expect "instrumental model" to characterise models that generate predictions but provide no information about the unobservable aspects of the target. Although intuitive, this is not how the term would seem to be used in the literature. Sometimes a data model cannot be constructed solely with statistical methods and a model is used to "fill the gaps" between data points. In the context of atmospheric science, this process is known as *data assimilation*; when data assimilation is applied to historical records with the aim of constructing long-term datasets for past periods, the process is known as *reanalysis*. The models used for this process are *reanalysis models*, and they belong to the group of *data analysis models*, which are the models that are used to process historical weather and climate records (Section 3.6).

16.4 The Nature of Carriers

In Section 6.2 we introduced the Problem of Carriers. The carrier of a representation is the thing that does the representing, and if the representation is a model, then the carrier is the object that serves as the model. Broadly speaking, the Problem of Carriers is to understand and characterise the objects that are used as representations. This problem can be broken down into two subproblems: the Problem of Ontology and the Problem of Handling (Frigg and Nguyen 2020, 15–16). The former concerns the ontology of the objects that are used as carriers, while the latter asks us to understand what is involved in handling these objects in the scientific process. We now discuss model types that pertain to these problems, beginning with the Problem of Ontology.

A model is an *abstract model* if it is an abstract entity (Section 8.2).[13] Abstract models fall into the group of *nonconcrete models*, or *non-material models*, which are models whose carriers are not material objects (Section 8.5); Rosenblueth and Wiener call them *intellectual models* (1945, 317). A *fictional model* is one that is akin to the objects and places of literary fiction (Section 14.5). At the most basic level, an *imaginary model* is a model that is imagined, which can happen, for instance, in an act of pretence (Section 14.6). Achinstein submits that the act of imagination is based on assumptions and says that we have an imaginary model if "an object or system is described by a set of assumptions" whereby the "proponent of the model does not commit himself to the truth, or even plausibility of the assumptions he makes" (1968, 220). The carrier of a *concrete model* or *material model*, by contrast, is a material object (Section 14.4). If the material carrier is an animal, then we speak of an *animal model* (Fülöp et al. 2013, 58); one can then also speak of *plant models* if the carrier is a plant. We speak of an *in vivo model* if the "whole living animal is used to investigate the effect of any therapeutic candidate or to study any biological process" (Khan et al. 2017, 432). So animal models and in vivo models are the same (as long as the animal is alive). We are dealing with *in vitro models* if the carriers are "microorganisms, isolated cells, biological molecules, cell culture systems, tissue slice preparations, or isolated organs in optimum conditions outside their normal biological context" (*ibid.*). These models contrast with so-called *in silico models*, which are computational models implemented on a computer (Leung et al. 2001, 622).[14]

Let us now turn to notions that pertain to the problem of handling. Achinstein says that if a material model is such that "by examining it one can ascertain facts about the object it represents", then it is a *tinkertoy model* (1968, 209). His examples are "models of molecules, models of the solar system found in science museums, engineering models of dams" (*ibid.*). Presumably the label is owed to the fact that these models can be explored by "tinkering around" with them. If the materials that are used to construct a material model are recycled bits that would otherwise have been thrown away, it is a *junk model*, although junk models predominantly seem to be toys rather than instruments for scientific research (Institute of Imagination 2021). If the material model is able to perform, on a small scale, the same task that the target itself performs (or is expected to perform), then it is a *working model*.[15] An example of such a model is a small locomotive that is capable of pulling small coaches.

A model that is either itself visual, or is presented in a visual manner, is a *visual model*. Giere discusses Wegener's maps picturing the breakup of continents and Holmes and Hess' visual representation of convection currents splitting a continent as examples of visual models (1996, 1999). Evagorou, Erduran, and Mäntylä emphasise that visual models can be both two-dimensional and three-dimensional, and discuss Faraday's field lines and Watson and Crick's model of DNA as a examples of visual models (2015). A closely related notion is that of a *graphical model*. The learning platform study.com defines graphical models as "visual representations, graphs depicting data, or charts simplifying the display of data for comparison purposes. All of these can be hand-drawn or made using a computer with appropriate software". According to that definition, graphical models are two-dimensional visual models. However, the term "graphical model" is also used in a more specific way, namely as referring to "a graph with vertices that are random variables, and an associated set of joint probability distributions over the random variables, all of which share a set of conditional independence relations" (Spirtes 2005, 1).

A model is a *mathematical model* if standard presentations of it in a scientific context employ mathematical tools (Section 14.5). This subsumes *symbolic models* and *numerical models*. Frey says that a "system of equations constitutes a symbolic model" and that such a model has "no immediate picturesque similarity with the represented object" (Frey 1961, 95, my translation). Bokulich and Oreskes say that "[n]umerical models are mathematical models that represent natural systems and their interactions by means of a system of equations" (2017, 895). In a broad sense, a *formal model* is a model that is formalised in some formalism, typically mathematics or formal logic. In this vein, Davidsson, Klügl, and Verhagen define a *formal model* as one that is "represented using a formal language with so clearly defined syntax and semantics that the model can be executed using a computer" (2017, 785). If the formalism is such that it represents "the functional dependence of parameters", then, according to Weinert, we have a *functional model* (1999, 315–316). If a model represents the structure of a target system, then we have a *structural model* (*ibid.*).

Sometimes the equations of a model cannot be solved analytically, or, more generally, the formal expressions of a model resist exploration with paper and pencil methods. A *computational model* is one that can be implemented on a computer, which can then be used to study the model's behaviour (Section 14.5). As we have seen, there is controversy over whether computational models are *sui generis* or whether they are a specific kind of mathematical model. The activity of carrying out model computations on a computer is also called a simulation, and for this reason models implemented on a computer are called *simulation models*.[16] Such models are also called *digital models* (Imbert 2017), although the term "digital model" is also used to refer to the process of creating an exact three-dimensional replica of the form of an object through a process in which the object is first measured up by laser scanners, then the data are processed in the computer, and then the result is printed with 3D printer. In this latter sense, a digital model is a computer-generated three-dimensional iconic model. Returning to mathematical models, a model is a *nonlinear model* if the equations that define the model are non-linear equations (Herfel 1995). A model is a *coupled model* if it consists of certain parts that interact with each other. The notion is frequently used in climate modelling, where models consist of different modules for different parts of climate system (for instance the atmosphere, the oceans, land masses, and ice), and these modules are coupled to each other to simulate the physical interaction between them (Bokulich and Oreskes 2017, 896).

A model is a *black-box model* if its carrier is (or is treated as) a single unit whose internal structure is either unknown or disregarded. A black-box model therefore correlates inputs with outputs without providing any information about its internal workings, which remain opaque to the user. Black-box models contrast with *white-box models*, which provide information about the inner workings of a system in a way that model users can grasp and that offers them an explanation of the manifest behaviour (Boumans 2009, 211). A *grey-box model* is a modular model, i.e. an assembly of modules that perform different tasks. The modules are self-contained black boxes, which are, however, connected to other modules in a known manner (*ibid.*, 212).

A *conceptual model* is a verbal description of a situation, usually in a natural language (Haefner 2005, 10). Conceptual models are also known as *verbal models* or *qualitative models* (*ibid.*, 10, 32). The purpose of a qualitative model is "to provide a conceptual framework for the attainment of the objectives", where the "framework summarizes the modeler's current thinking concerning the number and identity of necessary system components (objects) and the relationships among them" (*ibid.*, 32).[17] An example of such a model is a pricing model saying that the price of goods in an economy is determined by the amount of money that is in circulation in the economy (Section 13.4). As Haefner notes, a qualitative model "does not contain explicit equations, but its purpose is to provide enough detail and structure so that a consistent set of equations can be written", where we have to bear in mind that a "qualitative model does not uniquely determine the equations" (*ibid.*). When equations are formulated based on the relationships described in the qualitative model, we transform the qualitative model into *quantitative model*. Quantitative models have a mathematical structure and their outputs are mathematical in nature, often numbers (*ibid.*, 13). This conversion happened, for instance, when Fisher formulated his exchange equation based on the pricing model we have just seen (Section 13.4).[18]

16.5 Model Construction and Model-Theory Relations

We now turn to model types that pertain to how models are constructed and to how they relate to theory, beginning with the former. As we have seen in Section 13.2, a *bottom-up model* is one that was constructed departing only from what we know about the target and basic facts about the domain of interest while making few, if any, theoretical assumptions and not relying on general theories. Bottom-up models contrast with top-down models. A *top-down model* is one whose construction departed from a theoretical framework and then worked its way down from the general theory to the phenomena. A *hybrid model* has elements of both. On the one hand, a hybrid model includes a broad and well-corroborated theory like Newtonian mechanics; on the other hand, the model is not just applied theory, and it also contains elements that do not derive from theory such as empirical data and empirically determined functional dependencies (Katzav 2013, 114–115).[19] *Horizontal models* are constructed neither top-down nor bottom-up, nor by a blend of the two. A model is horizontal if, as Bokulich puts it, "the primary guiding principle in the model's construction came, not by way of theory or any particular set of experimental phenomena, but rather, by way of analogy with models belonging to neighboring theories" (2003, 611, cf. 623–624). Bokulich's examples of horizontal models are quantum versions of maps from classical chaos theory (like the horseshoe map in Section 13.3), which were developed by drawing analogies with their classical counterparts. A *generative model* is one that has the capacity to produce new models through a generative process (Tee 2020).[20] An *open model* is a computational model whose programming code is in the public domain and thereby available to everybody (see, for instance, openmod 2021).

Let us now look at the relation between models and theories. Broadly speaking, a *theoretical model* is a model that is closely related to a theory. Opinions differ on what exactly this means. A first option is to follow Hesse in saying that theoretical models "are models in something like the logical sense of being interpretations of a formal or semiformal theoretical system" (1967, 356). Giere agrees with this characterisation when he says that models are abstract objects that satisfy the equations of the theory (Giere 1988, 78–79). Theoretical models are closely related to *interpretative models* (Section 13.5) and *substitute models* (Groenewold 1961, 99), which ground the application of mathematical theories to real-world targets. Theoretical models are what Pincock calls *equation models*, a class of models "picked out" by an equation (2007, 961). Both theoretical models and equation models are instances of *logical models*, models that are collections of objects that make a formal sentence true if the terms of the sentence are interpreted as referring to these objects along with their properties and relations (Section 2.2). According to Hesse, a logical model is a *post hoc model* if it has been "invented to embody an existing mathematical theory largely or solely in order to make the mathematical theory easier to apply, or to demonstrate its consistency" (1961, 27). If the formal sentence is written in the data modelling language YANG, then it is a *yang model*. A *metamodel* is a modelling language definition (Dodig-Crnkovic and Cicchetti 2017, 710).

A second way to explicate the notion of a theoretical model is to follow Achinstein in saying that a "theoretical model is a set of assumptions about some object or system" (1968, 212). Often this amounts to attributing to the system "what might be called an inner structure, composition, or mechanism, reference to which will explain various properties exhibited by that object or system" (1965, 103). These assumptions, and the attributed structures, are often simplifications, which is why a "theoretical model is treated as a simplified approximation useful for certain purposes" (1968, 214).[21]

The second meaning of "phenomenological model" marks the antipode to theoretical models (we have discussed the first meaning in Section 16.3). On that reading, a *phenomenological model* is a model that is independent of theories. In Section 13.2 we called this an *independent model*. The question is how strong this independence is supposed to be, and different authors have given different answers. McMullin says that a phenomenological model is "an arbitrarily-chosen mathematically-expressed correlation of physical parameters from which the empirical laws of some domain can be derived" (1968, 390–391), and Wimsatt says that it is "derived solely to give descriptions and/or predictions of phenomena without making any claims as to whether the variables in the model exist" (1987, 29). This suggest that phenomenological models have complete independence from theory. This would make phenomenological models line up with bottom-up models, with what Bunge calls *behaviour models* (Section 16.3), and with what Basso, Lisciandra, and Marchionni call *empirical models*, i.e. models that "are built for testing and measuring relationships between variables and are based on empirical data" and that "do not describe hypothetical systems" (2017, 414). Hartmann opts for a more liberal reading of the relation between phenomenological models and theories. He sees phenomenological models as models that fail to be derivable from a theory and yet can incorporate principles and laws associated with theories. He says that the assumptions underlying the model "may be *inspired* by a theory" and that the models "mimic many of the features of theory, but are much easier to handle" (1999, 327, original italics). Yet, it can also be the case that the model's assumptions contradict the relevant theory (*ibid.*). In a similar vein, Portides says that phenomenological models "are constructed by the deployment of semi-empirical results, often by the use of ad hoc hypotheses, or by the use of a conceptual apparatus that is not directly related to fundamental theory and not always straightforwardly compatible with the theoretical calculus" (2011, 335). This distances phenomenological models from theory, but it does not make them completely independent from theory. In fact, it makes room for phenomenological models to be *inconsistent models*, i.e. models that are inconsistent with a background theory or, alternatively, with other models (Morrison 2011, 344).

Complementary models are important when theories are incompletely specified because they can then step in to provide what is missing (Section 13.4).[22] A *mediating model* acts as mediator between theories and the world (Section 13.6). A *floating model* is, in a sense, the opposite of a mediating model. A mediating model is anchored both in the theory and the target and thereby brings the two together. As Redhead describes them, floating models are disconnected from both (1980, 158–160). They are disconnected from theory through a computational gap in that the approximations that have to be made to get from the theory to the model cannot be justified. They are disconnected from the target in that their predictions fail. So the model "floats" at both ends.

Finally, Harré discusses the notion of a *sentential model* (1970, 36). Consider two theories T and T '. Assume that it is the case that for every sentence p in T there is sentence p' in T ' such that the following holds: if p' is acceptable then p is true and when p is false then p' is unacceptable. If this is the case, then T ' is a sentential model of T.

16.6   Uses and Functions of Models

The final group of model types we are looking at concerns the uses and functions of models in the process of scientific investigation. A first family of models concern the process of theory development and discovery. Something has a heuristic function if it serves the purpose of problem-solving, learning, and discovery. As Redhead points out, models can play a heuristic role in the development of new theories (1980, 155–156). A model that serves this purpose is a *heuristic model*.[23] Heuristic models thus understood are *developmental models* (Section 13.2). Sometimes the problem is the opposite: we have a theory but we do not know how the theory behaves. As Hartmann points out, physicists can then use simple models to probe the "qualitative type of behaviour of a given theory" (1995, 54). A model that serves this purpose is a *probing model*. Groenewold describes the same use of models to explore the properties of theories and calls these models *study models* because they serve the purpose of studying a theory (1961, 99). He mentions the example of quantum field theory, where difficulties with divergences, renormalisation, ghost states, and so on are studied in a simplified model which provides insight into the nature of the theory. Thus understood, study models are like toy models as characterised by Luczak (Section 16.3). Gelfert has recently introduced the notion of an *exploratory model* and characterises models of this kind through four functions. They (i) provide starting points; (ii) feature in a proof-of-principle; (iii) generate potential explanations; and (iv) assist in an assessment of the target, i.e. help identify a suitable target for a given model (2016, 83–94). Massimi argues that perspectival models are a special kind of exploratory models in that they also serve the purpose of providing knowledge of (v) "causal possibilities" and (vi) "objective possibilities for hypothetical entities" (Massimi 2019, 870).

An *explanatory model* is one that provides an explanation. There are varied views about how models do this, reflecting the many different accounts of explanation that have been proposed in the literature. Bokulich (2017) provides a survey of the different positions in the debate over the explanatory function of models. Among them are the kairetic account and the optimality account. According to Strevens' kairetic account, a model can be split into a part with difference-makers and a part with idealisations; the former is true and latter is false; the true part is explanatorily relevant while the false part is harmless but irrelevant (2008, 318). A model that explains in this way can be called a *kairetic model*. *Optimality models* are based on optimisation theory, which aims to identify the values of the control variables that optimise the values of some design variables under certain constraints, and the explanation lies in the identification of the optimum (Rice 2015, 591).

A prosthesis is a device that is able to replace a functional part of a system. A prosthetic arm, for instance can perform certain functions of a real arm, even though it bears little resemblance to a human arm. Mechanisms are usually parts of higher-level systems, and they interact with other parts through interfaces. According to Craver, a *prosthetic model* "is an engineered simulation of a mechanism causally integrated into a biological system to replace the function of the target", where the "goal of building a prosthetic model is to replace the behavior of the missing part in context while preserving the behavior of the system as a whole" (2010, 841–842).

An *experimental model* is a material model on which actual experiments are performed (Sterrett 2017, 391, Wilde and Williamson 2016, 272). Weisberg describes the case of the Army Corps of Engineers' model of the San Francisco Bay (2013, 1–3). The model is an immense water tank with the topography or the Bay. It occupies an area of about $6000m^2$, and a variety of hydraulic pumps allow engineers to simulate currents, tidal streams, and river flows in the Bay. Engineers performed experiments on this model. For instance, they built dams in it and studied what effect the dams would have on tidal streams. Indeed, most material models are also experimental models (Section 14.4). *A fortiori*, animal models and plant models (Section 16.4) are also experimental models because they are often used in laboratories to perform experiments on them. An animal model is a *xenodiagnostic model* if it can be used to diagnose the presence of an infectious disease. For instance, C3H/HeJ mice are used as xenodiagnostic models for the detection of Ehrlichia chaffeensis (Lockhart and Davidson 1999).

A *didactic model* is one that serves the purpose of teaching or communicating results, but that is not used as tool of investigation. The material model of the solar system in the science museum is a didactic model: school children can learn about the constitution of the solar system by engaging with the model, but the model is not involved in a process of research.[24] A specific example of a didactic model is the *zombie model*, which, as its name suggests, models a zombie invasion. The purpose of this is model is not to study such an event (which we rule out with confidence), but to provide an example that makes "mathematical modeling and infectious disease epidemiology more accessible to public health professionals, students, and the general public" (Lofgren et al. 2016). So by studying an invasion of zombies, students gain an understanding of basic mechanisms of disease transmission and the tools to model them mathematically.

A *support model* is a model whose aim it is to "generate support for the human by reasoning based on the domain model" (Gerritsen and Bosse 2017, 1055). An example is a model for crime prevention, which "takes as input certain information about the future scenario for which the user desires support" and then "generates advices about which strategies are recommended to prevent crime in this scenario" (*ibid.*, 1060).

16.7 Conclusion

Readers who have made it to the end of this chapter deserve an award for perseverance and determination. Ploughing one's way through this long list of distinction is not an easy task, and I am painfully aware of the fact that the text does not flow as naturally as it would if one were to develop an argument. I hope, however, that the effort was worth it and that the multiplicity of model types that populate philosophical discussions is now less bewildering.

Notes

1 The entry "Models in Science" in the Stanford Encyclopedia of Philosophy (Frigg and Hartmann 2020) features a list with different types of models. A Google search for this list in August 2021 returned over 500 results, and in many cases the discussions surrounding this list present the multiplicity of model types as a perplexity that needs to be dealt with; see, for instance, Gelfert's (2017, 6–7).

2 This is an extended version of the list in Frigg and Hartmann's (2020). For the last three letters of the alphabet, I have taken some liberties with regard to my own exclusion rules. Please contact me with better suggestions.

3 For a discussion of alternative classifications of models, see Downes' (2021, Ch. 3).

4 See Portides' (2017, 26). An alternative label is *representative model* (Groenewold 1961, 98; Cartwright 1999, 180). Achinstein provides a narrower definition according to which a representational model is "a three-dimensional physical representation of an object which is such that by examining it one can ascertain facts about the object it represents" (1968, 209). However, as we have seen in previous chapters, the notion of representation is not limited to three-dimensional physical objects and hence restricting representational models to such objects is unnecessary.

5 The Lotka-Volterra model was introduced in Section 13.2. For discussions of the other models, see, for instance, Lavis' (2015, Ch. 3) for the Ising model, Schelling's (1978) for the Schelling model, Akerlof's (1970) for the "market for lemons" model, Jebeile's (2020) for the Kac ring model, Karlin and McGregor's (1965) for the Ehrenfest urn model, and Tabor's (1989) for the baker's transformation and the Arnold cat map. Nowakowa and Nowak go a step further and say constructing caricature models is characteristic for all of science: "[s]cience consists of the same procedure which we find in caricature. Both deform the world which we inhabit" (2000, 9–10).

6 Reutlinger, Hangleiter, and Hartmann further distinguish between *embedded* and *autonomous* toy models. The former are embedded in an empirically well-confirmed theory, while the latter are not related to such a theory (2018, Sec. 2).

7 This notion of a toy model also seems to be at work in Hartmann's (1995, 57–58, 1999, 328).

8 Batterman (2002, 21–26) has also emphasised the caricature character of minimal models. The characterisation of minimal models in terms of universality and renormalisation originates in Batterman's (2002), and it is further developed in Batterman and Rice's (2014) and Rice's (2018, 2021, Ch. 3). Chirimuuta's (2014) discusses the use of minimal models in computational neuroscience; Fletcher's (2019) argues that the strategies underlying minimal models can be extended beyond models, in particular to the kind of approximations one finds in cases like Norton's (2008) dome; Shech's (2018) provides an explanation of the Aharonov-Bohm effect in terms of minimal models. For critical discussion of Batterman and Rice's analysis of minimal models, see Lange's (2015) and Povich's (2018). Batterman's (2019) and Rice's (2020) contain

discussions of minimal models that also respond to criticisms. For a comparison of minimal models and toy models, see Gelfert's (2019).

9 For further discussion see Grüne-Yanoff's (2013). A number of authors have pushed back against this account of minimal models by arguing, essentially, that there is no learning about the world without representation. For a discussions, see Casini's (2014) and Fumagalli's (2015, 2016).

10 Harré also notes that "the iconic model is imagined and its behavior studied in a *gedanken*-experiment" (1988, 121–122); Del Re observes that we explore physical models in thought experiments (2000, 6); and Cartwright urges that models "are often experiments *in thought*" (2010, 19, original emphasis). Murphy disagrees and argues that the use of the imagination in models is different from its use in thought experiments (2020a, Ch. 4, 2020b). For discussions of thought experiments, see, for instance, the contributions to Stuart et al. (2018).

11 In fact, there is third sense: in her (1983) Cartwright uses "phenomenological model" as synonym for "representative model"; for a discussion, see Cartwright's (1999, 180).

12 See Bokulich's (2011, 44), McMullin's (1968, 390–391), and Wimsatt's (1987, 29).

13 Note that this is the second meaning of "abstract model"; for the first meaning, see Section 16.3.

14 The expression refers to the chemical element silicon (the element with the symbol Si and with atomic number 14) because microchips are made from silicon. The Latin name for silicon is "silicium", which is why one also sees "in silicio" as variant of "in silico" (see, for instance, Gruner 2013, 251).

15 This definition is stated in the online version of the Merriam-Webster Dictionary.

16 For a discussion of computer simulations and the use of simulation models, see Humphreys' (2004) and Winsberg's (2010), although neither provides a definition of "simulation model". For a critical evaluation of some of the bold claims that have been made in connection with computer simulations, see Frigg and Reiss' (2009).

17 Weinert uses the term differently, namely as an umbrella term for analogue models and thought experiments (Weinert 2016, 37).

18 Discussing models in chemistry, Weisberg proposes drawing the line between qualitative and quantitative models differently. The distinction, says Weisberg, "is not about the use of numbers; both types of models can be numerical. Rather it is a distinction resting on degrees of approximation and idealization. Qualitative models contain more approximations and are more highly idealized than quantitative models" (2004, 1071–1072). However, this way of drawing the line would seem to be specific to chemistry.

19 In the case of climate models such non-theoretical features often appear in the form of parametrisations, which capture the supposed net effect of processes that cannot be resolved in the model (Katzav 2013, 117–118).

20 Note that this characterisation of a generative model is different from the one we have seen in Section 16.3.

21 Similar characterisations of theoretical models can be found in Black's (1962, 226–230) and Bunge's (1973, 97).

22 Hesse has an alternative reading of "complementary model": "there are complementary models such as the wave and particle models in quantum physics, which exclude each other in certain respects and which therefore limit each other's positive analogy, but whose potential positive analogy is unexhausted in other respects so that each can still function as a useful model in particular circumstances" (1961, 27). This reading is, however, specific to quantum theory and cannot be generalised to other domains of inquiry.

23 Although the term "heuristic model" can also be applied to any model that helps solving a problem. It is in this sense that, for instance, Grandori (2010) speaks of a "heuristic model" of economic decision making.

24 Although I have often heard the term being used in this way, I have not been able to trace it in the literature. Searches for "didactic model" invariably led me into the literature on teaching, where a didactic model is a way of teaching or a way of learning. Thus understood, the "didactic" in the model's name specifies the target of the model and is therefore not included in the list.

References

Achinstein, P. 1965. Theoretical Models. *The British Journal for the Philosophy of Science* 16: 102–120.

Achinstein, P. 1968. *Concepts of Science: A Philosophical Analysis*. Baltimore: Johns Hopkins Press.

Akerlof, G. A. 1970. The Market for 'Lemons': Quality Uncertainty and the Market Mechanism. *Quarterly Journal of Economics* 84: 488–500.

Ambrosio, C. 2014. Iconic Representations and Representative Practices. *International Studies in the Philosophy of Science* 28: 255–275.

Basso, A., C. Lisciandra, and C. Marchionni 2017. Hypothetical Models in Social Science. In L. Magnani and T. Bertolotti (eds.), *Springer Handbook of Model-Based Science*. Dordrecht and Heidelberg: Springer, pp. 413–433.

Batterman, R. W. 2002. Asymptotics and the Role of Minimal Models. *The British Journal for the Philosophy of Science* 53: 21–38.

Batterman, R. W. 2019. Universality and Rg Explanations. *Perspectives on Science* 27: 26–47.

Batterman, R. W. and C. C. Rice 2014. Minimal Model Explanations. *Philosophy of Science* 81: 349–376.

Black, M. 1962. Models and Archetypes. In *Models and Metaphors: Studies in Language and Philosophy*. Ithaca and New York: Cornell University Press, pp. 219–243.

Bokulich, A. 2003. Horizontal Models: From Bakers to Cats. *Philosophy of Science* 70: 609–627.

Bokulich, A. 2011. How Scientific Models Can Explain. *Synthese* 180: 33–45.

Bokulich, A. 2017. Models and Explanation. In L. Magnani and T. Bertolotti (eds.), *Springer Handbook of Model-Based Science*. Dordrecht, Heidelberg, London, and New York: Springer, pp. 103–118.

Bokulich, A. and N. Oreskes 2017. Models in Geosciences. In L. Magnani and T. Bertolotti (eds.), *Springer Handbook of Model-Based Science*. Dordrecht, Heidelberg, London, and New York: Springer, pp. 891–911.

Boumans, M. 2009. Understanding in Economics. Gray-Box Models. In H. W. de Regt, S. Leonelli, and K. Eigner (eds.), *Scientific Understanding, Philosophical Perspectives*. Pittsburgh: University of Pittsburgh Press, pp. 2011–2029.

Bunge, M. 1973. *Method, Model, and Matter*. Dordrecht: Reidel.

Cartwright, N. 1983. *How the Laws of Physics Lie*. Oxford: Oxford University Press.

Cartwright, N. 1999. *The Dappled World: A Study of the Boundaries of Science*. Cambridge: Cambridge University Press.

Cartwright, N. 2010. Models: Parables V Fables. In R. Frigg and M. C. Hunter (eds.), *Beyond Mimesis and Convention: Representation in Art and Science*. Berlin and New York: Springer, pp. 19–32.

Casini, L. 2014. Not-So-Minimal Models: Between Isolation and Imagination. *Philosophy of the Social Sciences* 44: 646–672.

Chirimuuta, M. 2014. Minimal Models and Canonical Neural Computations: The Distinctness of Computational Explanation in Neuroscience. *Synthese* 191: 127–153.

Craver, C. 2010. Prosthetic Models. *Philosophy of Science* 182: 840–851.

Davidsson, P., F. Klügl, and H. Verhagen 2017. Simulation of Complex Systems. In L. Magnani and T. Bertolotti (eds.), *Springer Handbook of Model-Based Science*. Dordrecht, Heidelberg, London, and New York: Springer, pp. 783–797.

Del Re, G. 2000. Models and Analogies in Science. *Hyle* 6: 5–15.

Dhaene, G., C. Gourieroux, and O. Scaillet 1998. Instrumental Models and Indirect Encompassing. *Econometrica* 66: 673–688.

Dodig-Crnkovic, G. and A. Cicchetti 2017. Computational Aspects of Model-Based Reasoning. In L. Magnani and T. Bertolotti (eds.), *Springer Handbook of Model-Based Science*. Dordrecht, Heidelberg, London, and New York: Springer, pp. 695–718.

Downes, S. M. 2021. *Models and Modeling in the Sciences: A Philosophical Introduction*. New York and London: Routledge.

Evagorou, M., S. Erduran, and T. Mäntylä 2015. The Role of Visual Representations in Scientific Practices: From Conceptual Understanding and Knowledge Generation to 'Seeing' How Science Works. *International Journal of STEM Education* 2: 1–13.

Fletcher, S. C. 2019. Minimal Approximations and Norton's Dome. *Synthese* 196: 1749–1760.

Frey, G. 1961. Symbolische Und Ikonische Modelle. In H. Freudenthal (ed.), *The Concept and the Role of the Model in Mathematics and Natural and Social Sciences*. Dordrecht: Reidel, pp. 89–97.

Frigg, R. and S. Hartmann 2020. Models in Science. In E. N. Zalta (ed.), *The Stanford Encyclopedia of Philosophy*. https://plato.stanford.edu/archives/spr2020/entries/models-science/.

Frigg, R. and J. Nguyen 2020. *Modelling Nature: An Opinionated Introduction to Scientific Representation* (Synthese Library). Berlin and New York: Springer.

Frigg, R. and J. Reiss 2009. The Philosophy of Simulation: Hot New Issues or Same Old Stew? *Synthese* 169: 593–613.

Fülöp, A., Z. Turócz, D. Garbaisz, L. Harsányi, and A. Szijártó 2013. Experimental Models of Hemorrhagic Shock: A Review. *European Surgical Research* 50: 57–70.

Fumagalli, R. 2015. No Learning from Minimal Models. *Philosophy of Science* 82: 798–809.

Fumagalli, R. 2016. Why We Cannot Learn from Minimal Models. *Erkenntnis* 81: 433–455.

Gelfert, A. 2016. *How to Do Science with Models: A Philosophical Primer*. Cham: Springer.

Gelfert, A. 2017. The Ontology of Models. In L. Magnani and T. Bertolotti (eds.), *Springer Handbook of Model-Based Science*. Dordrecht, Heidelberg, London, and New York: Springer, pp. 5–23.

Gelfert, A. 2019. Probing Possibilities: Toy Models, Minimal Models, and Exploratory Models. In Á. Nepomuceno-Fernández, L. Magnani, F. J. Salguero-Lamillar, C. Barés-Gómez, and M. Fontaine (eds.), *Model-Based Reasoning in Science and Technology: Inferential Models for Logic, Language, Cognition and Computation*. Cham: Springer, pp. 3–19.

Gerritsen, C. and T. Bosse 2017. Model-Based Reasoning in Crime Prevention. In L. Magnani and T. Bertolotti (eds.), *Springer Handbook of Model-Based Science*. Dordrecht and Heidelberg: Springer, pp. 1051–1063.

Gibbard, A. and H. R. Varian 1978. Economic Models. *The Journal of Philosophy* 75: 664–677.

Giere, R. N. 1988. *Explaining Science: A Cognitive Approach.* Chicago: Chicago University Press.

Giere, R. N. 1996. Visual Models and Scientific Judgement. In B. S. Baigrie (ed.), *Picturing Knowledge: Historical and Philosophical Problems Concerning the Use of Art in Science.* Toronto: University of Toronto Press, pp. 269–302.

Giere, R. N. 1999. Visual Models. In R. N. Giere (ed.), *Science without Laws.* Chicago: University of Chicago Press, pp. 118–146.

Grandori, A. 2010. A Rational Heuristic Model of Economic Decision Making. *Rationality and Society* 22: 477–504.

Grobler, A. 1995. The Representational and the Non-Representational in Models of Scientific Theories. In W. E. Herfel, W. Krajewski, I. Niiniluoto, and R. Wojcicki (eds.), *Theories and Models in Scientific Processes* (Poznań Studies in the Philosophy of Science and the Humanities 44). Amsterdam: Rodopi, pp. 37–48.

Groenewold, H. J. 1961. The Model in Physics. In H. Freudenthal (ed.), *The Concept and the Role of the Model in Mathematics and Natural and Social Sciences.* Dordrecht: Reidel, pp. 98–103.

Grüne-Yanoff, T. 2009. Learning from Minimal Economic Models. *Erkenntnis* 70: 81–99.

Grüne-Yanoff, T. 2013. Appraising Models Nonrepresentationally. *Philosophy of Science* 80: 850–861.

Gruner, S. 2013. Eric Winsberg: Science in the Age of Computer Simulation. *Minds & Machines* 23: 251–254.

Haefner, J. W. 2005. *Modeling Biological Systems: Principles and Applications.* New York: Springer.

Hansen, A. J. 1982. The Meeting of Parallel Lines: Science, Fiction, and Science Fiction. In G. E. Slusser, E. S. Rabkin, and R. Scholes (eds.), *Bridges to Fantasy.* Carbondale and Edwardsville: Southern Illinois University Press, pp. 51–58.

Harré, R. 1970. *The Principles of Scientific Thinking.* Chicago: The University of Chicago Press.

Harré, R. 1988. Where Models and Analogies Really Count. *International Studies in the Philosophy of Science* 2: 118–133.

Harré, R. 2004. *Modeling: Gateway to the Unknown.* Amsterdam: Elsevier.

Hartmann, S. 1995. Models as a Tool for Theory Construction: Some Strategies of Preliminary Physics. In W. E. Herfel, W. Krajewski, I. Niiniluoto, and R. Wojcicki (eds.), *Theories and Models in Scientific Processes* (Poznań Studies in the Philosophy of Science and the Humanities 44). Amsterdam: Rodopi, pp. 49–67.

Hartmann, S. 1999. Models and Stories in Hadron Physics. In M. Morgan and M. Morrison (eds.), *Models as Mediators: Perspectives on Natural and Social Science.* Cambridge: Cambridge University Press, pp. 326–346.

Hartshorne, C. and P. Weiss (eds.) 1931–1935. *Collected Papers of Charles Sanders Peirce* (Vols. I–VI). Cambridge, MA: Harvard University Press.

Herfel, W. E. 1995. Nonlinear Dynamical Models as Concrete Construction. In W. E. Herfel, W. Krajewski, I. Niiniluoto, and R. Wojcicki (eds.), *Theories and Models in Scientific Processes* (Poznań Studies in the Philosophy of Science and the Humanities 44). Amsterdam: Rodopi, pp. 69–84.

Hesse, M. B. 1961. *Forces and Fields: The Concept of Action at a Distance in the History of Physics.* London and Edinburgh: Thomas Nelson and Sons.

Hesse, M. B. 1967. Models and Analogy in Science. In P. Edwards (ed.), *Encyclopedia of Philosophy.* New York: Macmillan, pp. 354–359.

Humphreys, P. 2004. *Extending Ourselves: Computational Science, Empiricism, and Scientific Method*. Oxford: Oxford University Press.

Imbert, C. 2017. Computer Simulations and Computational Models in Science. In L. Magnani and T. Bertolotti (eds.), *Springer Handbook of Model-Based Science*. Dordrecht, Heidelberg, London, and New York: Springer, pp. 735–781.

Institute of Imagination 2021. *Try Out Junk Modelling at Home*. https://ioi.london/latest/new-video-try-out-junk-modelling-at-home/ (accessed 25 August 2021).

Jebeile, J. 2020. The Kac Ring or the Art of Making Idealisations. *Foundations of Physics* 50: 1152–1170.

Karlin, S. and J. McGregor 1965. Ehrenfest Urn Models. *Journal of Applied Probability* 2: 352–376.

Katzav, J. 2013. Hybrid Models, Climate Models, and Inference to the Best Explanation. *The British Journal for the Philosophy of Science* 64: 107–129.

Khan, A., K. Waqar, A. Shafique, R. Irfan, and A. Gul 2017. In Vitro and in Vivo Animal Models: The Engineering Towards Understanding Human Diseases and Therapeutic Interventions. In D. Barh and V. Azevedo (eds.), *Omics Technologies and Bio-Engineering: Towards Improving Quality of Life*. Amsterdam: Academic Press (Elsevier), pp. 431–448.

Kovaka, K. 2020. Mate Choice and Null Models. *Philosophy of Science* 87: 1096–1106.

Lange, M. 2015. On 'Minimal Model Explanations': A Reply to Batterman and Rice. *Philosophy of Science* 82: 292–305.

Lavis, D. A. 2015. *Equilibrium Statistical Mechanics of Lattice Models*. Cham: Springer.

Leung, Y. F., D. S. C. Lam, and C. P. Pang 2001. *In Silico* Biology: Observation, Modeling, Hypothesis and Verification. *TRENDS in Genetics* 17: 622–623.

Lockhart, J. M. and W. R. Davidson 1999. Evaluation of C3h/Hej Mice for Xenodiagnosis of Infection with *Ehrlichia Chaffeensis*. *Journal of Veterinary Diagnostic Investigation* 11: 55–59.

Lofgren, E. T., K. M. Collins, T. C. Smith, and R. A. Cartwright 2016. Equations of the End: Teaching Mathematical Modeling Using the Zombie Apocalypse. *Journal of Microbiology & Biology Education* 17: 137–142.

Luczak, J. 2017. Talk About Toy Models. *Studies in History and Philosophy of Modern Physics* 57: 1–7.

Mäki, U. 2009. Realistic Realism About Unrealistic Models. In H. Kincaid and D. Ross (eds.), *The Oxford Handbook of Philosophy of Economics*. Oxford: Oxford University Press, pp. 68–98.

Massimi, M. 2019. Two Kinds of Exploratory Models. *Philosophy of Science* 86: 869–881.

McMullin, E. 1968. What Do Physical Models Tell Us? In B. van Rootselaar and J. F. Staal (eds.), *Logic, Methodology and Science III*. Amsterdam: North Holland, pp. 385–396.

Morrison, M. 2011. One Phenomenon, Many Models: Inconsistency and Complementarity. *Studies in History and Philosophy of Science* 42: 342–353.

Murphy, A. 2020a. *Thought Experiments and the Scientific Imagination*. PhD Thesis, University of Leeds.

Murphy, A. 2020b. Towards a Pluralist Account of the Imagination in Science. *Philosophy of Science* 87: 957–967.

Nguyen, J. 2020. It's Not a Game: Accurate Representation with Toy Models. *The British Journal for the Philosophy of Science* 71: 1013–1041.

Norton, J. D. 2008. The Dome: An Unexpectedly Simple Failure of Determinism. *Philosophy of Science* 75: 786–798.

Nowakowa, I. and L. Nowak 2000. Introduction. Science as a Caricature of Reality. In I. Nowakowa and L. Nowak (eds.), *Idealization X: The Richness of Idealization* (Poznań Studies in the Philosophy of the Sciences and the Humanities 69). Amsterdam: Rodopi, pp. 9–14.

Ohsawa, Y., T. Hayashi, and H. Kido 2017. Restructuring Incomplete Models in Innovators Marketplace and Data Jackets. In L. Magnani and T. Bertolotti (eds.), *Springer Handbook of Model-Based Science*. Dordrecht, Heidelberg, London, and New York: Springer, pp. 1015–1031.

openmod 2021. *Open Models.* https://wiki.openmod-initiative.org/wiki/Open_Models (accessed 25 August 2021).

Pincock, C. 2007. Mathematical Idealization. *Philosophy of Science* 74: 957–967.

Portides, D. 2011. Seeking Representations of Phenomena: Phenomenological Models. *Studies in History and Philosophy of Science* 42: 334–341.

Portides, D. 2017. Models and Theories. In L. Magnani and T. Bertolotti (eds.), *Springer Handbook of Model-Based Science*. Dordrecht and Heidelberg: Springer, pp. 25–48.

Povich, M. 2018. Minimal Models and the Generalized Ontic Conception of Scientific Explanation. *The British Journal for the Philosophy of Science* 69: 117–137.

Redhead, M. 1980. Models in Physics. *The British Journal for the Philosophy of Science* 31: 145–163.

Reutlinger, A., D. Hangleiter, and S. Hartmann 2018. Understanding (with) Toy Models. *The British Journal for the Philosophy of Science* 69: 1069–1099.

Rice, C. 2015. Moving Beyond Causes: Optimality Models and Scientific Explanation. *Nous* 49: 589–615.

Rice, C. 2018. Idealized Models, Holistic Distortions, and Universality. *Synthese* 195: 2795–2819.

Rice, C. 2020. Universality and the Problem of Inconsistent Models. In M. Massimi and C. D. McCoy (eds.), *Understanding Perspectivism*. New York: Routledge, pp. 85–109.

Rice, C. 2021. *Leveraging Distortions: Explanation, Idealization, and Universality in Science*. Cambridge, MA: MIT Press.

Rosenblueth, A. and N. Wiener 1945. The Role of Models in Science. *Philosophy of Science* 12: 316–321.

Russo, F. 2017. Model-Based Reasoning in the Social Sciences. In L. Magnani and T. Bertolotti (eds.), *Springer Handbook of Model-Based Science*. Dordrecht, Heidelberg, London, and New York: Springer, pp. 953–970.

Schelling, T. C. 1978. *Micromotives and Macrobehavior*. New York: Norton.

Shech, E. 2018. Idealizations, Essential Self-Adjointness, and Minimal Model Explanation in the Aharonov – Bohm Effect. *Synthese* 195: 4839–4863.

Spirtes, P. 2005. Graphical Models, Causal Inference, Andeconometric Models. *Journal of Economic Methodology* 12: 1–22.

Sterrett, S. G. 2017. Physically Similar Systems – A History of the Concept. In L. Magnani and T. Bertolotti (eds.), *Springer Handbook of Model-Based Science*. Dordrecht, Heidelberg, London, and New York: Springer, pp. 377–411.

Strevens, M. 2008. *Depth: An Account of Scientific Explanation*. Cambridge, MA: Harvard University Press.

Stuart, M. T., Y. Fehige, and J. R. Brown (eds.) 2018. *The Routledge Companion to Thought Experiments*. London: Routledge.

Tabor, M. 1989. *Chaos and Integrability in Nonlinear Dynamics: An Introduction*. New York: Wiley.

Tee, S.-H. 2020. Generative Models. *Erkenntnis*: 1–19. https://doi.org/10.1007/s10670-020-00338-w.

Wartofsky, M. W. 1979. *Models: Representation and the Scientific Understanding*. Dordrecht: Reidel.

Weinert, F. 1999. Theories, Models and Constraints. *Studies in History and Philosophy of Science* 30: 303–333.

Weinert, F. 2016. *The Demons of Science: What They Can and Cannot Tell Us About Our World*. Cham: Springer.

Weisberg, M. 2004. Qualitative Theory and Chemical Explanation. *Philosophy of Science* 71: 1071–1081.

Weisberg, M. 2013. *Simulation and Similarity: Using Models to Understand the World*. Oxford: Oxford University Press.

Wilde, M. and J. Williamson 2016. Models in Medicine. In M. Solomon, J. R. Simon, and H. Kincaid (eds.), *The Routledge Companion to Philosophy of Medicine*. Abingdon: Routledge, pp. 271–284.

Williams, D. 2021. Imaginative Constraints and Generative Models. *Australasian Journal of Philosophy* 99: 68–82.

Wimsatt, W. C. 1987. False Models as Means to Truer Theories. In M. H. Nitecki, and A. Hoffman (eds.), *Neutral Models in Biology*. New York and Oxford: Oxford University Press, pp. 23–55.

Winsberg, E. 2010. *Science in the Age of Computer Simulation*. Chicago: University of Chicago Press.

Wylie, A. 2017. Representational and Experimental Modeling in Archaeology. In L. Magnani and T. Bertolotti (eds.), *Springer Handbook of Model-Based Science*. Dordrecht, Heidelberg, London, and New York: Springer, pp. 989–1002.

ENVOI

The nature of models and theories has occupied philosophers ever since the advent of modern science. In the 16 chapters of this book, we discussed core philosophical questions that arise in connection with models and theories, and we examined positions that were put forward in the debates since the 1920s. Providing a summary of the points made and the conclusions reached is neither desirable nor feasible. Our project in these final pages is to take a step back and reflect on the implications of the arguments we have seen, and to draw conclusions for where work on models and theories can, and should, go from here.

The perceived antagonism between the syntactic and the semantic views of theories (which we preferred to call the Linguistic View and the Model-Theoretical View) has been a *leitmotiv* in the philosophical engagement with models and theories over the last 60 years, and there was hardly a discussion of the topic in which the antagonism did not make an appearance in one way or another. The discussions were often uneven in that the syntactic view was considered dead from the outset and merely served as a foil against which the prowess of the semantic view could be showcased. It is time to change the tune. Not only have reports of the death of the syntactic view been premature; the entire debate is based on a false dichotomy. Any tenable account will have to see theories as consisting of both linguistic and non-linguistic elements, and no further ink should be spilled on the question of whether theories are either linguistic or non-linguistic entities. Leaving the syntax-semantics debate behind us does not, however, mark the end of the debate over the nature of theories. Saying that a theory consists of linguistic and non-linguistic elements leaves options wide open as to what these elements are and how they are integrated. A fruitful discussion of the nature of theories will focus on the questions of what the parts are, on how they come together to form a harmonious whole, and on what role each part plays in the seamless functioning of this whole.

DOI: 10.4324/9781003285106-22

Some progress towards this goal has been made in recent discussions about the nature of theories. These discussions have, however, focused predominantly on the formal structure of theories. Understanding the formalism of a theory is important, but it is only half the project. Theories are about a certain domain of objects and phenomena. They are about elementary particles, molecules, genes, microbes, animals, galaxies, populations, and so on. That is, theories have content. Understanding how theories acquire content requires going beyond a theory's formalism. This problem has two aspects. The first aspect is to understand how the formal language of a theory is interpreted in terms of a theory's subject matter, or, if one sees a theory as having both a formal language and an object language, to understand how these two languages function and interlock. This is a problem on which the philosophy of science can fruitfully collaborate with the philosophy of language. It is lamentable that these two branches of philosophy have drifted apart. To some extent this may be a consequence of growing professional specialisation within philosophy, but attitudes have played their part too. Seeing leading exponents of the philosophy of science insist that theories are extralinguistic entities and that matters of language have no philosophical significance does not create an environment that engenders productive collaborations with philosophers of language. It is time to push the reset button and to rediscover shared interests.

The second aspect of the problem is to understand how a theory's models represent. This problem has attracted some attention over the last decade, and a number of accounts of how models represent have been proposed. However, many of them operate at high levels of abstraction and ultimately remain programmatic. Abstract accounts can be fruitful in bringing questions into focus and directing research, but they cannot replace in-depth engagements with the details of actual representations. Discussions of idealisation, analogy, and robustness can be seen as being a productive part of this engagement. Yet not only are there still many open questions concerning these modes of representation; there are also representations that do not fit any of these moulds. The next step in a discussion of representation will be to get to a better understanding of particular representation relations and the styles to which they belong, as well as to integrate an account of how models represent into a broader understanding of the structure of theories.

A deeper understanding of representation will also assist research in other areas of philosophy. Questions concerning the use of symmetries in physical theories, theoretical and empirical equivalence, the contributions of theories/models to scientific explanation and understanding (and specifically the role that facticity plays in this), the articulation of selective realism, and the relation between science and art are but some areas of philosophical research that can benefit from a fine-grained understanding of scientific representation.

So far, the philosophy of models and the decision sciences have by and large gone about their own business without taking much note of each other, the former dealing with the issues covered in this book and the latter investigating methods of decision-making at different levels. In various domains of public life difficult policy decisions must be made, and there is a broad consensus that these decisions must be based on the best available scientific evidence. This is the guiding principle of evidence-based policy-making. In some domains, evidence comes in the form of experimental data and observed facts. But in other domains much, or at least important parts, of the evidence that feeds into a decision process takes the form of model outputs. Decisions concerning climate change, public health, and natural catastrophe protection are cases in point. How do, or should, model outputs feed into a decision process? If one could simply run models to forecast the relevant systems' behaviours, the answer to this question would be simple: modellers would run their best model, possibly with different initial and boundary conditions, and then hand over their results to the policy-maker who would use them as inputs to their decision algorithms. Alas, things are rarely, if ever, that simple. In particular in policy-relevant domains, models are often constructed under more or less severe uncertainty, and as a result the scientific community ends up producing an entire ensemble of different and often incompatible models rather than one "best" model. But how are we to make decisions that meet the standards of evidence-based policy-making if the best available evidence is ambiguous? An answer to this question will depend on a deeper understanding of what the models are, how they are constructed, how they operate, and what uncertainties they embody, as well as on having decision algorithms that can take such information as inputs. Neither the philosophy of modelling nor the decision sciences will be able to provide viable answers on their own. Decision-making under scientific uncertainty is a challenge that they will have to face together, and the time has come to make a collaborative effort.

INDEX